For UK order enquiries: please contact Bookpoint Ltd, 130 Milton Park, Abingdon, Oxon OX14 4SB. Telephone: +44 (0) 1235 827720. Fax: +44 (0) 1235 400454. Lines are open 09.00–18.00, Monday to Saturday, with a 24-hour message answering service. Details about our titles and how to order are available at www.teachyourself.co.uk.

For USA order enquiries: please contact McGraw-Hill Customer Services, PO Box 545, Blacklick, OH 43004-0545, USA. Telephone: 1-800-722-4726. Fax: 1-614-755-5645.

For Canada order enquiries: please contact McGraw-Hill Ryerson Ltd, 300 Water St, Whitby, Ontario L1N 9B6, Canada. Telephone: 905 430 5000. Fax: 905 430 5020.

Long renowned as the authoritative source for self-guided learning – with more than 30 million copies sold worldwide – the *Teach Yourself* series includes over 300 titles in the fields of languages, crafts, hobbies, business, computing and education.

British Library Cataloguing in Publication Data: a catalogue entry for this title is available from The British Library.

Library of Congress Catalog Card Number: on file.

First published in UK 1992 by Hodder Headline Ltd, 338 Euston Road, London, NW1 3BH.

First published in US 1993 by Contemporary Books, a Division of the McGraw-Hill Companies, 1 Prudential Plaza, 130 East Randolph Street, Chicago, IL 60601 USA.

This edition published 2003.

The 'Teach Yourself' name is a registered trade mark of Hodder & Stoughton Ltd.

Typeset by Transet Limited, Coventry, England.
Printed in Great Britain for Hodder & Stoughton Educational, a division
Ltd, 338 Euston Road, London NW1 3BH, by Cox & Wyman Ltd, Re⁻

Papers used in this book are natural, renewable and recyclab'
from wood grown in sustainable forests. The logging a⁻
conform to the environmental regulations of the country of or

Impression number   10 9 8 7 6 5 4 3 2 1
Year   2009 2008 2007 2006 2005 2004 2(

contents

foreword

The *Teach Yourself Welsh Dictionary* is a modern dictionary specifically designed for use by Welsh learners. The Welsh–English section is based on a basic vocabulary formulated to meet their particular needs. It differs significantly from the traditional type of dictionary, in as much as it also contains mutated forms of nouns, verbs, adjectives and prepositions integrated into the main alphabetical structure. Learners thereby are able to trace the standard form of a mutated word without difficulty. Irregularly formed plural nouns are systematically included, and each Welsh verb is complete with its first person singular form in the present tense. In addition, many of the prepositions governed by various verbs are included.

An attempt has been made to supply sufficient grammatical detail with each entry in the English–Welsh section to facilitate cross-reference and easy access to the fuller definition in the Welsh–English section.

Throughout, the dictionary is well illustrated with examples of language in action, with an emphasis on Welsh idiomatic usage.

The supplement contains a short introduction to some of the salient features of Welsh grammar including the conjugation of verbs and prepositions, the comparison of adjectives, forms of personal pronouns, and a summary of the main rules of consonantal mutation.

I am indebted to Mr Cennard Davies, M.A., for his sustained interest and encouragement during the preparation of the work, for reading the manuscript, and for his many valuable suggestions.

I gratefully acknowledge that a section of the dictionary was awarded First Prize at the 1989 Llanrwst National Eisteddfod. Its completion was commissioned by the Eisteddfod Council, and it is now published by kind permission of the National Eisteddfod Court.

Edwin C. Lewis

Llangyfelach
Swansea

Welsh–English dictionary

a.	ansoddair	*adjective*
a.b.	ansoddair benywaidd	*feminine adjective*
ad.	adferf	*adverb*
a.g.	ansoddair gwrywaidd	*masculine adjective*
ardd.	arddodiad	*preposition*
At.	Atodiad	*Supplement, Appendix*
b.	benywaidd	*feminine*
be.	berfenw	*verb-noun* (followed in brackets by the first person present tense)
bf.	berf	*verb*
c.	cysylltair	*conjunction*
D.C.	De Cymru	*South Wales (S.W.)*
e.b.	enw benywaidd	*feminine noun*
* *e.b.g.*	enw benywaidd/gwrywaidd	*feminine/masculine noun*
ebych	ebychiad	*interjection*
e.e.	er enghraifft	*for example*
e.g.	enw gwrywaidd	*masculine noun*
* *e.g.b.*	enw gwrywaidd/benywaidd	*masculine/feminine noun*
e.ll.	enw lluosog	*plural noun*
e.torf.	enw torfol	*collective noun*
g.	gwrywaidd	*masculine*
G.C.	Gogledd Cymru	*North Wales (N.W.)*
geir.	geiryn	*particle*
geir. gof.	geiryn gofynnol	*interrogative particle*
geir. perth.	geiryn perthynol	*relative particle*
gw.	gweler	*see*
lit.	yn llythrennol	*literally*
ll.	lluosog	*plural*
N.W.	Gogledd Cymru	*North Wales (dialect)*
[pron.]	dywedir	*[pronounced]*
rhag.	rhagenw	*pronoun*
rhagdd.	rhagddodiad	*prefix*
rhag. gof.	rhagenw gofynnol	*interrogative pronoun*
rhag. perth.	rhagenw perthynol	*relative pronoun*
S.W.	De Cymru	*South Wales (dialect)*
S.W.W.	De Orllewin Cymru	*South West Wales (dialect)*
y fan.	y fannod	*definite article*
ymad. ad.	ymadrodd adferfol	*adverbial phrase*

*The gender of some nouns varies in different dialects, for example: munud (*minute*); llygad (*eye*).

a   8

A

a *geir. gof. o flaen berf
(interrogative particle before
a verb)*. **A oes heddwch?** Is
there peace?

a *rhag. perth. (followed by
soft mutation)* who, whom,
which (**a** *is often omitted in
everyday speech, but the
mutated form of the verb
remains*). **Y ferch a welais**
The girl whom I saw; **y llyfr a
ddarllenais** the book which I
read

a:ac [**ac** *pron.* **ag**] *c.* (**a** *before
a consonant*, **ac** *before a
vowel*; **a** *followed by spirant
mutation*) and. **du a gwyn**
black and white; **pensil a
phapur** pencil and paper;
afal ac oren apple and
orange

â *bf.* he/she/it goes. *gw.*
mynd

â: ag 1 *ardd*, (**â** *before a
consonant*, **ag** *before a
vowel*; **â** *followed by spirant
mutation*) with (*an
instrument*), by means of.
torri cig â chyllell cutting
meat with a knife; **crynu ag
ofn** shivering with fear. 2 *c.*
(**â** before a consonant, **ag**
before a vowel; **â** followed by
spirant mutation) as. **cyn
goched â thân** as red as fire;
mor ysgafn â phluen as light
as a feather; **mor wyn ag eira**
as white as snow

aber *e.g.b. ll.* -**oedd** estuary,
mouth of river; confluence;
stream

aberth *e.g.b. ll.* -**au** sacrifice

aberth *be.* (**aberthaf**) to
sacrifice

absennol *a.* absent

ac *gw.* **a: ac**

acen *e.b. ll.* -**nau**, -**ion** accent;
intonation

act *e.b. ll.* -**au** act; statute

actio *be.* (**actiaf**) to act

acw: cw *ad.* (**cw** *in everyday
speech*) there, yonder

achlysur *e.g. ll.* -**on** occasion;
cause, opportunity

achos 1 *e.g. ll.* -**ion** reason,
cause; action; case, factor.
2 *ardd.* because, for

achosi *be.* (**achosaf**) to cause

achub *be.* (**achubaf**) to save.
achub bywyd to save life;
achub cyfle to seize an
opportunity

adael *gw.* **gadael**

adain: aden *e.b. ll.* **adenydd**
wing

adar *gw.* **aderyn**

adeg *e.b. ll.* -**au** opportunity;
period of time. **adeg y
Nadolig** Christmas time; **ar
adegau** at (certain) times

adeilad *e.g. ll.* -**au** building

adeiladu *be.* (**adeiladaf**) to
build, to construct

adeiladwr *e.g. ll.* **adeiladwyr**
builder

adenydd *gw.* **aden**

aderyn *e.g. ll.* **adar** bird

adfer *be.* (**adferaf**) to return; to

revive; to restore *(to health, former condition, etc.)*

adferf *e.f.* *ll.* **-au** adverb

adlais *e.g.* *ll.* **adleisiau** echo

adleisiau *gw.* **adlais**

adloniannau *gw.* **adloniant**

adloniant *e.g.* *ll.* **adloniannau** entertainment; recreation

adnabod *be.* **(adnabyddaf)** to recognise; to be familiar with; to identify; to know *(person or place)*; to diagnose

adnod *e.b.* *ll.* **-au** verse *(in Bible)*; clause; section

adran *e.b.* *ll.* **-nau** division, section; department. **Adran Addysg** Education Department

adref *ad.* homewards

adrodd *be.* **(adroddaf)** to relate; to recite; to report

adroddiad *e.g.* *ll.* **-au** account, report; recitation; narration

addas *a.* fitting, suitable, proper

addewid *e.g.b.* *ll.* **-ion** promise

addo (i), *be.* **(addawaf)** to promise. **Addewais iddo y byddwn yn mynd.** I promised him that I would go

addoldai *gw.* **addoldy**

addoldy *e.g.* *ll.* **addoldai** place of worship

addoli *be.* **(addolaf)** to worship

addoliad *e.g.* *ll.* **-au** worship; religious service

addysg *e.b.* *ll.* **-au** learning, knowledge; education,

instruction. **addysg grefyddol** religious education;
addysg gynradd primary education; **addysg uwchradd** secondary education

aeaf *gw.* **gaeaf**

aeddfed *a.* ripe, mature

ael *e.b.* *ll.* **-iau** brow

aelod *e.g.* *ll.* **-au** limb; member. **Aelod Seneddol** Member of Parliament

aelodaeth *e.b.* membership

aelwyd *e.b.* *ll.* **-ydd** hearth; home

aer 1 *e.g.* air, atmosphere. **2** *e.g.* *ll.* **-(i)on** heir

aeres *e.b.* *ll.* **-au** heiress

aerion *gw.* **aer**

aeron *gw.* **aer, aeronen**

aeronen *e.b.* *ll.* **aeron** berry, fruit. **aeron cochion** red berries

aeth *gw.* **mynd**

afael *gw.* **gafael**

afaelgar *gw.* **gafaelgar**

afal *e.g.* *ll.* **-au** apple

afan(s)en *e.b.* *ll.* **afan(s)** raspberry *(S.W.)*

afiach *a.* unhealthy, sick; dirty, unwholesome

afiechyd *e.g.* *ll.* **-on** disease, illness

afon *e.b.* *ll.* **-ydd** river; straits. **Afon Tawe** River Tawe; **Afon Menai** Menai Straits

afonydd *gw.* **afon**

afr *gw.* **gafr**

agor *be.* **(agoraf)** to open

agored *a.* open; unobstructed; liable

agoriad *e.g. ll.* **-au** key
(N.W.); opening, aperture.
  agoriad llygad eye-opener
agos *a.* (at *person*, **i** *place*)
  near. *gw. At. Ansoddeiriau*
agosach *gw.* **agos**
agosaf *gw.* **agos**
agosáu (at, i) *be.* **(agosâf)** to
  draw near to, to approach.
  agosáu at *(person);* **agosáu i**
  (place)
agosed *gw.* **agos**
agwedd *e.g. ll.* **-au** attitude
angau *e.g. ll.* **angheuoedd**
  death
angel *e.g. ll.* **angylion, engyl**
  angel
angenrheidiau *gw.* **anghenraid**
angenrheidiol *a.* necessary
anghenraid *e.g. ll.*
  angenrheidiau necessity
angheuoedd *gw.* **angau**
anghofio *be.* **(anghofiaf)** to
  forget
anghyfarwydd *a.* unfamiliar,
  unaccustomed.
  anghyfarwydd â unfamiliar
  with, unaccustomed to
anghywir *a.* inaccurate,
  wrong; false
angladd *e.g.b. ll.* **-au** funeral
angylion *gw.* **angel**
ai 1 *geir. gof. heb dreiglad ar
ei ôl, a geir o flaen enw,
rhagenw, berfenw ac
ansoddair (interrogative
particle not followed by
mutation, and used before a
noun, pronoun, verb-noun,
or adjective)* (**ai** *is often

omitted in spoken Welsh). **Ai
te sy'n y cwpan?** Is it tea in
the cup? **Ai Twm sy yno?** Is
it Twm that's there? 2 *c.*
either . . . or; **naill ai Marc
neu Ioan** Either Marc or
Ioan
âi *bf.* he/she/it was
going/would go/used to go;
gw. **mynd**
ail *a. (followed by soft
mutation)* second; like,
similar. **yr ail fachgen** the
second boy; **yr ail dŷ** the
second house; **yr ail gadair**
the second chair; **heb (ei) ail**
unequalled; **bob (yn) ail**
alternate, alternately
ail *rhagdd.* re-, second;
secondary. **ail achos**
secondary cause; **ailadroddiad**
repetition; **ailfeddwl** second
thought, afterthought;
ailgyfrif a recount; **ail-law**
second-hand; **ailystyried** to
reconsider
ailgylchu *be.* **(ailgylchaf)** to
recycle
air *gw.* **gair**
alar *gw.* **galar**
alarch *e.g. ll.* **-od, elyrch** swan
alaru *gw.* **galaru**
alaw *e.b. ll.* **-on** music; air,
melody, tune; lily. **alaw werin**
folk tune
Alban, Yr *eb.* Scotland
Almaen, Yr *eb.* Germany
alw *gw.* **galw**
alwad *gw.* **galwad**
alwedigaeth *gw.* **galwedigaeth**

alwyn *gw.* **galwyn**
allan *ad.* out, outside
allanfa *e.b.* *ll.* **allanfeydd** exit
allanfeydd *gw.* **allanfa**
allanol *a.* external, outward,
  exterior
allt *e.b.* *ll.* **elltydd** hill *(N.W.)*;
  cliff *(N.W.)*; wood *(S.W.)*
alltud *e.g.* *ll.* **-ion** exile; alien
alltudion *gw.* **alltud**
allu *gw.* **gallu**
alluog *gw.* **galluog**
allwedd *e.b.* *ll.* **-au, -i** key
  (S.W.); clef
allweddell *e.b.* *ll.* **-au**
  keyboard
am 1 *ardd. (followed by soft
  mutation) (personal forms:*
  **amdana, amdanat,
  amdano/amdani, amdanon,
  amdanoch, amdanyn)** about,
  at, around, for, on. **am ddeg
  o'r gloch** at ten o'clock;
  Galwodd am Emyr He called
  for Emyr; **am y tro** for the
  time being; *gw.* **At.
  Arddodiaid. 2** *c.* because, for,
  since; provided that
amaethwr *e.g.* *ll.* **amaethwyr**
  farmer; *gw.* **ffarmwr: ffermwr**
amaethyddiaeth *e.b.*
  agriculture
amau 1 *be.* **(amheuaf)** to
  doubt; to suspect; to dispute.
  2 *e.g.* *ll.* **amheuon** doubt
ambell *a. (followed by soft
  mutation)* occasional. **ambell
  waith** occasionally,
  sometimes; **ambell un** an
  occasional one

ambiwlans *e.g.* *ll.* **-ys**
  ambulance
amcan *e.g.* *ll.* **-ion** purpose,
  notion, guess
amcanion *gw.* **amcan**
amddiffyn 1 *be.* **(amddiffynnaf)**
  to defend; to protect. **2** *e.g.*
  ll. **-ion** defence
Americanwr *e.g.* *ll.*
  Americanwyr an American
amgaeëdig *a.* enclosed
amgáu *be.* **(amgaeaf)** to
  enclose; to envelop
amgueddfa *e.b.* *ll.*
  amgueddfeydd museum;
  Amgueddfa Genedlaethol
  National Museum;
  Amgueddfa Werin Folk
  Museum
amgueddfeydd *gw.*
  amgueddfa
amgylch *e.g.* *ll.* **-oedd** circuit,
  environs; **o amgylch** round
  about, about
amgylchedd *e.g.* *ll.* **-au, -ion**
  environment
amharod *a.* unprepared,
  unready, unwilling
amherffaith *a.* imperfect
amheuaeth *e.b.* *ll.* **-au** doubt,
  suspicion
amheuon *gw.* **amau**
amhosibl *a.* impossible
aml *a. (followed by soft
  mutation)* frequent,
  abundant; **aml (i) gyfle**
  frequent opportunity; **gan
  amlaf** most often, mostly
amlen *e.b.* *ll.* **-ni** envelope
amlenni *gw.* **amlen**

amlosgfa *e.b.* *ll.* **amlosgfeydd**
crematorium

amlosgfeydd *gw.* **amlosfga**

amlosgi *be.* **(amlosgaf)** to
cremate

amlwg *a.* evident, clear, plain;
famous; prominent

amod *e.g.b.* *ll.* **-au** condition;
term; proviso

amrwd *a.* raw, crude

amryw *a.* *(followed by soft
mutation)* several; various.
amryw fath various kinds

amrywiaeth *e.g.* *ll.* **-au** variety;
variation

amrywiol *a.* miscellaneous

amser *e.g.* *ll.* **-au, -oedd** time,
period; season; tense;
rhythm, measure *(in music
and poetry)*

amserau *gw.* **amser**

amserlen *e.b.* *ll.* **-ni** timetable

amseroedd *gw.* **amser**

amynedd *e.g.* patience

amyneddgar *a.* patient

anabl *a.* disabled

anabledd *e.g.* disability

anadl *[pron.* **anal** *in S.W.]*
e.g.b. *ll.* **-au, -on** breath

anadlu *be.* **(anadlaf)** to breathe

anaddas *a.* unfit, unsuitable

anafu *be.* **(anafaf)** to receive
hurt or injury; to injure, to
wound, to mutilate

anaml *a.* infrequent; scarce,
rare

anarferol *a.* unusual

anawsterau *gw.* **anhawster**

aned *gw.* **ganed**

aneffeithiol *a.* ineffectual

aneglur *a.* obscure

anerchion *gw.* **annerch**

anferth *a.* huge, gigantic,
monstrous, prodigious

anfodlon *a.* unwilling,
discontented

anfoesgar *a.* rude, ill-
mannered

anfon *be.* **(i** *place,* **at** *person)*
(anfonaf) to send; to transmit

anffodus *a.* unfortunate

anhapus *a.* unhappy; unlucky

anhawster *e.g.* *ll.* **anawsterau**
difficulty

anhwyldeb *e.g.* *ll.* **-au** sickness

anhwylder *e.g.* *ll.* **-au** sickness

anhwylus *a.* unwell;
inconvenient

anialwch *e.g.* desert,
wilderness

anifail *e.g.* *ll.* **anifeiliaid**
animal, beast. **anifail anwes**
pet

anifeiliaid *gw.* **anifail**

anlwcus *a.* unlucky

annerch 1 *be.* **(anerchaf)** to
greet; to address. 2 *e.g.* *ll.*
anerchion greetings
anerchiadau addresses,
speeches

annhebyg *a.* unlike, dissimilar,
different

annheg *a.* unfair, unjust

annheilwng *a.* unworthy

anniben *a.* untidy

annibyniaeth *e.b.*
independence

Annibynnwr *e.g.* *ll.*
Annibynwyr Independent,
Congregationalist

annoeth *a.* unwise

annwyd *e.g.* *ll.* -au, -on cold, chill. **Mae annwyd arno fe(fo)** He has a cold

annwyl *a. (when the adjective precedes the noun soft mutation occurs)* dear, beloved; precious. **Annwyl Blant** Dear Children; **Annwyl Gyfaill** Dear Friend *(used to begin a speech or a letter).*

anwylyd darling

anochel *a.* unavoidable, inevitable

anodd *a.* difficult, hard

anos *a.* more difficult, harder

anrheg *e.b.* *ll.* -ion gift, present

anrhydedd *e.g.* *ll.* -au honour

ansicr *a.* uncertain, doubtful

ansicrwydd *e.g.* uncertainty, doubt

ansoddair *e.g.* *ll.* **ansoddeiriau** adjective

ansoddeiriau *gw.* ansoddair

antur *e.g.b.* *ll.* -iau, -iaethau adventure; danger; risk

anturus *a.* adventurous

anweledig *a.* invisible, unseen

anwes *e.g.* *ll.* -au fondness, pampering, fondling; indulgence. **anifail anwes** pet

anwesu *be.* **(anwesaf)** to fondle, to cherish

anwiredd *e.g.* *ll.* -au untruth, iniquity

anwyd *gw.* **ganwyd**

anwylaf 1 *a.* dearest. 2 *e.g. b.* beloved one

anwyliaid *e.ll.* beloved ones

ar *ardd. (followed by soft mutation) (personal forms:* **arna, arnat, arno/arni, arnon, arnoch, arnyn)** on, upon; by, in, at. **ar fynydd Epynt** on Epynt mountain; **ar lawr y gegin** on the kitchen floor; **ar hap a damwain** by chance; *gw. At. Arddodiaid*

araf *a.* slow, leisurely. **yn araf deg** slowly, gently; by degrees

arafu *be.* **(arafaf)** to slow, to retard, to decelerate

araith *e.b.* *ll.* **areithiau** speech, address

arall *a.* *ll.* **eraill** another, other, else. **bachgen arall** another boy; **bechgyn eraill** other boys

arbed *be.* **(arbedaf)** to spare, to save. **arbed amser** to save time

arbennig *a.* specialist, distinct

arch 1 *e.b.* *ll.* **eirchion** request, petition. 2 *e.b.* *ll.* **eirch** coffin, ark

arch- *rhagdd.* chief, principal, high, arch-; worst. **archesgob** archbishop; **archdderwydd** archdruid; **archoffeiriad** chief priest; **archelyn** worst enemy

archeb *e.b.* *ll.* -ion order *(especially for goods)*

archebu *be.* **(archebaf)** to order

archfarchnad *e.b.* *ll.* -oedd hypermarket

ardal *e.b.* *ll.* -oedd region, district, area

ardd *gw.* **gardd**

arddangosfa 14

arddangosfa *e.b.* *ll.*
arddangosfeydd show,
exhibition
ardderchog *a.* excellent,
splendid
arddio *gw.* **garddio**
arddodiad *e.g.* *ll.* **arddodiaid**
preposition
arddodiaid *gw.* **arddodiad**
arddwr *gw.* **garddwr**
arddwrn *e.g.* *ll.* **arddyrnau**
wrist
areithiau *gw.* **araith**
arf *e.g.b.* *ll.* **-au** weapon; tool;
arfau arms
arfer 1 *be.* **(arferaf)** to use; to
practise; to accustom; to
partake of. 2 *e.g.b.* *ll.* **-ion**
usage, custom, practice; rule;
habit
arferion *gw.* **arfer**
arferol *a.* usual, customary
arfog *a.* armed
arfordir *e.g.* *ll.* **-oedd** seacoast,
maritime district
arglwydd *e.g.* *ll.* **-i** lord. **Tŷ'r
Arglwyddi** House of Lords
arglwyddes *e.b.* *ll.* **-au** lady
arglwyddi *gw.* **arglwydd**
argraff *e.b.* *ll.* **-iadau, -au**
impression, imprint
argraffiad *e.g.* *ll.* **-au** edition
argraffu *be.* **(argraffaf)** to
print, to impress
argymell *be.* **(argymhellaf)** to
urge
arholiad *e.g.* *ll.* **-au**
examination. **arholiad llafar**
oral examination; **arholiad
ysgrifenedig** written

examination; **sefyll arholiad**
to take *(sit)* an examination
arian *e.g.* silver; money, coin,
cash. **arian byw** quicksilver,
mercury; **arian gleision** small
change, **arian parod** cash;
arian pen exact money; **arian
poced** pocket money
arlleg *gw.* **garlleg**
arllwys *be.* **(arllwysaf)** to pour,
to empty. **arllwys y glaw** to
pour with rain *(S.W.)*
arogl *e.g.* *ll.* **-au** scent,
perfume *(N.W.)*
arogli: aroglu *be.* **(aroglaf)** to
scent, to smell *(N.W.)*.
aros (am) *be.* **(arhosaf)** to wait
(for), to stay; to stop, to
remain
arth *e.g.* *ll.* **eirth** bear
arw *gw.* **garw**
arwain *be.* **(arweiniaf)** to lead,
to guide, to conduct
arweinydd *e.g.* *ll.* **-ion** leader,
guide, conductor
arwydd *e.g.* *ll.* **-ion** sign
arwyddo *be.* **(arwyddaf)** to sign
asesu *be.* **(asesaf)** to assess
asgellwr *e.g.* *ll.* **asgellwyr**
wing: **blaenasgellwr** flanker
(rugby)
asgwrn *e.g.* *ll.* **esgyrn** bone
asiant *e.g.* *ll.* **-au** agent
asiantaeth *e.b.* *ll.* **-au** agency
asyn *e.g.* *ll.* **-nod** ass, donkey
asynnod *gw.* **asyn**
at *ardd.* *(followed by soft
mutation)* *(personal forms:*
**ata, atat, ato/ati, aton, atoch,
atyn)** to, towards, for, at, by.

gw. At. Arddodiaid
atal (rhag) *be.* **(ataliaf)** to stop;
to prevent; to withhold. **atal
dweud** to stammer
ateb 1 *be.* **(atebaf)** to answer,
to reply. **2** *e.g.* *ll.* **-ion**
answer, reply
atebion *gw.* **ateb**
atgoffa *be.* **(atgoffaf)** to recall,
to remind
atodiad *e.g.* *ll.* **-au** appendix
atyniadol *a.* attractive
athrawes *e.b.* *ll.* **-au** female
teacher
athrawon *gw.* **athro**
athro *e.g.* *ll.* **athrawon**
teacher, professor: **yr Athro
Thomas Parry** Professor
Thomas Parry
aur *e.g.* gold
awdur *e.g.* *ll.* **-on** author
awduraeth *e.b.* *ll.* **-au**
authorship
awdurdod *e.g.b.* *ll.* **-au**
authority. **awdurdod iechyd**
health authority
awduron *gw.* **awdur**
awel *e.b.* *ll.* **-on** breeze
awelon *gw.* **awel**
awgrymu *be.* **(awgrymaf)** to
suggest
awn *bf.* we go. *gw.* **mynd**
awr *e.b.* *ll.* **oriau** hour; time
Awst *e.g.* August
awyddus *a.* desirous, eager,
zealous. **yn awyddus i fynd**
eager to go
awyr *e.b.* air; sky. **awyr agored**
open air; **awyr iach** fresh air
awyren *e.b.* *ll.* **-nau** aeroplane

B

ba *gw.* **pa**
bab *gw.* **pab**
baban *e.g.* *ll.* **-od** baby
babanaidd *a.* babyish,
childish, puerile
babell *gw.* **pabell**
babi *e.g.* baby; *gw.* **pabi**
babydd *gw.* **pabydd**
bac *gw.* **pac**
baced *gw.* **paced**
bacio *be.* **(baciaf)** to back; to
move backward; to bet (on).
bacio car to reverse a car;
bacio ceffyl to bet on success
of a horse; *gw.* **pacio**
bach 1 *e.g.* *ll.* **-au** hook,
hinge. **2** *a.* small, little; dear.
araf bach slowly, very
slowly; **bore bach** very early
morning, crack of dawn
bachau *gw.* **bach; bachyn**
bachgen *e.g.* *ll.* **bechgyn** boy
bachgennaidd *a.* boyish,
childish, puerile
bachu *be.* **(bachaf)** to hook, to
grapple
bachyn *e.g.* *ll.* **bachau** hook
bad *e.g.* *ll.* **-au** boat. **bad
achub** lifeboat
badell *gw.* **padell**
bader *gw.* **pader**
bae *e.g.* *ll.* **-au** bay. **Bae
Abertawe** Swansea Bay
baent *gw.* **paent**
bafiliwn *gw.* **pafiliwn**
bafin *gw.* **pafin**
bag *e.g.* *ll.* **-iau** bag
bagan *gw.* **pagan**

bagiau *gw*. **bag**

bai *e.g. ll*. **beiau** fault, blame; defect

baich *e.g. ll*. **beichiau** load, burden

bais *gw*. **pais**

bâl *gw*. **pâl**

balas *gw*. **palas**

balch *a*. proud, fine, stately; glad. **Roedd e'n falch ein gweld ni** he was glad to see us

balchder *e.g*. pride, glory

baled *e.b. ll*. **-i** ballad

baledwr *e.g. ll*. **baledwyr** composer of ballads, balladmonger

balot *e.g. ll*. **-au** ballot

balu *gw*. **palu**

balŵn *e.b. ll*. **balwnau** balloon

ballu *gw*. **pallu**

bamffled *gw*. **pamffled**

ban *e.g.b. ll*. **-nau** peak, mountain, beacon, height; top, summit; corner, quarter; arm, branch; verse, section of line. **Bannau Brycheiniog** Brecon Beacons; **o bedwar ban y byd** from the four corners of the world

banana *e.g. ll*. **-s, bananâu** banana

banasen *gw*. **panasen**

banc 1 *e.g. ll*. **-iau** bank. **gŵyl banc** bank holiday. 2 *e.g. ll*. **bencydd** mound, bank, hillock

bancio *be*. **(banciaf)** to bank

band *e.g. ll*. **-au, -iau** band, binding. **band pres** brass band

banel *gw*. **panel**

baner *e.b. ll*. **-i** banner, flag

bannas *gw*. **panasen**

bannau *gw*. **ban**

bannod *e.b. ll*. **banodau** 1 line, clause, part. 2 definite article *gw*. **y, yr, 'r**

banodau *gw*. **bannod**

bant *gw*. **pant**

bapur *gw*. **papur**

bapuro *gw*. **papuro**

bar *e.g. ll*. **-rau** bar

bâr *gw*. **pâr**

bara *e.g*. bread. **bara brith** currant bread; **bara lawr** laver bread; **bara menyn** bread and butter. *gw*. **para**

baragraff *gw*. **paragraff**

baratoi *gw*. **paratoi**

barbeciw *e.g. ll*. **barbeciwiau** barbecue

barc *gw*. **parc**

barch *gw*. **parch**

barchedig *gw*. **parchedig**

barchu *gw*. **parchu**

barchus *gw*. **parchus**

bardwn *gw*. **pardwn**

bardd *e.g. ll*. **beirdd** bard, poet

barddoniaeth *e.b*. poetry

barf *e.b. ll*. **-au** beard

barhad *gw*. **parhad**

barhau *gw*. **parhau**

barn *e.b. ll*. **-au** opinion, judgement. **Dydd y Farn** the Day of Judgement

barnwr *e.g. ll*. **barnwyr** judge

barod *gw*. **parod**

barrau *gw.* **bar**
barsel *gw.* **parsel**
barti *gw.* **parti**
bas 1 *e.g.* bass *(voice)*; base. 2
a. shallow
Basg, Gwlad y *e.b.* the Basque
Country. *gw.* **Pasg**
basged *e.b.* *ll.* **-i** basket.
basgedaid basketful
basiant *gw.* **pasiant**
basn *e.g.* *ll.* **-au, -ys** basin.
basn siwgr sugar basin
basnau *gw.* **basn**
basnys *gw.* **basn**
baswn i. *bf.* I would (be). *gw.*
bod
baswr *e.g.* *ll.* **baswyr** bass
(singer)
bat *e.g.* *ll.* **-iau** bat
batrwm *gw.* **patrwm**
batrymau: batrynau *gw.*
patrwm
bath 1 *e.g.* *ll.* **-au** kind; bath;
such a. **Dim byd o'r fath**
nothing of the kind; **Welais i
erioed y fath le.** I never saw
such a place. 2 *a.* minted
bathdai *gw.* **bathdy**
bathdy *e.g.* *ll.* **bathdai** mint
bathodyn *e.g.* *ll.* **-nau** badge
bathu *be.* **(bathaf)** to form, to
shape, to coin, to mint. **bathu
gair** to coin a word
baw *e.g.* dirt *(S.W.)*, dung,
filth, mucus
bawb *gw.* **pawb**
bawd *e.g.* *ll.* **bodiau** thumb;
big toe. **bys bawd** thumb, big
toe
bawen *gw.* **pawen**

becso *be.* **(becsaf)** to worry,
to vex *(S.W.)*
becyn *gw.* **pecyn**
bechadur *gw.* **pechadur**
bechan *a.b.* little, small. *gw.*
bychan
bechgyn *gw.* **bachgen**
bechod *gw.* **pechod**
bechu *gw.* **pechu**
bedair *gw.* **pedair**
bedol *gw.* **pedol**
bedw *gw.* **bedwen**
bedwar *gw.* **pedwar**
bedwaredd *gw.* **pedwaredd**
bedwen *e.b.* *ll.* **bedw** birch.
gwialen fedw birch-rod
bedwerydd *gw.* **pedwerydd**
bedyddio *be.* **(bedyddiaf)** to
baptize
Bedyddiwr *e.g.* *ll.* **Bedyddwyr**
Baptist. **Ioan Fedyddiwr** John
the Baptist
bedd *e.g.* *ll.* **-au** grave, tomb
beg *gw.* **peg**
begwn *gw.* **pegwn**
beiau *gw.* **bai**
Beibl *e.g.* *ll.* **-au** Bible. **Y Beibl
Cymraeg Newydd** The New
Welsh Bible
beic *e.g.* *ll.* **-iau** bicycle
beicio *be.* **(beiciaf)** to cycle
beichiau *gw.* **baich**
beichiog *a.* pregnant;
burdened
beidio *gw.* **peidio (â)**
beiddio *be.* **(beiddiaf)** to dare,
to venture
beilot *gw.* **peilot**
beint *gw.* **peint**
beintio *gw.* **peintio**

beintiwr *gw.* **peintiwr**
beio *be.* (beiaf) to blame, to accuse, to censure
beirdd *gw.* **bardd**
beiriant *gw.* **peiriant**
beirniad *e.g. ll.* **beirniaid** adjudicator, critic
beirniadu *be.* (beirniadaf) to adjudicate, to criticize
beirniaid *gw.* **beirniad**
beisiau *gw.* **pais**
bêl *gw.* **pêl**
belydr *gw.* **pelydr**
bell *gw.* **pell**
bellach *ad.* now, at length, further. *gw.* **pell**
bellaf *gw.* **pell**
belled *gw.* **pell**
bellter *gw.* **pellter**
ben *gw.* **pen**
benaethiaid *gw.* **pennaeth**
benawdau *gw.* **pennawd**
ben-blwydd *gw.* **pen-blwydd**
bencadlys *gw.* **pencadlys**
bencampwr *gw.* **pencampwr**
bencydd *gw.* **banc**
bendant *gw.* **pendant**
benderfyniad *gw.* **penderfyniad**
benderfynol *gw.* **penderfynol**
benderfynu *gw.* **penderfynu**
bendigedig *a.* blessed, glorious, wonderful
bendith *e.b. ll.* **-ion** blessing
bendithio *b.e.* (bendithiaf) to bless
benelin *gw.* **penelin**
benfoel *gw.* **penfoel**
ben-glin *gw.* **pen-glin**
benigamp *gw.* **penigamp**

benillion *gw.* **pennill**
ben-lin *gw.* **pen-glin**
benlinio *gw.* **penlinio**
bennaeth *gw.* **pennaeth**
bennaf *gw.* **pennaf**
bennau *gw.* **pen**
bennawd *gw.* **pennawd**
bennill *gw.* **pennill**
bennod *gw.* **pennod**
benodau *gw.* **pennod**
benodi *gw.* **penodi**
benodiad *gw.* **penodiad**
benrhyn *gw.* **penrhyn**
bensaer *gw.* **pensaer**
bensil *gw.* **pensil**
bensiwn *gw.* **pensiwn**
bensiynau *gw.* **pensiwn**
bensiynwr *gw.* **pensiynwr**
benteulu *gw.* **penteulu**
bentref *gw.* **pentref**
bentwr *gw.* **pentwr**
bentyrrau *gw.* **pentwr**
benthyca *be.* (benthycaf) to borrow, to lend
benwythnos *gw.* **penwythnos**
benyw *e.b. ll.* **-od** woman, female
benywaidd *a.* female, feminine
ber *a.b.* short, brief. *gw.* **byr**
bêr *gw.* **pêr**
berchen: berchennog *gw.* **perchen**
beren *gw.* **peren**
bererin *gw.* **pererin**
berf *e.b. ll.* **-au** verb
berfa *e.b. ll.* **berfâu** wheelbarrow (*N.W.*); *gw.* **whilber**
berfedd *gw.* **perfedd**
berfenw *e.b. ll.* **-au** verb-noun

berffaith *gw.* perffaith
berffeithio *gw.* perffeithio
beri *gw.* peri
berl *gw.* perl
berlysiau *gw.* perlysiau
berllan *gw.* perllan
bersli *gw.* persli
berson *gw.* person
bersonol *gw.* personol
bersonoliaeth *gw.*
  personoliaeth
bert *gw.* pert
berth *gw.* perth
berthnasau *gw.* perthynas
berthnasol *gw.* perthnasol
berthyn *gw.* perthyn
berthynas *gw.* perthynas
berw 1 *e.g.* boiling, tumult,
  turmoil. 2 *a.* boiling,
  seething; **dŵr berw** boiling
  water. 3 *e.g.* cress: **berw'r**
  dŵr water cress
berwi *be.* (berwaf) to boil
bergyl *gw.* perygl
beryglus *gw.* peryglus
beswch *gw.* peswch
besychiad *gw.* pesychiad
betrol *gw.* petrol
beth *rhag.* what? **beth am**
  ginio? what about dinner?
  beth mae e'n wneud? what's
  he doing? **beth sydd yma?**
  what's here? **beth ydy ei**
  enw? what's his name? **beth**
  bynnag anyway. *gw.* peth
biano *gw.* piano
bianydd *gw.* pianydd
bib *gw.* pib
biben *gw.* piben
bicil: bicl *gw.* picil

bictiwr *gw.* pictiwr
bicwnen *gw.* picwnen
bigfain *gw.* pigfain
bigiad *gw.* pigiad
bigo *gw.* pigo
bigog *gw.* pigog
bil *e.g.* *ll.* -iau bill. *gw.* pil
biler *gw.* piler
bilio *gw.* pilio
bilion *gw.* pil
bili-pala *gw.* pili-pala
bilsen *gw.* pilsen
bilyn *gw.* pilyn
bin *e.g.* *ll.* -iau bin. *gw.* pin
bîn *gw.* pîn
bînafal *gw.* pînafal
binc *gw.* pinc
binnau *gw.* pin
binsio *gw.* pinsio
binwydden *gw.* pinwydden
bioden *gw.* pioden
bioleg *e.b.* biology
bisged *e.b.* *ll.* bisgedi biscuit
bisgïen *e.b.* *ll.* bisgis biscuit
bisyn *gw.* pisyn
biti *gw.* piti
bitw *a.* tiny. **bws bitw** minibus
blaen 1 *e.g.* *ll.* -au, -ion point,
  end, top, tip; front, van;
  edge; source, limit, lead. 2 *a.*
  foremost, front, first
blaendal *e.g.* *ll.* -iadau deposit
blaenor *e.g.* *ll.* -iaid leader;
  deacon; predecessor
blaenwr *e.g.* *ll.* blaenwyr
  forward (*rugby and soccer*);
  leader (*of orchestra*)
blaguro *be.* (blaguraf) to bud
blaguryn *e.g.* *ll.* blagur bud
blaid *gw.* plaid

blaidd *e.g. ll.* **bleiddiaid, bleiddiau** wolf

blan *gw.* **plan**

blanced *e.b. ll.* **-i** blanket. **blanced wlân** woollen blanket; **blanced drydan** electric blanket

blanhigyn *gw.* **planhigyn**

blannu *gw.* **plannu**

blant *gw.* **plant**

blas *e.g.* taste, flavour; fervour, zest. **colli blas ar** to lose one's taste for. *gw.* **plas**

blasty *gw.* **plasty**

blasu *be.* **(blasaf)** to taste, to relish

blasus *a.* tasty, delicious, savoury

blât *gw.* **plât**

blawd *e.g. ll.* **blodiau, blodion** flour, meal; **blawd codi** self-raising flour; **blawd llif** sawdust

ble *rhag.* where?

bleidiau *gw.* **plaid**

bleidlais *gw.* **pleidlais**

bleidleisio *gw.* **pleidleisio**

bleidleisiwr *gw.* **pleidleisiwr**

bleiddiaid: bleiddiau *gw.* **blaidd**

blentyn *gw.* **plentyn**

blentynnaidd *gw.* **plentynnaidd**

bleser *gw.* **pleser**

bleserus *gw.* **pleserus**

blesio *gw.* **plesio**

blew *gw.* **blewyn**

blewyn *e.g. ll.* **blew** hair (*on body, not on head*), fur; small fish bone. **hollti blew** to split hairs

blin *a.* tired, tiresome, cross; sorry

blinder *e.g. ll.* **-au** weariness, trouble, adversity

blinedig *a.* wearisome, tired

blino *be.* **(blinaf)** to tire, to vex, to weary. **Rydw i wedi blino** I am tired; **Mae e wedi blino** he is tired; **blino ar** to grow tired of

blisgyn *gw.* **plisgyn**

blisman: blismon *gw.* **plisman**

blith *gw.* **plith**

blodau *gw.* **blodyn**

blodeugerdd *e.b. ll.* **-i** anthology

blodfresychen *e.b. ll.* **blodfresych** cauliflower

blodiau: blodion *gw.* **blawd**

blodyn *e.g. ll.* **blodau** flower, blossom, bloom

bloedd *e.g. ll.* **-iau, -iadau** shout

bloeddio *be.* **(bloeddiaf)** to shout (*N.W.*)

blows *e.b. ll.* **-ys** blouse

blu *gw.* **pluen**

bluen *gw.* **pluen**

bluf *gw.* **plufyn**

blufyn *gw.* **plufyn**

blwc *gw.* **plwc**

blwch *e.g. ll.* **blychau** box, chest

blwg *gw.* **plwg**

blwm *gw.* **plwm**

blwydd 1 *e.b. ll.* **-i** year-old, year of age. **tair blwydd oed** three years of age. 2 *a.* year old. *gw. At. Treiglad-*

Trwynol
blwyddyn *e.b.* *ll.*
  blynyddoedd year. **dwy**
  flynedd two years; **tair**
  blynedd three years; **pedair**
  blynedd four years; **pum**
  mlynedd five years. *gw. At.*
  Treiglad Trwynol
blwyf *gw.* **plwyf**
blychau *gw.* **blwch**
blygu *gw.* **plygu**
blynedd *gw.* **blwyddyn**
blynedd *e.b.ll.* years (*used*
  usually after cardinal
  numbers)
blynyddoedd *gw.* **blwyddyn**
bob *gw.* **pob. bob bore** every
  morning; **bob nos** every
  night; **bob dydd** every day
bobi *gw.* **pobi**
bobl *gw.* **pobl**
boblogaeth *gw.* **poblogaeth**
boblogaidd *gw.* **poblogaidd**
bobman *gw.* **pobman**
bobydd *gw.* **pobydd**
boced *gw.* **poced**
bocedi *gw.* **poced**
bocs *e.g.* *ll.* **-ys** box
boch *e.b.* *ll.* **-au** cheek
bod 1 *e.g.* *ll.* **-au** existence;
  being. **Y Bod Mawr** God.
  2 *be.* (**rydw i**) to be; **rydw i**
  I am, **rwyt ti** you are, **mae e/o**
  he/it is, **mae hi** she/it is, *etc.*
  gw. At. Berfau
bodau *gw.* **bod**
bodiau *gw.* **bawd**
bodio *be.* (**bodiaf**) to thumb,
  to finger
bodlon: boddlon *a.* willing,

pleased, content. **bodlon ar**
  satisfied with
bodloni *be.* (**bodlonaf**) to
  please, to satisfy, to be
  contented
bodd *e.g.* will, pleasure;
  consent. **rhyngu bodd** to
  please; **trwy fodd** with
  consent or permission; **wrth
  ei fodd** happy, contented
boddhad *e.g.* satisfaction,
  pleasure
boddi *be.* (**boddaf**) to drown,
  to be drowned, to flood
boddlon *gw.* **bodlon**
boen *gw.* **poen**
boeni *gw.* **poeni**
boenus *gw.* **poenus**
boenydio *gw.* **poenydio**
boer: boeri *gw.* **poer, poeri**
boeth *gw.* **poeth**
boeth *gw.* **poethi**
bol *e.g.* *ll.* **-iau** belly,
  stomach, abdomen
bola *e.g.* *ll.* **bolâu, boliau**
  belly, stomach, abdomen
bolâu *gw.* **bola**
boliau *gw.* **bol, bola**
bolion *gw.* **polyn**
boliticaidd *gw.* **politicaidd**
bolyn *gw.* **polyn**
bollt *e.g.b.* *ll.* **-au, byllt** bolt,
  dart; thunderbolt
bolltau *gw.* **bollt**
bolltio *be.* (**bolltiaf**) to bolt
bom *e.g.* *ll.* **-iau** bomb
bôn *e.g.* *ll.* **bonau, bonion**
  base, trunk, stump,
  counterfoil. **yn y bôn**
  basically, in reality

boneddiges

boneddiges *e.b.* *ll.* **-au** lady
boneddigion *gw.* **bonheddwr**
bonheddig *a.* noble, gentle
bonheddwr *e.g.* *ll.*
  bonheddwyr, boneddigion
  gentleman, nobleman.
  foneddigion a boneddigesau
  ladies and gentlemen *(in
  addressing an audience)*
bonion *gw.* **bôn**
bont *gw.* **pont**
bontydd *gw.* **pont**
bopeth *g.w.* **popeth**
bopty *gw.* **popty**
bord *e.b.* *ll.* **-ydd, -au** table
  (*S.W.*), board (*S.W.*)
bordau: bordydd *gw.* **bord**
bore *e.g.* *ll.* **-au** morning. **yn
  fore** early; **bore trannoeth**
  next morning
borfa *gw.* **porfa**
borfeydd *gw.* **porfa**
borffor *gw.* **porffor**
bori *gw.* **pori**
bortread *gw.* **portread**
borth *gw.* **porth**
borthladd *gw.* **porthladd**
bos *e.g.* *ll.* **-ys** boss, chief.
  Pwy ydy'r bos yma? Who's
  the boss here?
bos *gw.* **pos**
bosibilrwydd *gw.*
  posibilrwydd
bosibl *gw.* **posibl**
bost *gw.* **post**
bostio *gw.* **postio**
bostman: bostmon *gw.*
  postman
bostmyn *gw.* **postman**
bostyn *gw.* **postyn**

bosys *gw.* **bos**
botel *gw.* **potel**
botwm *e.g.* *ll.* **botymau**
  button
botymu *be.* **(botymaf)** to
  button
bowdr: bowdwr *gw.* **powdr**
bowdrau *gw.* **powdr**
bowlen: powlen *e.b.* *ll.* **-ni,
  bowliau: powliau** bowl
braf *a.* fine, nice, pleasant.
  bore braf a fine morning;
  Mae hi'n braf *(no mutation)*,
  it is fine *(weather-wise)*
bragdy *e.g.* *ll.* **bragdai**
  brewery
braich *e.b.g.* *ll.* **breichiau** arm
braidd *ad.* near, almost, just,
  rather, scarcely. **o'r braidd**
  hardly. *gw.* **praidd**
brain *gw.* **brân**
braint *e.b.* *ll.* **breintiau,
  breiniau** privilege, right,
  honour, status.
bram *gw.* **pram**
brân *e.b.* *ll.* **brain** crow
bras *a.* thick, fat; greasy;
  coarse; rich; rough,
  approximate
braslun *e.g.* *ll.* **-iau** outline,
  sketch
braster *e.g.* *ll.* **-au** grossness,
  fat
braw *e.g.* *ll.* **-iau** terror, fright
brawd *e.g.* *ll.* **brodyr** brother
brawddeg *e.b.* *ll.* **-au** sentence
brawf *gw.* **prawf**
brawiau *gw.* **braw**
brecwast *e.g.* *ll.* **-au**
  breakfast. **wy i frecwast-**

egg for breakfast
brech *e.b. ll.* **-au** eruption,
vaccination, pox. **brech goch**
measles; **brech yr ieir**
chickenpox
brechdan *e.b. ll.* **-au** slice of
buttered bread, sandwich
brechiad *e.g. ll.* **-au**
inoculation, vaccination
bregeth *gw.* **pregeth**
bregethu *gw.* **pregethu**
bregethwr *gw.* **pregethwr**
breichiau *gw.* **braich**
breichled *e.b. ll.* **-au** bracelet,
bangle
breiddiau *gw.* **praidd**
breifat *gw.* **preifat**
breiniau: breintiau *gw.* **braint**
bren *gw.* **pren**
brenhines *e.b. ll.* **breninesau**
queen
brenhinoedd *gw.* **brenin**
brenhinol *a.* royal
brenin *e.g. ll.* **brenhinoedd**
king
brennau *gw.* **pren**
brentis *gw.* **prentis**
brentisiaeth *gw.* **prentisiaeth**
bres *e.g. ll.* **-i,-ys** brace. *gw.*
pres
breseb *gw.* **preseb**
bresennol *gw.* **presennol**
bresenoldeb *gw.* **presenoldeb**
bresgripsiwn *gw.*
presgripsiwn
brest *e.b. ll.* **-iau** breast; chest
breswyl: breswylfod *gw.*
preswyl
breswylfeydd *gw.* **preswyl**
bresychen *e.b. ll.* **bresych**

cabbage
brethyn *e.g. ll.* **-nau** cloth.
brethyn cartref home-spun
cloth
breuddwyd *e.b.g. ll.* **-ion**
dream
breuddwydio *be.*
(breuddwydiaf) to dream
breuddwydion *gw.* **breuddwyd**
bridwerth *gw.* **pridwerth**
bridd *gw.* **pridd**
brif *gw.* **prif**
brifardd *gw.* **prifardd**
brifathrawes *gw.* **prifathrawes**
brifathro *gw.* **prifathro**
brifddinas *gw.* **prifddinas**
brifeirdd *gw.* **prifardd**
brifio *gw.* **prifio**
brifo *be.* **(brifaf)** to hurt, to
wound; to crumble (*N.W.*)
brifysgol *gw.* **prifysgol**
briffordd *gw.* **priffordd**
briffyrdd *gw.* **priffordd**
brig *e.g. ll.* **-au** top, summit;
outcrop; twig(s). **brig y don**
crest of the wave; **brig y**
goeden the tree top; **brig y**
nos dusk; **brig y to** the roof-
top; **o'r brig i'r bôn** from top
to bottom; **glo brig** open-cast
coal
brigau *gw.* **brig, brigyn**
brigyn *e.g. ll.* **brigau** twig
brin *gw.* **prin**
brinder *gw.* **prinder**
brintio *gw.* **printio**
briod *gw.* **priod**
briodas *gw.* **priodas**
briodi *gw.* **priodi**
briodol *gw.* **priodol**

bris *gw.* **pris**

britho: brithio *be.* **(brithaf: brithiaf)** to turn grey (of hair, beard)

briwsionyn *e.g. ll.* **briwsion** crumb, fragment

bro *e.b. ll.* **bröydd** region, country, vale, lowland. **bro a bryn** vale and hill; **Bro Morgannwg** Vale of Glamorgan

broblem *gw.* **problem**

brodor *e.g. ll.* **-ion** native

brodorol *a.* native

brodyr *gw.* **brawd**

brofi *gw.* **profi**

brofiad *gw.* **profiad**

brofiadol *gw.* **profiadol**

brofion *gw.* **profion**

broffid *gw.* **proffid**

broffidiol *gw.* **proffidiol**

broffwyd *gw.* **proffwyd**

broffwydo *gw.* **proffwydo**

broga *e.g. ll.* **-od** frog. *gw.* **ffroga**

bron 1 *e.b. ll.* **-nau** breast. 2 *e.b. ll.* **-nydd** breast of hill. 3 *ad.* almost nearly, just about to

bronfraith *e.b. ll.* **bronfreithod** thrush

bronnau: bronnydd *gw.* **bron**

Brotestant *gw.* **Protestant**

brown *a.* brown

bröydd *gw.* **bro**

brudd *gw.* **prudd**

brwdfrydig *a.* enthusiastic

brwnt *a.* dirty (*S.W.*), foul, cruel (*N.W.*)

brws: brwsh *e.g. ll.* **brwsys:**

brwshys brush, broom

brwsio: brwshio *be.* **(brwsiaf: brwshiaf)** to sweep, to brush

brwsys: brwshys *gw.* **brws**

brwydr *e.b. ll.* **-au** battle, conflict

brwydrau *gw.* **brwydr**

bryd *e.g. ll.* **-iau** mind, thought, intent. *gw.* **pryd**

Brydain *gw.* **Prydain**

brydau *gw.* **pryd**

Brydeinig *gw.* **Prydeinig**

bryder *gw.* **pryder**

bryderu *gw.* **pryderu**

bryderus *gw.* **pryderus**

brydferth *gw.* **prydferth**

brydferthwch *gw.* **prydferthwch**

brydiau *gw.* **bryd, pryd**

brydlon *gw.* **prydlon**

bryf: bryfedyn: bryfyn *gw.* **pryf**

bryfed *gw.* **pryf**

bryfocio *gw.* **profocio**

bryfyn *gw.* **pryf**

bryn *e.g. ll.* **-iau** hill

brynhawn *gw.* **prynhawn**

bryniau *gw.* **bryn**

brynu *gw.* **prynu**

brynwr *gw.* **prynwr**

brys *e.g.* haste, hurry. **ar frys** in haste, hurriedly; **ar frys gwyllt** in a mad rush

brysio *be.* **(brysiaf)** to hasten, to hurry

brysurdeb *gw.* **prysurdeb**

brysuro *gw.* **prysuro**

brysur *gw.* **prysur**

buan *a.* swift, quick, fast; soon. *gw. At. Ansoddeiriau*

buarth *e.g. ll.* **-au** farmyard, yard

buchod *gw.* **buwch**

budr *a.* dirty (*N.W.*), nasty (*N.W.*), foul (*N.W.*), vile (*N.W.*). **bachgen budr** a bit of a lad (*S.W.*)

buddsoddi *be.* **(buddsoddaf)** to invest

buddugol *a.* victorious, winning

buddugoliaeth *e.b. ll.* **-au** victory

bues i *bf.* I was, I have been. *gw.* **bod**

bugail *e.g. ll.* **bugeiliaid** shepherd; pastor

bugeiliaid *gw.* **bugail**

bugeilio *be.* **(bugeiliaf)** to shepherd, to watch

bulpud *gw.* **pulpud**

bum: bump *gw.* **pump**

bûm: bues *bf.* I was, I have been. *gw.* **bod**

b'un *gw.* **p'un**

bunnau: bunnoedd *gw.* **punt**

bunt *gw.* **punt**

bupur *gw.* **pupur**

bur *gw.* **pur**

burfa *gw.* **purfa**

buro *gw.* **puro**

busnes *e.g.b. ll.* **-ion, -au** business, affairs

buwch *e.b. ll.* **buchod, da** (*S.W.*) cow

bwced *e.g.b. ll.* **-i** bucket

bwdin *gw.* **pwdin**

bwdr *gw.* **pwdr**

bwdryn *gw.* **pwdryn**

bwdu *gw.* **pwdu**

bwlch *e.g. ll.* **bylchau** gap, pass

bŵer *gw.* **pŵer**

bwll *gw.* **pwll**

bwmp *gw.* **pwmp**

bwnc *gw.* **pwnc**

bwrdd *e.g. ll.* **byrddau** table (*N.W.*); board, plank; deck. **bwrdd brecwast** breakfast table; **bwrdd du** blackboard

bwriad *e.g. ll.* **-au** purpose, intention, resolution

bwriadu *be.* **(bwriadaf)** to intend

bwrpas *gw.* **pwrpas**

bwrs *gw.* **pwrs**

bwrw *be.* **(bwriaf)** to cast; to shed; to strike. **bwrw glaw** to rain; **bwrw cesair** to hail; **bwrw eira** to snow

bws *e.g. ll.* **bysiau, bysys** bus

bwthyn *e.g. ll.* **bythynnod** cottage, cabin

bwy *gw.* **pwy**

bwyd *e.g. ll.* **-ydd** food

bwyda *gw.* **bwydo**

bwydlen *e.b. ll.* **-ni** menu

bwydo: bwyda *be.* **(bwydaf)** to feed, to nourish. **bwydo'r adar** to feed the birds

bwydydd *gw.* **bwyd**

bwyll *gw.* **pwyll**

bwyllgor *gw.* **pwyllgor**

bwyllo *gw.* **pwyllo**

bwynt *gw.* **pwynt**

bwys *gw.* **pwys**

bwysedd *gw.* **pwysedd**

bwysig *gw.* **pwysig**

bwysigrwydd *gw.* **pwysigrwydd**

bwyslais *gw.* **pwyslais**
bwyso *gw.* **pwyso**
bwyta: byta (*S.W.*) *be.*
(**bwytâf**) to eat; to consume,
to ravage; to corrode (*S.W.*).
Bwytâf ginio bob dydd I eat
dinner every day. *gw. At.*
Berfau
bwyty *e.g. ll.* **bwytai**
restaurant
bwyth *gw.* **pwyth**
bychan *a.g.* little, small,
petty. *gw.* **bechan**
byd *e.g. ll.* **-oedd** world; life;
state. **byd caled** a hard
struggle; **byd da** good living,
a sumptuous life; **byd o**
wahaniaeth a world of
difference; **gwyn ei fyd!**
blessed is he, how fortunate!
beth yn y byd. . .? what in
the world. . .? what on
earth. . .?
bydoedd *gw.* **byd**
bydru *gw.* **pydru**
bydd (e/hi) *bf.* he/she/it will
be. **Bydd Mair yno** Mair will
be there; **bydd plant yno**
hefyd children will be there
also. *gw.* **bod**
byddar 1 *e.g. ll.* **-iaid** deaf
person
2 *a.* deaf
byddin *e.b. ll.* **-oedd** army,
host
byddinoedd *gw.* **byddin**
byg *e.g. ll.* **bygiau** bug
bylchai *gw.* **bwlch**
byllau *gw.* **pwll, pyllyn**
byllt *gw.* **bollt**

byllyn *gw.* **pyllyn**
bymtheg: bymtheng *gw.*
pymtheg
bymthegfed *gw.* **pymthegfed**
bynciau *gw.* **pwnc**
bynnag *rhag.* -ever, -soever.
beth bynnag whatsoever; **ble**
bynnag wherever; **pryd**
bynnag whenever; **pwy**
bynnag whoever
byped *gw.* **pyped**
byr *a.g. ll.* **-ion** short, brief.
dyn byr a short man; **stori fer**
a short story; **straeon byrion**
short stories. *gw.* **ber**
byrbryd *e.g. ll.* **-iau** snack
byrddaid *e.g. ll.* **byrddeidiau**
tableful
byrddau *gw.* **bwrdd**
byrfodd *e.g. ll.* **-au**
abbreviation
byrsau *gw.* **pwrs**
byrth *gw.* **porth**
bys *e.g. ll.* **-edd** finger. **bys**
bawd thumb, big toe; **bysedd**
y blaidd lupins; **bysedd y**
cŵn foxgloves. *gw.* **pysen**
bysedd *gw.* **bys**
bysen *gw.* **pysen**
bysgod *gw.* **pysgodyn**
bysgodyn *gw.* **pysgodyn**
bysgota *gw.* **pysgota**
bysgotwr *gw.* **pysgotwr**
bysiau *gw.* **bws**
byst *gw.* **post**, *gw.* **postyn**
bysys *gw.* **bws**
byta (*S.W.*) *gw.* **bwyta**
byth 1 *ad.* ever, still, always.
am byth for ever; **byth a**
hefyd continually. 2 (**byth** *is*

*frequently used in negative
sentences in the present,
future, imperfect and
conditional tense to convey
the meaning* never). **Ddaw e
byth** He will never come;
Doedd hi byth yn hwyr She
was never late. 3 *e.g. ll.*
-oedd eternity. **byth
bythoedd** for ever and ever,
world without end
bythefnos *gw.* **pythefnos**
bythynnod *gw.* **bwthyn**
byw 1 *be.* **(bywiaf)** to live, to
exist, to dwell, to inhabit; to
animate, to revive, to restore
to life. **byw a bod** to be
habitually present; **Mae e'n
byw yma** He lives here.
2 *a.* alive, living. **Ydy e'n
fyw?** Is he alive? 3 *e.g.* life.
yn fy myw for the life of me
bywiog *a.* lively, vivacious
bywyd *e.g. ll.* **-au** life,
existence
bywydeg *e.b.* biology

C

caban *e.g. ll.* **-au** booth,
cabin, hut
cacen *e.b. ll.* **-nau, -ni** cake
(N.W.)
cacwn *gw.* **cacynen**
cacynen *e.b. ll.* **cacwn** wasp
(N.W.). **yn gacwn gwyllt**
furious
cadach *e.g. ll.* **-au** cloth, rag;
handkerchief, bandage

(N.W.). **cadach llawr** cloth
for wiping floor; **cadach
llestri** dish cloth
cadair *e.b. ll.* **cadeiriau** chair.
cadair esmwyth easy chair;
cadair freichiau arm chair
cadeirio *be.* **(cadeiriaf)** to
chair
cadeiriol *a.* chaired. **eglwys
gadeiriol** cathedral
cadeirydd *e.g. ll.* **-ion**
chairman
cadno *e.g. ll.* **cadnoaid,
cadnawon** fox. **cadnawes:
cadnöes** vixen *(S.W.)*
cadw **(rhag.)** *be.* **(cadwaf)** to
keep, to preserve (from).
cadw ar gof to keep on
record; **cadw draw** to stay
away; **cadw sŵn** to make a
noise, to complain; **cadw'n
heini** to keep fit; **cadw
ystafell** to reserve a room;
cadw-mi-gei money box;
cyfrif cadw deposit account
cadwrol *a.* conservative
cadwyn *e.b. ll.* **-au, -i** chain;
series
cadwyno *be.* **(cadwynaf)** to
chain, to enslave
cae *e.g. ll.* **-au** field
caeau *gw.* **cae**
cael *be.* **(caf)** to have, to find.
ar gael in existence,
available; **cael annwyd** to
catch a cold; **cael blas ar** to
enjoy; **cael a chael** a close
call. *gw. At. Berfau*
caer *a.b. ll.* **-au, ceyrydd** fort,
castle

Caer *e.b.* Chester
Caerdydd *e.b.* Cardiff
Caeredin *e.b.* Edinburgh
Caerfyrddin *e.b.* Carmarthen
Caergybi *e.b.* Holyhead
Caerloyw *e.b.* Gloucester
Caersalem: Jerwsalem *e.b.*
 Jerusalem
caets *e.g. ll.* **-ys** cage
caf *bf.* I have, I shall have.
 gw. **cael**
cafodd *bf.* he/she/it had. *gw.*
 cael
caffe *e.g. ll.* **-s** café
cangen *e.b. ll.* **canghennau**
 branch
canghennau *gw.* **cangen**
caiff *bf.* he/she/it will have.
 gw. **cael**
cais *e.g. ll.* **ceisiadau, ceisiau**
 attempt; try *(rugby)*; request;
 application. **gwneud cais** to
 make an application, to
 apply
calan *e.g. ll.* **-nau** first day
 (of month or season). **Dydd**
 Calan New Year's Day;
 Calan Gaeaf All Saints' Day;
 Calan Mai May Day
caled *a.* hard, hardy,
 difficult. *gw. At.*
 Ansoddeiriau
caledi *e.g.* hardship, severity
caledu *be.* **(caledaf)** to
 harden; to dry. **caledu dillad**
 to air clothes; **caledu gwely**
 to air a bed
caledwch *e.g.* hardness;
 difficulty
calendr *e.g. ll.* **-au** calendar

calenigion *gw.* **calennig**
calennig *e.g. ll.* **calenigion**
 New Year's gift
caletach *gw.* **caled**
caletaf *gw.* **caled**
caleted *gw.* **caled**
calon *e.b. ll.* **-nau** heart.
 diolch o galon heartfelt
 thanks; **calon lân** pure heart;
 calon y gwir the absolute
 truth. **trawiad ar y galon**
 heart attack
call *a.* wise, sensible, **hanner**
 call a chrac foolish, stupid.
 gw. At. Ansoddeiriau
callach *gw.* **call**
callaf *gw.* **call**
called *gw.* **call**
cam **1** *e.g. ll.* **-au** stride, step;
 injury. **o gam i gam** step by
 step. **2** *a.* crooked, false.
 coesgam bandy-legged
camarwain *be.* **(camarweiniaf)**
 to mislead
camddeall *be.* **(camddeallaf)**
 to misunderstand
camera *e.g. ll.* **camerâu**
 camera
camp *e.b. ll.* **-au** feat, game;
 excellence. **campau** sports
campfa *e.b. ll.* **campfeydd**
 gymnasium
campfeydd *gw.* **campfa**
campus *a.* excellent, splendid
campwaith *e.g. ll.*
 campweithiau masterpiece
campweithiau *gw.* **campwaith**
camsyniad *e.g. ll.* **-au**
 mistake *(S.W.)*
camu *be.* **(camaf)** to step, to

stride; to bend, to stoop
cân *e.b.* *ll.* **caniadau,**
caneuon song, poem. **cân**
actol action song; **cân bop**
pop song; **cân serch** love
song; **cân werin** folksong;
cân ysgafn ballad
can 1 *a.* white; hundred.
canpunt a hundred pounds
(sterling); **canmlwydd** a
hundred years old; **canmil** a
hundred thousand; **canrif** a
century. *gw.* **cant.**
2 *e.g.* white flour, flour;
bara cân white bread. 3 *e.g.*
ll. **-iau** *(tin)* can
caneuon *gw.* **cân**
canfed *a.* hundredth
canhwyllau *gw.* **cannwyll**
canhwyllbren *e.g.* *ll.* **-nau, -ni**
candlestick
caniad *e.g.* *ll.* **-au** song,
singing; ring *(telephone)*.
Rhowch ganiad i fi
Telephone me
caniadaeth *e.b.* music,
singing. **Caniadaeth y Cysegr**
Songs of Praise
caniadau *gw.* **cân, caniad**
caniatâd *e.g.* permission,
consent
caniatáu *be.* **(caniatâf)** to
allow
caniedydd *e.g.* *ll.* **-ion** song-
book, hymn-book
canmlwydd *e.ll. & e.b.* *ll.* **-i** a
hundred years old, hundred
years; century
canmlwyddiannau *gw.*
canmlwyddiant

canmlwyddiant *e.g.* *ll.*
canmlwyddiannau centenary
canmol 1 *be.* **(canmolaf)** to
praise. 2 *e.g.* praise
canmoliaeth *e.b.* *ll.* **-au** praise
cannoedd *gw.* **cant**
cannu *be.* to bleach, to
whiten
cannwyll *e.b.* *ll.* **canhwyllau**
candle. **cannwyll y llygad**
pupil of the eye; apple of the
eye
canol 1 *e.g.* *ll.* **-au** centre,
middle. **canol dydd** midday;
canol nos midnight. 2 *a.*
middle. **canol y ffordd**
middle of the road
canolbarth *e.g.* *ll.* **-au**
midland; **Canolbarth Cymru**
Mid Wales; **Canolbarth**
Lloegr The Midlands;
Canolbarth Ffrainc Central
France
canolbwyntio (ar) *be.*
(canolbwyntiaf) to
concentrate, to focus (on)
canoldir *e.g.* *ll.* **-oedd** inland
region. **Y Môr Canoldir**
Mediterranean Sea
canolfan *e.b.* *ll.* **-nau** centre.
canolfan ddinesig civic
centre; **canolfan hamdden**
leisure centre
canolog *a.* central
canolwr *e.g.* *ll.* **canolwyr**
referee, umpire
canradd *a.* centigrade
canran *e.b.* *ll.* **canrannau**
percentage
canrif *e.b.* *ll.* **canrifau,**

canrifoedd century
canrifau: canrifoedd *gw*.
  canrif
cant: can *e.g*. *ll*. **cannoedd**
  hundred. **cant a mil** a
  hundred and one, a large
  number; **cant y cant**
  hundred per cent; **deg y cant**
  ten per cent; **can diolch**
  many thanks; **canwaith** a
  hundred times
cantor *e.g*. *ll*. **-ion** precentor.
  gw. **cantores; canwr**
cantores *e.b*. *ll*. **-au** female
  singer, female vocalist. *gw*.
  cantor; canwr
canu *be*. **(canaf)** to sing, to
  play. **canu cloch** to ring a
  bell; **canu'n iach** to bid
  goodbye; **canu'r piano** to
  play the piano; **wedi canu ar**
  too late, all up. *gw*. **At.**
  Berfau
canŵ *e.g*. *ll*. **-od** canoe
canŵio *be*. **(canŵiaf)** to canoe
canwr *e.g*. *ll*. **canwyr** male
  singer, vocalist. *gw*. **cantor;**
  cantores
canwriad *e.g*. *ll*. **canwriaid**
  centurion
cap *e.g*. *ll*. **-iau** cap
capel *e.g*. *ll*. **-i, -au** chapel
capteiniaid *gw*. **capten**
capten *e.g*. *ll*. **-iaid,**
  capteiniaid captain
capteiniaid *gw*. **capten**
car *e.g*. *ll*. **ceir** car. **car**
  heddlu police car; **car rasio**
  racing car; **car llusg** sled
carafan *e.b*. *ll*. **-au** caravan

carafana *be*. **(carafanaf)** to go
  caravanning
carco *be*. **(carcaf)** to take care
  of *(S.W.)*
carcus *a*. careful *(S.W.)*
carchar *e.g*. *ll*. **-au** prison
carcharor *e.g*. *ll*. **-ion**
  prisoner
carcharu *be*. **(carcharaf)** to
  imprison
cardiau *gw*. **cerdyn**
caredig *a*. kind
caredigrwydd *e.g*. kindness
cariad *e.g.b*. *ll*. **-on** love,
  lover. **Dere 'ma, cariad!**
  Come here, love!
cariadon *gw*. **cariad**
cariadus *a*. beloved; loving
cario *be*. **(cariaf)** to carry
carlamu *be*. **(carlamaf)** to
  gallop
carol *e.b*. *ll*. **-au** carol. **carol**
  Nadolig Christmas carol
carped *e.g*. *ll*. **-i** carpet
carreg *e.b*. *ll*. **cerrig** stone.
  carreg aelwyd hearthstone;
  carreg fedd tombstone;
  carreg filltir milestone;
  carreg y drws doorstep;
  cerrig mân pebbles,
  chippings
cartref *e.g*. *ll*. **-i** home. **gartref**
  at home; **adref** homewards
cartrefi *gw*. **cartref**
cartrefu *be*. **(cartrefaf)** to
  dwell
caru *be*. **(caraf)** to love, to
  like, to court
carwriaeth *e.b*. *ll*.
  carwriaethau affair, romance

cas *e.g.* enmity, hated
person or thing; case. **2** *a.*
nasty

casáu *be.* **(casâf)** to detest

casgen *e.b. ll.* **casgenni**
barrel

casgenni *gw.* **casgen**

casgliad *e.g. ll.* **-au**
collection; gathering;
conclusion. **Fe ddaeth i'r
casgliad** He came to the
conclusion

casglu *be.* **(casglaf)** to collect,
to infer. **casglu dros** to
collect on behalf of

Cas-gwent *e.b.* Chepstow

Casllwchwr *e.b.* Loughor

Casnewydd *e.b.* Newport
(Mon.)

castell *e.g. ll.* **cestyll** castle

Castell-nedd *e.b.* Neath

cath *e.b. ll.* **-od** cat. **cath fach**
kitten; **cwrcath, cwrcyn**
tomcat

cau 1 *be.* **(caeaf)** to close.
2 *a.* enclosed; hollow

cawl 1 *e.g.* soup, broth. **cawl
cennin** leek broth; **cawl pys**
pea soup. **2** *e.g.* mess. **Fe
wnaeth e gawl o'r trefniadau**
He made a mess of the
arrangements

cawod *e.b. ll.* **cawodydd**
shower. **cawodydd Ebrill**
April showers

cawr *e.g. ll.* **cewri** giant. **cawr
o wleidydd** a great politician

caws *e.g.* cheese. **caws Caer**
Cheshire cheese; **caws
Caerffili** Caerffili cheese;

cael caws o fola ci to get
blood out of a stone. *gw.*
cosyn

cefn *e.g. ll.* **-au** back; ridge;
support. **cefn gwlad** heart of
the countryside. **Roedd e'n
gefn i'r teulu** He was a great
help to the family

cefnder *e.g. ll.* **-wyr, cefndyr**
cousin *(male)*; *gw.* **cyfnither**

cefnderwyr *gw.* **cefnder**

cefndir *e.g. ll.* **-oedd**
background

cefndiroedd *gw.* **cefndir**

cefndyr *gw.* **cefnder**

cefnogi *be.* **(cefnogaf)** to
support

cefnu (ar) *be.* **(cefnaf)** to turn
one's back upon, to forsake

cefnwr *e.g. ll.* **cefnwyr** back,
full-back

ceffyl *e.g. ll.* **-au** horse. **ceffyl
blaen** leading horse, pushy
person; **ceffyl brith** piebald
horse; **ceffyl gwinau** bay
(horse); **ceffyl siglo** rocking
horse; **ar gefn ei geffyl** on
his high horse, exultant

ceg *e.b. ll.* **-au** mouth. **(cael,
rhoi) llond ceg** *(to receive, to
give)* a telling off

cegin *e.b. ll.* **-au** kitchen
cegin fach kitchenette; **cegin
gefn** back kitchen

cei *e.g. ll.* **ceiau** quay. *gw.*
cael

ceidwad *e.g. ll.* **ceidwaid**
keeper.

ceiliog *e.g. ll.* **-od** cockerel.
ceiliog y gwynt weathercock;

ceiliog y rhedyn grasshopper
Ceinewydd *e.b.* Newquay
ceiniog *e.b. ll.* **-au** penny.
 heb geiniog goch without a
 brass farthing or penny
ceir *gw.* **car**
ceiriosen *e.b. ll.* **ceirios**
 cherry
ceisiadau: ceisiau *gw.* **cais**
ceisio *be.* **(ceisiaf)** to seek, to
 ask. **ceisio am** to try for, to
 apply for
celf *e.b. ll.* **-au** art, craft;
 Adran Celf Art Department
celfi *gw.* **celficyn**
celficyn *e.g. ll.* **celfi** a piece
 of furniture; a tool
Celtaidd *a.* Celtic
celwydd *e.g. ll.* **-au** lie,
 untruth. **celwydd golau**
 white lie; **celwydd noeth**
 barefaced lie; **celwyddgi** a
 liar
celwyddog *a.* untruthful
celyn *gw.* **celynnen**
celynnen *e.b. ll.* **celyn** holly.
 llwyn celyn holly bush
cell *e.b. ll.* **-oedd, -au** cell
cellau: celloedd *gw.* **cell**
cemeg *e.b.* chemistry
cenadaethau *gw.* **cenhadaeth**
cenedl *e.b. ll.* **cenhedloedd**
 nation; species, kind; gender
 (grammar). **Cenedl y Cymry**
 the Welsh nation; **Y**
 Cenhedloedd the Gentiles;
 y Cenhedloedd Unedig the
 United Nations; **cenedl**
 enwau gender of nouns
cenedlaethau *gw.* **cenhedlaeth**

cenedlaethol *a.* national.
 Llyfrgell Genedlaethol Cymru
 National Library of Wales
cenedlaetholdeb *e.b.*
 nationalism
cenedlaetholwr *e.g. ll.*
 cenedlaetholwyr a
 nationalist
cenedlaetholwyr *gw.*
 cenedlaetholwr
cenedligrwydd *e.g.*
 nationality
cenfigennus *a.* jealous
cenhadaeth *e.b. ll.*
 cenadaethau mission;
 embassy
cenhadol *a.* missionary
cenhadon *gw.* **cenhadwr**
cenhadu *be.* **(cenhadaf)** to
 conduct a mission
cenhadwr *e.g. ll.* **cenhadon** a
 missionary; **cenhades** a
 female missionary
cenhedlaeth *e.b. ll.*
 cenedlaethau generation;
 nation
cenhedloedd *gw.* **cenedl**
cenhinen *e.b. ll.* **cennin** leek.
 cenhinen Bedr daffodil
cenllysg *e.torf.* hailstones
cennin *gw.* **cenhinen**
cer *bf.* go! *(singular).* *gw.*
 mynd
cerdyn *e.g. ll.* **cardiau** card.
 cerdyn Nadolig Christmas
 card; **cerdyn pen-blwydd**
 birthday card
cerdd *e.b. ll.* **-i** song, poem;
 music. **cerdd dafod** poetic
 art, poetry; music; **cerdd**

dant instrumental music;
penillion singing
cerdded *be.* **(cerddaf)** to walk
cerddi *gw.* **cerdd**
cerddor *e.g. ll.* **-ion** musician
cerddorfa *e.b. ll.*
cerddorfeydd orchestra.
Cerddorfa leuenctid Youth
Orchestra
cerddorfeydd *gw.* **cerddorfa**
cerddoriaeth *e.b.* music
cerddorol *a.* musical
cerddwr *e.g. ll.* **cerddwyr**
walker. **Cymdeithas
Cerddwyr Llanelli** Llanelli
Ramblers' Association
cerddwyr *gw.* **cerddwr**
cerfio *be.* **(cerfiaf)** to carve
cerflun *e.g. ll.* **-iau** statue
cerrig *gw.* **carreg**
cerwch *bf.* go! *(plural). gw.*
mynd
ces *bf.* I had. *gw.* **cael**
cesair *e. torf.* hailstones
(S.W.)
cestyll *gw.* **castell**
ceubren *e.g. ll.* **-nau** hollow
tree
cewri *gw.* **cawr**
cewyn *e.g. ll.* **-nau, -ion**
napkin *(S.W.)*
ceyrydd *gw.* **caer**
ci *e.g. ll.* **cŵn** dog. **ci bach**
pup, **ci defaid** sheepdog; **ci
hela** hound; **corgi** corgi;
milgi greyhound
cig *e.g. ll.* **-oedd** meat; gum.
cig eidion beef; **cig oen**
lamb; **cig moch** bacon
cigydd *e.g. ll.* **-ion** butcher

cigyddion *gw.* **cigydd**
cilio (i, rhag.) *be.* **(ciliaf)** to
flee; to retreat (to, from).
cilio i to flee towards; **cilio
rhag** to flee from, to retreat
from
ciniawau *gw.* **cinio**
cinio *e.g.b. ll.* **ciniawau**
dinner
cipolwg *e.g. ll.* **cipolygon**
glance
cist *e.b. ll.* **-iau** chest, coffer
claf 1 *e.g. ll.* **cleifion** sick
person. **ystafell y cleifion**
sick-room. **2** *a.* ill
clai *e.g. ll.* **cleiau, cleion** clay.
traed o glai mortal
clasur *e.g. ll.* **-on** a classic
clasurol *a.* classical
clawdd *e.g. ll.* **cloddiau** wall
made of earth, ditch. **Clawdd
Offa** Offa's Dyke
clawr *e.g. ll.* **cloriau** cover,
lid. **ar glawr** on record
clebran *be.* **(clebraf)** to
chatter
cledr *e.b. ll.* **-au** pole, rafter;
rail; palm *(of hand).* **cledrau**
rails *(of railway)*
clefyd *e.g. ll.* **-au, -on**
sickness. **clefyd melyn**
jaundice; **clefyd melys/siwgr**
diabetes
cleifion *gw.* **claf**
clêr *gw.* **cleren**
clerc *e.g. ll.* **-od** clerk
cleren *e.b. ll.* **clêr** fly *(S.W.).*
cleren lwyd horse-fly
clir *a.* clear
clirio *be.* **(cliriaf)** to clear

clo *e.g. ll.* **-eau, -eon** lock. **ar glo** locked; **dan glo** locked, locked up, under lock and key; **yng nghlo** locked; **twll y clo** keyhole

cloc *e.g. ll.* **-iau** clock. **cloc larwm** alarm-clock

clocwedd *a.* clockwise

cloch *be. ll.* **clychau** bell. **cloch y llan** chuch-bell; **clychau'r gog** bluebells; **dau o'r gloch** two o'clock

clod *e.g.b. ll.* **-ydd** praise

clodfori *be.* **(clodforaf)** to praise

cloddiau *gw.* **clawdd**

cloeau *gw.* **clo**

cloeon *gw.* **clo**

cloff *a.* lame

cloffi 1 *be.* **(cloffaf)** to become lame. **cloffi rhwng dau feddwl** to hesitate. **2** *e.g.* lameness

clogwyn *e.g. ll.* **-au, -i** cliff, crag

clogwyni: clogwynau *gw.* **clogwyn**

clogyn *e.g. ll.* **-au** cloak

cloi *be.* **(cloaf, clof)** to lock; to conclude. **cloi allan** to lock out, to exclude; **cload allan** lock-out; **Nawr i gloi** Now to conclude

clorian *e.b. ll.* **-nau** scales

cloriau *gw.* **clawr**

clown *e.g. ll.* **-iaid** clown

clun *e.b. ll.* **-iau** hip; thigh; leg

clust *e.b. ll.* **-iau** ear. **bonclust** box on the ear

clustog *e.b. ll.* **-au** pillow, cushion

clwm *e.g. ll.* **clymau** knot; tie. *gw.* **cwlwm**

clwtyn *e.g. ll.* **clytiau** rag *(S.W.)*. **clwtyn llawr** floor cloth; **clwtyn llestri** dish cloth; **clwtyn ymolch** face cloth. **ar y clwt** stranded, abandoned; without work

Clwyd *e.b.* Former county in N.E. Wales

clwyd *e.b. ll.* **-i, -au** gate

clwydi: clwydau *gw.* **clwyd**

clwyf *e.g. ll.* **-au** wound, injury. **clwyf y traed a'r genau** foot and mouth disease

clychau *gw.* **cloch**

clymau *gw.* **clwm, cwlwm**

clymu *be.* **(clymaf)** to tie

clytiau *gw.* **clwtyn**

clyw 1 *e.g.* hearing, earshot. **trwm ei glyw** hard of hearing; **yn fy nghlyw** within my hearing. **2** *bf.* hear! *(singular)*, listen! *(singular)*, *gw.* **clywed**

clywed (am, oddi wrth) *be.* **(clywaf)** to hear (of, from); to feel; to taste; to smell. **Clywch, clywch!** Hear, hear!

cnau *gw.* **cneuen**

cneuen *e.b. ll.* **cnau** nut

cnoc *e.g.b. ll.* **-au** a knock; a fool *(S.W.)*. **tipyn o gnoc:** quite a fool; **cnocell y coed** woodpecker

cnocio; cnoco *be.* **(cnociaf: cnocaf)** to knock, to strike

cnoi *be.* **(cnoaf)** to bite, to chew. **cnoi cil** to chew the cud; to mull over

coban *e.b. ll.* **cobannau** night-shirt

cobannau *gw.* **coban**

coch *a. ll.* **-ion** red. **yn goch** obscene; of poor quality; **coch y berllan** bullfinch. *gw. At. Ansoddeiriau*

cochach *gw.* **coch**

cochaf *gw.* **coch**

coched *gw.* **coch**

cochen *e.b.* red-haired female

cochyn *e.b.* red-haired male

codi *be.* **(codaf)** to rise, to erect, to pick up; to withdraw *(money)*, to charge (fee)

coed *gw.* **coeden**

Coed-duon Blackwood

coeden *e.b. ll.* **coed** tree

coedwig *e.b. ll.* **-oedd** forest, wood

coes *e.b. ll.* **-au** leg. **tynnu coes** to leg pull

cof *e.g. ll.* **-ion** memory; remembrance. **er cof am** in memory of; **o fewn cof** within living memory; **o'i gof** angry; mad; **ar gof a chadw** recorded and preserved, on record; **cofion cynnes** warmest regards

cofio (am) *be.* **(cofiaf)** to remember

cofion *gw.* **cof**

cofleidio *be.* **(cofleidiaf)** to embrace

cofrestr *e.b. ll.* **-au, -i** register

cofrestru *be.* **(cofrestraf)** to register

coffi *e.g.* coffee; **noson goffi** coffee evening

cog 1 *e.b. ll.* **-au** cuckoo. *gw.* **cwcw**. 2 *e.g. ll.* **-au** cook

coginio *be.* **(coginiaf)** to cook

cogydd *e.g. ll.* **-ion** cook

coleg *e.g. ll.* **-au** college

coler *e.g.b. ll.* **-au, -i** collar

colofn *e.b. ll.* **-au** column, pillar

coluro *be.* **(coluraf)** to colour, to make up

colled *e.g.b. ll.* **-ion** loss. **Roedd colled arni** She was angry

collen *e.b. ll.* **cyll** hazel. **cnau cyll** hazelnuts

colli *be.* **(collaf)** to lose, to spill, to fail, to miss. **ar goll** lost, missing, mislaid

copi *e.g. ll.* **copïau** a copy

copïo *be.* **(copïaf)** to copy

copyn *e.g. ll.* **-nau, -nod** spider. **pryf copyn** spider

côr *e.g. ll.* **corau** choir; pew (in church or chapel); stall, crib. **côr cymysg** mixed choir; **côr merched** ladies' choir

corau *gw.* **côr**

cordyn *e.g. ll.* **-ion** cord, string

corff *e.g. ll.* **cyrff** body; corpse; capital. **Yr Hen Gorff** Calvinistic Methodists

corfforol *a.* bodily, physical. **Addysg Gorfforol** physical

education
corgi *e.g. ll.* **corgwn** corgi
corn *e.g. ll.* **cyrn** horn; corn; cairn; chimney. **corn simdde** chimney stack; **Siôn Corn** Father Christmas
cornel *e.b.g. ll.* **-au, -i** corner
coron *e.b. ll.* **-au** crown
coroni *be.* **(coronaf)** to crown. **i goroni'r cwbl** to cap it all
corryn *e.g. ll.* **corynnod** spider *(S.W.)*
corynnod *gw.* **corryn**
cosb *e.b. ll.* **-au** punishment, penalty. **y gosb eithaf** capital punishment; **cic gosb** penalty kick
cosbi *be.* **(cosbaf)** to punish
cosi 1 *be.* **(cosaf)** to itch. 2 *e.g.* itch
costus *a.* expensive
cosyn *e.g. ll.* **-nau** a small cheese. *gw.* **caws**
cot: côt *e.b. ll.* **cotau: cotiau** coat. **cot fawr** overcoat; **cot law** raincoat
cotau: cotiau *gw.* **cot**
cotwm *e.g. ll.* **cotymau** cotton
crac 1 *e.g. ll.* **-au, -iau** crack. 2 *a.* angry *(S.W.)*
crachach *e.ll.* snobs *(S.W.)*
crafu 1 *be.* **(crafaf)** to scratch; to scrape. 2 *e.g.* itch
crafiad *e.g. ll.* **-au** scratch
cragen *e.b. ll.* **cregyn** shell
craig *e.b. ll.* **creigiau** rock, cliff. **Mae e'n graig o arian.** He's very wealthy

cras *a. ll.* **creision** baked; scorched; harsh. **llai cras** not so highly baked; **tafod cras** a harsh tongue; **llais cras** a raucous voice. *gw.* **creisionyn**
crasu *be.* **(crasaf)** to bake; to scorch
credu (yn) *be.* **(credaf)** to believe, to trust (in)
crefydd *e.b. ll.* **-au** religion
crefft *e.b. ll.* **-au** skill, craft
crefftwr *e.g. ll.* **crefftwyr** craftsman
crefftwyr *gw.* **crefftwr**
cregyn *gw.* **cragen**
creigiau *gw.* **craig**
creigiog *a.* rocky
creision *gw.* **cras, creisionyn**
creisionyn *e.g. ll.* **creision** crisp, flake. **creision ŷd** corn flakes
crempog *e.b. ll.* **-au** pancake *(N.W.)*. *gw.* **ffroesen**
creulon *a.* cruel
creulondeb *e.g. ll.* **-au** cruelty
cri *e.g.b. ll.* **-au** cry, lament. **cri'r wylan** gull's cry
crib *e.b. ll.* **-au** comb; bird's comb; crest, summit, ridge. **crib y ceiliog** the cock's comb; **crib y mynydd** the mountain's ridge; **mynd â chrib fân** to examine minutely
cribo *be.* **(cribaf)** to comb; to card
criced *e.g.* cricket (game)
cricedwr *e.g. ll.* **cricedwyr** cricketer

cricsyn *e.g. ll.* **criciaid, crics**
a cricket *(insect)*

crio (am, ar) *be.* **(criaf)** to
shout, to weep *(N.W.)*

Cristion *e.g. ll.* **Cristnogion**
Christian

criw *e.g. ll.* **-iau** crew, crowd.
criw o bobl ifainc a gang of
young people

croen *e.g. ll.* **crwyn** skin,
hide; peel. **croendenau** thin-
skinned; sensitive; **croendew**
thick-skinned; insensitive;
croenddu black-skinned;
negroid; **croen ei din ar ei
dalcen** in a bad mood

croes *e.b. ll.* **-au** cross. **croes
Crist** Christ's cross

croesair *e.g. ll.* **croeseiriau**
crossword; **pos croeseiriau**
crossword puzzle

croesau *gw.* **croes**

croesawu *be.* **(croesawaf)** to
welcome

croesawus *a.* hospitable

croeseiriau *gw.* **croesair**

croesfan *e.g. ll.* **-nau** crossing

croesffordd *e.b. ll.* **croesffyrdd**
crossroad

croeshoelio *be.* **(croeshoeliaf)**
to crucify

croesholi *be.* **(croesholaf)** to
cross-examine. **croesholiad** a
cross-examination

croesi *be.* **(croesaf)** to cross,
to oppose

croeso *e.g.* welcome. **y
Bwrdd Croeso** the Welsh
Tourist Board

Croesoswallt *e.b.* Oswestry

cron *a.b.* round. *gw.* **crwn**

cronfa *e.b. ll.* **cronfeydd**
reservoir; fund

cronfeydd *gw.* **cronfa**

crud *e.g. ll.* **-au, -iau** cradle

crwn *a.g.* round. *gw.* **cron**

crwst *e.g. ll.* **crystiau** crust.
gw. **crystyn**

crwyn *gw.* **croen**

cryd *e.g. ll.* **-iau** shivering,
fever. **Mae'r cryd arna i** I've
got the shivers; **cryd y
cymalau** rheumatism

cryf *a. ll.* **-ion** strong,
powerful. *gw. At.
Ansoddeiriau*

cryfach *gw.* **cryf**

cryfaf *gw.* **cryf**

cryfed *gw.* **cryf**

crynhoi *be.* **(crynhoaf)** to
collect, to gather, to
summarize. **i grynhoi** to sum
up

cryno *a.* tidy; suitable;
compact. **ffurfiau cryno'r ferf**
compact forms of the verb;
cryno ddisg compact disc

crynodeb *e.g.b. ll.* **-au** precis,
summary; tidiness

crynu *be.* **(crynaf)** to shiver,
to quake. **daeargryn**
earthquake

crys *e.g. ll.* **-au** shirt. **crys T**
T-shirt; **Y Crysau Cochion**
The Welsh rugby team

crystiau *gw.* **crwst, crystyn**

crystyn *e.g. ll.* **crystiau**,
crust. *gw.* **crwst**

cu *a.* dear, fond, beloved.
mam-gu grandmother

(S.W.). **tad-cu** grandfather *(S.W.)*

cuddio (rhag) *be.* **(cuddiaf)** to hide (from), to cover, to bury

cul *a.* *ll.* **-ion** narrow, narrow-minded. **culfor** *e.g.* strait, channel

curo *be.* **(curaf)** to strike, to knock, to defeat. **curo dwylo** to clap hands

cusan *e.g.b.* *ll.* **-au** kiss

cusanu *be.* **(cusanaf)** to kiss

cw *gw.* **acw**

cwb *e.g.* *ll.* **cybiau** kennel, coop

cwbl 1 *a.* all, complete, entire. **cwbl iach** completely healthy; **cwbl gyfan** quite complete; **cwbl sicr** completely certain. **2** *e.g.* *ll.* *(used with the definite article)* all, everything. **y cwbl** everything, all: **y cwbl oll** everything, the whole lot; **dim o gwbl** nothing at all; **dyna'r cwbl** that's all; **Prynodd e'r cwbl** He bought everything

cwblhau *be.* **(cwblhaf)** to finish, to complete

cwcw *e.b.* *ll.* **cwcŵod** cuckoo *(S.W.).* *gw.* **cog**

cwch *e.g.* *ll.* **cychod** boat; hive. **cwch hwylio** sailing boat; **cwch modur** motor boat; **cwch pysgota** fishing boat; **cwch rhwyfo** rowing boat; **cwch gwenyn** beehive

cwd *e.g.* *ll.* **cydau** bag; purse; sack

cwdyn *e.g.* *ll.* **cydau** bag; purse; sack

cweryl *e.g.* *ll.* **-au, -on** quarrel

cweryla (â) *be.* **(cwerylaf)** to quarrel (with)

cwerylau: cwerylon *gw.* **cweryl**

cwestiwn *e.g.* *ll.* **cwestiynau** question

cwestiyna *be.* **(cwestiynaf)** to question

cwestiynau *gw.* **cwestiwn**

cwlwm *e.g.* *ll.* **clymau** knot; bunch. *gw.* **clwm**

cwm *e.g.* *ll.* **cymoedd** valley. **Cwm Tawe** Swansea Valley

cwmni *e.g.* *ll.* **cwmnïau, cwmnïoedd** company. **cwmni yswiriant** insurance company

cwmnïau *gw.* **cwmni**

cwmnïoedd *gw.* **cwmni**

cwmwl *e.g.* *ll.* **cymylau** cloud

cŵn *gw.* **ci**

cwningen *e.b.* *ll.* **cwningod** rabbit

cwningod *gw.* **cwningen**

cwpan *e.g.b.* *ll.* **-au** cup

cwpla *be.* **(cwplâf)** to finish *(S.W.)*

cwpwrdd *e.g.* *ll.* **cypyrddau** cupboard. **cwpwrdd cornel** corner cupboard

cwr *e.g.* *ll.* **cyrrau, cyrion** corner, end; edge, border; outskirts. **ar gwr y dref** on the outskirts of the town

cwrdd 1 *e.g.* *ll.* **cyrddau**

meeting *(S.W.)*, religious
service, congregation. **cwrdd
gweddi** prayer-meeting;
cyrddau mawr special
preaching meetings; **tŷ cwrdd**
chapel *(nonconformist)*.
2 *be.* **(cwrddaf)** to meet, to
come together; to touch.
cwrdd â to meet, meeting
cwrs *e.g. ll.* **cyrsau, cyrsiau**
course
cwrtais *a.* courteous
cwrw *e.g. ll.* **-au** beer
cwsg 1 *e.g.* sleep; numbness.
2 *a.* asleep; numb. **ynghwsg**
asleep; lifeless, numb
cwsmer *e.g. ll.* **-iaid** customer
cwstwm *e.g. ll.* **cystymau**
custom, patronage
cwt *e.b.g. ll.* **cytiau** hut, sty;
wound; tail; queue. **cwt ieir**
chicken coop
cwta *a.* short, abrupt
cwymp *e.g. ll.* **-au, -iau** fall,
slope; collapse
cwympo *be.* **(cwympaf)** to
fall; to fell
cwyn *e.b.g. ll.* **-au, -ion**
complaint
cwyno (am, i) *be.* **(cwynaf)** to
complain (about, to)
cwyr *e.g. ll.* **-au** beeswax;
wax
cychod *gw.* cwch
cychwyn 1 *e.g.* beginning,
start. 2 *be.* **(cychwynnaf)**
to begin, to start. **ar y
cychwyn** at first, at the
start
cydadrodd *be.* **(cydadroddaf)**

to recite together. **parti
cydadrodd** choral speaking
party
cydau *gw.* cwd, cwdyn
cydio (yn) *be.* **(cydiaf)** to join,
to connect, to couple, to take
hold (of)
cydnabod 1 *be.* **(cydnabyddaf)**
to acknowledge; to honour,
to remunerate. 2 *e.g.*
acquaintance
cydwybodol *a.* conscientious
cydymdeimlad *e.g. ll.*
cydymdeimladau sympathy
cyfagos *a.* neighbouring
cyfaill *e.g. ll.* **cyfeillion**
friend, companion. **Annwyl
Gyfeillion** Dear Friends
(form of address). gw.
cyfeilles
cyfan *e.g. ll.* **-ion** all, total,
entirety. **y cyfan** all, the lot,
everything: **ar y cyfan** on the
whole; **wedi'r cyfan** after all
cyfangwbl *a.* altogether,
complete, whole. **yn
gyfangwbl** completely,
wholly; **Roedd e'n gyfangwbl
ddu** He was completely
black
cyfansoddi *be.* **(cyfansoddaf)**
to compose; to establish
cyfansoddwr *e.g. ll.*
cyfansoddwyr composer
cyfanswm *e.g. ll.* **cyfansymiau**
total, amount
cyfarch *be.* **(cyfarchaf)** to
greet
cyfarchion *e.ll.* greetings
cyfarfod 1 *e.g. ll.* **-ydd**

meeting. 2 *be.* **(cyfarfyddaf)**
to meet, to encounter.
cyfarfod â to meet
cyfarfodydd *gw.* **cyfarfod**
cyfarth *be.* **(cyfarthaf)** to bark
cyfarwyddiadur *e.g. ll.* **-on**
directory
cyfarwyddo (â) *be.*
(cyfarwyddaf) to familiarize,
to instruct
cyfarwyddwr *e.g. ll.*
cyfarwyddwyr director
cyfeilles *e.b. ll.* **-au** female
friend. *gw.* **cyfaill**
cyfeillgar *a.* friendly, sociable.
gw. At. Ansoddeiriau
cyfeillgarwch *e.g.* friendship
cyfeillion *gw.* **cyfaill**
cyfeiriad *e.g. ll.* **-au** direction,
reference, address
cyfeirio (at, i) *be.* **(cyfeiriaf)** to
direct, to refer
cyfenw *e.g. ll.* **-au** surname.
cyfenwau Evans, Huws, Jones
cyferbyn (â) *a.* opposite,
contrary. **cyferbyn â**
opposite
cyfiawn *a.* righteous, just
cyfiawnder *e.g. ll.* **-au**
righteousness, justice
cyfieithiad *e.g. ll.* **-au**
translation
cyfieithu *be.* **(cyfieithaf)** to
translate
cyfieithydd *e.g. ll.* **-ion**
translator, interpreter
cyfle *e.g. ll.* **-oedd**
opportunity, chance
cyfleu *be.* **(cyfleaf)** to convey,
to imply

cyfleus *a.* convenient,
expedient
cyflog *e.b. ll.* **-au** salary,
wages, hire
cyflogi *be.* **(cyflogaf)** to
employ, to hire
cyflogwr *e.g. ll.* **cyflogwyr**
employer
cyflwr *e.g. ll.* **cyflyrau** state,
condition, case
cyflwyno (i) *be.* **(cyflwynaf)**
present (to), to dedicate (to)
cyflym *a.* quick, swift, speedy.
gw. At. Ansoddeiriau
cyflymach *gw.* **cyflym**
cyflymaf *gw.* **cyflym**
cyflymder *e.g. ll.* **-au** speed,
velocity, swiftness
cyflymed *gw.* **cyflym**
cyflymu *be.* **(cyflymaf)** to
accelerate, to hasten
cyflymydd *e.g. ll.* **-ion**
accelerator
cyflyrau *gw.* **cyflwr**
cyfnither *e.b. ll.* **-oedd** female
cousin. *gw.* **cefnder**
cyfnod *e.g. ll.* **cyfnodau**
period
cyfoeth *e.g.* wealth, riches
cyfoethog *a.* rich, wealthy
cyfradd *e.b. ll.* **-au** rate.
cyfraddau llog interest rates
cyfraith *e.b. ll.* **cyfreithiau**
law
cyfrannu (i, at) *be.* **(cyfrannaf)**
to contribute; to impart
cyfreithiwr *e.g. ll.* **cyfreithwyr**
solicitor, lawyer
cyfreithwyr *gw.* **cyfreithiwr**
cyfres *e.b. ll.* **-au, -i** series,

suite *(musical)*. **drama gyfres**
a serial
cyfresau: cyfresi *gw.* **cyfres**
cyfrif 1 *be.* **(cyfrifaf)** to count,
to reckon. **2** *e.g.* account,
reckoning. **cyfrif trafod**
current account; **cyfrif cadw**
deposit account
cyfrifiadur *e.g. ll.* **-on**
computer
cyfrifiannell *e.g. ll.*
cyfrifianellau calculator
cyfrifol *a.* responsible;
calculable. **cyfrifol am**
responsible for
cyfrifoldeb *e.g. ll.* **-au**
responsibility
cyfrifydd *e.g. ll.* **-ion**
accountant
cyfrinach *e.b. ll.* **-au** secret,
mystery
cyfrinachol *a.* secret,
confidential, private
cyfrol *e.b. ll.* **-au** volume,
book
cyfrwng *e.g. ll.* **cyfryngau**
agent; agency; medium;
means. **trwy gyfrwng** through
the medium of; **y cyfryngau**
the media
cyfrwys *a.* cunning, crafty
cyfryngau *gw.* **cyfrwng**
cyfun *a.* agreeing,
comprehensive, united. **Ysgol
Gyfun Treforys** Morriston
Comprehensive School
cyfuwch *gw.* **uchel**
cyfweld (â) *be.* **(cyfwelaf)** to
interview
cyfweliad *e.g. ll.* **-au**

interview
cyfyng *a.* narrow, confined,
restricted. **Mae hi'n gyfyng
arni** She is in dire straits
cyfyngu (ar) *be.* **(cyfyngaf)** to
narrow, to confine, to restrict
cyfystyr 1 *e.g. ll.* **-on**
synonym. **2** *a* synonymous.
cyfystyr â synonymous
with
cyfforddus: cyffyrddus *a.*
comfortable *(S.W.)*
cyffredin *a.* common,
ordinary, vulgar. **enw
cyffredin** common noun;
pobl gyffredin ordinary
people
cyffrous *a.* exciting, moving
cyffur *e.g. ll.* **-iau** drug,
medicine
cyffwrdd (â) *be.* **(cyffyrddaf)** to
touch, to contact, to meet
cyngerdd *e.g.b. ll.*
cyngherddau concert
cyngherddau *gw.* **cyngerdd**
cynghori (i) *be.* **(cynghoraf)** to
advise, to counsel, to exhort
cynghorion *gw.* **cyngor**
cynghorwr *e.g. ll.* **cynghorwyr**
adviser, councillor
cynghrair *e.g. ll.* **cynghreiriau**
alliance, league
cynghreiriad *e.g. ll.*
cynghreiriaid ally
cynghreiriau *gw.* **cynghrair**
cyngor 1 *e.g. ll.* **cynghorion**
advice, counsel. **2** *e.g. ll.*
cynghorau council. **cyngor
cymuned** community
council; **cyngor dosbarth**

district council; **cyngor sir**
county council; **Cyngor y
Celfyddydau** the Arts
Council

cyhoedd 1 *a.* public. **2** *e.g.*
public. **ar gyhoedd, ar goedd**
publicly; **y cyhoedd** the
public

cyhoeddi *be.* **(cyhoeddaf)** to
announce, to proclaim; to
publish

cyhoeddiad *e.g. ll.* **-au**
publication; announcement;
engagement

cyhoeddus *a.* public. **neuadd
gyhoeddus** public hall;
cyfarfod cyhoeddus public
meeting

cyhoeddusrwydd *e.g.*
publicity

cyhoeddwr *e.g. ll.*
cyhoeddwyr publisher;
announcer

cyhuddiad *e.g. ll.* **-au**
accusation

cyhuddo *be.* **(cyhuddaf)** to
accuse

cyhyd *gw.* **hir**

cyhyrog *a.* muscular, strong

cylch *e.g. ll.* **-au, -oedd** circle,
hoop; class; region. **o gylch**
around

cylchfan *e.g. ll.* **-nau**
roundabout

cylchgrawn *e.g. ll.*
cylchgronau magazine,
periodical

cylchgronau *gw.* **cylchgrawn**

cylchlythyr *e.g. ll.* **-au, -on** a
circular

cyll *bf.* he/she/it loses. *gw.*
collen, colli

cyllell *e.b. ll.* **cyllyll** knife.
cyllell boced penknife; **cyllell
fara** bread knife

cyllyll *gw.* **cyllell**

cymaint *gw.* **mawr**

cymal *e.g. ll.* **-au** joint; clause,
phrase

cymanfa *e.b. ll.* **-oedd**
assembly, singing festival

cymanfaoedd *gw.* **cymanfa**

cymar *e.g. ll.* **cymheiriaid**
partner

cymdeithas *e.b. ll.* **-au**
society, association

cymdogion *gw.* **cymydog**

cymeriad *e.g. ll.* **-au** character

cymryd *be.* **(cymeraf)** to
accept, to take. **cymryd ar** to
pretend *(N.W.)*

cymharu (â) *be.* **(cymharaf)** to
compare

cymhleth *a.* complex,
involved

cymhlethdod *e.g. ll.* **-au**
complication, complexity

cymhlethu *be.* **(cymhlethaf)** to
complicate

cymhorthion *gw.* **cymorth**

cymoedd *gw.* **cwm**

cymorth *e.g. ll.* **cymhorthion**
aid, assistance. **cymorth
cyntaf** first aid

Cymraeg 1 *e.b.g.* Welsh
(language). **2** *a.* Welsh *(in
language).* **Y Gymraeg** the
Welsh language; **yn Gymraeg**
in Welsh; **Cymraeg da**
good *(spoken or written)*

Welsh
Cymraes; Cymreiges *e.b. ll.*
-au Welshwoman
Cymreictod *e.g.* Welsh
quality, Welshness
Cymreig *a.* Welsh, pertaining
to Wales or to the Welsh.
arferion Cymreig Welsh
traditions; **brethyn Cymreig**
Welsh woollen cloth
Cymreiges *gw.* **Cymraes**
Cymro *e.g. ll.* **Cymry**
Welshman. **Cymro i'r carn**
thorough Welshman; **Cymro
uniaith** monoglot Welshman;
Cymry alltud exiled Welsh;
Cymry Llundain London
Welsh
Cymru *e.b.* Wales. **Cymru a'r
Cymry** Wales and the Welsh,
Wales and her people
Cymry *gw.* **Cymro**
cymryd *gw.* **cymeryd**
cymundeb *e.g. ll.* **-au**
communion, fellowship
cymuned *e.b. ll.* **-au**
community
cymwynas *e.b. ll.* **-au** favour,
kindness. **talu'r gymwynas
olaf** to pay the last respects
(attendance at funeral)
cymydog *e.g. ll.* **cymdogion**
neighbour
cymylau *gw.* **cwmwl**
cymylog *a.* cloudy
cymysg *a.* mixed
cymysgu (â) *be.* **(cymysgaf)** to
mix, to confuse
cymysgwch 1 *e.g.* jumble,
medley, mixture. **2** *bf.* mix!

(plural). gw. **cymysgu**
cyn 1 *ardd.* before, previous
to. **Dewch cyn cinio** Come
before dinner. **2** *rhagdd.*
(followed by soft mutation)
first, former, ex-;
cyn-brifathro former
headteacher; **cyn-löwr**
former miner; **cyn-ŵr**
former husband; **cyn-
weinidog** former minister.
3 *c. & ad. (followed by soft
mutation)* as. **cyn dewed â
mochyn** as fat as a pig; **cyn
ddued â'r frân** as black as
the crow; **cyn goched â thân**
as red as fire; *gw. At.
Treigladau*
cynaeafau *gw.* **cynhaeaf**
cynddrwg *gw.* **drwg**
cynffon *e.b. ll.* **-nau** tail
(N.W.). **cynffonnau ŵyn bach**
hazel catkins. *gw.* **cwt**
cynhadledd *e.b. ll.*
cynadleddau conference
cynhaeaf *e.g. ll.* **cynaeafau**
harvest
cynhesu *be.* **(cynhesaf)** to
warm, to get warm
cynhwysion *gw.* **cynnwys**
cynhyrfus *a.* exciting, agitated
cynigion *gw.* **cynnig**
cynilion *e.ll.* savings
cynilo *be.* **(cynilaf)** to save, to
economize
cynllun *e.g. ll.* **-iau** plan,
design, scheme, project
cynllunio *be.* **(cynlluniaf)** to
plan, to design
cynlluniwr: cynllunydd *e.g. ll.*

cynllunwyr planner, designer, architect

cynnal *be.* **(cynhaliaf)** to support, to hold, to maintain. **gwaith cynnal a chadw** maintenance work

cynnar *a.* early, soon. *gw. At. Ansoddeiriau*

cynnes *a.* warm

cynnig 1 *be.* **(cynigiaf)** to attempt, to try, to propose. **rhoi cynnig ar** to attempt to. **2** *e.g. ll.* **cynigion** attempt; offer, proposal; motion, bid

cynnwys 1 *e.g. ll.* **cynhwysion.** content, contents. **2** *be.* **(cynhwysaf)** to contain, to include. **gan gynnwys** including

cynnyrch *e.g. ll.* **cynhyrchion** produce

cynorthwy-ydd *e.g. ll.* **cynorthwywyr** helper, assistant

cynorthwywr *e.g. ll.* **cynorthwywyr** helper, assistant

cynradd *a.* primary. **ysgol gynradd** primary school

cynrychioli *be.* to represent

cynt: gynt *ad.* formerly, previously. *née.* **Siân Owen, gynt Lewis** Siân Owen, *née* Lewis; **y flwyddyn gynt** the previous year. *gw.* **buan, cynnar**

cyntaf *a.* first, chief, earliest. *gw.* **cynnar**

cynted *gw.* **cynnar**

cyntedd *e.g. ll.* **cynteddau,**

cynteddoedd porch, court, lobby, hall

cynteddau: cynteddoedd *gw.* **cyntedd**

cynulleidfa *e.b. ll.* **-oedd** congregation

cynulliad *e.g. ll.* **-au** assembly

Cynulliad Cenedlaethol Cymru National Assembly for Wales

cynwysedig *a.* included

cypyrddau *gw.* **cwpwrdd**

cyrddau *gw.* **cwrdd**

cyrff *gw.* **corff**

cyrion *gw.* **cwr**

cyrliog *a.* curly

cyrn *gw.* **corn**

cyrraedd *be.* **(cyrhaeddaf)** to reach, to arrive, to attain. **Cyrhaeddodd y tŷ** He arrived at the house

cyrrau *gw.* **cwr**

cyrsau *gw.* **cwrs**

cyrsiau *gw.* **cwrs**

cysglyd *a.* sleepy

cysgod *e.g. ll.* **-ion, -au** shadow; shelter

cysgodau *gw.* **cysgod**

cysgodi (rhag) *be.* **(cysgodaf)** to shade; to shelter

cysgodion *gw.* **cysgod**

cysgu *be.* **(cysgaf)** to sleep

cystadlaethau *gw.* **cystadleuaeth**

cystadleuaeth *e.b. ll.* **cystadlaethau** competition

cystadleuwr: cystadleuydd *e.g. ll.* **cystadleuwyr** competitor

cystadleuwyr *gw.* **cystadleuwr**

cystadlu (â) *be.* **(cystadlaf)** to compete

cystal *a.* as well. **yn ogystal**
in addition. *gw.* **da**

cystymau *gw.* **cwstwm**

cysur *e.g. ll.* **-on** comfort,
consolation

cysuro *be.* **(cysuraf)** to
comfort, to console

cysurus *a.* comfortable

cyswllt *e.g. ll.* **cysylltau** joint,
junction, connection

cytgan *e.b. ll.* **-au** chorus

cytsain 1 *e.b. ll.* **cytseiniaid**
consonant.
2 *e.b. ll.* **cytseiniau** harmony

cytseiniaid *gw.* **cytsain**

cytseiniau *gw.* **cytsain**

cytundeb *e.g. ll.* **-au**
agreement, pact, contract

cytuno (â) *be.* **(cytunaf)** to
agree (with), consent (to)

cyw *e.g. ll.* **-ion** chick. **cyw iâr**
chicken *(N.W.)*; *gw.* **ffowlyn**

cywaith *e.g. ll.* **cyweithiau**
project; collective work

cyweithiau *gw.* **cywaith**

cywilydd *e.g.* shame

cywion *gw.* **cyw**

cywir *a.* correct, sincere, true,
honest

cywiriad *e.g. ll.* **-au**
correction

cywiro *be.* **(cywiraf)** to
correct, to amend, to verify

CH

'ch *rhag.* you, your. *gw.* At.
Rhagenwau Personol

chaban *gw.* **caban**

chacen *gw.* **cacen**

chacwn *gw.* **cacwn**

chacynen *gw.* **cacynen**

chadach *gw.* **cadach**

chadair *gw.* **cadair**

chadeirio *gw.* **cadeirio**

chadeiriol *gw.* **cadeiriol**

chadeirydd *gw.* **cadeirydd**

chadnawes *gw.* **cadno**

chadno *gw.* **cadno**

chadnoaid *gw.* **cadno**

chadw *gw.* **cadw**

chadwyn *gw.* **cadwyn**

chadwyno *gw.* **cadwyno**

chae *gw.* **cae**

chael *gw.* **cael**

chaer *gw.* **caer**

Chaerdydd *gw.* **Caerdydd**

Chaerfyrddin *gw.* **Caerfyrddin**

Chaergybi *gw.* **Caergybi**

chaets *gw.* **caets**

chaf *gw.* **caf**

chafodd *gw.* **cafodd**

chaffe *gw.* **caffe**

changen *gw.* **cangen**

changhennau *gw.* **cangen**

chaiff *gw.* **caiff**

chais *gw.* **cais**

chalan *gw.* **calan**

chaled *gw.* **caled**

chaledi *gw.* **caledi**

chaledu *gw.* **caledu**

chaledwch *gw.* **caledwch**

chalendr *gw.* **calendr**

chalenigion *gw.* **calennig**

chalennig *gw.* **calennig**

chaletach *gw.* **caled**

chaletaf *gw.* **caled**

chaleted *gw.* **caled**

chalon *gw.* **calon**

chall *gw.* call
challach *gw.* call
challaf *gw.* call
challed *gw.* call
cham *gw.* cam
chamarwain *gw.* camarwain
chamddeall *gw.* camddeall
chamera *gw.* camera
champ *gw.* camp
champfa *gw.* campfa
champfeydd *gw.* campfa
champus *gw.* campus
champwaith *gw.* campwaith
chamsyniad *gw.* camsyniad
chamu *gw.* camu
chân *gw.* cân
chan *gw.* can, gan
chaneuon *gw.* cân
chanfed *gw.* canfed
chanhwyllau *gw.* cannwyll
chanhwyllbren *gw.*
 canhwyllbren
chaniad *gw.* caniad
chaniadaeth *gw.* caniadaeth
chaniadau *gw.* cân, caniad
chaniatâd *gw.* caniatâd
chaniatáu *gw.* caniatáu
chaniedydd *gw.* caniedydd
chanmlwydd *gw.* canmlwydd
chanmlwyddiannau *gw.*
 canmlwydd
chanmol *gw.* canmol
chanmoliaeth *gw.* canmoliaeth
channoedd *gw.* cant
channwyll *gw.* cannwyll
chanol *gw.* canol
chanolbarth *gw.* canolbarth
chanolbwyntio *gw.*
 canolbwyntio
chanoldir *gw.* canoldir

chanolfan *gw.* canolfan
chanolog *gw.* canolog
chanolwr *gw.* canolwr
chanradd *gws.* canradd
chanran *gw.* canran
chanrif *gw.* canrif
chanrifau: chanrifoedd *gw.*
 canrif
chant *gw.* cant
chantor *gw.* cantor
chantores *gw.* cantores
chanu *gw.* canu
chanŵ *gw.* canŵ
chanŵio *gw.* canŵio
chanwr *gw.* canwr
chap *gw.* cap
chapel *gw.* capel
chapteiniaid *gw.* capten
chapten *gw.* capten
chapteniaid *gw.* capten
char *gw.* car
charafán *gw.* carafán
charafana *gw.* carafana
charco *gw.* carco
charcus *gw.* carcus
charchar *gw.* carchar
charcharor *gw.* carcharor
charcharu *gw.* carcharu
chardiau *gw.* cerdyn
charedig *gw.* caredig
charedigrwydd *gw.*
 caredigrwydd
chariad *gw.* cariad
chariadon *gw.* cariad
chariadus *gw.* cariadus
chario *gw.* cario
charlamu *gw.* carlamu
charol *gw.* carol
charped *gw.* carped
charreg *gw.* carreg

chartref *gw.* cartref
chartrefi *gw.* cartref
chartrefu *gw.* cartrefu
charu *gw.* caru
charwriaeth *gw.* carwriaeth
chas *gw.* cas
chasáu *gw.* casáu
chasgen *gw.* casgen
chasgenni *gw.* casgen
chasgliad *gw.* casgliad
chasglu *gw.* casglu
Chas-gwent *gw.* Cas-gwent
Chasllwchwr *gw.* Casllwchwr
Chasnewydd *gw.* Casnewydd
chastell *gw.* castell
Chastell-nedd *gw.* Castell-
  nedd
chath *gw.* cath
chau *gw.* cau
chawl *gw.* cawl
chawod *gw.* cawod
chawr *gw.* cawr
chaws *gw.* caws
chefn *gw.* cefn
chefnder *gw.* cefnder
chefndir *gw.* cefndir
chefndiroedd *gw.* cefndir
chefndyr *gw.* cefnder
chefnogi *gw.* cefnogi
chefnu *gw.* cefnu
chefnwr *gw.* cefnwr
chefnwyr *gw.* cefnwr
cheffyl *gw.* ceffyl
cheg *gw.* ceg
chegin *gw.* cegin
chei *gw.* cael, cei
cheidwad *gw.* ceidwad
cheiliog *gw.* ceiliog
Cheinewydd *gw.* Ceinewydd
cheiniog *gw.* ceiniog

cheiriosen *gw.* ceiriosen
cheisio *gw.* ceisio
chelf *gw.* celf
chelfi *gw.* celficyn
chelficyn *gw.* celficyn
Cheltaidd *gw.* Celtaidd
chelwydd *gw.* celwydd
chelwyddog *gw.* celwyddog
chelyn *gw.* celynnen
chelynnen *gw.* celynnen
chell *gw.* cell
chellau: chelloedd *gw.* cell
chemeg *gw.* cemeg
chenadaethau *gw.* cenhadaeth
chenedl *gw.* cenedl
chenedlaethau *gw.*
  cenhedlaeth
chenedlaethol *gw.*
  cenedlaethol
chenedlaetholdeb *gw.*
  cenedlaetholdeb
chenedlaetholwr *gw.*
  cenedlaetholwr
chenedlaetholwyr *gw.*
  cenedlaetholwr
chenfigennus *gw.* cenfigennus
chenhadaeth *gw.* cenhadaeth
chenhadol *gw.* cenhadol
chenhadon *gw.* cenhadwr
chenhadu *gw.* cenhadu
chenhadwr *gw.* cenhadwr
chenhedlaeth *gw.* cenhedlaeth
chenhedloedd *gw.* cenedl
chenhinen *gw.* cenhinen
chennin *gw.* cenhinen
cher *gw.* mynd
cherdyn *gw.* cerdyn
cherdd *gw.* cerdd
cherdded *gw.* cerdded
cherddor *gw.* cerddor

cherddorfa *gw*. cerddorfa
cherddorfeydd *gw*. cerddorfa
cherddoriaeth *gw*.
 cerddoriaeth
cherddorol *gw*. cerddorol
cherddwr *gw*. cerddwr
cherddwyr *gw*. cerddwr
cherflun *gw*. cerflun
cherrig *gw*. carreg
cherwch *gw*. mynd
ches *gw*. ces
chesair *gw*. cesair
chestyll *gw*. castell
chewri *gw*. cawr
chewyn *gw*. cewyn
cheyrydd *gw*. caer
chi: chwi *rhag*. you. *gw*. ci
chig *gw*. cig
chigydd *gw*. cigydd
chigyddion *gw*. cigydd
chilio *gw*. cilio
chiniawau *gw*. cinio
chinio *gw*. cinio
chipolwg *gw*. cipolwg
chist *gw*. cist
chithau: chwithau *rhag*. you
 also
chlaf *gw*. claf
chlai *gw*. clai
chlasur *gw*. clasur
chlasurol *gw*. clasurol
chlawdd *gw*. clawdd
chlawr *gw*. clawr
chlebran *gw*. clebran
chledr *gw*. cledr
chlefyd *gw*. clefyd
chleifion *gw*. claf
chlêr *gw*. cleren
chlerc *gw*. clerc
chleren *gw*. cleren

chlir *gw*. clir
chlirio *gw*. clirio
chlo *gw*. clo, cloi
chloc *gw*. cloc
chloch *gw*. cloch
chlod *gw*. clod
chlodfori *gw*. clodfori
chloff *gw*. cloff
chloffi *gw*. cloffi
chlogwyn *gw*. clogwyn
chlogyn *gw*. clogyn
chloi *gw*. cloi
chlorian *gw*. clorian
chloriau *gw*. clawr
chlown *gw*. clown
chlun *gw*. clun
chlust *gw*. clust
chlustog *gw*. clustog
chlwm *gw*. clwm
chlwtyn *gw*. clwtyn
Chlwyd *gw*. Clwyd
chlwyd *gw*. clwyd
chlwydau: chlwydi *gw*. clwyd
chlwyf *gw*. clwyf
chlychau *gw*. cloch
chlymau *gw*. clwm
chlymu *gw*. clymu
chlytiau *gw*. clwtyn
chlyw *gw*. clyw
chlywed *gw*. clywed
chnau *gw*. cneuen
chneuen *gw*. cneuen
chnoc *gw*. cnoc
chnocio *gw*. cnocio
chnoi *gw*. cnoi
choban *gw*. coban
chobannau *gw*. coban
choch *gw*. coch
chochach *gw*. coch
chochaf *gw*. coch

choched *gw.* coch
chodi *gw.* codi
Choed-duon *gw.* Coed-duon
choeden *gw.* coeden
choedwig *gw.* coedwig
choes *gw.* coes
chof *gw.* cof
chofio *gw.* cofio
chofion *gw.* cof
chofleidio *gw.* cofleidio
chofrestr *gw.* cofrestr
chofrestru *gw.* cofrestru
choffi *gw.* coffi
chog *gw.* cog
choginio *gw.* coginio
chogydd *gw.* cogydd
choleg *gw.* coleg
choler *gw.* coler
cholofn *gw.* colofn
choluro *gw.* coluro
cholled *gw.* colled
chollen *gw.* collen
cholli *gw.* colli
chopïo *gw.* copïo
chopyn *gw.* copyn
chôr *gw.* côr
chorau *gw.* côr
chordyn *gw.* cordyn
chorff *gw.* corff
chorfforol *gw.* corfforol
chorgi *gw.* corgi
chorn *gw.* corn
chornel *gw.* cornel
choron *gw.* coron
choroni *gw.* coroni
chorryn *gw.* corryn
chorynnod *gw.* corryn
chosb *gw.* cosb
chosbi *gw.* cosbi
chostus *gw.* costus

chot *gw.* cot
chotau: chotiau *gw.* cot
chotwm *gw.* cotwm
chrac *gw.* crac
chrachach *gw.* crachach
chrafu *gw.* crafu
chragen *gw.* cragen
chraig *gw.* craig
chras *gw.* cras
chrasu *gw.* crasu
chredu *gw.* credu
chrefydd *gw.* crefydd
chrefft *gw.* crefft
chrefftwr *gw.* crefftwr
chrefftwyr *gw.* crefftwyr
chregyn *gw.* cragen
chreigiau *gw.* craig
chreigiog *gw.* creigiog
chreision *gw.* creisionyn
chrempog *gw.* crempog
chreulon *gw.* creulon
chreulondeb *gw.* creulondeb
chri *gw.* cri
chrib *gw.* crib
chribo *gw.* cribo
chriced *gw.* criced
chricedwr *gw.* cricedwr
chrio *gw.* crio
Christion *gw.* Cristion
Christnogion *gw.* Cristion
chriw *gw.* criw
chroen *gw.* croen
chroes *gw.* croes
chroesair *gw.* croesair
chroesau *gw.* croes
chroesawu *gw.* croesawu
chroesawus *gw.* croesawus
chroeseiriau *gw.* croesair
chroesfan *gw.* croesfan
chroesffordd *gw.* croesffordd

chroesholi *gw.* **croesholi**
chroesi *gw.* **croesi**
chroeso *gw.* **croeso**
chron *gw.* **cron**
chronfa *gw.* **cronfa**
chronfeydd *gw.* **cronfa**
chrud *gw.* **crud**
chrwn *gw.* **crwn**
chrwst *gw.* **crwst**
chryd *gw.* **cryd**
chryf *gw.* **cryf**
chryfach *gw.* **cryf**
chryfaf *gw.* **cryf**
chryfed *gw.* **cryf**
chrynhoi *gw.* **crynhoi**
chryno *gw.* **cryno**
chrynodeb *gw.* **crynodeb**
chrynu *gw.* **crynu**
chrys *gw.* **crys**
chrystiau *gw.* **crwst, crystyn**
chrystyn *gw.* **crystyn**
chu *gw.* **cu**
chuddio *gw.* **cuddio**
chul *gw.* **cul**
churo *gw.* **curo**
chusan *gw.* **cusan**
chusanu *gw.* **cusanu**
chwaer *e.b.* *ll.* **chwiorydd**
sister, maiden
chwain *gw.* **chwannen**
chwaith: ychwaith *ad.* neither,
nor . . . either, not . . . either
chwalu *be.* **(chwalaf)** to
crumble; to scatter, to
disperse. **chwalu cartref** to
break up a home; **chwalwr**
disperser, scatterer
chwaneg: ychwaneg *a. & e.g.*
more, additional
chwanegu *gw.* **ychwanegu**

chwannen *e.b.* *ll.* **chwain** flea
chwant *e.g.* *ll.* **-au** desire,
appetite; lust. **Mae chwant
bwyd arnaf i** I desire food;
Does dim chwant mynd arni
She doesn't feel like going
chwap *a. & ad.* at once,
instantly
chwarae: 1 *be.* **(chwaraeaf)** to
play, to perform. **2** *e.g.* *ll.*
-on game, sport; play. **amser
chwarae** playtime; **chwarae
teg** fair play; **meysydd
chwarae** playing fields
chwaraewr *e.g.* *ll.* **chwaraewyr**
player, actor
chwaraewyr *gw.* **chwaraewr**
chwarddaf *g.w.* **chwerthin**
chwarel 1 *e.b.g.* *ll* **-i, -au**
quarry. **2** *e.g.b.* *ll.* **-au, -i**
pane of glass
chwarelau: chwareli *gw.*
chwarel
chwarelwr *e.g.* quarryman
chwareus *a.* playful
chwarter *e.g.* *ll.* **-au, -i** quarter
chwb *gw.* **cwb**
chwbl *gw.* **cwbl**
chwcw *gw.* **cwcw**
chwch *gw.* **cwch**
chwd *gw.* **cwd**
chwdyn *gw.* **cwdyn**
chwe: chwech *a.* six. **chwe**
*before singular nouns
(followed by spirant
mutation);* **chwe bachgen,
chwe llyfr; chwech** *on its
own or with* **o** + *plural noun*
**chwech o dai, chwech o
blant; chwe deg** sixty

chweched *a.* sixth

chwedl *e.b. ll.* **-au, -euon** story, legend, fable; report, rumour; saying

chwedlau: chwedleuon *gw.* **chwedl**

Chwefror *e.g.* February

chwerthin 1 *be.* **(chwarddaf)** to laugh, to smile. **chwerthin am ei ben** to laugh at him. 2 *e.g.* laughter

chwerthinllyd *a.* laughable

chwerw *a.* bitter; severe, sharp, spiteful

chweryl *gw.* **cweryl**

chweryla *gw.* **cweryla**

chwerylau: chwerylon *gw.* **cweryl**

chwestiwn *gw.* **cwestiwn**

chwestiyna *gw.* **cwestiyna**

chwestiynau *gw.* **cwestiwn**

chwi *gw.* **chi**

chwiban *e.g. ll.* **-au** a whistling, whistle

chwiban: chwibanu (ar) *be.* **(chwibanaf)** to whistle

chwifio (at) *be.* **(chwifiaf)** to wave

chwilen *e.b. ll.* **chwilod** beetle. **Mae chwilen yn ei ben** He has a bee in his bonnet

chwilio (am) *be.* **(chwiliaf)** to search (for), to examine

chwiliwr *e.g. ll.* **chwilwyr** investigator, searcher

chwilod *gw.* **chwilen**

chwilota *be.* **(chwilotaf)** to rummage, to pry

chwilwyr *gw.* **chwiliwr**

chwilotwr *e.g. ll.* **chwilotwyr** rummager, one engaged in research

chwiorydd *gw.* **chwaer**

chwip 1 *e.b.g. ll.* **-au, -iau** whip. 2 *a.* swift, quick. 3 *ad.* instantly

chwipio *be.* **(chwipiaf)** to whip

chwistrelliad *e.g. ll.* **-au** injection

chwith *a.* left; strange; sad. **o chwith** the wrong way about, awkwardly; **tu chwith** inside out; **llaw chwith** left-handed

chwithau *gw.* **chithau**

chwithig *a.* strange; awkward

chwlwm *gw.* **cwlwm**

chwm *gw.* **cwm**

chwmni *gw.* **cwmni**

chwmnïau *gw.* **cwmni**

chwmnïoedd *gw.* **cwmni**

chwmwl *gw.* **cwmwl**

chwn *gw.* **ci**

chwningen *gw.* **cwningen**

chwningod *gw.* **cwningen**

chwpan *gw.* **cwpan**

chwpla *gw.* **cwpla**

chwpwrdd *gw.* **cwpwrdd**

chwr *gw.* **cwr**

chwrdd *gw.* **cwrdd**

chwrs *gw.* **cwrs**

chwrtais *gw.* **cwrtais**

chwrw *gw.* **cwrw**

chwsg *gw.* **cwsg**

chwsmer *gw.* **cwsmer**

chwstwm *gw.* **cwstwm**

chwt *gw.* **cwt**

chwta *gw.* **cwta**

chwydu *be.* **(chwydaf)** to vomit

chwyddiant *e.g. ll.*
 chwyddiannau inflation;
 inflammation
chwyddo *be.* (chwyddaf) to
 swell, to increase
chwyddwydr *e.g. ll.* -au
 magnifying glass
chwyldro: chwyldroad *e.g. ll.*
 chwyldroadau revolution.
 y Chwyldro Diwydiannol the
 Industrial Revolution; y
 Chwyldro Ffrengig the
 French Revolution
chwymp *gw.* cwymp
chwympo *gw.* cwympo
chwyn *e. torf.* weeds. *gw.*
 cwyn; *gw.* chwynnyn
chwynladdwr *e.g.* weedkiller
chwynnyn *e.g. ll. & e.torf.*
 chwyn weed
chwynnu *be.* (chwynnaf) to
 weed
chwyno *gw.* cwyno
chwyro *gw.* cwyro
chwyrnu *be.* (chwyrnaf) to
 snore, to snarl; to whirl
chwys *e.g.* perspiration,
 sweat. yn chwys domen
 dripping with perspiration
chwysu *be.* (chwysaf) to
 perspire, to sweat
chwythu *be.* (chwythaf) to
 blow
chychod *gw.* cwch
chychwyn *gw.* cychwyn
chydadrodd *gw.* cydadrodd
chydau *gw.* cwd; cwdyn
chydio *gw.* cydio
chydnabod *gw.* cydnabod
chydwybodol *gw.* cydwybodol

chydymdeimlad *gw.*
 cydymdeimlad
chyfagos *gw.* cyfagos
chyfaill *gw.* cyfaill
chyfan *gw.* cyfan
chyfangwbl *gw.* cyfangwbl
chyfansoddi *gw.* cyfansoddi
chyfansoddwr *gw.*
 cyfansoddwr
chyfanswm *gw.* cyfanswm
chyfarch *gw.* cyfarch
chyfarfod *gw.* cyfarfod
chyfarfodydd *gw.* cyfarfod
chyfarwyddiadur *gw.*
 cyfarwyddiadur
chyfarwyddo *gw.* cyfarwyddo
chyfarwyddwr *gw.*
 cyfarwyddwr
chyfeilles *gw.* cyfeilles
chyfeillgar *gw.* cyfeillgar
chyfeillgarwch *gw.*
 cyfeillgarwch
chyfeiriad *gw.* cyfeiriad
chyfeirio *gw.* cyfeirio
chyfenw *gw.* cyfenw
chyferbyn *gw.* cyferbyn
chyfiawn *gw.* cyfiawn
chyfiawnder *gw.* cyfiawnder
chyfieithiad *gw.* cyfieithiad
chyfieithu *gw.* cyfieithu
chyfieithydd *gw.* cyfieithydd
chyfle *gw.* cyfle
chyfleu *gw.* cyfleu
chyfleus *gw.* cyfleus
chyflog *gw.* cyflog
chyflogi *gw.* cyflogi
chyflogwr *gw.* cyflogwr
chyflwr *gw.* cyflwr
chyflwyno *gw.* cyflwyno
chyflym *gw.* cyflym

chyflymach *gw*. cyflym
chyflymaf *gw*. cyflym
chyflymder *gw*. cyflymder
chyflymed *gw*. cyflym
chyflymu *gw*. cyflymu
chyflymydd *gw*. cyflymydd
chyflyrau *gw*. cyflwr
chyfnither *gw*. cyfnither
chyfnod *gw*. cyfnod
chyfoeth *gw*. cyfoeth
chyfoethog *gw*. cyfoethog
chyfraith *gw*. cyfraith
chyfrannu *gw*. cyfrannu
chyfreithiwr *gw*. cyfreithiwr
chyfreithwyr *gw*. cyfreithiwr
chyfres *gw*. cyfres
chyfresau: chyfresi *gw*. cyfres
chyfrif *gw*. cyfrif
chyfrifiadur *gw*. cyfrifiadur
chyfrifiannell *gw*. cyfrifiannell
chyfrifol *gw*. cyfrifol
chyfrifoldeb *gw*. cyfrifoldeb
chyfrifydd *gw*. cyfrifydd
chyfrinach *gw*. cyfrinach
chyfrinachol *gw*. cyfrinachol
chyfrol *gw*. cyfrol
chyfrwng *gw*. cyfrwng
chyfrwys *gw*. cyfrwys
chyfryngau *gw*. cyfrwng
chyfun *gw*. cyfun
chyfuwch *gw*. uchel
chyfweld *gw*. cyfweld
chyfweliad *gw*. cyfweliad
chyfyng *gw*. cyfyng
chyfyngu *gw*. cyfyngu
chyfystyr *gw*. cyfystyr
chyfforddus *gw*. cyfforddus
chyffredin *gw*. cyffredin
chyffrous *gw*. cyffrous
chyffur *gw*. cyffur
chyffwrdd *gw*. cyffwrdd
chyffyrddus *gw*. cyffyrddus
chyngerdd *gw*. cyngerdd
chyngherddau *gw*. cyngerdd
chynghori *gw*. cynghori
chynghorion *gw*. cyngor
chynghorwr *gw*. cynghorwr
chynghrair *gw*. cynghrair
chynghreiriad *gw*.
  cynghreiriad
chyngor *gw*. cyngor
chyhoedd *gw*. cyhoedd
chyhoeddi *gw*. cyhoeddi
chyhoeddiad *gw*. cyhoeddiad
chyhoeddus *gw*. cyhoeddus
chyhoeddusrwydd *gw*.
  cyhoeddusrwydd
chyhoeddwr *gw*. cyhoeddwr
chyhuddiad *gw*. cyhuddiad
chyhuddo *gw*. cyhuddo
chyhyd *gw*. cyhyd
chyhyrog *gw*. cyhyrog
chylch *gw*. cylch
chylchfan *gw*. cylchfan
chylchgrawn *gw*. cylchgrawn
chylchgronau *gw*. cylchgrawn
chylchlythyr *gw*. cylchlythyr
chyll *gw*. collen; colli
chyllell *gw*. cyllell
chyllyll *gw*. cyllell
chymaint *gw*. cymaint
chymal *gw*. cymal
chymanfa *gw*. cymanfa
chymanfaoedd *gw*. cymanfa
chymar *gw*. cymar
chymdeithas *gw*. cymdeithas
chymdogion *gw*. cymydog
chymeriad *gw*. cymeriad
chymeryd *gw*. cymryd
chymharu *gw*. cymharu

chymhleth

chymhleth *gw.* cymhleth
chymhlethdod *gw.*
 cymhlethdod
chymhlethu *gw.* cymhlethu
chymhorthion *gw.* cymorth
chymoedd *gw.* cwm
chymorth *gw.* cymorth
Chymraeg *gw.* Cymraeg
Chymraes *gw.* Cymraes
Chymreictod *gw.* Cymreictod
Chymreig *gw.* Cymreig
Chymreiges *gw.* Cymreiges
Chymro *gw.* Cymro
Chymru *gw.* Cymru
Chymry *gw.* Cymro
chymryd *gw.* cymryd
chymundeb *gw.* cymundeb
chymuned *gw.* cymuned
chymwynas *gw.* cymwynas
chymydog *gw.* cymydog
chymylau *gw.* cwmwl
chymylog *gw.* cymylog
chymysg *gw.* cymysg
chymysgu *gw.* cymysgu
chymysgwch *gw.* cymysgwch
chyn *gw.* cyn
chynaeafau *gw.* cynhaeaf
chynddrwg *gw.* cynddrwg
chynffon *gw.* cynffon
chynhadledd *gw.* cynhadledd
chynhaeaf *gw.* cynhaeaf
chynhesu *gw.* cynhesu
chynhyrfus *gw.* cynhyrfus
chynigion *gw.* cynnig
chynilion *gw.* cynilion
chynilo *gw.* cynilo
chynllun *gw.* cynllun
chynllunio *gw.* cynllunio
chynlluniwr *gw.* cynlluniwr
chynllunydd *gw.* cynlluniwr

chynnal *gw.* cynnal
chynnar *gw.* cynnar
chynnes *gw.* cynnes
chynnig *gw.* cynnig
chynnwys *gw.* cynnwys
chynnyrch *gw.* cynnyrch
chynorthwywr *gw.*
 cynorthwywr
chynorthwy-ydd *gw.*
 cynorthwy-ydd
chynradd *gw.* cynradd
chynt *gw.* cynnar
chyntaf *gw.* cyntaf, cynnar
chynted *gw.* cynnar
chyntedd *gw.* cyntedd
chynteddau *gw.* cyntedd
chynteddoedd *gw.* cyntedd
chynulleidfa *gw.* cynulleidfa
chynwysiedig *gw.*
 cynwysiedig
chypyrddau *gw.* cwpwrdd
chyrddau *gw.* cwrdd
chyrff *gw.* corff
chyrion *gw.* cwr
chyrliog *gw.* cyrliog
chyrn *gw.* corn
chyrraedd *gw.* cyrraedd
chyrrau *gw.* cwr
chyrsau *gw.* cwrs
chyrsiau *gw.* cwrs
chysglyd *gw.* cysglyd
chysgod *gw.* cysgod
chysgodau *gw.* cysgod
chysgodi *gw.* cysgodi
chysgodion *gw.* cysgod
chysgu *gw.* cysgu
chystadlaethau *gw.*
 cystadleuaeth
chystadleuaeth *gw.*
 cystadleuaeth

chystadleuwr *gw*. cystadleuwr
chystadleuwyr *gw*.
  cystadleuwr
chystadleuydd *gw*.
  cystadleuwr
chystadlu *gw*. cystadlu
chystal *gw*. cystal
chystymau *gw*. cwstwm
chysur *gw*. cysur
chysuro *gw*. cysuro
chysurus *gw*. cysurus
chyswllt *gw*. cyswllt
chytgan *gw*. cytgan
chytsain *gw*. cytsain
chytseiniaid *gw*. cytsain
chytseiniau *gw*. cytsain
chytundeb *gw*. cytundeb
chytuno *gw*. cytuno
chyw *gw*. cyw
chywaith *gw*. cywaith
chyweithiau *gw*. cywaith
chywilydd *gw*. cywilydd
chywion *gw*. cyw
chywir *gw*. cywir
chywiriad *gw*. cywiriad
chywiro *gw*. cywiro

D

da 1 *a.* good, well. **bore da**
good morning; **da iawn** very
good, very well (*in health*);
Mae'n dda gen i weld I'm
glad to see. *gw.* At.
Ansoddeiriau. 2 *e.g.* good,
goodness. 3 *e. torf.* goods,
stock; cattle (*S.W.*)
dabl *gw.* tabl
dablet *gw.* tablet

dacl *gw.* tacl
daclo *gw.* taclo
daclu *gw.* taclu
daclus *gw.* taclus
dacluso *gw.* tacluso
daclwr *gw.* taclwr
dacsi *gw.* tacsi
dacw *ad.* There is/are, behold
  (*far away*) (*followed by soft
  mutation*)
Dachwedd *gw.* Tachwedd
dad *gw.* tad
dadansoddi *be.* (**dadansoddaf**)
  to analyse
dad-cu *gw.* tad-cu
dadl *e.b.* *ll.* **-euon** debate,
  argument, dispute
dadlau *be.* (**dadleuaf**) to
  argue, to debate, to dispute
dadrewi *be.* (**dadrewaf**) to
  defrost
daear *e.b.* *ll.* **-oedd** earth,
  ground, soil, land. **Beth ar y
  ddaear ydy e?** What on
  earth is it? **Ble ar y ddaear
  mae e?** Where on earth is
  he/it?
daeareg *e.b.* geology
daeargryn *e.g.b.* *ll.* **-fâu,
  -feydd** earthquake
daearyddiaeth *e.b.* geography
daeth *bf.* he/she/it came. *gw.*
  dod
dafad *e.b.* *ll.* **defaid** sheep,
  ewe; wart
dafarn *gw.* tafarn
dafarnwr *gw.* tafarnwr
dafell *gw.* tafell
daflegryn *gw.* taflegryn
daflen *gw.* taflen

daflu 56

daflu *gw.* taflu
dafod *gw.* tafod
dafodiaith *gw.* tafodiaith
dafol *gw.* tafol
dagfa *gw.* tagfa
dagrau *gw.* deigryn
dagu *gw.* tagu
dangnefedd *gw.* tangnefedd
daid *gw.* taid
dail *gw.* dalen, deilen
daioni *e.g.* goodness. **er**
 daioni for the good of. *gw.*
 da
dair *gw.* tair
daith *gw.* taith
dal *gw.* tal
dal: dala *(S.W.) be.* **(daliaf,**
 dalaf) to hold, to capture, to
 seize, to catch; to maintain;
 to keep, to wager, to bet; to
 continue; to rely, to trust.
 dal annwyd to catch a cold;
 dal ati to persevere, to stick
 at it; **dal dŵr** to hold water;
 dal dig to bear or retain a
 grudge; **dal ei dir** to hold his
 ground; **dal i fyny** to bear
 up, to uphold; **dal i lawr** to
 subjugate; **dal perthynas â** to
 be related to; **dal sylw** to
 take notice; **dal wrth/at** to
 adhere to, to persevere in;
 dal y slac yn dynn to
 pretend to work; **does dim**
 dal arno. He cannot be relied
 upon; **Ydy e'n dal i ganu?**
 Does he still sing?
dâl *gw.* tâl
dalai *gw.* talai
dalaith *gw.* talaith

dalcen *gw.* talcen
daleb *gw.* taleb
daleion *gw.* talai
dalen *e.g. ll.* **dail, -nau** leaf
 (*of a book*); sheet (*of paper*);
 leaf (*of tree, plant, etc.*). **troi**
 dalen newydd to turn over a
 new leaf; **ymyl y ddalen**
 margin of a page. *gw.* **deilen,**
 tudalen
dalent *gw.* talent
dalentog *gw.* talentog
dalgylch *e.g. ll.* **-oedd**
 catchment area
dalu *gw.* talu
dalwr *gw.* talwr
dalwrn *gw.* talwrn
dall 1 *a.* blind. 2 *e.g. ll.*
 deillion, deilliaid blind
 person(s)
dallu *be.* **(dallaf)** to blind, to
 dazzle
damaid *gw.* tamaid
dameg *e.b. ll.* **damhegion**
 parable
dameidiau *gw.* tamaid
damhegion *gw.* dameg
damwain *e.b. ll.* **damweiniau**
 accident; chance. **ar**
 ddamwain, trwy ddamwain,
 wrth ddamwain by chance
dan: tan *ardd.* **(dana, danat,**
 dano/dani, danon, danoch,
 danyn) under, until, as far;
 (*followed by soft mutation*).
 gw. At. Arddodiaid. **dan +**
 verb-noun: aeth adref dan
 ganu he went home singing;
 cododd hi dan chwerthin she
 got up laughing; **aethon nhw**

i'r capel dan wylo they went
to the chapel weeping
dân *gw.* **tân**
danau *gw.* **tân**
dancer *gw.* **tancer**
danddaear *gw.* **tanddaear**
danfon *be.* **(danfonaf)** to send,
to dispatch; to conduct, to
accompany. *gw.* **anfon**
danfor *gw.* **tanfor**
dangos (i) *be.* **(dangosaf)** to
show, to reveal
danio *gw.* **tanio**
danlinellu *gw.* **tanlinellu**
danlwybr *gw.* **tanlwybr**
danllyd *gw.* **tanllyd**
dannau *gw.* **tant**
dannedd *gw.* **dant**
dannoedd *e.b.* toothache
danseilio *gw.* **tanseilio**
dant *e.g.* *ll.* **dannedd** tooth;
cog; tine. **dant blaen** front
tooth; incisor; **dannedd
gosod/dodi** false teeth; **at ei
ddant** to his taste; **dant y
llew** dandelion. *gw.* **tant**
danwydd *gw.* **tanwydd**
dap *gw.* **tap**
dâp *gw.* **tâp**
daran *gw.* **taran**
daranu *gw.* **taranu**
darddiad *gw.* **tarddiad**
darddu *gw.* **tarddu**
darfod (i) *be.* **(darfodaf)** to
end; to finish, to die; to
waste away; to happen
(*N.W.*)
darganfod *be.* **(darganfyddaf)**
to discover
darged *gw.* **targed**

darian *gw.* **tarian**
darlith *e.b.* *ll.* **-iau, -oedd**
lecture
darlithio *be.* **(darlithiaf)** to
lecture
darlithiwr: darlithydd *e.g.* *ll.*
darlithwyr lecturer
darlun *e.g.* *ll.* **-iau** picture
darlunio *be.* **(darluniaf)** to
describe, to draw, to
illustrate
darlledu *be.* **(darlledaf)** to
broadcast
darllen *be.* **(darllenaf)** to read
darllenwr: darllenydd *e.g.* *ll.*
darllenwyr reader
darn *e.g.* *ll.* **-au** part, piece
daro *gw.* **taro**
darw *gw.* **tarw**
dasg *gw.* **tasg**
dasgu *gw.* **tasgu**
datblygiad *e.g.* *ll* **-au**
development, evolution
datblygu *be.* **(datblygaf)** to
develop, to evolve
daten *gw.* **taten**
datgan *be.* **(datganaf)** to
declare, to recite
datganiad *e.g.* *ll.* **-au**
declaration, rendering
datganoli *be.* **(datganolaf)** to
devolve, to decentralize
datgelu *be.* **(datgelaf)** to
reveal
datguddio *be.* **(datguddiaf)** to
reveal, to disclose
dato: datws *gw.* **taten**
datod *be.* **(datodaf)** to undo,
to solve, to loose; to dissolve
(*N.W.*)

datrys *be.* **(datrysaf)** to solve,
to unravel

datws *gw.* **taten**

dathliad *e.g. ll.* **dathliadau**
celebration

dathlu *be.* **(dathlaf)** to
celebrate

dau 1 *a.g.* (*followed by soft
mutation*) two. 2 *e.g. ll.*
deuoedd two. **y ddau** both.
gw. **dwy**

dawel *gw.* **tawel**

dawelu *gw.* **tawelu**

dawelwch *gw.* **tawelwch**

dawelydd *gw.* **tawelydd**

dawelyn *gw.* **tawelyn**

dawns *e.b. ll.* **-iau** dance.
dawns werin folk dance

dawnsio *be.* **(dawnsiaf)** to
dance. **dawnsio gwerin** folk
dancing

de 1 *a.* southern; right. **y llaw
dde** the right hand. 2 *e.g.*
south. **pegwn y de** south
pole. 3 *e.b.* right side.
ar y dde on the right (hand)
side. *gw.* **te**

deall 1 *be.* **(deallaf)** to
understand.
2 *e.g.* understanding,
intelligence, intellect

deallus *a.* intelligent

debot *gw.* **tebot**

debyg *gw.* **tebyg**

debygrwydd *gw.* **tebygrwydd**

decell *gw.* **tegell**

dechneg *gw.* **techneg**

dechnegol *gw.* **technegol**

dechnegwr *gw.* **technegwr**

dechnoleg *gw.* **technoleg**

dechrau 1 *be.* **(dechreuaf)** to
begin, originate. **Mae e'n
dechrau tyfu** He/it is
beginning to grow.
2 *e.g.* beginning, origin

dechreuad *e.g.* beginning.
'**Yn y dechreuad . . .**' 'In the
beginning . . .'

dedwydd *a.* happy, blessed

deddf *e.b. ll.* **-au** law, statute,
act. **Deddf Gwlad** law of the
land; **Deddf Uno 1536** Act of
Union 1536; **Deddf yr Iaith**
(Welsh) Language Act

deddfu *be.* **(deddfaf)** to
legislate

defnydd *e.g. ll.* **-iau** material,
cloth, fabric; use, purpose

defnyddio *be.* **(defnyddiaf)** to
use

defnyddiol *a.* useful

deffro *be.* **(deffroaf)** to awake,
to awaken

deg: deng 1 *a.* ten. **deng
mlynedd** ten years, decade;
deng mlwydd ten years (*of
age*); **deng niwrnod** ten days;
a'm deg ewin (*doing*) my
level best. *gw.* **At. Tr.
Trwynol.** 2 *e.g. ll.* **degau**
ten. *gw.* **teg**

degan *gw.* **tegan**

degawd *e.g. ll.* **-au** decade

degell *gw.* **tegell**

degwch *gw.* **tegwch**

deng *a.* ten; (*used before
blwydd, blynedd and
diwrnod*) (followed by nasal
mutation). *gw.* **deg**

deheuol *a.* southern

dei *gw.* tei
deialog *e.g.b. ll.* -au dialogue
deiar *gw.* teiar
deidiau *gw.* taid
deigr *gw.* teigr
deigryn *e.g. ll.* dagrau tear
deilen *e.b. ll.* dail leaf (*of tree*); *gw.* dalen
deiliwr *gw.* teiliwr
deilsen *gw.* teilsen
deilwng *gw.* teilwng
deilwres *gw.* teilwres
deilyngdod *gw.* teilyngdod
deilliaid: deillion *gw.* dall
deimlad *gw.* teimlad
deimlo *gw.* teimlo
deintydd *e.g. ll.* -ion dentist
deipiadur *gw.* teipiadur
deirgwaith *gw.* teirgwaith
deiseb *e.b. ll.* -au petition
deisen *gw.* teisen
deitl *gw.* teitl
deithio *gw.* teithio
deithiwr *gw.* teithiwr
del *a.* pretty, neat (*N.W.*)
deledu *gw.* teledu
deleffon *gw.* teleffon
delw *e.b. ll.* -au image, idol, form, manner. **ar ddelw** in the image of
delwi *be.* (**delwaf**) to become motionless, to be paralyzed with fright
delyn *gw.* telyn
delyneg *gw.* telyneg
delynor *gw.* telynor
delynores *gw.* telynores
deml *gw.* teml
denau *gw.* tenau
deniadol *a.* attractive, enticing
denu *be.* (**denaf**) to attract, to entice
derbyn *be.* (**derbyniaf, derbynnaf**) to receive
derbynebau: derbynebion *gw.* derbynneb
derbyniol *a.* acceptable, approved, receptive
derbynneb *e.g. ll.* derbynebau, derbynebion receipt, voucher
derbynnydd *e.g. ll.* derbynyddion receiver; receptionist. **derbynnydd swyddogol** official receiver
derfyn *gw.* terfyn
deri *e. ll.* oak trees, oak. *gw.* derwen
derm *gw.* term
derw *a.* of oak, oaken. *gw.* derwen
derwen *e.b. ll.* derw oak tree, oak. *gw.* deri, derw
des *gw.* tes
desg *e.b. ll.* -iau desk
desog *gw.* tesog
destun *gw.* testun
detholiad *e.g. ll.* -au selection, anthology
deuawd *e.g.b. ll.* -au duet
deuddeg 1 *a.* twelve. 2 *e.g.* twelve
deuddegfed *a.* twelfth
deugain 1 *a.* forty. **deugain mlynedd** forty years. 2 *e.g.* forty
deulu *gw.* teulu
deunaw 1 *a.* eighteen. **deunaw mlynedd** eighteen

years. 2 *e.g.* eighteen
deuoedd *gw.* **dau**
dew *gw.* **tew**
dewch *bf.* come! (*plural*). *gw.*
dod
dewin *e.g. ll.* **-iaid** magician,
wizard, diviner
dewis 1 *be.* **(dewisaf)** to
choose, to select. 2 *e.g. ll.*
-au choice, desire
dewr 1 *a. ll* **-ion** brave,
valiant. 2 *e.g. ll.* **-ion** brave
man, hero
deyrnas *gw.* **teyrnas**
di *gw.* **ti.** *gw. At. Rhagenwau*
diacon *e.g. ll.* **-iaid** deacon
diafol *e.g. ll.* **diawliaid** devil
dial (ar) 1 *be.* **(dialaf)** to
avenge; to revenge. 2 *e.g. ll.*
-au, -on vengeance; **dialedd**
vengeance, retribution
dianc (rhag) *be.* **(dihangaf)** to
escape, to avoid
diarfogi *be.* **(diarfogaf)** to
disarm
diarhebion *gw.* **dihareb**
diawl *e.g. ll.* **-iaid** devil. **Cer
i'r diawl!** To hell with you!
diawl o beth a devil of a
thing
diawledig *a.* devilish
diawliaid *gw.* **diafol, diawl**
di-baid *a.* unceasing, constant
diben *e.g. ll.* **-ion** end, object,
aim. **di-ben-draw** endless,
interminable
dibennu *be.* **(dibennaf)** to
end, to finish, to terminate
di-blwm *a.* unleaded. **petrol
di-blwm** unleaded petrol

dibynnu (ar) *be.* **(dibynnaf)** to
depend (on), to rely (on)
diced *gw.* **ticed**
diderfyn *a.* unlimited
diddordeb *e.g. ll.* **-au** interest,
hobby
diddorol *a.* interesting, of
interest
dieithr *a.* strange, unfamiliar
dieithryn *e.g. ll.* **dieithriaid**
stranger
diferyn *e.g. ll.* **-nau, diferion**
drop
difetha *be.* **(difethaf)** to
destroy, to spoil
diflannu *be.* **(diflannaf)** to
vanish, to disappear
diflas *a.* distasteful, dull
difrifol *a.* serious, earnest,
solemn
difyr: difyrrus *a.* pleasant,
amusing, entertaining
difyrru *be.* **(difyrraf)** to amuse,
to entertain
diffiniad *e.g. ll.* **-au** definition
diffinio *be.* **(diffiniaf)** to define
diffodd *be.* **(diffoddaf)** to
extinguish, to quench.
**diffodda'r golau/stôf/tân/
teledu** switch off the
light/stove/fire/television
diffuant *a.* genuine, sincere.
Yr eiddoch yn ddiffuant
Yours sincerely
diffyg *e.g. ll.* **-ion** defect,
want, lack, failure, flaw
digidol *a.* digital
digon 1 *e.g.* enough,
sufficiency; plenty.
2 *a.* enough; plentiful,

ample. 3 *ad.* enough,
sufficiently, adequately. **Dyna
ddigon!** That's enough! **yn
ddigon da** good enough (*no
mutation*)

digonedd *e.g.* abundance,
plenty

digrif *a.* merry, amusing

digwydd *be.* **(digwyddaf)** to
happen, to occur.
Digwyddodd hi weld y dyn.
She happened to see the man

digwyddiad *e.g.* *ll.* **-au**
happening, event

dihareb *e.b.* *ll.* **diarhebion**
proverb

diheintydd *e.g.* *ll.* **-ion**
disinfectant

dihuno *be.* **(dihunaf)** to
waken, to awaken (*S.W.*)

dileu *be.* **(dileaf)** to delete, to
abolish, to exterminate, to
erase

dilyn *be.* **(dilynaf)** to follow,
to pursue

dillad *gw.* **dilledyn**

dilledyn *e.g.* *ll.* **dillad**
garment, dress, item of
clothing. **dillad bob dydd**
everyday clothes; **dillad
diwedydd** clothes changed
into after work; **dillad gwaith**
working clothes; **dillad gwely**
bedclothes; **dillad isa(f)**
underclothing; **dillad nos**
pyjamas; **dillad parch**
Sunday best, best clothes

dim 1 *e.g.* any, anything,
nothing. 2 *a.* any, no. **am
ddim** for nothing, gratis; **dim**

byd nothing at all; **dim ond**
nothing but, only, merely;
dim un not a single one; **i'r
dim** exactly

dinas *e.b.* *ll.* **-oedd** city

dinasyddion *gw.* **dinesydd**

dinesig *a.* civic, urban

dinesydd *e.g.* *ll.* **dinasyddion**
citizen

dinistrio *be.* **(dinistriaf)** to
destroy

diniwed *a.* innocent,
harmless, simple

diod *e.b.* *ll.* **-ydd** drink,
beverage. **diod gadarn**
strong drink; **diod o ddŵr** a
drink of water

dioddef (o) 1 *be.* **(dioddefaf)**
to suffer, to endure, to
allow. 2 *e.g.* *ll.* **-au, -iadau**
suffering, passion

diofal *a.* careless

diog: dioglyd *a.* lazy,
sluggish, indolent

diogel *a.* safe, secure, certain

diogi 1 *be.* **(diogaf)** to be lazy
or idle, to laze. 2 *e.g.*
laziness

dioglyd *gw.* **diog**

diogyn *e.g.* *ll.* **-nod** idler,
sluggard

diolch (i, am) 1 *be.* **(diolchaf)**
to thank, to give thanks.
2 *e.g.* *ll.* **-iadau** thanks;
thanksgiving. **diolch byth!**
thank heaven! **diolch yn fawr**
many thanks (*to you*). **diolch
i'r nef (drefn)** thank
goodness

diolchgar *a.* thankful,

diolchgarwch

grateful
diolchgarwch *e.g.*
thankfulness, thanksgiving.
Cwrdd Diolchgarwch
Harvest thanksgiving service
diolchiadau *gw.* **diolch**
diota *be.* **(diotaf)** to drink
(*alcohol*)
dip *gw.* **tip**
dipyn *gw.* **tipyn**
dir *gw.* **tir**
dirgelwch *e.g.* *ll.* **dirgelion**
mystery, secret, secrecy
dirion *gw.* **tirion**
dirlun *gw.* **tirlun**
diroedd *gw.* **tiroedd**
dirprwy *e.g.* *ll.* **-on** deputy,
delegate, proxy, substitute.
dirprwy brifathro deputy
headmaster
dirprwyaeth *e.b.* *ll.* **-au**
deputation, delegation
dirwy *e.b.* *ll.* **-on** fine, penalty
disg *e.g.b.* *ll.* **-iau** disc,
record
disglair *a.* bright, brilliant
disgleirio *be.* **(disgleiriaf)** to
shine, to glitter
disgrifiad *e.g.* *ll.* **-au**
description
disgrifio *be.* **(disgrifiaf)** to
describe
disgwyl (am) *be.* **(disgwyliaf)**
to expect, to look, to wait
for. **Mae hi'n disgwyl baban**
She is expecting a baby. **Mae
e'n disgwyl bws.** He is
waiting for a bus
disgybl *g.* *ll.* **-ion** disciple,
pupil, novice, follower,

adherent
disgyblaeth *e.b.* *ll.* **-au**
discipline
disgyn *be.* **(disgynnaf)** to
descend, to fall
disian *gw.* **tisian**
distaw *a.* silent, calm, quiet
distawrwydd *e.g.* silence,
quiet
distewi *be.* **(distewaf)** to
silence, to be silent, to calm
diswyddo *be.* **(diswyddaf)** to
dismiss, to depose, to sack,
to make redundant
dithau *gw.* **tithau**
di-waith *a.* unemployed, idle
diwallu *be.* **(diwallaf)** to
satisfy, to supply
diwedd 1 *e.g.* *ll* **-ion, -au** end,
close, conclusion; death;
purpose. 2 *a.* last, final. **o'r
dechrau i'r diwedd** from
start to finish
diweddar *a.* recent; modern,
late (*S.W.*); late (*of person*);
lately, deceased. **y diweddar
Tom Jones** the late Tom
Jones. **Ydych chi wedi nofio'n
ddiweddar?** Have you been
swimming lately? **Cymraeg
Diweddar** Modern Welsh
diweddglo *e.g.* *ll.*
diweddgloeon conclusion,
close, epilogue
diweddarach *a.* later. *gw.*
diweddar
diwerth *a.* worthless
diwethaf *a.* last; previous;
latest. **Rydw i'n dal y trên
nesa achos collais yr un**

diwethaf I'm catching the next train because I missed the previous one

diwrnod *e.g. ll.* **-au** day. **diwrnod braf/teg** fine day; **diwrnod gwaith** working day; **diwrnod gŵyl** holy day, holiday; **diwrnod mawr** red letter day, 'big day'; **diwrnod i'r brenin** a thoroughly enjoyable day; **y diwrnod o'r blaen** the day before, the other day; **ers diwrnodau** for many days (*past*)

diwtor *gw.* **tiwtor**

diwydiant *e.g. ll.* **diwydiannau** industry. **diwydiant dur** steel industry; **diwydiant glo** coal industry; **diwydiant ymwelwyr** tourist industry; **diwydiant ysgafn** light industry

diwygiad *e.g. ll.* **-au** reform, reformation; revival. **Diwygiad Protestannaidd** Protestant Reformation

diwygio *be.* **(diwygiaf)** to amend, to reform, to revise

diwylliant *e.g. ll.* **diwylliannau** culture

dlawd *gw.* **tlawd**

dlodi *gw.* **tlodi**

dlodion *gw.* **tlawd**

dlos *gw.* **tlos**

dlws *gw.* **tlws**

dlysau *gw.* **tlws**

do *ad.* yes (*affirmative answer to questions using verbs in the past tense*). **Fuest ti'n siopa heddiw? Do** Were you shopping today? Yes. **Welaist ti'r dyn? Do** Did you see the man? Yes. *gw.* **to**

doc *e.g. ll.* **-iau** dock. **docfa berth**

doctor *e.g. ll.* **-iaid** doctor (always used in title); **Y Dr Tom Huws** Dr Tom Huws

docyn *gw.* **tocyn**

docynnwr *gw.* **tocynnwr**

dod: dyfod (at, dros, yn, i) *be.* **(deuaf)** to come, to arrive; to occur; to become. *gw. At. Berfau*

dodi *be.* **(dodaf)** to put, to place (*S.W.*); to give. **dodi ar ddeall** to explain to; **dodi bai ar** to blame; **dodi (un) ar waith** to set (one) to work

dodrefnyn *e.g. ll.* **dodrefn** piece of furniture (*N.W.*). *gw.* **celficyn**

dodwy *be.* **(dodwaf)** to lay eggs

doddi *gw.* **toddi**

doe *ad. & e.g.b.* yesterday. **bore ddoe** yesterday morning; **echdoe** the day before yesterday

does *gw.* **toes**

doeth *a.* wise. **Y Tri Gŵr Doeth** The Three Wise Men

doethineb *e.b. ll.* **-au** wisdom, discretion

dof *a. ll.* **-ion** tame, domesticated

dogfen *e.b. ll.* **-ni, -nau** document

doiled *gw.* **toiled**

dol *e.b. ll.* **-iau** doll

dôl *e.b. ll* **dolydd, dolau**
meadow
dôl *e.g.* dole. **ar y dôl** on the
dole
dolc *gw.* **tolc**
dolcio *gw.* **tolcio**
dolen *e.b. ll.* **-nau, -ni** handle,
link, ring. **dolen gydiol**
connecting link
dolur *e.g. ll.* **-iau** hurt,
ailment, pain, ache. **dolur**
rhydd diarrhoea; **dolur y**
galon heart disease
dolydd *gw.* **dôl**
doll *gw.* **toll**
dom *gw.* **tom**
don *gw.* **ton**
dôn *gw.* **tôn**
donau *gw.* **tôn**
donfedd *gw.* **tonfedd**
doniol *a.* witty, humorous
donnau *gw.* **ton**
dorch *gw.* **torch**
doreithiog *gw.* **toreithiog**
doreth *gw.* **toreth**
dorf *gw.* **torf**
dorfeydd *gw.* **torf**
dorheulo *gw.* **torheulo**
Dori *gw.* **Tori**
doriad *gw.* **toriad**
Dorïaid *gw.* **Torïaid**
Dorïaidd *gw.* **Torïaidd**
dorri *gw.* **torri**
dors *gw.* **tors**
dorth *gw.* **torth**
dosau *gw.* **tosyn**
dosbarth *e.g. ll.* **-au, -iadau**
class, standard; district.
dosbarth canol middle class;
dosbarth gweithiol working

class; **dosbarth isaf** lower
class; **dosbarth uchaf** upper
class; **dosbarthiadau meithrin**
nursery classes; **cyngor**
dosbarth district council;
dosbarth nos evening class
dost *gw.* **tost**
dostrwydd *gw.* **tostrwydd**
dosyn *gw.* **tosyn**
drachfen: trachefn *ad.* again
draddodiad *gw.* **traddodiad**
draddodiadol *gw.*
traddodiadol
draed *gw.* **traed**
draen *e.b. ll.* **-iau** drain.
draeniau dŵr water drains
draen: draenen *e.b. ll.* **drain**
thorn. **draenen ddu**
blackthorn; **draenen wen**
hawthorn; **ar bigau'r drain**
on tenterhooks
draenog *e.g. ll.* **-od, -iaid, -ion**
hedgehog
draeth *gw.* **traeth**
draethau *gw.* **traeth**
draethawd *gw.* **traethawd**
draethodau *gw.* **traethawd**
drafnidiaeth *gw.* **trafnidiaeth**
drafod *gw.* **trafod**
drafferth *gw.* **trafferth**
drafferthu *gw.* **trafferthu**
draffordd *gw.* **traffordd**
draffyrdd *gw.* **traffordd**
dragwyddol *gw.* **tragwyddol**
drai *gw.* **trai**
draig *e.b. ll.* **dreigiau** dragon.
Y Ddraig Goch the Red
Dragon.
drain *e. ll.* thorns; *gw.* **draen:**
draenen

drais *gw*. trais
drallod *gw*. trallod
drallwysiad *gw*. trallwysiad
drama *e.b. ll*. **dramâu** drama.
  drama radio radio play;
  drama deledu television
  play; **drama gyfres** serial;
  drama un act one-act play
dramodwr: dramodydd *e.g. ll*.
  dramodwyr dramatist
dramor *gw*. tramor
drannoeth *gw*. trannoeth
drap *gw*. trap
draul *gw*. traul
draw *ad*. yonder, there,
  beyond. **Mae'r tŷ draw fanna**
  The house is over there
drawsblannu *gw*. trawsblannu
drawst *gw*. trawst
drechu *gw*. trechu
dref: dre *gw*. tref
drefi *gw*. tref
drefn *gw*. trefn
drefnu *gw*. trefnu
drefnus *gw*. trefnus
dreigiau *gw*. draig
dreiglad *gw*. treiglad
dreiglo *gw*. treiglo
dreisio *gw*. treisio
dreisgar *gw*. treisgar
drem *gw*. trem
drên *gw*. trên
drenau *gw*. trên
drennydd *gw*. trennydd
dreser: dresel *e.g. ll*. **-i, -ydd**
  dresser
dreth *gw*. treth
drethdalwr *gw*. trethdalwr
drethu *gw*. trethu
dreuliau *gw*. traul

dreulio *gw*. treulio
drewdod *e.g.* stink, stench
drewi (o) 1 *be*. **(drewaf)** to
  stink. 2 *e.g.* stench
dri *gw*. tri
driawd *gw*. triawd
dric *gw*. tric
dridiau *gw*. tridiau
drigain *gw*. trigain
drigfan *w*. trigfan
drigo *gw*. trigo
drigolion *gw*. trigolion
dringo *be*. **(dringaf)** to climb
dringwr *e.g. ll*. **dringwyr**
  climber
drin *gw*. trin
drindod *gw*. trindod
drioedd *gw*. trioedd
driongl *gw*. triongl
drist *gw*. trist
dristwch *gw*. tristwch
dro *gw*. tro
drochi *gw*. trochi
droeau *gw*. tro
droed *gw*. troed
droedfedd *gw*. troedfedd
droedffordd *gw*. troedffordd
dröedig *gw*. tröedig
dröedigaeth *gw*. tröedigaeth
droedio *gw*. troedio
droednoeth *gw*. troednoeth
droeon *gw*. tro
drogylch *gw*. trogylch
droi *gw*. troi
dros: tros *ardd. (followed by
  soft mutation)* **(drosto,
  drostot/drosot, drosto/drosti,
  droston, drostoch, drostyn)**.
  over, for, instead of, on.
  dros Gymru for/over Wales

behalf of. **drosodd** finished;
drosodd a throsodd over
and over again; **dros ben**
exceedingly; **mynd dros ben
llestri** to go over the top;
dros dro temporary; **dros
nos** overnight; **dros y Sul**
over the weekend. *gw. At.
Arddodiaid*

drosedd *gw.* **trosedd**

droseddu *gw.* **troseddu**

droseddwr *gw.* **troseddwr**

drosgais *gw.* **trosgais**

drosglwyddo *gw.* **trosglwyddo**

drosi *gw.* **trosi**

drosiad *gw.* **trosiad**

droswr *gw.* **troswr**

drothwy *gw.* **trothwy**

drowsus *gw.* **trowsus**

druan *gw.* **truan**

drud *a.* expensive, dear,
precious, valuable

drudwy *e.g. ll.* **-od** starling

drueni *gw.* **trueni**

druenus *gw.* **truenus**

drugaredd *gw.* **trugaredd**

drugarhau *gw.* **trugarhau**

drwbl *gw.* **trwbl**

drwchus *gw.* **trwchus**

drwg 1 *e.g.* evil, iniquity,
wickedness. **o ddrwg i waeth**
from bad to worse; **y drwg
yn y caws** the source of the
evil. **2** *a.* evil; bad; wicked;
rotten. **afal drwg** rotten
apple; **wy drwg** rotten egg;
dyn drwg evil man. *gw. At.
Ansoddeiriau*

drwm *e.g. ll.* **drymiau** drum.
gw. **trwm**

drws *e.g. ll.* **drysau** door,
entrance, gap. **drws cefn** a
back door; **drws nesaf** next
door; **wrth y drws** at hand,
close, near; **carreg y drws**
doorstep

drwser *gw.* **trwser**

drwsio *gw.* **trwsio**

drwsiwr *gw.* **trwsiwr**

drwy: trwy *ardd. (followed by
soft mutation)* (**drwyddo,
drwyddot, drwyddo/drwyddi,
drwyddon, drwyddoch,
drwyddyn**) through, by, by
means of. *gw. At.
Arddodiaid*

drwydded *gw.* **trwydded**

drwyn *gw.* **trwyn**

drwynol *gw.* **trwynol**

drych *e.g. ll.* **-au** mirror;
image, form; spectacle;
vision

drychineb *gw.* **trychineb**

drychiolaeth *e.b. ll.* **-au**
apparition, illusion

drydan *gw.* **trydan**

drydanol *gw.* **trydanol**

drydanwr *gw.* **trydanwr**

drydedd *gw.* **trydedd**

drydydd *gw.* **trydydd**

drydyddol *gw.* **trydyddol**

drygioni *e.g.* evil, wickedness.
gw. **drwg**

drygionus *a.* bad, wicked.
gw. **drwg**

dryloyw *gw.* **tryloyw**

dryll *e.g.b. ll.* **-iau** gun
(*S.W.*), rifle (*S.W.*), cannon

drysau *gw.* **drws**

drysor *gw.* **trysor**

drysorfa *gw.* **trysorfa**

drysori *gw.* **trysori**

drysorydd *gw.* **trysorydd**

drysu *be.* **(drysaf)** to confuse, to entangle, to disarrange

dryw *e.g.b.* *ll.* **-od** wren

drywydd *gw.* **trywydd**

du *a.* *ll* **-on** black; dark

dudalen *gw.* **tudalen**

dueddiad *gw.* **tueddiad**

dull *e.g.* *ll* **-iau** form, mode, manner

dun *gw.* **tun**

dunnell *gw.* **tunnell**

duo *be.* **(duaf)** to blacken, to darken

duon *a.ll.* black. *gw.* **du**

dur 1 *e.g.* *ll.* **-oedd** steel. 2 *a.* steel

duw *e.g.* *ll.* **-iau** god. **Duw Dad** God the Father; **Duw Hollalluog** Almighty God; **Duw Tragwyddol** Eternal God; **bendith Duw** the blessing of God; **Duw Duw!** Good God!

duwies *e.b.* *ll.* **-au** goddess

duwiol *a.* devout, godly

dwbl *a.* double, twice

dweud (**am, wrth**) *be.* **(dwedaf, dywedaf)** to say, to speak; to mention. **dweud a dweud** to keep on saying; **dweud anwiredd** to tell a lie; **dweud ei feddwl** to say what one thinks; **dweud yn dda (am)** to speak well (of); **dweud yn ddrwg (am)** to speak ill (of); **dywedais wrtho am gau ei geg** I told him to shut up

dwfn *a.* deep; profound

dwfr *gw.* **dŵr**

dwl *a.* dull, foolish

dwlc *gw.* **twlc**

dwll *gw.* **twll**

dwmpath *gw.* **twmpath**

dwndis *gw.* **twndis**

dwnel *gw.* **twnel**

dwp *gw.* **twp**

dwpsyn *gw.* **twpsyn**

dŵr: dwfr *e.g.* *ll.* **dyfroedd** water. **dŵr berw(edig)** boiling water, **dŵr glaw** rainwater; **dŵr golchi llestri** dishwater; **dŵr (y) môr** sea water; **gwneud dŵr** to urinate. *gw.* **tŵr**

dwr *gw.* **twr**

dwrci *gw.* **twrci**

dwristiaeth *gw.* **twristiaeth**

dwrn *e.g.* *ll.* **dyrnau** fist

dwrw *gw.* **twrw**

dwsin *e.g.* *ll.* **-au** dozen

dwt *gw.* **twt**

dwy *a.b.* two. **y ddwy** the two, both (feminine). *gw.* **dau**

dwyieithog *a.* bilingual

dwyieithrwydd *e.g.* bilingualism

dwylo *e.ll.* hands. *gw.* **llaw**

dwyll *gw.* **twyll**

dwyllo *gw.* **twyllo**

dwym *gw.* **twym**

dwymo *gw.* **twymo**

dwymyn *gw.* **twymyn**

dwyn *be.* **(dygaf)** to take away, to bear, to convey; to bring; to steal. **dwyn ar gof** to bring to mind; **dwyn i ben**

to accomplish, to complete;
dwyn ffrwyth to bear fruit;
dwgyd to steal (*S.W.*)
dwyrain *e.g.* east. **y Dwyrain
Canol** the Middle East; **y
Dwyrain Pell** the Far East
dwys *a.* grave; intense;
profound; thick, dense,
concentrated. **cwrs dwys**
crash course
dwywaith *ad.* twice
dy *rhag.* (*followed by soft
mutation*) your (*singular*). **dy
chwaer** your sister; **dy lyfr**
your book; **dy hunan**
yourself
dŷ *gw.* **tŷ**
dybied: dybio *gw.* **tybied**
dychmygion *gw.* **dychymyg**
dychmygu *be.* (**dychmygaf**) to
imagine, to think, to contrive
dychrynllyd *a.* frightful,
dreadful, horrendous
dychwelyd *be.* (**dychwelaf**) to
return
dychymyg *e.g.* *ll.*
dychmygion imagination,
fancy; idea; riddle
dydy e/hi ddim *bf.* he/she/it
does not. *gw.* **bod**
dydd *e.g.* *ll.* **-iau** day. **Dydd
da!** Good day; **o ddydd i
ddydd** from day to day;
dyddiau'r wythnos days of
the week; **ers dyddiau** many
days ago; **Dydd Nadolig**
Christmas Day; **Dydd Gŵyl
Dewi** St David's Day; **Dydd
Gwener y Groglith** Good
Friday; **Dydd Llun (y) Pasg**

Easter Monday
dyddiad *e.g.* *ll.* **-au** date,
dating
dyddiau *gw.* **dydd**
dyddio *be.* (**dyddiaf**) to date
(*something*); to become
day
dyddyn *gw.* **tyddyn**
dyddynnwr *gw.* **tyddynnwr**
dyfalu *be.* (**dyfalaf**) to
conjecture, to guess; to
devise
dyfarniad *e.g.* *ll.* **-au** verdict,
decision
dyfarnu *be.* (**dyfarnaf**) to
adjudicate; to decide
dyfarnwr *e.g.* *ll.* **dyfarnwyr**
judge, umpire
dyfiant *gw.* **tyfiant**
dyfnder *e.g.* *ll.* **-au**, **-oedd**
deep, depth
dyfod *gw.* **dod**
dyfodol 1 *a.* future, coming.
2 *e.g.* future. **amser dyfodol**
future tense; **yn y dyfodol** in
the future; **dyfodol disglair** a
brilliant future
dyfroedd *gw.* **dŵr**
dyfu *gw.* **tyfu**
dyfyniad *e.g.* *ll.* **-au**
quotation
dyffryn *e.g.* *ll.* **-noedd** valley
dynged *gw.* **tynged**
dyngedfennol *gw.*
tyngedfennol
dyngu *gw.* **tyngu**
dylanwad *e.g.* *ll.* **-au**
influence
dyle *gw.* **tyle**
dyled *e.b.* *ll.* **-ion** debt, due,

claim, obligation

dyledus *a.* due, indebted,
obligatory

dyletswydd *e.b. ll.* -au duty,
obligation

dylino *gw.* tylino

dylwyth *gw.* tylwyth

dyllau *gw.* twll

dyllu *gw.* tyllu

dylluan *gw.* tylluan

dyma *ad.* here is/are; this is;
these are (*followed by soft
mutation*)

dymer *gw.* tymer

dymestl *gw.* tymestl

dymherau *gw.* tymheredd

dymheredd *gw.* tymheredd

dymhestlog *gw.* tymhestlog

dymhorau *gw.* tymor

dymor *gw.* tymor

dymuniad *e.g. ll.* -au wish,
desire; request. **gyda phob
dymuniad da** with all best
wishes; **dymuniadau gorau**
best wishes

dymuno *be.* (**dymunaf**) to
wish, to desire

dymunol *a.* desirable,
pleasant; desired

dyn *e.g. ll.* -ion man, person.
dyn cyffredin common man;
dyn dieithr stranger; **dyn eira**
snowman. *gw.* tyn(n)

dyna *ad.* there is/are
(*followed by soft mutation*).
dyna chi there you are; **dyna
dro** what bad luck! **dyna
drueni** what a pity! **dyna fe**
there it is

dyner *gw.* tyner

dynerwch *gw.* tynerwch

dynes *e.b. ll.* -au woman
(*N.W.*)

dynion *gw.* dyn

dyn(n) *gw.* tyn(n)

dynnu *gw.* tynnu

dyrau *gw.* twr

dyrfa *gw.* tyrfa

dyrfau *gw.* twrw

dyrnaid *e.g. ll.* dyrneidiau
handful, little, few

dyrnau *gw.* dwrn

dyrneidiau *gw.* dyrnaid

dyrrau *gw.* twr

dysgedig *a.* learned

dysgl *e.b. ll.* -au dish, plate;
cup; disk. **dysgl de** tea cup;
dysgl gawl soup-plate, soup-
bowl

dysgu (i) *be.* (**dysgaf**) to
learn, to teach, to educate;
dysgu ar gof to learn by
heart

dysgwr *e.g. ll.* dysgwyr
learner

dysgwyr *gw.* dysgwr

dyst *gw.* tyst

dystio *gw.* tystio

dystiolaeth *gw.* tystiolaeth

dystion *gw.* tyst

dystysgrif *gw.* tystysgrif

dywediad *e.g. ll.* -au saying

dyweddïad *e.g. ll.* -au
engagement, betrothal

dyweddïo *be.* (**dyweddïaf**) to
get engaged

dywel *gw.* tywel

dywod *gw.* tywod

dywydd *gw.* tywydd

dywyll *gw.* tywyll

dywyllu

dywyllu *gw*. tywyllu
dywyllwch *gw*. tywyllwch
dywys *gw*. tywys
dywysog *gw*. tywysog
dywysoges *gw*. tywysoges

DD

dda *gw*. da
ddadansoddi *gw*. dadansoddi
ddadl *gw*. dadl
ddadlau *gw*. dadlau
ddadrewi *gw*. dadrewi
ddaear *gw*. daear
ddaeareg *gw*. daeareg
ddaeargryn *gw*. daeargryn
ddaearyddiaeth *gw*.
  daearyddiaeth
ddaeth *gw*. daeth
ddafad *gw*. dafad
ddagrau *gw*. deigryn
ddail *gw*. deilen
ddaioni *gw*. daioni
ddal: ddala *gw*. dal
ddalen *gw*. dalen
ddalgylch *gw*. dalgylch
ddall *gw*. dall
ddallu *gw*. dallu
ddameg *gw*. dameg
ddamhegion *gw*. dameg
ddamwain *gw*. damwain
ddanfon *ge*. danfon
ddangos *gw*. dangos
ddannedd *gw*. dant
ddannoedd *gw*. dannoedd
ddant *gw*. dant
ddarfod *gw*. darfod
ddarganfod *gw*. darganfod
ddarlith *gw*. darlith

ddarlithio *gw*. darlithio
ddarlithiwr: darlithydd *gw*.
  darlithiwr
ddarlun *gw*. darlun
ddarlunio *gw*. darlunio
ddarlledu *gw*. darlledu
ddarllen *gw*. darllen
ddarllenwr: ddarllenydd *gw*.
  darllenwr
ddarn *gw*. darn
ddatblygiad *gw*. datblygiad
ddatblygu *gw*. datblygu
ddatgan *gw*. datgan
ddatganiad *gw*. datganiad
ddatganoli *gw*. datganoli
ddatgelu *gw*. datgelu
ddatguddio *gw*. datguddio
ddatod *gw*. datod
ddatrys *gw*. datrys
ddathliad *gw*. dathliad
ddathlu *gw*. dathlu
ddau *gw*. dau
ddawns *gw*. dawns
ddawnsio *gw*. dawnsio
dde *gw*. de
ddeall *gw*. deall
ddeallus *gw*. deallus
ddechrau *gw*. dechrau
ddechreuad *gw*. dechreuad
ddedwydd *gw*. dedwydd
ddeddf *gw*. deddf
ddeddfu *gw*. deddfu
ddefnydd *gw*. defnydd
ddefnyddio *gw*. defnyddio
ddefnyddiol *gw*. defnyddiol
ddeffro *gw*. deffro
ddeg: ddeng *gw*. deg
ddegawd *gw*. degawd
ddeheuol *gw*. deheuol
ddeialog *gw*. deialog

ddeigryn *gw.* deigryn
ddeilen *gw.* deilen
ddeilliaid: ddeillion *gw.* dall
ddeintydd *gw.* deintydd
ddeiseb *gw.* deiseb
ddel *gw.* del
ddelw *gw.* delw
ddelwi *gw.* delwi
ddeniadol *gw.* deniadol
ddenu *gw.* denu
dderbyn *gw.* derbyn
dderbyniol *gw.* derbyniol
dderbynneb *gw.* derbynneb
dderbynnydd *gw.* derbynnydd
dderi *gw.* deri
dderw *gw.* derwen
dderwen *gw.* derwen
ddesg *gw.* desg
ddetholiad *gw.* detholiad
ddeuawd *gw.* deuawd
ddeuddeg *gw.* deuddeg
ddeuddegfed *gw.* deuddegfed
ddeugain *gw.* deugain
ddeunaw *gw.* deunaw
ddeuoedd *gw.* deuoedd
ddewin *gw.* dewin
ddewis *gw.* dewis
ddewr *gw.* dewr
ddiacon *gw.* diacon
ddiafol *gw.* diafol
ddial *gw.* dial
ddianc *gw.* dianc
ddiarfogi *gw.* diarfogi
ddiawl *gw.* diawl
ddiawledig *gw.* diawledig
ddiawliaid *gw.* diafol, diawl
ddi-baid *gw.* di-baid
ddiben *gw.* diben
ddibennu *gw.* dibennu
ddi-blwm *gw.* di-blwm

ddibynnu *gw.* dibynnu
ddiderfyn *gw.* diderfyn
ddiddordeb *gw.* diddordeb
ddiddorol *gw.* diddorol
ddieithr *gw.* dieithr
ddieithryn *gw.* dieithryn
ddiferyn *gw.* diferyn
ddifetha *gw.* difetha
ddiflannu *gw.* diflannu
ddiflas *gw.* diflas
ddifrifol *gw.* difrifol
ddifyr: ddifyrrus *gw.* difyr
ddifyrru *gw.* difyrru
ddiffiniad *gw.* diffiniad
ddiffinio *gw.* diffinio
ddiffodd *gw.* diffodd
ddiffuant *gw.* diffuant
ddiffyg *gw.* diffyg
ddigon *gw.* digon
ddigonedd *gw.* digonedd
ddigrif *gw.* digrif
ddigwydd *gw.* digwydd
ddigwyddiad *gw.* digwyddiad
ddihareb *gw.* dihareb
ddiheintydd *gw.* diheintydd
ddihuno *gw.* dihuno
ddileu *gw.* dileu
ddilyn *gw.* dilyn
ddillad *gw.* dilledyn
ddilledyn *gw.* dilledyn
ddim *gw.* dim
ddinas *gw.* dinas
ddinasyddion *gw.* dinesydd
ddinesig *gw.* dinesig
ddinesydd *gw.* dinesydd
ddinistrio *gw.* dinistrio
ddiniwed *gw.* diniwed
ddiod *gw.* diod
ddioddef *gw.* dioddef
ddiofal *gw.* diofal

ddiog: ddioglyd *gw*. diog
ddiogel *gw*. diogel
ddiogi *gw*. diogi
ddioglyd *gw*. diog
ddiogyn *gw*. diogyn
ddiolch *gw*. diolch
ddiolchgar *gw*. diolchgar
ddiolchgarwch *gw*.
  diolchgarwch
ddiota *gw*. diota
ddirgelwch *gw*. dirgelwch
ddirprwy *gw*. dirprwy
ddirprwyaeth *gw*. dirprwyaeth
ddirwy *gw*. dirwy
ddisg *gw*. disg
ddisglair *gw*. disglair
ddisgleirio *gw*. disgleirio
ddisgrifiad *gw*.disgrifiad
ddisgrifio *gw*. disgrifio
ddisgwyl *gw*. disgwyl
ddisgybl *gw*. disgybl
ddisgyblaeth *gw*. disgyblaeth
ddisgyn *gw*. disgyn
ddistaw *gw*. distaw
ddistawrwydd *gw*.
  distawrwydd
ddistewi *gw*. distewi
ddiswyddo *gw*. diswyddo
ddi-waith *gw*. di-waith
ddiwallu *gw*. diwallu
ddiwedd *gw*. diwedd
ddiweddar *gw*. diweddar
ddiweddarach *gw*. diweddar
ddiweddglo *gw*. diweddglo
ddiwerth *gw*. diwerth
ddiwethaf *gw*. diwethaf
ddiwrnod *gw*. diwrnod
ddiwydiant *gw*. diwydiant
ddiwygiad *gw*. diwygiad
ddiwygio *gw*. diwygio

ddiwylliant *gw*. diwylliant
ddoc *gw*. doc
ddoctor *gw*. doctor
ddod: ddyfod *gw*. dod
ddodi *gw*. dodi
ddodrefnyn *gw*. dodrefnyn
ddodwy *gw*. dodwy
ddoe *gw*. doe
ddoeth *gw*. doeth
ddoethineb *gw*. doethineb
ddof *gw*. dof
ddogfen *gw*. dogfen
ddol *gw*. dol
ddôl *gw*. dôl
ddolen *gw*. dolen
ddolur *gw*. dolur
ddoniol *gw*. doniol
ddosbarth *gw*. dosbarth
ddraen: ddraenen *gw*. draen
ddraenog *gw*. draenog
ddraig *gw*. draig
ddrain *gw*. draen
ddrama *gw*. drama
ddramodwr *gw*. dramodwr
ddramodydd *gw*. dramodwr
ddreser: ddresel *gw*. dreser
ddrewdod *gw*. drewdod
ddrewi *gw*. drewi
ddringo *gw*. dringo
ddringwr *gw*. dringwr
ddrud *gw*. drud
ddrudwy *gw*. drudwy
ddrwg *gw*. drwg
ddrwm *gw*. drwm
ddrws *gw*. drws
ddrych *gw*. drych
ddrychiolaeth *gw*.
  drychiolaeth
ddrygioni *gw*. drygioni
ddrygionus *gw*. drygionus

ddryll *gw*. dryll
ddrylliau *gw*. dryll
ddrysau *gw*. drws
ddrysu *gw*. drysu
ddryw *gw*. dryw
ddu *gw*. du
ddull *gw*. dull
dduo *gw*. duo
ddur *gw*. dur
dduw *gw*. duw
dduwies *gw*. duwies
ddwbl *gw*. dwbl
ddweud *gw*. dweud
ddwfn *gw*. dwfn
ddwfr *gw*. dŵr
ddwl *gw*. dwl
ddŵr *gw*. dŵr
ddwrn *gw*. dwrn
ddwsin *gw*. dwsin
ddwy *gw*. dwy
ddwyieithog *gw*. dwyieithog
ddwyieithrwydd *gw*.
 dwyieithrwydd
ddwylo *gw*. dwylo
ddwyn *gw*. dwyn
ddwyrain *gw*. dwyrain
ddwys *gw*. dwys
ddwywaith *gw*. dwywaith
ddychmygion *gw*. dychymyg
ddychmygu *gw*. dychmygu
ddychrynllyd *gw*. dychrynllyd
ddychwelyd *gw*. dychwelyd
ddychymyg *gw*. dychymyg
ddydd *gw*. dydd
ddyddiad *gw*. dyddiad
ddyddiau *gw*. dydd
ddyfalu *gw*. dyfalu
ddyfarniad *gw*. dyfarniad
ddyfarnu *gw*. dyfarnu
ddyfarnwr *gw*. dyfarnwr

ddyfnder *gw*. dyfnder
ddyfod *gw*. dod
ddyfodol *gw*. dyfodol
ddyfroedd *gw*. dŵr
ddyfyniad *gw*. dyfyniad
ddyffryn *gw*. dyffryn
ddylanwad *gw*. dylanwad
ddyled *gw*. dyled
ddyledus *gw*. dyledus
ddyletswydd *gw*. dyletswydd
ddymuniad *gw*. dymuniad
ddymuno *gw*. dymuno
ddymunol *gw*. dymunol
ddyn *gw*. dyn
ddynes *gw*. dynes
ddyrnaid *gw*. dyrnaid
ddyrnau *gw*. dwrn
ddyrneidiau *gw*. dyrnaid
ddysgedig *gw*. dysgedig
ddysgl *gw*. dysgl
ddysgu *gw*. dysgu
ddysgwr *gw*. dysgwr
ddysgwyr *gw*. dysgwyr
ddywediad *gw*. dywediad
ddyweddïad *gw*. dyweddïad
ddyweddïo *gw*. dyweddïo

E

e: o *gw*. ef
eang *a*. broad, wide,
 extensive
eb: ebe: ebr *bf*. says, said (I,
 he/she, they, etc.)
ebol *e.g. ll*. -ion colt; buck
e-bost *e.g.ll*. e-bostiau e-mail
Ebrill *e.g.* April
economeg *e.b.* economics.
echdoe *e.g. ll. & ad.* the day
 before yesterday

echnos *e.b. ll. & ad.* the night before last

edau *e.b. ll.* **edafedd** thread

edifar: edifeiriol *a.* sorry, penitent, contrite. **Mae'n edifar gen i** I regret

edmygu *be.* **(edmygaf)** to admire

edrych *be.* **(edrychaf)** to look, to observe, to search, to examine; to expect. **edrych am** to look for, to expect; **edrych ar** to look on, to look upon; **edrych ar ôl** to look after, to mind; **edrych at** to look towards; **edrych dros** to overlook, to survey; **edrych allan** to look out, to seek; **edrych ymlaen** to look forward

ef: efe: efô *rhag.* he, him, it (*N.W.*)

efallai *ad.* perhaps

efengyl *e.b. ll.* **-au** gospel. **Efengyl Iesu Grist** the Gospel of Jesus Christ

efeilliaid *gw.* **gefell**

efo *ardd.* with, by means of (*N.W.*)

efô *gw.* **ef**

Efrog *e.b.* York

Efrog Newydd *e.b.* New York

effaith *e.b. ll.* **effeithiau** effect

effeithiau *gw.* **effaith**

effeithiol *a.* effective

effro *a.* awake (*N.W.*)

egin *gw.* **eginyn**

eginyn *e.g. ll.* **egin** shoot, sprout, (young) blade

eglur *a.* clear, evident, plain

egluro *be.* **(egluraf)** to reveal; to explain; to manifest

eglwys *e.b. ll.* **-i** church, the church

egni *e.g. ll.* **egnïon, egnïoedd** energy, might; effort, endeavour

egnïoedd *gw.* **egni**

egnïol *a.* vigorous, energetic

egnïon *gw.* **egni**

egwyddor *e.b. ll.* **-ion** principle; rudiment; alphabet

egwyddorol *a.* having principles. *gw.* **gwyddor**

egwyl *e.b. ll.* **-iau, -ion** break, interval; spell

enghraifft *e.b. ll.* **enghreifftiau** example, instance. **er enghraifft** for example

enghreifftiau *gw.* **enghraifft**

englyn *e.g. ll.* **-ion** an epigrammatic four-line stanza in Welsh poetry

engyl *gw.* **angel**

ehedydd *e.g. ll.* **-ion** lark

ei *rhag.* his, her, its. **ei hunan** himself/herself. *gw. At. Treigladau*

eich *rhag.* your. **eich hunan** yourself; **eich hunain** yourselves

Eidal, Yr *e.b.* Italy

Eidaleg *e.b.* Italian language

Eidales *e.b. ll.* **-au** Italian woman

Eidalwr *e.g. ll.* **Eidalwyr** Italian man

eiddo 1 *e.g.* possession(s), property, estate. **ei eiddo** his possession. **2** *ad.* his, hers, etc

eifr *gw.* **gafr**
Eingl-Gymro *e.g.* *ll.* **Eingl-Gymry** Anglo-Welshman
eiliad *e.g.b.* *ll.* **-au** second, moment. **dwy eiliad** two seconds
eilwaith *ad.* again, a second time
ein *rhag.* our. **ein hunain** ourselves
eira *e.g.* *ll.* **-oedd** snow
eirch *gw.* **arch**
eirchion *gw.* **arch**
eirfa *gw.* **geirfa**
eiriadur *gw.* **geiriadur**
eiriau *gw.* **gair**
eirin *gw.* **eirinen**
eirinen *e.b.* *ll.* **eirin** plum, damson; berry. **eirin gwlanog** peaches
eirio *gw.* **geirio**
eirlys *e.g.* *ll.* **-iau** snowdrop. *gw.* **tlws yr eira**
eirth *gw.* **arth**
eisiau *e.g.* need, want, lack, poverty. **Rydw i eisiau –** I need –, I want –. **Mae eisiau – arnaf i** I need –, I want –
eisoes *ad.* already
eistedd *be.* **(eisteddaf)** to sit, to seat
eisteddfod *e.b.* *ll.* **-au** eisteddfod
eisteddfodwr *e.g.* *ll.* **eisteddfodwyr** a frequenter of *eisteddfodau*
eitem *e.b.* *ll.* **-au** item
eithaf 1 *e.g.* *ll.* **-ion, -oedd, -edd** end, extremity, uttermost part. 2 *a.* farthest, surperlative. **y gosb eithaf** capital punishment. 3 *ad.* very, quite
eithafol *a.* extreme
eithr 1 *rhag.* except, besides. 2 *c.* but
eithrio *be.* **(eithriaf)** to except, to exclude. **ac eithrio** except, excepting
eleni *ad.* this year
elfen *e.b.* *ll.* **-nau** element, particle, factor, tendency. **yn fy elfen** in my element
elfennau *gw.* **elfen**
elfennol *a.* elementary, constituent, simple
eliffant *e.g.* *ll.* **-od** elephant
elw *e.g.* *ll.* **-on** profit, gain
elwa *be.* **(elwaf)** to profit, to gain
elyn *gw.* **gelyn**
elltydd *gw.* **allt**
em *gw.* **gem**
emyn *e.g.* *ll.* **-au** hymn. **emyn-dôn** hymn-tune
emynydd *e.g.* *ll.* **emynwyr** hymn-writer
ên *gw.* **gên**
enaid *e.g.* *ll.* **eneidiau** soul, spirit; life
enau *gw.* **genau**
enedigaeth *gw.* **genedigaeth**
eneidiau *gw.* **enaid**
eneth *gw.* **geneth**
eneuau *gw.* **genau**
enfawr *a.* enormous, vast, immense, huge
enfys *e.b.* *ll.* **-au** rainbow
eni *gw.* **geni**
enillwr: enillydd *e.g.* *ll.* **enillwyr**

earner; victor, winner

ennill 1 *be.* **(enillaf)** to gain,
to profit, to get; to win.
2 *e.g. ll.* **enillion** winnings;
salary; profit

ennyd *e.g.b.* a while, moment

enw *e.g. ll.* **-au** name; noun;
enw anwes pet name; **enw
benywaidd** feminine noun;
enw gwrywaidd masculine
noun; **enw torfol** collective
noun; **ffugenw** *nom de
plume*, pseudonym

enwad *e.g. ll.* **-au** religious
denomination

enwedig *a.* especial

enwi *be.* **(enwaf)** to name

enwog 1 *a.* famous
renowned, eminent. **2** *e.ll.*
-ion persons of renown or
fame; celebrities

enwogrwydd *e.g.* fame

enyn *gw.* **genyn**

eos *e.b. ll.* **-iaid** nightingale

epa *e.g. ll.* **-od** ape

er *ardd.* because of, for, in
order to; since (*a fixed point
in time*); despite. **er
anrhydedd** in honour; **er
bod** although; **er cof** in
memory, *in memoriam*; **er
gwaethaf** in spite of, despite;
er hynny yet, since then; **er
lles/budd** for the benefit of;
er mwyn for the sake of, in
order to; **er dydd Llun** since
Monday

eraill *gw.* **arall**

erbyn *ardd.* against, facing,
opposite; by, for, in

preparation for. **erbyn hyn**
by this time, by now; **mynd
yn erbyn** to oppose, to go
against; **erbyn meddwl**
coming to think of it

erchyll *a.* atrocious, terrible

erddi *gw.* **gardd**

erfin *gw.* **erfinen**

erfinen *e.b. ll.* **erfin** turnip,
swede

erfyn 1 *be.* **(erfyniaf)** to beg,
to entreat, to pray, to
implore. **2** *e.g. ll.* **arfau**
weapon, tool. *gw.* **arf**

ergyd *e.g.b. ll.* **-ion** blow,
knock, shot, hit, bang,
detonation

erioed *ad.* ever

erlid *be.* **(erlidiaf)** to pursue,
to persecute

erlyn *be.* **(erlynaf)** to
prosecute

erlyniad *e.g. ll.* **-au**
prosecution

erlynydd *e.g. ll.* **-ion**
prosecutor

ernes *e.b. ll.* **-au** security,
pledge; deposit

ers *ardd.* for, since (*a
continuing period*). **ers
pythefnos** for the last
fortnight. **ers tro** for some
time

erthygl *e.b. ll.* **-au** article,
literary composition; clause

erthyliad *e.g. ll.* **-au** abortion,
miscarriage

erthylu *be.* **(erthylaf)** to abort,
to miscarry

erw *e.b. ll.* **-au** acre

eryr *e.g. ll.* **-od** eagle
Eryri *e.b.* Snowdonia.
es i *bf.* I went. *gw.* **mynd**
esboniad *e.g. ll.* **-au**
commentary; explanation,
exposition
esbonio (i) *be.* **(esboniaf)** to
explain (to)
esgeulus *a.* negligent
esgeuluso *be.* **(esgeulusaf)** to
neglect
esgeulustod: esgeulustra *e.g.*
negligence
esgid *e.b. ll.* **-iau** boot; shoe:
esgidiau mawr/uchel high
boots; **esgidiau ysgafn** light
boots or shoes; **yr esgid yn
gwasgu** a difficult financial
situation
esgob *e.g. ll.* **-ion** bishop.
Esgob Tyddewi Bishop of St
David's; **esgobaeth** diocese;
Esgob! Oh Lord!
esgus *e.g. ll.* **-ion, -odion**
excuse; pretence (*S.W.*). **mae
e'n esgus cysgu** he's
pretending to sleep
esgusion *gw.* **esgus**
esgusodi *be.* **(esgusodaf)** to
make an excuse, to excuse;
Esgusodwch fi Excuse me
esgusodion *gw.* **esgus**
esgyrn *gw.* **asgwrn. Esgyrn
Dafydd!** Good heavens!
esiampl *e.b. ll.* **-au** example
esmwyth *a.* soft, easy,
comfortable
estron *e.g. ll.* **-iaid** foreigner,
alien, stranger
estyn *be.* **(estynnaf)** to

extend, to reach; to stretch,
to lengthen; to give
estyniad *e.g. ll.* **-au** extension
etifeddu *be.* **(etifeddaf)** to
inherit
eto *c. & ad.* again a second
time, yet, still, nevertheless
ethol *be.* **(etholaf)** to elect, to
choose, to select
etholaeth *e.b. ll.* **-au**
constituency; electorate
etholiad *e.g. ll.* **-au** election;
etholiad cyffredinol general
election; **is-etholiad** by-
election
eu *rhag.* (*words beginning
with a vowel are aspirated
when preceded by* **eu**) their.
eu hafalau their apples; **eu
hemynau** their hymns; **eu
hysgolion** their schools. **eu
hunain** themselves. *gw. At.
Rhagenwau*
euog *a.* guilty; **euog neu
ddieuog** guilty or not guilty
euogrwydd *e.g.* guilt
euraid: euraidd *a.* gold,
golden
ewch *bf.* go! (*plural*). *gw.*
mynd
ewin *e.g.b. ll.* **-edd** nail, claw,
talon; hoof. **â'i ddeg ewin**
with all his might
Ewrop *e.b.* Europe
ewyllys *e.b. ll.* **-iau, -ion** will;
desire; testament. **yn erbyn ei
ewyllys** against his will
ewyn *e.g.* foam, froth. *gw.*
gewyn
ewythr *e.g. ll.* **-edd, -od** uncle

F

fab *gw.* mab
faban *gw.* baban
fabanaidd *gw.* babanaidd
fabi *gw.* babi
fabolgamp *gw.* mabolgamp
facio *gw.* bacio
fach *gw.* bach
fachau *gw.* bach, bachyn
fachgen *gw.* bachgen
fachgennaidd *gw.*
  bachgennaidd
fachlud *gw.* machlud
fachu *gw.* bachu
fachyn *gw.* bach
fad *gw.* bad
fadarch *gw.* madarch
fae *gw.* bae
faer *gw.* maer
faeres *gw.* maeres
faes *gw.* maes
faestref *gw.* maestref
fafon *gw.* mafonen
fag *gw.* bag
fagddu, y *e.b.* utter darkness
fagiau *gw.* bag
fagu *gw.* magu
Fai *gw.* Mai
fai *gw.* bai
faich *gw.* baich
fain *gw.* main
faint *rhag. gof.* how much?
  how many? *gw.* maint
falch *gw.* balch
falchder *gw.* balchder
faldod *gw.* maldod
faldodi *gw.* maldodi
faled *gw.* baled
faledwr *gw.* baledwr

falot *gw.* balot
falu *gw.* malu
falŵn *gw.* balŵn
falwoden *gw.* malwoden
fam *gw.* mam
fam-gu *gw.* mam-gu
famiaith *gw.* mamiaith
fân *gw.* mân
fan *e.b. ll.* -iau van. *gw.* ban,
  man
fanana *gw.* banana
fanc *gw.* banc
fancio *gw.* bancio
fand *gw.* band
fandal *e.g. ll.* -iaid vandal
fandaleiddio *be.* (fandaleiddiaf)
  to vandalize
fandaliaeth *e.b.* vandalism
faneg *gw.* maneg
faner *gw.* baner
fannau *gw.* ban, man
fannod *gw.* bannod
fans *gw.* mans
fantais *gw.* mantais
fanteisio *gw.* manteisio
fanteision *gw.* mantais
fantell *gw.* mantell
fanwl *gw.* manwl
fanylion *gw.* manylyn
fanylu *gw.* manylu
fanylyn *gw.* manylyn
fap *gw.* map
far *gw.* bar
fara *gw.* bara
farbeciw *gw.* barbeciw
farc *gw.* marc
farcio *gw.* marcio
farchnad *gw.* marchnad
farchog *gw.* marchog
fardd *gw.* bardd

farddoniaeth *gw.* **barddoniaeth**

farf *gw.* **barf**

farn *gw.* **barn**

farnwr *gw.* **barnwr**

farrau *gw.* **bar**

fart *gw.* **mart**

farw *gw.* **marw**

farwaidd *gw.* **marwaidd**

farwol *gw.* **marwol**

farwolaeth *gw.* **marwolaeth**

fas *gw.* **bas**

fasged *gw.* **basged**

fasn *gw.* **basn**

fasnach *gw.* **masnach**

fasnachwr *gw.* **masnachwr**

fasnau: fasnys *gw.* **basn**

faswr *gw.* **baswr, maswr**

fat *gw.* **bat, mat**

fater *gw.* **mater**

fatsen: fatsien *gw.* **matsen**

fath *gw.* **bath, math**

fathdy *gw.* **bathdy**

fathemateg *gw.* **mathemateg**

fathemategol *gw.*
  mathemategol

fathemategwr *gw.*
  mathemategwr

fathodyn *gw.* **bathodyn**

fathu *gw.* **bathu**

faw *gw.* **baw**

fawd *gw.* **bawd**

fawl *gw.* **mawl**

fawn *gw.* **mawn**

fawr *gw.* **mawr**

fawredd *gw.* **mawredd**

Fawrth *be.* **Mawrth**

fe 1 *rhag.* he, him, it. **2** *geir.*
  particle (*may be used before
  verbs* (*S.W.*)). **fe welais; fe
  glywais; fe gwympodd.** *gw.*

At. Berfau – **Fe/Mi**

feallai *ad.* perhaps

fecso *gw.* **becso**

fechan *gw.* **bechan**

fechgyn *gw.* **bachgen**

fechnïaeth *gw.* **mechnïaeth**

Fedi *gw.* **Medi**

fedi *gw.* **medi**

fedru *gw.* **medru**

fedrus *gw.* **medrus**

fedwen *gw.* **bedwen**

fedyddio *w.* **bedyddio.**

Fedyddiwr *gw.* **Bedyddiwr**

fedd *gw.* **bedd, meddu**

feddal *gw.* **meddal**

feddalu *gw.* **meddalu**

feddalwedd *gw.* **meddalwedd**

feddu *gw.* **meddu**

feddw *gw.* **meddw**

feddwi *gw.* **meddwi**

feddwl *gw.* **meddwl**

feddyg *gw.* **meddyg**

feddygfa *gw.* **meddygfa**

feddyginiaeth *gw.*
  meddyginiaeth

feddylgar *gw.* **meddylgar**

feddyliau *gw.* **meddwl**

fefus *gw.* **mefusen**

Fehefin *gw.* **Mehefin**

feiau *gw.* **bai**

feibion *gw.* **mab**

Feibl *gw.* **Beibl**

feic *gw.* **beic**

feicrodon *gw.* **meicrodon**

feichiau *gw.* **baich**

feichiog *gw.* **beichiog**

feiddio *gw.* **meiddio**

feim *gw.* **meim**

feinir *gw.* **meinir**

feio *gw.* **beio**

feirdd

feirdd *gw*. bardd

feirioli *gw*. meirioli

feirniad *gw*. beirniad

feirniadu *gw*. beirniadu

feirniaid *gw*. beirniad

feistr *gw*. meistr

feistres *gw*. meistres

feistri: feistriaid *gw*. meistr

feistroli *gw*. meistroli

feithrin *gw*. meithrin

fel *c*. as, so, like. fel arfer as usual, usually; fel pe bai/petai/petasai as if

fêl *gw*. mêl

felen *gw*. melen

felin *gw*. melin

felyn *gw*. melyn

felys *gw*. melys

felysfwyd *gw*. melysfwyd

fellten *gw*. mellten

felltith *gw*. melltith

felly *ad*. so, thus

fendigedig *gw*. bendigedig

fendith *gw*. bendith

fenig *gw*. maneg

fenter *gw*. menter

fentrau *gw*. menter

fentro *gw*. mentro

fentrus *gw*. mentrus

fenthyca *gw*. benthyca

fenyn *gw*. menyn

fenyw *gw*. benyw, menyw

fenywaidd *gw*. benywaidd, menywaidd

fer *gw*. ber

fêr *gw*. mêr

ferch *gw*. merch

Fercher *gw*. Mercher

ferchetaidd *gw*. merchetaidd

ferf *gw*. berf

ferfa *gw*. berfa

ferfenw *gw*. berfenw

ferlod *gw*. merlyn

ferlota *gw*. merlota

ferlotwr *gw*. merlotwr

ferlyn *gw*. merlyn

fersiwn *e.g*. *ll*. fersiynau version

ferthyr *gw*. merthyr

ferw *gw*. berw

ferwi *gw*. berwi

fes *gw*. mesen

fesen *gw*. mesen

festri *e.b*. *ll*. festrïoedd vestry

fesul *gw*. mesul

fesur *gw*. mesur

fesurydd *gw*. mesurydd

fetel *gw*. metel

fetr *gw*. metr

fetrig *gw*. metrig

fethiant *gw*. methiant

fewn *gw*. mewn

fewnwr *gw*. mewnwr

feysydd *gw*. maes

fi: mi *rhag*. I, me. *gw*. mi

ficer *e.g*. *ll*. -iaid vicar

ficerdai *gw*. ficerdy

ficerdy *e.g*. *ll*. ficerdai vicarage

ficrodon *gw*. microdon

figwrn *gw*. migwrn

fil *gw*. mil

filfeddyg *gw*. milfeddyg

filgi *gw*. milgi

filiwn *gw*. miliwn

filoedd *gw*. mil

filwr *gw*. milwr

filltir *gw*. milltir

fin *gw*. bin

fin *gw*. min

finegr *e.g.* *ll.* -au vinegar
finiog *gw.* miniog
finlliw *gw.* minlliw
finnau *gw.* minnau
fiola *e.b.* *ll.* -s viola
fioled *e.b.* *ll.* -au violet
fioleg *gw.* bioleg
firi *gw.* miri
firws *e.g.* *ll.* -au virus
fis *gw.* mis
fisged *gw.* bisged
fisgïen *gw.* bisgïen
fisglwyf *gw.* misglwyf
fisoedd *gw.* mis
fisol *gw.* misol
fisolyn *gw.* misolyn
fitw *gw.* bitw
fiwsig *gw.* miwsig
flaen *gw.* blaen
flaendal *gw.* blaendal
flaenor *gw.* blaenor
flaenwr *gw.* blaenwr
flaguro *gw.* blaguro
flaguryn *gw.* blaguryn
flaidd *gw.* blaidd
flanced *gw.* blanced
flas *gw.* blas
flasu *gw.* blasu
flasus *gw.* blasus
flawd *gw.* blawd
fleiddiaid *gw.* blaidd
flew *gw.* blewyn
flewyn *gw.* blewyn
flin *gw.* blin
flinder *gw.* blinder
flinedig *gw.* blinedig
flino *gw.* blino
flodau *gw.* blodyn
flodeugerdd *gw.* blodeugerdd
flodfresychen *gw.*

blodfresychen
flodyn *gw.* blodyn
floedd *gw.* bloedd
floeddio *gw.* bloeddio
flows *gw.* blows
flwch *gw.* blwch
flwydd *gw.* blwydd
flwyddyn *gw.* blwyddyn
flychau *gw.* blwch
flynedd *gw.* blwyddyn
flynyddoedd *gw.* blwyddyn
fo *rhag.* he, him, it (*N.W.*)
focs *gw.* bocs
foch *gw.* boch, mochyn
fochyn *gw.* mochyn
fod *gw.* bod
fodau *gw.* bod
fodfedd *gw.* modfedd
fodiau *gw.* bodiau
fodio *gw.* bodio
fodlon: foddlon *gw.* bodlon
fodloni *gw.* bodloni
fodrwy *gw.* modrwy
fodryb *gw.* modryb
fodur *gw.* modur
fodurwr *gw.* modurwr
fodd *gw.* bodd, modd
foddhad *gw.* boddhad
foddi *gw.* boddi
foddion *gw.* moddion
foel *gw.* moel
foelni *gw.* moelni
foes *gw.* moes
foesol *gw.* moesol
foethus *gw.* moethus
fogi *gw.* mogi
fol *gw.* bol
fola *gw.* bola
foli *gw.* moli
foliau *gw.* bol

follt *gw*. bollt

folltau *gw*. bollt

fom *gw*. bom

Fôn *gw*. Môn

fôn *gw*. bôn

foneddiges *gw*. boneddiges

foneddigion *gw*. bonheddwr

fonheddig *gw*. bonheddig

fonheddwr *gw*. bonheddwr

fonion *gw*. bôn

fôr *gw*. môr

ford *gw*. bord

fordaith *gw*. mordaith

fordau: fordydd *gw*. bord

forddwyd *gw*. morddwyd

fore *gw*. bore

forfa *gw*. morfa

forfil *gw*. morfil

forgais *gw*. morgais

Forgannwg *gw*. Morgannwg

forgeisiau *gw*. morgais

forgrugyn *gw*. morgrugyn

forio *gw*. morio

fôr-leidr *gw*. môr-leidr

forio *gw*. morio

foroedd *gw*. môr

foron *gw*. moronen

foronen *gw*. moronen

forthwyl *gw*. morthwyl

forwr *gw*. morwr

forwyn *gw*. morwyn

fory: yfory *ad.* tomorrow

fos *gw*. bos

fotwm *gw*. botwm

fotymu *gw*. botymu

fowlen *gw*. bowlen

fragdy *gw*. bragdy

fraich *gw*. braich

fraint *bw*. braint

frân *gw*. brân

fras *gw*. bras

fraslun *gw*. braslun

fraster *gw*. braster

fraw *gw*. braw

frawd *gw*. brawd

frawddeg *gw*. brawddeg

frecwast *gw*. brecwast

frech *gw*. brech

frechdan *gw*. brechdan

frechiad *gw*. brechiad

freichiau *gw*. braich

freichled *gw*. breichled

freiniau: freintiau *gw*. braint

frenhines *gw*. brenhines

frenhinoedd *gw*. brenin

frenhinol *gw*. brenhinol

frenin *gw*. brenin

fres *gw*. bres

frest *gw*. brest

fresychen *gw*. bresychen

frethyn *gw*. brethyn

freuddwyd *gw*. breuddwyd

freuddwydio *gw*. breuddwydio

freuddwydion *gw*. breuddwyd

frifo *gw*. brifo

frig *gw*. brig

frigau *gw*. brig, brigyn

frigyn *gw*. brigyn

fritho: frithio *gw*. britho

friwsion *gw*. briwsionyn

friwsionyn *gw*. briwsionyn

fro *gw*. bro

frodor *gw*. brodor

frodyr *gw*. brawd

froga *gw*. broga

fron *gw*. bron

fronfraith *gw*. bronfraith

fronnau: fronnydd *gw*. bron

frown *gw*. brown

fröydd *gw*. bro

frwdfrydig *gw*. brwdfrydig

frwnt *gw*. brwnt

frws: frwsh *gw*. brws

frwsio: frwshio *gw*. brwsio

frwsys: frwshys *gw*. brws

frwydr *gw*. brwydr

frwydrau *gw*. brwydr

fryd *gw*. bryd

fryn *gw*. bryn

fryniau *gw*. bryn

frys *gw*. brys

frysio *gw*. brysio

fuan *gw*. buan

fuarth *gw*. buarth

fuchod *gw*. buwch

fud *gw*. mud

fudiad *gw*. mudiad

fudr *gw*. budr

fuddsoddi *gw*. buddsoddi

fuddugol *gw*. buddugol

fuddugoliaeth *gw*.
  buddugoliaeth

fues i *bf*. I was, I have been.
  gw. bod

fugail *gw*. bugail

fugeiliaid *gw*. bugail

fugeilio *gw*. bugeilio

ful *gw*. mul

fûm: fues *bf*. I was, I have
  been. *gw*. bod

funud *gw*. munud

fur *gw*. mur

fusnes *gw*. busnes

fuwch *gw*. buwch

fwced *gw*. bwced

fwg *gw*. mwg

fwgwd *gw*. mwgwd

fwlch *gw*. bwlch

fwnci *gw*. mwnci

fwrdeistref *gw*. bwrdeistref

fwrdd *gw*. bwrdd

fwriad *gw*. bwriad

fwriadu *gw*. bwriadu

fwrw *gw*. bwrw

fws *gw*. bws

fwstash *gw*. mwstash

fwstwr *gw*. mwstwr

fwthyn *gw*. bwthyn

fwy *gw*. mawr

fwyaf *gw*. mawr

fwyar *gw*. mwyaren

fwyaren *gw*. mwyaren

fwyd *gw*. bwyd

fwydo: fwyda *gw*. bwydo

fwydlen *gw*. bwydlen

fwydydd *gw*. bwyd

fwydyn *gw*. mwydyn

fwyn *gw*. mwyn

fwynhad *gw*. mwynhad

fwynhau *gw*. mwynhau

fwyta: fyta *gw*. bwyta

fwyty *gw*. bwyty

fy *rhag*. (*followed by nasal
  mutation*) my, of me. *gw*. At.
  Rhagenwau

fychan *gw*. bychan

fyd *gw*. byd

fydoedd *gw*. byd

fydd e/o/hi *bf*. he/she/it will
  be. *gw*. bod

fyddar *gw*. byddar

fyddin *gw*. byddin

fyddinoedd *gw*. byddin

fyfyrdod *gw*. myfyrdod

fyfyrio *gw*. myfyrio

fyfyriwr *gw*. myfyriwr

fyglyd *gw*. myglyd

fygu *gw*. mygu

fygydau *gw*. mwgwd

fylchau *gw*. bwlch

fynach *gw.* mynach
fynachlog *gw.* mynachlog
fynachod *gw.* mynach
fynaich *gw.* mynach
fynd: fyned *gw.* mynd
fynedfa *gw.* mynedfa
fynedfeydd *gw.* mynedfa
fynediad *gw.* mynediad
fynegai *gw.* mynegai
fynegeion *gw.* mynegai
fynegi *gw.* mynegi
fynnu *gw.* mynnu
fynwent *gw.* mynwent
fyny, i *ad.* up, upwards. **oddi
fyny** from above; **ar i fyny**
upwards; in good spirits, in a
cheerful mood
fynychu *gw.* mynychu
fynydd *gw.* mynydd
fynyddig: fynyddog *gw.*
mynyddig
fyr *gw.* byr
fyrbryd *gw.* byrbryd
fyrddau *gw.* bwrdd
fyrfodd *gw.* byrfodd
fyrr *gw.* myrr
fys *gw.* bys
fysedd *gw.* bys
fystyrau *gw.* mwstwr
fysys *gw.* bws
fyth, *gw.* byth, *gw.* myth
fythynnod *gw.* bwthyn
fyw *gw.* byw
fywiog *gw.* bywiog
fywyd *gw.* bywyd
fywydeg *gw.* bywydeg

FF

ffa *gw.* ffäen

ffäen: ffeuen *e.b. ll.* **ffa** bean.
ffa pob baked beans
ffactor *e.g.b. ll.* **-au** factor
ffaelu (â) *be.* **(ffaelaf)** to fail,
to miss, to mistake (*S.W.*)
ffafr *e.b. ll.* **-au** favour,
respect
ffair *e.b. ll.* **ffeiriau** fair. **ffair
haf** summer fair; **ffair lyfrau**
book fair; **ffair sborion**
jumble sale; **fel ffair** an utter
mess, very busy
ffaith *e.b. ll.* **ffeithiau** fact
ffarm: fferm *e.b. ll.* **ffermydd**
farm. **tŷ fferm** farmhouse
ffarmio: ffermio *be.* **(ffarmiaf:
ffermiaf)** to farm
ffarmwr: ffermwr *e.g. ll.*
ffermwyr farmer,
agriculturist
ffárwel: ffarwél *e.b.* farewell.
Ffárwel haf Michaelmas
daisy
ffarwelio (â) *be.* **(ffarweliaf)** to
bid farewell; to say goodbye
ffatri *e.b. ll.* **ffatrïoedd**
factory
ffau *e.b. ll.* **ffeuau** den, lair,
burrow, set
ffawydden *e.b. ll.* **ffawydd**
beech tree
ffefryn *e.g. ll.* **-nau** favourite
ffeiriau *gw.* ffair
ffeithiau *gw.* ffaith
ffel *a.* dear; knowing –
especially of a dog
ffenestr *e.b. ll.* **-i** window
fferm *gw.* ffarm
ffermdai *gw.* ffermdy
ffermdy *e.g. ll.* **ffermdai**

farmhouse

ffermio *gw.* **ffarmio**

ffermwr *gw.* **ffarmwr**

ffermwyr *gw.* **ffarmwr**

fferyllydd *e.g. ll.* **-ion** pharmacist, chemist

ffeuau *gw.* **ffau**

ffeuen *gw.* **ffäen**

ffiaidd *a.* foul, loathsome, odious

ffigur *e.g. ll.* **-au** figure, type, form; diagram

ffin *e.b. ll.* **-iau** boundary, border, frontier, limit

ffiniau *gw.* **ffin**

ffiniol *a.* bordering

ffiseg *e.b.* physics

fflachio *be.* (**fflachiaf**) to flash

fflam *e.b. ll.* **-au, -iau** flame, blaze

fflamau: fflamiau *gw.* **fflam**

ffoadur *e.g. ll.* **-iaid** fugitive, refugee; deserter

ffoaduriaid *gw.* **ffoadur**

ffodus *a.* fortunate, lucky, prosperous

ffoi (rhag) *be.* (**ffoaf**) to flee, to escape; to desert

ffôl *a.* foolish, unwise, silly, foolhardy

ffolineb *e.g. ll.* **-au** foolishness, folly

ffon *e.b. ll.* **ffyn** stick, walking-stick, staff; rod; club

ffôn *e.g. ll.* **ffonau** telephone, phone. **ffôn symudol** mobile phone. *gw.* **teleffon**

ffonio *be.* (**ffoniaf**) to phone

fforc *e.b. ll.* **ffyrc** fork

fforchio *be.* (**fforchiaf**) to

fork; to straddle

ffordd *e.b. ll.* **ffyrdd** road, way, street, route. **ffordd allan** exit; **ffordd fawr** highway; **ffordd osgoi** bypass; **priffordd** highway; **ffordd dda** good way; **traffordd** motorway; **ffordd ddeuol** dual carriageway; **pontffordd** viaduct; **trosffordd** fly-over

ffortiwn *e.b. ll.* **ffortiynau** fortune

ffortiynau *gw.* **ffortiwn**

ffos *e.b. ll.* **-ydd** ditch, trench

ffosydd *gw.* **ffos**

ffowls *gw.* **ffowlyn**

ffowlyn *e.g. ll.* **ffowls** chicken, fowl (*S.W.*)

ffraeo (â) *be.* (**ffraeaf**) to quarrel, to bicker

Ffrangeg *e.b.* French (language)

Ffrainc *e.b.* France

Ffrances *e.b. ll.* **-au** Frenchwoman

Ffrancod *gw.* **Ffrancwr**

Ffrancwr *e.g. ll.* **Ffrancwyr, Ffrancod** Frenchman

Ffrancwyr *gw.* **Ffrancwr**

Ffrengig *a.* French

ffres *a.* fresh

ffrind *e.g. ll.* **-iau** friend

ffrindiau *gw.* **ffrind**

ffrio *be.* (**ffriaf**) to fry

ffroen *e.b. ll.* **-au** nostril

ffroesen *e.b. ll.* **ffroes** pancake (*S.W.*). *gw.* **crempog**

ffrog: ffroc *e.b. ll.* **-iau** frock.

ffrog felen a yellow frock;
ffrog wen a white frock
ffroga *e.g. ll.* **ffrogaod** frog.
gw. **broga**
ffrwd *e.b. ll.* **ffrydiau** swift
stream; torrent, flood;
current
ffrwydro *be.* (**ffrwydraf**) to
explode
ffrwyth *e.g. ll.* **ffrwythau**
fruit; produce; result, effect
ffrwythlon *a.* fruitful, fertile
ffrwythloni *be.* (**ffrwythlonaf**)
to become or be fruitful; to
fertilize
ffrydiau *gw.* **ffrwd**
ffrynt *e.g.b. ll.* **-iau** front.
ffrynt gynnes warm front;
ffrynt oer cold front; **drws
(y) ffrynt** front door; **o'r
ffrynt** from the front
ffug *a.* deceptive, sham,
counterfeit, false. **dogfen ffug**
forged document
ffug-bas *e.b. ll.* **-ys** dummy-
pass (*rugby*)
ffugenw *e.g. ll.* **-au**
pseudonym, *nom de plume*
ffugio *be.* (**ffugiaf**) to pretend,
to disguise, to forge, to feign
ffuglen *e.b.* fiction. **ffuglen
wyddonol** *e.b.* science fiction
ffurf *e.b. ll.* **-iau** form, shape;
appearance, likeness;
substance
ffurfafen *e.b. ll.* **-nau** sky;
heavens
ffurfiau *gw.* **ffurf**
ffurfio *be.* (**ffurfiaf**) to form, to
fashion, to create

ffurflen *e.b. ll.* **-ni** form,
chart. **ffurflen gais**
application form
ffurflenni *gw.* **ffurflen**
ffwdan *e.g.* fuss, flurry
ffŵl *e.g. ll.* **ffyliaid** fool
ffwr *e.g. ll.* **ffyrrau** fur
ffwrdd, i *ad.* away. **ffwrdd-â-
hi** *a. & ad.* slapdash,
precipitate
ffwrn *e.b. ll.* **ffyrnau** oven,
furnace. **ffwrn microdon**
microwave oven
ffws *e.g.* fuss
ffydd *e.b. ll.* **-iau** faith, belief,
confidence
ffyddlon *a.* faithful, loyal
ffyliaid *gw.* **ffŵl**
ffyn *gw.* **ffon**
ffynhonnau *gw.* **ffynnon**
ffynhonnell *e.b. ll.* **ffynonellau**
source, spring, fount; origin
ffynidwydden *e.b. ll.*
ffynidwydd fir tree, pine tree
ffynnon *e.b. ll.* **ffynhonnau**
spring, fountain,well; source,
origin
ffynonellau *gw.* **ffynhonnell**
ffyrc *gw.* **fforc**
ffyrdd *gw.* **ffordd**
ffyrnau *gw.* **ffwrn**
ffyrnig *a.* fierce, savage,
furious, wild.
ffyrnigrwydd *e.g.* ferocity
ffyrrau *gw.* **ffwr**

G

ga i *bf.* may I . . .? *gw.* **cael**
gaban *gw.* **caban**

gacen *gw.* cacen
gacwn *gw.* cacynen
gacynen *gw.* cacynen
gadach *gw.* cadach
gadael *be.* (gadawaf) to leave,
to desert; to allow. gadewais
I left; gadewaist you left
gadair *gw.* cadair
gadeiriau *gw.* cadair
gadeirio *gw.* cadeirio
gadeiriol *gw.* cadeiriol
gadeirydd *gw.* cadeirydd
gadno *gw.* cadno
gadw *gw.* cadw
gadwyn *gw.* cadwyn
gadwyno *gw.* cadwyno
gae *gw.* cae
gaeaf *e.g.* *ll.* -au winter
gaeau *gw.* cae
gael *gw.* cael
gaer *gw.* caer
Gaer *gw.* Caer
Gaerdydd *gw.* Caerdydd
Gaeredin *gw.* Caeredin
Gaerfyrddin *gw.* Caerfyrddin
Gaergybi *gw.* Caergybi
gaets *gw.* caets
gaf *gw.* cael
gafael (yn) *be.* (gafaelaf) to
hold tight, to clutch; to grip.
Gafael yn fy llaw Take my
hand
gafaelgar *a.* gripping
gafodd *gw.* cael
gafr *e.b.* *ll.* geifr goat
gaffe *gw.* caffe
gangen *gw.* cangen
ganghennau *gw.* cangen
gaiff *gw.* caiff
gair *e.g.* *ll.* geiriau word. gair

bach short address, brief
note; geirda good report,
commendation, reference;
gair drwg bad reputation; ar
y gair instantly: cadw at ei
air to keep his word; dweud
gair to speak or address (a
meeting, etc.); Gair Duw
God's word; gair yn ei bryd
timely advice
gais *gw.* cais
galan *gw.* calan
galar *e.g.* mourning, grief
galaru *be.* (galaraf) to mourn
galed *gw.* caled
galedi *gw.* caledi
galedwch *gw.* caledwch
galendr *gw.* calendr
galennig *gw.* calennig
galetach *gw.* caled
galetaf *gw.* caled
galeted *gw.* caled
galon *gw.* calon
galw (ar, am) *be.* (galwaf) to
call, to summon; to visit; to
name
galwad *e.b.g.* *ll.* -au a call;
vocation, calling, profession.
Cafodd y gweinidog alwad i
Lanelli The minister received
a call to Llanelli
galwedigaeth *e.b.* *ll.* -au
occupation, vocation
galwyn *e.g.* *ll.* -i, -au gallon
gall *gw.* call
gallach *gw.* call
gallaf *gw.* call. *gw.* gallu
galled *gw.* call
gallu 1 *be.* (gallaf) to be able.
2 *e.g.* *ll.* -oedd ability,

galluog

power, wealth
galluog *a.* able, powerful
gam *gw.* cam
gamarwain *gw.* camarwain
gamddeall *gw.* camddeall
gamera *gw.* camera
gamp *gw.* camp
gampfa *gw.* campfa
gampfeydd *gw.* campfa
gampus *gw.* campus
gampwaith *gw.*campwaith
gampweithiau *gw.* campwaith
gamsyniad *gw.* camsyniad
gamu *gw.* camu
gan *ardd.* (*followed by soft mutation*) (*personal forms*: **gen i, gen ti, ganddo/ganddi, gennyn, gennych, ganddyn**). with, by, from, since. **gan amlaf** usually, mostly: **gan hynny** therefore; **gan mwyaf** mostly, almost. *gw. At. Arddodiaid; gw.* **can; cant**
gân *gw.* cân
ganddi: ganddo *gw.* gan
ganddyn *gw.* gan
ganed *bf.* he/she was born
ganeuon *gw.* cân
ganfed *gw.* canfed
ganhwyllbren *gw.*
  canhwyllbren
ganiad *gw.* caniad
ganiadaeth *gw.* caniadaeth
ganiadau *gw.* cân, caniad
ganiatâd *gw.* caniatâd
ganiatáu *gw.* caniatáu
ganiedydd *gw.* caniedydd
ganmlwydd *gw.* canmlwydd
ganmlwyddiannau *gw.*
  canmlwyddiant

ganmlwyddiant *gw.*
  canmlwyddiant
ganmol *gw.* canmol
ganmoliaeth *gw.* canmoliaeth
gannoedd *gw.* cant
gannwyll *gw.* cannwyll
ganhwyllau *gw.* cannwyll
ganol *gw.* canol
ganolbarth *gw.* canolbarth
ganolbwyntio *gw.*
  canolbwyntio
ganoldir *gw.* canoldir
ganolfan *gw.* canolfan
ganolog *gw.* canolog
ganolwr *gw.* canolwr
ganradd *gw.* canradd
ganran *gw.* canran
ganrif *gw.* canrif
ganrifau: ganrifoedd *gw.*
  canrif
gant *gw.* cant
gânt *gw.* cael
gantor *gw.* cantor
gantores *gw.* cantores
ganu *gw.* canu
ganŵ *gw.* canŵ
ganŵio *gw.* canŵio
ganwr *gw.* canwr
ganwriad *gw.* canwriad
ganwyd *bf.* he/she was born.
  Ganwyd ef yng Nghymru He
  was born in Wales. *gw.* **geni**
gap *gw.* cap
gapel *gw.* capel
gapten *gw.* capten
gar *gw.* car
garafán *gw.* carafán
garafana *gw.* carafana
garco *gw.* carco
garcus *gw.* carcus

garchar *gw*. carchar
garcharor *gw*. carcharor
garcharu *gw*. carcharu
gardiau *gw*. cerdyn
gardd *e.b*. *ll*. gerddi garden;
  Gardd Fotaneg Genedlaethol
  National Botanic Garden of
  Wales
garddio *be*. (**garddiaf**) to
  garden, to cultivate a garden
garddwr *e.g*. *ll*. **garddwyr**
  gardener
garedig *gw*. caredig
garedigrwydd *gw*.
  caredigrwydd
garej *e.g*. *ll*. **-ys** garage
gariad *gw*. cariad
gariadon *gw*. cariad
gariadus *gw*. cariadus
gario *gw*. cario
garlleg *e.g*. garlic. **ewin(-edd)**
  garlleg clove of garlic
garol *gw*. carol
garped *gw*. carped
garreg *gw*. carreg
gartref *ad*. at home. **Mae e'n**
  byw gartref He's living at
  home. *gw*. cartref
gartrefi *gw*. cartref
gartrefu *gw*. cartrefu
garu *gw*. caru
garw *a*. *ll*. **geirwon** coarse,
  rough, harsh
garwriaeth *gw*. carwriaeth
gas *gw*. cas
gasáu *gw*. casáu
gasgen *gw*. casgen
gasgenni *gw*. casgen
gasgliad *gw*. casgliad
gasglu *gw*. casglu

Gas-gwent *gw*. Cas-gwent
Gasllwchwr *gw*. Casllwchwr
Gasnewydd *gw*. Casnewydd
gastell *gw*. castell
Gastell-nedd *gw*. Castell-nedd
gât *e.b*. *ll*. **gatiau, gâts,**
  gatsys (*never undergoes soft*
  mutation) gate. **yr hen gât**
  the old gate; **dwy gât** two
  gates; **y gât wen** the white
  gate. *gw*. clwyd. *gw*. iet
gath *gw*. cath
gau *a*. (*precedes noun*) false.
  gau broffwyd a false
  prophet. *gw*. cau
gawl *gw*. cawl
gawod *gw*. cawod
gawr *gw*. cawr
gaws *gw*. caws
gefell *e.g.b*. *ll*. **gefeilliaid**
  twin. **gefell** twin brother;
  gefeilles twin sister; **yr**
  efeilliaid the twins
gefn *gw*. cefn
gefnder *gw*. cefnder
gefndir *gw*. cefndir
gefndiroedd *gw*. cefndir
gefndyr *gw*. cefnder
gefnogi *gw*. cefnogi
gefnu *gw*. cefnu
gefnwr *gw*. cefnwr
geffyl *gw*. ceffyl
geg *gw*. ceg
gegin *gw*. cegin
gei *gw*. cei
geidwad *gw*. ceidwad
geifr *gw*. gafr
geiliog *gw*. ceiliog
Geinewydd *gw*. Ceinewydd
geiniog *gw*. ceiniog

geir *gw.* car
geirfa *e.b.* *ll.* **-oedd**
  vocabulary
geiriadur *e.g.* *ll.* **-on**
  dictionary
geiriau *gw.* **gair**
geirio *be.* **(geiriaf)** to word, to
  phrase
geiriosen *gw.* **ceiriosen**
geirwon *gw.* **garw**
geisiadau: geisiau *gw.* **cais**
geisio *gw.* **ceisio**
gelf *gw.* **celf**
gelfi *gw.* **celficyn**
gelficyn *gw.* **celficyn**
Geltaidd *gw.* **Celtaidd**
gelwydd *gw.* **celwydd**
gelwyddog *gw.* **celwyddog**
gelyn *e.g.* *ll.* **-ion** enemy.
  gelyn pennaf chief enemy.
  gw. **celynnen**
gelynnen *gw.* **celynnen**
gell *gw.* **cell**
gellau: gelloedd *gw.* **cell**
gem *e.b.g.* *ll.* **-au** gem
gêm *e.b.* *ll.* **gêmau** (*doesn't
  mutate*) game. **Dyma gêm
  dda** Here's a good game;
  dwy gêm rygbi two rugby
  games; **dewch i gêmau'r
  ysgol** Come to the school's
  games
gemeg *gw.* **cemeg**
gen *gw.* **gan**
gên *e.b.* *ll.* **genau** chin, jaw
genau *e.g.* *ll.* **geneuau**
  mouth; *gw.* **gên**
genedigaeth *e.b.* *ll.* **-au** birth
genedl *gw.* **cenedl**
genedlaethol *gw.*

cenedlaethol
genedlaetholdeb *gw.*
  cenedlaetholdeb
genedlaetholwr *gw.*
  cenedlaetholwr
genetig: genetaidd: genynnol
  a. genetic
geneth *e.b.* *ll.* **-od** girl (*N.W.*)
geneuau *gw.* **genau**
genfigennus *gw.* **cenfigennus**
genhadaeth *gw.* **cenhadaeth**
genhadol *gw.* **cenhadol**
genhadu *gw.* **cenhadu**
genhadwr *gw.* **cenhadwr**
genhedlaeth *gw.* **cenhedlaeth**
genhedloedd *gw.* **cenedl**
genhinen *gw.* **cenhinen**
geni *be.* to be born, to give
  birth to. **dyddiad geni** date
  of birth
gennin *gw.* **cenhinen**
gennych *gw.* **gan**
gennym *gw.* **gan**
genyn *e.g.* *ll.* **-au** gene
ger *ardd.* at, by, near, before,
  in front of. **gerllaw** close to
gêr *e.ll.* gear, tackle; rubbish
gerbron *gw.* **ger**
gerdyn *gw.* **cerdyn**
gerdd *gw.* **cerdd**
gerdded *gw.* **cerdded**
gerddi *gw.* **cerdd, gardd**
gerddor *gw.* **cerddor**
gerddorfa *gw.* **cerddorfa**
gerddoriaeth *gw.* **cerddoriaeth**
gerddorol *gw.* **cerddorol**
gerddwr *gw.* **cerddwr**
gerddwyr *gw.* **cerddwr**
gerfio *gw.* **cerfio**
gerflun *gw.* **cerflun**

gerllaw *gw.* **ger**
gerrig *gw.* **carreg**
ges *gw.* **cael**
gesair *gw.* **cesair**
gestyll *gw.* **castell**
gewri *gw.* **cawr**
gewyn *gw. ll.* **-nau, -ion**
sinew, tendon, ligament;
nerve. *gw.* **cewyn**
geyrydd *gw.* **caer**
gi *gw.* **ci**
gig *gw.* **cig**
gigydd *gw.* **cigydd**
gilio *gw.* **cilio**
gilydd *rhag.* other, another,
another of the same class or
kind. **ei gilydd** each other;
gyda'i gilydd together (they);
gyda'ch gilydd together
(you); **gyda'n gilydd** together
(we)
ginio *gw.* **cinio**
gipolwg *gw.* **cipolwg**
gist *gw.* **cist**
glaf *gw.* **claf**
glai *gw.* **clai**
glan *e.b. ll.* **-nau, glennydd**
bank, shore. **glan y môr**
seashore; **glan yr afon** river's
bank; **glan y bedd** the grave-
side; **gwyliwr y glannau**
coastguard
glân *a.* clean, pure, holy;
beautiful, fair
glanhau *be.* **(glanhaf)** to
clean, to purify; to heal
glanio *be.* **(glaniaf)** to land, to
come or go ashore,
disembark; bring to land
glannau *gw.* **glan**

glas 1 *a. ll.* **gleision** blue,
green, grey, silver; wan,
pallid; raw. **arian gleision**
silver (money), silver coins;
glas y dorlan kingfisher.
2 *e.g.* blue
glaswelltyn *e.g. ll.* **glaswellt**
green grass
glasur *gw.* **clasur**
glasurol *gw.* **clasurol**
glaw *e.g. ll.* **-ogydd** rain.
bwrw glaw to rain; **eirlaw**
sleet; **glaw mân** drizzle
glawdd *gw.* **clawdd**
glawr *gw.* **clawr**
glebran *gw.* **clebran**
glefyd *gw.* **clefyd**
gleison *gw.* **glas**
glendid *e.g.* cleanness,
cleanliness, purity; beauty;
piety, holiness
glennydd *gw.* **glan**
glêr *gw.* **cleren**
glerc *gw.* **clerc**
gleren *gw.* **cleren**
glin *e.g.b. ll.* **-iau** knee
glir *gw.* **clir**
glirio *gw.* **clirio**
glo *e.g.* coal. **glo brig** open-
cast coal; **glo carreg**
anthracite coal; **glo mân**
small coal; **glo rhwym**
bituminous coal. *gw.* **clo**
gloc *gw.* **cloc**
glocwedd *gw.* **clocwedd**
gloch *gw.* **cloch**
glod *gw.* **clod**
glodfori *gw.* **clodfori**
gloddiau *gw.* **clawdd**
glofa *e.b. ll.* **glofeydd** colliery

glofeydd *gw*. **glofa**

gloff *gw*. **cloff**

gloffi *gw*. **cloffi**

glogwyn *gw*. **clogwyn**

glogyn *gw*. **clogyn**

gloi *gw*. **cloi**

glorian *gw*. **clorian**

glown *gw*. **clown**

glöwr *e.g*. *ll*. **glowyr** collier, coal-miner

glöyn byw *e.g*. *ll*. **glöynnod byw** butterfly (*N.W.*)

gloyw *a*. *ll*. **-on** clear, bright, shiny. **Cymro glân gloyw** a thoroughbred Welshman

glud *e.g*. *ll*. **-ion** glue

gludio: gludo *be*. **(gludiaf: gludaf)** to glue; to adhere

glun *gw*. **clun**

glust *gw*. **clust**

glustog *gw*. **clustog**

glwm *gw*. **clwm**

glwtyn *gw*. **clwtyn**

Glwyd *gw*. **Clwyd**

glwyd *gw*. **clwyd**

glwyf *gw*. **clwyf**

glychau *gw*. **cloch**

glymau *gw*. **clwm, cwlwm**

glymu *gw*. **clymu**

glyn *e.g*. *ll*. **-noedd** valley, glen

Glynebwy *e.b*. Ebbw Vale

glynu (wrth) *be*. **(glynaf)** to adhere, to cling

glyw *ge*. **clyw**

glywed *gw*. **clywed**

gnau *gw*. **cneuen**

gneuen *gw*. **cneuen**

gnoc *gw*. **cnoc**

gnocio *gw*. **cnocio**

gnoi *gw*. **cnoi**

go *ad*. (*precedes noun and causes soft mutation*) rather, somewhat; small, little, exceeding (*N.W.*). **go ddrud** somewhat expensive

gobaith *e.g*. *ll*. **gobeithion** hope

goban *gw*. **coban**

gobeithio *gw*. **(gobeithiaf)** to hope

gobeithion *gw*. **gobaith**

gobennydd *e.g*. *ll*. **gobenyddion** pillow, bolster

goch *gw*. **coch**

gochach *gw*. **coch**

gochaf *gw*. **coch**

goched *gw*. **coch**

godi *gw*. **codi**

godidog *gw*. excellent, splendid

godre *e.g*. *ll*. **-on** edge, hem, fringe; foot or bottom (*of mountain, hill, etc*.); foot (*of page*)

godro *be*. **(godraf)** to milk

goddef *be*. **(goddefaf)** to suffer, to bear, to endure, to tolerate

goddefgar *a*. tolerant

goddrych *e.g*. *ll*. **-au** subject

Goed-duon *gw*. **Coed-duon**

goeden *gw*. **coeden**

goedwig *gw*. **coedwig**

goes *gw*. **coes**

gof *e.g*. *ll*. **-aint** smith, blacksmith. *gw*. **cof**

gofal *e.g*. *ll*. **-on** care; charge

gofalu (am) *be*. **(gofalaf)** to take care; to worry, to vex

gofalus *a.* careful, anxious, worried

gofalwr *e.g.* *ll.* **gofalwyr** caretaker, custodian

gofid *e.g.* *ll.* **-iau** trouble, sorrow, grief, affliction

gofidio (am) *be.* **(gofidiaf)** to grieve, to vex

gofio *gw.* **cofio**

gofleidio *gw.* **cofleidio**

gofod *e.g.* *ll.* **-au** space, gap. *gw.* **gwagle**

gofodwr *e.g.* *ll.* **gofodwyr** astronaut

gofrestr *gw.* **cofrestr**

gofrestru *gw.* **cofrestru**

gofyn (am) 1 *be.* **(gofynnaf)** to ask (for). 2 *e.g.* *ll.* **-ion** request, requirement, demand. **yn ôl y gofyn** according to demand; **Gofyn bendith** to say grace

goffi *gw.* **coffi**

gog *gw.* **cog**

goginio *gw.* **coginio**

gogledd 1 *e.g.* north. 2 *a.* north, northern. **Pegwn y Gogledd** North Pole

gogleddol *a.* northern

gogleddwr *e.g.* *ll.* **gogleddwyr** northerner

gogleisio *be.* **(gogleisiaf)** to tickle

gogoniant *e.g.* *ll.* **gogoniannau** glory

gogydd *gw.* **cogydd**

gogystal *a.* comparable

gohirio *be.* **(gohiriaf)** to postpone

gôl *e.b.* *ll.* **goliau** goal

(*soccer*)

golau 1 *e.g.* light. 2 *a.* light, fair (*colour*). *gw.* **goleuni**. **golau diogelwch** safety light; **golau dydd** daylight; **golau (l)leuad** moonlight; **golau llachar** bright light

golchi *be.* **(golchaf)** to wash; to flow over or past

goleg *gw.* **coleg**

goler *gw.* **coler**

goleudy *e.g.* *ll.* **goleudai** lighthouse

goleuni *e.g.* light; *gw.* **golau**

goleuo *be.* **(goleuaf)** to light, to enlighten; to set fire to

goliau *gw.* **gôl**

golofn *gw.* **colofn**

golud *e.g.* *ll.* **-oedd** wealth, riches

goluro *gw.* **coluro**

golwg *e.g.b.* *ll.* **golygon** sight; appearance, view. **golygon** eyes; **i bob golwg** to all appearances; **o'r golwg** out of sight; **y fath olwg!** what a sight; **rhagolygon y tywydd** weather prospects; **roedd golwg wael arni** she looked ill; **allan o olwg** out of sight

golygfa *e.b.* *ll.* **golygfeydd** view, scenery, scene

golygon *gw.* **golwg**

golygu *be.* **(golygaf)** to view; to mean, to imply, to intend; to edit. **Beth rwyt ti'n ei olygu?** What do you mean?

golygus *a.* handsome

golygydd *e.g.* *ll.* **-ion** editor

golled *gw.* **colled**

gollen *gw.* **collen**

golli *gw.* **colli**

gollwng *be.* **(gollyngaf)** to release; to leak

gonest *a.* honest, sincere

gopïo *gw.* **copïo**

gopyn *gw.* **copyn**

gôr *gw.* **côr**

gorau *a.* best. **o'r gorau** okay. *gw.* **da.** *gw.* **côr**

gorchfygu *be.* **(gorchfygaf)** to defeat, to conquer, to subdue, to beat

gorchymyn (i) 1 *be.* **(gorchmynnaf)** to command, to order, to decree, to charge. 2 *e.g. ll.* **gorch(y)mynion** commandment, command, decree, order. **Y Deg Gorchymyn** The Ten Commandments

gordyn *gw.* **cordyn**

gorfod 1 *e.g.b. ll.* **-au** compulsion, obligation; victory, success. 2 *a.* enforced, compulsory, obligatory; conquering, victorious. 3 *be.* **(gorfodaf)** to be obliged, forced or compelled to, to have (to). **Rwyt ti'n gorfod mynd** You have to go

gorfodaeth *e.b.g. ll.* **-au** compulsion, obligation. **gorfodaeth filwrol** military conscription

gorfodi (i) *be.* **(gorfodaf)** to compel, to oblige; to conquer, to overcome

gorfodol *a.* compulsory, obligatory

gorfoleddus *a.* joyful

gorff *gw.* **corff**

gorffen *be.* **(gorffennaf)** to finish, to conclude

Gorffennaf *e.g.* July

gorffennol 1 *e.g.* the past. 2 *a.* past

gorfforol *gw.* **corfforol**

gorffwys *e.g.* rest

gorffwyso *be.* **(gorffwysaf)** to rest

gorgi *gw.* **corgi**

gorlawn *a.* overflowing, overcrowded

gorllewin *e.g.* west. **Gorllewin Cymru** West Wales

gormod 1 *e.g.* excess; too many. 2 *a. & ad.* too much, excessive. **gormod o gwynion** too many complaints; **gormod o straeon** too many stories; **gormod o stŵr** too much noise; **gormod o drafferth** too much trouble; **bwyta gormod** to eat too much

gorn *gw.* **corn**

gornel *gw.* **cornel**

gornest *e.b. ll.* **-au** contest, battle; match

goron *gw.* **coron**

goroni *gw.* **coroni**

gorryn *gw.* **corryn**

gorsaf *e.b. ll.* **-oedd** station. **gorsaf betrol** petrol station; **gorsaf bŵer** power station; **gorsaf dân** fire station

gorsedd *e.b. ll.* **-au** throne.
  Gorsedd y Beirdd the
  Gorsedd of Bards (*bardic
  institution*)
goruchaf *a.* most high,
  supreme
goruwchnaturiol *a.*
  supernatural
gorwedd *be.* (**gorweddaf**) to
  lie, to lie down
gorwel *e.g. ll.* **-ion** horizon
gorymdaith *e.b. ll.*
  gorymdeithiau procession
gosb *gw.* **cosb**
gosbi *gw.* **cosbi**
gosi *gw.* **cosi**
gosod 1 *be.* (**gosodaf**) to put;
  to plant; to let; to bestow; to
  fix. **gosod gerbron** to set
  before; **gosod mewn trefn** to
  set in order; **gosod pris** to
  fix a price; **gosod yr ardd** to
  plant the garden. **2** *a.* false,
  artificial, applied. **dannedd
  gosod** false teeth, denture.
  gwallt gosod false hair, wig
gostus *gw.* **costus**
gostwng *be.* (**gostyngaf**) to
  lower, to reduce; to
  diminish; to ease
gostyngedig *a.* humble
gostyngiad *e.g. ll.* **-au**
  reduction
gosyn *gw.* **cosyn**
got: gôt *gw.* **cot**
gotwm *gw.* **cotwm**
grac *gw.* **crac**
grachach *gw.* **crachach**
gradd *e.b. ll.* **-au** step, grade,
  degree, university degree.

gradd anrhydedd an
  honours degree; **i'r fath
  raddau** to such an extent;
  mewn graddau by degrees,
  gradually; **o radd i radd** step
  by step, by degrees
graddfa *e.b. ll.* **graddfeydd**
  scale. **ar raddfa eang** on a
  large scale; **graddfa Celsius**
  Celsius Scale
graddio *be.* (**graddiaf**) to
  graduate, to grade, to scale
graddol *a.* gradual. **yn raddol**
  by degrees
graenus *a.* of good quality,
  glossy, sleek
grafu *gw.* **crafu**
gragen *gw.* **cragen**
graig *gw.* **craig**
gramadeg *e.g. ll.* **-au**
  grammar. **llyfr gramadeg**
  grammar book
gramadegol *a.* grammatical
grant *e.g. ll.* **-iau** grant
gras *e.g. ll.* **-au, -usau** grace.
  gw. **cras**
grasu *bw.* **crasu**
grawnffrwyth *e.g. ll.* **-au**
  grapefruit
gredu *gw.* **credu**
grefydd *gw.* **crefydd**
grefft *gw.* **crefft**
grefftwr *gw.* **crefftwr**
gregyn *gw.* **cragen**
greigiau *gw.* **craig**
greigiog *gw.* **creigiog**
greision *gw.* **cras, creisionyn**
grempog *gw.* **crempog**
gresyn *e.g. ll.* **-au** pity
  (*N.W.*). **Gresyn iddo farw**

Pity that he died; **Gresyn o beth** It's a shame
gresynu *be.* **(gresynaf)** to deplore, to be sorry, to pity
greulon *gw.* **creulon**
greulondeb *gw.* **creulondeb**
gri *gw.* **cri**
grib *gw.* **crib**
gribo *gw.* **cribo**
griced *gw.* **criced**
gricedwr *gw.* **cricedwr**
grio *gw.* **crio**
gris *e.g.* *ll.* **-iau** step, stair
Gristion *gw.* **Cristion**
griw *gw.* **criw**
Groeg 1 *e.b.* Greece. 2 *e.b. & a.* the Greek language, Greek; pertaining to the Greek language, to Greece or to the Greeks
Groegaidd *a.* Grecian, Greek
Groeges *e.b.* *ll.* **-au** Greek female
Groegwr *e.g.* *ll.* **Groegwyr** Greek, Grecian
groen *gw.* **croen**
groes *gw.* **croes**
groesair *gw.* **croesair**
groesawu *gw.* **croesawu**
groesawus *gw.* **croesawus**
groesfan *gw.* **croesfan**
groesffordd *gw.* **croesffordd**
groesholi *gw.* **croesholi**
groesi *gw.* **croesi**
groeso *gw.* **croeso**
gron *gw.* **cron**
gronfa *gw.* **cronfa**
grud *gw.* **crud**
grudd *e.b.g.* *ll.* **-iau** cheek
grug *e.g.* heather

grwn *gw.* **crwn**
grŵp *e.g.* *ll.* **grwpiau** group. **grŵp pop** pop group
grwst *gw.* **crwst**
gryd *gw.* **cryd**
gryf *gw.* **cryf**
gryfach *gw.* **cryf**
gryfaf *gw.* **cryf**
gryfed *gw.* **cryf**
grym *e.g.* *ll.* **-oedd** force; energy; power
grymus *a.* powerful, strong, mighty
grynhoi *gw.* **crynhoi**
gryno *gw.* **cryno**
grynodeb *gw.* **crynodeb**
grynu *gw.* **crynu**
grys *gw.* **crys**
grystyn *gw.* **crystyn**
gu *gw.* **cu**
guddio *gw.* **cuddio**
gul *gw.* **cul**
guro *gw.* **curo**
gusan *gw.* **cusan**
gusanu *gw.* **cusanu**
gwadu *be.* **(gwadaf)** to deny, to disown
gwaed *e.g.* blood. **yn y gwaed** in the blood as a family trait; **Cymro o waed coch cyfan** a thoroughbred Welshman
gwaedu *be.* **(gwaedaf)** to bleed. **gwaedu fel mochyn** to bleed like a (slaughtered) pig
gwaedd *e.b.* *ll.* **-au** shout
gwael *a.* poor; miserable; sick; vile. **tro gwael â** an unworthy act (with)
gwaelod *e.g.* *ll.* **-ion** bottom, base, foundation. **ar waelod**

at the bottom; **yng ngwaelod**
in the bottom; **gwaelodion**
sediment, dregs
gwaeth *gw*. drwg
gwaethaf *gw*. drwg. **er
gwaethaf** in spite of;
gwaetha'r modd the more
the pity; worse luck
gwaethed *gw*. drwg
gwaethygu *be.* (**gwaethygaf**)
to worsen
gwag *a. ll.* **gweigion** empty;
desolate; vacant
gwagedd *e.g. ll.* **-au** vanity;
void
gwagio: gwagu *be.* (**gwagiaf:
gwagaf**) to empty
gwagle *e.g. ll.* **-oedd** space,
void. *gw*. **gofod**
gwagu *gw*. gwagio
gwahân *e.g.* separation;
difference. **ar wahân** apart;
separately; independently;
byw ar wahân to live apart
gwahaniaeth *e.g.* difference,
separation
gwahaniaethu *be.*
(**gwahaniaethaf**) to differ
gwahanol *a.* different, various
gwahanu *be.* (**gwahanaf**) to
separate
gwahardd *be.* (**gwaharddaf**) to
prohibit
gwahodd 1 *be.* (**gwahoddaf**)
to invite, to ask. 2 *e.g. ll.*
-ion invitation, bidding
gwahoddedig *e.g. ll.* **-ion**
invited, bidden, called.
gwahoddedigion guests
gwahoddiad *e.g. ll.* **-au**

invitation
gwahoddion *gw*. gwahodd
gwair *e.g. ll.* **gweiriau** grass
(*grown for harvesting*); hay
(*S.W.*)
gwaith 1 *e.g. ll.* **gweithiau**
work; composition; works.
gwaith annwyd cold sores;
gwaith cartref homework;
gwaith glo coal-mine,
colliery; **gwaith tŷ** house
work. 2 *e.b. ll.* **gweithiau**
time, occasion, turn. **unwaith**
once; **dwywaith** twice;
teirgwaith three times;
canwaith a hundred times;
y waith honno that occasion.
3 *c.* for, because
gwal *e.b. ll.* **gwaliau, gwelydd**
wall
gwâl *e.b. ll.* **gwalau** lair; bed
gwall *e.g. ll.* **-au** mistake,
defect, want
gwallgof *a.* insane, mad
gwallt *e.g. ll.* **-au, -iau** hair.
blewyn (*one*) hair
gwallus *a.* faulty, inaccurate,
erroneous
gwan *a. ll.* **gweiniaid,
gweinion** weak, feeble.
esgus wan a feeble excuse
gwanwyn *e.g. ll.* **-au** spring
gwar *e.b.g. ll.* **-rau** nape of
the neck
gwâr *a.* cultured
gwarchod *be.* (**gwarchodaf**) to
watch, to guard, to baby-sit
gwaredu (**rhag**) *be.* (**gwaredaf**)
to save, to redeem, to
deliver, to rid

gwaredwr *e.g. ll.* **gwaredwyr** saviour, deliverer

gwario *be.* **(gwariaf)** to spend (*money*)

gwarrau *gw.* **gwar**

gwartheg *e.ll.* cattle. *gw.* **buwch, da**

gwarthus *a.* shameful

gwas *e.g. ll.* **gweision** male servant; boy, lad. **gwas ffarm** farm labourer. *gw.* **morwyn**

gwasanaeth *e.g. ll.* **-au** service; use

gwasanaethu *be.* **(gwasanaethaf)** serve, to minister

gwasg 1 *e.b. ll.* **-au, -oedd, gweisg** press, pressure; waist. **gwasg argraffu** printing-press; **gwasg gaws** cheese-press; **gwŷr y wasg** the press (*reporters*). **2** *e.g. ll.* **-au, -oedd** stress; waist

gwasgedd *e.g. ll.* **-au** pressure. **gwasgedd isel** low pressure; **gwasgedd uchel** high pressure

gwasgfa *e.b. ll.* **gwasgfeydd** squeeze

gwasgod *e.b. ll.* **-au** waistcoat

gwasgu *be.* **(gwasgaf)** to press, to squeeze, to wring, to crush

gwastad 1 *e.g.ll.* **-au** plain. **2** *a.* flat, level, even; constant. **yn wastad** always (*S.W.*)

gwastraff *e.g. ll.* **-au, -oedd** waste. **gwastraff niwclear** nuclear waste

gwastraffu *be.* **(gwastraffaf)** to waste

gwau *be.* **(gweaf, gweuaf)** to weave; to knit. **dillad gwau** knitted garments. *gw.* **gweu**

gwaun *e.b. ll.* **gweunydd** meadow; moor

gwawd *e.g. ll.* **-iau, -ion** scorn, satire

gwawdio *be.* **(gwawdiaf)** to scorn, to mock, to jeer

gwawr *e.b.g. ll.* **-iau, -oedd** dawn; hue; shade. **ar doriad gwawr** at daybreak; **roedd gwawr las yn y brethyn** there was a shade of blue in the material

gwawrio *be.* **(gwawriaf)** to dawn

gwawroedd *gw.* **gwawr**

gwb *gw.* **cwb**

gwbl *gw.* **cwbl**

gwcw *gw.* **cwcw**

gwch *gw.* **cwch**

gwd *gw.* **cwd**

gwdihŵ *e.b. ll.* **-aid, -s** owl (*S.W.*). *gw.* **tylluan**

gwdyn *gw.* **cwdyn**

gwddf *e.g. ll.* **gyddfau** neck, throat; neckline. **gwddf crwn** round neck; **gwddf ffrog** neckline; **gwddf sgwâr** square neck; **gwddf V** V-neck

gwddwg *e.g. ll.* **gwddygau** neck, throat; neckline (*S.W.*)

gwe *e.b. ll.* **-oedd** web, cobweb. **gwe corryn: gwe pry' cop** cobweb; **safle ar y**

we: **gwefan** website
gweddi *e.b. ll.* **gweddïau**
prayer. **Gweddi'r Arglwydd**
The Lord's Prayer; **cwrdd
gweddi** prayer meeting
gweddill *e.g. ll.* **-ion** remnant
gweddïo *be.* **(gweddïaf)** to
pray
gweddol 1 *a.* fair. **pris
gweddol** a fairly good price;
cyflog gweddol a fairly good
wage. **2** *ad. (precedes the
adjective and is followed by
soft mutation).* **yn weddol
dawel** fairly quiet; **yn
weddol gyflym** fairly quick
gweddw 1 *e.b. ll.* **-on** widow.
2 *a.* widowed. **gŵr gweddw**
widower
gwefus *e.b. ll.* **-au** lip
gweiddi *be.* **(gwaeddaf)** to
shout
gweigion *gw.* **gwag**
gweiniaid *gw.* **gwan**
gweinidog *e.g. ll.* **-ion**
minister, servant. **Gweinidog
yr Efengyl** Minister of the
Gospel; **Prif Weinidog** Prime
Minister; **Gweinidog Gwladol**
Minister of State
gweinion *gw.* **gwan**
gweinydd *e.g. ll.* **-ion** waiter
gweinyddes *e.b. ll.* **-au**
waitress, female attendant;
nurse. **gweinyddes feithrin**
nursery nurse
gweiriau *gw.* **gwair**
gweisg *gw.* **gwasg**
gweision *gw.* **gwas**
gweithdy *e.g. ll.* **gweithdai**

workshop
gweithgar *a.* hardworking,
industrious
gweithiau *gw.* **gwaith**
gweithio *be.* **(gweithiaf)** to
work; to ferment; to operate
gweithiwr *e.g. ll.* **gweithwyr**
worker
gweithred *e.b. ll.* **-oedd** act,
deed
gweithredu *be.* **(gweithredaf)**
to act, to operate, to execute
gweithwyr *gw.* **gweithiwr**
gwelâu *gw.* **gwely**
gweld: gweled *be.* **(gwelaf)** to
see, to perceive. **gweler** see
(*when referring to
something*)
gwelw *a.* pale
gwely *e.g. ll.* **-au, gwelâu** bed
gwelydd *gw.* **gwal**
gwell *a.* better (*note: nouns
following* **gwell** *do not
mutate*)
gwella *be.* **(gwellaf)** to
improve, to better; to cure;
to mend
gwellt *e. torf.* grass, sward;
straw. *gw.* **gwelltyn**
gwelltyn *e.g. ll.* **gwellt** blade
of grass; a straw. *gw.* **gwellt**
gwen *a.b.* white. **ffrog wen** a
white frock; **torth wen** a
white loaf. *gw.* **gwyn**
gwên *e.b. ll.* **gwenau** smile
gwenau *gw.* **gwên**
gwendid *e.g. ll.* **-au**
weakness; wane (*of the
moon*). **y lleuad yn ei
gwendid** the wane of the

moon
Gwener *e.b.* Venus. **dydd
Gwener** Friday
gwenith *e.ll.* wheat.
gwenithen a grain of wheat
gwennol *e.b. ll.* **gwenoliaid**
swallow
Gwent *e.b.* a former county
in S.E. Wales, now
Monmouthshire
gwenu (ar) *be.* **(gwenaf)** to
smile
gwenwyn *e.g. ll.* **-au** poison;
venom; malice; spite
gwenwynig: gwenwynol *a.*
poisonous
gwenynen *e.b. ll.* **gwenyn**
bee
gwêr *e.g. ll.* **gwerau** tallow
gwerdd *a.b.* green. **ffrog
werdd** a green frock; **deilen
werdd** a green leaf; **y Blaid
Werdd** The Green Party. *gw.*
gwyrdd
gwerin *e.b. & e.torf. ll.*
-oedd, -edd ordinary people,
peasantry, folk; proletariat.
amgueddfa werin folk
museum; **cân werin** folk
song
gweriniaeth *e.b. ll.* **-au**
democracy, republic
Gweriniaeth Iwerddon *e.b.*
Eire
gwers *e.b. ll.* **-i** lesson; stanza
of poetry. **gwers Gymraeg**
Welsh lesson; **gwers hanes**
history lesson
gwerslyfr *e.g. ll.* **-au** textbook
gwersyll *e.g. ll.* **-oedd** camp

gwerth *e.g. ll.* **-oedd** worth,
value. **mae'n werth y
drafferth** it's worth the
trouble; **ar werth** for sale;
mae'n werth punt It's worth
a pound; **Ga i werth pum
punt o betrol?** May I have
five pounds' worth of petrol?
gwerthfawr *a.* valuable,
precious
gwerthfawrogi *be.*
(gwerthfawrogaf) to
appreciate
gwerthfawrogiad *e.g. ll.* **-au**
appreciation
gwerthiant *e.g. ll.*
gwerthiannau sale
gwerthoedd *gw.* **gwerth**
gwerthu *be.* **(gwerthaf)** to sell
gwerthwr *e.g. ll.* **gwerthwyr**
seller, salesman
gweryl *gw.* **cweryl**
gweryla *gw,* **cweryla**
gwestai *e.g. ll.* **gwesteion**
guest. *gw.* **gwesty**
gwesteion *gw.* **gwestai**
gwesteiwr *e.g. ll.* **gwesteiwyr**
host. **gwesteiwraig** hostess
gwestiwn *gw.* **cwestiwn**
gwestiyna *gw.* **cwestiyna**
gwestiynau *gw.* **cwestiwn**
gwesty *e.g. ll.* **gwestai,
gwestyau** hotel, inn
gweu *be.* **(gweuaf)** to weave;
to knit. *gw.* **gwau**
gweunydd *gw.* **gwaun**
gwg *e.g. ll.* **-on, gygau** frown,
scowl
gwgu (ar) *be.* **(gwgaf)** to
frown, to scowl, to glower

gwiail *gw.* **gwialen**
gwialen *e.b. ll.* **gwiail,**
 gwialennod rod, cane, stick.
 gwialen fedw birch-rod
gwialennod *gw.* **gwialen**
gwin *e.g. ll.* **-oedd** wine. **gwin**
 coch red wine; **gwin gwyn**
 white wine
gwir 1 *e.g.* truth. **yn wir** in
 truth, indeed. 2 *a.* true; real;
 net. **stori wir** a true story;
 (*the adjective may also*
 precede a noun and convey
 additional emphasis; it then
 causes a soft mutation). **gwir**
 bwysau net weight; **gwir**
 Gymro a real Welshman; **y**
 gwir ystyr the real meaning
gwirionedd *e.g. ll.* **-au** truth,
 reality
gwisg *e.b. ll.* **-oedd** dress.
 gwisg briodas wedding-
 dress; **gwisg nos** night-dress
gwisgo *be.* **(gwisgaf)** to dress;
 to wear
gwiwer *e.b. ll.* **-od** squirrel. **y**
 wiwer goch the red squirrel;
 y wiwer lwyd the grey
 squirrel
gwlad *e.b. ll.* **gwledydd**
 country, land. **gwlad fy**
 nhadau land of my fathers
Gwlad Belg *e.b.* Belgium
gwladfa *e.b. ll.* **gwladfaoedd,**
 gwladfeydd colony;
 settlement. **Y Wladfa**
 Patagonia
gwladgarwr *e.g. ll.*
 gwladgarwyr patriot
gwladol *a.* civil; country;

state; national. **Ysgrifennydd**
 Gwladol Secretary of State
Gwlad Pwyl *e.b.* Poland
Gwlad y Basg *e.b.* Basque
 Country
Gwlad yr Haf *e.b.* Somerset
Gwlad yr Iâ *e.b.* Iceland
gwlân *e.g. ll.* **gwlanoedd** wool
gwlanen *e.b. ll.* **-ni** home-
 spun, home-made cloth or
 flannel. **gwlanen goch** red
 flannel; **gwlanen wen** white
 flannel; **gwlanen ymolchi**
 face-cloth; **crys gwlanen**
 flannel shirt
gwledig *a.* rural; rustic;
 boorish. **Cymru Wledig**
 Rural Wales
gwledydd *gw.* **gwlad**
gwledd *e.b. ll.* **-oedd** feast;
 gwledd briodas marriage-
 feast
gwledda *be.* **(gwleddaf)** to
 feast
gwleidydd *e.g. ll.* **-ion**
 politician, statesman
gwleidyddiaeth *e.b.* politics
gwleidyddol *a.* political
gwlff *e.g. ll.* **gylffau** gulf
gwlith *e.g. ll.* **-oedd** dew
gwlwm *gw.* **cwlwm**
gwlyb *a. ll.* **-ion** wet
gwlybaniaeth *e.g.* moisture,
 wet, humidity
gwlychu *be.* **(gwlychaf)** to
 wet, to moisten; to get wet
gwm *e.g. ll.* **gymiau** gum.
 gw. **cwm**
gwmni *gw.* **cwmni**
gwmnïau *gw.* **cwmni**

gwmnïoedd *gw.* cwmni
gwmwl *gw.* cwmwl
gwn *e.g. ll.* **gynnau** gun. *gw.*
  gwybod
gŵn *e.g. ll.* **gynau** gown.
  gŵn gwisgo dressing gown;
  gŵn nos night-gown; *gw.* **ci**
gwneud: gwneuthur *be.*
  (gwnaf) to make; to do. *gw.*
  At. Berfau
gwningen *gw.* cwningen
gwniadyddes: gwniyddes *e.b.*
  ll. -au dressmaker,
  seamstress
gwnïo *be.* **(gwnïaf)** to sew, to
  stitch. **peiriant gwnïo** sewing
  machine
gwniyddes *gw.* gwniadyddes
gwobr *e.b. ll.* -au prize,
  reward. **y wobr gyntaf** the
  first prize; **gwobr gysur**
  consolation prize
gwobrwyo *be.* **(gwobrwyaf)** to
  reward, to award prize to
gwpan *gw.* cwpan
gwpla *gw.* cwpla
gwpwrdd *gw.* cwpwrdd
gwr *gw.* cwr
gŵr *e.g. ll.* **gwŷr** man;
  husband. **gŵr dieithr**
  stranger; **gŵr gwadd** guest,
  guest speaker; **gwŷr y wasg**
  pressmen, the press
gwrach *e.b. ll.* -od, -ïod hag,
  witch
gwragedd *gw.* gwraig
gwraidd *gw.* gwreiddyn
gwraig *e.b. ll.* gwragedd
  wife; woman
gwrandawiad *e.g. ll.* -au

listening, hearing
gwrandawr *e.g. ll.*
gwrandawyr listener, hearer
gwrando (ar) *be.* **(gwrandawaf)**
  to listen. **Gwrandewais ar** I
  listened to; **Gwrandewaist ar**
  You listened to
gwrdd *gw.* cwrdd
gwreichionen *e.b. ll.*
  gwreichion spark
gwreiddiau *gw.* gwreiddyn
gwreiddio *be.* **(gwreiddiaf)** to
  root, to ground
gwreiddiol *a.* original
gwreiddyn *e.g. ll.* **gwraidd,
  gwreiddiau** root; stock
gwres *e.g. ll.* -au heat,
  warmth; zeal. **gwres canolog**
  central heating
gwresog *a.* hot, warm;
  fervent
gwresogi *be.* **(gwresogaf)** to
  heat
gwresogydd *e.g. ll.* -ion
  heater
gwrido *be.* **(gwridaf)** to blush
gwridog *a.* rosy-cheeked,
  ruddy
gwrol *a.* brave, courageous
gwrs *gw.* cwrs
gwrtais *gw.* cwrtais
gwrtaith *e.g. ll.* **gwrteithiau**
  manure, fertilizer
gwrth *rhagdd.* (*Prefix with
  the sense 'against, contra-,
  counter-, anti-' in nouns,
  adjectives and verbs, and
  followed by soft mutation*).
  gwrth-ddweud to contradict
gwrthblaid *e.b. ll.*

gwrthbleidiau opposition (*party*)

gwrthchwyswr *e.b.* *ll.* **gwrthchwyswyr** antiperspirant

gwrthdaro *be.* **(gwrthdrawaf)** to clash, to collide

gwrthdystio *be.* **(gwrthdystiaf)** to protest

gwrthglocwedd *a.* anticlockwise

gwrthod *be.* **(gwrthodaf)** to refuse; to reject. **Fe wrthododd e fynd adref** He refused to go home

gwrthrych *e.g.* *ll.* **-au** object

gwrthrychol *a.* objective

gwrthryfel *e.g.* *ll.* **-oedd** rebellion, mutiny, insurrection

gwrthryfela *be.* **(gwrthryfelaf)** to rebel

gwrthwyneb 1 *e.g.* *ll.* **-au** in opposition to. 2 *a.* contrary, opposite. **i'r gwrthwyneb** to the contrary, in the opposite direction.

gwrthwynebu *be.* **(gwrthwynebaf)** to oppose; to object

gwrthwynebwr: **gwrthwynebydd** *e.g.* *ll.* **gwrthwynebwyr** opponent; objector; antagonist. **gwrthwynebydd cydwybodol** conscientious objector

gwrw *gw.* **cwrw**

gwrych *e.g.* *ll.* **-oedd** hedge; *e.ll.* bristles

gwryw 1 *e.g.* *ll.* **-od** male.

gwryw a benyw male and female. 2 *a.* male

gwrywaidd: gwrywol *a.* male

gwrywgydiaeth *e.b.* homosexuality. **gwrywgydiwr** homosexual

gwsg *gw.* **cwsg**

gwsmer *gw.* **cwsmer**

gwstwm *gw.* **cwstwm**

gwt *gw.* **cwt**

gwta *gw.* **cwta**

gwthiad *e.g.* *ll.* **-au** heave, thrust

gwthio *be.* **(gwthiaf)** to push, to thrust

gwthiwr *e.g.* *ll.* **gwthwyr** pusher

gwybedyn *e.g.* *ll.* **gwybed** gnat

gwybod (am) 1 *be.* **(gwn)** to know. *gw. At. Berfau.* 2 *e.g.* *ll.* **-au** knowledge. **heb yn wybod (i)** without knowing, unwittingly

gwybodaeth *e.b.* *ll.* **-au** knowledge

gwych *a.* fine, splendid; brilliant

gwydr *e.g.* *ll.* **-au** glass. **gwydr gwin** wineglass; **gwydr lliw** coloured glass, stained glass; **gwydr nadd** cut-glass; **tŷ gwydr** glasshouse

gwydrau *gw.* **gwydr, gwydryn**

gwydryn *e.g.* *ll.* **gwydrau** drinking-glass. **gwydraid** glassful

gŵydd 1 *e.b.* *ll.* **gwyddau** goose. **croen gŵydd** goose-flesh. 2 *e.g.* presence. **yng**

ngŵydd fy ngelynion in the presence of my enemies

gwyddbwyll *e.b.* chess

Gwyddel *e.g.* *ll.* **-od, Gwyddyl** Irishman

Gwyddeleg *e.g.* Irish language

Gwyddeles *e.b.* *ll.* **-au** Irishwoman

Gwyddelig *a.* Irish

gwyddoniaeth *e.b.* science

gwyddonol *a.* scientific

gwyddonydd *e.g.* *ll.* **gwyddonwyr** scientist

gwyddor *e.b.* *ll.* **-ion** rudiment, science: **yr wyddor** the alphabet

gwyfyn *e.g.* *ll.* **-od** moth

gŵyl *e.b.* *ll.* **gwyliau** feast, festival; holiday. **Gŵyl Dewi** Saint David's Day. **gŵyl y banc** bank holiday

gwylan *e.b.* *ll.* **-od** gull

gwyliadwrus *a.* watchful, cautious

gwyliau *gw.* **gŵyl**

gwylio (dros) *be.* **(gwyliaf)** to mind; watch (over); to guard

gwyliwr *e.g.* *ll.* **gwylwyr** sentry, guard, watchman

gwylnos *e.b.* *ll.* **-au** vigil, watchnight

gwylwyr *gw.* **gwyliwr**

gwyll *e.g.* darkness

gwyllt *a.* wild, mad. **yn wyllt gacwn** furiously cross, in a mad rage

gwylltio: gwylltu *be.* **(gwylltiaf: gwylltaf)** to lose one's temper, to excite violently

gwymon *e.g.* seaweed

gwymp *gw.* **cwymp**

gwympo *gw.* **cwympo**

gwyn *a.* *ll.* **-ion** white; holy. **Gwlad y menig gwynion** Land of the white gloves (*alluding to the frequent presentation of white gloves to assize judges in Wales, when there were no cases for trial*). *gw.* **cwyn.** *gw.* **gwen**

Gwynedd *e.b.* council and local authority in N. W. Wales

gwynegon *e.g.* rheumatism (*S.W.*)

gwynegu *be.* **(gwynegaf)** to ache (*S.W.*)

gwynfa *e.b.* paradise

gwynfyd *e.g.* *ll.* **-au** blessedness, bliss. **Y Gwynfydau** The Beatitudes

gwyngalch *e.g.* white-lime, whitewash

gwynion *gw.* **cwyn.** *gw.* **gwyn**

gwynnu *be.* **(gwynnaf)** to whiten, to bleach

gwynt *e.g.* *ll.* **-oedd** wind; smell. **a'i wynt yn ei ddwrn** breathless, panting, having one's heart in one's mouth; **prin ei wynt** short of breath

gwyntog *a.* windy; bombastic; **hirwyntog** longwinded

gwyr *gw.* **cwyr**

Gŵyr *e.b.* Gower

gŵyr 1 *a.* crooked, inclined, aslant. 2 *bf.* he/she/it knows. *gw.* **gwybod**

gwŷr *gw.* gŵr

gwyrdd 1 *a. ll.* -ion green.
 2 *e.g.* green. *gw.* gwerdd

gwyriad *e.g. ll.* -au deviation

gwyro: gwyrio *be.* (gwyraf:
 gwyriaf) to bend, to deviate,
 to incline, to swerve

gwyrth *e.b. ll.* -iau miracle

gwyrthiol *a.* miraculous.
 Roedd hi'n wyrthiol ei weld
 It was miraculous to see him

gwyryf *e.b. ll.* -on virgin

gwysion *gw.* gwŷs

gwŷs *e.b. ll.* gwysion
 summons

gwystl *e.g. ll.* -on hostage;
 pledge.

gwywo *be.* (gwywaf) to
 wither, to fade

gychod *gw.* cwch

gychwyn *gw.* cychwyn

gyd, i *ad.* (*always immediately
 follows the noun to which it
 refers*) all. **Roedd y plant i
 gyd yn dost** All the children
 were ill; **Mae'r cŵn i gyd yma**
 All the dogs are here

gyda: gydag *ardd.* together
 with; in company of

gydadrodd *gw.* cydadrodd

gydio *gw.* cydio

gydnabod *gw.* cydnabod

gyddfau *gw.* gwddf

gyfaill *gw.* cyfaill

gyfan *gw.* cyfan

gyfangwbl *gw.* cyfangwbl

gyfansoddi *gw.* cyfansoddi

gyfansoddwr *gw.*
 cyfansoddwr

gyfanswm *gw.* cyfanswm

gyfarch *gw.* cyfarch

gyfarfod *gw.* cyfarfod

gyfarwyddiadur *gw.*
 cyfarwyddiadur

gyfarwyddo *gw.* cyfarwyddo

gyfarwyddwr *gw.*
 cyfarwyddwr

gyfeilles *gw.* cyfeilles

gyfeillgar *gw.* cyfeillgar

gyfeillgarwch *gw.*
 cyfeillgarwch

gyfeillion *gw.* cyfaill

gyfeiriad *gw.* cyfeiriad

gyfeirio *gw.* cyfeirio

gyfenw *gw.* cyfenw

gyferbyn (â) *ardd.* opposite.
 yn y tŷ gyferbyn in the
 opposite house; **gyferbyn â'n
 tŷ ni** opposite our house

gyfiawn *gw.* cyfiawn

gyfiawnder *gw.* cyfiawnder

gyfieithiad *gw.* cyfieithiad

gyfieithu *gw.* cyfieithu

gyfieithydd *gw.* cyfieithydd

gyfle *gw.* cyfle

gyfleu *gw.* cyfleu

gyfleus *gw.* cyfleus

gyflog *gw.* cyflog

gyflogi *gw.* cyflogi

gyflogwr *gw.* cyflogwr

gyflwr *gw.* cyflwr

gyflwyno *gw.* cyflwyno

gyflym *gw.* cyflym

gyflymach *gw.* cyflym

gyflymaf *gw.* cyflym

gyflymder *gw.* cyflymder

gyflymed *gw.* cyflym

gyflymu *gw.* cyflymu

gyflymydd *gw.* cyflymydd

gyfnither *gw.* cyfnither

gyfnod

gyfnod *gw*. cyfnod
gyfoeth *gw*. cyfoeth
gyfoethog *gw*. cyfoethog
gyfraith *gw*. cyfraith
gyfrannu *gw*. cyfrannu
gyfreithiwr *gw*. cyfreithiwr
gyfres *gw*. cyfres
gyfrif *gw*. cyfrif
gyfrifiadur *gw*. cyfrifiadur
gyfrifol *gw*. cyfrifol
gyfrifoldeb *gw*. cyfrifoldeb
gyfrifydd *gw*. cyfrifydd
gyfrinach *gw*. cyfrinach
gyfrinachol *gw*. cyfrinachol
gyfrol *gw*. cyfrol
gyfrwng *gw*. cyfrwng
gyfrwys *gw*. cyfrwys
gyfun *gw*. cyfun
gyfuwch *gw*. uchel
gyfweld *gw*. cyfweld
gyfweliad *gw*. cyfweliad
gyfyng *gw*. cyfyng
gyfyngu *gw*. cyfyngu
gyfystyr *gw*. cyfystyr
gyfforddus *gw*. cyfforddus.
gyffredin *gw*. cyffredin
gyffrous *gw*. cyffrous
gyffur *gw*. cyffur
gyffwrdd *gw*. cyffwrdd
gygau *gw*. gwg
gyngerdd *gw*. cyngerdd
gynghori *gw*. cynghori
gynghorwr *gw*. cynghorwr
gyngor *gw*. cyngor
gyhoedd *gw*. cyhoedd
gyhoeddi *gw*. cyhoeddi
gyhoeddiad *gw*. cyhoeddiad
gyhoeddus *gw*. cyhoeddus
gyhoeddusrwydd *gw*.
  cyhoeddusrwydd

gyhoeddwr *gw*. cyhoeddwr
gyhyd *gw*. cyhyd
gyhyrog *gw*. cyhyrog
gylch *gw*. cylch
gylchgrawn *gw*. cylchgrawn
gylchlythyr *gw*. cylchlythyr
gyll *gw*. cyll
gyllell *gw*. cyllell
gyllyll *gw*. cyllell
gymaint *gw*. mawr
gymal *gw*. cymal
gymanfa *gw*. cymanfa
gymdeithas *gw*. cymdeithas
gymdogion *gw*. cymydog
gymeriad *gw*. cymeriad
gymharu *gw*. cymharu
gymhleth *gw*. cymhleth
gymhlethdod *gw*.
  cymhlethdod
gymhlethu *gw*. cymhlethu
gymoedd *gw*. cwm
gymorth *gw*. cymorth
Gymraeg *gw*. Cymraeg
Gymraes *gw*. Cymraes
Gymreictod *gw*. Cymreictod
Gymreig *gw*. Cymreig
Gymreiges *gw*. Cymraes
Gymro *gw*. Cymro
Gymru *gw*. Cymru
Gymry *gw*. Cymro
gymryd *gw*. cymryd
gymundeb *gw*. cymundeb
gymuned *gw*. cymuned
gymwynas *gw*. cymwynas
gymydog *gw*. cymydog
gymylau *gw*. cwmwl
gymylog *gw*. cymylog
gymysg *gw*. cymysg
gymysgu *gw*. cymysgu
gymysgwch *gw*. cymysgwch

gyn *gw.* cyn
gynaeafau *gw.* cynhaeaf
gynau *gw.* gŵn
gynddrwg *gw.* cynddrwg
gynffon *gw.* cynffon
gynhadledd *gw.* cynhadledd
gynhaeaf *gw.* cynhaeaf
gynhesu *gw.* cynhesu
gynhyrfus *gw.* cynhyrfus
gynigion *gw.* cynnig
gynilion *gw.* cynilion
gynilo *gw.* cynilo
gynllun *gw.* cynllun
gynllunio *gw.* cynllunio
gynlluniwr *gw.* cynlluniwr
gynllunydd *gw.* cynlluniwr
gynnal *gw.* cynnal
gynnar *gw.* cynnar
gynnau *ad.* a short while ago, just now. *gw.* gwn
gynnes *gw.* cynnes
gynnig *gw.* cynnig
gynradd *gw.* cynradd
gynt *ad.* formerly; *née*; long since; ages ago. **Rhian Smith (gynt Jones)** Rhian Smith (*née* Jones); **yr hen ddyddiau gynt** the old days, ages ago. *gw.* cynnar
gyntaf *gw.* cynnar
gynted *gw.* cynnar
gyntedd *gw.* cyntedd
gynulleidfa *gw.* cynulleidfa
gynulliad *gw.* cynulliad
gyrddau *gw.* cwrdd
gyrfa *e.b.* *ll.* -oedd, gyrfeydd race; career; course
gyrfeydd *gw.* gyrfa
gyrff *gw.* corff
gyrion *gw.* cwr
gyrliog *gw.* cyrliog
gyrn *gw.* corn
gyrraedd *gw.* cyrraedd
gyrrau *gw.* cwr
gyrru *be.* **(gyrraf)** to drive; to send; to push
gyrrwr *e.g.* *ll.* **gyrwyr** driver; sender
gyrwyr *gw.* gyrrwr
gysglyd *gw.* cysglyd
gysgod *gw.* cysgod
gysgodi *gw.* cysgodi
gysgu *gw.* cysgu
gystadleuaeth *gw.* cystadleuaeth
gystadleuwr *gw.* cystadleuwr
gystadleuydd *gw.* cystadleuwr
gystadlu *gw.* cystadlu
gystal *gw.* da
gystymau *gw.* cwstwm
gysur *gw.* cysur
gysuro *gw.* cysuro
gysurus *gw.* cysurus
gyswllt *gw.* cyswllt
gytgan *gw.* cytgan
gytsain *gw.* cytsain
gytundeb *gw.* cytundeb
gytuno *gw.* cytuno
gyw *gw.* cyw
gywaith *gw.* cywaith
gywir *gw.* cywir
gywiriad *gw.* cywiriad
gywiro *gw.* cywiro

NG

ngadael *gw.* gadael
ngaeaf *gw.* gaeaf
ngafael *gw.* gafael
ngafr *gw.* gafr

ngair *gw.* gair
ngalar *gw.* galar
ngalw *gw.* galw
ngalwad *gw.* galwad
ngalwedigaeth *gw.*
 galwedigaeth
ngalwyn *gw.* galwyn
ngallu *gw.* gallu
ngardd *gw.* gardd
ngarddio *gw.* garddio
ngarddwr *gw.* garddwr
ngarej *gw.* garej
ngarlleg *gw.* garlleg
ngat *gw.* gât
ngefeilliaid *gw.* gefell
ngeirfa *gw.* geirfa
ngeiriadur *gw.* geiriadur
ngeiriau *gw.* gair
ngelyn *gw.* gelyn
ngên *gw.* gên
ngenau *gw.* gên, genau
ngenetaidd *gw.* genetig
ngenetig *gw.* genetig
ngeneth *gw.* geneth
ngeneuau *gw.* genau
ngeni *gw.* geni
ngenyn *gw.* genyn
ngenynnol *gw.* genetig
ngêr *gw.* gêr
ngewyn *gw.* gewyn
nghaban *gw.* caban
nghacen *gw.* cacen
nghacwn *gw.* cacynen
nghacynen *gw.* cacynen
nghadach *gw.* cadach
nghadair *gw.* cadair
nghadeirio *gw.* cadeirio
nghadeirydd *gw.* cadeirydd
nghadnawes *gw.* cadno
nghadno *gw.* cadno

nghadw *gw.* cadw
nghadwyn *gw.* cadwyn
nghadwyno *gw.* cadwyno
nghae *gw.* cae
nghael *gw.* cael
Nghaer *gw.* Caer
nghaer *gw.* caer
Nghaerdydd *gw.* Caerdydd
Nghaerfyrddin *gw.*
 Caerfyrddin
Nghaergybi *gw.* Caergybi
Nghaerloyw *gw.* Caerloyw
Nghaersalem *gw.* Caersalem
nghaets *gw.* caets
nghaffe *gw.* caffe
nghangen *gw.* cangen
nghais *gw.* cais
nghalan *gw.* calan
nghaledi *gw.* caledi
nghaledu *gw.* caledu
nghaledwch *gw.* caledwch
nghalendr *gw.* calendr
nghalennig *gw.* calennig
nghalon *gw.* calon
ngham *gw.* cam
nghamarwain *gw.* camarwain
nghamddeall *gw.* camddeall
nghamera *gw.* camera
nghamp *gw.* camp
nghampfa *gw.* campfa
nghampwaith *gw.* campwaith
nghamsyniad *gw.* camsyniad
nghan *gw.* can
nghân *gw.* cân
nghaneuon *gw.* cân
nghanfed *gw.* canfed
nghanhwyllau *gw.* cannwyll
nghanhwyllbren *gw.*
 canhwyllbren
nghaniad *gw.* caniad

nghaniadaeth *gw.* caniadaeth
nghaniadau *gw.* cân. *gw.*
 caniad
nghaniatâd *gw.* caniatâd
nghaniatáu *gw.* caniatáu
nghaniedydd *gw.* caniedydd
nghanmlwydd *gw.* canmlwydd
nghanmol *gw.* canmol
nghanmoliaeth *gw.*
 canmoliaeth
nghannoedd *gw.* cant
nghannwyll *gw.* cannwyll
nghanol *gw.* canol
nghanolbarth *gw.* canolbarth
nghanoldir *gw.* canoldir
nghanolfan *gw.* canolfan
nghanolwr *gw.* canolwr
nghanradd *gw.* canradd
nghanran *gw.* canran
nghanrif *gw.* canrif
nghanrifau: nghanrifoedd *gw.*
 canrif
nghant *gw.* cant
nghantor *gw.* cantor
nghantores *gw.* cantores
nghanu *gw.* canu
nghanŵ *gw.* canŵ
nghanŵio *gw.* canŵio
nghanwr *gw.* canwr
nghap *gw.* cap
nghapel *gw.* capel
nghapten *gw.* capten
nghar *gw.* car
ngharafán *gw.* carafán
ngharafana *gw.* carafana
ngharco *gw.* carco
ngharchar *gw.* carchar
ngharcharor *gw.* carcharor
ngharcharu *gw.* carcharu
nghardiau *gw.* cerdyn

ngharedigrwydd *gw.*
 caredigrwydd
nghariad *gw.* cariad
nghariadon *gw.* cariad
nghariadus *gw.* cariadus
nghario *gw.* cario
ngharol *gw.* carol
ngharped *gw.* carped
ngharreg *gw.* carreg
nghartref *gw.* cartref
nghartrefi *gw.* cartref
nghartrefu *gw.* cartrefu
ngharu *gw.* caru
ngharwriaeth *gw.* carwriaeth
nghas *gw.* cas
nghasáu *gw.* casáu
nghasgen *gw.* casgen
nghasgliad *gw.* casgliad
nghasglu *gw.* casglu
Nghas-gwent *gw.* Cas-gwent
Nghasllwchwr *gw.* Casllwchwr
Nghasnewydd *gw.*
 Casnewydd
nghastell *gw.* castell
Nghastell-nedd *gw.* Castell-
 nedd
nghath *gw.* cath
nghau *gw.* cau
nghawl *gw.* cawl
nghawod *gw.* cawod
nghawr *gw.* cawr
nghaws *gw.* caws
nghefn *gw.* cefn
nghefnder *gw.* cefnder
nghefndir *gw.* cefndir
nghefndiroedd *gw.* cefndir
nghefndyr *gw.* cefnder
nghefnogi *gw.* cefnogi
nghefnu *gw.* cefnu
nghefnwr *gw.* cefnwr

nghefnwyr *gw.* cefnwr

ngheffyl *gw.* ceffyl

ngheg *gw.* ceg

nghegin *gw.* cegin

nghei *gw.* cei

ngheidwad *gw.* ceidwad

ngheiliog *gw.* ceiliog

Ngheinewydd *gw.* Ceinewydd

ngheiniog *gw.* ceiniog

ngheiriosen *gw.* ceiriosen

ngheisio *gw.* ceisio

nghelf *gw.* celf

nghelfi *gw.* celficyn

nghelficyn *gw.* celficyn

nghelwydd *gw.* celwydd

nghelyn *gw.* celynnen

nghelynnen *gw.* celynnen

nghell *gw.* cell

nghellau: nghelloedd *gw.* cell

nghemeg *gw.* cemeg

nghenedl *gw.* cenedl

nghenedlaetholdeb *gw.*
  cenedlaetholdeb

nghenedlaetholwr *gw.*
  cenedlaetholwr

nghenhadaeth *gw.*
  cenhadaeth

nghenhadon *gw.* cenhadwr

nghenhadu *gw.* cenhadu

nghenhadwr *gw.* cenhadwr

nghenhedlaeth *gw.*
  cenhedlaeth

nghenhinen *gw.* cenhinen

nghennin *gw.* cennin

ngherdyn *gw.* cerdyn

ngherdd *gw.* cerdd

ngherddor *gw.* cerddor

ngherddorfa *gw.* cerddorfa

ngherddoriaeth *gw.*
  cerddoriaeth

ngherddwr *gw.* cerddwr

ngherfio *gw.* cerfio

ngherflun *gw.* cerflun

ngherrig *gw.* carreg

nghesair *gw.* cesair

nghestyll *gw.* castell

nghewri *gw.* cawr

nghewyn *gw.* cewyn

ngheyrydd *gw.* caer

nghi *gw.* ci

nghig *gw.* cig

nghigydd *gw.* cigydd

nghinio *gw.* cinio

nghipolwg *gw.* cipolwg

nghist *gw.* cist

nghlaf *gw.* claf

nghlai *gw.* clai

nghlasur *gw.* clasur

nghlawdd *gw.* clawdd

nghlawr *gw.* clawr

nghlebran *gw.* clebran

nghledr *gw.* cledr

nghlefyd *gw.* clefyd

nghleifion *gw.* claf

nghlêr *gw.* cleren

nghlerc *gw.* clerc

nghleren *gw.* cleren

nghlirio *gw.* clirio

nghlo *gw.* clo

nghloc *gw.* cloc

nghloch *gw.* cloch

nghlod *gw.* clod

nghlodfori *gw.* clodfori

nghloddiau *gw.* clawdd

nghloffi *gw.* cloffi

nghlogwyn *gw.* clogwyn

nghlogyn *gw.* clogyn

nghloi *gw.* cloi

nghlorian *gw.* clorian

nghloriau *gw.* clawr

nghlown *gw*. clown
nghlun *gw*. clun
nghlust *gw*. clust
nghlustog *gw*. clustog
nghlwm *gw*. clwm
nghlwtyn *gw*. clwtyn
Nghlwyd *gw*. Clwyd
nghlwyd *gw*. clwyd
nghlwydau: nghlwydi *gw*.
 clwyd
nghlwyf *gw*. clwyf
nghlychau *gw*. cloch
nghlymau *gw*. clwm
nghlymu *gw*. clymu
nghlytiau *gw*. clwtyn
nghlyw *gw*. clyw
nghlywed *gw*. clywed
nghnau *gw*. cneuen
nghneuen *gw*. cneuen
nghnoc *gw*. cnoc
nghnocio *gw*. cnocio
nghnoi *gw*. cnoi
nghoban *gw*. coban
nghoch *gw*. coch
nghodi *gw*. codi
nghoed *gw*. coeden
Nghoed-duon *gw*. Coed-duon
nghoeden *gw*. coeden
nghoedwig *gw*. coedwig
nghoes *gw*. coes
nghof *gw*. cof
nghofion *gw*. cof
nghofleidio *gw*. cofleidio
nghofrestr *gw*. cofrestr
nghofrestru *gw*. cofrestru
nghoffi *gw*. coffi
nghog *gw*. cog
nghoginio *gw*. coginio
nghogydd *gw*. cogydd
ngholeg *gw*. coleg

ngholer *gw*. coler
ngholofn *gw*. colofn
ngholuro *gw*. coluro
ngholled *gw*. colled
nghollen *gw*. collen
ngholli *gw*. colli
nghopïo *gw*. copïo
nghopyn *gw*. copyn
nghôr *gw*. côr
nghorau *gw*. côr
nghordyn *gw*. cordyn
nghorff *gw*. corff
nghorgi *gw*. corgi
nghorn *gw*. corn
nghornel *gw*. cornel
nghoron *gw*. coron
nghoroni *gw*. coroni
nghorryn *gw*. corryn
nghosb *gw*. cosb
nghosbi *gw*. cosbi
nghot *gw*. cot
nghôt *gw*. cot
nghotwm *gw*. cotwm
nghrac *gw*. crac
nghrachach *gw*. crachach
nghrafu *gw*. crafu
nghragen *gw*. cragen
nghraig *gw*. craig
nghrasu *gw*. crasu
nghredu *gw*. credu
nghrefydd *gw*. crefydd
nghrefft *gw*. crefft
nghrefftwr *gw*. crefftwr
nghregyn *gw*. cragen
nghreigiau *gw*. craig
nghreision *gw*. creision
nghrempog *gw*. crempog
nghreulondeb *gw*.
 creulondeb
nghri *gw*. cri

nghrib *gw*. crib
nghribo *gw*. cribo
nghriced *gw*. criced
nghricedwr *gw*. cricedwr
nghricsyn *gw*. cricsyn
nghrio *gw*. crio
Nghristion *gw*. Cristion
Nghristnogion *gw*. Cristion
nghriw *gw*. criw
nghroen *gw*. croen
nghroes *gw*. croes
nghroesair *gw*. croesair
nghroesau *gw*. croes
nghroesawu *gw*. croesawu
nghroesfan *gw*. croesfan
nghroesffordd *gw*.
 croesffordd
nghroesholi *gw*. croesholi
nghroesi *gw*. croesi
nghroeso *gw*. croeso
nghronfa *gw*. cronfa
nghronfeydd *gw*. cronfa
nghrud *gw*. crud
nghrwst *gw*. crwst
nghrwyn *gw*. croen
nghryd *gw*. cryd
nghrynodeb *gw*. crynodeb
nghrynu *gw*. crynu
nghrys *gw*. crys
nghrystiau *gw*. crwst, crystyn
nghrystyn *gw*. crystyn
nghuddio *gw*. cuddio
nghuro *gw*. curo
nghusan *gw*. cusan
nghusanu *gw*. cusanu
nghwb *gw*. cwb
nghwbl *gw*. cwbl
nghwcw *gw*. cwcw
nghwch *gw*. cwch
nghwd *gw*. cwd

nghwdyn *gw*. cwdyn
nghweryl *gw*. cweryl
nghwestiwn *gw*. cwestiwn
nghwestiyna *gw*. cwestiyna
nghwestiynau *gw*. cwestiwn
nghwlwm *gw*. cwlwm
nghwm *gw*. cwm
nghwmni *gw*. cwmni
nghwmnïau: nghwmnïoedd
 gw. cwmni
nghwmwl *gw*. cwmwl
nghŵn *gw*. ci
nghwningen *gw*. cwningen
nghwningod *gw*. cwningen
nghwpan *gw*. cwpan
nghwpla *gw*. cwpla
nghwpwrdd *gw*. cwpwrdd
nghwr *gw*. cwr
nghwrdd *gw*. cwrdd
nghwrs *gw*. cwrs
nghwrw *gw*. cwrw
nghwsg *gw*. cwsg
nghwsmer *gw*. cwsmer
nghwstwm *gw*. cwstwm
nghwt *gw*. cwt
nghwymp *gw*. cwymp
nghwyn *gw*. cwyn
nghwyno *gw*. cwyno
nghwyr *gw*. cwyr
nghychod *gw*. cwch
nghychwyn *gw*. cychwyn
nghydadrodd *gw*. cydadrodd
nghydau *gw*. cwd, cwdyn
nghydnabod *gw*. cydnabod
nghyfaill *gw*. cyfaill
nghyfan *gw*. cyfan
nghyfansoddi *gw*. cyfansoddi
nghyfansoddwr *gw*.
 cyfansoddwr
nghyfanswm *gw*. cyfanswm

nghyfarch *gw*. cyfarch
nghyfarfod *gw*. cyfarfod
nghyfarfodydd *gw*. cyfarfod
nghyfarwyddiadur *gw*.
 cyfarwyddiadur
nghyfarwyddo *gw*.
 cyfarwyddo
nghyfarwyddwr *gw*.
 cyfarwyddwr
nghyfeilles *gw*. cyfeilles
nghyfeillgarwch *gw*.
 cyfeillgarwch
nghyfeillion *gw*. cyfaill
nghyfeiriad *gw*. cyfeiriad
nghyfeirio *gw*. cyfeirio
nghyfenw *gw*. cyfenw
nghyfiawnder *gw*. cyfiawnder
nghyfieithiad *gw*. cyfieithiad
nghyfieithu *gw*. cyfieithu
nghyfieithydd *gw*. cyfieithydd
nghyfle *gw*. cyfle
nghyflog *gw*. cyflog
nghyflogi *gw*. cyflogi
nghyflogwr *gw*. cyflogwr
nghyflwr *gw*. cyflwr
nghyflwyno *gw*. cyflwyno
nghyflymder *gw*. cyflymder
nghyflymu *gw*. cyflymu
nghyflymydd *gw*. cyflymydd
nghyfnither *gw*. cyfnither
nghyfoeth *gw*. cyfoeth
nghyfraith *gw*. cyfraith
nghyfreithiwr *gw*. cyfreithiwr
nghyfres *gw*. cyfres
nghyfrif *gw*. cyfrif
nghyfrifiadur *gw*. cyfrifiadur
nghyfrifiannell *gw*.
 cyfrifiannell
nghyfrifoldeb *gw*. cyfrifoldeb
nghyfrifydd *gw*. cyfrifydd

nghyfrinach *gw*. cyfrinach
nghyfrol *gw*. cyfrol
nghyfrwng *gw*. cyfrwng
nghyfweliad *gw*. cyfweliad
nghyfyngu *gw*. cyfyngu
nghyffur *gw*. cyffur
nghyffwrdd *gw*. cyffwrdd
nghyngerdd *gw*. cyngerdd
nghynghori *gw*. cynghori
nghynghorwr *gw*. cynghorwr
nghynghrair *gw*. cynghrair
nghyngor *gw*. cyngor
nghyhoeddi *gw*. cyhoeddi
nghyhoeddiad *gw*.
 cyhoeddiad
nghyhoeddusrwydd *gw*.
 cyhoeddusrwydd
nghyhoeddwr *gw*. cyhoeddwr
nghylch *gw*. cylch
nghylchfan *gw*. cylchfan
nghylchgrawn *gw*.
 cylchgrawn
nghylchgronau *gw*.
 cylchgrawn
nghylchlythyr *gw*. cylchlythyr
nghyll *gw*. collen
nghyllell *gw*. cyllell
nghyllyll *gw*. cyllell
nghymal *gw*. cymal
nghymanfa *gw*. cymanfa
nghymdeithas *gw*.
 cymdeithas
nghymdogion *gw*. cymydog
nghymeriad *gw*. cymeriad
nghymharu *gw*. cymharu
nghymhlethdod *gw*.
 cymhlethdod
nghymoedd *gw*. cwm
nghymorth *gw*. cymorth
Nghymraeg *gw*. Cymraeg

Nghymraes *gw*. Cymraes

Nghymreictod *gw*. Cymreictod

Nghymreiges *gw*. Cymreiges

Nghymro *gw*. Cymro

Nghymru *gw*. Cymru

Nghymry *gw*. Cymro

nghymryd *gw*. cymryd

nghymundeb *gw*. cymundeb

nghymwynas *gw*. cymwynas

nghymydog *gw*. cymydog

nghymylau *gw*. cwmwl

nghymysgu *gw*. cymysgu

nghymysgwch *gw*.
  cymysgwch

nghyn- *gw*. cyn-

nghynaeafau *gw*. cynhaeaf

nghynffon *gw*. cynffon

nghynhadledd *gw*.
  cynhadledd

nghynhaeaf *gw*. cynhaeaf

nghynhesu *gw*. cynhesu

nghynilion *gw*. cynilion

nghynllun *gw*. cynllun

nghynllunio *gw*. cynllunio

nghynlluniwr *gw*. cynlluniwr

nghynnal *gw*. cynnal

nghynnig *gw*. cynnig

nghynnwys *gw*. cynnwys

nghynorthwywr *gw*.
  cynorthwywr

nghynorthwy-ydd *gw*.
  cynorthwy-ydd

nghyntaf *gw*. cyntaf

nghyntedd *gw*. cyntedd

nghynulleidfa *gw*. cynulleidfa

nghypyrddau *gw*. cwpwrdd

nghyrddau *gw*. cwrdd

nghyrff *gw*. corff

nghyrn *gw*. corn

nghyrraedd *gw*. cyrraedd

nghyrsau: nghyrsiau *gw*. cwrs

nghysgod *gw*. cysgod

nghysgodi *gw*. cysgodi

nghysgodion *gw*. cysgod

nghysgu *gw*. cysgu

nghystadlaethau *gw*.
  cystadleuaeth

nghystadleuaeth *gw*.
  cystadleuaeth

nghystadleuwr *gw*.
  cystadleuwr

nghystadlu *gw*. cystadlu

nghystymau *gw*. cwstwm

nghysur *gw*. cysur

nghysuro *gw*. cysuro

nghyswllt *gw*. cyswllt

nghytgan *gw*. cytgan

nghytsain *gw*. cytsain

nghytundeb *gw*. cytundeb

nghytuno *gw*. cytuno

nghyw *gw*. cyw

nghywaith *gw*. cywaith

nghywiriad *gw*. cywiriad

nghywiro *gw*. cywiro

nglan *gw*. glan

nglân *gw*. glân

nglanhau *gw*. glanhau

nglanio *gw*. glanio

nglannau *gw*. glan

nglas *gw*. glas

nglaswelltyn *gw*. glaswelltyn

nglaw *gw*. glaw

nglendid *gw*. glendid

nglin *gw*. glin

nglo *gw*. glo

nglofa *gw*. glofa

nglöwr *gw*. glöwr

nglöyn byw *gw*. glöyn byw

nglud *gw*. glud

ngludio *gw*. gludio

ngludo *gw.* gludio
nglyn *gw.* glyn
nglynu *gw.* glynu
ngobaith *gw.* gobaith
ngobeithion *gw.* gobaith
ngobennydd *gw.* gobennydd
ngodre *gw.* godre
ngodro *gw.* godro
ngoddef *gw.* goddef
ngoddrych *gw.* goddrych
ngof *gw.* gof
ngofaint *gw.* gof
ngofal *gw.* gofal
ngofalwr *gw.* gofalwr
ngofid *gw.* gofid
ngofidio *gw.* gofidio
ngofod *gw.* gofod
ngofodwr *gw.* gofodwr
ngofynion *gw.* gofyn
ngogledd *gw.* gogledd
ngogleisio *gw.* gogleisio
ngogogiant *gw.* gogoniant
ngôl *gw.* gôl
ngolau *gw.* golau
ngolchi *gw.* golchi
ngoleudy *gw.* goleudy
ngoleuni *gw.* goleuni
ngoleuo *gw.* goleuo
ngolud *gw.* golud
ngolwg *gw.* golwg
ngolygfa *gw.* golygfa
ngolygfeydd *gw.* golygfa
ngolygon *gw.* golwg
ngolygydd *gw.* golygydd
ngollwng *gw.* gollwng
ngorau *gw.* gorau
ngorchfygu *gw.* gorchfygu
ngorchymyn *gw.* gorchymyn
ngorfodaeth *gw.* gorfodaeth
ngorfodi *gw.* gorfodi

Ngorffennaf *gw.* Gorffennaf
ngorffennol *gw.* gorffennol
ngorffwys *gw.* gorffwys
ngorffwyso *gw.* gorffwyso
ngorllewin *gw.* gorllewin
ngornest *gw.* gornest
ngorsaf *gw.* gorsaf
ngorsedd *gw.* gorsedd
ngorwel *gw.* gorwel
ngosod *gw.* gosod
ngostwng *gw.* gostwng
ngostyngiad *gw.* gostyngiad
ngradd *gw.* gradd
ngraddfa *gw.* graddfa
ngramadeg *gw.* gramadeg
ngrant *gw.* grant
ngras *gw.* gras
ngrawnffrwyth *gw.*
  grawnffrwyth
ngris *gw.* gris
Ngroeg *gw.* Groeg
ngrudd *gw.* grudd
ngrug *gw.* grug
ngrŵp *gw.* grŵp
ngrym *gw.* grym
ngwadu *gw.* gwadu
ngwaed *gw.* gwaed
ngwaedu *gw.* gwaedu
ngwaedd *gw.* gwaedd
ngwaelod *gw.* gwaelod
ngwaelodion *gw.* gwaelod
ngwaethaf *gw.* gwaethaf
ngwagedd *gw.* gwagedd
ngwagle *gw.* gwagle
ngwahanol *gw.* gwahanol
ngwahodd *gw.* gwahodd
ngwahoddedigion *gw.*
  gwahoddedig
ngwahoddiad *gw.*
  gwahoddiad

ngwair *gw*. gwair
ngwaith *gw*. gwaith
ngwal *gw*. gwal
ngwâl *gw*. gwâl
ngwalau *gw*. gwâl
ngwaliau *gw*. gwal
ngwall *gw*. gwall
ngwallt *gw*. gwallt
ngwanwyn *gw*. gwanwyn
ngwar *gw*. gwar
ngwarchod *gw*. gwarchod
ngwaredu *gw*. gwaredu
ngwaredwr *gw*. gwaredwr
ngwario *gw*. gwario
ngwartheg *gw*. gwartheg
ngwas *gw*. gwas
ngwasanaeth *gw*. gwasanaeth
ngwasanaethu *gw*.
　gwasanaethu
ngwasg *gw*. gwasg
ngwasgedd *gw*. gwasgedd
ngwasgfa *gw*. gwasgfa
ngwasgod *gw*. gwasgod
ngwasgu *gw*. gwasgu
ngwastraff *gw*. gwastraff
ngwastraffu *gw*. gwastraffu
ngwau *gw*. gwau
ngwaun *gw*. gwaun
ngwawdio *gw*. gwawdio
ngwawr *gw*. gwawr
ngwdihŵ *gw*. gwdihŵ
ngwddf *gw*. gwddf
ngwddwg *gw*. gwddwg
ngweddi *gw*. gweddi
ngweddill *gw*. gweddill
ngweddïo *gw*. gweddïo
ngwefus *gw*. gwefus
ngweiddi *gw*. gweiddi
ngweigion *gw*. gwag
ngweiniaid *gw*. gwan

ngweinidog *gw*. gweinidog
ngweinion *gw*. gwan
ngweinydd *gw*. gweinydd
ngweinyddes *gw*. gweinyddes
ngweiriau *gw*. gwair
ngweisg *gw*. gwasg
ngweision *gw*. gwas
ngweithdy *gw*. gweithdy
ngweithiau *gw*. gwaith
ngweithio *gw*. gweithio
ngweithiwr *gw*. gweithiwr
ngweithred *gw*. gweithred
ngweithwyr *gw*. gweithiwr
ngwelâu *gw*. gwely
ngweld *gw*. gweld
ngwely *gw*. gwely
ngwelyau *gw*. gwely
ngwell *gw*. da
ngwella *gw*. gwella
ngwellt *gw*. gwellt, gwelltyn
ngwelltyn *gw*. gwelltyn
ngwên *gw*. gwên
ngwenau *gw*. gwên
ngwendid *gw*. gwendid
Ngwener *gw*. Gwener
ngwenith *gw*. gwenith
ngwennol *gw*. gwennol
Ngwent *gw*. Gwent
ngwenu *gw*. gwenu
ngwenwyn *gw*. gwenwyn
ngwenynen *gw*. gwenynen
ngwêr *gw*. gwêr
ngwerin *gw*. gwerin
ngweriniaeth *gw*. gweriniaeth
ngwers *gw*. gwers
ngwerslyfr *gw*. gwerslyfr
ngwersyll *gw*. gwersyll
ngwerth *gw*. gwerth
ngwerthfawrogi *gw*.
　gwerthfawrogi

ngwerthfawrogiad *gw.*
  gwerthfawrogiad
ngwerthiant *gw.* gwerthiant
ngwerthu *gw.* gwerthu
ngwerthwr *gw.* gwerthwr
ngwestai *gw.* gwestai, gwesty
ngwesteion *gw.* gwestai
ngwesteiwr *gw.* gwesteiwr
ngwesteiwraig *gw.* gwesteiwr
ngwesty *gw.* gwesty
ngweu *gw.* gweu
ngweunydd *gw.* gwaun
ngwg *gw.* gwg
ngwgu *gw.* gwgu
ngwiail *gw.* gwialen
ngwialen *gw.* gwialen
ngwialennod *gw.* gwialen
ngwin *gw.* gwin
ngwir *gw.* gwir
ngwirionedd *gw.* gwirionedd
ngwisg *gw.* gwisg
ngwisgo *gw.* gwisgo
ngwiwer *gw.* gwiwer
ngwlad *gw.* gwlad
ngwladfa *gw.* gwladfa
ngwladgarwyr *gw.*
  gwladgarwr
ngwlân *gw.* gwlân
ngwlanen *gw.* gwlanen
ngwledydd *gw.* gwlad
ngwledd *gw.* gwledd
ngwledda *gw.* gwledda
ngwleidydd *gw.* gwleidydd
ngwleidyddiaeth *gw.*
  gwleidyddiaeth
ngwlff *gw.* gwlff
ngwlith *gw.* gwlith
ngwlybaniaeth *gw.*
  gwlybaniaeth
ngwlychu *gw.* gwlychu

ngwn *gw.* gwn
ngŵn *gw.* gŵn
ngwneud *gw.* gwneud
ngwyniadyddes *gw.*
  gwniadyddes
ngwnïo *gw.* gwnïo
ngwniadyddes *gw.*
  gwniadyddes
ngwobr *gw.* gwobr
ngwobrwyo *gw.* gwobrwyo
ngŵr *gw.* gŵr
ngwrach *gw.* gwrach
ngwragedd *gw.* gwraig
ngwraidd *gw.* gwreiddyn
ngwraig *gw.* gwraig
ngwrandawiad *gw.*
  gwrandawiad
ngwrandawr *gw.* gwrandawr
ngwrando *gw.* gwrando
ngwreichion *gw.*
  gwreichionen
ngwreiddiau *gw.* gwreiddyn
ngwreiddio *gw.* gwreiddio
ngwreiddyn *gw.* gwreiddyn
ngwres *gw.* gwres
ngwresogi *gw.* gwresogi
ngwresogydd *gw.*
  gwresogydd
ngwrtaith *gw.* gwrtaith
ngwrthblaid *gw.* gwrthblaid
ngwrthdystio *gw.* gwrthdystio
ngwrthod *gw.* gwrthod
ngwrthrych *gw.* gwrthrych
ngwrthryfel *gw.* gwrthryfel
ngwrthwyneb *gw.*
  gwrthwyneb
ngwrthwynebu *gw.*
  gwrthwynebu
ngwrthwynebwr *gw.*
  gwrthwynebwr

ngwrthwynebydd *gw.*
  gwrthwynebwr
ngwrywgydiaeth *gw.*
  gwrywgydiaeth
ngwthiad *gw.* gwthiad
ngwthio *gw.* gwthio
ngwthiwr *gw.* gwthiwr
ngwybod *gw.* gwybod
ngwybodaeth *gw.*
  gwybodaeth
ngwydr *gw.* gwydr
ngwydrau *gw.* gwydr,
  gwydryn
ngwydryn *gw.* gwydryn
ngŵydd *gw.* gŵydd
ngwyddbwyll *gw.* gwyddbwyll
Ngwyddel *gw.* Gwyddel
Ngwyddeleg *gw.* Gwyddeleg
ngwyddoniaeth *gw.*
  gwyddoniaeth
ngwyddonydd *gw.*
  gwyddonydd
ngwyddor *gw.* gwyddor
ngwyfyn *gw.* gwyfyn
ngŵyl *gw.* gŵyl
ngwylan *gw.* gwylan
ngwyliau *gw.* gŵyl
ngwylio *gw.* gwylio
ngwyliwr *gw.* gwyliwr
ngwylnos *gw.* gwylnos
ngwylwyr *gw.* gwyliwr
ngwyll *gw.* gwyll
ngwylltio *gw.* gwylltio
ngwymon *gw.* gwymon
ngwyn *gw.* gwyn
Ngwynedd *gw.* Gwynedd
ngwynegon *gw.* gwynegon
ngwynfa *gw.* gwynfa
ngwynfyd *gw.* gwynfyd
ngwyngalch *gw.* gwyngalch

ngwynt *gw.* gwynt
ngwŷr *gw.* gŵr
ngwyrdd *gw.* gwyrdd
ngwyriad *gw.* gwyriad
ngwyro *gw.* gwyro
ngwyrth *gw.* gwyrth
ngwŷs *gw.* gwŷs
ngwystion *gw.* gwystl
ngynau *gw.* gŵn
ngynnau *gw.* gwn
ngyrfa *gw.* gyrfa
ngyrfeydd *gw.* gyrfa
ngyrru *gw.* gyrru
ngyrrwr *gw.* gyrrwr
ngyrwyr *gw.* gyrrwr

H

In certain circumstances **h** is
prefixed to words beginning
with a vowel. If the word you
require does not appear in
this section ignore the initial
h and look it up in the
appropriate section, for
example, **hawr**, see **awr**. See
Personal Pronouns in the
Supplement.

had *e. torf.* seed. *gw.* **hadyn,**
  hedyn
hadu *be.* **(hadaf)** to sow, to
  propagate; to run to seed
hadyn; hedyn *e.g.* *ll.* **had** a
  seed. *gw.* **had**
haearn 1 *e.g.* *ll.* **heyrn** iron.
  2 *a.* of iron, iron
haeddu *be.* **(haeddaf)** to
  deserve, to merit. **haeddu**
  ennill to deserve to win;

haeddu clod to deserve praise

hael *a.* generous, liberal

haelioni *e.g.* generosity, liberality

haelionus *a.* generous, liberal

haenen *e.b. ll.* **haenau** layer, stratum, seam (*of rock*)

haerllug *a.* impudent

haerllugrwydd *e.g.* cheek, impudence

haeru *be.* (**haeraf**) to assert, to affirm

haf *e.g. ll.* **-au** summer, summertime

hafaidd *a.* summer-like, summery

hafal *a.* like, similar, equal

hafaliad *e.g. ll.* **-au** equation. **hafaliad cydamserol** simultaneous equation; **hafaliad dwyradd** quadratic equation; **hafaliad syml** simple equation; **hafaliad unradd** linear equation

hafan *e.b. ll.* **-au** haven, port, harbour

hafdy *e.g. ll.* **hafdai** summerhouse. **tŷ haf** holiday cottage

hafddydd *e.g. ll.* **-iau** summer's day

hafod *e.g. ll.* **-ydd** (*often seen in place names*) summer residence formerly occupied by the family and its stock during the summer months only. *gw.* **hendref**

hafoty *e.g. ll.* **hafotai** chalet, holiday cottage

Hafren *e.b.* Severn. **Afon Hafren** River Severn, the Severn; **Pont Hafren** Severn Bridge

hagr *a.* ugly, unsightly (*N.W.*)

hagrwch *e.g.* ugliness

haid *e.b. ll.* **heidiau** swarm, flock, drove. **haid o wenyn** swarm of bees

haidd *e. torf.* barley. *gw.* **heidden**

haig *e.b. ll.* **heigiau** shoal. **haig o bysgod** shoal of fish

haint *e.b. ll.* **heintiau** disease, infection, plague; faint, fit. **Fe ges i haint pan welais i'r ysbryd** I had a fit when I saw the ghost

hala *be.* (**halaf**) to spend; to send; to drive; to spread (*S.W.*)

halen *e.g. ll.* **-au** salt, brine. **halen y ddaear** salt of the earth

hallt *a.* salty, briny; harsh, severe. **talu'n hallt** to pay dearly

halltu *be.* (**halltaf**) to salt, to cure

hamdden *e.g.b.* leisure, respite. **canolfan hamdden** leisure centre; **oriau hamdden** leisure hours, spare time

hamddena *be.* (**hamddenaf**) to concern oneself with leisure pursuits

hamddenol *a.* leisurely

hances *e.b. ll.* **-i** handkerchief

hanerau *gw.* **hanner**

haneri *gw.* **hanner**

hanerwr *e.g. ll.* **hanerwyr** half-back (games)

hanes *e.g. ll.* **-ion** history; story of the past, tale, record, report. **Glywaist ti'r hanes am Wil?** Did you hear the tale about Wil?

haneswyr *gw.* **hanesydd**

hanesydd: haneswr *e.g. ll.* **hanesyddion: haneswyr** historian

hanesyn *e.g. ll.* **-nau** story, anecdote, tale

hanfodol *a.* essential; integral

haniaethol *a.* abstract

hanner *e.g. ll.* **hanerau, haneri** half. **hanner awr** half an hour; **hanner call** foolish, half-witted; **hanner cylch** semicircle; **hanner dydd** midday, noon; **hanner munud!** half-a-minute! half-a-moment! **hanner nos** midnight; **hanner-pan** half-soaked; half-wit; **hanner pris** half-price

hap *e.b. ll.* **-au, -iau** chance, luck, fortune. **chwarae hap** to gamble. **ar hap a damwain** by chance, by luck

hapus *a.* happy, cheerful

hapusrwydd *e.g.* happiness, bliss, blessedness

harbwr *e.g. ll.* **-s** harbour, port

hardd *a. ll.* **heirdd** beautiful, comely, handsome, fine, splendid (*of person or object*)

harddwch *e.g.* beauty, fairness, comeliness

hau: heu *be.* **(heuaf)** to sow, to scatter; to disseminate

haul *e.g. ll.* **heuliau** sun

hawdd *a.* easy. **Mae'n hawdd gweld** It is easy to see; **Mae'n hawdd nofio** It is easy to swim; **Mae'n hawdd siopa** It is easy to shop. *gw. At. Ansoddeiriau*

hawl *e.b.g. ll.* **-iau** legal claim, right, demand; question. **hawliau dyn/dynol** the rights of man, human rights; **hawliau sifil** civil rights

hawlfraint *e.b. ll.* **hawlfreintiau** privilege; copyright

hawlio *be.* **(hawliaf)** to claim, to demand

haws *gw.* **hawdd**

hawsaf *gw.* **hawdd**

hawsed *gw.* **hawdd**

heb *ardd.* (*followed by soft mutation*) **(hebddo, hebddot, hebddo/hebddi, hebddon, hebddoch, hebddyn)** without, minus, free from, besides. *gw. At. Arddodiaid*

heblaw *ardd.* besides, without

hebog *e.g. ll.* **-au, -iaid** hawk, falcon. **gwylio fel hebog** to watch like a hawk, to watch intensely

Hebraeg *e.g.* Hebrew language

Hebreig *a.* Hebrew

Hebrĕwr *e.g.* *ll.* **Hebrĕwyr**
Hebrew; **Hebrĕes** female
Hebrew

hebrwng *be.* **(hebryngaf)** to
lead, to accompany, to
escort. **cynhebrwng** funeral,
funeral procession; **tŷ
hebrwng** funeral home,
chapel of rest

hecsagon *e.g.* *ll.* **-au**
hexagon

hedeg *be.* **(hedaf)** to fly

hedfan *be.* **(hedfanaf)** to fly

hedydd *e.g.* *ll.* **-ion** lark. *gw.*
ehedydd

hedyn *gw.* **hadyn**

hedd *e.g.b.* *ll.* **-au** peace,
tranquillity, serenity, calm

heddiw *ad.* today

heddlu *e.g.* *ll.* **-oedd** police
force

heddwas *e.g.* *ll.* **heddweision**
policeman

heddwch *e.g.* peace,
tranquillity, stillness

heddweision *gw.* **heddwas**

hefo *gw.* **efo** (*N.W.*)

hefyd *c. & ad.* also, too, in
addition; likewise

heibio *ad.* past; aside, beside,
by. **heibio i'r tŷ** past the
house

heidiau *gw.* **haid**

heidden *e.b.* *ll.* **haidd** grain of
barley

heigiau *gw.* **haig**

heini *a.* active, lively, agile,
nimble. **dosbarth cadw'n
heini** keep fit class

heintiau *gw.* **haint**

heintus *a.* diseased,
infectious, contagious

heirdd *gw.* **hardd**

hel: hela *be.* **(heliaf: helaf)** to
drive; to chase, to pursue; to
send; to hunt; to gather, to
collect; to fetch. **hel achau**
to genealogize (*N.W.*). **hel
straeon** to gossip (*N.W.*)

helaeth *a.* ample, large,
broad; plentiful

helfa *e.b.* *ll.* **helfâu, helfeydd**
a hunting, hunt, chase,
catch. **helfa drysor** treasure
hunt; **helfa dda** a good catch

helgi *e.g.* *ll.* **helgwn** hound

heliwr *e.g.* *ll.* **helwyr**
huntsman, gatherer

help *e.g.b.* help, aid;
assistance; support. **help llaw**
helping hand

help (i) *be.* **(helpaf)** to help, to
assist

helygen *e.b.* *ll.* **helyg** willow

helynt *e.g.* *ll.* **-ion** course or
way (*of life, etc.*); fuss,
bother; business. **Beth yw ei
hynt a'i helynt?** What has
become of him?

hem *e.b.* *ll.* **-iau** hem, border,
seam

hen *a.* old, aged; ancient
(*precedes the noun and
causes soft mutation*) **hen
bryd** high time; **hen ddigon**
quite enough; **henffasiwn**
old-fashioned; **hen gariad**
former sweetheart, 'old
flame'; **hen gownt**

outstanding account, debit; grudge; **hen lanc** (old) bachelor; **wedi hen farw** long since dead; **yr Hen Wlad** the Old Country, term of endearment for Wales. *gw. At. Ansoddeiriau*

henach *gw.* **hen**

henaf *gw.* **hen**

henaidd *a.* oldish, old-fashioned

henaint *e.g.* old age; senility

hendaid *e.g. ll.* **hendeidiau** great-grandfather; forefather, ancestor

hendeidiau *gw.* **hendaid**

hendref *e.b. ll.* **hendrefi, hendrefydd** winter dwelling located in the valley, to which the family and its stock returned after the summer months in the **hafod** on the mountain. *gw.* **hafod**

hendrefi *gw.* **hendref**

hendrefydd *gw.* **hendref**

henebion *e.ll.* ancient monuments

hened *gw.* **hen**

heneiddio *be.* **(heneiddiaf)** to grow old, to become old

heneiniau *gw.* **hennain**

henffasiwn *gw.* **hen**

hennain *e.b. ll.* **heneiniau** great-grandmother (*N.W.*)

heno *ad.* tonight, (on) this night

henoed *e.g. & e.torf. & a.* old age, great age; old person; old people, old, elderly. **cartref henoed** old

people's home

henwr *e.g. ll.* **henwyr** old man

heol: hewl *e.b. ll.* **-ydd** street, road, way. **heol ddeuol** dual carriageway; **heol fawr** highway; **heol gefn** back-road, byway

heolydd *gw.* **heol**

her *e.b. ll.* **-iau** challenge, defiance, provocation

hercyd *be.* **(hercaf)** to fetch, to reach (*S.W.*)

herio *be.* **(heriaf)** to challenge, to defy, to dare

herwfilwr *e.g. ll.* **herwfilwyr** guerilla

herwgipiad *e.g. ll.* **-au** hijack

herwgipio *be.* **(herwgipiaf)** to hijack

herwgipiwr *e.g. ll.* **herwgipwyr** hijacker

herwgydiad *e.g. ll.* **-au** kidnap

herwgydio *be.* **(herwgydiaf)** to kidnap

herwgydiwr *e.g. ll.* **herwgydwyr** kidnapper

herwydd *ardd.* according to, by. **o'r herwydd** on account of that

het *e.b. ll.* **-au, -iau** hat

heu *gw.* **hau**

heuad *e.g.* a sowing

heulog *a.* sunny

heuliau *gw.* **haul**

heulwen *e.b.* sunshine; a girl's name. **Heulwen ydy enw'r ferch** The girl's name is Heulwen heuwr *e.g. ll.* **heuwyr** sower

hewl *gw.* heol

hewlydd *gw.* heol

heyrn *gw.* haearn

hi *rhag.* she, her, it

hidio (am) *be.* (hidiaf) to heed, to care, to mind (*S.W.*)

hil *e.b. ll.* -ion, -iau race, lineage; offspring, descendants

hiliol *a.* racial

hin *e.b. ll.* -oedd weather

hindda *e.b.* fine weather. **hindda a drycin** fair weather and foul

hinsawdd *e.b. ll.* **hinsoddau** climate

hir *a. ll.* -ion long, lengthy. *gw. At. Ansoddeiriau*

hirach *gw.* hir

hiraeth *e.g. ll.* -au longing, nostalgia, homesickness, grief

hiraethu (am) *be.* (hiraethaf) to long (for), to yearn (for), to sorrow, to grieve

hiraf *gw.* hir

hirbell *a.* distant, remote. **o hirbell** from afar; **dysgu o hirbell** distance learning

hired *gw.* hir

hirgylch *e.g. ll.* -au, -oedd ellipse

hirion *gw.* hir

hirlwm *e.g.* lean period at the end of winter

hirnod *e.g. ll.* -au circumflex accent (^)

hithau *rhag.* she, she too

hiwmor *e.g.* humour

hoe *e.g. ll.* -au pause, break, respite. **Sioni hoe** a layabout (*S.W.*)

hoel: hoelen *e.g.b. ll.* **hoelion, hoelon** nail. **taro'r hoelen ar ei phen** to comment appropriately with a fitting remark; to hit the nail on the head

hoelio *be.* (hoeliaf) to nail

hofrennydd *e.g. ll.* **hofrenyddion** helicopter

hoff *a.* (*precedes the noun and causes soft mutation*) dear, beloved, favourite. **fy hoff le bwyta** my favourite eating place

hoffi *be.* (hoffaf) to like, to be pleased (with)

hoffter *e.g. ll.* -au liking, fondness

hogen *e.b. ll.* -nod girl, lass (*N.W.*)

hogi *be.* (hogaf) to sharpen, to whet. **carreg hogi** whetstone

hogiau *gw.* hogyn

hogyn *e.g. ll.* hogiau, hogynnau boy, lad (*N.W.*)

hongian *be.* (hongiaf) to hang, to suspend

hôl *be.* (holaf) to fetch (*S.W.*). *gw.* holi, nôl

holi *be.* (holaf) to question, to inquire, to ask (about). **holi am** to ask about, to ask after

holiadur *e.g. ll.* -on questionnaire

holwr *e.g. ll.* **holwyr**

questioner, examiner,
interrogator
holwyddoreg *e.b. ll.* -au
catechism
holl *a.* (*precedes the noun and
causes soft mutation*) all,
whole. **yr holl bobl** all the
people; **yr holl fyd** the whole
world
hollalluog *a.* almighty
hollfyd *e.g.* universe
holliach *a.* whole, sound (of
health)
hollol *a. & ad.* (*precedes the
adjective and causes soft
mutation*) whole, entire,
complete. **yn hollol dawel**
completely quiet; **yn hollol
gywir** wholly correct
hollt *e.g. ll.* -au a split
hollti *be.* (**holltaf**) to split
hon *a.b. & rhag.* this (one),
she (her), it
honedig *a.* alleged, reputed
honiad *e.g. ll.* -au assertion,
claim
honni *be.* (**honnaf**) to allege,
to assert, to profess, to
pretend, to claim
honno, honna *a.b. & rhag.*
that (one), she (her), it. *gw.*
hwnnw
hosan *e.b. ll.* -au stocking,
sock
hoyw *a.* lively, sprightly; gay,
homosexual
hud *e.g. ll.* -ion magic,
charm, spell
hudo *be.* (**hudaf**) to charm, to
allure

hudol *a.* enchanting
huddygl *e.g.* soot
hufen *e.g. ll.* -nau cream.
hufen iâ ice-cream
hugain *gw.* **ugain**
hun: hunan 1 *rhag. ll.* **hunain**
self. **fi fy hun(an)** I myself; **ti
dy hun(an)** you yourself; **ef
ei hun(an)** he himself; **nhw
eu hunain** they themselves;
ei hunan bach alone. 2 *a.*
self-. **hunanwasanaeth** self-
service
hunain *gw.* **hun**
hunanarlwyol *a.* self-catering
hunan-barch *e.g.* self-respect
hunangofiant *e.g.*
autobiography
hunanhyderus *a.* self-
confident
hunanladdiad *e.g. ll.* -au
suicide
hunanlanhaol *a.* self-cleaning
hunanol *a.* selfish
hunllef *e.b.* nightmare
huno *be.* (**hunaf**) to sleep, to
fall asleep
Hunodd, 5 Mai 1940 Died 5
May 1940 (*on gravestones*)
hurt *a.* stupid, dull, stunned.
hurtyn stupid person,
blockhead
hwch *e.b. ll.* **hychod** sow.
Mae hi'n hen hwch She is
slovenly
hwiangerdd *e.b. ll.* -i lullaby;
nursery-rhyme
hwn *a.g. & rhag.* this (one)
hwnnw, hwnna *a.g. & rhag.*
that (one). *gw.* **honno**

hwnt *ad.* beyond, aside, away. **tu hwnt** beyond; **yn gyflym tu hwnt** exceedingly fast

hwp *e.g.* push, thrust, shove

hwrdd *e.g.* *ll.* **hyrddod.** ram (*S.W.*)

hwrê *ebych. & e.b.* hooray!

hwy: hwynt: nhw *rhag.* they, them. *gw.* **hir**

hwyaf *gw.* **hir**

hwyad: hwyaden *e.b.* *ll.* **hwyaid** duck

hwyaid *gw.* **hwyad**

hwyl *e.b.* *ll.* **-iau** sail; journey; religious fervour; mood; fun; goodbye. **mewn hwyliau da** in a good mood; **hwyl!** bye! **Pob hwyl ichi** All the best

hwyliau *gw.* **hwyl**

hwylio *be.* **(hwyliaf)** to sail, to set out on a journey

hwylus *a.* ease, comfortable, expedient, convenient

hwyluso *be.* **(hwylusaf)** to facilitate

hwylustod *e.g.* ease, convenience, facility, expediency

hwynt *gw.* **hwy**

hwyr 1 *a.* late. 2 *e.g.* (late) evening

hwyrach *ad.* perhaps (*N.W.*). *gw.* At. *Ansoddeiriau*

hwythau *rhag.* they, they also

hyblyg *a.* flexible, pliable, pliant

hybu *be.* **(hybaf)** to recover; to promote

hychod *gw.* **hwch**

hyd 1 *ardd.* (*followed by soft mutation*) to, till, for, as far as. **hyd yn hyn** up till now; **hyd at bum punt** up to £5. *gw.* At. *Treigladau.* 2 *e.g.* *ll.* **-au, -oedd, -ion** length; while

hyder *e.g.* confidence, trust

hyderu *be.* **(hyderaf)** to be confident; to trust, rely or depend (on)

hyderus *a.* confident

Hydref *e.g.* October

hydref *e.g.* *ll.* **-au** autumn

hydrefol *a.* autumnal

hydrogen *e.g.* hydrogen

hydd *e.g.* *ll.* **-od** stag

hyddysg *a.* learned, well-versed

hyf *a.* bold

hyfdra *e.g.* boldness

hyfryd *a.* pleasant, delightful, fine, agreeable

hyfrydwch *e.g.* delight, pleasure

hyfforddi *be.* **(hyfforddaf)** to train, to direct, to instruct

hyfforddiant *e.g.* *ll.* **hyfforddiannau** training, instruction

hyfforddwr *e.g.* *ll.* **hyfforddwyr** instructor, guide, trainer, coach

hyhi *rhag.* she, her (*emphatic*)

hylif *a. & e.g.* *ll.* **-au** liquid, flowing; fluid; a liquid, a fluid; a flow

hyll *a.* ugly, hideous

hyn *a. & rhag.* this, these

hŷn *gw.* **hen**

hynaf *gw.* **hen**

hynafiad *e.g. ll.* **hynafiaid**
ancestor

hynafol *a.* ancient

hyned *gw.* **hen**

hynny *a. & rhag.* that, those

hynod *a.* remarkable,
notable; exceptional. **yn
hynod o dda** exceptionally
well; **yn hynod o gyfoethog**
exceptionally rich

hynt *e.b. ll.* **-au, -oedd** way,
course, journey; career;
(one's) fate or lot, condition,
state. **Beth yw ei hynt erbyn
hyn?** What's his fate by
now?

hyrddod *gw.* **hwrdd**

hysbyseb *e.b.g. ll.* **-ion**
advertisement,
announcement

hysbysebiad *e.g. ll.* **-au**
advertisement

hysbysebu *be.* (**hysbysebaf**)
to advertise

hysbysebwr *e.g. ll.*
hysbysebwyr advertiser

hysbysfwrdd *e.g. ll.*
hysbysfyrddau noticeboard

hysbysiad *e.g. ll.* **-au**
announcement, notice,
advertisement

hysbysu *be.* (**hysbysaf**) to
announce, to inform; to
advertise

hytrach *ad.* rather; more so

I

i 1 *ardd.* (*followed by soft*

mutation)
(**i fi/mi, i ti, iddo/iddi, i ni, i
chi, iddyn nhw**) to, into, for.
i'r dim exactly, precisely; **i
fyny** up, upwards; **i ffwrdd**
away; **i gyd** all; **i lawr** down;
i mewn into; **i fod i**
supposed to; **i'w gilydd** to
each other. *gw. At.
Arddodiaid.* **2** *rhag.* I, me.
gw. At. Rhagenwau Personol

iâ *e.g.* ice. **cloch iâ** icicle

iach *a.* healthy, well

iacháu *be.* (**iachâf**) to heal, to
cure

iachawdwr *e.g. ll.* **iachawdwyr**
saviour

iachawdwriaeth:
iechydwriaeth *e.b.* salvation,
healing

iachus *a.* healthy, wholesome

iaith *e.b. ll.* **ieithoedd**
language. **iaith lafar** spoken
language; **mamiaith** first
language, mother tongue; **ail
iaith** second language;
dwyieithog bilingual

iâr *e.b. ll.* **ieir** hen. **iâr fach yr
haf** butterfly

iard *e.b. ll.* **ierdydd** yard (of
school, etc.)

iarll *e.g. ll.* **ieirll** earl

iarlles *e.b. ll.* **-au** countess

ias *e.b. ll.* **-au** thrill, shiver;
temper

iasol *a.* thrilling; intensely
cold

Iau *e.g.* Thursday

iau 1 *e.g. ll.* **ieuau** liver. **2**
e.b. ll. **ieuau** yoke. *gw.*

ieuanc
iawn 1 *ad.* very. **yn dda iawn**
very good. **2** *e.g.* rightness,
truth; compensation;
atonement; **talu'r iawn am** to
compensate. **3** *a.* right, true,
correct
iawndal *e.g. ll.* **-oedd**
compensation, damages,
indemnity
iawnder *e.g. ll.* **-au** justice,
right, rightness. **iawnderau
dynol: iawnderau sifil** civil
rights, civil liberties
idiom *e.b. ll.* **-au** idiom
Iddew *e.g. ll.* **-on** Jew
Iddewes *e.b. ll.* **-au** Jewess
Iddewig *a.* Jewish
Iddewaeth *e.b.* Judaism
ie *ad.* yes (*positive response
to a question that does not
begin with a verb*)
iechyd *e.g.* health, soundness,
well-being
iechyd da! good health! (*in
drinking a toast*)
ieir *gw.* iâr
ieirll *gw.* iarll
ieithoedd *gw.* iaith
ierdydd *gw.* iard
Iesu *e.g.* Jesus. **Iesu Grist**
Jesus Christ; **Iesu Mab Duw**
Jesus Son of God
iet *e.b. ll.* **-au, -iau** gate. *gw.*
clwyd
ieuangach *gw.* ieuanc
ieuangaf *gw.* ieuanc
ieuanged *gw.* ieuanc
ieuainc *gw.* ieuanc
ieuanc: ifanc *a. ll.* ieuainc:

ifainc. young. *gw. At.*
Ansoddeiriau
ieuau *gw.* iau
ieuenctid *e.g. & e.ll.* youth.
côr ieuenctid youth choir
ifainc *gw.* ieuanc
ifanc *gw.* ieuanc
ifancach *gw.* ieuanc
ifancaf *gw.* ieuanc
ig *e.b. ll.* **-ion** hiccup
igam-ogam *a.* zigzag
igian *be.* (igiaf) to hiccup
ing *e.g. ll.* **-oedd** anguish,
agony, distress
ildio *be.* (ildiaf) to yield
ill *rhag.* both, they, them. **ill
dau (dwy)** both of them
imwnedd *e.g.* immunity
imwneiddiad *e.g. ll.* **-au**
immunisation
imwneiddio *be.* (imwneiddiaf)
to immunise
incwm *e.g.* income. **Treth
Incwm** Income Tax
India, Yr *e.b.* India
Indiad *e.g. ll.* Indiaid an
Indian. **Un o'r India yw e/hi**
He/she is Indian
injan: injin *e.b. ll.* **-s** engine
Ionawr *e.g.* January
iorwg *e.g.* ivy (*S.W.*)
iro *be.* (iraf) to grease; to
anoint; to oil; to lubricate
is 1 *ardd.* below, under. *gw.*
isel. 2 *rhagdd.* (*followed by
soft mutation*) sub-, under-,
vice-
isaf *gw.* isel
ised *gw.* isel
isel *a.* low; humble; base;

Iseldiroedd

depressed. *gw. At. Ansoddeiriau*

Iseldiroedd, Yr *e.b.* The Netherlands

is-etholiad *e.g. ll.* **-au** by-election

is-gadeirydd *e.g. ll.* **-ion** vice-chairman

islaw *ardd.* below, beneath

is-lywydd *e.g. ll.* **-ion** vice-president

israddol *a.* inferior; subordinate

isymwybod *e.g.* subconscious

Iwerddon *e.b.* Ireland. **byw yn Iwerddon** to live in Ireland; **dod o Iwerddon** to come from Ireland; **mynd i Iwerddon** to go to Ireland

J

jac: Jac *e.g. ll.* **-s** jack

jac-codi-baw *e.g.* 'J.C.B.', mechanical excavator

jac-do: jac-y-do *e.g. ll.* **-s** jackdaw

jac-y-do *gw.* **jac-do**

jam *e.g. ll.* **-iau** jam

Japan *e.b.* Japan

Japanead *e.g. ll.* **Japaneaid** a Japanese

Japaneaidd *a.* Japanese

Japanaeg *e.b.* Japanese (language)

jar: jâr *e.b. ll.* **jariau, jarrau** jar

jas *e.g.* jazz

jeli *e.g. ll.* **-s, jeliau** jelly

jersi: jyrsi: siersi *e.b. ll.* **-s** jersey

jet *e.g. ll.* **-iau** jet (of water, gas, etc.); jet (nozzle); jet plane. **awyren jet** jet aircraft, jet plane; **peiriant jet** jet engine

ji-binc *e.b. ll.* **-od** chaffinch

jig-so *e.g.* jigsaw: **pos jig-so** jigsaw puzzle

jîns *e.g.* jeans

jîp *e.g.* jeep

jiráff *e.g. ll.* **jiraffod** giraffe

jiwbilî: jubilî *e.b. ll.* **jiwbilïau** jubilee, occasion or season of rejoicing

job *e.g.b. ll.* **-iau, -s** job, piece of work; occupation

jobyn *e.g. ll.* **jobiau** a small job. **Jobyn da!** Good job!

jôc *e.b. ll.* **-s** a joke, witticism; object of ridicule

jocan *bf.* **(jocaf)** to joke (*S.W.*)

joio *bf.* **(joiaf)** to enjoy

jubilî *gw.* **jiwbilî**

jwg: siwg *e.b. ll.* **jygiau: siygiau** jug. **jwg laeth** milk jug

jygiau *gw.* **jwg**

jyngl *e.b. ll.* **-oedd** jungle

jyrsi *gw.* **jersi**

L

labed *gw.* **llabed**

label *e.g. ll.* **-i** label

labelu *be.* **(labelaf)** to label

labordy *e.g. ll.* **labordai** laboratory

labrwr *e.g. ll.* **labrwyr**

labourer
lac *gw.* **llac**
lacio *gw.* **llacio**
lacs *gw.* **llacs**
lacsog *gw.* **llacsog**
lachar *gw.* **llachar**
Ladin *gw.* **Lladin**
ladrad *gw.* **lladrad**
ladrata *gw.* **lladrata**
ladron *gw.* **lleidr**
ladd *gw.* **lladd**
ladd-dy *gw.* **lladd-dy**
laes *gw.* **llaes**
laesu *gw.* **llaesu**
laeth *gw.* **llaeth**
lafant *e.g.* lavender
lafar *gw.* **llafar**
lafariad *gw.* **llafariad**
lafn *gw.* **llafn**
lafur *gw.* **llafur**
lafurio *gw.* **llafurio**
lafurus *gw.* **llafurus**
lafurwr *gw.* **llafurwr**
lai *gw.* **llai**
lain *gw.* **llain**
lais *gw.* **llais**
laith *gw.* **llaith**
lam *gw.* **llam**
lamp *e.b. ll.* **-au** lamp. **lamp
ôl** rear-lamp, tail-light of
vehicle; **lamp olew** oil lamp
lamplen *e.b.* lampshade
lamu *gw.* **llamu**
lan *ad.* up; *gw.* **glan, llan**
lân *gw.* **glân**
lanastr *gw.* **llanastr**
lanc *gw.* **llanc**
lances *gw.* **llances**
lanciau *gw.* **llanc**
lanhau *gw.* **glanhau**

lanio *gw.* **glanio**
lannau *gw.* **glan, llan**
lanw *gw.* **llanw**
lapio (am) *be.* (**lapiaf**) to lap,
to wrap. **papur lapio**
wrapping paper
larwm *e.g.* alarm: **cloc larwm**
alarm-clock
las *gw.* **glas**
laswelltyn *gw.* **glaswelltyn**
lathen *gw.* **llathen**
lau *gw.* **lleuen**
law *gw.* **glaw, llaw**
lawdriniaeth *gw.* **llawdriniaeth**
lawen *gw.* **llawen**
lawenhau *gw.* **llawenhau**
lawenydd *gw.* **llawenydd**
lawer *gw.* **llawer**
lawes *gw.* **llawes**
lawfeddyg *gw.* **llawfeddyg**
lawfeddygaeth *gw.*
  llawfeddygaeth
lawfeddygol *gw.* **llawfeddygol**
lawlif *gw.* **llawlif**
lawlyfr *gw.* **llawlyfr**
lawn *gw.* **llawn**
lawnder *gw.* **llawnder**
lawnt *e.g.b. ll.* **-iau, -ydd**
  lawn
lawr, i *ad.* down. *gw.* **llawr**
lawysgrif *gw.* **llawysgrif**
lawysgrifen *gw.* **llawysgrifen**
le *gw.* **lle**
lecyn *gw.* **llecyn**
lechen *gw.* **llechen**
lechi *gw.* **llechen**
led *gw.* **lled**
ledled *gw.* **lledled**
ledr *gw.* **lledr**
ledrith *gw.* **lledrith**

ledu 130

ledu *gw*. lledu
lef *gw*. llef
lefain *e.g.b.* leaven. *gw*.
  llefain
lefaru *gw*. llefaru
lefarwr *gw*. llefarwr
lefarwyr *gw*. llefarwr
lefarydd *gw*. llefarydd
lefau *gw*. llef
lefel *e.b.g. ll*. -au, -ydd, leflau
  level. lefel y môr sea-level
lefelyn *gw*. llefelyn
leflau *gw*. lefel
lefrith *gw*. llefrith
lefydd *gw*. lle
leiaf *gw*. bach
leiafrif *gw*. lleiafrif
leian *gw*. lleian.
leidr *gw*. lleidr
leihau *gw*. lleihau
lein *e.b. ll*. -iau, leins line,
  cord; telephone line; line-out.
  lein ddillad clothes line; lein
  fach narrow-gauge railway
leiniau *gw*. lein, llain
leinio *be*. (leiniaf) to line up;
  to form a line-out; to thrash,
  to give (one) a hiding (*N.W.*)
leisiau *gw*. llais
leisio *gw*. lleisio
leithder *gw*. lleithder
len *gw*. llen
lên *gw*. llên
lencyndod *gw*. llencyndod
lendid *gw*. glendid
lenni *gw*. llen
lennydd *gw*. glan
lenor *gw*. llenor
lenwi *gw*. llenwi
lenyddiaeth *gw*. llenyddiaeth

lenyddol *gw*. llenyddol
leoedd *gw*. lle
leol *gw*. lleol
leoli *gw*. lleoli
leoliad *gw*. lleoliad
Lerpwl *e.b.* Liverpool
les 1 *e.b. ll*. -oedd lease.
  2 *e.b. ll*. -au lace. *gw*. lles
lesol *gw*. llesol
lestr *gw*. llestr
letchwith *gw*. lletchwith
lety *gw*. llety
letya *gw*. lletya
letys *gw*. letysen
letysen *e.b. ll*. letys lettuce
leuad *gw*. lleuad
leuen *gw*. lleuen
lew *gw*. llew
lewygu *gw*. llewygu
lewyrch *gw*. llewyrch
lewyrchu *gw*. llewyrchu
lewyrchus *gw*. llewyrchus
lewys *gw*. llawes
liain *gw*. lliain
lid *gw*. llid
lieiniau *gw*. lliain
lif *gw*. llif
lifio *gw*. llifio
lifo *gw*. llifo
lifogydd *gw*. llif
lifft *e.g. ll*. -iau lift
lili *e.b. ll*. -s, liliau lily; lili
  wen fach snowdrop
lin *gw*. glin
lindysyn *e.g.* (*b.* lindysen)
  ll. lindys caterpillar
linell *gw*. llinell
linyn *gw*. llinyn
lipa *gw*. llipa
litr *e.g. ll*. -au litre

lithren *gw.* llithren
lithriad *gw.* llithriad
lithrig *gw.* llithrig
lithro *gw.* llithro
liw *gw.* lliw
liwgar *gw.* lliwgar
liwiau *gw.* lliw
liwio *gw.* lliwio
liwiog *gw.* lliwiog
liwo *gw.* lliwo
lo *gw.* glo, llo
loches *gw.* lloches
lochesu *gw.* llochesu
Loegr *gw.* Lloegr
loer *gw.* lloer
loeren *gw.* lloeren
lofa *gw.* glofa
lofnod *gw.* llofnod
lofnodi *gw.* llofnodi
lofrudd *gw.* llofrudd
lofruddiaeth *gw.* llofruddiaeth
lofruddio *gw.* llofruddio
lofft *gw.* llofft
log *gw.* llog
logi *gw.* llogi
long *gw.* llong
longddrylliad *gw.*
  llongddrylliad
longwr *gw.* llongwr
loi *gw.* llo
lol *e.b.* frivolity; nonsense.
  Paid â siarad lol! Don't talk
  nonsense!.
lolfa *e.b.* *ll.* lolfeydd lounge,
  sitting-room
lolian: lolian *be.* (lolaf: loliaf)
  to lounge; to joke, to talk
  nonsense (*S.W.*)
lon *gw.* llon
lôn *e.b.* *ll.* lonydd lane, road.

y Lôn Goed the Tree-Lined
  Way (*place name in N.W.*
  Wales); y lôn gefn the back-
  lane; lôn ddianc escape lane
loncian *be.* (lonciaf) to jog
lonciwr *e.g.* *ll.* loncwyr
  jogger
lond *gw.* llond
longyfarch *gw.* llongyfarch
longyfarchiad *gw.*
  llongyfarchiad
lonydd *gw.* lôn. *gw.* llonydd
lonyddwch *gw.* llonyddwch
loriau *gw.* llawr
lorïau *gw.* lorri
lorri *e.b.* *ll.* lorïau, lorris
  lorry. lorri laeth milk-lorry;
  lorri lo coal-lorry; lorri
  wartheg cattle-lorry
losg *gw.* llosg
losgi *gw.* llosgi
losin *gw.* losinen
losinen: losen *e.b.* *ll.* losin
  sweet, lozenge
lôwr *gw.* glôwr
löyn byw *gw.* glöyn byw
loyw *gw.* gloyw
lu *gw.* llu
lud *gw.* glud
ludio: ludo *gw.* gludio
ludw *gw.* lludw
Lun *gw.* Llun
lun *gw.* llun
Lundain *gw.* Llundain
luniaidd *gw.* lluniaidd
lunio *gw.* llunio
luoedd *gw.* llu
luosi *gw.* lluosi
luosog *gw.* lluosog
lusern *gw.* llusern

lusgo *gw.* **llusgo**
luwch *gw.* **lluwch**
luwchfa *gw.* **lluwchfa**
lw *gw.* **llw**
lŵans: lwfans *e.g.b.*
    allowance, concession
lwc *e.b.g.* luck, fate, chance.
    Pob lwc i ti! Good luck to
    you! **Lwc dda!** Good luck!
    Prosperity! Success!
lwcus *a.* lucky, fortunate
lwch *gw.* **llwch**
lwfans *gw.* **lŵans**
lwfr *gw.* **llwfr**
lwgu *gw.* **llwgu**
lwnc *gw.* **llwnc**
lwncdestun *gw.* **llwncdestun**
lwon *gw.* **llw**
lwy *gw.* **llwy**
lwyaid *gw.* **llwyaid**
lwybr *gw.* **llwybr**
lwyd *gw.* **llwyd**
lwydo *gw.* **llwydo**
lwydrew *gw.* **llwydrew**
lwydrewi *gw.* **llwydrewi**
lwydd *gw.* **llwydd**
lwyddiannus *gw.*
    llwyddiannus
lwyddiant *gw.* **llwydd**
lwyddo *gw.* **llwyddo**
lwyfan *gw.* **llwyfan**
lwyfannu *gw.* **llwyfannu**
lwyn *gw.* **llwyn**
lwynog *gw.* **llwynog**
lwyr *gw.* **llwyr**
lwyrymwrthodwr *gw.*
    llwyrymwrthodwr
lwyth *gw.* **llwyth**
lwytho *gw.* **llwytho**
lwythog *gw.* **llwythog**

lydan *gw.* **llydan**
lydanu *gw.* **llydanu**
Lydaw *gw.* **Llydaw**
lyfelyn *gw.* **llyfelyn**
lyfn *gw.* **llyfn**
lyfr *gw.* **llyfr**
lyfrgell *gw.* **llyfrgell**
lyfrgellydd *gw.* **llyfrgellydd**
lyfryn *gw.* **llyfryn**
lyfu *gw.* **llyfu**
lyffant *gw.* **llyffant**
lygad *gw.* **llygad**
lygadu *gw.* **llygadu**
lygaid *gw.* **llygad**
lygod *gw.* **llygoden**
lygoden *gw.* **llygoden**
lygredig *gw.* **llygredig**
lygredd *gw.* **llygredd**
lygru *gw.* **llygru**
lynges *gw.* **llynges**
lyn *gw.* **glyn, llyn**
lynciau *gw.* **llwnc**
lyncu *gw.* **llyncu**
lynnau *gw.* **llyn**
lynnoedd *gw.* **glyn, llyn**
lynu *gw.* **glynu**
lys *gw.* **llys**
lysenw *gw.* **llysenw**
lysenwi *gw.* **llysenwi**
lysfam *gw.* **llysfam**
lysfwytäwr *gw.* **llysfwytäwr**
lysgenhadaeth *gw.*
    llysgenhadaeth
lysgennad *gw.* **llysgennad**
lysiau *gw.* **llysieuyn**
lysieuol *gw.* **llysieuol**
lysieuyn *gw.* **llysieuyn**
lythrennau *gw.* **llythyren**
lythrennog *gw.* **llythrennog**
lythyr *gw.* **llythyr**

llain

lythyren *gw.* **llythyren**
lyw *gw.* **llyw**
lywio *gw.* **llywio**
lywodraeth *gw.* **llywodraeth**
lywodraethu *gw.* **llywodraethu**
lywodraethwr *gw.*
  llywodraethwr
lywydd *gw.* **llywydd**
lywyddu *gw.* **llywyddu**

LL

llabed *e.b.* *ll.* **-au** lapel, flap
llac *a.* slack, loose; lax
llacio *be.* **(llaciaf)** to slacken;
  to loosen; to relax
llacs *e.g.* mud, dirt (*S.W.*)
llacsog *a.* muddy, dirty
  (*S.W.*)
llachar *a.* bright, brilliant,
  dazzling
Lladin *e.b. & a.* Latin.
  America Ladin Latin
  America
lladrad *e.g.* *ll.* **-au** theft,
  robbery
lladrata *be.* **(lladrataf)** to rob,
  to steal, to thieve
lladron *gw.* **lleidr**
lladd *be.* **(lladdaf)** to kill, to
  slay, to slaughter; to cut, to
  mow, to fell. **lladd ar** to run
  down, to criticize adversely;
  lladd gwair to mow (*hay*);
  lladd mawn to cut peat; **fel
  lladd nadroedd** at full speed,
  with might and main (*lit.
  like killing snakes*)
lladd-dy *e.g.* *ll.* **lladd-dai**
  slaughterhouse

llaes *a.* loose, long, flowing
llaesu *be.* **(llaesaf)** to slacken,
  to loosen, to relax. **llaesu
  dwylo** to become idle, weak
  or indifferent, to stay one's
  hand(s)
llaeth *e.g.* *ll.* **-au** milk (*S.W.*)
  llaeth y fuwch cow's milk.
  gw. **llefrith**
llafar 1 *e.g.* (*verbal*)
  expression, spoken or
  colloquial language. **iaith
  lafar** the spoken language.
  2 *a.* loud, clear, vociferous;
  pertaining to the voice; oral
  arholiad llafar oral (*as
  opposed to written*)
  examination
llafariad *e.b.* *ll.* **llafariaid**
  vowel
llafn *e.g.* *ll.* **-au** blade
llafur *e.g.* *ll.* **-iau** labour, toil;
  tillage; corn. **llafur cariad**
  labour of love; **Y Blaid Lafur**
  The Labour Party
llafurio: llafuro *be.* **(llafuriaf:
  llafuraf)** to labour, to toil, to
  work
llafurus *a.* laborious,
  painstaking, industrious
llafurwr *e.g.* *ll.* **llafurwyr**
  labourer, worker,
  husbandman
llai *gw.* **bach**
llain *e.b.* *ll.* **lleiniau** (*long
  narrow*) strip of land, cloth
  &c., piece, patch, pitch,
  wicket (*cricket*), plot (*of
  land*). **llain galed** hard
  shoulder (*of motorway*); **llain**

lanio landing-strip, airstrip;
llain o dir strip of land,
isthmus

llais *e.g. ll.* **lleisiau** voice,
sound

llaith *a.* damp, moist, dank

llall *rhag. ll.* **lleill** the other
(*one*), another. **y llall** the
other (*person, thing*); **y lleill**
the others, the other
persons/things

llam *e.g. ll.* **-au** leap, jump,
bound, stride

llamu *be.* **(llamaf)** to leap, to
jump, to bound, to stride

llan *e.b. ll.* **-nau** (parish)
church, churchyard;
enclosure, yard

llanast(r) *e.g.* mess

llanc *e.g. ll.* **-iau** youth, lad

llances *e.b. ll.* **-i, -au** young
woman, lass

llanciau *gw.* **llanc**

llannau *gw.* **llan**

llanw 1 *e.g. ll.* **-au** flow (of
tide). **trai a llanw** ebb and
flow. 2 *be.* **(llanwaf)** to fill,
to fill up

llathen *e.b. ll.* **-ni** yard,
yardstick. **Doedd e ddim yn
llawn llathen** He wasn't all
there

llau *gw.* **lleuen**

llaw *e.b. ll.* **dwylo** hand. **i law**
to hand: **llawchwith** left-
handed; **llawdde** skilful,
dextrous; **llawfer** shorthand;
llaw galed trouble, rough
time, hard time (*especially
with sick person*); **llaw yn**

llaw hand in hand; **ail-law**
second hand; **hen law ar** one
who possesses the 'know
how', (*lit. an old hand*); **rhoi
help llaw** to give a helping
hand

llawdriniaeth *e.b. ll.* **-au**
surgery

llawen *a.* cheerful, merry,
glad. **Nadolig Hawen!** Merry
Christmas!

llawenhau (yn) *be.* **(llawenhaf)**
to rejoice, to be joyful

llawenydd *e.g.* joy, jubilation,
rejoicing

llawer 1 *e.g. ll.* **-oedd** many,
much; abundant. 2 *ad.* by
far, much (*with comparative
adjective*). **o lawer** by far, by
a great deal, by much; **llawer
gwaith** many times; **yn
llawer gwell** much better;
llawer tro many a time

llawes *e.b. ll.* **llewys** sleeve

llawfeddyg *e.g. ll.* **-on**
surgeon

llawfeddygaeth *e.b.* surgery

llawfeddygol *a.* surgical

llawlif *e.b. ll.* **-iau** hand-saw

llawlyfr *e.g. ll.* **-au** handbook,
manual

llawn *a. ll.* **-ion** full; **yn llawn
bryd** high time

llawnder *e.g.* abundance,
fullness

llawnion *gw.* **llawn**

llawr *e.g. ll.* **lloriau** floor,
ground; storey; earth. **ar lawr**
down, exhausted, on (to) the
ground, on the ground floor,

downstairs, up (*from bed*),
not yet gone to bed; **ar lawr
gwlad** on the lowlands; **y
llawr cyntaf** the first floor
llawysgrif *e.g. ll.* **-au**
manuscript
llawysgrifen *e.b. ll.*
llawysgrifennau handwriting
lle *e.g. ll.* **-oedd, llefydd**
place, room, accommodation
lle bwyd café, restaurant. **lle
chwech** toilet; **lle tân**
fireplace; **o'i le** out of (its)
place or order, wrong,
inappropriate
llecyn *e.g. ll.* **-nau** spot, place
llechen *e.b. ll.* **llechi** slate
llechi *gw.* **llechen**
lled 1 *e.g. ll.* **-au** breadth,
width. **Mae stori ar led yn a
pentref** There is a story
going around the village.
2 *ad.* rather, partly, almost
lledled *ardd.* throughout.
lledled y byd throughout the
world
lledr *e.g. ll.* **-au** leather
lledrith *e.g. ll.* **-oedd** magic,
enchantment; spectre;
fantasy: **hud a lledrith** magic
and fantasy
lledu *be.* **(lledaf)** to spread, to
widen, to open, to expand
llef *e.g. ll.* **-au** voice, cry
llefain *be.* **(llefaf)** to cry
(*S.W.*)
llefaru *be.* **(llefaraf)** to speak,
to utter
llefarwr *e.g. ll.* **llefarwyr**
speaker

llefarwyr *gw.* **llefarwr**
llefarydd *e.g. ll.* **-ion** speaker,
spokesman. **Y Llefarydd**
(the) Speaker of the House
of Commons
llefau *gw.* **llef**
llefelyn *e.g. ll* **-od** stye (*in
eye*). *gw.* **llyfelyn, llefrithen**
llefrith *e.g.* milk (*N.W.*). *gw.*
llaeth
llefrithen *e.b.* stye (in eye)
(*N.W.*); *gw.* **llefelyn, llyfelyn**
llefydd *gw.* **lle**
lleiaf *a.* smallest, least. **o leiaf**
at least; **gorau po leiaf** the
fewer the better
lleiafrif *e.g. ll.* **-au, -oedd**
minority
lleian *e.b. ll.* **-od** nun
lleidr *e.g. ll.* **lladron** thief,
robber, bandit. **lleidr pen
ffordd** highwayman
lleihau *be.* **(lleihaf)** to become
smaller, to diminish, to
shrink
lleill *gw.* **llall**
lleiniau *gw.* **llain**
lleisiau *gw.* **llais**
lleisio *be.* **(lleisiaf)** to use the
voice (*in speaking, shouting,
etc.*), to sound, to cry out
lleithder *e.g. ll.* **-au** damp,
moisture
llen *e.b. ll.* **-ni** curtain, veil,
sheet. **Y Llen Haearn** The
Iron Curtain
llên *e.b.* literature. **llên
gwerin** folklore; **ffuglen**
fiction
llencynnod *e.g.* adolescence

llenni *gw.* **llen**

llenor *e.g. ll.* **-ion** author, writer, literary person

llenwi *be.* **(llenwaf)** to fill

llenyddiaeth *e.b. ll.* **-au** literature

llenyddol *a.* literary

lleoedd *gw.* **lle**

lleol *a.* local. **llywodraeth leol** local government

lleoli *be.* **(lleolaf)** to locate, to localise, to place

lleoliad *e.g. ll.* **-au** location, setting.

lles *e.g. ll.* **-au** benefit, profit, advantage, welfare. **er lles** for the benefit of, to the advantage of: **o les** of benefit; **Y Wladwriaeth Les** The Welfare State

llesol *a.* beneficial, profitable, advantageous

llestr *e.g. ll.* **-i** vessel; cup, dish, pot

lletchwith *a.* awkward, clumsy

llety *e.g. ll.* **-au** lodging(s)

lletya *be.* **(lletyaf)** to lodge

lleuad *e.b. ll.* **-au** moon. **lleuad lawn** full moon; **lleuad newydd** new moon. *gw.* **lloer**

lleuen *e.b. ll.* **llau** louse

llew *e.g. ll.* **-od** lion. **llewes** lioness

llewygu *be.* **(llewygaf)** to faint, to swoon

llewyrch *e.g.* brightness, light, gleam, lustre

llewyrchu *be.* **(llewyrchaf)** to shine, to gleam

llewyrchus *a.* bright, prosperous

llewys *gw.* **llawes**

lliain *e.g. ll.* **llieiniau** line, cloth, towel, napkin

llid *e.g. ll.* **-iau, -ion** wrath; irritation, inflammation; passion. **llid yr ymennydd** meningitis

llieiniau *gw.* **lliain**

llif 1 *e.g. ll.* **-ogydd** stream, flow, flood, deluge, current. 2 *e.b. ll.* **-iau** saw. **llif gadwyn** chainsaw

llifio *be.* **(llifiaf)** to saw; to rasp, to file

llifo *be.* **(llifaf)** to flow, to stream, to flood

llifogydd *gw.* **llif**

llinell *e.b. ll.* **-au** line, axis; line-out. **llinell gam** crooked line; **llinell syth** straight line

llinyn *e.g. ll* **-nau** line, string, cord, tape, twine. **llinyn mesur** measuring tape

llipa *a.* limp, flaccid, weak

llithren *e.b. ll.* **-nau** chute, slide

llithriad *e.g. ll.* **-au** a slip, glide, slur; error, mistake

llithrig *a.* slippery; fluent

llithro *be.* **(llithraf)** to slip, to slide; to slur

lliw *e.g. ll.* **-iau** colour, countenance, hue. **lliw dydd** by day; **lliw nos** by night; **lliwiau'r hydref** autumn colours; **lliw llachar** bright colour

lliwgar *a.* colourful

lliwiau *gw.* **lliw**

lliwio: lliwo *be.* (**lliwiaf: lliwaf**) to colour, to dye

lliwiog *a.* coloured, tinted

lliwo *gw.* **lliwio**

llo *e.g. ll.* **lloi, lloeau** calf; **fel llo** gormless

lloches *e.g. ll.* **-au** refuge, shelter, lair

llochesu *be.* (**llochesaf**) to harbour, to shelter

lloeau *gw.* **llo**

Lloegr *e.b.* England

lloer *e.b. ll.* **-au** moon (*literary usage*); *gw.* **lleuad**

lloeren *e.b. ll.* **-ni, -nau** satellite, sputnik

llofnod *e.b. ll.* **-au, -ion** signature

llofnodi *be.* (**llofnodaf**) to sign

llofrudd *e.g. ll.* **-ion** murderer

llofruddiaeth *e.g. ll.* **-au** murder

llofruddio *be.* (**llofruddiaf**) to murder

llofft *e.b. ll.* **-ydd** loft, upstairs; gallery; bedroom: **ar y llofft** upstairs; **lan llofft** upstairs (*S.W.*)

llog *e.g. ll.* **-au** interest, hire; **ar log** for hire

llogi *be.* (**llogaf**) to hire

llong *e.b. ll.* **-au** ship. **llong hwyliau** sailing ship; **llong danfor** submarine; **llong ryfel** warship

llongddrylliad *e.g. ll.* **-au** shipwreck

llongwr *e.g. ll.* **llongwyr** sailor

lloi *gw.* **llo**

llon *a.* merry, cheerful

llond *e.g.* as much as something will hold; fullness, sufficiency. **llond llwy de o siwgr** a teaspoonful of sugar; **llond tŷ o blant** a houseful of children

llongyfarch (ar) *be.* (**llongyfarchaf**) to congratulate

llongyfarchiad *e.g. ll.* **-au** congratulation. **Llongyfarchiadau!** Congratulations!

llonydd *a.* quiet, still, calm; **Gad lonydd i fi!** Let me have some peace!

llonyddwch *e.g.* stillness, tranquillity, quietness; peace

lloriau *gw.* **llawr**

llosg 1 *e.g. ll.* **-iadau** burning, arson. 2 burning, burnt. **llosgfynydd** volcano; **pwnc llosg** burning issue

llosgi *be.* (**llosgaf**) to burn, to scorch, to smart

llosgydd *e.g. ll.* **-ion** incinerator, burner

llu *e.g. ll.* **-oedd** host, multitude; (*follows plural noun and undergoes soft mutation*) crowd. **Daeth milwyr lu o rywle** A host of soldiers came from somewhere

lluched *e. torf.* flash of lightning; lightning flashes

lludw *e.g.* ash, ashes. **lludw i ludw** ashes to ashes; **dydd Mercher y Lludw** Ash Wednesday; **lorri ludw** ashcart

Llun *e.g.* Monday. **Llun y Pasg** Easter Monday

llun *e.g.* *ll.* **-iau** picture, drawing, image

Llundain *e.b.* London

lluniaidd *a.* shapely, graceful

lluniau *gw.* **llun**

llunio *be.* (**lluniaf**) to form, to fashion, to shape

lluoedd *gw.* **llu**

lluosi *be.* (**lluosaf**) to multiply

lluosog *a.* numerous, plural

llusern *e.b.* *ll.* **-au** lamp, lantern

llusgo *be.* (**llusgaf**) to drag, to trail, to draw, to crawl: **llusgo traed** to drag (one's) feet

lluwch *e.g.* *ll.* **-au** snowdrift; dust, specks

lluwchfa *e.b.* *ll.* **lluwchfeydd** snowdrift

llw *e.g.* *ll.* **-on** oath; curse. **ar fy llw** on oath, on my word; **cymryd llw** to take an oath

llwch *e.g.* *ll.* **llychau** dust, powder; ashes; lake, loch

llwfr *a.* cowardly, timid

llwgu *be.* (**llwgaf**) to starve, to be ravenously hungry

llwm *a.* poor, bare

llwnc *e.g.* *ll.* **llynciau** gullet, throat; draught, gulp

llwncdestun *e.g.* *ll.* **-au** toast (health)

llwon *gw.* **llw**

llwy *e.b.* *ll.* **-au** spoon. **llwy bren** wooden spoon; **llwy de** teaspoon; **llwy gawl** soup-spoon; **llwy garu** love-spoon; **llwy arian** silver spoon

llwyaid *e.b.* *ll.* **llwyeidiau** spoonful

llwybr *e.g.* *ll.* **-au** path, track, route. **llwybr tarw** straight path, short cut; **ar y llwybr iawn** on the right track

llwyd *a.* grey, pale, hoary. **Brawd Llwyd** Grey Friar, Cistercian Friar

llwydo *be.* (**llwydaf**) to turn grey; to become mouldy

llwydrew *e.g.* *ll.* **-ogydd** hoarfrost (*S.W.*)

llwydrewi *be.* (**llwydrewaf**) to cast a hoarfrost, to be frosty (*S.W.*)

llwydd: llwyddiant *e.g.* *ll.* **llwyddiannau** success, prosperity

llwyddiannus *a.* successful, prosperous

llwyddo (i) *be.* (**llwyddaf**) to succeed, to prosper

llwyfan *e.g.b.* *ll.* **-nau** platform, stage. **llwyfan olew** oil rig

llwyfannu *be.* (**llwyfannaf**) to stage

llwyn 1 *e.g.* *ll.* **-i** grove, bush. **o lech i lwyn** furtively, stealthily, slyly (*literally from rock to bush*). 2 *e.b.* *ll.* **-au** loin

llwynog *e.g.* *ll.* **-od** fox

(*N.W.*). **llwynoges** vixen
llwyr 1 *a.* complete, entire,
utter, total. 2 *ad.* entirely,
altogether, utterly. 3 *rhagdd.*
total
llwyrymwrthodwr *e.g. ll.*
llwyrymwrthodwyr teetotaller
llwyth *e.g. ll.* -**au** tribe, clan;
e.g. ll. -**i** load, burden,
freight
llwytho *be.* (**llwythaf**) to load,
to burden
llwythog *a.* laden, burdened
llydan *a.* wide, broad
llydanu *be.* (**llydanaf**) to
widen
Llydaw *e.b.* Britanny
Llydäwr *e.g.* Breton
Llydawes *e.b.* Breton woman
Llydaweg *e.b.* Breton
language
llyfelyn *e.g. ll.* **llyfelod** stye
(in eye). *gw.* **llefelyn,
llefrithen**
llyfn *a.* smooth, sleek
llyfr *e.g. ll.* -**au** book. **llyfr
emynau** hymn-book; **llyfr
gosod** set book (*in syllabus*);
llyfr lloffion scrapbook; **llyfr
lluniau** picture book; **llyfr
sieciau** cheque book;
llawlyfr handbook, manual
llyfrgell *e.b. ll.* -**oedd** library.
llyfrgell y sir county library
llyfrgellydd *e.g. ll.* -**ion,
llyfrgellwyr** librarian
llyfryn *e.g. ll.* -**nau** booklet,
pamphlet
llyfu *be.* (**llyfaf**) to lick
llyffant *e.g. ll.* -**od, llyffaint**

toad. **caws llyffant** toadstool
llygad *e.g.b. ll.* **llygaid** eye.
llygad tro squint; **llygad y
ffynnon** fountain head,
original source of
information; **yn llygad ei le**
perfectly right, quite correct.
yn llygaid i gyd all eyes, all
attention; (**dim ond**) **dau
lygad a thrwyn** '(only) two
eyes and a nose', said of a
thin person
llygadu *be.* (**llygadaf**) to eye,
to watch, to have (one's) eye
upon
llygaid *gw.* **llygad**
llygod *gw.* **llygoden**
llygoden *e.b. ll.* **llygod**
mouse. **llygoden fach** mouse;
llygoden fawr/Ffrengig rat
llygredig *a.* corrupt,
degraded, defiled
llygredd *e.g. ll.* -**au**
corruption; pollution,
contamination
llygru *be.* (**llygraf**) to corrupt,
to pollute, to contaminate
llynges *e.b. ll.* -**au** fleet,
navy. **Y Llynges** The Navy
llym *a.* sharp, keen, severe
llyn *e.g.b. ll.* -**noedd, -nau**
lake, pool
llynciau *gw.* **llwnc**
llyncu *be.* (**llyncaf**) to
swallow, to devour, to gulp
llynedd *ad.* (*the definite
article is used with the
adverb*) last year. **Gwelais ef
y llynedd** I saw him last year
llynnau *gw.* **llyn**

llynnoedd *gw.* **llyn**

llyo *be.* **(llyaf)** to lick (*S.W.*)

llys *e.g. ll.* **-oedd** court, hall, place. **Llys y Goron** The Crown Court; **Llys yr Ynadon** The Magistrates' Court; **Yr Uchel Lys** The High Court

llysenw *e.g. ll.* **-au** nickname

llysenwi *be.* **(llysenwaf)** to nickname

llysfam *e.b. ll.* **-au** stepmother

llysfwytäwr *e.g. ll.* **llysfwytawyr** vegetarian (male). **llysfwytäwraig** vegetarian (female)

llysgenhadaeth *e.b. ll.* **llysgenadaethau** embassy

llysgennad *e.g. ll.* **llysgenhadon** ambassador

llysiau *gw.* **llysieuyn**

llysieuol *a.* herbal, vegetable, botanical; spiced. **te llysieuol** herbal tea

llysieuyn *e.g. ll.* **llysiau** vegetable, herb

llythrennau *gw.* **llythyren**

llythrennog *a.* literate

llythyr *e.g. ll.* **-au, -on** letter, epistle. **llythyr caru** love-letter; **llythyr cyfreithiwr** solicitor's letter

llythyren *e.b. ll.* **llythrennau** letter of the alphabet. **llythrennau'r abiec** letters of the alphabet; **priflythrennau** capital letters; **llythyren y ddeddf** letter of the law

llyw *e.g. ll.* **-iau** leader, ruler; rudder, helm. **(bod) wrth y llyw** (to be) at the helm, (to be) in charge

llywio *be.* **(llywiaf)** to govern, to rule; to steer, to pilot

llywodraeth *e.b. ll.* **-au** government. **llywodraeth ganolog** central government; **llywodraeth leol** local government

llywodraethu *be.* **(llywodraethaf)** to govern, to rule, to control

llywodraethwr *e.g. ll.* **llywodraethwyr** governor

llywydd *e.g. ll.* **-ion** president (*of society*). *gw.* **arlywydd**

llywyddu *be.* **(llywyddaf)** to preside

M

mab *e.g. ll.* **meibion** boy, son, man, male

maban *gw.* **baban**

mabi *gw.* **babi**

mabolgamp *e.b. ll.* **-au** game, sport, feat. **mabolgampau'r ysgol** school sports

mach *gw.* **bach**

machau *gw.* **bach; bachyn**

machgen *gw.* **bachgen**

machlud *e.g. ll.* **-oedd** setting (*of the sun*), going down. **machlud haul** sunset

machu *gw.* **bachu**

machyn *gw.* **bachyn**

mad *gw.* **bad**

madarch *e. torf.* mushroom(s); toadstool(s);

madarchen *e.b.* mushroom;
toadstool

mae *gw.* **bae, bod**

maer *e.g. ll.* **meiri** mayor.
maer y dre the town mayor

maeres *e.b. ll.* **-au** mayoress

maes *e.g. ll.* **meysydd** field,
square; syllabus. **maes
chwarae** playing field; **maes
o law** shortly

maestref *e.b. ll.* **-i, -ydd**
suburb

mafonen *e.b. ll.* **mafon**
raspberry

mag *gw.* **bag**

magiau *gw.* **bag**

magu *be.* **(magaf)** to breed, to
nurse, to gain. **magu bola** to
acquire a pot belly; **magu
hyder** to gain confidence

Mai *e.g.* May

mai *c.* that (*emphatic*). **rwy'n
sicr mai Tom yw e** I'm sure
that it is Tom (and nobody
else). *gw.* **bai**

maich *gw.* **baich**

main *a.* thin, lean, slim, shrill,
fine

maint *e.g.b. ll.* **meintiau** size,
dimension; magnitude;
amount, quantity; extent

malchder *gw.* **balchder**

maldod *e.g.* indulgence,
pampering, spoiling;
caresses; affectation

maldodi *be.* **(maldodaf)** to
pamper, to fondle, to pet

maled *gw.* **baled**

maledwr *gw.* **baledwr**

malot *gw.* **balot**

malu *be.* **(malaf)** to grind, to
crush, to smash. **malu awyr**
to talk nonsense, to talk idly

malŵn *gw.* **balŵn**

malwen: (*N.W.*) **malwoden**
(*S.W.*) *e.b. ll.* **malwod** snail,
slug

malwoden (*S.W.*) *gw.* **malwen**

mam *e.b. ll.* **-au** mother.
mam faeth foster-mother;
mam-yng-nghyfraith mother-
in-law

mam-gu *e.b. ll.* **mam-guod**
grandmother (*S.W.*); *gw.*
nain

mamiaith *e.b. ll.*
mamieithoedd mother
tongue

mân *a.* tiny, small, minute;
fine; petty. **arian mân** small
change, small coin; **glaw mân**
fine rain, drizzle; **glo mân**
small coal, slack; **yn fân ac
yn fuan** quickly and in short
gasps (*of breath*); with small
quick steps or movements

man *e.g.b. ll.* **-nau** place,
spot; mark; blemish. **man a
man (i fi, i ti . . .)** (it is) all the
same (to me, to you . . .), (it
makes) no difference; **man
cychwyn** starting-point; **man
cyfarfod** meeting place; **man
gwan** weak spot; **yn y fan a'r
lle** in the (very) place, on the
(very) spot; **yn y man** soon,
before (very) long, presently;
on the spot, immediately, at
once, now. *gw.* **ban**

manana *gw.* **banana**

manc *gw.* **banc**

mancio *gw.* **bancio**

mand *gw.* **band**

mandiau *gw.* **band**

maneg *e.b.* *ll.* **menig** glove, gauntlet. **Gwlad y menig gwynion** Land of the white gloves (alluding to the frequent presentation of white gloves to assize judges in Wales, when there were no cases for trial)

maner *gw.* **baner**

mannau *gw.* **ban, man**

mans *e.g.* manse

mantais *e.b.* *ll.* **manteision** advantage. **o fantais** of advantage; **cymryd mantais (ar)** to take advantage (of)

manteisio (ar) *be.* **(manteisiaf)** to take advantage, to profit (from)

manteision *gw.* **mantais**

mantell *e.b.* *ll.* **-oedd, mentyll** mantle, cloak, robe

manwl *a.* exact, careful, strict; fine; particular; **yn fanwl** in detail

manylion *e.ll.* details, particulars

manylu (ar) *be.* **(manylaf)** to particularize, to go into detail (about), to be exact

manylyn *e.g.* *ll.* **manylion** detail

map *e.g.* *ll.* **-iau** map

mar *gw.* **bar**

mara *gw.* **bara**

marbeciw *gw.* **barbeciw**

marc *e.g.* *ll.* **-iau, -au** mark.

gwneud marc to make one's mark

marcio *be.* **(marciaf)** to mark, to mark out

marchnad *e.b.* *ll.* **-oedd** market.

y Farchnad Gyffredin the Common market; **y farchnad rydd** the free market

marchog *e.g.* *ll.* **-ion** horseman, rider; knight

mardd *gw.* **bardd**

marddoniaeth *gw.* **barddoniaeth**

marf *gw.* **barf**

marn *gw.* **barn**

marnwr *gw.* **barnwr**

mart *e.g.* *ll.* **-iau** mart (*S.W.*)

marw 1 *be.* **(marwaf)** to die; **wedi marw: yn farw** dead. 2 *a.* *ll.* **meirw, meirwon** dead, deceased. 3 *e.g.* *ll.* **meirw, meirwon** the dead

marwaidd *a.* lifeless, listless, sluggish

marwol *a.* deadly, fatal, mortal. **ergyd farwol** mortal blow

marwolaeth *e.b.* *ll.* **-au** death

mas *gw.* **bas**

masged *gw.* **basged**

masn *gw.* **basn**

masnach *e.b.* *ll.* **-au** trade, commerce

masnachwr *e.g.* *ll.* **masnachwyr** merchant, tradesman, dealer

masnau: masnys *gw.* **basn**

maswr *e.g.* *ll.* **maswyr** outside-half (*rugby*)

meddygfa

mat *e.g. ll.* **-iau** mat. *gw.* **bat**
mater *e.g. ll.* **-ion** matter,
subject
matsen: matsien *e.b. ll.*
matsys match. **fel matsien**
wild tempered, fiery (*lit. like
a match*)
math *e.g. ll.* **-au** sort, kind,
species. *gw.* **bath**
mathemateg *e.g.* mathematics
mathemategol
a. mathematical
mathemategwr *e.g.*
ll. **mathemategwyr**
mathematician
mathodyn *gw.* **bathodyn**
maw *gw.* **baw**
mawd *gw.* **bawd**
mawl *e.g.* praise
mawn *e.g.* peat. **lladd mawn**
to cut peat
mawnog *e.b. ll.* **-ydd** a peat
bog
mawr *a. ll.* **-ion** great, big,
large. *gw. At. Ansoddeiriau*
mawredd *e.g.* greatness,
majesty, grandeur. **Mawredd
mawr!** Good gracious!
Mawrth *e.g.* March; Tuesday;
Mars. **Mawrth y Cyntaf** St
David's Day
mecso *gw.* **becso**
mechan *gw.* **bechan**
mechgyn *gw.* **bachgen**
mechnïaeth *e.b.* bail,
suretyship
Medi *e.g.* September
medi *be.* **(medaf)** to reap, to
harvest, to cut
medru *be.* **(medraf)** to be able

to do or accomplish (*a
thing*); to be able to speak,
know (*a language*); to hit, to
strike, to shoot. **medru'r
Gymraeg** to know Welsh, to
be able to speak Welsh
medrus *a.* skilful, able, clever
(*with one's hand*); correct
medw *gw.* **bedwen**
medwen *gw.* **bedwen**
medyddio *gw.* **bedyddio**
medd *e.g.* mead. *gw.* **bedd,
meddaf**
meddaf *bf.* I say, I said.
meddwn i I would say; **medd**
he/she/it says/said. *gw.*
meddu
meddai *bf.* he/she/it was
saying, he/she/it was used to
saying
meddal *a.* soft, tender, pliable
meddalu *be.* **(meddalaf)** to
soften, to become soft; to
thaw
meddalwedd *e.b.* software
meddu *be.* **(meddaf)** to
possess, to own
meddw *a. ll.* **-on** drunk. **yn
feddw gaib** blind drunk
meddwi (ar) *be.* **(meddwaf)** to
be drunk, to become drunk
meddwl (am) 1 *be.* **(meddyliaf,
meddylaf)** to think, to mean,
to intend. **meddwl y byd o** to
think the world of. 2 *e.g. ll.*
meddyliau thought, mind,
meaning, opinion
meddyg *e.g. ll.* **-on** doctor of
medicine
meddygfa *e.b.*

ll. **meddygfeydd** surgery

meddyginiaeth *e.b.* *ll.* **-au** remedy, medicine

meddylgar *a.* thoughtful, pensive

meddyliau *gw.* **meddwl**

mefusen *e.b.* *ll.* **mefus** strawberry

Mehefin *e.g.* June

meiau *gw.* **bai**

meibion *gw.* **mab**

Meibl *gw.* **Beibl**

meic *e.g.* *ll.* **-iau** microphone. *gw.* **beic**

meicrodon *gw.* **microdon**

meichiau *gw.* **baich**

meiddio *be.* **(meiddiaf)** to dare, to venture. *gw.* **beiddio**

meim *e.g.b.* *ll.* **-iau** mime

meinir *e.b.* maiden

meintiau *gw.* **maint**

meio *gw.* **beio**

meirdd *gw.* **bardd**

meiri *gw.* **maer**

meirioli *be.* **(meiriolaf)** to thaw, to melt

meirniad *gw.* **beirniad**

meirniadu *gw.* **beirniadu**

meirniaid *gw.* **beirniad**

meistr *e.g.* *ll.* **-i**, **-iaid** master, owner

meistres *e.b.* *ll.* **-i** mistress

meistri: meistriaid *gw.* **meistr**

meistroli *be.* **(meistrolaf)** to master

meithrin *be.* **(meithrinaf)** to nurture, to rear, to foster. **meithrinfa** nursery; **ysgol feithrin** nursery school

mêl *e.g.* honey. **mis mêl**

honeymoon; **yn fêl ar ei fysedd** music to his ears, to his extreme gratification

melen *a.b.* yellow: **ffrog felen** yellow frock. *gw.* **melyn**

melin *e.b.* *ll.* **-au** mill: **melin ddŵr** water mill; **melin wlân** woollen mill; **melin wynt** windmill; **gwneud melin ac eglwys** to make a great to-do of, to make a fuss about nothing

melyn *a.g.* yellow. **crys melyn** yellow shirt, **cyw melyn olaf** youngest child of family, last of the brood; **melynwy** yolk of an egg. *gw.* **melen**

melys *a.* sweet; **melysion** sweets

melysfwyd *e.g.* *ll.* **-ydd** dessert

mellt *gw.* **mellten**

mellten *e.b.* *ll.* **mellt** lightning. **fel mellten** like a flash (*of lightning*), fast

melltith *e.b.* *ll.* **-ion** curse. **Melltith arno!** Curse him!

menig *gw.* **maneg**

menter *e.b.* *ll.* **mentrau** venture, hazard

mentrau *gw.* **menter**

mentro (ar) *be.* **(mentraf)** to venture.

mentrus *a.* venturesome

mentyll *gw.* **mantell**

menthyca *gw.* **benthyca**

menyn: ymenyn *e.g.* butter. **blodau menyn** buttercups

menyw 1 *e.b.* *ll.* **-od** woman. 2 *a.* female (*S.W.*)

mêr *e.g.* *ll.* **merion** marrow (*bone*)

merch *e.b.* *ll.* **-ed** girl, daughter

Mercher *e.g.* Wednesday; Mercury. **Dydd Mercher Lludw** Ash Wednesday

merchetaidd *a.* effeminate

merf *gw.* **berf**

merfa *gw.* **berfa**

merfenw *gw.* **berfenw**

merlod *gw.* **merlyn**

merlota *bf.* to go pony-trekking

merlotwr *e.g.* *ll.* **merlotwyr** pony-trekker

merlyn *e.g.* *ll.* **-nod, merlod** pony

merthyr *e.g.* *ll.* **-on** martyr. **Merthyr Tudful** town & county borough (S. W.)

merw *gw.* **berw**

merwi *gw.* **berwi**

mesen *e.b.* *ll.* **mes** acorn

mesul *ad.* in the measure of. **Daeth y plant i mewn fesul un** The children came in one by one; **fesul tri** three at a time

mesur 1 *e.g.* *ll.* **-au** measure, metre. **ffon fesur** rule, ruler. **2** *be.* to measure

mesurydd *e.g.* *ll.* **-ion** measurer, meter, gauge. **mesurydd glaw** rain gauge

metel *e.g.* *ll.* **-oedd, -au** metal; mettle

metr *e.g.* *ll.* **-au** metre. **metr sgwâr** square metre

metrig *a.* metric

methiant *e.g.* *ll.* **methiannau** failure

methu (â) *be.* **(methaf)** to fail

meudwy *e.g.* *ll.* **-aid, -od** hermit, recluse

mewian *be.* **(mewiaf)** to mew

mewn *ardd.* in, within. **i mewn: i fewn** in, inward(s): **mewn a maes** in and out; **mewn bod** in being, extant; **mewn cariad** in love; **mewn eiliad** in a moment, at once, instantly; **mewn gwaith** in work, employed; **mewn llaw** in hand, receiving attention, under consideration; **mewn trefn** in order; **o fewn y mis** within the month; **y tu mewn: y tu fewn** inside

mewnwr *e.g.* *ll.* **mewnwyr** scrum-half (*rugby*), inside-forward (*soccer*)

meysydd *gw.* **maes**

mha *gw.* **pa**

Mhab *gw.* **Pab**

mhabell *gw.* **pabell**

mhabi *gw.* **pabi**

mhabydd *gw.* **pabydd**

mhac *gw.* **pac**

mhaced *gw.* **paced**

mhacio *gw.* **pacio**

mhadell *gw.* **padell**

mhader *gw.* **pader**

mhaent *gw.* **paent**

mhafiliwn *gw.* **pafiliwn**

mhafin *gw.* **pafin**

mhagan *gw.* **pagan**

mhais *gw.* **pais**

mhâl *gw.* **pâl**

mhalas *gw.* **palas**

mhalau: mhalod *gw.* pâl
mhalu *gw.* palu
mhamffled *gw.* pamffled
mhamffledyn *gw.* pamffledyn
mhanasen *gw.* panasen
mhanel *gw.* panel
mhannas *gw.* panasen
mhant *gw.* pant
mhapur *gw.* papur
mhapuro *gw.* papuro
mhâr *gw.* pâr
mharadwys *gw.* paradwys
mharagraff *gw.* paragraff
mharatoi *gw.* paratoi
mharc *gw.* parc
mharch *gw.* parch
mharchu *gw.* parchu
mharchus *gw.* parchus
mhardwn *gw.* pardwn
mharhad *gw.* parhad
mharsel *gw.* parsel
mharti *gw.* parti
Mhasg *gw.* Pasg
mhasiant *gw.* pasiant
mhatrwm *gw.* patrwm
mhatrwn *gw.* patrwn
mhatrymau *gw.* patrwm
mhatrynau *gw.* patrwn
mhawb *gw.* pawb
mhawen *gw.* pawen
mhebyll *gw.* pabell
mhecyn *gw.* pecyn
mhechadur *gw.* pechadur
mhechod *gw.* pechod
mhedair *gw.* pedair
mhedol *gw.* pedol
mhedwar *gw.* pedwar
mhedwaredd *gw.* pedwaredd
mhedwerydd *gw.* pedwerydd
mheg *gw.* peg

mhegwn *gw.* pegwn
mhegynau *gw.* pegwn
mheilot *gw.* peilot
mheint *gw.* peint
mheintio *gw.* peintio
mheintiwr *gw.* peintiwr
mheiriannau *gw.* peiriant
mheiriannydd *gw.* peiriannydd
mheiriant *gw.* peiriant
mheisiau *gw.* pais
mhêl *gw.* pêl
mhelydr *gw.* pelydr
mhellter *gw.* pellter
mhen *gw.* pen
mhenaethiaid *gw.* pennaeth
mhenawdau *gw.* pennawd
mhen-blwydd *gw.* pen-blwydd
mhencadlys *gw.* pencadlys
mhencampwr *gw.* pencampwr
mhenderfyniad *gw.*
  penderfyniad
mhenelin *gw.* penelin
mhenillion *gw.* pennill
mhennaeth *gw.* pennaeth
mhennau *gw.* pen
mhennawd *gw.* pennawd
mhennill *gw.* pennill
mhennod *gw.* pennod
mhenodau *gw.* pennod
mhenodi *gw.* penodi
mhenodiad *gw.* penodiad
mhenrhyn *gw.* penrhyn
mhensaer *gw.* pensaer
mhensil *gw.* pensil
mhensiwn *gw.* pensiwn
mhensiynwr *gw.* pensiynwr
mhenteulu *gw.* penteulu
mhentref *gw.* pentref
mhentwr *gw.* pentwr
mhenwythnos *gw.*

penwythnos
mhêr *gw.* pêr
mherchen: mherchennog *gw.*
 perchen
mheren *gw.* peren
mhererin *gw.* pererin
mherfedd *gw.* perfedd
mherffaith *gw.* perffaith
mherffeithio *gw.* perffeithio
mheri *gw.* peri
mherl *gw.* perl
mherlysiau *gw.* perlysiau
mherllan *gw.* perllan
mhersli *gw.* persli
mherson *gw.* person
mhersonoliaeth *gw.*
 personoliaeth
mherth *gw.* perth
mherthynas *gw.* perthynas
mherygl *gw.* perygl
mheswch *gw.* peswch
mhesychiad *gw.* pesychiad
mheth *gw.* peth
mhiano *gw.* piano
mhianydd *gw.* pianydd
mhib *gw.* pib
mhiben *gw.* piben
mhicil *gw.* picil
mhictiwr *gw.* pictiwr
mhicwn *gw.* picwnen
mhicwnen *gw.* picwnen
mhigiad *gw.* pigiad
mhigo *gw.* pigo
mhil *gw.* pil
mhiler *gw.* piler
mhilion *gw.* pil
mhili-pala *gw.* pili-pala
mhilsen *gw.* pilsen
mhilyn *gw.* pilyn
mhin *gw.* pin

mhîn *gw.* pîn
mhînafal *gw.* pînafal
mhinnau *gw.* pin
mhinsio *gw.* pinsio
mhinwydden *gw.* pinwydden
mhioden *gw.* pioden
mhisyn *gw.* pisyn
mhlaid *gw.* plaid
mhlan *gw.* plan
mhlanced *gw.* blanced,
 planced
mhlanhigyn *gw.* planhigyn
mhlannu *gw.* plannu
mhlant *gw.* plant
mhlas *gw.* plas
mhlasty *gw.* plasty
mhlât *gw.* plât
mhlatiau *gw.* plât
mhleidiau *gw.* plaid
mhleidlais *gw.* pleidlais
mhleidleisiau *gw.* pleidlais
mhleidleisio *gw.* pleidleisio
mhleidleisiwr *gw.* pleidleisiwr
mhlentyn *gw.* plentyn
mhleser *gw.* pleser
mhleserus *gw.* pleserus
mhlesio *gw.* plesio
mhlisgyn *gw.* plisgyn
mhlisman: mhlismon *gw.*
 plisman
mhlu *gw.* pluen
mhluen *gw.* pluen
mhluf *gw.* plufyn
mhlufyn *gw.* plufyn
mhlwc *gw.* plwc
mhlwg *gw.* plwg
mhlwm *gw.* plwm
mhlwyf *gw.* plwyf
mhlygu *gw.* plygu
mhob *gw.* pob

mhobi *gw*. pobi.
mhobl *gw*. pobl
mhoblogaeth *gw*. poblogaeth
mhobman *gw*. pobman
mhobydd *gw*. pobydd
mhoced *gw*. poced
mhoen *gw*. poen
mhoeni *gw*. poeni
mhoenus *gw*. poenus
mhoenydio *gw*. poenydio
mhoer: mhoeri *gw*. poer, poeri
mhoethi *gw*. poethi
mholyn *gw*. polyn
mhont *gw*. pont
mhopeth *gw*. popeth
mhopty *gw*. popty
mhorfa *gw*. porfa
mhorfeydd *gw*. porfa
mhorffor *gw*. porffor
mhortread *gw*. portread
mhorth *gw*. porth
mhorthladd *gw*. porthladd
mhos *gw*. pos
mhosibilrwydd *gw*.
  posibilrwydd
mhost *gw*. post
mhostman: mhostmon *gw*.
  postman
mhostyn *gw*. postyn
mhotel *gw*. potel
mhowdr: mhowdwr *gw*. powdr
mhowdrau *gw*. powdr
mhowlen *gw*. bowlen
mhraidd *gw*. praidd
mhram *gw*. pram
mhrawf *gw*. prawf
mhregeth *gw*. pregeth
mhregethu *gw*. pregethu
mhregethwr *gw*. pregethwr
mhreiddiau *gw*. praidd

mhren *gw*. pren
mhrennau *gw*. pren
mhrentis *gw*. prentis
mhrentisiaeth *gw*. prentisiaeth
mhrentisiaid *gw*. prentis
mhres *gw*. pres
mhreseb *gw*. preseb
mhresennol *gw*. presennol
mhresenoldeb *gw*.
  presenoldeb
mhresgripsiwn *gw*.
  presgripsiwn
mhreswyl: mhreswylfod *gw*.
  preswyl
mhridwerth *gw*. pridwerth
mhridd *gw*. pridd
mhrifardd *gw*. prifardd
mhrifathrawes *gw*.
  prifathrawes
mhrifathro *gw*. prifathro
mhrifddinas *gw*. prifddinas
mhrifeirdd *gw*. prifardd
mhrifysgol *gw*. prifysgol
mhriffordd *gw*. priffordd
mhrinder *gw*. prinder
mhrintio *gw*. printio
mhriod *gw*. priod
mhriodas *gw*. priodas
mhriodi *gw*. priodi
mhriodol *gw*. priodol
mhris *gw*. pris
mhroblem *gw*. problem
mhrofi *gw*. profi
mhrofiad *gw*. profiad
mhrofion *gw*. prawf
mhrofocio : mhryfocio *gw*.
  profocio
mhroffid *gw*. proffid
mhroffwyd *gw*. proffwyd
mhryd *gw*. pryd

Mhrydain *gw*. Prydain
mhrydau *gw*. pryd
mhryder *gw*. pryder
mhrydferthwch *gw*.
 prydferthwch
mhrydiau *gw*. pryd
mhryf: mhryfedyn: mhryfyn
 gw. pryf
mhryfocio *gw*. profocio
mhrynhawn *gw*. prynhawn
mhrynu *gw*. prynu
mhrynwr *gw*. prynwr
mhrysurdeb *gw*. prysurdeb
mhulpud *gw*. pulpud
mhum: mhump *gw*. pum
mhunnau *gw*. punt
mhunnoedd *gw*. punt
mhunt *gw*. punt
mhupur *gw*. pupur
mhurfa *gw*. purfa
mhuro *gw*. puro
mhwdin *gw*. pwdin
mhwdryn *gw*. pwdryn
mhŵer *gw*. pŵer
mhwll *gw*. pwll
mhwllyn *gw*. pwllyn
mhwmp *gw*. pwmp
mhwnc *gw*. pwnc
mhwrpas *gw*. pwrpas
mhwrs *gw*. pwrs
mhwyll *gw*. pwyll
mhwyllgor *gw*. pwyllgor
mhwynt *gw*. pwynt
mhwys *gw*. pwys
mhwysedd *gw*. pwysedd
mhwysigrwydd *gw*.
 pwysigrwydd
mhwyslais *gw*. pwyslais
mhwyso *gw*. pwyso
mhwyth *gw*. pwyth

mhyllau *gw*. pwll *gw*. pyllyn
mhyllyn *gw*. pyllyn
mhymtheg *gw*. pymtheg
mhymthegfed *gw*. pymthegfed
mhynciau *gw*. pwnc
mhyped *gw*. pyped
mhyrsau *gw*. pwrs
mhyrth *gw*. porth
mhys *gw*. pysen
mhysen *gw*. pysen
mhysgodyn *gw*. pysgodyn
mhysgota *gw*. pysgota
mhysgotwr *gw*. pysgotwr
mhyst *gw*. postyn
mhythefnos *gw*. pythefnos
mi *gw*. fi; geiryn (*particle used
 before a verb*) (N.W.). *gw*. fe
microdon: meicrodon *e.b.g.*
 microwave; microwave oven
migwrn *e.g*. *ll*. migyrnau.
 ankle, knuckle
mil *e.b*. *ll*. -oedd thousand
mil *gw*. bil
milfeddyg *e.g*. *ll*. -on
 veterinary surgeon
milgi *e.g*. *ll*. milgwn
 greyhound. fel milgi swift,
 like a greyhound
miliwn *e.b*. *ll*. miliynau
 million. miliynydd
 millionaire
miloedd *gw*. mil
milwr *e.g*. *ll*. milwyr soldier
milltir *e.b*. *ll*. -oedd mile.
 milltir sgwâr square mile;
 immediate locality
min *e.g*. *ll*. -ion lip; side,
 bank; (cutting) edge (of
 blade). min y gyllell the edge
 of the knife; min y ffordd the

wayside; **min y môr** the sea-shore, seaside; **byw wrth fin y gyllell** to live from hand to mouth. *gw.* **bin**

miniog *a.* sharp, keen, edged

minlliw *e.g.* lipstick

minnau *rhag.* I also, me

mioleg *gw.* bioleg

miri *e.g.* merriment, fun

mis *e.g.* *ll.* **-oedd** month.

 Mis Bach February

misged *gw.* bisged

misgedi *gw.* bisgedi

misgïen *gw.* bisgïen

misglwyf *e.g.* menstruation, period

misoedd *gw.* mis

misol *a.* monthly

misolyn *e.g.* *ll.* **misolion** monthly (magazine)

miwsig *e.g.* music

mlaen *gw.* blaen

mlaendal *gw.* blaendal

mlaenor *gw.* blaenor

mlaenwr *gw.* blaenwr

mlagur *gw.* blaguryn

mlaguryn *gw.* blaguryn

mlaidd *gw.* blaidd

mlanced *gw.* blanced

mlas *gw.* blas

mlasu *gw.* blasu

mlawd *gw.* blawd

mleiddiaid *gw.* blaidd

mlew *gw.* blewyn

mlewyn *gw.* blewyn

mlinder *gw.* blinder

mlino *gw.* blino

mlodau *gw.* blodyn

mlodeugerdd *gw.* blodeugerdd

mlodfresychen *gw.* blodfresychen

mlodyn *gw.* blodyn

mloedd *gw.* bloedd

mloeddio *gw.* bloeddio

mlows *gw.* blows

mlwch *gw.* blwch

mlwydd *gw.* blwydd

mlwyddyn *gw.* blwyddyn

mlychau *gw.* blwch

mlynedd *gw.* blwyddyn

mlynyddoedd *gw.* blwyddyn

mocs *gw.* bocs

moch *gw.* boch, mochyn

mochyn *e.g.* *ll.* **moch** pig. **fel mochyn** dirty, filthy, fat, like a pig

mod *gw.* bod

modfedd *e.b.* *ll.* **-i** inch

modiau *gw.* bawd

modloni *gw.* bodloni

modrwy *e.b.* *ll.* **-on** ring. **modrwy aur** gold ring; **modrwy briodas** wedding-ring; **modrwy glust** earring

modryb *e.b.* *ll.* **-edd** aunt

modur *e.g.* *ll.* **-on** motor

modurwr *e.g.* *ll.* **modurwyr** motorist

modd *e.g.* *ll.* **-ion** manner; means, wealth. **gwaetha'r modd** worse luck; **modd bynnag** however; **pa fodd?** how? *gw.* **bodd**

moddhad *gw.* boddhad

moddi *gw.* boddi

moddion *e.ll.* means; medicine: **moddion gras** means of grace. *gw.* **modd**

moel *a.* bare; bald
moelni *e.g.* bareness; baldness
moes *e.b.* *ll.* **-au** usual
behaviour, habit, wont; *in
plural:* manners; morals.
moesau da good manners;
good morals
moesol *a.* ethical; moral
moethus *a.* luxurious,
comfortable
mogi *be.* **(mogaf)** to suffocate,
to smother; **Brawd mogi yw
tagu** Suffocating is akin to
choking, one is as bad as the
other
mol *gw.* **bol**
mola *gw.* **bola**
moli *be.* **(molaf)** to praise
moliau *gw.* **bol**
mollt *gw.* **bollt**
mom *gw.* **bom**
Môn, Ynys *e.b.* Anglesey. **Môn
Mam Cymru** Anglesey
Mother of Wales
môn *gw.* **bôn**
moneddiges *gw.* **boneddiges**
moneddigion *gw.* **bonheddwr**
monheddwr *gw.* **bonheddwr**
môr *e.g.* *ll.* **moroedd** sea,
ocean. **Y Môr Canoldir**
Mediterranean Sea; **Môr
Iwerydd** Atlantic Ocean; **Môr
Tawel** Pacific Ocean
mor *ad.* (*followed by soft
mutation, except for
adjectives beginning with* **ll**
and **rh**) as, so, how. **mor dew
â mochyn** as fat as a pig;
mor ddu â'r nos as black as
the night; **mor goch â thân**

as red as fire; **mor wyn ag
eira** as white as snow
mord *gw.* **bord**
mordaith *e.b.* *ll.* **mordeithiau**
(sea) voyage
mordau: mordydd *gw.* **bord**
morddwyd *e.b.* *ll.* **-ydd** thigh
more *gw.* **bore**
morfa *e.b.g.* *ll.* **morfeydd** sea-
marsh, bog, fen
morfeydd *gw.* **morfa**
morfil *e.g.* *ll.* **-od** whale
morgais *e.g.* *ll.* **morgeisiau**
mortgage
Morgannwg *e.b.* Glamorgan.
De Morgannwg South
Glamorgan; **Gorllewin
Morgannwg** West
Glamorgan; **Morgannwg
Ganol** Mid Glamorgan
(*1974–96*)
morgeisiau *gw.* **morgais**
morgrugyn *e.g.* *ll.* **morgrug**
ant
morio *be.* **(moriaf)** to sail
môr-leidr *e.g.* *ll.* **môr-ladron**
pirate
morlo *e.g.* *ll.* **morloi** seal
moroedd *gw.* **môr**
moron *gw.* **moronen**
moronen *e.b.* *ll.* **moron**
carrot
morthwyl *e.g.* *ll.* **-ion** hammer
morwr *e.g.* *ll.* **morwyr** sailor,
seaman
morwyn *e.b.* *ll.* **morynion**
maid, girl, virgin. **y Forwyn
Fair** the Virgin Mary
morwyr *gw.* **morwr**
mos *gw.* **bos**

mosys *gw.* bos
motwm *gw.* botwm
motymau *gw.* botwm
mowlen *gw.* bowlen
mragdy *gw.* bragdy
mraich *gw.* braich
mrain *gw.* brân
mraint *gw.* braint
mrân *gw.* brân
mraslun *gw.* braslun
mraster *gw.* braster
mraw *gw.* braw
mrawd *gw.* brawd
mrawddeg *gw.* brawddeg
mrecwast *gw.* brecwast
mrech *gw.* brech
mrechdan *gw.* brechdan
mrechiad *gw.* brechiad
mreichiau *gw.* braich
mreichled *gw.* breichled
mrenhines *gw.* brenhines
mrenin *gw.* brenin
mres *gw.* bres
mrest *gw.* brest
mresychen *gw.* bresychen
mrethyn *gw.* brethyn
mreuddwyd *gw.* breuddwyd
mreuddwydio *gw.*
  breuddwydio
mreuddwydion *gw.*
  breuddwyd
mrifo *gw.* brifo
mrig *gw.* brig
mrigau *gw.* brig, brigyn
mrigyn *gw.* brigyn
mriwsionyn *gw.* briwsionyn
mro *gw.* bro
mrodorion *gw.* brodor
mrodyr *gw.* brawd
mroga *gw.* broga

mron *gw.* bron
mronfraith *gw.* bronfraith
mronnau: mronnydd *gw.* bron
mrown *gw.* brown
mröydd *gw.* bro
mrws: mrwsh *gw.* brws
mrwsio: mrwsho *gw.* brwsio
mrwsys: mrwshys *gw.* brws
mrwydr *gw.* brwydr
mrwydrau *gw.* brwydr
mryd *gw.* bryd
mryn *gw.* bryn
mryniau *gw.* bryn
mrys *gw.* brys
mrysio *gw.* brysio
muarth *gw.* buarth
muchod *gw.* buwch
mud *a.* dumb, mute
mudiad *e.g.* *ll.* -au
  movement. **Mudiad Ysgolion**
  Meithrin (Welsh) Nursery
  Schools' Movement
muddugoliaeth *gw.*
  buddugoliaeth
mugail *gw.* bugail
mugeiliaid *gw.* bugail
mugeilio *gw.* bugeilio
mul *e.g.* *ll.* -od donkey; mule
munud *e.g.b.* *ll.* -au minute.
  Arhoswch funud! Wait a
  minute! **ugain munud** twenty
  minutes
mur *e.g.* *ll.* -iau wall
musnes *gw.* busnes
muwch *gw.* buwch
mwced *gw.* bwced
mwg *e.g.* smoke
mwgwd *e.g.* *ll.* **mygydau**
  mask
mwlch *gw.* bwlch

mwnci *e.g. ll.* **mwncïod** monkey

mwrdeistref *gw.* **bwrdeistref**

mwrdd *gw.* **bwrdd**

mwriad *gw.* **bwriad**

mws *gw.* **bws**

mwstash *e.g. ll.* **mwstashis** moustache

mwstwr *e.g. ll.* **mystyrau** noise, commotion, bustle (*S.W.*)

mwthyn *gw.* **bwthyn**

mwy 1 *a.* bigger, larger, greater, more, louder, longer, further. **2** *ad.* more (*often followed by* **na**). **mwy na** more than. **mwy na digon** too much, excessive; **mwy na mwy** a lot, a great deal, very many, too much, exceedingly; **mwy na thebyg** more than likely; **mwy neu lai** more or less. *gw.* **mawr**

mwyach *ad.* any more, any longer, again, henceforth

mwyaf *gw.* **mawr**

mwyar *gw.* **mwyaren**

mwyaren *e.b. ll.* **mwyar** blackberry

mwyd *gw.* **bwyd**

mwydlen *gw.* **bwydlen**

mwydo: mwyda *gw.* **bwydo**

mwydod *gw.* **mwydyn**

mwydyn *e.g. ll.* **mwydod** worm

mwyn 1 *e.g. ll.* **-au** mineral; ore. **2** *e.g.* sake. **er mwyn** for the sake of; **er mwyn Duw** for God's sake. **3** *a.* gentle, mild, dear

mwynhad *e.g.* enjoyment, pleasure

mwynhau *be.* (**mwynhaf**) to enjoy; to become mild

mwyta: myta *gw.* **bwyta**

mwyty *gw.* **bwyty**

mychan *gw.* **bychan**. *gw.* **bechan**

myd *gw.* **byd**

myddin *gw.* **byddin**

myfi *rhag.* I, me, myself

myfyrdod *e.g. ll.* **-au** meditation

myfyrio *be.* (**myfyriaf**) to study, to meditate

myfyriwr *e.g. ll.* **myfyrwyr** student. **myfyriwr hŷn** mature student

myglyd *a.* smoky, close, stifling

mygu *be.* (**mygaf**) to smoke; to smother; to suffocate

mygydau *gw.* **mwgwd**

mylchau *gw.* **bwlch**

mynach *e.g. ll.* **-od, mynaich** monk

mynachlog *e.b. ll.* **-ydd** monastery

mynachod *gw.* **mynach**

mynaich *gw.* **mynach**

mynd: myned *be.* (**af**) to go, to proceed. *gw.* **At. Berfau**

mynedfa *e.b. ll.* **mynedfeydd** entrance, passage

mynedfeydd *gw.* **mynedfa**

mynediad *e.g. ll.* **-au** admission, access, entry; going. **mynediad am ddim** admission free

mynegai *e.g. ll.* **mynegeion**

index, concordance
mynegeion *gw.* **mynegai**
mynegi (i) *be.* **(mynegaf)** to tell, to indicate
mynnu *be.* **(mynnaf)** to will, to insist, to wish, to obtain
mynwent *e.b.* *ll.* **-ydd** graveyard, churchyard, cemetery
mynychu *be.* **(mynychaf)** to attend
mynydd *e.g.* *ll.* **-oedd** mountain; **llosgfynydd** volcano
mynyddig: mynyddog *a.* mountainous
myrbryd *gw.* **byrbryd**
myrddau *gw.* **bwrdd**
myrfodd *gw.* **byrfodd**
myrfoddau *gw.* **byrfodd**
myrr *e.g.* myrrh
mys *gw.* **bys**
mysedd *gw.* **bys**
mysiau *gw.* **bws**
mystyrau *gw.* **mwstwr**
mysys *gw.* **bws**
myta *gw.* **bwyta**
myth *e.g.* *ll.* **-au** myth
mythynnod *gw.* **bwthyn**
myw *gw.* **byw**
mywyd *gw.* **bywyd**
mywydeg *gw.* **bywydeg**

N

na 1 *c.* (*followed by spirant mutation*) nor, neither, than. **2** *ad.* no, not. *gw.* **da.** *gw. At.* **Treigladau**
nabod *gw.* **adnabod**

nac 1 *c.* neither, nor. **2** *ad.* no, not
nad *ad.* not
nadansoddi *gw.* **dadansoddi**
nadl *gw.* **dadl**
nadlau *gw.* **dadlau**
Nadolig *e.g.* *ll.* **-au** Christmas. **Nadolig Llawen** Merry Christmas
nadredd: nadroedd *gw.* **neidr**
naddo *ad.* no (*negative answer to questions using verbs in the past tense*) **Fuest ti yn y dre ddoe? Naddo** Were you in the town yesterday? No. **Ganodd e gyda'r côr? Naddo** Did he sing with the choir? No. **Fuoch chi yn Rhos erioed? Naddo** Were you ever in Rhos? No
naddu *be.* **(naddaf)** to chip, to hew, to whittle
naear *gw.* **daear**
naeareg *gw.* **daeareg**
naeargryn *gw.* **daeargryn**
naearyddiaeth *gw.* **daearyddiaeth**
nafad *gw.* **dafad**
nag *c.* than
nage *ad.* not so, no
nagrau *gw.* **deigryn**
nai *e.g.* *ll.* **neiaint** nephew
naid *e.g.* *ll.* **neidiau** jump, leap, bound
nail *gw.* **dalen, deilen**
naill *rhag.* the one, either: **y naill neu'r llall** the one or the other; **naill ai Ebrill neu Fai** either April or May

nain *e.b.* *ll.* **neiniau**
grandmother (*N.W.*). *gw.*
mam-gu

naioni *gw.* **daioni**

nal: nala *gw.* **dal**

nalen *gw.* **dalen**

nalgylch *gw.* **dalgylch**

nallu *gw.* **dallu**

nam *e.g.* *ll.* **-au** flaw, blemish,
mark

nameg *gw.* **dameg**

namhegion *gw.* **dameg**

namwain *gw.* **damwain**

nanfon *gw.* **danfon**

nangos *gw.* **dangos**

nannedd *gw.* **dannedd**

nannoedd *gw.* **dannoedd**

nant *e.b.* *ll.* **nentydd** brook,
stream. *gw.* **dant**

narganfod *gw.* **darganfod**

narlith *gw.* **darlith**

narlithio *gw.* **darlithio**

narlithiwr: narlithydd *gw.*
darlithiwr

narlun *gw.* **darlun**

narlunio *gw.* **darlunio**

narlledu *gw.* **darlledu**

narllen *gw.* **darllen**

narllenwr: narllenydd *gw.*
darllenwr

narn *gw.* **darn**

natblygiad *gw.* **datblygiad**

natblygu *gw.* **datblygu**

natgan *gw.* **datgan**

natganiad *gw.* **datganiad**

natganoli *gw.* **datganoli**

natguddio *gw.* **datguddio**

natod *gw.* **datod**

natrys *gw.* **datrys**

natur *e.b.* nature; temper

naturiol *a.* natural

nathliad *gw.* **dathliad**

nathlu *gw.* **dathlu**

nau *gw.* **dau**

naw 1 *a.* nine. 2 *e.g.* nine.
naw deg ninety; **naw deg un**
ninety one; **deunaw** eighteen;
naw wfft ichi! blow you!

nawdd *e.g.* refuge; patronage,
support

nawns *gw.* **dawns**

nawnsio *gw.* **dawnsio**

nawr *ad.* now. *gw.* **rŵan**

naws *e.b.* *ll.* **-au** feeling,
nature, tingle, disposition,
nuance. **naws y gaeaf** feeling
of winter; **naws oer** cold
feeling

ne *gw.* **de**

neall *gw.* **deall**

neb *e.g.* anyone, no one.
Does neb yma There's no
one here

nechrau *gw.* **dechrau**

nechreuad *gw.* **dechreuad**

neddf *gw.* **deddf**

neddfu *gw.* **deddfu**

nef: nefoedd *e.b.* heaven.
Nefoedd Wen! Good
heavens!

nefol: nefolaidd *a.* heavenly

nefnydd *gw.* **defnydd**

nefnyddio *gw.* **defnyddio**

neffro *gw.* **deffro**

neg: neng *gw.* **deg**

negawd *gw.* **degawd**

neges *e.b.* *ll.* **-au, -euon**
message, errand. **negesydd**
messenger

negyddol *a.* negative

neiaint *gw.* **nai**
neialog *gw.* **deialog**
neidiau *gw.* **naid**
neidio *be.* **(neidiaf)** to jump, to leap
neidiwr *e.g. ll.* **neidwyr** jumper, leaper
neidr *e.b. ll.* **nadroedd, nadredd** snake
neidwyr *gw.* **neidiwr**
neigryn *gw.* **deigryn**
neilen *gw.* **deilen**
neilliaid: neillion *gw.* **dall**
neilltu *e.g.* one side. **o'r neilltu** apart, aside
neilltuo *be.* **(neilltuaf)** to reserve, to set aside, to earmark
neilltuol *a.* special, particular, peculiar. **yn neilltuol o oer** particularly cold
neiniau *gw.* **nain**
neintydd *gw.* **deintydd**
neis *a.* nice
neiseb *gw.* **deiseb**
neithiwr *ad.* last night
nelw *gw.* **delw**
nen *e.b. ll.* **-nau, -noedd** ceiling; heaven, sky
nenfwd *e.g. ll.* **nenfydau** ceiling
nentydd *gw.* **nant**
nenu *gw.* **denu**
nerbyn *gw.* **derbyn**
nerbynneb *gw.* **derbynneb**
nerbynnydd *w.* **derbynnydd**
nerf *e.b. ll.* **-au** nerve
nerfus *a.* nervous
neri *gw.* **deri**
nerth *e.g. ll.* **-oedd** strength,

might, power
nerthoedd *gw.* **nerth**
nerw *gw.* **derw**
nerwen *gw.* **derwen**
nes *c. & ardd.* until. *gw.* **agos**
nesaf *a.* next. *gw.* **agos**
nesáu (at) *be.* **(nesâf)** to approach, to draw near
nesed *gw.* **agos**
nesg *gw.* **desg**
netholiad *gw.* **detholiad**
neu *c. (followed by soft mutation)* or. **bachgen neu ferch** boy or girl; **eira neu law** rain or snow. (*Note: conjugated forms of verbs do not mutate after* **neu**) **Rhedodd neu cerddodd** He walked or ran; **Holais neu gofynnais** I questioned or asked
neuadd *e.b. ll.* **-au** hall: **Neuadd Gyhoeddus** Public Hall; **Neuadd Les** Welfare Hall
neuawd *gw.* **deuawd**
neuddeg *gw.* **deuddeg**
neuddegfed *gw.* **deuddegfed**
neugain *gw.* **deugain**
neunaw *gw.* **deunaw**
neuoedd *gw.* **dau**
newid 1 *be.* **(newidiaf)** to change, to alter. **2** *e.g. ll.* **-iadau** change
newin *gw.* **dewin**
newis *gw.* **dewis**
newydd 1 *a.* new. **newydd sbon** brand new. **2** *e.g. ll.* **-ion** news. **papur newydd**

newspaper. **Mae e newydd
ganu.** He has just sung
newydd-ddyfodiad *e.g. ll.*
  newydd-ddyfodiaid
  newcomer
newyddiadurwr *e.g. ll.*
  newyddiadurwyr journalist
newyddion *gw.* **newydd**
newyn *e.g.* famine, hunger
nhabl *gw.* **tabl**
nhabled *gw.* **tabled**
nhacl *gw.* **tacl**
nhaclo *gw.* **taclo**
nhaclu *gw.* **taclu**
nhaclwr *gw.* **taclwr**
nhacsi *gw.* **tacsi**
Nhachwedd *gw.* **Tachwedd**
nhad *gw.* **tad**
nhad-cu *gw.* **tad-cu**
nhafarn *gw.* **tafarn**
nhafarnwr *gw.* **tafarnwr**
nhafell *gw.* **tafell**
nhaflegryn *gw.* **taflegryn**
nhaflen *gw.* **taflen**
nhaflu *gw.* **taflu**
nhafod *gw.* **tafod**
nhafodiaieth *gw.* **tafodiaith**
nhafol *gw.* **tafol**
nhagfa *gw.* **tagfa**
nhagu *gw.* **tagu**
nhangnefedd *gw.* **tangnefedd**
nhai *gw.* **tŷ**
nhaid *gw.* **taid**
nhair *gw.* **tair**
nhaith *gw.* **taith**
nhâl *gw.* **tâl**
nhalai *gw.* **talai**
nhalaith *gw.* **talaith**
nhalcen *gw.* **talcen**
nhaleb *gw.* **taleb**

nhalent *gw.* **talent**
nhaloedd *gw.* **tâl**
nhalu *gw.* **talu**
nhalwr *gw.* **talwr**
nhalwrn *gw.* **talwrn**
nhamaid *gw.* **tamaid**
nhameidiau *gw.* **tamaid**
nhân *gw.* **tân**
nhanau *gw.* **tân**
nhancer *gw.* **tancer**
nhanio *gw.* **tanio**
nhannau *gw.* **tant**
nhanseilio *gw.* **tanseilio**
nhant *gw.* **tant**
nhanwydd *gw.* **tanwydd**
nhap *gw.* **tap**
nhâp *gw.* **tâp**
nhapiau *gw.* **tap, tâp**
nharan *gw.* **taran**
nharddiad *gw.* **tarddiad**
nharged *gw.* **targed**
nharian *gw.* **tarian**
nhariannau *gw.* **tarian**
nharo *gw.* **taro**
nharw *gw.* **tarw**
nhasg *gw.* **tasg**
nhasgu *gw.* **tasgu**
nhaten *gw.* **taten**
nhato: nhatws *gw.* **taten**
nhawelu *gw.* **tawelu**
nhawelwch *gw.* **tawelwch**
nhawelydd *gw.* **tawelydd**
nhawelyn *gw.* **tawelyn**
nhe *gw.* **te**
nhebot *gw.* **tebot**
nhebygrwydd *gw.* **tebygrwydd**
nhecell *gw.* **tecell**
nhechneg *gw.* **techneg**
nhechnegwr *gw.* **technegwr**
nhechnoleg *gw.* **technoleg**

nhegan *gw.* tegan
nhegell *gw.* tecell
nhegwch *gw.* tegwch
nhei *gw.* tei
nheiar *gw.* teiar
nheidiau *gw.* taid
nheigr *gw.* teigr
nheiliwr *gw.* teiliwr
nheilsen *gw.* teilsen
nheilwres *gw.* teilwres
nheilyngdod *gw.* teilyngdod
nheimlad *w.* teimlad
nheimlo *gw.* teimlo
nheipiadur *gw.* teipiadur
nheisen *gw.* teisen
nheitl *gw.* teitl
nheithiau *gw.* taith
nheithio *gw.* teithio
nheithiwr *gw.* teithiwr
nhelediad *gw.* telediad
nheledu *gw.* teledu
nheleffon *gw.* teleffon
nhelyn *gw.* telyn
nhelyneg *gw.* telyneg
nhelynor *gw.* telynor
nhelynores *gw.* telynores
nhelynorion *gw.* telynor
nheml *gw.* teml
nherfyn *gw.* terfyn
nherfysg *gw.* terfysg
nherfysgaeth *gw.* terfysgaeth
nherfysgwr *gw.* terfysgwr
nherm *gw.* term
nhes *gw.* tes
nhestun *gw.* testun
nheulu *gw.* teulu
nheyrnas *gw.* teyrnas
nhiced *gw.* ticed
nhîm *gw.* tîm
nhip *gw.* tip

nhipyn *gw.* tipyn
nhir *gw.* tir
nhirlun *gw.* tirlun
nhiroedd *gw.* tir
nhiwtor *gw.* tiwtor
nhlodi *gw.* tlodi
nhlws *gw.* tlws
nhlysau *gw.* tlws
nho *gw.* to
nhocyn *gw.* tocyn
nhocynnwr *gw.* tocynnwr
nhoddi *gw.* toddi
nhoes *gw.* toes
nhoiled *gw.* toiled
nholc *gw.* tolc
nholl *gw.* toll
nhon *gw.* ton
nhôn *gw.* tôn
nhonau *gw.* tôn
nhonfedd *gw.* tonfedd
nhonnau *gw.* ton
nhorch *gw.* torch
nhorf *gw.* torf
nhorfeydd *gw.* torf
nhoriad *gw.* toriad
nhorri *gw.* torri
nhors *gw.* tors
nhorth *gw.* torth
nhosau *gw.* tosyn
nhost *gw.* tost
nhostrwydd *gw.* tostrwydd
nhosyn *gw.* tosyn
nhrachwant *gw.* trachwant
nhraddodiad *gw.* traddodiad
nhraed *gw.* troed
nhraeth *gw.* traeth
nhraethau *gw.* traeth
nhraethawd *gw.* traethawd
nhrafnidiaeth *gw.* trafnidiaeth
nhrafod *gw.* trafod

nhrafferth *gw.* trafferth
nhrafferthu *gw.* trafferthu
nhraffordd *gw.* traffordd
nhraffyrdd *gw.* traffordd
nhrai *gw.* trai
nhrais *gw.* trais
nhrallod *gw.* trallod
nhrallwysiad *gw.* trallwysiad
nhrap *gw.* trap
nhraul *gw.* traul
nhrawsblannu *gw.*
  trawsblannu
nhrawst *gw.* trawst
nhrechu *gw.* trechu
nhref: nhre *gw.* tref
nhrefn *gw.* trefn
nhrefnu *gw.* trefnu
nhrefnydd *gw.* trefnydd
nhrefydd *gw.* tref
nhreial *gw.* treial
nhreiglad *gw.* treiglad
nhreiglo *gw.* treiglo
nhreisio *gw.* treisio
nhrên *gw.* trên
nhrenau *gw.* trên
nhreth *gw.* treth
nhrethdalwr *gw.* trethdalwr
nhrethu *gw.* trethu
nhreuliau *gw.* traul
nhreulio *gw.* treulio
nhri *gw.* tri
nhriawd *gw.* triawd
nhric *gw.* tric
nhrigain *gw.* trigain
nhrigfan *gw.* trigfan
nhrigolion *gw.* trigolion
nhrin *gw.* trin
nhrindod *gw.* trindod
nhrioedd *gw.* trioedd
nhriongl *gw.* triongl

nhristwch *gw.* tristwch
nhro *gw.* tro
nhrochi *gw.* trochi
nhroeau *gw.* tro
nhroed *gw.* troed
nhroedfedd *gw.* troedfedd
nhroedffordd *gw.* troedffordd
nhröedigaeth *gw.* tröedigaeth
nhroedio *gw.* troedio
nhroeon *gw.* tro
nhrogylch *gw.* trogylch
nhroi *gw.* troi
nhrosedd *gw.* trosedd
nhroseddwr *gw.* troseddwr
nhrosgais *gw.* trosgais
nhrosglwyddo *gw.*
  trosglwyddo
nhrosiad *gw.* trosiad
nhroswr *gw.* troswr
nhrothwy *gw.* trothwy
nhrowsus *gw.* trowsus
nhruan *gw.* truan
nhrueni *gw.* trueni
nhrugaredd *gw.* trugaredd
nhrwbl *gw.* trwbl
nhrwser *gw.* trwser
nhrwsiwr *gw.* trwsiwr
nhrwydded *gw.* trwydded
nhrwyn *gw.* trwyn
nhrychineb *gw.* trychineb
nhrydan *gw.* trydan
nhrydanwr *gw.* trydanwr
nhrydedd *gw.* trydedd
nhrydydd *gw.* trydydd
nhrysor *gw.* trysor
nhrysorfa *gw.* trysorfa
nhrysori *gw.* trysori
nhrysorydd *gw.* trysorydd
nhrywydd *gw.* trywydd
nhudalen *gw.* tudalen

nhueddiad *gw.* tueddiad

nhun *gw.* tun

nhunnell *gw.* tunnell

nhw: hwy *rhag.* they, them.
 Ble maen nhw? Where are
 they? **Gwelodd nhw** He/she
 saw them

nhwlc *gw.* twlc

nhwll *gw.* twll

nhwmpath *gw.* twmpath

nhwndis *gw.* twndis

nhwnel *gw.* twnel

nhwpsyn *gw.* twpsyn

nhŵr *gw.* tŵr

nhwr *gw.* twr

nhwrci *gw.* twrci

nhwristiaeth *gw.* twristiaeth

nhwrw *gw.* twrw

nhwyll *gw.* twyll

nhwyllo *gw.* twyllo

nhwymo *gw.* twymo

nhwymyn *gw.* twymyn

nhŷ *gw.* tŷ

nhybied: nhybio *gw.* tybied

nhyddyn *gw.* tyddyn

nhyddynnwr *gw.* tyddynnwr

nhyfiant *gw.* tyfiant

nhyfu *gw.* tyfu

nhynged *gw.* tynged

nhyle *gw.* tyle

nhylwyth *gw.* tylwyth

nhyllau *gw.* twll

nhyllu *gw.* tyllu

nhylluan *gw.* tylluan

nhymer *gw.* tymer

nhymestl *gw.* tymestl

nhymheredd *gw.* tymheredd

nhymhorau *gw.* tymor

nhymor *gw.* tymor

nhyner *gw.* tyner

nhynerwch *gw.* tynerwch

nhynnu *gw.* tynnu

nhyrfa *gw.* tyrfa

nhyst *gw.* tyst

nhystiolaeth *gw.* tystiolaeth

nhystysgrif *gw.* tystysgrif

nhywel *gw.* tywel

nhywod *gw.* tywod

nhywydd *gw.* tywydd

nhywyllu *gw.* tywyllu

nhywyllwch *gw.* tywyllwch

nhywys *gw.* tywys

nhywysog *gw.* tywysog

nhywysoges *gw.* tywysoges

ni *rhag.* we, us

ni: nid *ad.* not

niacon *gw.* diacon

niafol *gw.* diafol

nial *gw.* dial

nianc *gw.* dianc

niawl *gw.* diawl

niawliaid *gw.* diafol, diawl

niben *gw.* diben

nid *gw.* ni

niddordeb *gw.* diddordeb

nieithryn *gw.* dieithryn

nifer (o) *e.g.b.* *ll.* -oedd, -i
 number, quantity. **nifer o
 fechgyn** a number of boys

niferyn *gw.* diferyn

nifetha *gw.* difetha

nifyrru *gw.* difyrru

niffiniad *gw.* diffiniad

niffinio *gw.* diffinio

niffodd *gw.* diffodd

niffyg *gw.* diffyg

nigon *gw.* digon

nigonedd *gw.* digonedd

nigwyddiad *gw.* digwyddiad

nihareb *gw.* dihareb

niheintydd *gw.* **diheintydd**
nihuno *gw.* **dihuno**
nileu *gw.* **dileu**
nilyn *gw.* **dilyn**
nillad *gw.* **dilledyn**
nilledyn *gw.* **dilledyn**
nim *gw.* **dim**
ninas *gw.* **dinas**
ninasyddion *gw.* **dinesydd**
ninesydd *gw.* **dinesydd**
ninistrio *gw.* **dinistrio**
ninnau *rhag.* we also
niod *gw.* **diod**
nioddef *gw.* **dioddef**
niogi *gw.* **diogi**
niogyn *gw.* **diogyn**
niolch *gw.* **diolch**
niolchgarwch *gw.*
  diolchgarwch
nirgelwch *gw.* **dirgelwch**
nirprwy *gw.* **dirprwy**
nirprwyaeth *gw.* **dirprwyaeth**
nirwy *gw.* **dirwy**
nis *ad.* not . . . him/her/it/
  them. **nis gwelais** I did not
  see him/etc
nisg *gw.* **disg**
nisgrifiad *gw.* **disgrifiad**
nisgrifio *gw.* **disgrifio**
nisgwyl *gw.* **disgwyl**
nisgybl *gw.* **disgybl**
nisgyblaeth *gw.* **disgyblaeth**
nisgyn *gw.* **disgyn**
nistawrwydd *gw.* **distawrwydd**
nistewi *gw.* **distewi**
niswyddo *gw.* **diswyddo**
nith *e.b.* *ll.* **-oedd** niece
niwallu *gw.* **diwallu**
niwed *e.g.* *ll.* **niweidiau** harm,
  damage, injury. **gwneud**

niwed i to harm
niwedd *gw.* **diwedd**
niweddglo *gw.* **diweddglo**
niweidiau *gw.* **niwed**
niwl *e.g.* *ll.* **-oedd** mist, haze.
  niwl trwchus fog
niwlog *a.* misty, foggy, hazy
niwrnod *gw.* **diwrnod**
niwydiant *gw.* **diwydiant**
niwygiad *gw.* **diwygiad**
niwygio *gw.* **diwygio**
niwylliant *gw.* **diwylliant**
noc *gw.* **doc**
noctor *gw.* **doctor**
nod *e.g.b.* *ll.* **-au, -ion** note;
  mark, token, aim
nodau *gw.* **nod, nodyn**
nodedig *a.* remarkable, noted,
  appointed, specified
nodi *be.* **(nodaf)** to note, to
  mark, to appoint, to state.
  gw. **dodi**
nodrefn *gw.* **dodrefnyn**
nodrefnyn *gw.* **dodrefnyn**
nodwedd *e.b.* *ll.* **-ion**
  character, feature,
  characteristic. **rhaglen
  nodwedd** feature programme
nodweddiadol *a.*
  characteristic, typical
nodwydd *e.b.* *ll.* **-au** needle
nodyn *e.g.* *ll.* **nodau** note
noddwr *e.g.* *ll.* **noddwyr**
  protector, patron
noe *gw.* **doe**
noeth *a.* naked, bare,
  exposed, raw, sheer
noethineb *gw.* **doethineb**
nofel *e.b.* *ll.* **-au** novel
nofelwr: nofelydd *e.g.*

ll. **nofelwyr** novelist
nofiad *e.g.* a swim
nofio *be.* **(nofiaf)** to swim
nogfen *gw.* **dogfen**
nol *gw.* **dol**
nôl: hôl *be.* **(nolaf: holaf)** to
fetch; *gw.* **dôl**
nolen *gw.* **dolen**
nolur *gw.* **dolur**
Norman *e.g. ll.* **-iaid** Norman.
castell **Normanaidd** Norman
castle
nos *e.b. ll.* **-au** night. **nos da**
good night; **nos Sul** Sunday
night; **nos yfory** tomorrow
night; **nos dywyll** dark
night
nosbarth *gw.* **dosbarth**
noson: noswaith *e.b. ll.*
nosweithiau evening:
noswaith dda good evening;
noson lawen merry evening;
am ddwy noson for two
evenings
nosweithiau *gw.* **noson**
nraen: nraenen *gw.* **draen**
nraenog *gw.* **draenog**
nraig *gw.* **draig**
nrain *gw.* **draen**
nrama *gw.* **drama**
nramodwr *gw.* **dramodwr**
nramodydd *gw.* **dramodwr**
nreigiau *gw.* **draig**
nreser: nresel *gw.* **dreser**
nrewdod *gw.* **drewdod**
nringwr *gw.* **dringwr**
nrudwy *gw.* **drudwy**
nrwg *gw.* **drwg**
nrwm *gw.* **drwm**
nrws *gw.* **drws**

nrych *gw.* **drych**
nrychiolaeth *gw.* **drychiolaeth**
nrygioni *gw.* **drygioni**
nryll *gw.* **dryll**
nryllau *gw.* **dryll**
nrysau *gw.* **drws**
nrysu *gw.* **drysu**
nryw *gw.* **dryw**
null *gw.* **dull**
nuo *gw.* **duo**
nur *gw.* **dur**
nuw *gw.* **duw**
nuwies *gw.* **duwies**
nwfr *gw.* **dŵr**
nŵr *gw.* **dŵr**
nwrn *gw.* **dwrn**
nwsin *gw.* **dwsin**
nwy *e.g. ll.* **-on, -au** gas. **Nwy
Môr y Gogledd** North Sea
gas. *gw.* **dwy**
nwyau *gw.* **nwy**
nwydd *e.g. ll.* **-au** material,
article. **nwyddau** goods (*note:
only the plural form is used*)
nwyon *gw.* **nwy**
nwyieithrwydd *gw.*
dwyieithrwydd
nwylo *gw.* **dwylo**
nwyn *gw.* **dwyn**
nwyrain *gw.* **dwyrain**
nychmygion *gw.* **dychymyg**
nychmygu *gw.* **dychmygu**
nychymyg *gw.* **dychymyg**
nydd *gw.* **dydd**
nyddiad *gw.* **dyddiad**
nyfarniad *gw.* **dyfarniad**
nyfarnu *gw.* **dyfarnu**
nyfarnwr *gw.* **dyfarnwr**
nyfnder *gw.* **dyfnder**
nyfodol *gw.* **dyfodol**

nyfroedd *gw.* **dŵr**
nyfyniad *gw.* **dyfyniad**
nyffryn *gw.* **dyffryn**
nylanwad *gw.* **dylanwad**
nyled *gw.* **dyled**
nyletswydd *gw.* **dyletswydd**
nymuniad *gw.* **dymuniad**
nyn *gw.* **dyn**
nynes *gw.* **dynes**
nyni *rhag.* we, us
nyrnaid *gw.* **dyrnaid**
nyrnau *gw.* **dwrn**
nyrs *e.g.b.* *ll.* **-ys** nurse
nyrsio *be.* **(nyrsiaf)** to nurse
nysgl *gw.* **dysgl**
nysgu *gw.* **dysgu**
nysgwr *gw.* **dysgwr**
nyth *e.b.* *ll.* **-od** nest. **nyth y dryw** the wren's nest
nywediad *gw.* **dywediad**
nyweddïad *gw.* **dyweddïad**
nyweddïo *gw.* **dyweddïo**

O

o *ardd.* *(followed by soft mutation)* *(personal forms:* **ohono, ohonot, ohono/ohoni, ohonon, ohonoch, ohonyn)** from, of, out of. **o amgylch** around; **o chwith** wrongly, the wrong way about; **o flaen** before, ahead of; **o gwbl** at all; **o gwmpas** around, round about; **o hyd** still; **o'r blaen** beforehand, earlier, previously; **o'r diwedd** at last; **o'r gloch** o'clock; **o'r gorau** very well. *gw. At. Arddodiaid. gw.* **ef**

obaith *gw.* **gobaith**
obeithio *gw.* **gobeithio**
obeithion *gw.* **gobaith**
obennydd *gw.* **gobennydd**
oblegid *c. & ardd.* because, for
ochenaid *e.b.* *ll.* **ocheneidiau** sigh
ochneidio *be.* **(ochneidiaf)** to sigh, to groan
ochr *e.b.* *ll.* **-au** side. **ochr yn ochr** side by side; **wrth ochr** beside; **yr ochr draw i** (on) the other side to
od *a.* odd, bizarre; remarkable
odidog *gw.* **godidog**
odl *e.b.* *ll.* **-au** rhyme; ode, song
odli *be.* **(odlaf)** to rhyme
odre *gw.* **godre**
odro *gw.* **godro**
oddef *gw.* **goddef**
oddefgar *gw.* **goddefgar**
oddeutu *ardd. & ad.* about, around
oddi *ardd.* out of, from. **oddi allan** outside; **oddi ar** from off; since; **oddieithr** except, unless; **oddi mewn** within; **oddi wrth** from; **oddi yma** from here
oddrych *gw.* **goddrych**
oed *e.g.* *ll.* **-au** age; time. **blwydd oed** year old; **saith oed** seven years of age; **gwneud oed â** to arrange a tryst, to make a date
oedfa *e.b.* *ll.* **-on, oedfeuon** service, meeting

oedi *be.* **(oedaf)** to delay, to postpone; to linger

oedolion *gw.* **oedolyn**

oedolyn *e.g. ll.* **oedolion** adult

oedran *e.g. ll.* **-nau** age

oedrannus *a.* aged, elderly

oedd *bf.* was, were. *gw.* **bod**

oen *e.g. ll.* **ŵyn** lamb

oer *a.* cold, chill, chilly; frigid

oerfel *e.g.* cold

oergell *e.b. ll.* **-oedd** refrigerator

oeri *be.* **(oeraf)** to cool, to become cold

oes 1 *e.b. ll.* **-au, -oedd** age, lifetime. **ers oes** from an age; **o oes i oes** from age to age; **yn oes oesoedd** for ever and ever. **2** *bf.* is, are. *gw.* **bod.** *gw. At. Berfau – Affirmative & Negative answers*

of *gw.* **gof**

ofal *gw.* **gofal**

ofalu *gw.* **gofalu**

ofalus *gw.* **gofalus**

ofalwr *gw.* **gofalwr**

ofer *a.* vain; prodigal; waste. **ymgais ofer** a vain attempt

oferedd *e.g.* vanity, dissipation, frivolity

ofergoel *e.b. ll.* **-ion** superstition

ofergoeledd: ofergoeliaeth *e.g.* superstition

ofergoelus *a.* superstitious

ofid *gw.* **gofid**

ofidio *gw.* **gofidio**

ofn *e.g. ll.* **-au** fear, terror, dread. **Mae ofn arno fe** He is afraid; **Mae ofn llygod arna i** I am afraid of mice

ofnadwy *a.* awful, dreadful, horrendous

ofnau *gw.* **ofn**

ofni *be.* **(ofnaf)** to fear, to dread

ofnus *a.* timid, nervous

ofod *gw.* **gofod**

ofodwr *gw.* **gofodwr**

ofyn *gw.* **gofyn**

offeiriad *e.g. ll.* **offeiriaid** priest, parson

offer *gw.* **offeryn**

offeren *e.b.* mass (*Roman Catholic*)

offeryn *e.g. ll.* **-nau, offer** instrument, tool, apparatus, equipment. **offeryn cerdd** musical instrument; **offeryn chwyth** wind instrument; **offeryn llinynnol** stringed instrument; **offerynnau taro** percussion instruments

offerynnol *a.* instrumental. **darn offerynnol** instrumental piece (*of music*)

ogledd *gw.* **gogledd**

ogleddol *gw.* **gogleddol**

ogleddwr *gw.* **gogleddwr**

ogleisio *gw.* **gogleisio**

ogof *e.b. ll.* **-âu, -eydd** cave, cavern; den

ogoniant *gw.* **gogoniant**

ogylch *ardd.* about

ogystal *gw.* **gogystal**

ongl *e.b. ll.* **-au** angle. **ongl sgwâr** right angle; **triongl** triangle

onglog *a.* angular

oherwydd *c. & ardd.*
because, for

ohirio *gw.* **gohirio**

ôl 1 *e.g. ll.* **olion** mark, print;
track; trace. **ôl bysedd**
finger-marks; **ôl traed**
footprints. 2 *a.* back, hind:
ar ôl after; **pen ôl** behind,
bottom (buttocks); **yn ôl**
according to; ago; **y tu ôl**
behind

olaf *a.* last (*the very last*). *gw.*
hwyr

olau *gw.* **golau**

olchi *gw.* **golchi**

oleudy *gw.* **goleudy**

oleuni *gw.* **goleuni**

oleuo *gw.* **goleuo**

olew *e.g. ll.* **-au** oil. **maes
olew** oilfield

olion *gw.* **ôl**

ôl-nodiad *e.g. ll.* **ôl-nodiadau**
postscript

ôl-ofal *e.g. ll.* **ôl-ofalon** aftercare

olrhain *be.* **(olrheiniaf)** to
trace, to track

olud *gw.* **golud**

olwg *gw.* **golwg**

olwr *e.g. ll.* **olwyr** back
(*rugby, etc.*)

olwyn *e.b. ll.* **-ion** wheel.
cadair olwyn/olwynion
wheelchair; **olwyn fesur**
trundle wheel

olwyr *gw.* **olwr**

olygfa *gw.* **golygfa**

olygon *gw.* **golwg**

olygu *gw.* **golygu**

oll *ad.* all, wholly; ever, at all

ollwng *gw.* **gollwng**

ond 1 *c.* but, only. 2 *ardd.*
except; save; but

onest *gw.* **gonest**

oni: onid 1 *ad.* not? is it not?
2 *c.* if not, unless. 3 *ardd.*
except; save; but: **onid e?**
otherwise; else; is it not?

onibai (am) *c.* were it not
(for)

onid *gw.* **oni**

onnen *e.b. ll.* **ynn** ash tree

opera *e.b. ll.* **operâu** opera.
opera ddigri comic opera;
opera fawreddog grand
opera; **opera ysgafn** light
opera; **opera sebon** soap
opera

optegwr: optegydd *e.g. ll.*
optegwyr optician

orau *gw.* **da**

orchfygu *gw.* **gorchfygu**

orchymyn *gw.* **gorchymyn**

oren *e.g. ll.* **-au** orange

orfod *gw.* **gorfod**

orfodaeth *gw.* **gorfodaeth**

orfodi *gw.* **gorfodi**

orfodol *gw.* **gorfodol**

orfoleddus *gw.* **gorfoleddus**

orffen *gw.* **gorffen**

Orffennaf *gw.* **Gorffennaf**

orffennol *gw.* **gorffennol**

orffwys *gw.* **gorffwys**

orffwyso *gw.* **gorffwyso**

organ *e.g.b. ll.* **-au** organ.
organ geg mouth-organ

organig *a.* organic

organydd *e.g. ll.* **-ion**
organist

oriau *gw.* **awr**

oriel *e.b.* *ll.* **-au** gallery
orlawn *gw.* **gorlawn**
orllewin *gw.* **gorllewin**
ormod *gw.* **gormod**
ornest *e.b.* *ll.* **-au** contest,
combat, duel, match. *gw.*
gornest
orsaf *gw.* **gorsaf**
orsedd *gw.* **gorsedd**
oruchaf *gw.* **goruchaf**
oruwchnaturiol *gw.*
goruwchnaturiol
orwedd *gw.* **gorwedd**
orwel *gw.* **gorwel**
orymdaith *gw.* **gorymdaith**
os *c.* if (*definite not
conjecture*). **Os daw Tom, dof
i hefyd** If Tom comes, I will
come too
osgoi *be.* **(osgoaf)** to avoid,
to swerve, to evade; to shirk.
ffordd-osgoi bypass
osod *gw.* **gosod**
ostwng *gw.* **gostwng**
ostyngedig *gw.* **gostyngedig**
ostyngiad *gw.* **gostyngiad**
owns *e.b.* *ll.* **-ys** ounce; **dwy
owns** two ounces

P

pa *a.* Which? What? **(Pa)
beth?** What (thing)? **Pa
bryd? Pryd?** When? **Pa
fodd?** How? **P'un?** Which
one? *gw.* **pam**
Pab *e.g.* *ll.* **-au** Pope
pabell *e.b.* *ll.* **pebyll** tent,
pavilion
pabi *e.b.* *ll.* **pabïau** poppy

pabydd *e.g.* *ll.* **-ion** papist
pac *e.g.* *ll.* **-au, -iau** pack,
bundle
paced *e.g.* *ll.* **-i** packet,
package
paciau *gw.* **pac**
pacio *be.* **(paciaf)** to pack
padell *e.b.* *ll.* **-i** bowl, pan
pader *e.g.* *ll.* **-au** the Lord's
prayer, prayers. **dweud
pader/dysgu pader i berson**
'*to teach your grandmother
to suck eggs*'
paent *e.g.* *ll.* **-iau** paint
pafiliwn *e.g.* pavilion
pafin *e.g.* *ll.* **-au** pavement
(*S.W*)
pagan *e.g.* **-iaid** pagan
paham *gw.* **pam**
pais *e.b.* *ll.* **peisiau** petticoat
pâl 1 *e.b.* *ll.* **palau** spade
(*S.W.*). 2 *e.g.* *ll.* **palod**
puffin
palas *e.g.* *ll.* **-au, -oedd**
palace
palau *gw.* **pâl**
palmant *e.g.* *ll.* **-au** pavement
(*N.W.*)
palod *gw.* **pâl**
palu *be.* **(palaf)** to dig over
(*not down*)
pallu *be.* **(pallaf)** to refuse, to
fail, to cease, to lack
pam: paham: pa *ad.* why?
pamffled *e.g.* *ll.* **-i, -au**
pamphlet
pamffledyn *e.g.* pamphlet
pan *c.* when
panasen *e.b.* *ll.* **pannas**
parsnip

panel *e.g. ll.* **-i** panel
pannas *gw.* **panasen.**
pant *e.g. ll.* **-au, -iau** valley, hollow; *dent. undergoing soft mutation after* **i** > **i bant, bant** *ad.* away, off. **Mae e bant** He's away; **o bant** from away; **o bant i bentan** everywhere, from pillar to post
papur *e.g. ll.* **-au** paper. **papur newydd** newspaper; **papur deg punt** ten-pound note; **papur wal** wallpaper
papuro *be.* **(papuraf)** to paper
pâr *e.g. ll.* **parau** pair
para (i): parhau (i) *be.* **(paraf)** to continue (to)
paradwys *e.b. ll.* **-au** paradise
paragraff *e.g. ll.* **-au** paragraph
paratoi *be.* **(paratoaf)** to prepare to. **paratoi i fynd** to prepare to go
parau *gw.* **pâr**
parc *e.g. ll.* **-au, -iau** park; field *(S.W.W.)*
parch *e.g.* respect. **dillad parch** Sunday best, best clothes *(lit. the clothes of respect)*
parchedig *a. ll.* **-ion** *(often abbreviated to* **y parchg)** reverend, reverent. **Y Parchedig Ifan Rhys** Reverend Ifan Rhys
parchu *be.* **(parchaf)** to respect
parchus *be.* respectable,

respectful
pardwn *e.g. ll.* **pardynau** pardon
parhad *e.g.* continuation
parhau *gw.* **para**
parod *a.* ready, willing, prepared. **yn barod** already; **arian parod** ready cash
parsel *e.g. ll.* **-au, -i** parcel
parti *e.g. ll.* **-ion** party
Pasg *e.g.* Easter. **Dydd Llun y Pasg** Easter Monday; **wy Pasg** Easter egg; **Gwyliau'r Pasg** Easter holidays; **y Pasg** Easter
pasiannau *gw.* **pasiant**
pasiant *e.g. ll.* **pasiannau** pageant
patrwm *e.g. ll.* **patrymau** pattern
patrwn *e.g. ll.* **patrynau** pattern
patrymau *gw.* **patrwm**
patrynau *gw.* **patrwn**
pawb *e.g.* everybody, all
pawen *e.b. ll.* **-nau** paw
pe *c.* if. **Pe bawn i yno** If I were there
pebyll *gw.* **pabell**
pecyn *e.g. ll.* **-nau** package, packet
pechadur *e.g. ll.* **-iaid** sinner
pechod *e.g. ll.* **-au** sin: **Dyna bechod!** What a pity!
pechu *be.* **(pechaf)** to sin; **pechu yn erbyn** to sin against
pedair *eb. & a.b. (adjective placed before feminine noun)* four. **pedair merch** four

girls; **pedair cadair** four
chairs. *gw.* **pedwar**
pedol *e.b. ll.* **-au** horseshoe
pedwar *e.g. ll. & a.g.* four.
gw. **pedair**
pedwaredd *a.b.* fourth. **y
bedwaredd ferch** the fourth
girl
pedwerydd *a.g.* fourth. **y
pedwerydd bachgen** the
fourth boy
peg *e.g. ll.* **-iau** peg
pegwn *e.g. ll.* **pegynau** pole.
Pegwn y De South Pole;
Pegwn y Gogledd North
Pole
pegynau *gw.* **pegwn**
peidio (â) *be.* **(peidiaf)** to
cease, to stop. **Paid (â) siarad**
Don't talk
peilot *e.g. ll.* **-iaid** pilot
peint *e.g. ll.* **-iau** pint. **peint a
hanner** a pint and a half
peintio *be.* **(peintiaf)** to paint
peintiwr *e.g. ll.* **peintwyr**
painter
peiriannau *gw.* **peiriant**
peiriannydd: peiriannwr *e.g.
ll.* **peirianwyr** engineer
peiriant *e.g. ll.* **peiriannau**
engine, machine. **peiriant
golchi** washing machine;
peiriant car car engine;
peiriant gwnïo sewing
machine
peisiau *gw.* **pais**
pêl *e.b. ll.* **peli, pelau** ball.
pêl-droed football; **pêl rygbi**
rugby ball
pelydr *e.g. ll.* **-au** ray, beam.

pelydr X X ray
pell *a.* far. *gw. At.
Ansoddeiriau.*
pellach *gw.* **pell**
pellaf *gw.* **pell**
pelled *gw.* **pell**
pellter *e.g. ll.* **-au, -oedd**
distance. **yn y pellter** in the
distance. **o bellter** from a
distance
pen 1 *e.g. ll.* **-nau** head, top,
end, mouth. **ar ben** on top
of, ended; **ar ei phen ei hun**
by herself; **pen y bryn** top of
the hill; **pen ôl** behind,
bottom (buttocks). **2** *a.*
chief, supreme
penaethiaid *gw.* **pennaeth**
penawdau *gw.* **pennawd**
pen-blwydd *e.g. ll.* **-i**
birthday
pencadlys *e.g. ll.* **-oedd**
headquarters
pencampwr *e.g. ll.*
pencampwyr champion
pendant *a.* positive, definite,
emphatic
penderfyniad *e.g. ll.* **-au**
resolution, determination
penderfynol *a.* resolute,
determined. **yn benderfynol o**
determined to
penderfynu *be.* **(penderfynaf)**
to decide, to resolve: **Fe
benderfynodd fynd** He
decided to go
penelin *e.g.b. ll.* **-oedd** elbow
penfoel *a.* bald-headed
pen-glin: pen-lin *e.b. ll.*
pengliniau: penliniau knee

penigamp *a.* splendid, excellent

penillion *gw.* pennill

pen-lin *gw.* pen-glin

penlinio *be.* (penliniaf) to kneel

pennaeth *e.g. ll.* penaethiaid chief

pennaf *a.* principal, chief

pennau *gw.* pen

pennawd *e.g. ll.* penawdau heading; headline; **penawdau'r newyddion** the news headlines

pennill *e.g. ll.* penillion stanza, verse

pennod *e.b. ll.* penodau chapter

penodau *gw.* pennod

penodi *be.* (penodaf) to appoint

penodiad *e.g. ll.* -au appointment

penrhyn *e.g. ll.* -au promontory, headland

pensaer *e.g. ll.* penseiri architect

penseiri *gw.* pensaer

pensil *e.g. ll.* -iau pencil

pensiwn *e.g. ll.* pensiynau pension

pensiynau *gw.* pensiwn

pensiynwr *e.g. ll.* pensiynwyr pensioner

penteulu *e.g. ll.* -oedd head of family

pentref *e.g. ll.* -i village

pentwr *e.g. ll.* pentyrrau heap, mass, pile

pentyrrau *gw.* pentwr

penwythnos *e.g. ll.* -au weekend

pêr *a.* sweet *(of sound). gw.* peren

perlysiau *e.ll.* herbs

perchen: perchennog *e.g. ll.* perchenogion owner, proprietor. **Roedd e'n berchen ar dŷ** He was a house owner

perchenogaeth *e.b.* ownership

perchenogi *be.* to own

peren *e.b. ll.* pêr pear

pererin *e.g. ll.* -ion pilgrim

perfedd *e.g. ll.* -ion entrails, guts, middle. **perfedd gwlad** heart of countryside; **perfedd nos** dead of night

perffaith *a.* perfect

perffeithio *be.* (perffeithiaf) to perfect

peri (i) *be.* (peraf) to cause

perl *e.g. ll.* -au pearl

perllan *e.b. ll.* -nau orchard

persawr *e.g. ll.* -au perfume, fragrance

persli *e.g.* parsley

person 1 *e.g. ll.* -au person. **2** *e.g. ll.* -iaid parson

personol *a.* personal

personoliaeth *e.b. ll.* -au personality

pert *a.* pretty

perth *e.b. ll.* -i bush; hedge *(S.W.)*

perthnasau *gw.* perthynas

perthnasol *a.* relevant

perthyn (i) *be.* (perthynaf) to belong, to be related

perthynas

perthynas *e.b.g. ll.*
perthnasau relation;
relationship

perygl *e.g. ll.* **peryglon**
danger

peryglus *a.* dangerous

peswch 1 *be.* **(pesychaf)** to
cough. 2 *e.g.* a cough

pesychiad *e.g. ll.* **-au** cough

petai *bf.* if it were
(conjecture). **pe bai** if; **pe
basai** if

petrol *e.g. ll.* **-au** petrol.
petrol di-blwm unleaded
petrol

peth *e.g. ll.* **-au** thing, some,
part. **pa beth?** what (thing)?
oes peth ar ôl is there some
left?

piano *e.g.b. ll.* **-s** piano

pianydd *e.g. ll.* **-ion** pianist

pib *e.b. ll.* **-au: pibell** *e.b. ll.*
-au, -i pipe *(smoking,
musical variety).* **canu'r
pibau** to play the pipes;
tanio pib to light a pipe

piben *e.b. ll.* **-ni** pipe
(drainpipe, etc.)

picil *e.g.* pickle, trouble.
mewn picil in trouble

pictiwr *e.g. ll.* **pictiyrau**
picture

picwn *gw.* **picwnen**

picwnen *e.b. ll.* **picwn** wasp
(S.W.). **nyth picwn** wasps'
nest. *gw.* **cacynen**

pigfain *a.* tapering

pigiad *e.g. ll.* **-au** prick, sting;
injection

pigo *be.* **(pigaf)** to pick, to

sting, to prick, to peck

pigog *a.* prickly, irritable

pil *e.g. ll.* **-ion** peel

piler *e.g. ll.* **-au** pillar,
column **o biler i bost** from
pillar to post

pilio *be.* **(piliaf)** to peel

pilion *gw.* **pil**

pili-pala *e.g. ll.* **pili-palod**
butterfly *(S.W.)*

pilsen *e.b. ll.* **pils** pill

pilyn *e.g. ll.* **-nau** garment
(S.W.) rag. **pilyn gorau** best
garment; **pilyn parch** Sunday
garment, best garment

pin *e.g. ll.* **-nau** pin; pen. **pin
ysgrifennu** writing pen;
pinnau bawd drawing pins

pîn *gw.* **pinwydden**

pînafal *e.g. ll.* **-au** pineapple

pinc *a.* pink: **yn y pinc** in
very good health

pinnau *gw.* **pin**

pinsio *be.* **(pinsiaf)** to pinch

pinwydden *e.b. ll.* **pîn,
pinwydd** pine

piod *gw.* **pioden**

pioden *e.b. ll.* **piod** magpie

pisyn *e.g. ll.* **-nau** piece
(S.W.). **Mae hi'n bisyn!** She's
good looking!

piti *e.g.* pity

plaid *e.b. ll.* **pleidiau** party,
side. **o blaid** in favour; **Y
Blaid Geidwadol** The
Conservative Party; **Y Blaid
Lafur** The Labour Party; **Y
Blaid (Plaid Cymru)** The
Welsh Nationalist Party; **Y
Blaid Werdd** The Green

Party
plan *e.g. ll.* **-iau** plan
planced *e.b. ll.* **-i** blanket.
gw. **blanced**
planhigyn *e.g. ll.* **planhigion**
plant
planiau *gw.* **plan**
plannu *be.* **(plannaf)** to plant
plant *gw.* **plentyn**
plas *e.g. ll.* **-au** palace,
mansion
plastai *gw.* **plasty**
plasty *e.g. ll.* **plastai** palace,
mansion
plât *e.g. ll.* **platiau** plate
platiau *gw.* **plât**
pleidiau *gw.* **plaid**
pleidlais *e.b. ll.* **pleidlesiau**
vote
pleidleisiau *gw.* **pleidlais**
pleidleisio *be.* **(pleidleisliaf)** to
vote. **bwrw pleidlais** to cast
a vote
pleidleisiwr *e.g. ll.*
pleidleiswyr voter
plentyn *e.g. ll.* **plant** child
plentynnaidd *a.* childish
pleser *e.g. ll.* **-au** pleasure.
rhoi pleser i to give pleasure
to
pleserus *a.* pleasant,
pleasurable
plesio *be.* **(plesiaf)** to please
plisgyn *e.g. ll.* **plisg** shell,
pod, casing
plisman: plismon *e.g. ll.*
plismyn policeman
plismyn *gw.* **plisman**
plith *e.g.* midst. **i blith** into
the midst of; **o blith** from

among; **ymhlith** among; **blith
draphlith** in confusion,
intermingled
plu *gw.* **pluen**
pluen *e.b. ll.* **plu** feather; fly
(fishing-bait). **clymu plu** to
fashion fishing-flies; **yn
ysgafn fel pluen** light as a
feather
pluf *gw.* **plufyn**
plufyn *e.g. ll.* **pluf** feather
(S.W.)
plwc *e.g. ll.* **plyciau** pull, jerk
plwg *e.g. ll.* **plygiau** plug
plwm 1 *e.g.* lead; 2 *a.* leaden;
vertical
plwyf *e.g. ll.* **-i** parish. **ar y
plwyf** on the parish,
destitute
plyciau *gw.* **plwc**
plygiau *gw.* **plwg**
plygu *be.* **(plygaf)** to fold, to
bend, to stoop, to bow, to
submit
pob *a.* each, every, all; roast.
pob cynnig every attempt,
every offer; **pob dydd** every
day; **pob tro** every occasion;
pob un everyone; **tatws pob**
roast potatoes
pobi *be.* **(pobaf)** to bake, to
roast
pobl *e.b. ll.* **-oedd** people. **y
bobl hyn** these people
poblogaeth *e.b. ll.* **-au**
population
poblogaidd *a.* popular
pobman *ad.* everywhere
pobydd *e.g. ll.* **-ion** baker
poced *e.b. ll.* **-i** pocket

poen *e.g.b. ll.* **-au** pain, ache, agony

poeni *be.* **(poenaf)** to pain, to worry, to tease. **Paid poeni!** Don't worry!

poenus *a.* painful

poenydio *be.* **(poenydiaf)** to torture, to torment

poer: poeri *e.g.* spittle, saliva

poeri (at, i'r) *be.* **(poeraf)** to spit. *gw.* **poer**

poeth *a.* hot

poethi *be.* **(poethaf)** to heat, to be heated

polion *gw.* **polyn**

politicaidd *a.* political

polyn *e.g. ll.* **polion** pole, stake

pont *e.b. ll.* **-ydd** bridge

pontydd *gw.* **pont**

Pont-y-pŵl *e.b.* Pontypool

popeth *e.g.* everything

poptai *gw.* **popty**

popty *e.g. ll.* **poptai** bakehouse; oven

porfa *e.b. ll.* **porfeydd** pasture; grass *(S.W.)*

porfeydd *gw.* **porfa**

porffor *e.g. & a.* purple

pori *be.* **(poraf)** to graze

portread *e.g. ll.* **-au** portrait, portrayal

porth *e.g. ll.* **pyrth** door; porch

porthladd *e.g. ll.* **-oedd** harbour

pos *e.g. ll.* **posau** puzzle, riddle. **pos croeseiriau** crossword puzzle

posibilrwydd *e.g.* possibility

posibl *a.* possible

post 1 *e.g. ll.* **pyst** post, pillar. 2 *e.g. ll.* **-iau** post, mail; **blwch postio/llythyrau** post box

postio *be.* **(postiaf)** to post

postman: postmon *e.g. ll.* **postmyn** postman

postmyn *gw.* **postman**

postyn *e.g. ll.* **pyst** post. **fel postyn** deaf *(as a post)*

potel *e.b. ll.* **-i** bottle. **potel ddŵr poeth** hotwater bottle

powdr: powdwr *e.g. ll.* **powdrau** powder

powdrau *gw.* **powdr**

powlen *gw.* **bowlen**

praidd *e.g. ll.* **preiddiau** flock

pram *e.g. ll.* **-iau** pram

prawf *e.g. ll.* **profion** trial, test, proof. **prawf darllen** reading test; **prawf gyrru** driving test; **ar brawf** on trial, on probation; **blwyddyn brawf** probationary year; **Gwasanaeth Prawf** Probation Service; **swyddog prawf** probation officer

pregeth *e.b. ll.* **-au** sermon

pregethu *be.* **(pregethaf)** to preach

pregethwr *e.g. ll.* **pregethwyr** preacher

preiddiau *gw.* **praidd**

preifat *a.* private

pren *e.g. ll.* **-nau** tree, wood, timber. **pren afalau** apple tree; **pren caled** hardwood; **pren meddal** softwood; **llwy**

bren a wooden spoon
prennau *gw.* pren
prentis *e.g. ll.* **-iaid**
apprentice
prentisiaeth *e.b. ll.* **-au**
apprenticeship
prentisiaid *gw.* prentis
pres 1 *e.g.* brass, bronze;
money. 2 *a.* brass. **band**
pres brass band; **jwg bres**
brass jug
preseb *e.g. ll.* **-au** crib, stall,
manger
presennol *a.* present. **yr**
amser presennol the present
tense
presenoldeb *e.g. ll.* **-au**
presence, attendance
presgripsiwn *e.g. ll.*
presgripsiynau prescription
preswyl: preswylfod *e.g. ll.*
preswylfeydd dwelling place.
preswylfan dwelling place;
ysgol breswyl boarding
school; **neuadd breswyl** hall
of residence
pridwerth *e.g.* ransom
pridd *e.g. ll.* **-oedd** soil, earth
prif *a. (precedes the noun it*
qualifies and is followed by
soft mutation) prime, chief,
major, principal. **prif**
ddiddordeb chief interest;
prif westeion principal
guests; **Prif Weinidog** Prime
Minister
prifardd *e.g. ll.* **prifeirdd** chief
bard *(one who has won*
chair or crown at National
Eisteddfod)

prifathrawes *e.b. ll.* **-au**
headmistress, principal
prifathro *e.g. ll.* **prifathrawon**
headmaster, principal
prifddinas *e.b. ll.* **-oedd**
capital city
prifeirdd *gw.* prifardd
prifio *be.* **(prifiaf)** to grow
(S.W.)
prifysgol *e.b. ll.* **-ion**
university: **Prifysgol Cymru**
University of Wales
priffordd *e.b. ll.* **priffyrdd**
highway
priffyrdd *gw.* priffordd
prin *a.* rare, scarce, hardly
prinder *e.g. ll.* **-au** scarcity
printio *be.* **(printiaf)** to print
priod 1 *a.* own, proper;
married. 2 *e.g.b.* husband or
wife. **ei phriod** her husband;
fy mhriod my partner
(husband/wife). **ei briod le**
his proper place; **priodfab**
bridegroom; **priodferch**
bride; **gŵr priod** married
man; **gwraig briod** married
woman; **Ydych chi'n briod?**
Are you married?
priodas *e.b. ll.* **-au** marriage,
wedding
priodi (â) *be.* **(priodaf)** to
marry
priodol *a.* appropriate,
proper
pris *e.g. ll.* **-iau, -oedd** price
problem *e.g. ll.* **-au** problem
profi *be.* **(profaf)** to prove, to
test, to taste
profiad *e.g. ll.* **-au** experience

profiadol *a.* experienced
profion *gw.* prawf
profocio: pryfocio *be.*
 (profociaf: pryfociaf) to
 provoke
proffid *e.b.* *ll.* **-iau** profit
proffiddiol *a.* profitable
proffwyd *e.g.* *ll.* **-i** prophet;
 proffwydes prophetess
proffwydo *be.* **(proffwydaf)** to
 prophesy
Protestant *e.g.* *ll.*
 Protestaniaid Protestant
prudd *a.* sad, grave, serious
pryd 1 *e.g.* *ll.* **-au** meal.
 byrbryd snack; **tamaid i aros
 pryd** temporary provision
 while awaiting arrival of
 something more substantial.
 2 *e.g.* *ll.* **-iau** time, season:
 Pryd? Pa bryd? What time?
 mewn pryd in time; **ar y pryd**
 at the time; impromptu; **hen
 bryd** about time
Prydain *e.b.* Britain
prydau *gw.* pryd
Prydeinig *a.* British
pryder *e.g.* *ll.* **-on** anxiety,
 care, worry
pryderu *be.* **(pryderaf)** to be
 anxious
pryderus *a.* anxious
prydferth *a.* beautiful,
 handsome
prydferthwch *e.g.* beauty
prydiau *gw.* pryd
prydlon *a.* punctual
pryf: pryfedyn: pryfyn *e.g.* *ll.*
 pryfed insect; vermin;
 animal; worm. **pryf copyn**

 spider *(N.W.)*
pryfed *gw.* pryf
pryfocio *gw.* profocio
pryfyn *gw.* pryf
prynhawn *e.g.* *ll.* **-au**
 afternoon. **prynhawn da!**
 good afternoon!
prynu *be.* **(prynaf)** to buy
prynwr *e.g.* *ll.* **prynwyr**
 buyer, redeemer
prysur *a.* busy, hasty;
 diligent, serious
prysurdeb *e.g.* haste, hurry;
 busyness
prysuro (i) *be.* **(prysuraf)** to
 hasten (to), to hurry. **Rwy'n
 prysuro i esbonio** I hasten to
 explain
pulpud *e.g.* *ll.* **-au** pulpit
pum: pump *e.g.* *ll.* & *a.* five.
 pumed fifth
p'un *gw.* pa
punnau *gw.* punt
punnoedd *gw.* punt
punt *e.b.* *ll.* **punnau,
 punnoedd** pound *(£)*
pupur *e.g.* *ll.* **-au** pepper. **fel
 melin bupur** very talkative
pur 1 *a.* pure, sincere. **Yr
 eiddoch yn bur** Yours
 sincerely. 2 *ad.* very, fairly.
 yn bur wael very poorly; **yn
 bur dda** fairly good
purfa *e.b.* *ll.* **purfeydd**
 refinery. **purfa olew** oil
 refinery
puro *be.* **(puraf)** to purify
pwdin *e.g.* *ll.* **-au** pudding,
 sweet *(after dinner)*. **Bydd
 pwdin yn dilyn** There's a

sweet to follow

pwdr *a.* rotten, corrupt, lazy *(S.W.)*

pwdryn *e.g* idler, sluggard *(S.W.)*

pwdu *be.* **(pwdaf)** to sulk, to pout

pŵer *e.g. ll.* **-au** power

pwll *e.g. ll.* **pyllau** pit, pool, pond. **pwll glo** coal-pit, coal-mine

pwmp *e.g. ll.* **pympiau** pump

pwnc *e.g. ll.* **pynciau** subject, topic. **pynciau craidd** core subjects; **pynciau sylfaen** foundation subjects; **Cymanfa Bwnc** assembly for cathechizing and discussing prepared portions of Scripture

pwrpas *e.g. ll.* **-au** purpose

pwrs *e.g. ll.* **pyrsau** purse

pwy *rhag. gof.* who? **pwy bynnag** whosoever

pwyll *e.g.* sense, discretion. **colli ei bwyll** to lose his senses, to become enraged; **cymryd pwyll** to take time; **mynd gan bwyll** to go steadily

pwllgor *e.g. ll.* **-au** committee. **pwllgor addysg** education committee; **pwyllgor brys** emergency committee; **pwyllgor gwaith** executive committee

pwyllo *be.* **(pwyllaf)** to pause, to consider, to reflect

pwynt *e.g. ll.* **-iau** point. **dau bwynt pump** 2.5 (two point

five); **rhewbwynt** freezing-point

pwys 1 *e.g. ll.* **-au** weight, importance. **ar bwys** near; **ennill pwysau** to put on weight; **o bwys** important; **codi pwys ar** to make one feel sick. 2 *e.g. ll.* **-i** pound *(lb)*

pwysedd *e.g.* pressure. **pwysedd gwaed** blood pressure

pwysig *a.* important

pwysigrwydd *e.g.* importance

pwyslais *e.g. ll.* **pwysleisiau** emphasis

pwyso (ar) *be.* **(pwysaf)** to weigh, to lean (on), to rest

pwyth *e.g. ll.* **-au** stitch. **talu'r pwyth** to avenge; retaliate

pydru *be.* **(pydraf)** to rot, to decay

pyllau *gw.* **pwll**, *gw.* **pyllyn**

pyllyn *e.g. ll.* **pyllau** pool, pond

pympiau *gw.* **pwmp**

pymtheg 1 *e.g. ll.* **-au** fifteen 2 *a.* fifteen

pymthegfed *a.* fifteenth

pynciau *gw.* **pwnc**

pyped *e.g. ll.* **-au** puppet

pyrsau *gw.* **pwrs**

pyrth *gw.* **porth**

pys *gw.* **pysen**

pysen *e.b. ll.* **pys** pea. **pys pêr** sweet peas

pysgod *gw.* **pysgodyn**

pysgodyn *e.g. ll.* **pysgod** a fish. **pysgodyn aur** a goldfish

pysgota *be.* **(pysgotaf)** to fish
pysgotwr *e.g.* *ll.* **pysgotwyr**
 fisherman
pyst *gw.* **post, postyn**
pythefnos *e.g.b.* *ll.* **-au**
 fortnight

PH

pha *gw.* **pa**
Phab *gw.* **Pab**
phabell *gw.* **pabell**
phabi *gw.* **pabi**
phabydd *gw.* **pabydd**
phac *gw.* **pac**
phaced *gw.* **paced**
phacio *gw.* **pacio**
phadell *gw.* **padell**
phader *gw.* **pader**
phaent *gw.* **paent**
phafiliwn *gw.* **pafiliwn**
phafin *gw.* **pafin**
phagan *gw.* **pagan**
phaham *gw.* **paham**
phais *gw.* **pais**
phâl *gw.* **pâl**
phalas *gw.* **palas**
phalau *gw.* **pâl**
phalod *gw.* **pâl**
phalu *gw.* **palu**
phallu *gw.* **pallu**
pham *gw.* **pam**
phamffled *gw.* **pamffled**
phamffledyn *gw.* **pamffled**
phan *gw.* **pan**
phanasen *gw.* **panasen**
phanel *gw.* **panel**
phannas *gw.* **panasen**
phant *gw.* **pant**
phapur *gw.* **papur**

phapuro *gw.* **papuro**
phâr *gw.* **pâr**
phara *gw.* **para**
pharadwys *gw.* **paradwys**
pharagraff *gw.* **paragraff**
pharatoi *gw.* **paratoi**
pharc *gw.* **parc**
pharch *gw.* **parch**
pharchedig *gw.* **parchedig**
pharchu *gw.* **parchu**
pharchus *gw.* **parchus**
pharhad *gw.* **parhad**
pharhau *gw.* **parhau**
pharod *gw.* **parod**
pharsel *gw.* **parsel**
pharti *gw.* **parti**
Phasg *gw.* **Pasg**
phasiannau *gw.* **pasiant**
phasiant *gw.* **pasiant**
phatrwm *gw.* **patrwm**
phatrwn *gw.* **patrwn**
phatrymau *gw.* **patrwm**
phatrynau *gw.* **patrwn**
phawb *gw.* **pawb**
phawen *gw.* **pawen**
phe *gw.* **pe**
phebyll *gw.* **pabell**
phecyn *gw.* **pecyn**
phechadur *gw.* **pechadur**
phechod *gw.* **pechod**
phechu *gw.* **pechu**
phedair *gw.* **pedair**
phedol *gw.* **pedol**
phedwar *gw.* **pedwar**
phedwaredd *gw.* **pedwaredd**
phedwerydd *gw.* **pedwerydd**
pheg *gw.* **peg**
phegwn *gw.* **pegwn**
phegynau *gw.* **pegwn**
pheidio *gw.* **peidio**

pheilot *gw*. peilot
pheint *gw*. peint
pheintio *gw*. peintio
pheintiwr *gw*. peintiwr
pheiriannydd: pheiriannwr *gw*.
 peiriannydd
pheiriannau *gw*. peiriant
pheiriant *gw*. peiriant
pheisiau *gw*. pais
phêl *gw*. pêl
phelydr *gw*. pelydr
phell *gw*. pell
phellach *gw*. pell
phellaf *gw*. pell
phelled *gw*. pell
phellter *gw*. pellter
phen *gw*. pen
phenaethiaid *gw*. pennaeth
phenawdau *gw*. pennawd
phen-blwydd *gw*. pen-blwydd
phencadlys *gw*. pencadlys
phencampwr *gw*. pencampwr
phendant *gw*. pendant
phenderfyniad *gw*.
 penderfyniad
phenderfynol *gw*. penderfynol
phenderfynu *gw*. penderfynu
phenelin *gw*. penelin
phenfoel *gw*. penfoel
phen-glin *gw*. pen-glin
phenigamp *gw*. penigamp
phenillion *gw*. pennill
phen-lin *gw*. pen-glin
phenlinio *gw*. penlinio
phennaeth *gw*. pennaeth
phennaf *gw*. pennaf
phennau *gw*. pen
phennawd *gw*. pennawd
phennill *gw*. pennill
phennod *gw*. pennod

phenodau *gw*. pennod
phenodi *gw*. penodi
phenodiad *gw*. penodiad
phenrhyn *gw*. penrhyn
phensaer *gw*. pensaer
phenseiri *gw*. pensaer
phensil *gw*. pensil
phensiwn *gw*. pensiwn
phensiynau *gw*. pensiwn
phensiynwr *gw*. pensiynwr
phenteulu *gw*. penteulu
phentref *gw*. pentref
phentwr *gw*. pentwr
phenwythnos *gw*.
 penwythnos
phêr *gw*. pêr
pherchen *gw*. perchen
pherchennog *gw*. perchen
pheren *gw*. peren
phererin *gw*. pererin
pherfedd *gw*. perfedd
pherffaith *gw*. perffaith
pherffeithio *gw*. perffeithio
pheri *gw*. peri
pherl *gw*. perl
pherlysiau *gw*. perlysiau
pherllan *gw*. perllan
phersli *gw*. persli
pherson *gw*. person
phersonol *gw*. personol
phersonoliaeth *gw*.
 personoliaeth
phert *gw*. pert
pherth *gw*. perth
pherthnasau *gw*. perthynas
pherthnasol *gw*. perthnasol
pherthyn *gw*. perthyn
pherthynas *gw*. perthynas
pherygl *gw*. perygl
pheryglus *gw*. peryglus

pheswch *gw*. peswch
phesychiad *gw*. pesychiad
phetai *gw*. petai
phetrol *gw*. petrol
pheth *gw*. peth
phiano *gw*. piano
phianydd *gw*. pianydd
phib *gw*. pib
phiben *gw*. piben
phicil *gw*. picil
phictiwr *gw*. pictiwr
phicwn *gw*. picwnen
phicwnen *gw*. picwnen
phigfain *gw*. pigfain
phigiad *gw*. pigiad
phigo *gw*. pigo
phigog *gw*. pigog
phil *gw*. pil
philer *gw*. piler
philio *gw*. pilio
philion *gw*. pil
phili-pala *gw*. pili-pala
philsen *gw*. pilsen
philyn *gw*. pilyn
phin *gw*. pin
phîn *gw*. pîn
phînafal *gw*. pînafal
phinc *gw*. pinc
phinnau *gw*. pin
phinsio *gw*. pinsio
phinwydden *gw*. pinwydden
phioden *gw*. pioden
phisyn *gw*. pisyn
phiti *gw*. piti
phlaid *gw*. plaid
phlan *gw*. plan
phlanced *gw*. blanced
phlanhigyn *gw*. planhigyn
phlaniau *gw*. plan
phlannu *gw*. plannu

phlant *gw*. plant
phlas *gw*. plas
phlastai *gw*. plasty
phlasty *gw*. plasty
phlât *gw*. plât
phlatiau *gw*. plât
phleidiau *gw*. plaid
phleidlais *gw*. pleidlais
phleidleisiau *gw*. pleidlais
phleidleisio *gw*. pleidleisio
phleidleisiwr *gw*. pleidleisiwr
phlentyn *gw*. plentyn
phlentynnaidd *gw*.
 plentynnaidd
phleser *gw*. pleser
phleserus *gw*. pleserus
phlesio *gw*. plesio
phlisgyn *gw*. plisgyn
phlisman: phlismon *gw*.
 plisman
phlismyn *gw*. plisman
phlu *gw*. pluen
phluen *gw*. pluen
phluf *gw*. plufyn
phlufyn *gw*. plufyn
phlwc *gw*. plwc.
phlwg *gw*. plwg
phlwm *gw*. plwm
phlwyf *gw*. plwyf
phlyciau *gw*. plwc
phlygiau *gw*. plwg
phlygu *gw*. plygu
phob *gw*. pob
phobi *gw*. pobi
phobl *gw*. pobl
phoblogaeth *gw*. poblogaeth
phoblogaidd *gw*. poblogaidd
phobman *gw*. pobman
phobydd *gw*. pobydd
phoced *gw*. poced

phoen *gw.* poen
phoeni *gw.* poeni
phoenus *gw.* poenus
phoenydio *gw.* poenydio
phoer *gw.* poer
phoeri *gw.* poer, poeri (at, i'r)
phoeth *gw.* poeth
phoethi *gw.* poethi
pholion *gw.* polyn
pholiticaidd *gw.* politicaidd
pholyn *gw.* polyn
phont *gw.* pont
phontydd *gw.* pont
Phont-y-pŵl *gw.* Pont-y-pŵl
phopeth *gw.* popeth
phoptai *gw.* popty
phopty *gw.* popty
phorfa *gw.* porfa
phorfeydd *gw.* porfa
phorffor *gw.* porffor
phori *gw.* pori
phortread *gw.* portread
phorth *gw.* porth
phorthladd *gw.* porthladd
phos *gw.* pos
phosibilrwydd *gw.* posibilrwydd
phosibl *gw.* posibl
phost *gw.* post
phostio *gw.* postio
phostman: phostmon *gw.* postman
phostmyn *gw.* postman
phostyn *gw.* postyn
photel *gw.* potel
phowdr: phowdwr *gw.* powdr
phowdrau *gw.* powdr
phowlen *gw.* bowlen
phraidd *gw.* praidd
phram *gw.* pram

phrawf *gw.* prawf
phregeth *gw.* pregeth
phregethu *gw.* pregethu
phregethwr *gw.* pregethwr
phreiddiau *gw.* praidd
phreifat *gw.* preifat
phren *gw.* pren
phrennau *gw.* pren
phrentis *gw.* prentis
phrentisiaeth *gw.* prentisiaeth
phrentisiaid *gw.* prentis
phres *gw.* pres
phreseb *gw.* preseb
phresennol *gw.* presennol
phresenoldeb *gw.* presenoldeb
phresgripsiwn *gw.* presgripsiwn
phreswyl: phreswylfod *gw.* preswyl
phridwerth *gw.* pridwerth
phridd *gw.* pridd
phrif *gw.* prif
phrifardd *gw.* prifardd
phrifathrawes *gw.* prifathrawes
phrifathro *gw.* prifathro
phrifddinas *gw.* prifddinas
phrifeirdd *gw.* prifardd
phrifio *gw.* prifio
phrifysgol *gw.* prifysgol
phriffordd *gw.* priffordd
phriffyrdd *gw.* priffordd
phrin *gw.* prin
phrinder *gw.* prinder
phrintio *gw.* printio
phriod *gw.* priod
phriodas *gw.* priodas
phriodi *gw.* priodi
phriodol *gw.* priodol

phris *gw*. pris
phroblem *gw*. problem
phrofi *gw*. profi
phrofiad *gw*. profiad
phrofiadol *gw*. profiadol
phrofion *gw*. prawf
phrofocio *gw*. profocio
phroffid *gw*. proffid
phroffidiol *gw*. proffidiol
phroffwyd *gw*. proffwyd
phroffwydo *gw*. proffwydo
Phrotestant *gw*. Protestant
phrudd *gw*. prudd
phryd *gw*. pryd
Phrydain *gw*. Prydain
phrydau *gw*. pryd
Phrydeinig *gw*. Prydeinig
phryder *gw*. pryder
phryderu *gw*. pryderu
phryderus *gw*. pryderus
phrydferth *gw*. prydferth
phrydferthwch *gw*.
  prydferthwch
phrydiau *gw*. pryd
phrydlon *gw*. prydlon
phryf: phryfedyn: phryfyn *gw*.
  pryf
phryfed *gw*. pryf
phryfocio *gw*. profocio
phryfyn *gw*. pryf
phrynhawn *gw*. prynhawn
phrynu *gw*. prynu
phrynwr *gw*. prynwr
phrysur *gw*. prysur
phrysurdeb *gw*. prysurdeb
phrysuro *gw*. prysuro
phulpud *gw*. pulpud
phum: phump *gw*. pum
ph'un *gw*. pa
phunnau *gw*. punt

phunnoedd *gw*. punt
phunt *gw*. punt
phupur *gw*. pupur
phur *gw*. pur
phurfa *gw*. purfa
phuro *gw*. puro
phwdin *gw*. pwdin
phwdr *gw*. pwdr
phwdryn *gw*. pwdryn
phwdu *gw*. pwdu
phŵer *gw*. pŵer
phwll *gw*. pwll
phwllyn *gw*. pwllyn
phwmp *gw*. pwmp
phwnc *gw*. pwnc
phwrpas *gw*. pwrpas
phwrs *gw*. pwrs
phwy *gw*. pwy
phwyll *gw*. pwyll
phwyllgor *gw*. pwyllgor
phwyllo *gw*. pwyllo
phwynt *gw*. pwynt
phwys *gw*. pwys
phwysedd *gw*. pwysedd
phwysig *gw*. pwysig
phwysigrwydd *gw*.
  pwysigrwydd
phwyslais *gw*. pwyslais
phwyso *gw*. pwyso
phwyth *gw*. pwyth
phwytho *gw*. pwytho
phydru *gw*. pydru
phyllau *gw*. pwll, pyllyn
phyllyn *gw*. pyllyn
phympiau *gw*. pwmp
phymtheg *gw*. pymtheg
phymthegfed *gw*. pymthegfed
phynciau *gw*. pwnc
phyped *gw*. pyped
phyrsau *gw*. pwrs

phyrth *gw.* porth
phys *gw.* pysen
physgod *gw.* pysgodyn
physgodyn *gw.* pysgodyn
physgota *gw.* pysgota
physgotwr *gw.* pysgotwr
physt *gw.* post, postyn
phythefnos *gw.* pythefnos

R

raca *gw.* rhaca
raced *e.b.g. ll.* -i racket
racs *gw.* rhecsyn
rad *gw.* rhad
radio *e.g. ll.* -s radio
radd *gw.* gradd
raddfa *gw.* graddfa
raddio *gw.* graddio
raddol *gw.* graddol
raeadr *gw.* rhaeadr
raenus *gw.* graenus
raff *gw.* rhaff
ragair *gw.* rhagair
ragbrawf *gw.* rhagbrawf
ragbrofion *gw.* rhagbrawf
ragenw *gw.* rhagenw
ragfarn *gw.* rhagfarn
ragfarnllyd *gw.* rhagfarnllyd
ragflas *gw.* rhagflas
Ragfyr *gw.* Rhagfyr
raglen *gw.* rhaglen
raglenni *gw.* rhaglen
ragor *gw.* rhagor
ragori *gw.* rhagori
ragorol *gw.* rhagorol
rai *gw.* rhai
raid *gw.* rhaid
ramadeg *gw.* gramadeg
ramadegol *gw.* gramadegol

ramantaidd *gw.* rhamantus
ramantus *gw.* rhamantus
ran *gw.* rhan
ranbarth *gw.* rhanbarth
randir *gw.* rhandir
raniad *gw.* rhaniad
rannau *gw.* rhan
rannu *gw.* rhannu
ras *e.b. ll.* -ys race
(competitive). ras-gyfnewid
relay race. *gw.* gras
raw *gw.* rhaw
rawnffrwyth *gw.* grawnffrwyth
record *e.b. ll.* -iau record
recsyn *gw.* rhecsyn
redeg *gw.* rhedeg
redwr *gw.* rhedwr
redyn *gw.* rhedynen
redynen *gw.* rhedynen
reg *gw.* rheg
regfeydd *gw.* rheg
regi *gw.* rhegi
reidiau *gw.* rhaid
reilffordd *gw.* rheilffordd
reilffyrdd *gw.* rheilffordd
reis *e.g.* rice. pwdin reis rice
pudding
reol *gw.* rheol
reolaidd *gw.* rheolaidd
reoli *gw.* rheoli
reolwr *gw.* rheolwr
reolwyr *gw.* rheolwr
res *gw.* rhes
resi *gw.* rhes
restr *gw.* rhestr
restrau *gw.* rhestr
restri *gw.* rhestr
reswm *gw.* rheswm
resymau *gw.* rheswm
resynu *gw.* gresynu

rew

rew *gw.* rhew
rewgell *gw.* rhewgell
rewi *gw.* rhewi
rewlif *gw.* rhewlif
rëydr *gw.* rhaeadr
riant *gw.* rhiant
rieni *gw.* rhiant
rif *gw.* rhif
rifau *gw.* rhif
rifo *gw.* rhifo
rifyddeg *gw.* rhifyddeg
rifyn *gw.* rhifyn
rifynnau *gw.* rhifyn
riffl *e.g. ll.* -au rifle
rigwm *gw.* rhigwm
rigymau *gw.* rhigwm
rihyrsal *e.b. ll.* -s rehearsal
rinwedd *gw.* rhinwedd
ris *gw.* gris
risiau *gw.* gris
riw *gw.* rhiw
robin goch *e.g.* robin
roced *e.b. ll.* -i, -au rocket
rodd *gw.* rhodd
roddi *gw.* rhoddi
roddion *gw.* rhodd
roedd -e/-hi *bf.* he/she/it/was. *gw.* bod
Roeg *gw.* Groeg
Roegaidd *gw.* Groegaidd
Roegwr *gw.* Groegwr
rofiau *gw.* rhaw
roi *gw.* rhoddi
Romania *e.b.* Romania
rolio *gw.* rholio
ros *gw.* rhos
rosydd *gw.* rhos
rosyn *gw.* rhosyn
rosynnau *gw.* rhosyn
ruban *e.g. ll.* -au ribbon

rudd *gw.* grudd
Rufain *gw.* Rhufain
Rufeinig *gw.* Rhufeinig
rug *gw.* grug
ruo *gw.* rhuo
ruthro *gw.* rhuthro
rŵan *ad.* now *(N.W.). gw.* nawr
rwbio *gw.* rhwbio
rwber *e.g.* rubber
Rwsia *e.b.* Russia
Rwsiad *e.g. ll.* **Rwsiaid** a Russian
Rwsieg *e.g.* Russian (language)
rwyd *gw.* rhwyd
rwydi *gw.* rhwyd
rwydd *gw.* rhwydd
rwyfo *gw.* rhwyfo
rwyfus *gw.* rhwyfus
rwygo *gw.* rhwygo
rwymo *gw.* rhwymo
rwystr *gw.* rhwystr
rybudd *gw.* rhybudd
rybuddio *gw.* rhybuddio
ryd *gw.* rhyd
rydw i *bf.* I am. *gw.* bod
Rydychen *gw.* Rhydychen
rydd *gw.* rhydd
ryddhau *gw.* rhyddhau
ryddid *gw.* rhyddid
ryddion *gw.* rhydd
ryfedd *gw.* rhyfedd
ryfeddod *gw.* rhyfeddod
ryfeddol *gw.* rhyfeddol
ryfeddu *gw.* rhyfeddu
ryfel *gw.* rhyfel
ryngwladol *gw.* rhyngwladol
rym *gw.* grym
rymus *gw.* grymus

rysáit *eb.* *ll.* **-s.** recipe,
prescription

ryw *gw.* **rhyw**

rywbeth *gw.* **rhywbeth**

rywbryd *gw.* **rhywbryd**

rywdro *gw.* **rhywdro**

rywfaint *gw.* **rhywfaint**

rywiol *gw.* **rhywiol**

rywle *gw.* **rhywle**

rywrai *gw.* **rhywun**

rywsut *gw.* **rhywsut**

rywun *gw.* **rhywun**

RH

rhaca *e.b.* *ll.* **-nau** rake. **fel
rhaca** very thin, like a rake

rhacs *gw.* **rhecsyn**

rhad 1 *a.* cheap; free. **yn rhad
ac am ddim** absolutely free.
2 *e.g.* *ll.* **-au** blessing, grace

rhaeadr *e.b.* *ll.* **-au, rhëydr**
cataract, waterfall

rhaff *e.b.* *ll.* **-au** rope

rhag 1 *ardd.* before; lest;
against, from. 2 *rhagdd.*
pre-, for-, ante-

rhagair *e.g.* preface

rhagbrawf *e.g.* *ll.* **rhagbrofion**
preliminary test; foretaste

rhagbrofion *gw.* **rhagbrawf**

rhagenw *e.g.* *ll.* **-au** pronoun.
rhagenw gofynnol
interrogative pronoun;
rhagenw perthynol relative
pronoun

rhagfarn *e.b.* *ll.* **-au** prejudice

rhagfarnllyd *a.* prejudiced

rhagflas *e.g.* foretaste

Rhagfyr *e.g.* December

rhaglen *e.b.* *ll.* **-ni**
programme. **rhaglen deledu**
television programme;
rhaglen fyw live programme;
rhaglen nodwedd feature
programme

rhaglenni *gw.* **rhaglen**

rhagor *e.g.* *ll.* **-au, -ion**
difference, more, excess.
rhagor o fwyd more food

rhagori (ar) *be.* **(rhagoraf)** to
excel, to surpass

rhagorol *a.* excellent,
splendid

rhai 1 *rhag.* ones. **y rhai da**
the good ones. 2 *a.* some.
Mae rhai pobl yn oer Some
people are cold

rhaid *e.g.* *ll.* **rheidiau**
necessity, need. **Mae rhaid i ti
fynd** You must go

rhain, y *rhag.* these. **Ble mae'r
rhain i fod?** Where are these
to go? **y rheina** those

rhamantus: rhamantaidd *a.*
romantic

rhan *e.b.* *ll.* **-nau** part, share;
rôle. **y rhan fwyaf** the
greatest part

rhanbarth *e.g.* *ll.* **-au**
division, region, area, district

rhandir *e.g.* *ll.* **-oedd** region,
division, district; allotment

rhandiroedd *gw.* **rhandir**

rhaniad *e.g.* *ll.* **-au** division;
parting

rhannau *gw.* **rhan**

rhannu *be.* **(rhannaf)** to
divide, to share, to distribute

rhaw *e.b.* *ll.* **-iau, rhofiau**

shovel; spade
rhecsyn *e.g. ll.* **rhacs** rag
rhedeg *be.* **(rhedaf)** to run; to
flow
rhedwr *e.g. ll.* **rhedwyr**
runner
rhedyn *e.ll.* fern, bracken.
gw. **rhedynen**
rhedynen *e.b. ll.* **rhedyn** fern
rheg *e.b. ll.* **-feydd** curse,
swearword
rhegfeydd *gw.* **rheg**
rhegi *be.* **(rhegaf)** to curse, to
swear
rheidiau *gw.* **rhaid**
rheiddiadur *e.g. ll.* **-on**
radiator
rheilffordd *e.b. ll.* **rheilffyrdd**
railway
rheiffyrdd *gw.* **rheilffordd**
rheina, y *gw.* **rhain**
rheini, y *rhag.* those (*not
present.*)
rheol *e.b. ll.* **-au** rule, order.
Rheolau'r Ffordd Fawr the
Highway Code
rheolaidd *a.* regular,
constant, orderly, proper
rheoli *be.* **(rheolaf)** to control,
to manage
rheolwr *e.g. ll.* **rheolwyr**
manager, ruler, controller,
governor; referee
rheolwyr *gw.* **rheolwr**
rhes *e.b. ll.* **-i** row, rank;
stripe, line
rhesi *gw.* **rhes**
rhestr *e.b. ll.* **-au, -i** row,
rank; list. **rhestr fer** short list
rhestrau *gw.* **rhestr**

rhestri *gw.* **rhestr**
rheswm *e.g. ll.* **rhesymau**
reason, cause. **y rheswm dros**
the reason for
rhesymau *gw.* **rheswm**
rhesymol *a.* reasonable
rhew *e.g. ll.* **-iau, -ogydd**
frost, ice. **rhewbwynt**
freezing-point. **rhewfwyd**
frozen food; **rhewlif** glacier;
Siôn Rhew Jack Frost
rhewgell *eb. ll.* **-oedd** deep
freeze cabinet, freezer
rhewi *be.* **(rhewaf)** to freeze
rhewiau *gw.* **rhew**
rhewlif *e.g. ll.* **-iau** glacier
rhewogydd *gw.* **rhew**
rhëydr *gw.* **rhaeadr**
rhiant *e.g. ll.* **rhieni** parent
rhieni *gw.* **rhiant**
rhif *e.g. ll.* **-au** number,
numeral
rhifau *gw.* **rhif**
rhifo *be.* **(rhifaf)** to count, to
number, to reckon
rhifyddeg *e.b.g.* arithmetic
rhifyn *e.g. ll.* **-nau** number
(*of magazine*)
rhifynnau *gw.* **rhifyn**
rhigwm *e.g. ll.* **rhigymau**
rhyme; rigmarole
rhigymau *gw.* **rhigwm**
rhiniog *e.b. ll.* **-au** threshold
rhinwedd *e.b.g. ll.* **-au** virtue
rhisgl *e.ll.* bark (*of tree*)
rhiw *e.b. ll.* **-iau** hill, ascent,
slope (*S.W.*)
rhodd *e.b. ll.* **-ion** gift,
donation
rhoddi: rhoi *be.* **(rhoddaf:**

rhoiaf) to give, to bestow, to put. **rhoi benthyg** to lend; **rhoi'r gorau i** to relinquish. *gw. At. Berfau*

rhoddion *gw.* **rhodd**

rhofion *gw.* **rhaw**

rhoi *gw.* **rhoddi**

rholio *be.* (**rholiaf**) to roll

rhos *e.b. ll.* **-ydd.** moor, heath, plain. *gw.* **rhosyn**

rhosod *gw.* **rhosyn**

rhosydd *gw.* **rhos**

rhosyn *e.g. ll.* **-nau, rhos, rhosod** rose

rhosynnau *gw.* **rhosyn**

Rhufain *e.b.* Rome

Rhufeinig *a.* Roman

rhugl *a.* fluent

rhuo *be.* (**rhuaf**) to roar, to bellow

rhuthro *be.* (**rhuthraf**) to rush

rhwbio *be.* (**rhwbiaf**) to rub

rhwng *ardd.* (*personal forms:* **rhyngo, rhyngot, rhyngddo/rhyngddi, rhyngom, rhyngoch, rhyngddyn**) between, among. *gw. At. Arddodiaid*

rhwyd *e.b. ll.* **-au, -i** net, snare

rhwydd *a.* easy; fluent; generous; fast (*S.W.*)

rhwyfo *be.* (**rhwyfaf**) to row

rhwyfus *a.* restless

rhwygo *be.* (**rhwygaf**) to tear, to rip

rhwym *a.* bound, tied; constipated

rhwymo *be.* (**rhwymaf**) to bind, to tie; to constipate

rhwystr *e.g. ll.* **-au** hindrance, obstacle

rhwystrau *gw.* **rhwystr**

rhy 1 *e.g.* excess. 2 *ad.* too. **yn rhy drwm** too heavy

rhybudd *e.g. ll.* **-ion** warning, notice, caution

rhybuddio (**rhag**) *be.* (**rhybuddiaf**) to warn, to caution

rhyd *e.b. ll.* **-au** ford

Rhydychen *e.b.* Oxford

rhydd *a. ll.* **-ion** free, liberal. **Y Seiri Rhyddion** Freemasons

rhyddhau *be.* (**rhyddhaf**) to free, to release, to loose

rhyddid *e.g.* freedom, liberty

rhyddion *gw.* **rhydd**

rhyfedd: rhyfeddol *a.* wonderful, strange

rhyfeddod *e.g. ll.* **-au** wonder, surprise

rhyfeddol *gw.* **rhyfedd**

rhyfeddu (**at**) *be.* (**rhyfeddaf**) to wonder, to marvel

rhyfel *e.g.b. ll.* **-oedd** war, warfare. **Rhyfel y Gwlff** The Gulf War; **Yr Ail Ryfel Byd** The Second World War; **Y Rhyfel Mawr** The Great War

rhyngo i *gw.* **rhwng**

rhyngrwyd *e.b.* internet

rhyngwladol *a.* international

rhyw 1 *e.b.g. ll.* **-au** sort, kind; sex; gender. 2 *a.* some, certain. **Roedd rhyw ddyn yma ddoe** A certain man was here yesterday

rhywbeth *e.g.* something

rhywbryd *ad.* sometime
rhywdro *ad.* sometime
rhywfaint *e.g.* some amount
rhywiol *a.* sexual
rhywle *ad.* somewhere, anywhere
rhywrai *gw.* **rhywun**
rhywsut *ad.* somehow, anyhow
rhywun *e.g.* *ll.* **rhywrai** someone, anyone. **rhywun neu'i gilydd** someone or other; **rhywrai** some

S

Sabath: Saboth *e.g.* *ll.* **-au** Sabbath
sach *e.b.* *ll.* **-au** sack. **sach gysgu** sleeping bag
Sadwrn *e.g.* *ll.* **Sadyrnau.** Saturn; Saturday
saer *e.g.* *ll.* **seiri** carpenter, joiner; wright; mason. **saer coed** carpenter; **saer maen** stonemason; **pensaer** architect
Saesneg 1 *e.b.* English (*language*). 2 *a.* English (*in language*)
Saesnes *e.b.* *ll.* **-au** Englishwoman.
Saeson *gw.* **Sais**
saeth *e.b.* *ll.* **-au** arrow
saethu (at) *be.* **(saethaf)** to shoot, to fire
saethwr *e.g.* *ll.* **saethwyr** shooter; archer; goal shooter
safbwynt *e.g.* *ll.* **-iau** standpoint, viewpoint, perspective
safle *e.g.* *ll.* **-oedd** position, station, situation, rank
safon *e.b.* *ll.* **-au** standard, class; criterion. **Y Safon Aur** The Gold Standard; **Safon A** A level
safonol *a.* standard
saib *e.g.* *ll.* **seibiau** pause, rest
sail *e.b.* *ll.* **seiliau** base, foundation; ground. **ar sail** on the basis of
saim *e.g.* *ll.* **seimiau** grease, fat. **saim gŵydd** goose grease
sain *e.b.* *ll.* **seiniau** sound, tone
saint *gw.* **sant**
Sais *e.g.* *ll.* **Saeson** Englishman
saith *a. & e.g.* seven
sâl 1 *a.* poorly, sick; mean. 2 *e.g.* sale (*N.W.*)
salm *e.b.* *ll.* **-au** psalm. **salmdôn** chant
salw *a.* ugly, vile, mean (*S.W.*)
salwch *e.g.* illness
sanctaidd *a.* holy
sant *e.g.* *ll.* **saint, seintiau** saint. **Dewi Sant** Saint David; **Sant Ioan** Saint John
santes *e.b.* *ll.* **-au** female saint; **Santes Dwynwen** Saint Dwynwen, patron saint of lovers
sarff *e.b.* *ll.* **seirff** serpent
sarhad *e.g.* *ll.* **-au** insult, disgrace

sarnu (ar) *be.* **(sarnaf)** to trample, to litter, to spill (*S.W.*)

sathru (ar) *be.* **(sathraf)** to trample, to tread. **sathru dan draed** to trample underfoot; **sathru ar gyrn** to offend

sawdl *e.g.b. ll.* **sodlau** heel

sawl *rhag. & ad. (followed by a singular noun)* he that, *(the one)* who, that which; several, a number (of); how many? many. **Sawl car sy 'da chi?** How many cars do you have? **Sawl tŷ sy ar y bryn?** How many houses are there on the hill? **Roedd sawl llyfr yn y pentwr** There were many books in the pile; **Y sawl a gododd a gollodd ei le** The one that got up lost his seat

saws *e.g. ll.* **-iau** sauce

Sbaen *e.g.* Spain

Sbaeneg *e.b.* Spanish language

Sbaenes *e.b. ll.* **-au** Spanish woman

Sbaenwr *e.g. ll.* **-wyr** Spanish man, Spaniard

sbardun *e.g. ll.* **-au** accelerator; spur

sbectol *e.b.* spectacles

sbon *ad. (as used with the adjective* **newydd**) wholly. **newydd sbon** brand new

sbot: sbotyn *e.g. ll.* **sbotiau** spot

sebon *e.g. ll.* **-au** soap. **sebon dannedd** toothpaste

sedd *e.b. ll.* **-au** seat, pew. **sedd fawr** deacon's pew

sef *c.* namely, that is to say

sefydliad *e.g. ll.* **-au** establishment, institution, induction

sefydlog *a.* fixed, settled, stationary

sefydlu *be.* **(sefydlaf)** to establish, to settle

sefyll (am) *be.* **(safaf)** to stand; to stop; to stay, to wait (for) (*S.W.*). **sefyll arholiad** to sit an examination

sefyllfa *e.b. ll.* **-oedd** situation, position

segur *a.* idle

segura *be.* **(seguraf)** to idle

segurdod *e.g.* idleness

sengl *a.* single

seiat *e.b. ll.* **seiadau** fellowship, meeting, society

seibiant *e.g. ll.* **-au, seibiannau** leisure, respite, pause

seibiannau *gw.* **seibiant**

seibiau *gw.* **saib**

seicoleg *e.b.g.* psychology

seiliau *gw.* **sail**

seilio *be.* **(seiliaf)** to base, to found, to grov nd

seimiau *gw.* **saim**

seimlyd: seimllyd *a.* greasy

seiniau *gw.* **sain**

seindorf *eb. ll.* **-eydd, seindyrf.** band (*musical*). **seindorf bres** brass band; **band un dyn** one-man band

seintiau *gw.* **sant**

seirff *gw.* **sarff**

seiri *gw.* **saer**

Seisnig *a.* English, pertaining to England

Seisnigeiddio: Seisnigo *be.* **(Seisnigeiddiaf: Seisnigaf)** to Anglicize

seithfed *a.* seventh

sêl *e.b.* zeal

Seland Newydd *e.b.* New Zealand

seld *e.b. ll.* **-au** dresser

sen *e.b. ll.* **-nau** rebuke, snub, censure. **bwrw sen ar** to cast a rebuke at

senedd *e.b. ll.* **-au** parliament, senate

sennau *gw.* **sen**

sêr *gw.* **seren**

serch 1 *e.g. ll.* **-iadau** love. 2 *c.* & *ardd.* although, notwithstanding. **serch ei fod e'n briod** although he was married

serchog *a.* affectionate, loving

serchus *a.* affectionate, loving; pleasant

seremoni *e.b. ll.* **seremonïau** ceremony

seren *e.b. ll.* **sêr** star; asterisk. **seren wib** shooting star

serennog *a.* starry

serth *a.* steep; unclean; obscene

set *e.b. ll.* **-iau** set. **set deledu** television set

sêt *e.b. ll.* **seti** seat, pew: **sêt fawr** deacons' seat

seti *gw.* **sêt**

setiau *gw.* **set**

setlo *be.* **(setlaf)** to settle

sgarff *e.b. ll.* **-iau** scarf

sgert *e.b. ll.* **-i, -iau** skirt. *gw.* **sgyrt**

sgets *e.b. ll.* **-ys** sketch

sgi *e.b.g.* ski

sgil *e.g. ll.* **-iau** skill, device, trick

sgil *ad.* in the wake of, behind. **Daeth tlodi yn sgil y rhyfel** There was poverty in the wake of the war

sgïo *be.* **(sgïaf)** to ski

sgipio *be.* **(sgipiaf)** to skip

sgiw 1 *e.b. ll.* **-iau** settle. 2 *a.* askew

sgïwr *e.g. ll.* **sgïwyr** skier

sglefrio *be.* **(sglefriaf)** to skate, to slide

sglodion *gw.* **sglodyn**

sglodyn *e.g. ll.* **sglodion** chips. **pysgod a sglodion** fish and chips

sgôr *e.b. ll.* **sgoriau** score

sgorio *be.* **(sgoriaf)** to score

sgrech *e.b. ll.* **-iadau** yell, scream. **sgrech y coed** jay

sgrechain: sgrechian *be.* **(sgrechaf: sgrechiaf)** to yell, to scream

sgrifennu: ysgrifennu (ar, at) *be.* **(sgrifennaf: ysgrifennaf)** to write

sgript *e.b. ll.* **-iau** script

sgrym *e.b. ll.* **-iau** scrum (*rugby*)

sgrymio *be.* **(sgrymiaf)** to scrum

sgubo *be.* **(sgubaf)** to sweep, to brush

sgwâr *e.g.b.* *ll.* **-iau** square

sgwd *e.g.* *ll.* **sgydau** waterfall, cataract

sgwrs *e.b.* *ll.* **sgyrsiau** talk, chat; conversation

sgwrsio (â) *be.* **(sgwrsiaf)** to talk, to chat

sgydau *gw.* **sgwd**

sgyrsiau *gw.* **sgwrs**

sgyrt *e.b.* *ll.* **-iau, -is** skirt. *gw.* **sgert**

si *e.g.* *ll.* **sïon** buzz, rumour, murmur

siaced *e.b.* *ll.* **-i** jacket, coat

sialc *e.g.* *ll.* **-iau** chalk. **sialciau lliw** coloured chalks

siampl *e.b.* *ll.* **-au** example

sianel *e.b.* *ll.* **-i** channel. **Sianel Pedwar Cymru** S4C (Welsh TV Channel 4)

siâp *e.g.* *ll.* **-iau** shape

siâr *e.b.* share. **Ga i siâr o'r bwyd?** May I have a share of the food?

siarad *be.* **(siaradaf)** to talk, to speak. **siarad â** to speak with; **siarad am** to speak about

siaradwr *e.g.* *ll.* **siaradwyr** talker, speaker

sibrwd *be.* **(sibrydaf)** to whisper

sicr: siŵr *a.* sure, certain; secure

sicrhau *be.* **(sicrhaf)** to assure, to confirm, to obtain, to fix, to secure.

sicrwydd *e.g.* certainty,

assurance, security

sidan *e.g.* *ll.* **-au** silk

siswrn *e.g.* *ll.* **sisyrnau** scissors

siwd *gw.* **sut**

siwg: jwg *e.g.* *ll.* **-iau** jug. **siwg laeth** milk jug

siwgr *e.g.* sugar; **siwgr brown** brown sugar

siŵr *gw.* **sicr**

siwrnai 1 *e.g.* *ll.* **siwrneiau, siwrneion** journey. **Siwrnai dda ichi!** Have a good trip! 2 *ad.* once. **Siwrnai roedd tawelwch, fe gododd i siarad** Once there was silence he rose to speak *(S.W.)*

sliper *e.b.* *ll.* **-i** slipper

smotyn *e.g.* *ll.* **smotiau** spot

sodlau *gw.* **sawdl**

sôn (am) 1 *be.* **(soniaf)** to mention, to talk, to rumour. 2 *e.g.* mention, talk, rumour: **Does dim sôn amdani** There is no sign of her

sosban *e.b.* *ll.* **-au, sosbenni** saucepan

sosbenni *gw.* **sosban**

soser *e.b.* *ll.* **-i** saucer

sosialaeth *e.b.* socialism

sosialaidd *a.* socialist

sosialwyr *gw.* **sosialydd**

sosialydd *e.g.* *ll.* **sosialwyr** socialist

sothach *e.torf.* trash, rubbish

stabl *e.b.* *ll.* **-au** stable

stafell: ystafell *e.b.* *ll.* **-oedd** room. **stafell ffrynt** front room; **stafell gefn** back

room; **stafell wely** bedroom;
stafell ymolchi bathroom
stamp *e.g. ll.* **-iau** stamp
stampio *be.* **(stampiaf)** to
stamp
stôl *e.b. ll.* **stolau** stool
stondin *e.b. ll.* **-au** stall.
stondin farchnad market
stall
stopio *be.* **(stopiaf)** to stop
stôr *e.g. ll.* **storau** store. **stôr
celfi** furniture store
stordy *e.g. ll.* **stordai**
storehouse, warehouse
storfa *e.b. ll.* **storfeydd** store;
storage
stori *eb. ll.* **storiáu, storïau,
straeon** story. **stori arswyd**
horror story; **stori fer** short
story
storiáu: storïau *gw.* **stori**
storïwr *e.g. ll.* **storïwyr**
storyteller
storm *e.b. ll.* **-ydd** storm
stormus *a.* stormy,
tempestuous
stormydd *gw.* **storm**
straeon *gw.* **stori**
strategaeth *e.b.* strategy
streic *e.b. ll.* **-iau** strike
strwythur *e.g. ll.* **-au**
structure
strwythuro *be.* **(strwythuraf)**
to structure
stryd *e.b. ll.* **-oedd** street
stumog *e.b. ll.* **-au** stomach
stumogi *be.* **(stumogaf)** to
stomach
stŵr *e.g.* stir, noise, bustle,
fuss

su *e.g. ll.* **suon** buzz,
murmur, rumour. *gw.* **si**
suddo *be.* **(suddaf)** to sink, to
dive; to invest
sugno *be.* **(sugnaf)** to suck,
to absorb
Sul *e.g. ll.* **-iau** Sunday. **Dydd
Sul** Sunday; **Sul y Blodau**
Palm Sunday; **Sul y Mamau**
Mothering Sunday
Sulgwyn *e.g.* Whitsunday
Suliau *gw.* **Sul**
suo *be.* **(suaf)** to hum, to
buzz; to lull
suon *gw.* **su**
sur *a. ll.* **-ion** sour, bitter,
acid
suro *be.* **(suraf)** to sour
sut: siwd *rhag.gof.* how?
Sut/Siwd mae? How are
things?
sŵ *e.g.* zoo
swil *a.* shy, bashful
Swistir Y, *e.b.* Switzerland
swm *e.g. ll.* **symiau** sum
sŵn *e.g. ll.* **synau** sound,
noise
swnio *be.* **(swniaf)** to sound,
to pronounce
swper *e.g.b. ll.* **-au** supper: **Y
Swper Olaf** The Last Supper
sws *e.g.* kiss (*N.W.*)
swydd *e.b. ll.* **-i** post, office,
job; county (*in England*).
gw. **sir. Swydd Gaerloyw**
Gloucestershire; **swydd
Buckingham**
Buckinghamshire
swyddfa *e.b. ll.* **swyddfeydd**
office. **Y Swyddfa Gymreig**

The Welsh Office
swyddfeydd *gw.* **swyddfa**
swyddi *gw.* **swydd**
swyddog *e.g. ll.* **-ion** officer,
official. **swyddog prawf**
probation officer. **swyddog y
llys** officer of the court
swyddogol *a.* official. **llythyr
swyddogol** official letter
swyn *e.g. ll.* **-ion** charm,
magic, spell
swyno *be.* **(swynaf)** to charm,
to enchant, to bewitch
swynol *a.* charming,
fascinating
sy: sydd *bf.* is, are. *gw.* **bod**
sych *a.* dry. **tywydd sych** dry
weather
syched *e.g.* thirst: **mae
syched ar Tom** Tom is
thirsty
sychedig *a.* thirsty, parched
sychu *be.* **(sychaf)** to dry, to
dry up; to wipe
sydyn *a.* sudden, abrupt
sydd *gw.* **sy**
syfrdanol *a.* stupefying,
stunning
sylfaen *e.b. ll.* **sylfeini**
foundation, base
sylfaenol *a.* basic,
fundamental
sylfeini *gw.* **sylfaen**
sylw *e.g. ll* **-adau** notice,
remark, observation,
attention. **Gadewch e dan
sylw.** Don't take notice of
him
sylwadau *gw.* **sylw**
sylwebaeth *e.b. ll.* **-au**
commentary
sylwebu (ar) *be.* **(sylwebaf)** to
give a commentary (on)
sylwebydd: sylwebwr *e.g. ll.*
sylwebwyr commentator
sylwedd *e.g. ll.* **-au**
substance, foundation
sylweddol *a.* substantial
sylweddoli *be.* **(sylweddolaf)**
to realize
sylwi (ar) *be.* **(sylwaf)** to
observe, to notice. **Sylwch
arnyn nhw** Notice them
syllu (ar) *be.* **(syllaf)** to gaze
symiau *gw.* **swm**
syml *a.* simple
symud 1 *be.* **(symudaf)** to
move, to remove; **2** *e.g.*
movement, action
symudiad *e.g. ll.* **-au**
movement, removal
symudol *a.* mobile, portable.
ffôn symudol mobile phone
syn *a.* amazed, astonishing,
surprising
synau *gw.* **sŵn**
syndod *e.g. ll.* **-au** surprise,
amazement
synhwyrau *gw.* **synnwyr**
synhwyro *be.* **(synhwyraf)** to
sense; to sniff, to smell
synhwyrol *a.* sensible
syniad *e.g. ll.* **-au** idea,
notion, thought
synnu (at) *be.* **(synnaf)** to be
surprised, to marvel, to
wonder. **Rwy'n synnu atoch
chi** I'm surprised at you
synnwyr *e.g. ll.* **synhwyrau**
sense

syr *e.g.* sir. **Annwyl Syr** Dear Sir.

syrcas *e.b.* *ll.* **-au** circus

syrffed *e.g.* surfeit

syrffedu (ar) *be.* **(syrffedaf)** to surfeit, to be fed up (with)

syrthio *be.* **(syrthiaf)** to fall. **syrthio mewn cariad** to fall in love; **syrthio ar fai** to admit to blame

syth *a.* stiff, straight, erect. **Dewch yn syth** Come at once

sythlyd *a.* cold, chilled

sythu *a.* to become chilled, to straighten (*S.W.*). **Rwyf bron â sythu** I'm perished

T

tabl *e.g.* *ll.* **-au** table

tabled *e.b.* *ll.* **-au, -i** tablet

tacl *e.b.g.* *ll.* **-au** tackle, gear

taclo *be.* **(taclaf)** to tackle

taclu *be.* **(taclaf)** to put in order; to dress (*S.W.*)

taclus *a.* neat, tidy

tacluso *be.* **(taclusaf)** to trim, to tidy

taclwr *e.g.* *ll.* **taclwyr** tackler (*rugby*)

tacsi *e.g.* *ll.* **-s** taxi

Tachwedd *e.g.* November

tad *e.g.* *ll.* **-au** father: **tad maeth** foster-father; **llystad** stepfather; **tad-yng-nghyfraith** father-in-law

tad-cu *e.g.* *ll.* **tad-cuod** grandfather (*S.W.*). *gw.* **taid**

tafarn *e.g.b.* *ll.* **tafarnau** tavern, public house, inn

tafarnwr *e.g.* *ll.* **tafarnwyr** publican, inn-keeper

tafell *e.b.* *ll.* **-au, -i, tefyll** slice, slab

taflegryn *e.g.* *ll.* **taflegrau** missile

taflen *e.b.* *ll.* **-ni** leaflet, list, table. **taflen amser** timetable

taflu (at) *be.* **(taflaf)** to throw (to), to fling, to cast; to dislocate

tafod *e.g.* *ll.* **-au** tongue, tang, spit. **tafod llym** sharp tongue

tafodiaith *e.b.* *ll.* **tafodieithoedd** dialect

tafodieithoedd *gw.* **tafodiaith**

tafol *e.b.* *ll.* **-au** scales

tagfa *e.b.* *ll.* **tagfeydd** strangulation, choking; bottleneck

tagu *be.* **(tagaf)** to strangle, to choke

tangnefedd *e.g.b.* peace

tai *gw.* **tŷ**

taid *e.g.* *ll.* **teidiau** grandfather (*N.W.*); *gw.* **tad-cu** (*S.W.*)

tair *a.b. & e.b.* three. **tair merch** three girls. *gw.* **tri**

taith *e.b.* *ll.* **teithiau** journey, tour, voyage

tal *a.* tall, lofty, high

tâl 1 *e.g.* *ll.* **taloedd, taliadau** pay, payment, charge, rates. **Tâl Cymunedol** Community Charge. **2** *e.g.* *ll.* **talau** forehead, front, end

talai *e.g. ll.* **taleion** payee
talaith *e.b. ll.* **taleithiau**
province, state. **Yr Unol
Daleithiau** The United States
talcen *e.g. ll.* **-nau, -ni**
forehead; gable, pine-end.
talcen tŷ pine-end of house
talcennau *gw.* **talcen**
talcenni *gw.* **talcen**
taleb *e.b. ll.* **-au, -ion** receipt
taleion *gw.* **talai**
taleithiau *gw.* **talaith**
talent *e.b. ll.* **-au** talent
talentog *a.* gifted, talented
talfyriad *e.g. ll.* **-au**
abbreviation
taliadau *gw.* **tâl**
taloedd *gw.* **tâl**
talu (am) *be.* **(talaf)** to pay
talwr *e.g. ll.* **talwyr** payer
talwrn *e.g. ll.* **talyrnau** spot,
place; cock-fighting pit:
Talwrn y Beirdd the Poet's
Place (*for competition*)
tamaid *e.g. ll.* **tameidiau**
piece, bit, bite. **tamaid i aros
pryd** temporary provision
while awaiting arrival of
something more substantial
tameidiau *gw.* **tamaid**
tan *ardd. (followed by soft
mutation)* until, as far as;
under. *gw.* **dan**
tân *e.g. ll.* **tanau** fire, light.
tân siafins short-lived
enthusiasm and transitory
zeal (*lit.* a blaze of wood
shavings)
tanau *gw.* **tân**
tanbaid *a.* hot, fervent, fiery,

brilliant
tanc *e.g. ll.* **-iau** tank
tancer *e.g. ll.* **-i** tanker
tanddaear: tanddaearol *a.*
subterranean, underground
tanfor *a.* submarine. **llong
danfor** submarine
tanio *be.* **(taniaf)** to ignite, to
fire, to stoke, to light. **tanio'r
dychymyg** to fire the
imagination
tanlinellu *be.* **(tanlinellaf)** to
underline
tanlwybr *e.g. ll.* **-au** subway
tanllyd *a.* fiery, fervent
tannau *gw.* **tant**
tanseilio *be.* **(tanseiliaf)** to
sap, to undermine
tant *e.g. ll.* **tannau** chord,
string. **tant telyn** harp string
tanwydd *e.g.* fuel, firewood
tap *e.g. ll.* **-iau** tap. **tap dŵr
oer** cold water tap
tâp *e.g. ll.* **tapiau** tape
tapiau *gw.* **tap, tâp**
taran *e.b. ll.* **-au** (peal of)
thunder. **mellt a tharanau**
thunder and lightning
taranu *be.* **(taranaf)** to
thunder, to threaten
tarddiad *e.g. ll.* **-au** source,
derivation
tarddu *be.* **(tarddaf)** to spring,
to sprout, to derive from, to
issue
targed *e.g. ll.* **-au** target
tarian *e.b. ll.* **tariannau** shield
tariannau *gw.* **tarian**
taro 1 *be.* **(trawaf)** to strike,
to hit, to tap; to suit. **Mae**

e'n dy daro'n iawn It suits you well. 2 *e.g.* difficulty, crisis; **mewn taro** in an emergency

tarw *e.g. ll.* **teirw** bull. **llwybr tarw** a short cut

tasg *e.b. ll.* **-au**

tasgu *be.* **(tasgaf)** to splash, to start, to bolt; to spark; to lose one's temper. **Roedd e'n tasgu pan glywodd e** He was mad when he heard

taten *e.b.* **tatws, tato** potato. **tatws drwy'r croen/pil** jacket potatoes; **tatws rhost** roast potatoes; **tatws wedi'u berwi** boiled potatoes; **tatws wedi'u ffrio** fried potatoes; **creision tatws** potato crisps

tato: tatws *gw.* **taten**

tawel *a.* quiet, calm, still, peaceful

tawelu *be.* **(tawelaf)** to calm, to grow calm

tawelwch *e.g.* quiet, calm, stillness, tranquillity

tawelydd *e.g. ll.* **-ion** tranquillizer

tawelyddion *gw.* **tawelydd**

tawelyn *e.g. ll.* **-nau** tranquillizer

tawelynnau *gw.* **tawelyn**

te *e.g.* tea

tebot *e.g. ll.* **-au** teapot

tebyg *a.* like, similar, likely. **yn debyg i** like, similar to; **yn debyg o** likely to

tebygol *a.* likely, probable. **yn debygol o ennill** likely to win

tebygrwydd *e.g.* likeness, similarity, resemblance

tecell: tegell *e.g. ll.* **-au, -i** kettle

techneg *e.b. ll.* **-au** technique

technegol *a.* technical

technegwr *e.g. ll.* **technegwyr** technician

technoleg *e.b.* technology

teg *a.* fair, fine, beautiful. **chwarae teg** fair play; **teg o bryd** beautiful in appearance

tegan *e.g. ll.* **-au** toy, plaything

tegell *gw.* **tecell**

tegwch *e.g.* beauty, fairness

tei *e.g.b. ll.* **teis** tie

teiar *e.g. ll.* **-s** tyre

teidiau *gw.* **taid**

teigr *e.g. ll.* **-od** tiger

teiliwr *e.g. ll.* **teilwriaid** tailor

teilsen *e.b. ll.* **teils** tile

teilwng *a.* worthy, deserved. **yn deilwng o** worthy of

teilwres *e.b. ll.* **-au** tailoress

teilwriaid *gw.* **teiliwr**

teilyngdod *e.g. ll.* **-au** merit, worthiness

teimlad *e.g. ll.* **-au** feel, emotion, feeling, sensation

teimlo *be.* **(teimlaf)** to feel, to handle, to touch. **teimlo fel** to feel like

teipiadur *e.g. ll.* **-on** typewriter

teirgwaith *ad.* three times

teirw *gw.* **tarw**

teis *gw.* **tei**

teisen *e.b. ll.* **-nau** cake, tart. **teisen ddwbl** sandwich cake;

teisen ffrwythau fruit cake;
teisennau cri Welsh cakes
teitl *e.g. ll.* **-au** title
teithiau *gw.* **taith**
teithio *be.* **(teithiaf)** to travel,
to journey
teithiwr *e.g. ll.* **teithwyr**
traveller
telediad *e.g. ll.* **-au** telecast
teledu 1 *be.* **(teledaf)** to
televise. **2** *e.g.* television. **set
deledu lliw** colour television
set
teleffon: ffôn *e.g. ll.* **-au**
telephone. *gw.* **ffôn**
teleffonio: ffonio *be.*
(teleffoniaf: ffoniaf) to
telephone, to phone
telyn *e.b. ll.* **-au** harp
telyneg *e.b. ll.* **-ion** lyric
telynor *e.g. ll.* **-ion** harpist
telynores *e.b. ll.* **-au** female
harpist
telynorion *gw.* **telynor**
teml *e.b. ll.* **-au** temple
tenau *a.* thin, slender, lean;
rare
terfyn *e.g. ll.* **-au** end,
boundary, extremity
terfynol *a.* ultimate, last. **y
taliad terfynol** the last
instalment
terfysg *e.g. ll.* **-oedd** tumult,
commotion, riot
terfysgaeth *e.g.* terrorism
terfysgwr *e.g. ll.* **terfysgwyr**
terrorist
term *e.g. ll.* **-au** term. **termau
technegol** technical terms
tes *e.g.* heat, sunshine, haze

tesog *a.* hot, sunny
testun *e.g. ll.* **-au** text,
subject. **testun sgwrs** subject
for debate; **testun siarad**
subject of gossip
teulu *e.g. ll.* **-oedd** family
tew *a.* fat
teyrnas *e.b. ll.* **-oedd**
kingdom. **Teyrnas Nefoedd**
Kingdom of Heaven; **Y
Deyrnas Unedig** The United
Kingdom
ti *rhag.* you *(singular)*
ticed *e.g. ll.* **-i** ticket
tîm *e.g. ll.* **timau** team
tip *e.g. ll.* **-iau** tip
tipiau *gw.* **tip, tipyn**
tipyn *e.g. ll.* **-nau, tipiau** little,
bit. **tipyn bach** a little; **bob
yn dipyn** little by little
tir *e.g. ll.* **-oedd** land, earth,
ground, territory. **tir neb** no
man's land; **colli tir** to lose
ground
tirion *a.* tender, kind, gentle,
gracious
tirlun *e.g. ll.* **-iau** landscape
tiroedd *gw.* **tir**
tisian *be.* **(tisiaf)** to sneeze
tithau *rhag.* you also
(singular)
tiwtor *e.g. ll.* **-iaid** tutor
tlawd *a. ll.* **tlodion** poor,
needy. **y tlodion** the poor
tlodi *e.g.* poverty
tlodion *gw.* **tlawd**
tlos *a.b.* pretty. **merch dlos**
a pretty girl *(N.W.). gw.*
tlws.
tlws 1 *e.g. ll.* **tlysau** gem,

jewel, brooch. **tlws aur** a
gold brooch; **tlws yr eira**
snowdrop; **clustlysau** ear-
rings. 2 *a.g.* pretty. *gw.* **tlos**
tlysau. *gw.* **tlws**
to 1 *e.g.* *ll.* **-eau, -eon** roof.
2 *e.g.b.* generation. **y to sy'n**
codi the rising generation
tocyn *e.g.* *ll.* **-nau** ticket,
token. **tocyn dwyffordd**
return ticket
tocynnau *gw.* **tocyn**
tocynnwr *e.g.* *ll.* **tocynwyr**
ticket collector, conductor
tocynwyr *gw.* **tocynnwr**
toddi *be.* **(toddaf)** to melt, to
thaw, to dissolve
toeau *gw.* **to**
toeon *gw.* **to**
toes *e.g.* dough. **toesenni**
doughnuts; **tylino toes** to
knead dough
toiled *e.g.* *ll.* **-au** toilet
tolc *e.g.* *ll.* **-iau** dent
tolcio *be.* **(tolciaf)** to dent
toll *e.b.* *ll.* **-au** toll, custom,
duty. **tollborth/tollglwyd** tollgate
tom *e.b.* manure
ton *e.b.* *ll.* **tonnau** wave,
breaker
tôn *e.b.* *ll.* **tonau** tune. **tôn**
gron a round (tune)
tonau *gw.* **tôn**
tonfedd *e.b.* *ll.* **-i** wavelength
tonnau *gw.* **ton**
torch *e.b.* *ll.* **-au** wreath, coil,
torque
toreithiog *a* abundant,
teeming

toreth *e.b.* abundance
torf *e.b.* *ll.* **-eydd** crowd,
multitude
torfeydd *gw.* **torf**
torfol *a.* collective, mass. **enw**
torfol collective noun
torheulo *be.* **(torheulaf)** to
sunbathe
Tori *e.g.* *ll.* **Torïaid** Tory
toriad *e.g.* *ll.* **-au** break, cut
Torïaid *gw.* **Tori**
Torïaidd *a.* Tory,
Conservative
torri *be.* **(torraf)** to break, to
cut, to sever; to go bankrupt.
torri ar draws to interrupt;
torri enw to sign; **torri gwynt**
to break wind
tors *e.g.b.* *ll.* **tyrs** torch
torth *e.b.* *ll.* **-au** loaf. **torth**
wen white loaf
tosau *gw.* **tosyn**
tost 1 *a.* severe, sharp, sore;
ill *(S.W.)*. 2 *e.g.* toast
(bread)
tostrwydd *e.g.* illness, severity
tosyn *e.g.* *ll.* **tosau** pimple
(S.W.)
tra 1 *ad.* extremely, over,
very. **Dw i'n dra diolchgar**
I'm very grateful; 2 *c.* while,
whilst. **Ewch tra bod**
heddwch Go whilst there is
peace
trachefn *gw.* **drachefn**
trachwant *e.g.* *ll.* **-au** lust,
greed, covetousness
trachwantus *a.* covetous,
lustful
traddodiad *e.g.* *ll.* **-au**

tradition; delivery
traddodiadol *a.* traditional
traed *gw.* **troed**
traeth *e.g. ll.* **-au** beach, shore
traethau *gw.* **traeth**
traethawd *e.g. ll.* **traethodau** essay, treatise, tract
traethodau *gw.* **traethawd**
trafnidiaeth *e.b.* traffic, commerce
trafod *be.* (**trafodaf**) to handle, to discuss, to negotiate, to transact. **cylch trafod** discussion group
trafferth *e.b.g. ll.* **-ion** trouble, toil, bother
trafferthu (i) *be.* (**trafferthaf**) to trouble, to bother, to take pains
trafferthus *a.* troublesome, laborious; troubled
traffordd *e.b. ll.* **traffyrdd** motorway
traffyrdd *gw.* **traffordd**
tragwyddol *a.* eternal, everlasting.
o dragwyddol bwys of everlasting importance
trai *e.g. ll.* **treiau** ebb, decrease. **trai a llanw** ebb and flow
trais *e.g. ll.* **treisiau** violence, oppression; rape
trallod *e.g. ll.* **-au, -ion** tribulation, trouble
trallodau *gw.* **trallod**
trallodion *gw.* **trallod**
trallwysiad *e.g. ll.* **-au** transfusion. **Gwasanaeth**

Trallwyso Gwaed Blood Transfusion Service
tramor *a.* overseas, foreign
trannoeth *ad.* next day. **Daeth e drannoeth** He came the next day
trap *e.g. ll.* **-iau** trap
traul *e.b. ll.* **treuliau** wear; cost, expense
trawsblannu *be.*
(**trawsblannaf**) to transplant
trawst *e.g. ll.* **-iau** beam, crossbar
tre *gw.* **tref**
trechu *be.* (**trechaf**) to overcome, to defeat
tref: tre *e.b. ll.* **trefi, trefydd** town, home. **tua thre** homeward: **tre farchnad** market town
trefi *gw.* **tref**
trefn *e.b. ll.* **-au** order, arrangment, system, method. **dweud y drefn** to scold
trefnu (i) *be.* (**trefnaf**) to order, to arrange, to organize, to sort
trefnus *a.* orderly, methodical
trefnydd *e.g. ll.* **-ion** organizer
trefol *a.* urban
trefydd *gw.* **tref**
treial *e.g. ll.* **-on** trial, contest. **treialon cŵn defaid** sheepdog trials
treiglad *e.g. ll.* **-au** mutation; rolling. **treiglad llaes** spirant mutation; **treiglad meddal** soft mutation; **treiglad trwynol** nasal mutation

treiglo *be.* **(treiglaf)** to mutate; to roll

treisgar *a.* violent

treisiau *gw.* **trais**

treisio *be.* **(treisiaf)** to force, to violate, to oppress; to rape.

trem *e.b. ll.* **-iau** sight, look

trên *e.g. ll.* **trenau** train

trenau *gw.* **trên**

trennydd *ad.* two days hence

treth *e.b. ll.* **-i** rate, tax, levy; strain. **treth ar werth** value added tax; **treth incwm** income tax; **treth y pen** community charge/poll tax; **treth gyngor** council tax; **Roedd e'n dreth ar fy amynedd** He was a strain on my patience

trethdalwr *e.g. ll.* **trethdalwyr** ratepayer

trethu *be.* **(trethaf)** to tax, to rate

treuliau *gw.* **traul**

treulio *be.* **(treuliaf)** to wear; to spend; to digest

tri *a.g. & e.g.* **-oedd** *(followed by spirant mutation)* three. **tri chap** three caps; **tri pheint** three pints; **tri thŷ** three houses; **tri chynnig i Gymro** three tries for a Welshman. *gw. At. Treigladau. gw.* **tair**

triawd *e.g. ll.* **-au** trio, threesome

tric *e.g. ll.* **-iau** trick

tridiau *e.ll.* three days

trigain *a. & e.g.* sixty. **trigain mlynedd yn ôl** sixty years

ago. *gw. At. Treiglad Trwynol*

trigfan *e.b. ll.* **-nau** dwelling-place

trigo *be.* **(trigaf)** to dwell, to reside; to die (of animal)

trigolion *e.ll.* inhabitants

trin *be.* **(triniaf)** to treat; to handle; to dress; to till; to revile. **siop trin gwallt** hairdresser's shop; **trin y tir** to cultivate the land

trindod *e.b. ll.* **-au** trinity. **Coleg y Drindod** Trinity College

trioedd *e.ll.* triads

triongl *e.g.b. ll.* **-au** triangle

trist *a.* sad, sorrowful, unhappy

tristwch *e.g.* sadness, sorrow. **tristwch o'r mwyaf** the greatest sorrow

tro *e.g. ll.* **troeau, troeon** turn, twist, bend; conversion. **gweld tro ar fyd** to experience a change in circumstances. **llygad tro** a squint; **tro gwael** an unworthy act; **tro yn ei gwt** a twist in his tail

trochi *be.* **(trochaf)** to dip, to plunge; to soil *(S.W.);* to bathe *(N.W.)*

troeau *gw.* **tro**

troed *e.g.b. ll.* **traed** foot, base; handle

troedfedd *e.b. ll.* **-i** foot *(measure)*

troedffordd *e.g. ll.* **troedffyrdd** footpath

tröedig *a.* turned, converted

tröedigaeth *e.b.* *ll.* -au conversion, turning

troedio *be.* (**troediaf**) to walk, to tread, to trudge

troednoeth *a.* barefooted

troeon *gw.* **tro**

trogylch *e.g.* *ll.* -oedd, -au roundabout

troi *be.* (**troaf**) to turn, to revolve, to convert; to plough; to translate. *gw. At. Berfau*

tros *gw.* **dros**

trosedd *e.b.* *ll.* -au crime, offence, transgression

troseddu *be.* (**troseddaf**) to offend, to transgress

troseddwr *e.g.* *ll.* **troseddwyr** criminal, transgressor

trosgais *e.g.* *ll.* **trosgeisiau** converted try *(rugby)*

trosglwyddo *be.* (**trosglwyddaf**) to convey, to transfer

trosi *be.* (**trosaf**) to turn, to translate, to transfer; to convert *(rugby)*

trosiad *e.b.* *ll.* -au translation; conversion *(rugby)*

troswr *e.g.* *ll.* **troswyr** switch *(electricity)*

trothwy *e.g.* *ll.* -au, -on threshold. **ar drothwy'r Nadolig** on the threshold of Christmas

trowsus *e.g.* *ll.* -au trousers. **trowsus byr** short trousers

truan *e.g.* *ll.* **trueiniaid**

wretch. **Druan ohono!** Poor fellow! **Jac druan!** Poor Jack!

trueiniad *gw.* **truan**

trueni *e.g.* wretchedness, pity, misery. **trueni ei fod** a pity that; **trueni iddo** a pity that

truenus *a.* wretched, pitiful

trugaredd *e.g.* *ll.* -au mercy, compassion. **drwy drugaredd** fortunately

trugarhau (wrth) *be.* (**trugarhaf**) to be merciful (to), to take pity (on)

trwbl *e.g.* trouble

trwchus *a.* thick; dense

trwm *a.* *ll.* **trymion** heavy, sad, wretched

trwser *e.g.* *ll.* -i trousers. *gw.* **trowsus**

trwsio *be.* (**trwsiaf**) to mend, to trim, to dress

trwsiwr *e.g.* *ll.* **trwswyr** repairer

trwy *gw.* **drwy**

trwydded *e.b.* *ll.* -au licence, dispensation. **trwydded yrru** driving licence

trwyn *e.g.* *ll.* -au nose, snout; point, cape

trwynol *a.* nasal. **treiglad trwynol** nasal mutation

trychineb *e.g.b.* *ll.* -au disaster, calamity

trydan 1 *e.g.* electricity. 2 *a.* electric. **Y Bwrdd Trydan** The Electricity Board

trydanol *a.* electrical

trydanwr *e.g.* *ll.* **trydanwyr** electrician

trydedd *a.b. (used before feminine nouns)* third. **y drydedd bennod** the third chapter

trydydd *a.g. (used before masculine nouns)* third. **y trydydd tro** the third time

trydyddol *a.* tertiary. **Coleg Trydyddol** Tertiary College

tryloyw *a.* transparent

trymaidd *a.* heavy, close, sultry

trymion *gw.* **trwm**

trysor *e.b. ll.* **-au** treasure

trysorfa *e.b. ll.* **trysorfeydd** treasury, fund

trysori *be.* **(trysoraf)** to treasure

trysorydd *e.g. ll.* **-ion** treasurer

trywydd *e.g. ll.* **-ion** scent, trail.
ar drywydd on the trail of

tu *e.g.* side, region. **tu draw i: tu hwnt** beyond; **tu fewn: tu mewn** inside; **tu faes** *(S.W.):* **tu allan** *(N.W.).* outside

tua: tuag *ardd. (followed by spirant mutation)* towards; about. **tua thre: adre** homewards; **tuag at** towards; **tua mis** about a month

tudalen *e.g.b. ll.* **-nau** page. **tudalen flaen** front page. *gw.* **dalen.**

tueddiad *e.g. ll.* **-au** tendency, proneness

tun 1 *e.g.* **-iau** tin, can. 2 *a.* tin

tunnell *e.g. ll.* **tunelli** ton

twlc *e.g. ll.* **tylciau** sty. **twlc mochyn** pigsty

twll *e.g. ll.* **tyllau** hole

twmffat *e.g.* funnel

twmpath *e.g. ll.* **-au** tump, hillock. **Twmpath Dawns** folk dancing event

twndis *e.g. ll.* **-au** funnel

twnel *e.g. ll.* **-au, -i** tunnel

twp *a.* dull, stupid *(S.W.)*

twpsyn *e.g.* stupid person

twr *e.g. ll.* **tyrrau** heap; group; crowd

twˆr *e.g. ll.* **tyrau** tower

twrci *e.g. ll.* **twrcïod, tyrcwn** turkey

twristiaeth *e.b.* tourism. **Y Bwrdd Croeso** The Tourist Board

twrw *e.g. ll.* **tyrfau** noise, tumult, roar, crash. **tyrfau: taranau** thunder

twt *a.* neat, tidy. **tŷ bach twt** a Wendy house *(lit. a neat little house);* **twt a lol** nonsense, rubbish

twyll *e.g.* deceit, fraud, treachery

twyllo *be.* **(twyllaf)** to deceive, to cheat, to defraud

twyllodrus *a.* deceitful, false, fraudulent

twym *a.* warm *(S.W.).* **twym iawn** hot *(S.W.)*

twymo *be.* **(twymaf)** to warm

twymyn *e.b. ll.* **-au** fever

tŷ *e.g. ll.* **tai** house. **tŷ newydd** new house; **tŷ bach** toilet; **tŷ tafarn** public house;

tŷ cwrdd religious meeting house

tybed *ad.* I wonder: is that so? **Tybed a ddaw hi?** I wonder whether she will come?

tybied: tybio *be.* **(tybiaf)** to suppose, to think, to imagine

tydi *rhag.* you yourself

tyddyn *e.g. ll.* **-nod, -nau** small holding, small farm, croft. **ty'n cwm: tyddyn y cwm** the valley smallholding; **ty'n y waun** the moor croft

tyddynnwr *e.g. ll.* **tyddynwyr** smallholder, crofter

tyddynwyr *gw.* **tyddynnwr**

tyfiannau *gw.* **tyfiant**

tyfiant *e.g. ll.* **tyfiannau** growth, increase

tyfu *be.* **(tyfaf)** to grow, to increase

tynged *e.b. ll.* **tynghedau** destiny, fate

tyngedfennol *a.* fateful, fatal

tynghedau *gw.* **tynged**

tyngu *be.* **(tyngaf)** to swear, to vow

tylciau *ge.* **twlc**

tyle *e.g. ll.* **-au** hill, ascent, slope *(S.W.)*

tylino *be.* **(tylinaf)** to knead *(dough)*

tylwyth *e.g. ll.* **-au** family, ancestry, kindred. **Tylwyth Teg** fairies

tyllau *gw.* **twll**

tyllu *be.* **(tyllaf)** to hole, to bore, to perforate

tylluan *e.b. ll.* **-od** owl *(N.W.). gw.* **gwdihŵ**

tymer *e.b. ll.* **tymherau** temper, temperament

tymereddau *gw.* **tymheredd**

tymestl *e.b. ll.* **tymhestloedd** tempest, storm

tymherau *gw.* **tymer**

tymheredd *e.g. ll.* **tymereddau** temperature, temperament

tymhestloedd *gw.* **tymestl**

tymhestlog *a.* tempestuous, stormy

tymhorau *gw.* **tymor**

tymor *e.g. ll.* **tymhorau** season, term. **Tymor yr Haf** Summer Term; **yn ei thymor** in season *(of animal)*

tyn 1 *a.* tight, mean, perverse. **2** *bf.* pull! tighten! *gw.* **tynnu**

tyner *a.* gentle, tender

tynerwch *e.g.* gentleness, tenderness

tynnu *be.* **(tynnaf)** to pull, to draw, to remove; take off. **Tynnwch eich cot** Take off your coat

tyrau *gw.* **twr**

tyrfa *e.b. ll.* **-oedd** crowd, multitude

tyrfau *gw.* **twrw**

tyrrau *gw.* **twr**

tyst *e.g. ll.* **-ion** witness

tystio *be.* **(tystiaf)** to testify, to witness. **tystio bod** to testify that

tystiolaeth *e.b. ll.* **-au** evidence; testimony

tystion *gw.* **tyst**

tystysgrif *e.b.* *ll.* **-au**
certificate. **tystysgrif geni**
birth certificate; **tystysgrif
marwolaeth** death certificate;
tystysgrif priodi marriage
certificate
tywel *e.g.* *ll.* **-ion** towel
tywod *e.g.* sand
tywydd *e.g.* weather. **tywydd
mawr** stormy weather;
tywydd teg fair weather
tywyll *a.* dark, obscure; blind,
sad
tywyllu *be.* **(tywyllaf)** to
darken
tywyllwch *e.g.* darkness
tywys *be.* **(tywysaf)** to lead,
to guide
tywysydd *e.g.* *ll.* **-ion** guide.
tywysog *e.g.* *ll.* **-ion** prince.
Tywysog Cymru Prince of
Wales
tywysoges *e.b.* *ll.* **-au**
princess. **Tywysoges Cymru**
Princess of Wales

TH

thabl *gw.* **tabl**
thabled *gw.* **tabled**
thacl *gw.* **tacl**
thaclo *gw.* **taclo**
thaclu *gw.* **taclu**
thaclus *gw.* **taclus**
thacluso *gw.* **tacluso**
thaclwr *gw.* **taclwr**
thacsi *gw.* **tacsi**
Thachwedd *gw.* **Tachwedd**
thad *gw.* **tad**
thad-cu *gw.* **tad-cu**

thafarn *gw.* **tafarn**
thafarnwr *gw.* **tafarnwr**
thafell *gw.* **tafell**
thaflegryn *gw.* **taflegryn**
thaflen *gw.* **taflen**
thaflu *gw.* **taflu**
thafod *gw.* **tafod**
thafodiaith *gw.* **tafodiaith**
thafodieithoedd *gw.* **tafodiaith**
thafol *gw.* **tafol**
thagfa *gw.* **tagfa**
thagu *gw.* **tagu**
thangnefedd *gw.* **tangnefedd**
thai *gw.* **tŷ**
thaid *gw.* **taid**
thair *gw.* **tair**
thaith *gw.* **taith**
thai *gw.* **tai**
thâl *gw.* **tâl**
thalai *gw.* **talai**. *gw.* **talu**
thalaith *gw.* **talaith**
thalcen *gw.* **talcen**
thalcennau: thalcenni *gw.*
 talcen
thaleb *gw.* **taleb**
thalent *gw.* **talent**
thalentog *gw.* **talentog**
thaliadau: thaloedd *gw.* **tâl**
thalu *gw.* **talu**
thalwr *gw.* **talwr**
thalwrn *gw.* **talwrn**
thamaid *gw.* **tamaid**
thameidiau *gw.* **tamaid**
than *gw.* **dan**
thân *gw.* **tân**
thanau *gw.* **tân**
thanbaid *gw.* **tanbaid**
thanc *gw.* **tanc**
thancer *gw.* **tancer**
thanddaear *gw.* **tanddaear**

thanddaearol *gw.* tanddaear
thanfor *gw.* tanfor
thanio *gw.* tanio
thanlinellu *gw.* tanlinellu
thanlwybr *gw.* tanlwybr
thanllyd *gw.* tanllyd
thannau *gw.* tant
thanseilio *gw.* tanseilio
thant *gw.* tant
thanwydd *gw.* tanwydd
thap *gw.* tap
thâp *gw.* tâp
thapiau *gw.* tap. *gw.* tâp
tharan *gw.* taran
tharanu *gw.* taranu
tharddiad *gw.* tarddiad
tharddu *gw.* tarddu
tharged *gw.* targed
tharian *gw.* tarian
tharianau *gw.* tarian
tharo *gw.* taro
tharw *gw.* tarw
thasg *gw.* tasg
thasgu *gw.* tasgu
thaten *gw.* taten
thato *gw.* taten
thatws *gw.* taten
thawel *gw.* tawel
thawelu *gw.* tawelu
thawelwch *gw.* tawelwch
thawelydd *gw.* tawelydd
thawelyddion *gw.* tawelydd
thawelyn *gw.* tawelyn
the *gw.* te
theatr *eb. ll.* -au theatre,
  playhouse
thebot *gw.* tebot
thebyg *gw.* tebyg
thebygrwydd *gw.* tebygrwydd
thecell *gw.* tecell

thechneg *gw.* techneg
thechnegol *gw.* technegol
thechnegwr *gw.* technegwr
thechnoleg *gw.* technoleg
theg *gw.* teg
thegan *gw.* tegan
thegell *gw.* tecell
thegwch *gw.* tegwch
thei *gw.* tei
theiar *gw.* teiar
theidiau *gw.* taid
theigr *gw.* teigr
theiliwr *gw.* teiliwr
theilsen *gw.* teilsen
theilwng *gw.* teilwng
theilwres *gw.* teilwres
theilwriaid *gw.* teiliwr
theilyngdod *gw.* teilyngdod
theimlad *gw.* teimlad
theimlo *gw.* teimlo
theipiadur *gw.* teipiadur
theirgwaith *gw.* teirgwaith
theirw *gw.* tarw
theis *gw.* tei
theisen *gw.* teisen
theitl *gw.* teitl
theithiau *gw.* taith
theithio *gw.* teithio
theithiwr *gw.* teithiwr
thelediad *gw.* telediad
theledu *gw.* teledu
theleffon *gw.* teleffon
theleffonio *gw.* teleffonio
thelyn *gw.* telyn
thelyneg *gw.* telyneg
thelynor *gw.* telynor
thelynores *gw.* telynores
thelynorion *gw.* telynor
thema *e.b ll.* themâu theme
theml *gw.* teml

thenau

thenau *gw.* tenau
therapydd *e.g. ll.* -ion
  therapist
therfyn *gw.* terfyn
therfysg *gw.* terfysg
therfysgaeth *gw.* terfysgaeth
therfysgwr *gw.* terfysgwr
therm *gw.* term
thermomedr *e.g. ll.* -au
  thermometer
thes *gw.* tes
thesog *gw.* tesog
thestun *gw.* testun
theulu *gw.* teulu
thew *gw.* tew
theyrnas *gw.* teyrnas
thi *gw.* ti
thiced *gw.* ticed
thîm *gw.* tîm
thipiau *gw.* tip. *gw.* tipyn
thipyn *gw.* tipyn
thir *gw.* tir
thirion *gw.* tirion
thirlun *gw.* tirlun
thiroedd *gw.* tir
thisian *gw.* tisian
thithau *gw.* tithau
thiwtor *gw.* tiwtor
thlawd *gw.* tlawd
thlodi *gw.* tlodi
thlodion *gw.* tlawd
thlos *gw.* tlos
thlws *gw.* tlws
thlysau *gw.* tlws
tho *gw.* to
thocyn *gw.* tocyn
thocynnau *gw.* tocyn
thocynnwr *gw.* tocynnwr
thocynwyr *gw.* tocynnwr
thoddi *gw.* toddi

thoeau *gw.* to
thoeon *gw.* to
thoes *gw.* toes
thoiled *gw.* toiled
tholc *gw.* tolc
tholcio *gw.* tolcio
tholl *gw.* toll
thom *gw.* tom
thon *gw.* ton
thôn *gw.* tôn
thonau *gw.* tôn
thonfedd *gw.* tonfedd
thonnau *gw.* ton
thorch *gw.* torch
thoreithiog *gw.* toreithiog
thoreth *gw.* toreth
thorf *gw.* torf
thorfeydd *gw.* torf
thorfol *gw.* torfol
thorheulo *gw.* torheulo
Thori *gw.* Tori
thoriad *gw.* toriad
Thorïaid *gw.* Tori
Thorïaidd *gw.* Torïaidd
thorri *gw.* torri
thors *gw.* tors
thorth *gw.* torth
thosau *gw.* tosyn
thost *gw.* tost
thostrwydd *gw.* tostrwydd
thosyn *gw.* tosyn
thrachefn *gw.* trachefn
thrachwant *gw.* trachwant
thrachwantus *gw.*
  trachwantus
thraddodiad *gw.* traddodiad
thraddodiadol *gw.*
  traddodiadol
thraed *gw.* troed
thraeth *gw.* traeth

thraethau *gw*. traeth
thraethawd *gw*. traethawd
thraethodau *gw*. traethawd
thrafnidiaeth *gw*. trafnidiaeth
thrafod *gw*. trafod
thrafferth *gw*. trafferth
thrafferthu *gw*. trafferthu
thrafferthus *gw*. trafferthus
thraffordd *gw*. traffordd
thraffyrdd *gw*. traffordd
thragwyddol *gw*. tragwyddol
thrai *gw*. trai
thrais *gw*. trais
thrallod *gw*. trallod
thrallodau *gw*. trallod
thrallodion *gw*. trallod
thrallwysiad *gw*. trallwysiad
thramor *gw*. tramor
thrannoeth *gw*. trannoeth
thrap *gw*. trap
thraul *gw*. traul
thrawsblannu *gw*.
 trawsblannu
thrawst *gw*. trawst
thre *gw*. tref
threchu *gw*. trechu
thref *gw*. tref
threfi *gw*. tref
threfn *gw*. trefn
threfnu *gw*. trefnu
threfnus *gw*. trefnus
threfnydd *gw*. trefnydd
threfol *gw*. trefol
threfydd *gw*. tref
threial *gw*. treial
threiau *gw*. trai
threiglad *gw*. treiglad
threiglo *gw*. treiglo
threisgar *gw*. treisgar
threisiau *gw*. trais

threisio *gw*. treisio
threm *gw*. trem
thrên *gw*. trên
threnau *gw*. trên
thrennydd *gw*. trennydd
threth *gw*. treth
threthdalwr *gw*. trethdalwr
threthu *gw*. trethu
threuliau *gw*. traul
threulio *gw*. treulio
thri *gw*. tri
thriawd *gw*. triawd
thric *gw*. tric
thridiau *gw*. tridiau
thrigain *gw*. trigain
thrigfan *gw*. trigfan
thrigo *gw*. trigo
thrigolion *gw*. trigolion
thrin *gw*. trin
thrindod *gw*. trindod
thrioedd *gw*. trioedd
thriongl *gw*. triongl
thrist *gw*. trist
thristwch *gw*. tristwch
thro *gw*. tro
throchi *gw*. trochi
throeau *gw*. tro
throed *gw*. troed
throedfedd *gw*. troedfedd
throedffordd *gw*. troedffordd
thröedig *gw*. tröedig
thröedigaeth *gw*. tröedigaeth
throedio *gw*. troedio
throednoeth *gw*. troednoeth
throeon *gw*. tro
throgylch *gw*. trogylch
throi *gw*. troi
thros *gw*. tros
throsedd *gw*. trosedd
throseddu *gw*. troseddu

throseddwr *gw.* troseddwr
throsgais *gw.* trosgais
throsglwyddo *gw.*
  trosglwyddo
throsi *gw.* trosi
throsiad *gw.* trosiad
throswr *gw.* troswr
throthwy *gw.* trothwy
throwsus *gw.* trowsus
thruan *gw.* truan
thrueiniaid *gw.* truan
thrueni *gw.* trueni
thruenus *gw.* truenus
thrugaredd *gw.* trugaredd
thrugarhau *gw.* trugarhau
thrwbl *gw.* trwbl
thrwchus *gw.* trwchus
thrwm *gw.* trwm
thrwser *gw.* trwser
thrwsio *gw.* trwsio
thrwsiwr *gw.* trwsiwr
thrwy *gw.* drwy
thrwydded *gw.* trwydded
thrwyn *gw.* trwyn
thrwynol *gw.* trwynol
thrychineb *gw.* trychineb
thrydan *gw.* trydan
thrydanol *gw.* trydanol
thrydanwr *gw.* trydanwr
thrydedd *gw.* trydedd
thrydydd *gw.* trydydd
thrydyddol *gw.* trydyddol
thryloyw *gw.* tryloyw
thrymaidd *gw.* trymaidd
thrymion *gw.* trwm
thrysor *gw.* trysor
thrysorfa *gw.* trysorfa
thrysorydd *gw.* trysorydd
thrywydd *gw.* trywydd
thu *gw.* tu

thua *gw.* tua
thuag *gw.* tua
thudalen *gw.* tudalen
thueddiad *gw.* tueddiad
thun *gw.* tun
thunnell *gw.* tunnell
thus *e.g.* frankincense
thwlc *gw.* twlc
thwll *gw.* twll
thwmpath *gw.* twmpath
thwndis *gw.* twndis
thwnel *gw.* twnel
thwp *gw.* twp
thwpsyn *gw.* twpsyn
thwr *gw,* twr
thŵr *gw.* tŵr
thwrci *gw.* twrci
thwristiaeth *gw.* twristiaeth
thwrw *gw.* twrw
thwt *gw.* twt
thwyll *gw.* twyll
thwyllo *gw.* twyllo
thwyllodrus *gw.* twyllodrus
thwym *gw.* twym
thwymo *gw.* twymo
thwymyn *gw.* twymyn
thŷ *gw.* tŷ
thybied *gw.* tybied
thybio *gw.* tybied
thydi *gw.* tydi
thyddyn *gw.* tyddyn
thyddynnwr *gw.* tyddynnwr
thyddynwyr *gw.* tyddynnwr
thyfiannau *gw.* tyfiant
thyfiant *gw.* tyfiant
thyfu *gw.* tyfu
thynged *gw.* tynged
thyngedfennol *gw.*
  tyngedfennol
thynghedau *gw.* tynged

thyngu *gw.* tyngu
thylciau *gw.* twlc
thyle *gw.* tyle
thylino *gw.* tylino
thylwyth *gw.* tylwyth
thyllau *gw.* twll
thyllu *gw.* tyllu
thylluan *gw.* tylluan
thymer *gw.* tymer
thymereddau *gw.* tymheredd
thymestl *gw.* tymestl
thymherau *gw.* tymer
thymheredd *gw.* tymheredd
thymhestloedd *gw.* tymestl
thymhestlog *gw.* tymhestlog
thymhorau *gw.* tymor
thymor *gw.* tymor
thyn *gw.* tyn
thyner *gw.* tyner
thynerwch *gw.* tynerwch
thynnu *gw.* tynnu
thyrau *gw.* tŵr
thyrfa *gw.* tyrfa
thyrfaoedd *gw.* tyrfa
thyrfau *gw.* twrw
thyrrau *gw.* twr
thyst *gw.* tyst
thystio *gw.* tystio
thystiolaeth *gw.* tystiolaeth
thystion *gw.* tyst
thystysgrif *gw.* tystysgrif
thystysgrifau *gw.* tystysgrif
thywel *gw.* tywel
thywod *gw.* tywod
thywydd *gw.* tywydd
thywyll *gw.* tywyll
thywyllu *gw.* tywyllu
thywyllwch *gw.* tywyllwch
thywys *gw.* tywys
thywysog *gw.* tywysog

thywysoges *gw.* tywysoges

U

uchaf *a.* uppermost, highest; loudest. **am yr uchaf** for the loudest
uchafbwynt *e.g.* *ll.* -iau climax; zenith
uchder *e.g.* *ll.* -au height, altitude
uchel *a.* high; loud
uchelder *e.g.* *ll.* -au highness
ucheldir *e.g.* *ll.* -oedd highland
uchelgais *e.g.b.* *ll.* uchelgeisiau ambition
uchelgeisiol *a.* ambitious
uchelion *e.ll.* heights
uchelwr *e.g.* *ll.* uchelwyr gentleman, nobleman
uchod *ad.* above. **yn y rhestr uchod** in the above list
udo *be.* **(udaf)** to howl, to moan, to wail
ufudd *a.* obedient
ufuddhau (i) *be.* **(ufuddhâf)** to obey
uffern *e.b.* *ll.* -au hell. **Uffern dân!** Hell fire!
uffernol *a.* infernal, hellish. **Roedd hi'n ddrud uffernol** It was extremely expensive.
ugain *a. & e.g.* *ll.* ugeiniau twenty. **tri ar hugain** twenty-three; **deg ar hugain** thirty
ugeinfed *a.* twentieth. **yr ugeinfed ganrif** the 20th century
ugeiniau *gw.* ugain

un *a. & e.g. ll.* -au one. **un tro** one turn; once; **yr un** the one, the same; **yr un faint** as much, the same; **yr un pryd** the same time

unawd *e.g. ll.* -au solo

unawdwr: unawdydd *e.g. ll.* unawdwyr soloist

unben *e.g. ll.* -iaid dictator, despot

undeb *e.g. ll.* -au union, unity. **Undeb yr Athrawon** the Teachers' Union; **Undeb y Mamau** the Mothers' Union

undebwr *e.g. ll.* undebwyr unionist

undod *e.g. ll.* -au unit, unity

Undodwr *e.g. ll.* Undodwyr Unitarian

undonog *a.* monotonous

undydd *a.* one-day. **ysgol undydd** a one-day school

uned *e.b. ll.* -au unit

unedig *a.* united

unfarn *a.* unanimous

unfryd: unfrydol *a.* unanimous

unffordd *a.* one-way. **stryd unffordd** one-way street

uniaethu (â) *be.* (uniaethaf) to identify (with)

unig *a. (precedes noun and causes soft mutation)* only, sole; alone, lonely. **yr unig fab** the only son; **mab unig** lonely son

unigol *a.* singular; individual

unigolyn *e.g. ll.* unigolion individual

unigrwydd *e.g.* loneliness

unigryw *a.* unique

union *a.* direct, straight; exact. **yr union fan** the exact place

unioni *be.* (unionaf) to rectify, to straighten

unman *ad.* anywhere

unnos *a.* of or for one night. **tŷ unnos** habitable cabin built between dusk and dawn

uno *be.* (unaf) to unite, to join

unrhyw *a.* same; any; homogeneous. **mewn unrhyw wlad** in any country; **unrhyw beth** anything

unwaith *ad.* once. **ar unwaith** at once; **unwaith ac am byth** once and for all

urdd *e.b. ll.* -au order, guild. **Urdd Gobaith Cymru** Welsh League of Youth

urddas *e.g. ll.* -au dignity, honour

urddo *be.* (urddaf) to ordain, to bestow honour on

us *e.ll.* chaff

ustus *e.g. ll.* -iaid magistrate

uwch *a.* higher, senior, superior; advanced. **uwchgapten** major (army officer); **uwchnormal** superior. *gw.* **uchel**

uwchben *ardd. & ad.* above

uwchfarchnad *e.b. ll.* -oedd supermarket

uwchlaw *ardd.* above

uwchradd *a.* secondary. **ysgol uwchradd** secondary school

uwd *e.g. ll.* -iau porridge

W

wadu *gw.* gwadu
waed *gw.* gwaed
waedu *gw.* gwaedu
waedd *gw.* gwaedd
wael *gw.* gwael
waelod *gw.* gwaelod
waeth *gw.* drwg
waethaf *gw.* drwg
waethed *gw.* drwg
waethygu *gw.* gwaethygu
wag *gw.* gwag
wagedd *gw.* gwagedd
wagio *gw.* gwagio
wagle *gw.* gwagle
wagu *gw.* gwagio
wahân *gw.* gwahân
wahanlaeth *gw.* gwahaniaeth
wahaniaethu *gw.*
  gwahaniaethu
wahanol *gw.* gwahanol
wahanu *gw.* gwahanu
wahardd *gw.* gwahardd
wahodd *gw.* gwahodd
wahoddedig *gw.*
  gwahoddedig
wahoddedigion *gw.*
  gwahoddedig
wahoddiad *gw.* gwahoddiad
wahoddion *gw.* gwahodd
wair *gw.* gwair
waith *gw.* gwaith
wal *e.b.* *ll.* -au wall. *gw.* gwal
wâl *gw.* gwâl
walau *gw.* gwâl
waliau *gw.* gwal, wal
wall *gw.* gwall
wallgof *gw.* gwallgof
wallt *gw.* gwallt

wallus *gw.* gwallus
wan *gw.* gwan
wanwyn *gw.* gwanwyn
war *gw.* gwar
wâr *gw.* gwâr
warchod *gw.* gwarchod
waredu *gw.* gwaredu
waredwr *gw.* gwaredwr
wario *gw.* gwario
warrau *gw.* gwar
wartheg *gw.* gwartheg
warthus *gw.* gwarthus
was *gw.* gwas
wasanaeth *gw.* gwasanaeth
wasanaethu *gw.* gwasanaethu
wasg *gw.* gwasg
wasgedd *gw.* gwasgedd
wasgfa *gw.* gwasgfa
wasgod *gw.* gwasgod
wasgu *gw.* gwasgu
wastad *gw.* gwastad
wastraff *gw.* gwastraff
wastraffu *gw.* gwastraffu
wats *e.g.* *ll.* -ys watch
wau *gw.* gwau
waun *gw.* gwaun
wawd *gw.* gwawd
wawdio *gw.* gwawdio
wawr *gw.* gwawr
wawrio *gw.* gwawrio
wawroedd *gw.* gwawr
wdihŵ *gw.* gwdihŵ
wddf *gw.* gwddf
wddwg *gw.* gwddwg
we *gw.* gwe
wedi *ardd.* after. **wedi deg**
after ten; **Mae wedi chwech
arno** He has lost his chance;
*the preposition is also used
as follows:* (forms of **bod**) +

(wedi) + *(be.)*; **Rydw i wedi
blino** I am tired; **Dwyt ti
ddim wedi cysgu** You have
not slept; **Roedd ef wedi troi**
He turned; **Maen nhw wedi
marw** They are dead
wedyn *ad.* afterwards, then
weddi *gw.* **gweddi**
weddïau *gw.* **gweddi**
weddill *gw.* **gweddill**
weddïo *gw.* **gweddïo**
weddol *gw.* **gweddol**
weddw *gw.* **gweddw**
wefus *gw.* **gwefus**
weiddi *gw.* **gweiddi**
weigion *gw.* **gwag**
weiniaid *gw.* **gwan**
weinidog *gw.* **gweinidog**
weinion *gw.* **gwan**
weinydd *gw.* **gweinydd**
weinyddes *gw.* **gweinyddes**
weiriau *gw.* **gwair**
weisg *gw.* **gwasg**
weision *gw.* **gwas**
weithdy *gw.* **gweithdy**
weithgar *gw.* **gweithgar**
weithiau *ad.* sometimes. *gw.*
 gwaith
weithio *gw.* **gweithio**
weithiwr *gw.* **gweithiwr**
weithred *gw.* **gweithred**
weithredu *gw.* **gweithredu**
weithwyr *gw.* **gweithiwr**
wel *ebych.* well!
welâu *gw.* **gwely**
weld *gw.* **gweld**
wele *ebych.* behold!
weled *gw.* **gweld**
welw *gw.* **gwelw**
wely *gw.* **gwely**

welyau *gw.* **gwely**
welydd *gw.* **gwal**
well *gw.* **gwell**
wella *gw.* **gwella**
wellt *gw.* **gwellt**
welltyn *gw.* **gwelltyn**
wen *gw.* **gwen**
wên *gw.* **gwên**
wenau *gw.* **gwên**
wendid *gw.* **gwendid**
Wener *gw.* **Gwener**
wenith *gw.* **gwenith**
wennol *gw.* **gwennol**
Went *gw.* **Gwent**
wenu *gw.* **gwenu**
wenwyn *gw.* **gwenwyn**
wenwynig *gw.* **gwenwynig**
wenwynol *gw.* **gwenwynig**
wenyn *gw.* **gwenynen**
wenynen *gw.* **gwenynen**
wêr *gw.* **gwêr**
werdd *gw.* **gwerdd**
werin *gw.* **gwerin**
weriniaeth *gw.* **gweriniaeth**
wers *gw.* **gwers**
werslyfr *gw.* **gwerslyfr**
wersyll *gw.* **gwersyll**
werth *gw.* **gwerth**
werthfawr *gw.* **gwerthfawr**
werthfawrogi *gw.*
 gwerthfawrogi
werthfawrogiad *gw.*
 gwerthfawrogiad
werthiant *gw.* **gwerthiant**
werthu *gw.* **gwerthu**
werthwr *gw.* **gwerthwr**
werthwyr *gw.* **gwerthwr**
westai *gw.* **gwestai.** *gw.*
 gwesty
westeion *gw.* **gwestai**

westeiwr *gw*. **gwesteiwr**
westeiwyr *gw*. **gwesteiwr**
westy *gw*. **gwesty**
weu *gw*. **gweu**
weunydd *gw*. **gwaun**
wg *gw*. **gwg**
wgu *gw*. **gwgu**
whilber *e.b*. *ll*. **-au**
  wheelbarrow. *gw*. **berfa**
wiail *gw*. **gwialen**
wialen *gw*. **gwialen**
wialennod *gw*. **gwialen**
wiced *e.b*. *ll*. **-i** wicket
wicedwr *e.g*. *ll*. **wicedwyr**
  wicket-keeper
widw *e.b*. *ll* **-od** widow
  (S.W.)
win *gw*. **gwin**
winwnsyn *e.g*. *ll*. **winwns**
  onion
wir *gw*. **gwir**
wirionedd *gw*. **gwirionedd**
wisg *gw*. **gwisg**
wisgo *gw*. **gwisgo**
wiwer *gw*. **gwiwer**
wlad *gw*. **gwlad**
wladfa *gw*. **gwladfa**
wladgarwr *gw*. **gwladgarwr**
wladol *gw*. **gwladol**
wlân *gw*. **gwlân**
wlanen *gw*. **gwlanen**
wledig *gw*. **gwledig**
wledydd *gw*. **gwlad**
wledd *gw*. **gwledd**
wledda *gw*. **gwledda**
wleidydd *gw*. **gwleidydd**
wleidyddiaeth *gw*.
  gwleidyddiaeth
wleidyddol *gw*. **gwleidyddol**
wlith *gw*. **gwlith**

wlyb *gw*. **gwlyb**
wlybaniaeth *gw*. **gwlybaniaeth**
wlychu *gw*. **gwlychu**
wn *gw*. **gwn**
ŵn *gw*. **gŵn**
wneud *gw*. **gwneud**
wneuthur *gw*. **gwneud**
wniadyddes *gw*. **gwniadyddes**
wnïo *gw*. **gwnïo**
wniyddes *gw*. **gwniadyddes**
wobr *gw*. **gwobr**
wobrwyo *gw*. **gwobrwyo**
ŵr *gw*. **gŵr**
wrach *gw*. **gwrach**
wragedd *gw*. **gwraig**
wraidd *gw*. **gwreiddyn**
wraig *gw*. **gwraig**
wrandawiad *gw*. **gwrandawiad**
wrandawr *gw*. **gwrandawr**
wrando *gw*. **gwrando**
wreichion *gw*. **gwreichionen**
wreichionen *gw*.
  gwreichionen
wreiddiau *gw*. **gwreiddyn**
wreiddio *gw*. **gwreiddio**
wreiddiol *gw*. **gwreiddiol**
wreiddyn *gw*. **gwreiddyn**
wres *gw*. **gwres**
wresog *gw*. **gwresog**
wresogi *gw*. **gwresogi**
wresogydd *gw*. **gwresogydd**
wrido *gw*. **gwrido**
wridog *gw*. **gwridog**
wrol *gw*. **gwrol**
wrtaith *gw*. **gwrtaith**
wrth *ardd*. by; with; to;
  because; since. **wrth gwrs** of
  course; **wrth law** at hand, in
  reserve; **wrth lwc** luckily
wrthblaid *gw*. **gwrthblaid**

wrthchwyswr *gw.*
  gwrthchwyswr
wrthdaro *gw.* gwrthdaro
wrthdystio *gw.* gwrthdystio
wrthglocwedd *gw.*
  gwrthglocwedd
wrthod *gw.* gwrthod
wrthrych *gw.* gwrthrych
wrthrychol *gw.* gwrthrychol
wrthryfel *gw.* gwrthryfel
wrthryfela *gw.* gwrthryfela
wrthwyneb *gw.* gwrthwyneb
wrthwynebu *gw.*
  gwrthwynebu
wrthwynebwr *gw.*
  gwrthwynebwr
wryw *gw.* gwryw
wrywaidd *gw.* gwrywaidd
wrywgydiaeth *gw.*
  gwrywgydiaeth
wrywol *gw.* gwrywaidd
wthiad *gw.* gwthiad
wthio *gw.* gwthio
wthiwr *gw.* gwthiwr
wy *e.g. ll.* -au *egg.* wy clwc
  addled egg; wy Pasg Easter
  egg; wy wedi'i falu beaten
  egg; wy wedi'i ferwi boiled
  egg; wy wedi'i ffrio fried egg
wybedyn *gw.* gwybedyn
wybod *gw.* gwybod
wybodaeth *gw.* gwybodaeth
wybren *e.b. ll.* -nau, -nydd
  sky, firmament *(literary
  usage)*
wybrennau *gw.* wybren
wybrennydd *gw.* wybren
wych *gw.* gwych
wydr *gw.* gwydr
wydrau *gw.* gwydr. *gw.*

gwydryn
wydryn *gw.* gwydryn
ŵydd *gw.* gŵydd
wyddau *gw.* gŵydd
wyddbwyll *gw.* gwyddbwyll
Wyddel *gw.* Gwyddel
Wyddeleg *gw.* Gwyddeleg
Wyddeles *gw.* Gwyddeles
Wyddelig *gw.* Gwyddelig
Wyddfa, Yr *e.b.* Snowdon
Wyddgrug, Yr *e.b.* Mold
wyddoniaeth *gw.*
  gwyddoniaeth
wyddonol *gw.* gwyddonol
wyddonydd *gw.* gwyddonydd
wyddor *gw.* gwyddor
wyf (i) *bf.* I am. *gw.* bod
wyfyn *gw.* gwyfyn
ŵyl *gw.* gŵyl
wylan *gw.* gwylan
wyliadwrus *gw.* gwyliadwrus
wyliau *gw.* gŵyl
wylio *gw.* gwylio
wyliwr *gw.* gwyliwr
wylnos *gw.* gwylnos
wylo *be.* (wylaf) to weep, to
  cry *(N.W.)*
wylwyr *gw.* gwyliwr
wyll *gw.* gwyll
wyllt *gw.* gwyllt
wylltio *gw.* gwylltio
wylltu *gw.* gwylltio
wymon *gw.* gwymon
wyn *gw.* gwyn
ŵyn *gw.* oen
wyneb *e.g. ll.* -au face;
  surface. dauwynebog
  deceitful; wyneb-ddalen title
  page; wynebgaled barefaced;
  wyneb i waered upside-

down
wynebu *be.* **(wynebaf)** to face, to confront
Wynedd *gw.* Gwynedd
wynegon *gw.* gwynegon
wynegu *gw.* gwynegu
wynfa *gw.* gwynfa
wynfyd *gw.* gwynfyd
wyngalch *gw.* gwyngalch
wynion *gw.* gwyn
wynnu *gw.* gwynnu
wynt *gw.* gwynt
wyntog *gw.* gwyntog
wŷr *gw.* gwŷr
ŵyr *e.g. ll.* **wyrion** grandson
wyrion *gw.* ŵyr
wyrdd *gw.* gwyrdd
wyres *e.b. ll.* **-au** grand-daughter
wyresau *gw.* wyres
wyriad *gw.* gwyriad
wyrio *gw.* gwyro
wyro *gw.* gwyro
wyrth *gw.* gwyrth
wyrthiol *gw.* gwyrthiol
wyryf *gw.* gwyryf
wŷs *gw.* gwŷs
Wysg *e.b.* Usk (river)
wystl *gw.* gwystl
wyt (ti) *bf.* you are *(singular).* **Wyt ti gartref?** Are you at home? *gw.* **bod.**
wyth *a. & e.g.* eight. **wyth deg** eighty
wythawd *e.g. ll.* **-au** octave; octet
wythfed *a.* eighth
wythnos *e.b. ll.* **-au** week. **yr wythnos diwethaf** last week; **yr wythnos hon** this week; **yr**

wythnos nesaf next week
wythnosol *a.* weekly. **cyfarfod wythnosol** weekly meeting; **papur wythnosol** weekly paper
wythwr *e.g. ll.* **wythwyr** number eight *(rugby forward)*
wythwyr *gw.* wythwr
wywo *gw.* gwywo

Y

y: yr: 'r, 1 *y fan.* the. **y** *before a consonant:* **y dyn** the man; **y ferch** the girl; **y tai** the houses; **yr** *before a vowel and h:* **yr afal** the apple; **yr esgid** the shoe; **yr haul** the sun; **yr heol** the road; **'r** *after a vowel:* **a'r plant** and the children; **o'r llyfr** from the book; **i'r cae** to the field; **y** *and* **'r** *are followed by soft mutation of feminine singular nouns:* **y dorth** the loaf; **tŷ'r fam** the mother's house; **gyda'r gath** with the cat; *nouns beginning with ll and rh do not mutate after* **y** *and* **'r.** *gw. At.* Treiglad Meddal. 2 *geir. used with forms of the verb* **bod: y mae...; yr oedd...; rwyf...**
y: yr *geir. perth.* **Dyma'r tŷ y trigaf ynddo** Here is the house in which I live
ychwaith *gw.* chwaith
ychwaneg *gw.* chwaneg
ychwanegu: chwanegu *be.*

(ychwanegaf: chwanegaf) to
add, to augment
ychydig *a.* little, few. **ychydig
o lyfrau** a few books;
ychydig fara a little bread;
ychydig lai a little less
ŷd *e.g. ll.* **ydau** corn. **creision
ŷd** cornflakes
ydy *bf.* is, are. *gw.* **bod**
yddfau *gw.* **gwddf**
yfed *be.* **(yfaf)** to drink
yfory: fory *ad.* tomorrow
yfflon *e.ll.* fragments, pieces,
bits *(S.W.).* **yn yfflon racs** in
smithereens. *gw.* **yfflyn**
yfflyn *e.g. ll.* **yfflon** fragment,
piece, bit. **heb yfflyn o
wahaniaeth** without a scrap
of difference
ygau *gw.* **gwg**
yng *gw.* **yn**
ynghanol *ardd.* in the midst
of
ynghyd *ad.* together. **ynghyd
â** together with
ynghylch *ardd.* about,
concerning
ynglŷn (â) *ad.* in connection
(with), concerning
ym *gw.* **yn**
yma *ad.* here, this
ymadael (â) *be.* **(ymadawaf)**
to depart
ymadrodd *e.g. ll.* **-ion** speech,
saying, expression
ymaelodi (â) *be.* **(ymaelodaf)**
to become a member, to join
ymaith *ad.* away
ymarfer (â) 1 *be.* **(ymarferaf)**
to practise. 2 *e.b.g. ll.* **-ion**

practice, exercise. **ymarfer
corff** physical exercise
ymarferiad *e.g. ll.* **-au**
practice, exercise
ymarferol *a.* practical
ymateb 1 *be.* **(ymatebaf)** to
respond. 2 *e.g. ll.* **-ion**
reaction; response
ymbelydredd *e.g.* radiation
ymbelydrol *a.* radioactive
ymchwil *e.b.* research, search,
quest
ymchwiliad *e.g. ll.* **-au**
investigation; inquiry
ymchwilio (i) *be.* **(ymchwiliaf)**
to research; to search
ymdaith 1 *e.b. ll.* **ymdeithiau**
journey, march. 2 *be.*
(ymdeithiaf) to travel, to
march
ymdrech *e.b. ll.* **-ion** effort,
endeavour, struggle:
ymdrech deg valiant effort
ymdrechu (i) *be.* **(ymdrechaf)**
to strive, to endeavour
ymdrin (â) *be.* **(ymdriniaf)** to
deal (with)
ymddangos (i) *be.*
(ymddangosaf) to appear, to
seem
ymddangosiad *e.g. ll.* **-au**
appearance
ymddeol *be.* **(ymddeolaf)** to
retire
ymddeoliad *e.g. ll.* **-au**
retirement
ymddiheuriad *e.g. ll.* **-au**
apology
ymddiheuro *be.* **(ymddiheuraf)**
to apologize

ymddiried (yn) *be.*
(ymddiriedaf) to trust, to
confide *(in)*
ymddirledaeth *e.b. ll.* **-au**
trust, confidence
ymddiriedolaeth *e.b. ll.* **-au**
trust *(charity)*;
Ymddiriedolaeth
Genedlaethol National Trust
ymddiriedolwr *e.b. ll.*
ymddiriedolwyr trustee
ymddiswyddiad *e.g. ll.* **-au**
resignation
ymddiswyddo *be.*
(ymddiswyddaf) to resign
ymddwyn *be.* **(ymddygaf)** to
behave
ymddygiad *e.g. ll.* **-au**
behaviour
ymennydd *e.g. ll.*
ymenyddion brain
ymenyddion *gw.* **ymennydd**
ymenyn: menyn *e.g.* butter.
bara menyn bread and
butter
ymerodraeth *e.b. ll.* **-au** empire
ymestyn (at) *be.* **(ymestynnaf)**
to stretch, to reach, to
extend
ymfudo *be.* **(ymfudaf)** to
emigrate
ymfudwr *e.g. ll.* **ymfudwyr**
emigrant
ymffrost *e.g.* boast
ymffrostio (yn) *be.*
(ymffrostiaf) to boast
ymffrostiwr *e.g. ll.*
ymffrostwyr boaster
ymffrostwyr *gw.* **ymffrostiwr**
ymgais *e.b.* effort, attempt

ymgeiswyr *gw.* **ymgeisydd**
ymgeisydd *e.g. ll.* **ymgeiswyr**
candidate, applicant.
ymgeisydd seneddol
parliamentary candidate
ymgeledd *e.g. ll.* **-au** care,
succour. **ymgeledd parod**
first aid
ymgom *e.b. ll.* **-ion**
conversation, chat. **ymgom â**
a conversation with
ymgomio (â) *be.* **(ymgomiaf)**
to chat, to converse
ymgorffori *be* **(ymgorfforaf)** to
incorporate
ymgrymu *be.* **(ymgrymaf)** to
stoop, to bow down
ymgynghori (â) *be.*
(ymgynghoraf) to consult, to
confer
ymgymryd (â) *be.*
(ymgymeraf) to undertake
ymgyrch *e.g.b. ll.* **-oedd**
campaign, expedition
ymhel (â) *be.* **(ymhəlaf)** to be
concerned; to meddle *(with)*
ymhell *ad.* far, afar
ymhellach *ad.* furthermore,
further
ymhlith *ardd.* among
ymholi *be.* **(ymholaf)** to
inquire
ymholiad *e.g. ll.* **-au** inquiry
ymlacio *be.* **(ymlaciaf)** to relax
ymladd (â) 1 *be.* **(ymladdaf)** to
fight (with). 2 *e.g. ll.* **-au**
fight, battle
ymladdwr *e.g. ll.* **ymladdwyr**
fighter
ymlaen *ad.* on, onward. **yn ôl**

ac ymlaen backward and forward

ymolch: ymolchi *be.* **(ymolchaf)** to wash oneself

ymosod (ar) *be.* **(ymosodaf)** to attack

ymosodiad *e.g. ll.* **-au** attack. **ymosodiadau awyr** air attacks

ymosodwr *e.g. ll.* **ymosodwyr** attacker

ymosodwyr *gw.* **ymosodwr**

ymostwng (i) *be.* **(ymostyngaf)** to stoop; to submit, to capitulate

ymryson (â) 1 *be.* **(ymrysonaf)** to contend; to strive, to compete. 2 *e.g. ll.* **-au** competition, rivalry; strife, contention. **Ymryson y Beirdd** poets' contest

ymuno (â) *be.* **(ymunaf)** to unite; to join

ymweld (â) *be.* **(ymwelaf)** to visit

ymweliad *e.g. ll.* **-au** visit, visitation

ymwelwr: ymwelydd *e.g. ll.* **ymwelwyr** visitor

ymwelwyr *gw.* **ymwelwr**

ymwelydd *gw.* **ymwelwr**

ymwneud (â) *be.* **(ymwnaf)** to deal (with), to be connected (with)

ymyl *e.g.b. ll.* **-on** edge, border, margin. **ymyl y ddalen** edge of the page; **yn ymyl** close by, near

ymyrraeth *e.b. ll.* **ymyrraethau** interference, intervention

ymyrru: ymyrryd (â) *be.* **(ymyrraf)** to interfere, to intervene, to meddle

ymysg *ardd.* among, amid

yn:'n:yng: ym 1 *ardd.* *(personal forms:* **yno, ynot, ynddo/ynddi, ynom, ynoch, ynddyn)** in, at, into; for; *the prepostion* **yn** *is followed by nasal mutation:* **yn** + Corwen **yng Nghorwen** in Corwen; **yn** + Pen-bre **ym Mhen-bre** in Pen-bre; **yn** + Treorci **yn Nhreorci** in Treorchy; **yn** + Gŵyr **yng Ngŵyr** in Gower; **yn** + Dinbych **yn Ninbych** in Denbigh; **yn** + Bangor **ym Mangor** in Bangor. *gw. At. Treiglad Trwynol.* 2 *geiryn.* (not translated). *An adjective or noun following the predicative particle* **yn** *takes soft mutation:* **Mae Twm yn ddoniol** Tom is amusing; **Ydy Alun yn ddyn da?** Is Alun a good man? *gw. At. Treiglad Meddal. No mutation occurs when* **yn** *is followed by a be.* (verb-noun): **Mae'r ci yn cyfarth** The dog is barking; **Mae'r gath yn cysgu** The cat is sleeping; **Mae Mair yn canu** Mair is singing; **Rydw i'n darllen** I am reading; **Maen nhw'n gwrando** They are listening

yna *ad.* there; then; thereupon; that

ynad *e.g. ll.* **-on** judge, justice, magistrate. **Ynad Heddwch (Y.H.)** Justice of the Peace (J.P.). **Llys yr Ynadon** the Magistrates' Court

ynau *gw.* **gŵn**

yn awr *ymadrodd ad.* now, at present. *gw.* **rwan**

ynn *gw.* **onnen**

ynnau *gw.* **gwn**

ynni *e.g.* energy, vigour

yno *ad.* there. *gw.* **yn**

yntau *rhag.* he, he also

ynte: ynteu *c.* or, or else, otherwise; then

ynys *e.b. ll.* **-oedd** island. **Ynys Bŷr** Caldey Island; **Ynys Enlli** Bardsey Island; **Ynys Wyth** Isle of Wight; **Ynysoedd Heledd** the Hebrides

ynysoedd *gw.* **ynys**

yr *gw.* **y**

yrfa *gw.* **gyrfa**

yrfeydd *gw.* **gyrfa**

yrru *gw.* **gyrru**

yrrwr *gw.* **gyrrwr**

yrwyr *gw.* **gyrrwr**

ysbardun *e.g. ll.* **-au** spur, accelerator *(in car)*

ysbïo *be.* **(ysbïaf)** to spy, to look

ysbïwr *e.g. ll.* **ysbïwyr** spy

ysbïwyr *gw.* **ysbïwr**

ysblander *e.g.* splendour, glory

ysbryd *e.g. ll* **-ion, -oedd** spirit, ghost. **Yr Ysbryd Glân** The Holy Spirit

ysbrydion *gw.* **ysbryd**

ysbrydoedd *gw.* **ysbryd**

ysbrydol *a.* spiritual; high-spirited.

ysbrydoli *be.* **(ysbrydolaf)** to inspire; to spiritualise

ysbwriel *e.g.* refuse, rubbish

ysbytai *gw.* **ysbyty**

ysbyty *e.g. ll.* **ysbytai** hospital, hospice

ysfa *e.b. ll.* **ysfeydd** itching; hankering; urge

ysfeydd *gw.* **ysfa**

ysgafn *a.* light *(weight)*

ysgafnhau: ysgafnu *be.* **(ysgafnhaf: ysgafnaf)** to lighten

ysgall *gw.* **ysgallen**

ysgallen *e.b. ll.* **ysgall** thistle

ysgariad *e.g. ll.* **-au** divorce

ysgol *e.b. ll.* **-ion** school; ladder. **ysgol annibynnol** independent school; **ysgol arbennig** special school; **ysgol breifat** private school; **ysgol breswyl** boarding school; **ysgol feithrin** nursery school; **ysgol gyfun** comprehensive school; **ysgol Gymraeg** Welsh medium school; **ysgol gynradd** primary school; **ysgol iau** junior school; **ysgol nos** night-school; **ysgol Sul** Sunday school; **ysgol uwchradd** secondary school

ysgolfeistr *e.g. ll.* **-i** schoolmaster

ysgolfeistres *e.b. ll.* **-au** schoolmistress

ysgolhaig *e.g. ll.*
 ysgolheigion scholar
ysgolheigion *gw.* **ysgolhaig**
ysgolor *e.g. ll.* **-ion** scholar
ysgoloriaeth *e.b. ll.* **-au**
 scholarship
ysgolorion *gw.* **ysgolor**
ysgrech *e.b. ll.* **-feydd**
 scream, shriek
ysgrechfeydd *gw.* **ysgrech**
ysgrif *e.b. ll.* **-au** article,
 essay
ysgrifennu (ar, at) *be.*
 (ysgrifennaf) to write
ysgrifennydd *e.g. ll.*
 ysgrifenyddion secretary
ysgrifenyddes *e.b. ll.* **-au**
 female secretary
ysgrifenyddion *gw.*
 ysgrifennydd
ysgrythur *e.b. ll.* **-au**
 scripture
ysgubo *be.* **(ysgubaf)** to
 sweep
ysgubor *e.b. ll.* **-iau** barn
ysgwyd *be.* **(ysgydwaf)** to
 shake, to sway, to wag
ysgwydd *e.b. ll.* **-au** shoulder
ysgyfaint *e.ll.* lungs
ysgyfarnog *e.b. ll.* **-od** hare.
 codi ysgyfarnog to raise a
 red herring *(fig. – irrelevant
 diversion)*
ysgytwad *e.g. ll* **-au** shock,
 shaking
ysmala *a.* funny, amusing;
 droll
ystadegau *e.ll.* statistics
ystafell *e.b. ll.* **-oedd** room.
 ystafell ddosbarth

classroom; **ystafell wely**
bedroom; **ystafell ymolchi**
bathroom
ystlum *e.g. ll.* **-od** bat
(animal)
ystlys *e.b. ll.* **-au** side, flank;
touchline
ystlyswr *e.g. ll.* **ystlyswyr**
linesman; sidesman
ystod *e.b. ll.* **-ion, -au** course,
space of time, span, range;
swath. **yn ystod** during;
ystod oed age range
ystrydeb *e.b. ll.* **-au** cliché;
stereotype
ystwyth *a.* flexible, supple,
agile, pliant
ystyr *e.g.b. ll.* **-on** sense,
meaning
ystyriaeth *e.b. ll.* **-au**
consideration, heed
ystyried *be.* **(ystyriaf)** to
consider, to heed
ystyriol *a.* heedful, mindful
ystyrlon *a.* meaningful
ysu *be.* **(ysaf)** to consume, to
crave, to itch. **yn ysu am
wybod** itching to know
yswiriannau *gw.* **yswiriant**
yswiriant *e.g. ll.* **yswiriannau**
insurance. **yswiriant cyfun**
comprehensive insurance;
yswiriant trydydd person
third-party insurance
yswirio: yswiro *be.* **(yswiriaf:
yswiraf)** to insure
yw *bf.* is, are. *gw.* **bod.** *gw.*
ywen
ywen *e.b. ll.* **yw** yew.

English–Welsh
dictionary

abbreviations

a.	adjective	*ansoddair*
ad.	adverb	*adferf*
c.	conjunction	*cysylltair*
def. art.	definite article	*y fannod*
e.g. (exempli gratia)	for example	*er enghraifft*
i.	interjection	*ebychiad*
int. pn.	interrogative pronoun	*rhagenw gofynnol*
n.	noun	*enw*
coll.	collective	*torfol*
f.	feminine	*benywaidd*
m.	masculine	*gwrywaidd*
n.pl.	noun plural	*enw lluosog*
N.W.	North Wales	*Gogledd Cymru*
pn.	pronoun	*rhagenw*
prp.	preposition	*arddodiad*
px.	prefix	*rhagddodiad*
rel. pn.	relative pronoun	*rhagenw perthynol*
S.W.	South Wales	*De Cymru*
v.	verb	*berf*

If the gender of the Welsh noun is not specified, that noun has the same gender as the noun(s) immediately following it in the definition.

A

abbreviation *n.* byrfodd, talfyriad *m.*
abdomen *n.* bol *m.*
ability *n.* gallu *m.*
able *a.* galluog, medrus. **to be able** gallu, medru
abode *n.* cartref, preswyl, preswylfod *m.*
abolish *v.* dileu
abort *v.* erthylu
abortion *n.* erthyliad *m.*
about *prp.* & *ad.* am, o gwmpas, oddeutu, tua, ogylch, ynghylch
above 1 *prp.* dros, i fyny, uwchben, uwchlaw. 2 *ad.* uchod
abrupt *a.* sydyn, cwta. **abrupt reply** ateb cwta
absent *a.* absennol
abstract *a.* haniaethol
abundance *n.* toreth *f.*
abundant *a.* helaeth, aml, toreithiog
accelerate *v.* cyflymu
accelerator *n.* cyflymydd, sbardun *m.*
accent *n.* acen *f.*
accept *v.* derbyn, cymryd
acceptable *a.* derbyniol
access *n.* mynedfa *f.* mynediad *m.*
accident *n.* damwain *f.*
accommodation *n.* llety, lle *m.*
accomplish *v.* cyflawni, gorffen
account *n.* cyfrif, cownt; adroddiad *m.*
accountant *n.* cyfrifydd *m.*
accusation *n.* cyhuddiad
accuse *v.* cyhuddo
accustom *v.* cyfarwyddo, arfer
ache 1 *n.* poen *mf,* dolur *m.* 2 *v.* poeni, brifo, gwynegu
acid 1 *n.* asid *m.* 2 *a.* sur
acknowledge *v.* cydnabod
acorn *n.* mesen *f.*
acquaintance *n.* cydnabod *m.*
acre *n.* erw, acer *f.*
across *prp.* draw, ar draws
act 1 *n.* act *(drama)*; deddf *(law)*; gweithred *f.* 2 *v.* actio *(drama)*; gweithredu
active *a.* bywiog, heini
actor *n.* actor, chwaraewr *m.*
add *v.* ychwanegu, chwanegu
address 1 *n.* cyfeiriad. *m.* 2 *n.* annerch
adequately *ad.* digonol
adhere *v.* glynu wrth
adjective *n.* ansoddair *m.*
adjudge *v.* dyfarnu
adjudicate *v.* beirniadu
adjudicator *n.* beirniad *m.*
admire *v.* edmygu
admit *v.* derbyn, cyfaddef
adolescence *n.* llencyndod *m.*
adult *n.* oedolyn *m.*
advantage *n.* mantais *f.* **to take advantage** manteisio
advantageous *a.* llesol, manteisiol
adventure *n.* antur *mf.*
adventurous *a.* anturus
advertise *v.* hysbysebu

advertisement *n.* hysbyseb *f.*
advertiser *n.* hysbysebwr *m.*
advice *n.* cyngor *m.*
advise *v.* cynghori
adviser *n.* ymgynghorwr *m.*
aeroplane *n.* awyren *f.*
afar *ad.* ymhell
affair *n.* carwriaeth; **mater, peth, busnes; helynt**
affectation *n.* maldod *m.*
affection *n.* cariad, serch *m.*
affectionate *a.* serchus, serchog, cariadus
after 1 *ad.* wedyn, yna. 2 *prp.* ar ôl, wedi
aftercare *n.* ôl-ofal *m.*
afternoon *n.* prynhawn *m.*
afterwards *ad.* wedyn, wedi hynny
again *ad.* eto, drachefn, eilwaith
against *prp.* erbyn, yn erbyn
age 1 *n.* oed, oedran *m;* oes *f.* 2 *v.* heneiddio
aged *a.* hen, oedrannus. **the aged** yr oedrannus, yr henoed
agency *n.* cyfrwng *m,* asiantaeth *f.*
agent *n.* asiant, cyfrwng *m.*
agile *a.* heini
agitated *a.* cynhyrfus
ago *ad.* yn ôl
agony *n.* ing, poen mawr *m.*
agree *v.* cytuno (â)
agreement *n.* cytundeb *m.*
agriculturalist *n.* ffarmwr, ffermwr, amaethwr *m.*
agriculture *n.* amaethyddiaeth *f.*
aid 1 *n.* cymorth, help *m.* 2 *v.* helpu. **First Aid** Cymorth Cyntaf.

ailment *n.* afiechyd, dolur *m.*
aim *n.* amcan, bwriad, diben, nod *m.*
air *n.* awyr; aer; alaw *f.* **fresh air** awyr iach
alarm *n.* braw, ofn; larwm *m.* **alarm-clock** cloc larwm
alien *n.* & *a.* estron *m.*
all 1 *n.* pawb; y cwbl, y cyfan *m.* 2 *a.* holl, i gyd, pob. 3 *ad.* yn hollol
allege *v.* honni
alleged *a.* honedig
alliance *n.* cynghrair *m.*
allotment *n.* rhandir *m.*
allow *v.* caniatáu, goddef, gadael (i)
allowance *n.* lŵans, lwfans *m.*
allure *v.* hudo
ally *n.* cynghreiriad *m.*
almighty *a.* hollalluog. **Almighty God** Hollalluog Dduw
almost *ad.* bron, braidd, lled
alone *a.* unig, ar ei ben ei hun, wrtho'i hun
along 1 *ad.* ymlaen; ar hyd. 2 *prp.* ar hyd. **all along** o'r cychwyn
alphabet *n.* yr wyddor, abiéc *f.*
already *ad.* eisoes, yn barod
also *ad.* & *c.* hefyd
alter *v.* newid
although *prp.* & *c.* serch, er
altitude *n.* uchder *m.*
altogether *ad.* yn gyfan gwbl, i gyd
always *ad.* bob amser, yn wastad
am, I *v.* rydw i, dw i
amazed *a.* syn

amazement *n.* syndod *m.*
amazing *a.* rhyfedd, rhyfeddol
ambassador *n.* llysgennad *m.*
ambition *n.* uchelgais *m.*
ambitious *a.* uchelgeisiol
ambulance *n.* ambiwlans *m.*
amend *v.* gwella, diwygio, cywiro
American 1 *n.* Americanwr *m,* Americanes *f.* **2** *a.* Americanaidd
amid *prp.* ymhlith, rhwng, ynghanol, ymysg
among *prp.* rhwng, ymhlith, ymysg
amount *n.* swm, cyfanswm, cyfrif *m.*
ample *a.* helaeth, digon, digonedd
amuse *v.* difyrru
amusing *a.* difyr, difyrrus, digrif, ysmala
analyse *v.* dadansoddi
ancestor *n.* hynafiad *m.*
ancient *a.* hynafol, hen iawn. **ancient monument** henebyn
and *c.* a, ac
anecdote *n.* hanesyn *m.*
angel *n.* angel *m.*
angle *n.* ongl *m.* **right angle** ongl sgwâr
Anglesey *n.* Môn *f.*
Anglicize *v.* Seisnigeiddio, Seisnigo
Anglo- *a.* Eingl-
Anglo-Welshman *n.* Eingl-Gymro *m.*
angry *a.* crac, dig
anguish *n.* ing *m.*
angular *a.* onglog
animal *n.* anifail *m.*
animate *a.* byw

ankle *n.* migwrn, pigwrn *m.*
announce *v.* cyhoeddi; datgan; hysbysu
announcement *n.* cyhoeddiad, hysbysiad *m.*
announcer *n.* cyhoeddwr *m.*
anoint *v.* iro
another *a.* & *pn.* arall, llall
answer *n.* & *v.* ateb *m.*
ant *n.* morgrugyn *m.*
antagonist *n.* gwrthwynebwr, gwrthwynebydd *m.*
anthology *n.* blodeugerdd *f,* detholiad *m.*
anti- *px.* gwrth-, yn erbyn
anticlockwise *a.* gwrthglocwedd
antiperspirant *n.* gwrthchwyswr
anxiety *n.* pryder *m.*
any *a.* unrhyw, rhyw, peth, dim. **I don't see her any longer/more** Ni fyddaf yn ei gweld mwyach
anyone *n.* & *pn.* rhywun, unrhyw un, neb *m.*
anywhere *ad.* unman, rhywle, unrhyw le
apart *ad.* ar wahân, o'r neilltu
ape *n.* epa *m.*
aperture *n.* agoriad, twll *m.*
apologize *v.* ymddiheuro
apology *n.* ymddiheuriad *m.*
apparatus *n.* offer *m.*
apparition *n.* drychiolaeth *f,* ysbryd *m.*
appear *v.* ymddangos
appearance *n.* ymddangosiad *m.*
appendix *n.* atodiad *m.*
apple *n.* afal *m.*
applicant *n.* ymgeisydd *m.*

appoint *v.* penodi; trefnu, nodi

appointed *a.* penodedig

appointment *n.* penodiad *m.*

appreciate *n.* gwerthfawrogi

appreciation *n.* gwerthfawrogiad *m.*

apprentice *n.* prentis *m.*

apprenticeship *n.* prentisiaeth *f.*

approach *v.* agosáu, nesáu

appropriate *a.* addas, priodol

approximate *a.* bras, agos

April *n.* Ebrill *m.*

archer *n.* saethwr *m.*

architect *n.* pensaer, cynlluniwr, cynllunydd *m.*

are *v.* mae, maen, maent, oes, sy, sydd, ydy, ydynt, ydyw, yw. *see* **bod**

argue *v.* dadlau

argument *n.* dadl *f.*

arithmetic *n.* rhifyddeg *f.*

ark *n.* arch *f.* **Noah's Ark** Arch Noa

arm *n.* braich *f;* arf *m.* **nuclear arms** arfau niwclear

armed *a.* arfog. **armed forces** lluoedd arfog

army *n.* byddin *f.*

around *ad.* & *prp.* am, o amgylch, o gwmpas, o gylch

arrange *v.* trefnu

arrive at *v.* cyrraedd

arrow *n.* saeth *f.*

art *n.* celf *f.* **art exhibition** arddangosfa gelf

article *n.* erthygl, ysgrif *f;* nwydd *m.* **definite article** y fannod (y, yr, 'r)

as *c.* & *ad.,* â, ag, fel, mor, cyn. **as if** fel pe bai, fel petai, fel petasai

ascent *n.* rhiw *f,* tyle *m.*

ash *n.* lludw *m;* onnen *f.*

ashes *n.* llwch, lludw *m.*

aside *ad.* o'r neilltu

ask *v.* gofyn, holi, gwahodd

askew *a.* ar gam, gŵyr

asleep *ad.* yn cysgu, yng nghwsg

ass *n.* asyn *m.*

assembly *n.* cymanfa *f.* cynulliad *m.*

assert *v.* honni, haeru

assertion *n.* honiad *m.*

assess *v.* asesu

assist *v.* helpu

assistance *n.* cymorth, help *m.*

assistant *n.* cynorthwywr, cynorthwy-ydd *m.*

association *n.* cymdeithas *f.*

assurance *n.* sicrwydd *m.*

assure *v.* sicrhau

asterisk *n.* seren *f.*

astonishing *a.* rhyfedd, rhyfeddol, syn

astronaut *n.* gofodwr *m,* gofodwraig *f.*

at *prp.* am, ar, ger, wrth, yn, yng, ym

atonement *n.* iawn *m.*

atrocious *a.* erchyll

attack 1 *n.* ymosodiad *m.* **2** *v.* ymosod (ar)

attacker *n.* ymosodwr *m.*

attain *v.* ennill, cyrraedd

attempt 1 *n.* cais, cynnig *m;* ymgais *f.* **2** *v.* ceisio, cynnig.

attend *v.* mynychu

attendance *n.* presenoldeb *m.*

attention *n.* sylw *m.*

attitude *n.* agwedd *m.*

attract *v.* denu, tynnu
attractive *a.* deniadol, atyniadol
augment *v.* ychwanegu at, chwanegu at
August *n.* Awst *m.*
aunt *n.* modryb *f.*
author *n.* awdur, llenor *m.*
authoress *n.* awdures, llenores, *f.*
authority *n.* awdurdod *m:*
Education Authority Awdurdod Addysg
autobiography *n.* hunangofiant *m.*
autumn *n.* hydref *m.*
autumnal *a.* hydrefol
avenge *v.* dial (ar)
avoid *v.* osgoi
awake 1 *v.* deffro, dihuno, 2 *a.* effro
away *ad.* ymaith, i ffwrdd
awful *a.* ofnadwy
awkward *a.* lletchwith; chwithig

B

baby *n.* baban, babi *m.*
baby-sit *v.* gwarchod.
babysitter *n.* gwarchodwr babanod *m.*
bachelor *n.* dyn dibriod, hen lanc *m.*
back 1 *n.* cefn; cefnwr *m.* 2 *ad.* yn ôl
background *n.* cefndir *m.*
bacon *n.* cig moch, bacwn *m.*
bad *a.* drwg, drygionus; sâl, gwael
badge *n.* bathodyn *m.*

bag *n.* bag, cwd, cwdyn *m.*
bail *n.* mechnïaeth *f.*
bake *v.* crasu, pobi
baked *a.* cras, pob
bakehouse *n.* popty *m.*
baker *n.* pobydd *m.*
bald *a.* moel, penfoel. **bald-headed** penfoel
baldness *n.* moelni *m.*
ball *n.* dawns; pêl *f.* **football** pêl droed; **rugby ball** pêl rygbi
ballad *n.* balad *f.* **ballad-monger** baledwr
ballot *n.* balot *m.*
banana *n.* banana *m.*
band *n.* band *m.;* seindorf *f.* **brass band** band pres
bangle *n.* breichled *f.*
bank 1 *n.* glan *f.;* clawdd; banc *m.* 2 *v.* bancio. **bank statement** adroddiad banc
banner *n.* baner *f.*
banquet 1 *n.* gwledd *f.* 2 *v.* gwledda
Baptist *n.* Bedyddiwr *m.*
baptize *v.* bedyddio
bar 1 *n.* bar *m.* 2 *v.* atal
barbecue *n.* barbeciw *m.*
bard *n.* bardd *m.*
bare *a.* noeth, llwm, moel, prin
barefooted *a.* troednoeth
barely *ad.* prin
bareness *n.* moelni *m.*
bark 1 *n.* cyfarthiad; rhisgl *m.* 2 *v.* cyfarth
barley *n.* haidd, barlys *m.coll.*
barn *n.* ysgubor *f.*
barrel *n.* casgen *f*, baril *mf.*
barrow *n.* berfa, whilber *f.*
base 1 *n.* bôn, gwaelod; sail,

sylfaen; canolfan *m*. 2 *a*. isel.
3 *v*. seilio

bashful *a*. swil

basic *a*. sylfaenol

basin *n*. basn *m*.

basket *n*. basged *f*.

Basque Country *n*. Gwlad y
Basg *f*.

bass *n*. bas, baswr *m*.

baste *v*. iro

bat 1 *n*. ystlum; bat *m*. 2 *v*.
batio

bath *n*. bath, baddon *m*.

bathe *v*. ymolch, ymolchi,
golchi

bathroom *n*. ystafell ymolchi *f*.

battle 1 *n*. ymladdfa *m*,
brwydr *f*. 2 *v*. ymladd *m*.

bay *n*. bae *m*. **Swansea Bay**
Bae Abertawe

be *v*. bod

beach *n*. traeth *m*, glan y
môr *f*.

beam *n*. pelydr: trawst *m*.

bean *n*. ffäen, ffeuen *f*.

bear 1 *n*. arth *m*, arthes *f*.
2 *v*. cario; geni; goddef.
  polar bear arth gwyn

beard *n*. barf *f*.

beat *v*. taro; gorchfygu

beautiful *a*. hardd, glân, teg,
prydferth

beauty *n*. harddwch,
prydferthwch, tegwch *m*.

because *prp*. er, oherwydd, o
achos, gan, am, oblegid

become *v*. dyfod, dod yn

bed *n*. gwely *m*.

bedding *n*. dillad gwely *m*.

bedroom *n*. ystafell wely,
llofft *f*.

bedsitter *n*. ystafell un gwely *f*.

bee *n*. gwenynen *f*.

beech *n*. ffawydden *f*.

been, I have *v*. bues i, fues i,
bûm, *see* bod

beer *n*. cwrw *m*.

beeswax *n*. cwyr *m*.

beetle *n* chwilen *f*.

before 1 *prp*. cyn, gerbron, o
flaen, rhag. 2 *ad*. o'r blaen.

before long cyn bo hir

beforehand *ad*. ymlaen llaw

beg *v*. erfyn (ar)

begin *v*. cychwyn, dechrau

beginning *n*. dechreuad *m*.

behave *v*. ymddwyn

behaviour *n*. ymddygiad *m*.

behind 1 *prp*. tu ôl (i), tu cefn
(i), 2 *ad*. ar ôl

behold 1 *i*. wele! 2 *v*. gweld,
edrych

being *n*. bod *m*.

Belgium *n*. Gwlad Belg *f*.

believe *v*. credu (yn)

bell *n*. cloch *f*.

bellow *v*. rhuo

belly *n*. bol, bola *m*.

belong *v*. perthyn (i)

beloved 1 *n*. anwylyd *mf*. 2 *a*.
annwyl, anwylaf, cariadus,
cu, hoff. **beloved ones**
anwyliaid

below *prp*. islaw, dan

bend 1 *n*. tro *m*. 2 *v*. plygu

beneath *prp*. islaw, dan.

beneficial *a*. llesol

benefit 1 *n*. elw, lles *m*. 2 *v*.
elwa

berry *n*. aeronen, mwyaren *f*.

berserk *a*. gwyllt.

beside *prp*. ger, gerllaw,
wrth, heibio, yn ymyl

besides *prp*. heb, heblaw

best *a.* gorau

bestow *v.* rhoddi, rhoi, cyflwyno

betrothal *n.* dyweddïad *m.*

better 1 *a.* gwell. 2 *ad.* yn well

between *prp.* rhwng

beverage *n.* diod *f.*

bewitch *v.* swyno

beyond *prp.* draw, dros, tu hwnt

Bible *n.* Beibl *m.*

bicker *v.* cweryla, ffraeo

bicycle *n.* beic *m.*

bid *n* & *v.* cynnig *m.*

bide *v.* aros, disgwyl

big *a.* mawr. **bigger** mwy; **biggest** mwyaf

bilingual *a.* dwyieithog. **bilingual education** addysg ddwyieithog

bilingualism *n.* dwyieithrwydd *m.*

bill *n.* bil; mesur *m;* rhaglen *f.*

bin *n.* bin *m.* **rubbish bin** bin ysbwriel

bind *v.* rhwymo, clymu

biological *a.* biolegol

biology *n.* bioleg, bywydeg *f.*

birch *n.* bedwen, bedw *f.*

bird *n.* aderyn *m.*

birthday *n.* pen-blwydd *m.* **birthday card** cerdyn pen-blwydd

biscuit *n.* bisged, bisgïen *f.*

bishop *n.* esgob *m.*

bit *n.* tamaid, darn, tipyn, yfflyn *m.*

bite 1 *n.* tamaid *m.* 2 *v.* cnoi

bitter *a.* chwerw, sur

bizarre *a.* od, rhyfedd, chwithig

black 1 *n.* du; dyn du *m.* 2 *a.* du, tywyll. 3 *v.* duo

blackberry *n.* mwyaren *f.*

blackbird *n.* aderyn du *m.*

blackboard *n.* bwrdd du *m.*

blacken *v.* duo

blacksmith *n.* gof *m.*

Blackwood *n.* Y Coed-duon *f.*

blade *n.* eginyn; llafn *m.*

blame 1 *n.* bai *m.* 2 *v.* beio

blameless *a.* di-fai

blanch *v.* gwynnu

blank *a.* gwag; syn. **blank cheque** siec wag

blanket *n.* blanced, planced *f.*

blaze *n.* fflam *f.*

bleach 1 *n.* cannydd *m.* 2 *v.* cannu, gwynnu

bleed *v.* gwaedu

blemish *n.* nam; bai *m.*

blend *v.* cymysgu

blessed *a.* bendigedig

blessedness *n.* gwynfyd *m.*

blessing *n.* bendith *f.*

blind 1 *a.* dall, tywyll. 2 *n.* person dall *m.* 3 *v.* dallu

bliss *n.* gwynfyd *f.*

blizzard *n.* storm o wynt ac eira *f.*

blood *n.* gwaed *m.* **blood pressure** pwysedd gwaed

bloom *n.* blodyn *m.*

blossom *n.* blodyn *m.*

blouse *n.* blows, blowsen *f.*

blow 1 *n.* ergyd *mf.* 2 *v.* chwythu

blow-dry *v.* chwythu'n sych

blue *n.* & *a.* glas *m.*

blush *v.* gwrido, cochi

blushing *a.* gwridog

blustery *a.* stormus

board *n.* bwrdd *m,* bord *f;*
bwyd *m.*

boarding house *n.* llety *m.*

boast 1 *n.* ymffrost *m.* 2 *v.*
ymffrostio

boaster *n.* ymffrostiwr *m.*

boat *n.* bad, cwch *m.*

bodily *a.* corfforol

body *n.* corff *m.*

boil *v.* berwi

boiling *n.* & *a.* berw *m.*

bold *a.* hyf

boldness *n.* hyfdra *m.*

bolster *n.* clustog hir *f,*
gobennydd mawr *m.*

bolt 1 *n.* bollt *m.* 2 *v.*
bolltio

bomb 1 *n.* bom *m.* 2 *v.*
bomio

bone *n.* asgwrn *m.*

book *n.* llyfr *m;* cyfrol *f.*

booklet *n.* llyfryn *m.*

boot *n.* esgid *f.*

booth *n.* caban *m.* stondin *f.*

border *n.* ffin *f,* ymyl *mf.*
border *m.*

bordering *a.* ffiniol

bore 1 *n.* twll; dyn diflas *m.*
2 *v.* tyllu; blino

boring *a.* diflas

born *a.* wedi ei eni; ganed

borough *n.* bwrdeistref *f.*
Borough Council Cyngor
Bwrdeistref

borrow *v.* benthyca, cael
benthyg

boss *n.* meistr, pennaeth, bos
m.

botanical *a.* llysieuol

both *a.* & *ad.* & *pn.* y ddau,
y ddwy. **they both** ill dau, ill
dwy

bother 1 *n.* helynt *f,* trafferth
m. 2 *v.* trafferthu

bottle *n.* potel *f.*

bottleneck *m.* tagfa *f.*

bottom *n.* gwaelod: godre *m.*

boulder *n.* carreg fawr *f.*

bound 1 *n.* llam; terfyn *m,*
ffin *f.* 2 *v.* llamu, neidio;
ffinio

boundary *n.* ffin *f,* terfyn *m.*

bow 1 *n.* bwa; clwm *m.* 2 *v.*
plygu, ymgrymu

bowl 1 *n.* bowlen, powlen *f.*
2 *v.* bowlio

box *n.* blwch, bocs; pren bocs
m. **box office** swyddfa
docynnau

boy *n.* bachgen, hogyn, mab;
gwas *m.*

boyish *a.* bachgennaidd

brace *n.* bres; pâr *m.*

braces *n.* bresys *m.*

bracelet *n.* breichled *f.*

brain *n.* ymennydd *m.*

branch *n.* cangen *f.*

brandy *n.* brandi *m.*

brass *n.* pres *m.*

brave *a.* dewr, gwrol

bread *n.* bara *m.* **daily bread**
bara beunyddiol

breadth *n.* lled *m.*

break 1 *n.* egwyl, hoe *f,*
toriad *m.* 2 *v.* torri

breaker *n.* ton *f.*

breakfast *n.* brecwast *m.*

breast *n.* bron; brest *f.*

breath *n.* anadl *mf,* gwynt *m.*

breathe *v.* anadlu, chwythu

breed *v.* magu, bridio

breeze *n.* awel *f.*

brewery *n.* bragdy *m.*

bride *n.* priodferch *f.*

bridge 1 *n.* pont *f.* 2 *v.* pontio
brief *a.* byr, cryno
bright *a.* disglair, gloyw,
llachar, llewyrchus
brightness *n.* llewyrch,
disgleirdeb *m.*
brilliant 1 *n.* gem *f.* 2 *a.*
disglair, llachar; gwych
bring *v.* dwyn, dod (â)
brink *n.* ymyl *mf,* min *m.*
Britain *n.* Prydain *f.*
British *a.* Prydeinig
Brittany *a.* Llydaw *f.*
broad *a.* llydan, eang, bras
broadcast 1 *n.* darllediad *m.*
2 *v.* darlledu
brochure *n.* llyfryn *m.*
bronze *n.* pres, efydd *m.*
brooch *n.* tlws *m.*
brook *n.* nant *f.*
broom *n.* brws, brwsh *m,*
ysgub *f.*
broth *n.* cawl *m.*
brother *n.* brawd *m.* **brother-
in-law** brawd-yng-nghyfraith
brow *n.* ael *f,* talcen *m;* crib
mf.
brown *a.* brown
brush 1 *n.* brws, brwsh *m,*
ysgub *f.* 2 *v.* brwsio,
brwshio, sgubo, ysgubo.
paint brush brws paent,
brwsh paent
bucket *n.* bwced *m.*
bud 1 *n.* blaguryn *m.* 2 *v.*
blaguro.
bug *n.* byg *m.*
build *v.* adeiladu, codi
builder *n.* adeiladwr *m.*
building *n.* adeilad *m.*
bull *n.* tarw *m.* **bulldozer**
tarw dur

bungalow *n.* tŷ unllawr,
byngalo *m.*
burden 1 *n.* baich, llwyth *m.*
2 *v.* llwytho
burdened *a.* llwythog
bureau *n.* swyddfa *f.*
burglar *n.* lleidr tŷ *m.*
burn 1 *n.* llosg *m;* nant *f.* 2 *a.*
llosg. 3 *v.* llosgi
burner *n.* llosgydd *m.*
burrow 1 *n.* twll cwningen *m.*
2 *v.* tyllu
bus *n.* bws *m.* **bus-stop**
arhosfan *f.* bysus.
bush *n.* llwyn *m,* perth *f.*
business *n.* busnes *m.*
busy *a.* prysur
but *c.* ond, onid
butcher *n.* cigydd
butter *n.* menyn, ymenyn *m.*
butterfly *n.* glöyn byw *m,* iâr
fach yr haf, pili-pala *f.*
button 1 *n.* botwm *m.* 2 *v.*
botymu
buy *v.* prynu
buyer *n.* prynwr *m.*
buzz 1 si, su, sŵn gwenyn *n.*
2 *v.* sio, suo
by *prp.* erbyn, ger, gerllaw,
drwy, trwy, gan, heibio,
wrth, â
by-election *n.* is-etholiad *m.*
bypass *n.* ffordd osgoi *f.*

C

cabbage *n.* bresychen;
bresych *f.*
cabin *n.* caban *m .*
café *n.* caffe *m.*
cake *n.* cacen, teisen *f.*

birthday cake teisen pen-
blwydd
calamity *n.* trychineb *mf.*
calculate *v.* cyfrif, rhifo
calculation *n.* cyfrif *m.*
calculator *n.* cyfrifiannell *m.*
calendar *n.* calendar *m.*
calf *n.* llo (anifail) *m;* croth
(coes) *f.*
call 1 *n.* galwad *mf,* galw *m.*
2 *v.* galw, ymweld (â)
calling *n.* galwad *mf;*
galwedigaeth *f.*
calm 1 *n.* tawelwch; hedd *m.*
2 *a.* tawel; 3 *v.* tawelu,
distewi
camera *n.* camera *m.*
camp 1 *n.* gwersyll *m.* 2 *v.*
gwersyllu
campaign *n.* ymgyrch *mf.*
can *n.* can, tun *m.*
candidate *n.* ymgeisydd *m.*
candle *n.* cannwyll *f.*
candlestick *n.* canhwyllbren
m.
cane *n.* gwialen *f.*
canoe 1 *n.* canŵ *m.* 2 *v.*
canŵio
cap *n.* cap *m.*
capital 1 *n.* prifddinas *f;* corff
(arian), cyfalaf *m;*
priflythyren *f.* 2 *a.* prif, pen
capitulate *v.* ymostwng, ildio
captain *n.* capten *m.*
captivate *v.* swyno, hudo,
denu
capture *v.* dal, dala
car *n.* car *m.* **car park** maes
parcio
caravan *n.* carafan *f.* **caravan
site** maes carafanau *m.*
card *n.* cerdyn *m,* carden *f.*

Cardiff *n.* Caerdydd *f.*
care 1 *n.* gofal, pryder *m.*
2 *v.* gofalu, carco, hidio,
pryderu
career 1 *n.* gyrfa *f.* 2 *v.*
rhuthro
careful *a.* carcus, gofalus,
manwl
careless *a.* diofal, esgeulus
caretaker *n.* gofalwr *m.*
caring *a.* gofalus
Carmarthen *n.* Caerfyrddin *f.*
carol *n.* carol *f.*
carpenter *n.* saer coed *m.*
carpet 1 *n.* carped *m.* 2 *v.*
carpedu
carrot *n.* moronen *f.*
carry *v.* cario
carve *v.* cerfio
case *n.* cas; achos; cyflwr *m;*
dadl *f.*
cash 1 *n.* arian parod *m.* 2 *v.*
newid
casing *n.* plisgyn; casin *m.*
cast *v.* taflu
castle *n.* castell *m.*
cat *n.* cath *f.*
catalogue *n.* catalog *m.*
cataract *n.* rhaeadr *f,* sgwd *m;*
pilen *(ar lygad) f.*
catch *v.* dal, dala
catchment *n.* dalgylch;
catchment area dalgylch
catechism *n.* holwyddoreg *f.*
caterpillar *n.* lindysen *m.*
cathedral *n.* eglwys gadeiriol
f.
catholic 1 *n.* pabydd *m.*
2 *a.* pabyddol; catholig
cattle *n.pl.* gwartheg, da
cauliflower *n.* blodfresychen *f.*
cause 1 *n.* achos; achlysur;

rheswm *m.* 2 *v.* achosi, peri

caution 1 *n.* pwyll; rhybudd *m.* 2 *v.* rhybuddio

cautious *a.* gofalus, gwyliadwrus

cave *n.* ogof *f.*

cavity *n.* gwagle *m.*

cease *v.* peidio (â)

ceaseless *a.* di-baid

ceiling *n.* nen *f.*

celebrate *v.* dathlu

celebrated *a.* enwog

celebration *n.* dathliad *m.*

cell *n.* cell *f.*

Celtic *a.* Celtaidd

cemetery *n.* mynwent *f.*

censure 1 *n.* cerydd *m,* sen *f.* 2 *v.* ceryddu.

centenary *n.* canmlwyddiant *m.*

centigrade *a.* canradd, sentigred. **20°C** ugain gradd Celsius

central *a.* canol, canolog. **central heating** gwres canolog

centre *n.* canol *m;* canolfan *f;* canolwr *m.* **shopping centre** canolfan siopa; **job centre** canolfan gwaith.

centurion *n.* canwriad *m.*

century *n.* cant *m;* canrif *f.*

ceremony *n.* seremoni *f.*

certain *a.* sicr, siŵr; rhyw, rhai

certainly *ad.* yn sicr, yn siŵr

certainty *n.* sicrwydd *m.*

certificate *n.* tystysgrif *f.*

chaff *n.* us *m.coll.*

chaffinch *n.* ji-binc, asgell fraith *f.*

chain 1 *n.* cadwyn *f.* 2 *v.* cadwyno

chair 1 *n.* cadair, stôl *f.* 2 *v.* cadeirio, llywyddu. **Chairing of the Bard** Cadeirio'r Bardd

chaired *a.* cadeiriol

chairman *n.* cadeirydd *m.*

chalet *n.* hafoty, bwthyn (haf) *m.*

chalk 1 *n.* sialc *m.* 2 *v.* sialcio

challenge 1 *n.* her *f.* 2 *v.* herio

chamber *n.* ystafell, siambr *f.* **chamber orchestra** cerddorfa siambr

champion *n.* pencampwr *m.*

chance 1 *n.* hap, siawns, lwc *f,* cyfle *m,* damwain *f.* 2 *v.* digwydd

change *n.* & *v.* newid *m.*

changing-room *n.* ystafell newid *f.*

channel *n.* sianel *f.* gwely *m.*

chapel *n.* capel *m.*

chapter *n.* pennod *f.*

character *n.* cymeriad, nod *m;* llythyren *f.*

characteristic 1 *n.* nodwedd *f.* 2 *a.* nodweddiadol

charge 1 *n.* gofal; gorchymyn; pris, tâl; ergyd *m.* 2 *v.* gofalu, gorchymyn; codi

charm 1 *n.* hud, swyn *m.* 2 *v.* hudo, swyno

charming *a.* swynol

chase 1 *n.* helfa *f.* 2 *v.* hel, hela, erlid

chat 1 *n.* sgwrs *f,* siarad, sôn *m,* ymgom *mf.* 2 *v.* sgwrsio, siarad, ymgomio

chatter *v.* clebran

cheap *a.* rhad

cheat 1 *n.* twyllwr *m.* **2** *v.* twyllo

cheek *n.* grudd *mf*, boch *f*, haerllugrwydd *m.*

cheerful *a.* llawen, llon, siriol

cheese *n.* caws *m.*

cheers! *i.* iechyd da!

chemist *n.* fferyllydd; cemegwr *m.*

chemistry *n.* cemeg *f.*

Chepstow *n.* Cas-Gwent *f.*

cheque *n.* siec *f.* **cheque book** llyfr sieciau; **cheque card** cerdyn sieciau

cherry *n.* ceiriosen *f.*

chest *n.* cist; brest *f*;

Chester *n.* Caer *f.*

chew *v.* cnoi

chick *n.* cyw *m.*

chicken *n.* cyw iâr *m.* ffowlyn *f.* **chickenpox** brech yr ieir

chief 1 *n.* pen, pennaeth *m.* **2** *a.* prif, pen, pennaf. **chief bard** prifardd

child *n.* plentyn *m.*

childish *a.* plentynnaidd

chill 1 *a.* oer. **2** *v.* oeri

chilled *a.* sythlyd, wedi ei oeri

chilly *a.* oer, oerllyd

chimney *n.* simdde, simnai *f.*, corn (mwg) *m.*

chin *n.* gên *f.*

China *n.* Tseina, China *f.*

china *n.* llestri te *m.*

chip *n.* sglodyn *m.* **fish and chips** pysgod a sglodion

chocolate *n.* siocled *m.*

choice *n.* dewis *m.*

choir *n.* côr *m.*

choke *v.* tagu

choose *v.* dewis, ethol

chop *v.* torri

chord *n.* tant, cord *m.*

chorus *n.* cytgan *f*; côr, corws *m.*

Christ *n.* Crist *m.*

christen *v.* bedyddio, enwi.

Christian 1 *n.* Cristion *m.* **2** *a.* Cristnogol. **Christian Aid** Cymorth Cristnogol; **Christian name** enw bedydd

Christmas *n.* y Nadolig *m.* **Christmas Day** Dydd Nadolig; **Christmas Eve** Noswyl Nadolig; **Christmas Holidays** gwyliau'r Nadolig; **Christmas presents** anrhegion Nadolig; **Christmas tree** coeden Nadolig

chum *n.* cyfaill, ffrind *m.*

church *n.* eglwys, llan *f.*

churchyard *n.* mynwent *f.*

chute *n.* llithren *f.*

cigar *n.* sigâr *f.*

cigarette *n.* sigarét *f.*

cinema *n.* sinema *f.*

circle *n.* cylch *m.*

circular 1 *n.* cylchlythyr *m.* **2** *a.* cylchog.

circumflex *n.* hirnod *mf.*

circus *n.* syrcas *f.*

citizen *n.* dinesydd *m.*

city *n.* dinas *f.*

civic *a.* dinesig

civil *a.* gwladol; cwrtais

civilian *n.* dinesydd *m.*

civil war *n.* rhyfel cartref *mf.*

claim 1 *n.* hawl *m.* **2** *v.* hawlio

clamber *v.* dringo

clash *v.* gwrthdaro

class 1 *n.* dosbarth *m;* adran *f,* cylch *m,* safon *f.* 2 *v.* dosbarthu

classic *n.* clasur, campwaith *m.*

classical *a.* clasurol

classics *n.* clasuron *m.pl.*

clause *n.* cymal *m.* adnod, adran *f.*

clay *n.* clai *m.*

clean 1 *a.* glân. 2 *v.* glanhau

cleanliness *n.* glendid *m.*

cleanly *ad.* yn lân

clear 1 *a.* amlwg, clir, eglur, gloyw. 2 *v.* clirio

clef *n.* allwedd *f,* cleff *m.*

clerk *n.* clerc *m.*

clever *a.* medrus, clyfar

cliché *n.* ystrydeb *f.*

cliff *n.* clogwyn *m,* craig *f.*

climate *n.* hinsawdd *f.*

climax *n.* uchafbwynt *m.*

climb *v.* dringo

climber *n.* dringwr *m.*

cling *v.* glynu, cydio

clinic *n.* meddygfa *f,* clinig *m.*

cloak *n.* clogyn *m,* mantell *f.*

clock *n.* cloc *m.* **o'clock** o'r gloch; **six o'clock** chwech o'r gloch; **alarm clock** cloc larwm

clockwise *a.* clocwedd

close 1 *n.* diwedd, terfyn *m.* 2 *v.* cau

close 1 *n.* clos, buarth *m,* iard *f.* 2 *a.* agos, clòs, tyn

cloth *n.* brethyn, defnydd, lliain, clwtyn *m.*

clothes *n.pl.* dillad *m.pl.,* gwisgoedd *f.pl.*

clothing *n.* dillad *m.*

cloud 1 *n.* cwmwl *m.* 2 *v.* cymylu

cloudy *a.* cymylog

clown *n.* clown *m.*

clumsy *a.* lletchwith

coach 1 *n.* hyfforddwr *m;* coets *f.* 2 *v.* hyfforddi

coal *n.* glo *m.*

coalfield *n.* maes glo *m.*

coarse *a.* garw, bras

coast *n.* arfordir *m,* glan môr *f.*

coat *n.* cot, siaced *f.*

cobweb *n.* gwe. *f.*

cockerel *n.* ceiliog *m.*

coffee *n.* coffi *m.*

coffin *n.* arch, coffin *f.*

cog *n.* dant, còg *m.*

coil 1 *n.* torch *m.* 2 *v.* torchi

coin 1 *n.* darn arian *m.* 2 *v.* bathu; **pound coin** darn punt

cold 1 *n.* oerfel; annwyd *m.* 2 *a.* oer, sythlyd. **to become cold** oeri; **to catch a cold** dal annwyd

collar *n.* coler *f.* **collar bone** pont yr ysgwydd

collect 1 *n.* colect *m* *(gweddi).* 2 *v.* casglu, crynhoi, hel

collection *n.* casgliad *m.*

college *n.* coleg *m.*

collide *n.* gwrthdaro

collier *n.* glöwr *m;* llong lo *f.*

colliery *n.* glofa *f,* pwll glo, gwaith glo *m.*

colloquial *a.* llafar

colony *n.* gwladfa *f.*

colour 1 *n.* lliw *m.* 2 *v.* lliwio, lliwo, coluro

coloured *a.* lliwiog

colourful *a.* lliwgar

colt *n* . ebol *m.*

column *n.* colofn *f,* piler *m.*

columnist *n.* newyddiadurwr *m.*

comb 1 *n.* crib *mf.* **2** *v.* cribo

combat *n.* gornest, brwydr *f.*

come *v.* dod, dyfod. **to come across** dod ar draws; **to come to an end** dod i ben

comely *a.* teg, glân, hardd

comfort 1 *n.* cysur *m.* **2** *v.* cysuro

comfortable *a.* cyfforddus, cyffyrddus, cysurus

command *n.* & *v.* gorchymyn *m.* **commandment** *n.* gorchymyn *m:* **The Ten Commandments** Y Deg Gorchymyn

commence *v.* dechrau

commend *v.* canmol

comment 1 *n.* sylw *m.* **2** *v.* sylwi, esbonio

commentary *n.* sylwebaeth *f;* esboniad *m.* **to commentate** sylwebu

commentator *n.* sylwebydd, sylwebwr *m.*

committee *n.* pwyllgor *m.*

common *a.* cyffredin. **common sense** synnwyr cyffredin

commons *n.* y cyffredin *m.pl.* **House of Commons** Tŷ'r Cyffredin

commotion *n.* terfysg *m.*

communion *n.* cymun, cymundeb *m.*

community *n.* cymdeithas, cymuned *f.*

compact *a.* cryno. **compact disc** cryno ddisg

companion *n.* cyfaill *m*, cyfeilles *f.*

company *n.* cwmni *m.*

compare *v.* cymharu (â)

compassion *n.* trugaredd *f.*

compel *v.* gorfodi

compensate *v.* talu iawn

compensation *n.* iawn, iawndal *m.*

compete *v.* cystadlu

competition *n.* cystadleuaeth *f*, ymryson *m.*

competitor *n.* cystadleuwr, cystadleuydd *m.*

complain *v.* cwyno

complaint *n.* cwyn *mf.*

complete *a.* hollol, llwyr

completely *ad.* yn hollol, yn llwyr

complex *a.* cymhleth

complexity *m.* cymhlethdod *m.*

complicate *v.* cymhlethu

complicated *a.* cymhleth

complication *n.* cymhlethdod *m.*

compose *v.* cyfansoddi

composer *n.* cyfansoddwr *m.*

comprehensive *a.* cyfun, cynhwysfawr. **Comprehensive School** Ysgol Gyfun

compulsion *n.* gorfod *m*, gorfodaeth *f.*

compulsory *a.* gorfodol

computer *n.* cyfrifiadur *m.*

conceal *v.* cuddio

concentrate *v.* canolbwyntio

concerning *prp.* ynglŷn â, ynghylch

concert *n.* cyngerdd *mf.*

concession *n.* lŵans, lwfans *m.*

conclude *v.* gorffen

conclusion *n.* casgliad;
diwedd, diweddglo *m.*

concrete *n.* concrit *m.*

condition *n.* cyflwr *m;* amod
mf.

conduct 1 *n.* ymddygiad *m.*
2 *v.* arwain

conductor *n.* arweinydd;
tocynnwr *m.*

cone *n.* côn *m.*

confer *v.* ymgynghori

conference *n.* cynhadledd *f.*

confide *v.* ymddiried (yn)

confidence *n.* hyder *m,*
ymddiriedaeth *f.* **self-
confidence** hunanhyder

confident *a.* hyderus: **to be
confident** hyderu

confidential *a.* cyfrinachol

confine *v.* cyfyngu, carcharu

confined *a.* cyfyng

confluence *n.* cymer *m.*

confront *v.* wynebu

confuse *v.* drysu, cymysgu

congratulate *v.* llongyfarch

congratulation *n.*
llongyfarchiad *m.*
Congratulations!
Llongyfarchiadau!

congregation *n.* cynulleidfa *f.*

Congregationalist *n.*
Annibynnwr *m.*

conjecture *v.* dychmygu,
dyfalu

conjunction *n.* cysylltair *m.*

connection *n.* cysylltiad *m,*
perthynas *mf.* **in connection
with** ynglŷn â

conquer *v.* gorchfygu, trechu

conquest *n.* buddugoliaeth,
concwest *f.*

conscientious *a.* cydwybodol

conscription *n.* gorfodaeth
filwrol *f.*

consent 1 *n.* caniatâd *m.* 2 *v.*
caniatáu

conservative 1 *n.* ceidwadwr;
Tori *m.* 2 *a.* cadwrol,
ceidwadol.

conservatory *n.* tŷ gwydr *m.*

conserve *v.* cadw, amddiffyn

consider *v.* ystyried

considerable *a.* cryn

consideration *n.* ystyriaeth *f.*

considering *prp.* ag ystyried

consolation *n.* cysur *m.*
consolation prize gwobr
gysur

console *v.* cysuro

consonant *n.* cytsain *f.*

constituency *n.* etholaeth *f.*

construct *v.* ffurfio, llunio,
adeiladu

consult *v.* ymgynghori (â)

consume *v.* bwyta;
defnyddio; treulio

contact *v.* cyffwrdd (â)

contain *v.* cynnwys, dal

contaminate *v.* llygru

contamination *n.* llygredd *m.*

content *n.* cynnwys *m.*

content 1 *a.* bodlon. 2 *v.*
bodloni

contention *n.* ymryson *m.*

contents *n.* cynnwys *m.pl.*

contest 1 *n.* gornest, ornest,
cystadleuaeth, ymryson *f.*
2 *v.* ymryson; ymladd

contestant *n.* cystadleuwr,
cystadleuydd *m.*

context *n.* cyd-destun *m.*

continual *a.* parhaus

continually *ad.* byth a hefyd

continuation *n.* parhad *m.*

continue v. para, parhau, dal (ati)

continuous a. parhaol

contra- px. gwrth-, croes- (*followed by soft mutation*).

contradiction n. gwrthddywediad m.

contract n. cytundeb m.

contrary a. gwrthwyneb, croes. **on the contrary** i'r gwrthwyneb

contribute v. cyfrannu

contrite a. edifeiriol

control v. rheoli

controller n. rheolwr m.

convenient a. cyfleus, hwylus

conversation n. ymgom mf, sgwrs f.

converse 1 n. gwrthwyneb m. 2 v. ymgomio, sgwrsio, ymddiddan

conversion n. trosiad m; tröedigaeth f.

convert v. troi, newid, trosi

converted a. wedi ei addasu. **converted try** trosgais

convey v. cyfleu; trosglwyddo

cook 1 n. cogydd m; cogyddes f. 2 v coginio, gwneud bwyd.

cool 1 a. oer. 2 v. oeri

copy 1 n. copi m. 2 v. copïo

copyright n. hawlfraint f.

cord n. cordyn m; lein f, llinyn m.

corgi n. corgi m.

corn n. llafur, corn, ŷd m.

corner n. cornel mf, cwr m, congl f.

cornflakes n. creision ŷd m.pl.

corpse n. corff m.

correct 1 a. cywir, iawn, priodol. 2 v. cywiro

correction n. cywiriad m.

corrupt 1 a. llygredig. 2 v. llygru

corruption n. llygredd, llygredigaeth m.

cost 1 n. pris m, traul, cost f. 2 v. costio

costume n. gwisg f.

cottage n. bwthyn m.

cotton n. cotwm m; edau f. **cotton wool** gwlân cotwm

cough 1 n. peswch, pesychiad m. 2 v. peswch

council n. cyngor m. **council house** tŷ cyngor; **county council** cyngor sir

councillor n. cynghorwr m. **County Councillor** Cynghorwr Sir

counsel 1 n. cyngor m. 2 v. cynghori

count 1 n. cyfrif; iarll m. 2 v. rhifo; cyfrif

counter- px. gwrth- (*followed by soft mutation*): **counteract** gwrthweithio; **counterclockwise** gwrthgloc

counterfeit n. & a. ffug m.

counterfoil n. bôn m (*siec/ derbynneb . . .*)

countess n. iarlles f.

country n. gwlad, bro f. **Country Music** Canu Gwlad

county n. sir, swydd (*English county*) f: **Carmarthenshire** Sir Gaerfyrddin, Sir Gâr; **Lancashire** Swydd Gaerhirfryn; **Yorkshire** Swydd Efrog; **Buckinghamshire** Swydd

Buckingham
courageous *a.* dewr, gwrol
course *n.* cwrs *m*, hynt; ystod; gyrfa *f.* **in the course of** yn ystod; **of course** wrth gwrs; **crash course** cwrs carlam
court 1 *n.* llys *m.* 2 *v.* caru, canlyn. **Magistrates' Court** Llys ynadon
courteous *a.* cwrtais
cousin *n.* cefnder *m*; cyfnither *f.*
cover 1 *n.* clawr *m.* 2 *v.* gorchuddio
covetous *a.* trachwantus
covetousness *n.* trachwant *m.*
cow *n.* buwch *f.*
cowardly *a.* llwfr
crack 1 *n.* crac *m.* 2 *v.* cracio
cradle *n.* crud *m.*
craft *n.* crefft; llong; awyren *f.*
craftsman *n.* crefftwr *m.*
crafty *a.* cyfrwys
crag *n.* craig *f*, clogwyn *m.*
cream *n.* hufen *m.*
crematorium *n.* amlosgfa *f.*
cress *n.* berw *m.*
crest *n.* brig *m*, crib *mf.*
crew *n.* criw *m.*
crib *n.* preseb *m.*
cricket *n.* criced; cricsyn *m.*
cricketer *n.* cricedwr *m.*
crime *n.* trosedd *f.*
criminal *n.* troseddwr *m.*
crisps *n.* creision (tatws) *m.pl.*
critic *n.* beirniad *m.*
criticize *v.* beirniadu
crockery *n.* llestri *pl.m.*
croft *n.* tyddyn *m.*

crook *n.* troseddwr; ffon fugail *m.*
crooked *a.* cam
cross 1 *n.*, croes *f.* 2 *v.* croesi
cross-examine *v.* croesholi
crossing *n.* croesfan *f.*
crossroad *n.* croesffordd *f.*
crossword *n.* croesair, pos croeseiriau *m.*
crow *n.* brân *f.*
crowd *n.* torf *f*, twr *m*, tyrfa *f*, llu *m.*
crown 1 *n.* coron *f.* 2 *v.* coroni: **Crown land** tir y Goron; **Triple Crown** Coron Driphlyg
cruel *a.* creulon
cruelty *n.* creulondeb *m.*
crumb *n.* briwsionyn *m.*
crumble *v.* chwalu; briwsioni
crush *v.* malu, gwasgu
crust *n.* crwst, crystyn *m.*
cry 1 *n.* cri *mf*, llef, sgrech *f.* 2 *v.* crio, llefain, wylo
cuckoo *n.* cog, cwcw *f.*
cultured *a.* gwâr
cunning *a.* cyfrwys
cup *n.* cwpan *mf*, dysgl *f.*
cupboard *n.* cwpwrdd *m.*
cure *v.* gwella, iacháu
curly *a.* cyrliog
current 1 *n.* ffrwd *f.* llif *m.* 2 *a.* cyfoes: **current affairs** materion cyfoes
currently *ad.* ar hyn o bryd
curse 1 *n.* llw *m*, melltith, rheg *f.* 2 *v.* rhegi
curtain *n.* llen *f.*
cushion *n.* clustog *f.*
custom *n.* arfer, cwstwm *m*; toll *f.*

customary *a.* arferol
customer *n.* cwsmer *m.*
customs *n.* y tollau *f.pl.*
 customs officer swyddog
 tollau
cut 1 *n.* toriad *m.* **2** *v.* torri
cycle 1 *n.* cylch; beic *m.* **2** *v.*
 seiclo
cylinder *n.* silindr *m.*
cylindrical *a.* silindrog

D

dad: daddy *n.* tad *m.*
daffodil *n.* cenhinen Bedr *f*,
 daffodil *m.*
daisy *n.* llygad y dydd *m.*
dale *n.* cwm, dyffryn *m*, dôl,
 bro *f.* **hill and dale** bryn a
 dôl
damage *n.* niwed, difrod *m.*
damages *n.pl.* iawndal, iawn
 m.
damp *a.* llaith
damson *n.* eirinen ddu *f.*
dance 1 *n.* dawns *f.* **2** *v.*
 dawnsio. **public folk dance**
 twmpath dawns; **folk dancing**
 dawnsio gwerin
dandelion *n.* dant y llew *m.*
danger *n.* perygl *m.*
dangerous *a.* peryglus
dank *a.* llaith, gwlyb
dare *v.* beiddio, meiddio,
 mentro
dark *a.* tywyll
darkness *n.* tywyllwch, gwyll
 m.
darling 1 *n.* anwylyd *mf*,
 cariad *m.* **2** *a.* annwyl
date *n.* dyddiad *m.*
daughter *n.* merch *f.*

dawn 1 *n.* gwawr *f.* **2** *v.*
 gwawrio
day *n.* diwrnod, dydd *m.* **day
 before yesterday** echdoe;
 yesterday doe, ddoe; **today**
 heddiw; **tomorrow** yfory; **day
 after tomorrow** trennydd;
 three days hence tradwy; **by
 day** liw dydd; **next day**
 trannoeth; **Good day!** Dydd
 da!
daybreak *n.* gwawr *f*, toriad
 dydd *m.*
daylight *n.* golau dydd *m.*
dazzle *v.* dallu; disgleirio
dazzling *a.* llachar, disglair
deacon *n.* diacon; blaenor *m.*
 deaconess diacones
dead *n.* & *a.* marw, meirw,
 meirwon *m.pl.*
deadly *a.* marwol
deaf *n.* & *a.* byddar *m.*
deal *v.* ymwneud (â), delio
 (â), ymdrin (â)
dear 1 *n.* anwylyd *mf*, cariad
 m. **2** *a.* annwyl, bach, cu,
 ffel, hoff; drud
dearest *n.* & *a.* anwylaf *mf*.
 dearest ones anwyliaid
death *n.* angau *m*,
 marwolaeth *f.*
debate 1 *n.* dadl *f.* **2** *v.*
 dadlau, ymryson
debt *n.* dyled *f.*
decade *n.* degawd *m.*
decay *v.* pydru
deceased *a.* y diweddar
deceit *n.* twyll *m.*
deceitful *a.* twyllodrus
deceive *v.* twyllo
decelerate *v.* arafu
December *n.* Rhagfyr *m.*

decentralize *v.* datganoli

decide *v.* penderfynu, dyfarnu

decision *n.* penderfyniad, dyfarniad *m.*

deck *n.* bwrdd; dec *m.*

declaration *n.* datganiad *m.*

declare *v.* datgan, mynegi

decompose *v.* pydru

decree *n.* gorchymyn *m.*

dedicate *v.* cyflwyno; cysegru

deed *n.* gweithred *f.*

deep 1 *n.* dyfnder *m.* **2** *a.* dwfn. **deep freeze cabinet** rhewgell

Deeside *n.* Glannau Dyfrdwy *f.*

defeat *v.* gorchfygu, trechu

defect *n.* nam, diffyg, gwall *m.*

defence *n.* amddiffyn, amddiffyniad *m;* amddiffynfa *f.*

defend *v.* amddiffyn

defiance *n.* her *f.*

define *v.* diffinio

definite *a.* pendant

definitely *ad.* yn bendant

definition *n.* diffiniad *m.*

defraud *v.* twyllo

defrost *v.* dadrewi

deft *a.* medrus

degree *n.* gradd *f.*

de-ice *v.* toddi

deity *n.* duwdod; duw *m.*

delay *v.* oedi

delectable *a.* hyfryd

delegate 1 *n.* dirprwy *m.* **2** *v.* dirprwyo

delegation *n.* dirprwyaeth *f.*

delete *v.* dileu

delicious *a.* blasus

delightful *a.* hyfryd, braf

deliver *v.* gwaredu (rhag); danfon, trosglwyddo

deliverer *n.* gwaredwr

demand 1 *n.* gofyn, galw *m.* arch; gofynneb *f.* **2** *v.* mynnu, gofyn

demi- *px.* hanner

demise *n.* marwolaeth *f.*

den *n.* ffau *f.*

denomination *n.* enwad *m.*

dense *a.* trwchus; hurt

dent 1 *n.* pant, tolc *m.* **2** *v.* tolcio

dentist *n.* deintydd *m.*

dentures *n.* dannedd gosod, dannedd dodi *m.pl.*

deny *v.* gwadu, gwrthod

depart *v.* ymadael (â); cychwyn

department *n.* adran *f.* dosbarth *m.*

depend *v.* dibynnu (ar)

deplore *v.* gresynu

depose *v.* diswyddo; tystio

deposit *n.* ernes *f.* blaendal *m.*

depressed *a.* isel, digalon.

depth *n.* dyfnder *m.*

deputation *n.* dirprwyaeth *f.*

deputy *n.* dirprwy *m.* **Deputy Director** Dirprwy Gyfarwyddwr; **Deputy Headteacher** Dirprwy Brifathro, Dirprwy Brifathrawes

derivation *n.* tarddiad *m.*

derive *v.* derbyn, cael; tarddu

descend *v.* disgyn

describe *v.* disgrifio, darlunio

description *n.* disgrifiad *m.*

desert *n.* anialwch *m.*

desert *v.* cilio, ffoi (rhag)

deserter *n.* ffoadur *m.*

deserve v. haeddu
deserved a. teilwng
design 1 n. cynllun m.
 2 v. cynllunio
designer n. cynlluniwr,
 cynllunydd m.
desirable a. dymunol
desire 1 n. dymuniad,
 chwant, ewyllys m.
 2 v. dymuno
desirous a. awyddus
desk n. desg f.
desolate a. gwag
despite prp. er, er gwaethaf
despot n. unben m.
dessert n. pwdin, melysfwyd
 m.
destiny n. tynged f.
destroy v. dinistrio, difetha
detached a. ar wahân
detail 1 n. manylyn m. 2 v.
 manylu. **details** manylion; **in
 detail** yn fanwl
detective n. ditectif m.
 detective story stori dditectif
determination n. penderfyniad
 m.
determine v. penderfynu
determined a. penderfynol
detest v. casáu
develop v. datblygu
development n. datblygiad m.
deviate v. gwyro, gwyrio
deviation n. gwyriad m.
devil n. diafol, diawl m.
devilish a. diawledig
devolution n. datganoli m.
devolve v. datganoli
devour v. llyncu, ysu
dew 1 n. gwlith m. 2 v.
 gwlitho
diagnose v. adnabod

diagnosis n. diagnosis m.
dialect n. tafodiaith f.
dialogue n. deialog, sgwrs f.
diarrhoea n. dolur rhydd m.
diary n. dyddiadur m.
dictator n. unben m.
dictionary n. geiriadur m.
die v. marw, darfod, trigo
differ v. gwahaniaethu
difference n. gwahaniaeth m.
different a. gwahanol
difficult a. anodd, caled
difficulty n. anhawster m.
dig v. palu
digest v. treulio
digital a. digidol
dignity n. urddas m.
diligent a. prysur, diwyd
dimension n. maint m.
diminish v. lleihau
diminutive a. bychan
dingle n. cwm, glyn, pant m.
dinner n. cinio mf.
dip v. trochi, golchi
direct 1 a. union. 2 v.
 cyfeirio
direction n. cyfeiriad;
 hyfforddiant m.
directly ad. yn union
director n. cyfarwyddwr m.
directory n. cyfarwyddiadur m.
dirt n. baw, llacs m.
dirty a. brwnt, budr
disability n. anabledd m.
disabled a. anabl, methedig
disappear v. diflannu
disappoint v. siomi
disappointed a. siomedig
disappointing a. siomedig
disappointment n. siom mf.
disarm v. diarfogi
disaster n. trychineb mf.

disc *n.* disg *mf.*
disciple *n.* disgybl *m.*
discipline *n.* disgyblaeth *f.*
disclaim *v.* gwadu
disclose *v.* datguddio
discontented *a.* anfodlon
discover *v.* darganfod
discretion *n.* doethineb, pwyll *m.*
discuss *v.* trafod
discussion *n.* trafodaeth, sgwrs *f.*
disease *n.* afiechyd, clefyd, dolur *m.* haint *f.*
disembark *v.* glanio
dish *n.* dysgl *f.*
disinfectant *n.* diheintydd *m.*
disk *n.* disg *mf.*
dislike *v.* casáu
dismiss *v.* diswyddo; rhyddhau; gwrthod
disown *v.* gwadu, diarddel
dispatch 1 *n.* neges *f.* **2** *v.* anfon, danfon
dispute 1 *n.* dadl *f.* **2** *v.* dadlau, amau, ymryson
disseminate *v.* hau
dissimilar *a.* annhebyg, gwahanol
dissolve *v.* toddi; datod
distance *n.* pellter *m.*
distant *a.* pell, hirbell. **from far** o hirbell
distasteful *a.* diflas
distinct *a.* arbennig; eglur; gwahanol
distribute *v.* rhannu, dosbarthu
district *n.* ardal *f.* dosbarth, cylch, rhanbarth, rhandir *m.*
ditch *n.* ffos *f.*
diverse *a.* gwahanol

divide *v.* rhannu
diviner *n.* dewin, dyn hysbys *m.*
division *n.* adran, rhan *f,* rhaniad, rhanbarth, rhandir *m.*
divorce *n.* ysgariad *m.*
do *v.* gwneud, gwneuthur
dock *n.* doc *m.*
doctor *n.* meddyg, doctor *m.*
Dr John Jones y Dr John Jones
document *n.* dogfen *f.*
dog *n.* ci *m.*
doll *n.* dol *f.*
domesticated *a.* dof
donation *n.* rhodd *f,* cyfraniad *m.*
donkey *n.* asyn, mul *m.*
door *n.* drws, porth *m.*
double *a.* dwbl
doubt 1 *n.* amheuaeth, amau. **2** *v.* amau.
dough *n.* toes *m.*
down *ad.* i lawr
dozen *n.* dwsin, deuddeg *m.*
drag *v.* llusgo
dragon *n.* draig *f.*
drama *n.* drama *f.* **drama festival** gŵyl ddrama
dramatist *n.* dramodydd *m.*
draw *v.* darlunio, llunio, tynnu; llusgo
drawing *n.* llun *m.*
dread 1 *n.* ofn *m.* **2** *v.* ofni
dreadful *a.* ofnadwy
dream 1 *n.* breuddwyd *mf.* **2** *v.* breuddwydio
dregs *n.* gwaelodion *m.pl.,* gwaddodd *m.*
dress 1 *n.* gwisg *f,* dilledyn *m,* ffrog *f.* **2** *v.* gwisgo, taclu;

trin

dresser *n.* seld, dreser, dresel *f*; gwisgwr *m.*

dressmaker *n.* gwniadyddes, gwniyddes *f.*

drink 1 *n.* diod *f.* **2** *v.* yfed; diota

drive 1 *n.* dreif *m.* **2** *v.* gyrru, hala

driver *n.* gyrrwr *m.*

driving licence *n.* trwydded yrru *f.*

droll *a.* ysmala, digrif

drop 1 *n.* cwymp; diferyn *m.* **2** *v.* cwympo. **drop goal** gôl adlam

drown *v.* boddi

drug *n.* cyffur *m.*

drum *n.* drwm

drunk *a.* meddw. **to get drunk** meddwi

drunkard *n.* meddwyn *m.*

dry 1 *a.* sych, cras. **2** *v.* sychu

Dublin *n.* Dulyn *f.*

duck *n.* hwyad, hwyaden *f.* **duckling** cyw hwyaden *m.*

due 1 *n.* dyled, hawl *f*, tâl *m.* **2** *a.* dyledus

duel *n.* gornest *f.*

duet *n.* deuawd *mf.*

dull *a.* dwl, hurt; diflas, cymylog. **dull man** dyn dwl; **dull day** diwrnod cymylog

dumb *a.* mud

dummy-pass *n.* ffug-bas *f.*

during *prp.* yn ystod

dust *n.* llwch, dwst *m.* **dustbin** bin ysbwriel *m.*

duty *n.* dyletswydd; toll *f.*

dwell *v.* cartrefu, trigo, byw

dwelling *n.* preswylfa, trigfa, trigfan *f.*

dye *v.* lliwio, lliwo

dyke *n.* clawdd, morglawdd *m.* **Offa's Dyke** Clawdd Offa

E

each *a.* & *pn* pob un, pob

eager *a.* awyddus

eagle *n.* eryr *m.*

ear *n.* clust *f.*

earl *n.* iarll *m.*

earliest *a.* cyntaf

early 1 *a.* cynnar, bore, boreol. **2** *a.* yn fore

earmark 1 *n.* clustnod *mf.* **2** *v.* clustnodi, neilltuo

earn *v.* ennill

earner *n.* enillwr, enillydd *m.*

earnings *n.* enillion *pl.*

earring *n.* clustlws *m.*

earshot *n.* clyw *m.*

earth *n.* daear, Y Ddaear *f*, pridd, tir, y byd *m.*

earthquake *n.* daeargryn *mf.*

earthwork *n.* clawdd *m.*

east 1 *n.* dwyrain *m.* **2** *a.* dwyreiniol

Easter *n.* y Pasg *m.* **Easter egg** wy Pasg; **Easter holidays** gwyliau'r Pasg

easy *a.* hawdd, rhwydd

easy chair *n.* cadair esmwyth *f.*

eat *v.* bwyta.

ebb *n.* trai *m.*

echo *n.* adlais, atsain *m.* carreg ateb *f.*

economics *n.* economeg *f.*

economize *v.* cynilo

edge *n.* cwr, blaen, min *m*, ymyl *mf.*

Edinburgh *n.* Caeredin *f.*

edit *v.* golygu

edition *n.* argraffiad *m.*
editor *n.* golygydd *m.*
education *n.* addysg *f.*
effect 1 *n.* effaith *f.* **2** *v.*
effeithio
effective *a.* effeithiol
effeminate *a.* merchetaidd
effort *n.* ymdrech, ymgais *f.*
e.g. *(exempli gratia), ad.*
er enghraifft *(e.e.)*
egg *n.* wy *m.*
egg cup *n.* cwpan wy *mf.*
eight *n.* & *a.* wyth *m.*
eighteen *n.* & *a.* deunaw, un
deg wyth *m.*
eighth *n.* & *a.* wythfed *m.*
eighty *n.* & *a.* wyth deg,
pedwar ugain *m.*
either 1 *a.* & *pn.* un o'r ddau,
naill ai . . . neu. **2** *ad.* & *c.*
na, nac, chwaith, ychwaith
elbow *n.* penelin *mf.*
elderly *a.* oedrannus
elect *v.* ethol, dewis
election *n.* etholiad *m.*
electorate *n.* etholaeth *f.*
electric *n.* & *a.* trydan *m.*
  electric fire tân trydan
electrical *a.* trydanol
electrician *n.* trydanwr *m.*
electricity *n.* trydan *m.*
element *n.* elfen *f.*
elementary *a.* elfennol
elephant *n.* eliffant
eleven *n.* & *a.* un ar ddeg *m.*
eleventh *n.* & *a.* unfed ar
ddeg *m.*
ellipse *n.* hirgylch *m.*
else *ad.* arall
e-mail *n.* e-bost *m.*
embankment *n.* clawdd, cob
m.

embassy *n.* llysgenhadaeth *f.*
embrace *v.* cofleidio
emigrant *n.* ymfudwr *m.*
emigrate *v.* ymfudo
eminent *a.* enwog, amlwg
emphasis *n.* pwys, pwyslais
m.
emphatic *a.* pendant
empire *n.* ymerodraeth *f.*
employ *v.* cyflogi
employee *n.* gŵr cyflog *m.*
employer *n.* cyflogwr *m.*
employment *n.* gwaith *m.*
empty 1 *a.* gwag. **2** *v.*
gwagio, arllwys. **empty-
handed** gwaglaw
enchant *v.* swyno, hudo
enchanting *a.* hudol, swynol
enchantment *n.* lledrith, swyn
m.
enclose *v.* amgáu
enclosed *a.* amgaeëdig
encore 1 *n.* encôr *m.* **2** *ad.*
eto
end 1 *n.* diwedd, diben, pen,
terfyn *m.* **2** *v.* dibennu,
gorffen
endeavour 1 *n.* ymdrech *f.*
2 *v.* ymdrechu
endless *a.* diddiwedd
endure *v.* dioddef, goddef
enemy *n.* gelyn *m.*
energetic *a.* egnïol
energy *n.* egni, ynni *m.*
enforce *v.* gorfodi
enforced *a.* gorfod
enforcement *n.* gorfodaeth *f.*
engagement *n.* dyweddïad;
ymrwymiad *m.*
engine *n.* peiriant *m*, injan,
injin *f.*
England *n.* Lloegr *f.*

English 1 *n.* Saesneg *f.* **2** *a.*
Saesneg, Seisnig
Englishman *n.* Sais *m.*
Englishwoman *n.* Saesnes *f.*
enjoy *v.* mwynhau, joio
enjoyment *n.* mwynhad *m.*
enlighten *v.* goleuo; hysbysu
enormous *a.* enfawr, anferth
enough 1 *n.* digon, digonedd
m. **2** *a.* & *ad.* digon
enquire *v.* gofyn, holi
entangle *v.* drysu
enter *v.* mynd i mewn
entertain *v.* difyrru
entertaining *a.* difyr, difyrrus
entertainment *n.* adloniant *m.*
enthusiastic *a.* brwdfrydig
entice *v.* denu, hudo
enticing *a.* deniadol, dengar
entire *a.* cyfan, hollol, llwyr
entirely *ad.* yn gyfan gwbl, yn
hollol, yn llwyr
entrails *n.* perfedd *pl.*
entrance *n.* mynedfa *f.*
mynediad, drws, porth; tâl *m.*
entrance *v.* swyno
entreat *v.* erfyn
entry *n.* mynediad *m,*
mynedfa *f.*
envelop *v.* amgáu
envelope *n.* amlen *f.*
environment *n.* amgylchedd
m.
environs *n.* amgylchoedd *pl.*
envoy *n.* negesydd, cennad *m.*
epilogue *n.* diweddglo, epilog
m.
epistle *n.* llythyr, epistol *m.*
equal *a.* cydradd, yr un faint,
hafal
equation *n.* hafaliad *m.*
  simple equation hafaliad

syml
equipment *n.* offer *m.pl.*
erase *v.* dileu.
erect 1 *a.* syth. **2** *v.* codi
errand *n.* neges *f.*
error *n.* camsyniad; bai, gwall
m.
escape *v.* dianc, ffoi
escort *v.* hebrwng
especial *a.* arbennig,
enwedig, neilltuol
especially *ad.* yn arbennig, yn
enwedig
essay *n.* traethawd *m.* ysgrif
mf.
essential *a.* hanfodol
establish *v.* sefydlu
establishment *n.* sefydliad *m.*
estate *n.* eiddo *m,* ystad, stad
f.
estuary *n.* aber *m.*
eternal *ad.* yn dragwyddol, yn
oes oesoedd
Europe *n.* Ewrop *f.*
evade *v.* osgoi
eve *n.* min nos *m,* noswyl *f.*
Christmas Eve Noswyl
Nadolig
even 1 *n.* yr hwyr *m.* **2** *a.*
gwastad, llyfn; tawel. **3** *ad.*
hyd yn oed
evening *n.* hwyr *m,* noson,
noswaith *f.* **evening class**
dosbarth nos
event *n.* digwyddiad *m.*
eventually *ad.* o'r diwedd
ever *ad.* byth, erioed
evergreen *n.* & *a.* bythwyrdd
m.
everlasting *a.* tragwyddol
evermore *ad.* byth, byth
bythoedd

every *a.* pob
everybody *pn.* pawb, pob un
everyday *a.* bob dydd
everyone *pn* pawb, pob un
everything *pn.* pob peth,
popeth
everywhere *ad.* ym mhobman
evidence *n.* tystiolaeth *f*,
prawf *m.*
evident *a.* amlwg, eglur
evil 1 *n.* drwg, drygioni *m.*
2 *a.* drwg, drygionus
evolve *v.* datblygu; esblygu
ewe *n.* dafad, mamog *f.*
ex- *px.* cyn-
exact *a.* cywir, manwl, union.
to be exact manylu
exactly *ad.* yn union, i'r dim
examination *n.* arholiad,
archwiliad *m.*
examine *v.* arholi, chwilio,
archwilio
examiner *n.* arholwr, holwr
m.
example *n.* enghraifft,
esiampl *f.* **for example, e.g.**
er enghraifft, e.e
excavator *n.* jac-codi-baw *m.*
excel *v.* rhagori
excellent *a.* ardderchog,
campus, godidog, gwych,
penigamp, rhagorol
excellently *ad.* yn ardderchog
except 1 *v.* eithrio. 2 *prp.* ac
eithrio. 3 *pn.* eithr
excess *n.* gormod
exciting *a.* cyffrous,
cynhyrfus
exclaim *v.* llefain, gweiddi,
bloeddio
exclamation *n.* llef, gwaedd *f.*
exclude *v.* eithrio, cau allan

excuse 1 *n.* esgus *m.* 2 *v.*
esgusodi
execute *v.* gweithredu;
dienyddio
exercise 1 *n.* ymarfer *f*,
ymarferiad *m.* 2 *v.* ymarfer.
exercise book llyfr ymarfer,
llyfr ysgrifennu
exile 1 *n.* alltud *m.* 2 *v.*
alltudio
exist *v.* bod
existence *n.* bod *m*,
bodolaeth *f.*
exit 1 *n.* allanfa *f*, mynediad
allan *m.* 2 *v.* mynd allan
expect *v.* disgwyl
expediency *n.* hwylustod *m.*
expedient *a.* hwylus, cyfleus
expense *n.* traul, cost *f.*
expenses *n.* treuliau *f.pl.*
expensive *a.* costus, drud
experience *n.* profiad *m.*
experienced *a.* profiadol
explain *v.* egluro, esbonio
explanation *n.* esboniad,
eglurhad *m.*
explode *v.* ffrwydro
expose *v.* amlygu, dinoethi
exposed *a.* agored, noeth
exposition *n.* esboniad *m.*
express 1 *a.* cyflym. 2 *v.*
mynegi. 3 *n.* trên cyflym *m.*
extend *v.* estyn, ymestyn
extension *a.* estyniad *m.*
extensive *a.* eang, helaeth
extent *n.* maint, hyd,
mesur *m.* **to some extent**
i raddau
exterior 1 *n.* y tu allan *m.*
2 *a.* allanol
external *a.* allanol. **external
exam** arholiad allanol

extinguish *v.* diffodd; dileu
extreme 1 *n.* eithaf *m.* **2** *a.*
eithafol
extremely *ad.* dros ben, gor-
extremity *n.* eithaf, terfyn,
pen *m.*
eye 1 *n.* llygad *mf.* **2** *v.*
llygadu, sylwi ar
eyesight *n.* golwg *mf.*
eyewitness *n.* llygad-dyst *m.*

F

fable *n.* chwedl *f.*
fabric *n.* defnydd *m.*
face 1 *n.* wyneb *m.* **2** *v.*
wynebu. **face-cloth** clwtyn
ymolch
facilitate *v.* hwyluso
fact *n.* ffaith *f*, gwirionedd *m.*
as a matter of fact mewn
gwirionedd
factor *n.* elfen, ffactor *f.*
factory *n.* ffatri *f.*
fade *v.* gwywo, colli lliw
fail *v.* methu, ffaelu
failure *n.* methiant *m.*
faint 1 *a.* gwan. **2** *v.* llewygu.
fair 1 *n.* ffair *f.* **2** *a.* teg, glân;
gweddol; golau
fairly *ad.* yn deg, yn lân, yn
weddol, eithaf-, go-, lled-.
fairly good eithaf da, go dda,
lled dda. **fairly rare** go brin.
fairly quiet lled dawel;
*see Appendix for mutation of
Adjectives following certain
Adverbs.*
fairness *n.* harddwch; tegwch
m.
faith *n.* ffydd *f.*

faithful *a.* ffyddlon, cywir
faithfully *ad.* yn ffyddlon, yn
gywir. **Yours faithfully** Yr
eiddoch yn gywir
fake 1 *a.* ffug. **2** *v.* ffugio
falcon 1 *n.* hebog *m.*
fall 1 *n.* cwymp *m.* **2** *v.*
cwympo, syrthio
false *a.* ffug, gau, twyllodrus.
false teeth dannedd gosod,
dannedd dodi
fame *n.* enwogrwydd, clod *m.*
familiarize *v.* cyfarwyddo
family *n.* teulu *m.*
famine *n.* newyn *m.*
famish *v.* llwgu
famous *a.* enwog
fanciful *a.* ffansïol
fancy 1 *n.* dychymyg *m*,
ffansi *f*, serch *m.* **2** *v.*
dychmygu, ffansïo, serchu
fantasy *n.* ffantasi *f.*
far *a.* & *ad.* pell, ymhell. **as
far as** hyd at: **from afar** o
hirbell
farewell 1 *n.* ffárwel, ffarwél *f.*
2 *v.* ffarwelio. **to bid farewell**
canu'n iach
farm 1 *n.* ffarm, fferm *f.* **2** *v.*
ffarmio, ffermio
farmer *n.* amaethwr, ffarmwr,
ffermwr *m.*
farmhouse *n.* ffermdy, tŷ
ffarm *m.*
farming *n.* ffermio, gwaith
ffarm *m*, amaethyddiaeth *f.*
farmyard *n.* buarth, clos *m.*
farthest *a.* pellaf, eithaf
fascinate *v.* hudo, swyno
fascinating *a.* hudol, swynol
fashion 1 *n.* llun, ffasiwn *m*;
arfer *mf.* **2** *v.* llunio, ffurfio,

gwneud.

fast *a.* cyflym, buan; tyn

fat 1 *n.* braster, saim *m.* **2** *v.* bras, tew. **fat meat** cig bras, cig gwyn

fatal *a.* marwol

fatality *n.* marwolaeth *f.*

fate *n.* tynged *f.*

fateful *a.* tyngedfennol

father *n.* tad *m.* **father-in-law** tad-yng-nghyfraith; **stepfather** llystad. **Father Christmas** *n.* Siôn Corn *m.*

fault *n.* bai, nam, diffyg *m.*

faultless *a.* di-fai

faulty *a.* gwallus

favour *n.* cymwynas, ffafr *f.*

favourite 1 *n.* ffefryn *m.* **2** *a.* hoff

fear 1 *n.* ofn, braw *m.* **2** *v.* ofni

feast 1 *n.* gwledd, gŵyl *f.* **2** *v.* gwledda

feat *n.* camp *f.*

feather 1 *n.* pluen, plufyn *m.* **2** *v.* pluo, plufio

feature *n.* nodwedd

fee *n.* tâl *m*, cyflog *mf*, ffi *f.*

February *n.* Chwefror, Mis Bach *m.*

feeble *a.* gwan, egwan, bregus

feed *v.* bwydo, bwyda; bwyta

feel 1 *n.* teimlad *m.* **2** *v.* teimlo, clywed

feeling *n.* teimlad *m*, naws *f.*

feign *v.* cymryd ar; ffugio

fell *v.* cwympo, syrthio, torri

female 1 *n.* benyw, menyw *f.* **2** *a.* benywaidd, menywaidd

feminine *a.* benywaidd, menywaidd

fence 1 *n.* clawdd *m*, ffens *f.* **2** *v.* cau, amgáu

fern *n.* rhedynen *f*, rhedyn *pl.*

ferocious *a.* ffyrnig, gwyllt

fertile *a.* ffrwythlon, bras, toreithiog

fertilize *v.* ffrwythloni; gwrteithio

fertilizer *n.* gwrtaith *m.*

fervent *a.* gwresog, tanllyd, tanbaid, selog

festival *n.* gŵyl, dydd gŵyl *m.* **singing festival** cymanfa ganu

fetch *v.* hôl, nôl, hercyd

fever *n.* twymyn *f*, clefyd, gwres *m.*

few *a.* ychydig

fiancé *n.* darpar-ŵr, dyweddi *m.*

fiancée *n.* darpar wraig, dyweddi *f.*

fiction *n.* ffuglen *f.*

fictitious *a.* ffug, ffugiol

field *n.* cae, maes, parc *m.*

fierce *a.* ffyrnig

fiery *a.* tanllyd, tanbaid

fifteen *n.* & *a.* pymtheg *m.*

fifteenth *n.* & *a.* pymthegfed *m.*

fifth *n.* & *a.* pumed *m.*

fifty *n.* & *a.* hanner cant, pum deg *m.*

fight 1 *n.* brwydr *f.* ymladd *m.* **2** *v.* brwydro, ymladd

fighter *n.* ymladdwr *m.*

fighting *n.* ymladd *m.*

figure 1 *n.* ffigur *mf;* ffurf *f*, llun *m.* **2** *v.* ffurfio; rhifo

fill 1 *n.* digon, digonedd *m.* **2** *v.* llanw, llenwi

film 1 *n.* ffilm *f.* **2** *v.* ffilmio

filth *n.* baw, budreddi, mochyndra *m.*

final 1 *n.* rownd derfynol *f.* **2** *a.* terfynol, olaf

finale *n.* diweddglo

finally *ad.* o'r diwedd, yn olaf

find *v.* darganfod, cael, dod o hyd

fine 1 *n.* dirwy *f.* **2** *v.* dirwyo. **3** *a.* mân, manwl; main; braf; gwych; hardd, hyfryd, teg

finger *n.* bys *m.* **fingerprint** ôl bys

finish 1 *n.* diwedd, terfyn *m.* **2** *v.* gorffen, dibennu, cwpla

fir *n.* ffynidwydden *f.*

fire 1 *n.* tân *m.* **2** *v.* tanio; saethu. **fire-brigade** brigâd dân *f.* **fire exit** allanfa dân *f.*

fireplace *n.* lle tân *m.*

firewood *n.* coed tân *f.pl.*

fireworks *n.* tân gwyllt *m.pl.*

firm 1 *n.* cwmni, ffyrm *m.* **2** *a.* cadarn, cryf. **3** *v.* nerthu, cryfhau.

firmament *n.* ffurfafen *f.*

first 1 *n. & a.* cyntaf *m.* **2** *ad.* yn gyntaf

fish 1 *n.* pysgodyn *m.* **2** *v.* pysgota

fisherman *n.* pysgotwr *m.*

fishing *n.* pysgota *m.*

fist *n.* dwrn *m.*

fitting *a.* addas, priodol

five *n. & a.* pump *m.*

fix *v.* gosod, sicrhau, sefydlu

fixed *a.* sefydlog

flabby *a.* llac, llipa, llaes

flag *n.* baner *f.* **Union Jack** Jac-yr-Undeb

flakes *n.* creision *m.pl.* **cornflakes** creision ŷd; **snowflakes** plu eira

flame 1 *n.* fflam *f.* **2** *v.* fflamio

flank *n.* ystlys, ochr *f.*

flannel *n.* gwlanen *f.*

flap 1 *n.* llabed *f.* fflap *m.* **2** *v.* fflapio

flash 1 *n.* fflach *f.* **2** *v.* fflachio

flat 1 *n.* fflat *f.* **2** *a.* fflat, gwastad

flavour 1 *n.* blas *m.* **2** *v.* blasu

flaw *n.* bai, diffyg, nam *m.*

flea *n.* chwannen *f.*

flee *v.* cilio, dianc, ffoi

fleet *n.* llynges *f.*

flesh *n.* cig, cnawd *m.* **flesh and blood** cig a gwaed

flexible *a.* hyblyg, ystwyth

fling *v.* taflu

flock *n.* haid *f*; praidd *m.*

flood 1 *n.* llif *m.* **2** *v.* llifo, gorlifo

floor *n.* llawr *m.*

flour *n.* blawd, can *m.*

flow 1 *n.* llif *m.* **2** *v.* llifo, rhedeg

flower *n.* blodyn *m.* **flower pot** pot blodau

flowing *a.* llithrig; llaes, llac, rhydd

fluent *a.* rhwydd, llithrig, rhugl

fluid *n. & a.* hylif *m.*

fly 1 *n.* cleren *f*, pryf, gwybedyn *m.* **2** *v.* hedfan

foam *n.* ewyn *m.* **sea-foam** ewyn môr

focus 1 *n.* canolbwynt, ffocws

m. 2 *a.* canolbwyntio

foe *n.* gelyn *m.*

fog *n.* niwl, ffog *m.* **thick fog** niwl trwchus

foggy *a.* niwlog

fold *v.* plygu

folk *n.* gwerin *coll.f.,* pobl *f.*

folklore *n.* llên gwerin

folksong *n.* cân werin *f.*

follow *v.* dilyn

follower *n.* dilynwr *m.*

folly *n.* ffolineb *m.*

fond *a.* hoff, cu, annwyl

fondle *v.* anwesu, anwylo

fondness *n.* hoffter; anwes *m.*

food *n.* bwyd *m.*

fool 1 *n.* ffŵl *m.* 2 *v.* twyllo

foolish *a.* ffôl, dwl

foolishness *n.* ffolineb, dwli *m.*

foot *n.* troed *mf;* troedfedd *f.*

football *n.* pêl-droed *f.*
  footballer pêldroediwr *m.*

footpath *n.* troedffordd *f,* llwybr *m.* **public footpath** llwybr cyhoeddus

footprint *n.* ôl troed *m.*

for 1 *prp.* am, dros, tros, er, ers, erbyn, hyd, i, yn, lle. 2 *c.* achos, gan, oblegid, oherwydd

force *n.* grym; llu *m.* **armed forces** lluoedd arfog

ford *n.* rhyd *f.* **Ammanford** Rhydaman: **Oxford** Rhydychen

forehead *n.* talcen, tâl *m.*

foreign *a.* estron, tramor. **foreign affairs** materion tramor

foreigner *n.* estron *m.*

forest *n.* coedwig, fforest *f.*

foretaste *n.* rhagflas, rhagbrawf *m.*

forge 1 *n.* gefail *f.* 2 *v.* ffugio, twyllo

forget *v.* anghofio. **forget-me-not** glas y gors

forgive *v.* maddau

fork *n.* fforc, fforch *f.*

form 1 *n.* ffurf *f;* modd, dull *m;* ffurflen *f;* dosbarth *m.* 2 *v.* ffurfio, llunio. **application form** ffurflen gais *f.*

former *px.* cyn

formerly *ad.* gynt

fort *n.* caer *f.*

forthcoming *a.* ar ddod, gerllaw

fortnight *n.* pythefnos *mf.*

fortnightly *ad.* bob pythefnos

fortunate *a.* ffodus, lwcus

fortunately *ad.* yn ffodus, yn lwcus

fortune *n.* ffortiwn *f.*

forty *n.* & *a.* deugain, pedwar deg *m.*

forward 1 *n.* blaenwr *m.* 2 *a.* blaen; eofn. 3 *ad.* ymlaen. 4 *v.* anfon ymlaen. **wing forward** blaenasgellwr: **number eight** wythwr

foster *v.* meithrin, rhoi ar faeth

foster-mother *n.* mam-faeth *f.*

foul *a.* brwnt, budr, ffiaidd

found *v.* dechrau, sefydlu

foundation *n.* sail *f,* sylfaen *mf.*

fountain *n.* ffynnon, ffynhonnell *f.*

four *n.* & *a.* pedair, pedwar *m.*

fourteen *n.* & *a.* pedwar ar ddeg, pedair ar ddeg, un deg pedwar *m.*

fourth *n.* & *a.* pedwaredd, pedwerydd *m.*

fowl *n.* ffowlyn *m.*

fox *n.* cadno, llwynog. **vixen** cadnawes, cadnöes, llwynoges

fraction *n.* ffracsiwn *m.*

fragment *n.* darn, tamaid *m,* yfflyn *m.*

France *n.* Ffrainc *f.*

frankincense *n.* thus *m.*

fraud *n.* twyll *m.*

fraudulent *a.* twyllodrus

free 1 *a.* rhad, rhydd, di-dâl. **2** *v.* rhyddhau. **free kick** cic rydd. **free phone** rhadffôn; **freepost** rhadbost

freedom *n.* rhyddid *m.*

freely *ad.* yn rhydd

freeze *v.* rhewi

freezer *n.* rhewgell *f.*

freight *n.* llwyth *m.*

French 1 *n.* Ffrangeg *f.* **2** *a.* Ffrengig

Frenchman *n.* Ffrancwr *m.*

Frenchwoman *n.* Ffrances *f.*

frequent *a.* aml

fresh *a.* ffres, newydd

Friday *n.* dydd Gwener

friend *n.* cyfaill *m,* cyfeilles *f,* ffrind *m.*

friendly *a.* cyfeillgar

friendship *n.* cyfeillgarwch *m.*

fright *n.* braw, ofn *m.*

frighten *v.* codi ofn ar, brawychu

frightful *a.* dychrynllyd

frigid *a.* oer, rhewllyd

frivolity *n.* lol *f.*

frock *n.* ffrog *f.*

frog *n.* broga, ffroga *m.*

from *prp.* o, oddi, gan, oddi wrth, rhag

front 1 *n.* ffrynt, talcen, tu blaen *m.* **2** *a.* ffrynt, blaen. **front door** drws ffrynt: **front page** tudalen flaen; **front room** ystafell flaen: **front row** rhes flaen: **cold front** ffrynt oer: **warm front** ffrynt cynnes

frontier *n.* ffin *f.*

frost *n.* rhew *m.* **hoarfrost** barrug; **to cast hoar frost** llwydrewi

frosty *a.* rhewllyd

froth *n.* ewyn *m.*

frown 1 *n.* gwg *m.* **2** *v.* gwgu

frozen *a.* wedi rhewi

fruit *n.* ffrwyth *m,* ffrwythau *pl.* **fruit juice** sudd ffrwythau *m.*

fruitful *a.* ffrwythlon

fry *v.* ffrio

frying pan *n.* padell ffrio *f.*

fuel *n.* tanwydd *m.*

fugitive *n.* ffoadur *m.*

full *a.* llawn

full-back *n.* cefnwr *m.*

fullness *n.* llawnder, cyflawnder *m.*

fully *ad.* yn gyfan gwbl, yn hollol

fun *n.* hwyl *f,* miri *m.*

fund *n.* cronfa *f.*

fundamental *a.* sylfaenol

funeral *n.* angladd *mf.*

funnel *n.* twndis, corn, twmffat *m.*

funny *a.* digrif, ysmala,

doniol
fur *n.* ffwr, blew *m.*
furious *a.* ffyrnig, yn gacwn
wyllt, crac
furnace *n.* ffwrn, ffwrnais *f.*
furnishings *n.* dodrefn *pl.*
furniture *n.* celfi, dodrefn *pl.*
piece of furniture celficyn,
dodrefnyn.
furry *a.* blewog
further *ad.* bellach,
ymhellach. **further education**
addysg bellach
fuss *n.* helynt *f*, trafferth,
ffws, stŵr *m.* ffwdan *f.*
fussy *a.* ffyslyd, ffwdanus
future *n.* & *a.* dyfodol *m.*

G

gain 1 *n.* elw, ennill *m,*
enillion *pl.* 2 *v.* elwa, ennill
gale *n.* gwynt cryf *m.* tymestl
f.
gallery *n.* oriel *f*, galeri *m,*
llofft *f.*
gallon *n.* galwyn *m.*
gallop *v.* carlamu
gamble *v.* hapchwarae,
gamblo
game *n.* gêm *f*, chwarae *m,*
camp *f.*
gang *n.* mintai *f*, torf, haid,
gang *f.*
gaol 1 *n.* carchar *m.* 2 *v.*
carcharu
gap *n.* bwlch, adwy *m.*
garage *n.* garej *f.*
garbage *n.* ysbwriel, sothach
m.
garden 1 *n.* gardd *f.* 2 *v.*

garddio; **National Botanic
Garden of Wales** Gardd
Fotaneg Genedlaethol
gardener *n.* garddwr *m.*
garlic *n.* garlleg *m.*
garment *n.* pilyn *m*, gwisg *f,*
dilledyn *m.*
gas *n* nwy *m.* **Gas Board**
Bwrdd Nwy **gas mask**
mwgwd nwy
gate *n.* clwyd, gât, iet, llidiart
f.
gateway *n.* mynedfa *f.*
gather *v.* casglu, crynhoi,
cynnull, hel
gathering *n.* casgliad,
cynulliad *m.*
gaunt *a.* llwm, tenau
gauntlet *n.* maneg *f.*
gay *a.* llon, bywiog, hoyw
gaze *v.* edrych, syllu, rhythu
gear *n.* gêr *mf*, offer *pl.*
gem *n.* gem *f*, tlws *m.*
gender *n.* rhyw *mf*, cenedl *f.*
gene *n.* genyn *m.*
general 1 *n.* cadfridog *m.*
2 *a.* cyffredin, cyffredinol.
general election etholiad
cyffredinol
generally *ad.* yn gyffredinol
generation *n.* cenhedlaeth, to
m.
generosity *n.* haelioni *m.*
generous *a.* hael, haelionus
genetic *a.* genetig
genial *a.* tyner, tirion, hynaws
genteel *a.* bonheddig
gentle *a.* tyner, mwyn
gentleman *n.* bonheddwr,
gŵr bonheddig, uchelwr *m.*
gentleness *n.* tynerwch,

addfwynder *m.*

gently *ad.* yn dyner, yn
addfwyn; gan bwyll

gents *n.* toiledau dynion
m.pl.

genuine *a.* diffuant, cywir,
pur

geography *n.* daearyddiaeth *f.*

geology *n.* daeareg *f.*

geometry *n.* geometreg *mf.*

German 1 *n.* Almaeneg *(iaith)*
f. Almaenwr *(person) m.*
2 *a.* Almaenaidd

Germany *n.* yr Almaen *f.*

get *v.* cael, ennill

ghost *n.* ysbryd *m,*
drychiolaeth *f.*

giant *n.* cawr *m.*

gift *n.* anrheg, rhodd *f.*

gifted *a.* talentog, dawnus

gigantic *a.* anferth

gipsy *n.* sipsi *m.*

giraffe *n.* jiráff *m.*

girder *n.* trawst *m.*

girl *n.* merch, geneth, croten,
hogen, llances *f.*

give *v.* rhoddi, rhoi. **to give
generously** rhoi'n hael. **to
give up** rhoi'r gorau i

glad *a.* llawen, llon, balch

gladly *ad.* yn llawen, â
phleser

Glamorgan *n.* Morgannwg *f.*
Mid Glamorgan Morgannwg
Ganol; **South Glamorgan** De
Morgannwg; **West
Glamorgan** Gorllewin
Morgannwg *(1974–1996)*

glance *n.* cipolwg *m,* trem *f,*
cip *m.*

glass *n.* gwydr, gwydryn *m.*

gleam 1 *n.* llewyrch *m.* 2 *v.*
llewyrchu

glen *n.* glyn, cwm, dyffryn *m.*

glide 1 *n.* llithriad *m.* 2 *v.*
llithro dros

glitter *v.* disgleirio, serennu

glorious *a.* gogoneddus

glory *n.* gogoniant, ysblander
m.

Gloucester *n.* Caerloyw *f.*

glove *n.* maneg *f.*

glower *v.* gwgu, cuchio

glue 1 *n.* glud *m.* 2 *v.* gludo,
gludio, glynu

gnat *n.* gwybedyn *m.*

go *v.* cer! dos! *(unigol)*;
cerwch! ewch! *(lluosog); see*
mynd

goal *n.* gôl *f.* **goalkeeper**
golgeidwad, golwr *m.*

goat *n.* gafr *f.*

god *n.* duw *m.* **God** Duw

goddess *n.* duwies *f.*

godly *a.* duwiol

gold *n.* aur *m.*

golden *a.* euraid, euraidd

goldfish *n.* pysgod aur *m.pl.*

golf *n.* golff *m.* **golf course**
maes golffio

golfer *n.* golffwr *m.*

good *n. & a.* da. **good
afternoon** prynhawn da;
good day dydd da; **good
evening** noswaith dda; **good
morning** bore da; **good
night** nos da; **good luck** lwc
dda; **good weather** tywydd
da; **Good gracious!** Bobol
annwyl! **Good health!**
Iechyd da!

goodbye 1 *n.* ffarwél *m.*
2 *i.* da bo chi! hwyl! yn iach!

goodness *n.* daioni *m.*

goods *n.* eiddo *m*, nwyddau, da *m.pl.*

goodwill *n.* ewyllys da *m.*

goose *n.* gŵydd *f.*

gosling *n.* cyw gŵydd *m.*

gospel *n.* efengyl *f.* **the Gospel according to John** yr Efengyl yn ôl Ioan

govern *v.* llywodraethu, rheoli

government *n.* llywodraeth *f.*

governor *n.* llywodraethwr, rheolwr

Gower *n.* Gŵyr *f.*

gown *n.* gŵn *f.*

grace *n.* gras *m.*

graceful *a.* lluniaidd, urddasol

grade 1 *n.* gradd, safon *f.* 2 *v.* graddio

gradual *a.* graddol

graduate 1 *n.* gŵr gradd *m.* 2 *v.* graddio

gram *n.* gram *m.*

grammar *n.* gramadeg *m.* **Grammar School** Ysgol Ramadeg

grammatical *a.* gramadegol

grand *a.* mawreddog, ardderchog, crand; prif, uchel. **grand concert** cyngerdd mawreddog

grandchild *n.* ŵyr *m*, wyres *f.*

granddaughter *n.* wyres *f.*

grandeur *n.* mawredd *m.*

grandfather *n.* tad-cu, taid *m.*

grandmother *n.* mam-gu, nain *f.*

grandson *n.* ŵyr *m.*

grant 1 *n.* rhodd *f*, grant, cymhorthdal *m.* 2 *v.* caniatáu.

grapefruit *n.* grawnffrwyth *m.*

grapes *n.pl.* grawnwin

grass *n.* glaswellt *m*, porfa *f*: **grasshopper** ceiliog y rhedyn, sioncyn y gwair

grateful *a.* diolchgar

gratefulness *n.* diolchgarwch *m.*

gratitude *n.* diolchgarwch *m.*

grave 1 *n.* bedd *m.* 2 *a.* difrifol, dwys, prudd

gravestone *n.* carreg fedd *f.*

graveyard *n.* mynwent *f.*

graze *v.* pori

grease 1 *n.* saim *m.* 2 *v.* iro

greasy *a.* seimlyd, seimllyd

great *a.* mawr. **a great many** llawer iawn

great-grandfather *n.* hen dad-cu, hendaid *m.*

great-grandmother *n.* hen fam-gu, hennain *f.*

greatly *ad.* yn fawr

greatness *n.* mawredd *m.*

Grecian 1 *n.* Groegwr *m.* 2 *v.* Groegaidd

Greece *n.* Groeg, Gwlad Groeg *f.*

greed *n.* trachwant *m.*

greedy *a.* trachwantus

Greek 1 *n.* Groeg *f* (*iaith*); Groegwr *m.* (*person*). 2 *a.* Groeg, Groegaidd

green 1 *a.* gwyrdd, gwerdd, glas. 2 *v.* glasu

greenhouse *n.* tŷ gwydr *m.*

greet *v.* cyfarch, annerch

greeting *n.* cyfarchiad *m.*

grey *a.* llwyd, glas: **to turn grey** llwydo, britho, brithio

greyhound *n.* milgi *m.*

grief *n.* galar, gofid, hiraeth *m.*

grievance *n.* cwyn *mf.*
grieve *v.* gofidio, hiraethu
grievous *a.* gofidus, poenus, blin, difrifol
grind *v.* malu
grip 1 *n.* gafael *f.* 2 *v.* gafael (yn), gwasgu
gripping *a.* gafaelgar
groan *v.* ochneidio, griddfan
gross 1 *n.* gros *m.* 2 *a.* bras.
  gross weight pwysau gros
ground 1 *n.* daear *f*, tir *m*; sail *f*; cae chwarae *m.* 2 *v.* gwreiddio, seilio
groundless *a.* di-sail
group *n.* grŵp, twr *m.*
grove *n.* llwyn *m*, celli *f.*
grow *v.* tyfu, prifio, codi
growing *a.* yn tyfu
growth *n.* tyfiant *m.*
grubby *a.* brwnt, budr
guard 1 *n.* gwyliwr, gard *m.* 2 *v.* gwarchod, gwylio
guerilla *n.* herwfilwr *m.*
guess 1 *n.* amcan, dyfaliad *m.* 2 *v.* dyfalu
guest *n.* gwestai, gŵr gwadd *m*, gwraig wadd *f.*
guests *n.* gwesteion, gwahoddedigion *m.pl.*
guide 1 *n.*, arweinydd, hyfforddwr, tywysydd *m.* 2 *v.* arwain, tywys
guild *n.* cymdeithas, urdd *f.*
guilt *n.* euogrwydd, bai *m.*
guilty *a.* euog
guitar *n.* gitâr *m.*
gulf *n.* gwlff *m.*
gull *n.* gwylan *f.*
gulp *v.* llyncu, traflyncu
gum *n.* gwm, glud; cig (y dannedd) *m.*

gun *n.* dryll, gwn *m.*
guts *n.* perfedd *m.*
gymnasium *n.* campfa *f.*

H

habit *n.* arfer *mf*; gwisg *f.*
had, he/she/it *v.* cafodd. **I had** ces i, cefais: *see* cael
hag *n.* gwrach *f.*
hail 1 *n.* cesair, cenllysg *coll.& pl.* 2 *v.* bwrw cesair; cyfarch, galw. 3 *i.* henffych well!
hailstones *n.* cesair *coll. & pl.*
hair *n.* gwallt; blewyn *m.*
hairbrush *n.* brwsh gwallt *m.*
hairy *a.* blewog
half *n.* hanner *m.*
half-back *n.* hanerwr *m.*
hall *n.* neuadd *f*, llys, plas; cyntedd *m.*
Hallowe'en *n.* Nos Galan Gaeaf *f.*
hammer 1 *n.* morthwyl *m.* 2 *v.* morthwylio
hand *n.* llaw *f*; *(of clock)* bys *m.* **hands** dwylo. **in hand** mewn llaw, ar waith
handbag *n.* bag llaw *m.*
handbook *n.* llawlyfr *m.*
handful *n.* dyrnaid *m*, llond llaw *f.*
handkerchief *n.* cadach *m*, hances, neisied *f*, macyn *m.*
handle *n.* dolen *f.* 2 *v.* trafod, trin
handsome *a.* hardd, glân, prydferth, golygus
handwork *n.* gwaith llaw *m.*
handwriting *b.* llawysgrifen *f.*

hang v. hongian; crogi
hankering n. ysfa f.
happen v. digwydd
happening n. digwyddiad m.
happily ad. yn hapus
happiness n. hapusrwydd, llawenydd m.
happy a. dedwydd, hapus, llawen, wrth ei fodd, wrth ei bodd
harbour 1 n. harbwr m, hafan f, porth, porthladd m. **2** v. llochesu
hard a. caled, anodd
harden v. caledu
hardly ad. o'r braidd
hardness n. caledwch m.
hardship n. caledi m.
hard shoulder n. llain galed f.
hard-up a. prin o arian
hardwood n. pren caled m.
hardworking a. gweithgar
hardy a. caled
hare n. ysgyfarnog f.
harm n. cam, drwg, niwed m.
harmless a. diniwed
harp 1 n. telyn f. **2** v. canu'r delyn
harpist n. telynor m., telynores f.
harsh a. llym, garw, cras
harvest n. cynhaeaf
haste 1 n. brys, prysurdeb m. **2** v. brysio, prysuro, cyflymu
hasten v. brysio
hastily ad. yn frysiog
hasty a. brysiog
hat n. het f.
hate 1 n. cas, casineb m. **2** v. casáu
hatred n. cas, casineb m.
haul v. tynnu, llusgo

have, I v. caf. **he/she/it will have** caiff; see cael
haven n. hafan f.
hawk n. hebog m.
hawthorn n. draenen wen f.
hay n. gwair m, porfa f.
hazard n. perygl m, antur mf.
haze n. niwl, tawch m.
hazel n. collen f.
hazy a. niwlog
he pn. ef, fe, efe, efô, fo, yntau
head 1 n. pen, pennaeth m. **2** a. prif
headache n. pen tost, cur yn y pen m.
heading n. pennawd, teitl m.
headland n. penrhyn m.
headline n. pennawd, teitl m. **news headlines** penawdau'r newyddion
headmaster n. prifathro m.
headmistress n. prifathrawes f.
headquarters n. pencadlys m.
heal v. iacháu, gwella
health n. iechyd. **Health Service** Gwasanaeth Iechyd
healthy a. iach, iachus
heap n. pentwr, twr m.
hear v. clyw! (unigol), clywch! (lluosog); see clywed
hearer n. gwrandawr m.
hearing n. clyw; gwrandawiad m. **hearing aid** cymorth clywed
heart n. calon f. **heart attack** trawiad ar y galon
hearth n. aelwyd f.
heat 1 n. gwres m. **2** v. poethi, twymo, gwresogi
heater n. gwresogydd m.

heath n. rhos f, rhostir m.
heather n. grug m.
heave 1 n. gwthiad, hwb m.
2 v. gwthio, codi
heaven n. nef, nefoedd, nen f.
heavenly a. nefol, nefolaidd
heavens n. ffurfafen, wybren f.
heavy a. trwm, trymaidd
Hebrew 1 n. Hebraeg f.
(iaith); Hebrëwr, m. Hebrëes
f. 2 a. Hebraeg, Hebreig
hedge n. perth f, clawdd, gwrych m.
hedgehog n. draenog m.
heed 1 n. sylw m. ystyriaeth f.
2 v. sylwi, ystyried, hidio
heedful a. ystyriol, gofalus
heel 1 n. sawdl mf. 2 v. sodli
height n. uchder, uchelder m.
heir n. aer, etifedd m.
heiress n. aeres, etifeddes f.
helicopter n. hofrennydd f.
hell n. uffern f.
hellish a. uffernol
hello i. helô! hylô! clyw! gwrando!
helm n. llyw m.
help 1 n. cymorth, help m.
2 v. cynorthwyo, helpu
helper n. cynorthwywr, cynorthwy-ydd, helpwr m.
hem n. hem f, godre m, ymyl mf.
hen n. iâr f.
henceforth ad. mwyach, o hyn ymlaen
her pn. ei, hi, hithau
herb n. llysieuyn m.
herbal a. llysieuol
herbs n. llysiau pêr, perlysiau m.pl.

herd n. gyr m, cenfaint f.
here ad. yma, yn y man hwn
hermit n. meudwy m.
hero n. arwr m.
heroine n arwres f.
hers pn. ei, ei heiddo
hew v. torri, naddu
hexagon n. hecsagon m.
hiccup n. yr ig m.
hide 1 n. croen m. 2 v.
cuddio. **hide and seek**
chwarae mig
high a. uchel; mawr; cryf;
llawn. **most high** goruchaf
higher a. uwch
highest a. uchaf
highland n. ucheldir m.
highly ad. yn fawr, yn uchel
highness n. uchder, uchelder;
mawrhydi m. **His Highness**
Ei Fawrhydi
highway n. priffordd f.
highwayman n. lleidr
penffordd m.
hijack 1 n. herwgipiad m. 2 v.
herwgipio
hill n. allt f, bryn m, rhiw f,
tyle m.
hillock n. bryncyn, twmpath
m.
him pn. ef, fe, efe, efô, fo,
yntau
hindrance n. rhwystr m.
hint 1 n. awgrym m. 2 v.
awgrymu.
hip n. clun f.
hire 1 n. cyflog mf. 2 v.
cyflogi, llogi
his pn. ei, ei eiddo
historian n. hanesydd,
haneswr m.
history n. hanes m. **History of**

Wales Hanes Cymru
hit 1 *n.* ergyd *mf,* trawiad *m.*
2 *v.* taro
hoarfrost *n.* llwydrew, barrug
m.
hoary *a.* llwyd
hoax 1 *n.* tric, twyll *m.* 2 *v.*
twyllo
hold 1 *n.* gafael *f.* 2 *v.* dal,
dala, gafael
hole 1 *n.* twll *m;* ffau *f.* 2 *v.*
tyllu
holiday *n.* gŵyl *f.*
holidays *n.* gwyliau *pl.*
Christmas holidays gwyliau
Nadolig: **summer holidays**
gwyliau haf
hollow 1 *n.* pant *m.* 2 *a.*
gwag, cau
holly *n.* celyn *pl,* celynnen *f.*
holly bush llwyn celyn
holy *a.* sanctaidd, glân, gwyn:
Holy Spirit Ysbryd Glân
Holyhead *n.* Caergybi *f.*
home 1 *n.* cartref *m,* aelwyd *f.*
2 *ad.* adref, tua thref. **at**
home gartref: **going home**
mynd adref, mynd tua thref
homeless *a.* digartref
homesick *a.* hiraethus
homesickness *n.* hiraeth *m.*
homestead *n.* tyddyn *m.*
homeward *ad.* adref, tua thref
homework *n.* gwaith cartref
m. **homework book** llyfr
gwaith cartref
homosexuality *n.*
gwrywgydiaeth *f.*
honest *a.* cywir, gonest, onest
honesty *n.* gonestrwydd,
onestrwydd *m.*
honey *n.* mêl *m.*

honeymoon *n.* mis mêl
honour 1 *n.* anrhydedd *mf.*
2 *v.* anrhydeddu; urddo;
cydnabod
hook 1 *n.* bach, bachyn;
cryman *m.* 2 *v.* bachu
hoop *n.* cylch *m.*
hooray *i.* & *n.* hwrê
hope 1 *n.* gobaith *m.* 2 *v.*
gobeithio
horizon *n.* gorwel *m.*
horn *n.* corn *m.* (*automobile*).
horrendous *a.* dychrynllyd,
ofnadwy
horrible *a.* ofnadwy
horse *n.* ceffyl, march *m.*
horseman *n.* marchog *m.*
horseshoe *n.* pedol *f.*
hospice *n.* ysbyty, llety *m.*
hospitable *a.* croesawus,
lletygar
hospital *n.* ysbyty *m.*
host *n.* llu *m,* byddin *f;*
gwesteiwr, lletywr *m.*
hostage *n.* gwystl *m.*
hostel *n.* neuadd breswyl *f.*
hostess *n.* gwesteiwraig *f.*
hot *a.* twym, poeth, gwresog.
hot-water bottle potel ddŵr
twym/poeth
hotel *n.* gwesty *m.*
hotelier *n.* gwestywr *m.*
hound 1 *n.* ci hela, helgi *m.*
2 *v.* hela, erlid
hour *n.* awr *f.*
hourly *ad.* bob awr
house *n.* tŷ *m.*
housework *n.* gwaith tŷ *m.*
housewife *n.* gwraig tŷ *f.*
housing *n.* tai *pl.*
how *ad.* sut, pa fodd, pa. **how**
many? faint?

however *ad.* sut bynnag, er hynny, pa fodd bynnag

howl *v.* udo

hue *n.* lliw *m.* gwawr *f.*

hug *v.* cofleidio, gwasgu

huge *a.* anferth, enfawr

hum 1 *n.* si, sibrwd *m.* **2** *v.* mwmian

humble *a.* gostyngedig, isel

humorous *a.* doniol

humour *n.* hiwmor *m*, hwyl *f.*

hundred 1 *n.* cant *m.* **2** *a.* can. **hundred years old** canmlwydd

hundredth *n.* & *a.* canfed

hunger 1 *n.* newyn, chwant bwyd *m.* **2** *v.* newynu

hunt *n.* helfa *f.* **2** *v.* hel, hela, erlid

hunter *n.* heliwr; ceffyl hela *m.*

hunting *n.* hela *m.* **hunting horn** corn hela

hurricane *n.* corwynt *m.*

hurry 1 *n.* brys, prysurdeb *m.* **2** *v.* brysio, prysuro

hurt 1 *n.* niwed, dolur *m.* **2** *v.* anafu, brifo

husband *n.* gŵr, priod, gŵr priod *m.*

hut *n.* caban, cwt *m.*

hutch *n.* cwt, cwb *m.*

hydrogen *n.* hydrogen *m.*

hymn *n.* emyn, hymn *m.*

hymnal *n.* llyfr emynau *m.*

hymn-tune *n.* emyn-dôn *f.*

hypermarket *n.* archfarchnad *f.*

hyphen *n.* cyplysnod, cysylltnod *m.*

I

I *pn.* mi, myfi; fi, i; minnau, innau

ice *n.* iâ, rhew *m.* **Ice Age** Oes yr Iâ

iceberg *n.* mynydd iâ *m.*

ice-cream *n.* hufen iâ *m.*

Iceland *n.* Gwlad yr Iâ *f.*

icy *a.* rhewllyd.

idea *n.* syniad *m.*

identical *a.* yr un *(fath).*

identify *v.* abnabod *(fel yr un un),* enwi, nodi; uniaethu (â)

idiom *n.* priod-ddull, idiom *f.*

idle 1 *a.* segura, diog, dioglyd. **2** *v.* segur, diogi

idler *n.* diogyn, pwdryn *m.*

idol *n.* delw *f.*

if *c.* os, pe

ignite *v.* tanio

ill *a.* claf, gwael, sâl, tost; drwg

ill-mannered *a.* anfoesgar

illness *n.* afiechyd, clefyd, dolur, salwch, tostrwydd *m.*

illustrate *v.* darlunio; egluro, esbonio

illustration *n.* darlun *m.*

image *n.* delw, llun *m.*

imagination *n.* dychymyg *m.*

imagine *v.* dychmygu, tybied, tybio

immediately *ad.* ar unwaith, yn union, yn y man

immense *a.* anferth, eang

imminent *a.* agos, gerllaw, wrth y drws

immunization *n.* imwneiddiad *m.*

immunize *v.* imwneiddio

immunity *n.* imwnedd *m.*

impart *v.* cyfrannu, rhoi
imperative 1 *n.* gorchymyn *m.*
  2 *a.* gorchmynnol, gorfodol
imperfect *a.* amherffaith
impinge *v.* taro yn erbyn,
  cyffwrdd â
implement 1 *n.* offeryn. arf *m.*
  2 *v.* gweithredu
implore *v.* erfyn (ar)
imply *v.* cyfleu, awgrymu
importance *n.* pwys,
  pwysigrwydd *m.*
important *a.* pwysig
impossible *a.* amhosibl
impress 1 *n.* argraff *f.* **2** *v.*
  argraffu, pwyso (ar)
impression *n.* argraff
imprison *v.* carcharu
improve *v.* gwella
impudence *n.* haerllugrwydd
  m.
impudent *a.* haerllug, eofn
in 1 *prp.* yn, yng, ym, mewn.
  2 *ad.* i mewn. **in the midst of**
  ynghanol: **in time** mewn
  pryd
inaccurate *a.* anghywir,
  gwallus
inasmuch *ad.* yn gymaint (â)
inch *n.* modfedd *f.*
incident *n.* digwyddiad *m.*
incinerator *n.* llosgydd *m*,
  ffwrnais *f.*
include *v.* cynnwys
included *a.* cynwysedig
including *prp.* gan gynnwys
inclusive *a.* gan gynnwys,
  cynwysedig
income *n.* enillion *pl*, incwm
  m. **Income Tax** Treth Incwm
incorporate *v.* ymgorffori
incorrect *a.* anghywir

indebted *a.* dyledus
indeed *ad.* yn wir, iawn
indemnity *n.* iawndal *m.*
independence *n.*
  annibyniaeth *f.*
independent *n.* annibynnwr *m.*
independent *a.* annibynnol
independently *ad.* yn
  annibynnol, ar wahân
index *n.* mynegai *m.*
India *n.* Yr India *f.*
Indian 1 *n.* Indiad *m.* **2** *a.*
  Indiaidd
indicate *v.* dangos, mynegi
indigestion *n.* diffyg traul *m.*
individual 1 *n.* un, unigolyn *n.*
  2 *a.* unigol
indolent *a.* diog, dioglyd,
  segur, pwdr
indoor *a.* i mewn, dan do
induct *v.* sefydlu
induction *n.* sefydliad *m.*
indulgence *n.* maldod *m.*
industrious *a.* gweithgar
industry *n.* diwydiant;
  diwydrwydd *m.*
ineffectual *a.* aneffeithiol
inevitable *a.* anochel
inexpensive *a.* rhad
inexperience *n.* diffyg profiad
  m.
inexperienced *a.* dibrofiad
infant *n.* baban, maban *m.*
  Infants' school ysgol
  fabanod: **Infants' teacher**
  athrawes fabanod
infection *n.* haint *f.*
inferior *a.* is, israddol
infinitive *n.* berfenw *m.*
infirm *a.* gwan
infirmity *n.* gwendid, llesgedd
  m.

inflammation *n.* llid *m.*

inflate *v.* chwyddo, rhoi awyr yn

inflation *n.* chwyddiant *m.*

influence 1 *n.* dylanwad *m.* 2 *v.* dylanwadu

influenza *n.* ffliw *m.*

inform *v.* hysbysu

information *n.* gwybodaeth *f.*

infrequent *a.* anaml

ingredients *n.* defnyddiau, cynhwysion *m.pl.*

inhabitants *n.* trigolion, preswylwyr *m.pl.*

inhale *v.* anadlu

inherit *v.* etifeddu

iniquity *n.* drwg, drygioni, anwiredd *m.*

injection *n.* chwistrelliad, pigiad *m.*

injure *v.* anafu, niweidio

injury *n.* niwed, cam, clwyf, anaf *m.*

inn *n.* tafarn *mf*, gwesty *m.*

inner *a.* mewnol

inn-keeper *n.* tafarnwr, gwestywr *m.*

innocent *a.* diniwed

inoculation *n.* brechiad *m.*

inquire *v.* gofyn, holi, ymholi

inquiry *n.* ymchwiliad, ymholiad *m.*

inquisition *n.* ymchwiliad *m.*

insane *a.* gwallgof

insect *n.* pryf, pryfedyn, pryfyn *m.*

in-service *a.* mewn swydd. **in-service training** hyfforddiant mewn swydd

inside 1 *n.* tu mewn *m.* 2 *a.* mewnol. 3 *ad.* i mewn, o fewn. 4 *prp.* y tu mewn

inside-out *ad.* o chwith

insist *v.* mynnu

insolence *n.* haerllugrwydd *m.*

insolent *a.* haerllug

inspire *v.* ysbrydoli

instantaneous *a.* yn y man

instead *ad.* yn lle

institution *n.* sefydliad *m.*

instruct *v* . cyfarwyddo, dysgu, hyfforddi

instruction *n.* hyfforddiant *m.*

instructor *n.* hyfforddwr *m.*

instrument *n.* offeryn, arf *m.* **musical instrument** offeryn cerdd

instrumental *a.* offerynol; yn gyfrwng

insult *n.* sarhad *m.*

insurance *n.* yswiriant *m.*

insure *v.* yswiro, yswirio

insurrection *n.* terfysg, gwrthryfel *m.*

intellect *n.* deall *m.*

intelligent *a.* deallus

intelligentsia *n.* y deallus *m*, deallusion *m.pl.*

intend *v.* bwriadu, golygu

intense *a.* dwys

intent *n.* bwriad, amcan; diben *m.*

intention *n.* bwriad *m.*

interest *n.* diddordeb; llog; budd *m.* **interest rates** cyfraddau llog

interests *n.pl.* diddordebau *m.*

interfere *v.* ymhel, ymyrru, ymyrryd

interference *n.* ymyrraeth *f.*

interior 1 *n.* tu mewn, canol *m.* 2 *a.* mewnol

intermediate *a.* canol,
canolradd
internal *a.* mewnol
international *a.* rhyngwladol
international eisteddfod
eisteddfod tyngwladol
internet *n.* rhyngrwyd *f.*
interpreter *n.* cyfieithydd *m.*
interrogate *v.* holi
interrogator *n.* holwr *m.*
interrupt *v.* torri ar, torri ar
draws, ymyrru, ymyrryd
interval *n.* egwyl *f,* saib *m.*
intervene *v.* ymyrru, ymyrryd
interview 1 *n.* cyfweliad *m.*
2 *v.* cyfweld
into *prp.* i, i mewn
intoxicate *v.* meddwi
invalid *n.* un afiach, un
methedig *mf.*
invalid *a.* di-rym
invest *v.* buddsoddi
investigate *v.* ymchwilio,
chwilio
investigation *n.* ymchwiliad *m.*
investigator *n.* ymchwiliwr,
ymchwilydd *m.*
invisible *a.* anweledig
invitation *n.* gwahoddiad,
gwahodd *m.*
invite *v.* gwahodd
invited *a.* gwahoddedig
involved *a.* cymhleth, astrus,
cywrain
inward *a.* mewnol
Ireland *n.* Iwerddon, Yr Ynys
Werdd *f.*
Irish 1 *n.* Gwyddeleg *f. (iaith).*
2 *a.* Gwyddelig
Irishman *n.* Gwyddel *m.*
Irishwoman *n.* Gwyddeles *f.*
iron 1 *n.* & *a.* haearn *m.* 2 *v.*

smwddio
ironing board *n.* bwrdd
smwddio *m.*
irritable *a.* pigog, piwis
irritation *n.* poen *mf,* llid, *m,*
enynfa *f.*
is *v.* ydy, yw, mae, oes, sy,
sydd
island *n.* ynys *f.* **Caldy Island**
Ynys Bŷr: **Bardsey Island**
Ynys Enlli
Israel *n.* Israel *f.*
Israelite *n.* Israeliad *m.*
issue 1 *n.* llif, tarddiad;
plant; cyhoeddiad *m.* 2 *v.*
tarddu; cyhoeddi
it *pn.* ef, efe, fe, efo, fo; hi
Italian *n.* Eidaleg *f. (iaith);*
Eidalwr *m,* Eidales *f.*
Italy *n.* Yr Eidal *f.*
itch 1 *n.* crafu *m,* ysfa *f.* 2 *v.*
cosi, ysu
item *n.* eitem *f.*
its *pn.* ei
itself *pn.* ei hun, ei hunan
ivy *n.* iorwg, eiddew *m.*

J

jackdaw *n.* jac-y-do *m.*
jacket *n.* siaced *f.*
jail *n.* carchar *m.*
jam 1 *n.* jam *m.;* tagfa *f.* 2 *v.*
gwasgu, tagu
January *n.* Ionawr *m.*
Japan *n.* Japan *f.*
Japanese 1 *n.* Japanaeg *f.*
(iaith); Japanead *m.* 2 *a.*
Japaneaidd
jar 1 *n* jar, jâr *f.* 2 *v.* ysgwyd
jaundice *n.* y clefyd melyn *m.*

jaw *n.* gên, cern *f.*

jay *n.* sgrech y coed *m.*

jealous *a.* cenfigennus

jeer 1 *n.* gwawd *m.* 2 *v.* gwawdio

jelly *n.* jeli *m.*

jerk 1 *n.* plwc *m.* 2 *v.* plycio

jersey *n.* jersi, jyrsi, siersi *f.*

Jerusalem *n.* Caersalem, Jerwsalem *f.*

Jesus *n.* Iesu *m.* **Jesus Christ** Iesu Grist: **Jesus Son of God** Iesu Mab Duw

Jew *n.* Iddew *m.*

Jewess *n.* Iddewes *f.*

jewel *n.* gem *f,* tlws *m.*

Jewish *a.* Iddewig

jingle *n.* rhigwm; tinc *m.*

job *n.* job, jobyn, gwaith *m,* swydd *f.* **Job Centre** Canolfan Gwaith *mf.*

jobless *a.* diwaith

jog *v.* loncian

jogger *n.* lonciwr *m.*

join *v.* cydio; ymuno; uno; ymaelodi

joiner *n.* saer coed *m.*

joint 1 *n.* cyswllt, cymal *m.* 2 *a.* cyd. **joint of meat** darn o gig *m.*

joke 1 *n.* jôc *f.* 2 *v.* jocan, cellwair

jolly *a.* braf, llawen, llon

journalist *n.* newyddiadurwr *m.*

journey 1 *n.* hynt, siwrnai, taith *f.* 2 *v.* teithio

joy *n.* llawenydd *m.*

joyful 1 *a.* llawen, llon. 2 *v.* llawenhau

jubilation *n* . llawenydd, gorfoledd *m.*

jubilee *n.* jiwbilî *f.*

Judaism *n.* Iddewaeth *f.*

judge 1 *n.* barnwr; beirniad; dyfarnwr *m.* 2 *v.* beirniadu; dyfarnu

judgement *n.* barn *f.* dyfarniad *m.*

jug *n.* jwg, siwg *f.*

juice *n.* sudd *m.*

juicy *a.* llawn sudd

July *n.* Gorffennaf *m.*

jumble 1 *n.* cymysgwch *m,* cymysgfa *f.* 2 *v.* cymysgu: **jumble sale** ffair sborion *f.*

jump 1 *n.* naid *f.* llam *m.* 2 *v.* neidio, llamu

jumper *n.* neidiwr *m;* jersi, jyrsi, siwmper *f.*

junction *n.* cydiad *m;* cyffordd *f.*

June *n.* Mehefin *m.*

junior *a.* iau; ieuaf. **junior school** ysgol iau

just 1 *a.* cyfiawn, cywir, iawn, teg. 2 *ad.* braidd, yn union, newydd. **just now** gynnau (fach)

justice *n.* cyfiawnder; ynad *m.* **Justice of the Peace** Ynad Heddwch

juvenile *a.* ieuanc, ifanc

K

kangaroo *n.* cangarŵ *m.*

keep 1 *n.* cadw *m;* amddiffynfa *f.* 2 *v.* cadw; cynnal

keeper *n.* ceidwad *m.*

kennel *n.* cwb, cenel *m.*

kerchief *n.* cadach *m,* hances

f, macyn *m*, neisied *f*.
kettle *n*. tegell *m*.
key *n*. agoriad *m*, allwedd *f*; cywair *m*. **keyhole** twll clo
kick 1 *n*. cic *f*. **2** *v*. cicio. **drop kick** cic adlam
kidnap 1 *n*. herwgydiad *m*. **2** *v*. herwgydio
kidnapper *n*. herwgydiwr *m*.
kidney beans *n.pl*. ffa dringo, cidnabêns *pl*.
kill *v*. lladd
killer *n*. lladdwr *m*.
kilogram *n*. kilogram (kg.) *m*.
kilometre *n*. kilometr (km.) *m*.
kilowatt *n*. kilowat (kW.) *m*.
kin *n*. perthynas *mf*.
kind *n*. math, rhyw *m*.
kind *a*. caredig
kindergarten *n*. ysgol feithrin *f*.
kindliness *n*. caredigrwydd *m*.
kindly *a*. caredig, tirion
kindness *n*. caredigrwydd *m*; cymwynas *f*.
kindred *n*. perthynas *mf*; perthnasau *pl*.
king *n*. brenin *m*.
kingdom *n*. teyrnas *f*. **Kingdom of Heaven** Teyrnas Nefoedd: **United Kingdom** Teyrnas Unedig
kingfisher *n*. glas y dorlan *m*.
kingly *a*. brenhinol
kipper *n*. ciper *m*.
kiss 1 *n*. cusan *mf*, sws *m* **2** *v*. cusanu
kitchen *n*. cegin *f*.
kitchenette *n*. cegin fach *f*.
kitchen garden *n*. gardd lysiau *f*.

kitten *n*. cath fach *f*.
knead *v*. tylino
knee *n*. glin *mf*, pen-glin, pen-lin *m*.
kneel *v*. penlinio
knife *n*. cyllell *f*. **bread knife** cyllell fara: **pocket knife** cyllell boced
knight *n*. marchog *m*.
knit *v*. gwau
knock 1 *n*. cnoc, ergyd *mf*. **2** *v*. cnocio, curo, taro
knot 1 *n*. clwm, cwlwm *m*. **2** *v*. clymu
know *v*. adnabod; gwybod: **I know** gwn, mi wn, rydw i'n gwybod; **to know well** gwybod yn iawn
knowing *a*. gwybodus; ffel
knowingly *ad*. yn fwriadol
knowledge *n*. gwybodaeth *f*.
knuckle *n*. migwrn, cymal *m*.

L

label 1 *n*. llabed, label, *f*. **2** *v*. labelu
laboratory *n* labordy *m*. **language laboratory** labordy iaith
laborious *a*. llafurus
labour 1 *n*. llafur, gwaith *m*. **2** *v*. llafurio, gweithio. **the Labour Party** y Blaid Lafur
labourer *n*. labrwr, gweithiwr *m*.
lace 1 *n*. les *m*. **2** *v*. cau *(esgidiau)*.
lack 1 *n*. eisiau, diffyg *m*. **2** *v*. bod mewn eisiau
lad *n*. llanc, hogyn, gwas,

bachgen *m.*
ladder *n.* ysgol *f.*
laden *a.* llwythog
ladies *n.* arglwyddesau;
boneddigesau; toiledau
merched *pl.*
lady *n.* arglwyddes;
boneddiges *f.*
lair *n.* ffau, gwâl, lloches *f.*
lake *n.* llyn *m.*
lamb *n.* oen *m.* **Paschal Lamb**
Oen y Pasg.
lame 1 *a.* cloff. 2 *v.* cloffi
lameness *n.* cloffi, cloffni *m.*
lamp *n.* lamp *f:* **lampshade**
lamplen *f.*
lamp post *n.* postyn lamp,
polyn lamp *m.*
land 1 *n.* tir *m,* daear, gwlad,
glan *f.* 2 *v.* glanio
landlady *n.* gwraig llety *f.*
landlord *n.* meistr tir, lletywr,
tafarnwr *m.*
landscape *n.* tirlun *m.*
lane *n.* lôn *f.* **escape lane** lôn
ddianc
language *n.* iaith *f.* **first
language** iaith gyntaf,
mamiaith; **second language**
ail iaith; **foreign language**
iaith dramor, iaith estron
lantern *n.* llusern *f.*
lap 1 *n.* arffed *f,* glin *mf.* 2 *v.*
lapio
lapel *n.* llabed *f.*
large *a.* mawr; eang; helaeth
largely *ad.* gan mwyaf
lark *n.* ehedydd, hedydd,
uchedydd *m.*
laryngitis *n.* llwnc tost *m.*
lass *n.* geneth, hogen, llances,
merch *f.*

last 1 *a.* diwethaf; olaf. 2 *ad.*
yn ddiwethaf, yn olaf. 3 *v.*
para, parhau, dal, dala. **last
night** neithiwr; **last week** yr
wythnos diwethaf; **last month**
mis diwethaf; **last year** y
llynedd; **at last** o'r diwedd;
the last word y gair olaf
late *a.* hwyr; diweddar
lately *ad.* yn ddiweddar
later *ad.* wedyn, eto, yn
ddiweddarach
latest *a.* diweddaraf
Latin *n.* Lladin *f.*
latter *a.* diwethaf, olaf
laugh *n.* & *v.* chwerthin *m.*
laughable *a.* chwerthinllyd
laughter *n.* chwerthin *m.*
launderette *n* . golchdy *m.*
lavatory *n.* tŷ-bach *m,* ystafell
ymolchi *f,* toiled *m.*
lavender *n.* lafant *m.*
law *n.* cyfraith, deddf *f.*
lawn *n.* lawnt *f.*
lawyer *n.* cyfreithiwr *m.*
lax *a.* llac; esgeulus
lay *v.* gosod, dodi; dodwy
layer *n.* haenen *f.*
laze *v.* diogi, segura
laziness *n.* diogi *m.*
lazy *a.* diog, dioglyd, pwdr
lead *n.* plwm *m.*
lead *v.* arwain, tywys
leaden *a.* plwm
leader *n.* arweinydd; blaenwr
m.
leaf *n.* deilen; dalen *f.*
leaflet *n.* taflen *f.*
league *n.* cynghrair *m.*
leak *v.* gollwng, colli, diferu
lean 1 *n.* cig coch *m.* 2 *a.*
main, tenau. 3 *v.* pwyso (ar)

leap 1 *n.* llam *m*, naid *f.* **2** *v.* llamu, neidio. **leap year** blwyddyn naid

learn *u.* dysgu

learned *a.* dysgedig, hyddysg

learner *n.* dysgwr *m.*

learning 1 *n.* dysg *f.* **2** *v.* dysgu

lease *n.* les, prydles *f.*

least *a.* lleiaf; *see* bach. **at least** o leiaf

leather *n.* lledr *m.*

leave 1 *n.* caniatâd *m.* **2** *v.* gadael, ymadael

leaven *n.* lefain *m.*

lecture 1 *n.* darlith *f.* **2** *v.* darlithio

lecturer *n.* darlithiwr, darlithydd *m.*

ledge *n.* silff *f*; crib *mf.*

leek *n.* cenhinen *f.*

left *a.* chwith. **left-handed** llawchwith

leg *n.* coes *f.*

legend *n.* chwedl *f.*

legislate *v.* deddfu

leisure *n.* hamdden *f.*

leisurely *a.* hamddenol

lemon *n.* lemwn *m.* **lemonade** diod lemwn; **lemon juice** sudd lemwn

lend *v.* benthyca, rhoi benthyg

length *n.* hyd *m.* **at length** o'r diwedd

lengthen *v.* estyn, ymestyn

lengthy *a.* hir

less 1 *a.* & *n.* llai *m.* **2** *ad.* yn llai

lesson *n.* gwers *f.* **history lesson** gwers hanes; **Welsh lesson** gwers Gymraeg

lest *c.* rhag, rhag ofn, fel na

let *v.* caniatáu; gadael; gosod ar rent

lethal *a.* marwol

letter *n.* llythyr *m*; llythyren *f.*

lettuce *n.* letysen *f.*

level *n.* & *a.* gwastad *m.* lefel *f.* **spirit level** lefelydd

level crossing *n.* croesfan *f.*

liable *a.* agored, atebol

liar *n.* celwyddgi *m.*

liberal *a.* hael, haelionus

liberty *n.* rhyddid *m.*

librarian *n.* llyfrgellydd *m.*

library *n.* llyfrgell *f.*

licence *n.* trwydded *f.* **driving licence** trwydded yrru

lick *v.* llyfu, llio

lid *n.* clawr *m.* **saucepan lid** clawr sosban

lie 1 *n.* celwydd, anwiredd *n.* **2** *v.* dweud celwydd, dweud anwiredd; gorwedd

life *n.* bywyd, byw *m.*

lifeboat *n.* bad achub *m.*

life insurance *n.* yswiriant bywyd *m.*

lifeless *a.* marwaidd

lifetime *n.* oes *f.*

lift 1 *n.* lifft *m.* **2** *v.* codi

ligament *n.* gewyn

light 1 *n.* golau, goleuni, llewyrch *m.* **2** *a.* golau; ysgafn. **3** *v.* goleuo; tanio

lighten *v.* ysgafnhau, ysgafnu

lighthouse *n.* goleudy *m.*

lightning *n.* mellt, lluched *pl.*

like 1 *a.* tebyg. **2** *prp.* fel. **3** *v.* hoffi, caru

likeable *a.* dymunol

likely *a.* & *ad.* tebygol, tebyg

likeness *n.* tebygrwydd *m.*

likewise 1 *n.* yn yr un modd.
2 *c.* hefyd

liking *n.* hoffter *m.*

lily *n.* lili *f.* **lily of the valley**
lili'r dyffrynnoedd

limb *n.* aelod *m;* cangen *f;*
cymal *m.*

limit *n.* ffin *f,* terfyn *m.*

limp 1 *a.* llipa. **2** *v.* cloffi

line *n.* llinell *f,* llinyn *m,* lein
f.

linen *n.* lliain *m.*

linesman *n.* llinellwr, ystlyswr
m.

link 1 *n.* dolen *f.* **2** *v.* cydio

lion *n.* llew *m.*

lioness *n.* llewes *f.*

lip *n.* gwefus *f,* min *m.*

lipstick *n.* minlliw *m.*

liquid 1 *n.* hylif *m.* **2** *a.* hylif;
gwlyb

list *n.* rhestr *f.*

listen *v.* gwrando

listener *n.* gwrandawr *m.*

literary *a.* llenyddol

literate *a.* llythrennog

literature *n.* llên, llenyddiaeth
f.

litre *n.* litr *m.*

litter 1 *n.* sbwriel, ysbwriel *m.*
2 *v.* sarnu

littérateur *n.* llenor *m.*

little *a.* bach, bychan, bechan;
mân, tamaid, ychydig

live *a.* & *v.* byw

lively *a.* bywiog, heini

liver *n.* iau *m,* afu *mf.*

Liverpool *n.* Lerpwl *f.*

living *a.* byw, yn fyw

load 1 *n.* baich, llwyth *m.*
2 *v.* llwytho

loaf *n.* torth *f.*

loathsome *a.* ffiaidd

lobby *n.* cyntedd, porth *m.*

local *a.* lleol. **Local**
Government Llywodraeth
Leol

locality *n.* lle *m,* ardal,
cymdogaeth *f.*

localize *v.* lleoli

locate *v.* lleoli, gosod

location *n.* lleoliad *m.*

loch *n.* llyn, llwch *m.*

lock 1 *n.* clo *m.* **2** *v.* cloi

locked *a.* ar glo, dan glo,
ynghlo

lodge 1 *n.* llety *m.* **2** *v.* lletya

lodger *n.* lletywr *m.*

lodging(s) *n. (pl).* llety *m.*

loft *n.* llofft *f.*

loin *n.* llwyn *f.*

London *n.* Llundain *f.*

loneliness *n.* unigrwydd *m.*

lonely *a.* unig

long 1 *n.* hir, maith. **2** *v.*
hiraethu. **long since** ers
amser

longing *n.* hiraeth *m.*

look 1 *n.* golwg *mf,* trem **2** *v.*
edrych, ysbïo

loose 1 *a.* llac, llaes, rhydd.
2 *v.* datod, llacio, rhyddhau

loosen *v.* llacio, rhyddhau,
datod

lord *n.* arglwydd *m.* **The Lord**
Yr Arglwydd; **the Lord's**
Prayer Gweddi'r Arglwydd;
House of Lords Tŷ'r
Arglwyddi

lord mayor *n.* arglwydd faer
m.

lorry *n.* lorri *f.*

lorry driver *n.* gyrrwr lorri *m.*

lose *v.* colli

loss *n.* colled *mf.*
loud *a.* uchel
loudest *a.* uchaf
Loughor *n.* Casllwchwr *f.*
lounge 1 *n.* lolfa *f.* 2 *v.* lolian
louse *n.* lleuen *f.*
love 1 *n.* cariad, serch *m.* 2 *v.* caru: **love-letter** llythyr caru
lovely *a.* hyfryd, teg, prydferth; braf
lover *n.* cariad *mf,* carwr *m.*
loving *a.* cariadus, serchus, serchog
low *a.* isel
lower 1 *a.* is. 2 *v.* gostwng, gollwng
lowest *a.* isaf; lleiaf
loyal *a.* ffyddlon, teyrngar
lozenge *n.* losinen, losen *f.*
luck *n.* lwc, ffortiwn *f.* **best of luck** lwc dda, pob hwyl
luckily *ad.* yn ffodus, yn lwcus
lucky *a.* ffodus, lwcus
lull 1 *n.* gosteg *m.* 2 *v.* suo
lullaby *n.* hwiangerdd *f.*
luminous *a.* golau, disglair, llachar
lungs *n.* ysgyfaint *pl.*
lupins *n.* bysedd y blaidd *pl.*
lust *n.* chwant, trachwant *m.*
lustful *a.* trachwantus
lustre *n.* llewyrch *m.*
luxurious *a.* moethus
lyric *n.* telyneg *f.*

M

machine *n.* peiriant *m.*
machinery peiriannau
mackintosh *n.* cot law *f.*

mad *a.* gwyllt, gwallgof
magazine *n.* cylchgrawn *m.*
magic *n.* hud, lledrith, swyn *m.*
magician *n.* dewin *m.*
magistrate *n.* ustus, ynad *m.*
magnificent *a.* gwych
magnifying glass *n.* chwyddwydr *m.*
magnitude *n.* maint, ehangder *m.*
magpie *n.* pioden *m.*
maid *n.* morwyn, merch *f.* **old maid** hen ferch
mail 1 *n.* y post *m.* 2 *v.* postio
main *a.* pennaf, prif, mwyaf. **main road** ffordd fawr, priffordd; **mainland** y tir mawr
mainly *ad.* yn bennaf
majesty *n.* mawredd; mawrhydi *m.* **Her Majesty** Ei Mawrhydi
major 1 *n.* uwchgapten *m.* 2 *a.* prif, mwyaf
majority *n.* mwyafrif; oedran llawn *m.*
make *v.* gwneud, gwneuthur
make-up *n.* & *v.* coluro *m.*
male *n.* gwryw *m.*
man *n.* dyn, gŵr, mab *m.* **man of letters** llenor
manage *v.* rheoli, trin; llwyddo
manager *n.* rheolwr *m.*
manger *n.* preseb *m.*
manifest *v.* dangos, egluro
manipulate *v.* trin, trafod
manner *n.* modd, dull *m.*
manners *n.* moesau *pl.* **good manners** moesau da
manse *n.* tŷ gweinidog, mans *m.*

mansion n. plas, plasty m.
mantle n. mantell f.
manual 1 n. llawlyfr m.
2 a. perthynol i'r llaw
manure n. gwrtaith, tail m.
tom f.
manuscript n. llawysgrif f.
many 1 n. llawer m. 2 a.
llawer, aml, sawl. **how many**
sawl. **too many** gormod
map n. map n.
March n. Mawrth m.
march 1 n. ymdaith f.
2 v. ymdeithio
margin n. ffin f, ymyl mf.
mariner n. llongwr, morwr m.
mark 1 n. nod, nam, ôl, marc
m. 2 v. nodi, marcio
market 1 n. marchnad f.
2 v. marchnata
marriage n. priodas f.
married a. priod
marrow n. mêr m. **vegetable
marrow** pwmpen f.
marry v. priodi
Mars n. Mawrth m.
mart n. mart m.
martyr n. merthyr m.
marvel 1 n. rhyfeddod m.
2 v. rhyfeddu, synnu
marvellous a. rhyfeddol,
gwych
masculine a. gwryw,
gwrywaidd, gwrywol
mask 1 n. mwgwd m. 2 v.
cuddio
mass n. pentwr m; pwysau
pl; offeren f.
massive a. anferth
master 1 n. meistr, capten
(llong) m. 2 v. meistroli
masterpiece n. campwaith m.

mat n. mat m.
match n. matsien; gêm;
gornest; priodas f.
material n. defnydd, nwydd
m.
mathematical a.
mathemategol
mathematician n.
mathemategwr m.
mathematics n. mathemateg
f.
matrimony n. priodas f.
matter n. mater m. **What's the
matter?** Beth sy'n bod?
mature 1 a. aeddfed. 2 v.
aeddfedu
maximum n. uchafswm,
uchafrif, uchafbwynt m.
May n. Mai m. **May Day**
Calan Mai
maybe ad. efallai, hwyrach
mayor n. maer f.
mayoress n. maeres f.
me pn. myfi, mi, fi, i; minnau
mead n. medd m.
meadow n. dôl, gwaun f, maes
m.
meagre a. cul, llwm, tenau,
prin
meal n. pryd o fwyd; blawd
m.
mean 1 n. cyfrwng, modd;
canol m. 2 a. sâl; gwael;
tynn. 3 v. bwriadu, golygu,
meddwl
meaning n. ystyr mf, meddwl
m.
meaningful a. ystyrlon
means n. modd, moddion,
cyfrwng; cyfoeth m. **by all
means** ar bob cyfrif, wrth
gwrs

measles *n.* y frech goch *f.*

measure *n.* mesur *m.*

meat *n.* cig *m.*

medal *n.* bathodyn *m,* medal *f.*

meddle *v.* ymhél, ymyrru, ymyrryd

media *n.* cyfryngau *pl.*

medicine *n.* moddion, ffisig *m;* meddyginiaeth *f.*

meditate *v.* myfyrio

meditation *n.* myfyrdod *m.*

medium 1 *n.* cyfrwng; canol *m.* 2 *a.* canol

medley *n.* cadwyn o alawon *f;* cymysgwch *m.*

meet *v.* cyfarfod, cwrdd (â); cyffwrdd

meeting *n.* cyfarfod, cwrdd *m;* oedfa *f.*

melody *n.* alaw, tôn *f.*

melt *v.* toddi

member *n.* aelod *m.* **to become a member** ymaelodi: **Member of Parliament (M.P.)** Aelod Seneddol (A.S.)

membership *n.* aelodaeth *f.*

memory *n.* cof *m.*

mend *v.* gwella, trwsio, cyweirio

meningitis *n.* llid yr ymennydd *m.*

menstruation *n.* y misglwyf *m.*

mention *n.* & *v.* sôn (am) *mf.*

menu *n.* bwydlen *f.*

merchant *n.* masnachwr *m.*

merciful *a.* trugarog

mercifully *ad.* drwy drugaredd

Mercury *n.* Mercher *m.*

mercury *n.* arian byw, mercwri *m.*

mercy *n.* trugaredd *f.* **to be merciful** trugarhau

merit 1 *n.* teilyngdod *m.* 2 *v.* haeddu

mermaid *n.* môr-forwyn *f.*

merriment *n.* miri *m.*

merry *a.* llawen, llon

mess *n.* llanast(r) *m.*

message *n.* neges *f.*

messenger *n.* negesydd *m.*

metal *n.* metel *m.*

meteor *n.* seren wib *f.*

meter *n.* mesurydd *m.*

method *n.* dull, modd *m,* trefn *f.* **new methods** dulliau newydd

methodical *a.* trefnus

metre *n.* mesur; metr *m.* **kilometre** kilometr (km.)

metric *a.* metrig. **metric scale** graddfa fetrig

mew *v.* mewian

micro-chip *n.* meicro-sglodyn *m.*

microphone *n.* meic, meicroffon *m.*

microscope *n.* meicrosgop *m.*

microwave *n.* meicrodon *f.*

mid *a.* canol

midday *n.* canol dydd, hanner dydd *m.*

middle *n.* canol *m.*

middle-aged *a.* canol oed

midland *n.* canolbarth *m.* **the Midlands** Canolbarth Lloegr: **Mid Wales** Canolbarth Cymru

midnight *n.* canol nos, hanner nos *f.*

midst 1 *n.* canol, plith *m.* 2 *prp.* rhwng

might *n.* nerth, gallu *m.*

mighty *a.* grymus
mild *a.* mwyn, tyner, meddal, gwan. **become mild** mwynhau, tyneru
mile *n.* milltir *f:* **milestone** carreg filltir *f.*
milk 1 *n.* llaeth, llefrith *m.* **2** *v.* godro. **milkman** dyn llaeth
mill *n.* melin *f.*
million *n.* miliwn *m.* **millionaire** miliynydd
mime 1 *n.* meim *m.* **2** *v.* meimio
mind 1 *n.* meddwl, bryd, bwriad *m.* **2** *v.* gwylio, gofalu, hidio
mindful *a.* gofalus, ystyriol
mine 1 *n.* pwll, mwynglawdd *m.* **2** *pn.* fy, yr eiddof i
miner *n.* glöwr, mwynwr *m.*
mineral *n.* mwyn *m.*
minimum *n.* lleiafswm, isafrif, isafbwynt *m.*
minister 1 *n.* gweinidog *m.* **2** *v.* gwasanaethu
minority *n.* lleiafrif *m.*
mint *n.* bathdy; mint, mintys *m.* **Royal Mint** Bathdy Brenhinol
minute *n.* munud *mf;* cofnod *m.* **minute book** llyfr cofnodion
minute *a.* bach, mân, manwl
miracle *n.* gwyrth *f.*
miraculous *a.* gwyrthiol
mirror *n.* drych *m.*
miscarriage *n.* erthyliad *m.*
miscarry *v.* erthylu; colli
mischief *n.* drwg, drygioni *m.*
mischievous *a.* drygionus
miserable *a.* gwael, truenus, diflas

misery *n.* trallod, trueni, diflastod *m.*
mislead *v.* camarwain, twyllo
miss *v.* colli, methu, gweld eisiau
missile *n.* taflegryn *m.*
mission *n.* cenhadaeth *f.*
missionary 1 *n.* cenhadwr *m;* cenhades *f.* **2** *a.* cenhadol
mist *n.* niwl *m.*
mistake *n.* camsyniad, gwall, camgymeriad *m.*
mistress *n.* meistres, athrawes *f:* **headmistress** prifathrawes
misty *a.* niwlog
misunderstand *v.* camddeall
mix *v.* cymysgu
mixed *a.* cymysg
mob *n.* torf, tyrfa, haid *f.*
mobile *a.* symudol. **mobile phone** ffôn symudol
mock *v.* gwawdio.
mode *n.* modd, dull *m.*
modern *a.* diweddar, modern
moist *a.* llaith, gwlyb
moisten *v.* gwlychu
moisture *n.* gwlybaniaeth *f.*
Mold *n.* Yr Wyddgrug *f.*
moment *n.* eiliad *f*, ennyd *mf*, moment *f.*
monarch *n.* brenin *m.*
monastery *n.* mynachlog *f.*
Monday *n.* dydd Llun *m.*
money *n.* arian, pres *m.*
monk *n.* mynach *m.*
monkey *n.* mwnci *m.*
monoglot 1 *n.* person uniaith *m.* **2** *a.* uniaith
monotonous *a.* undonog
monstrous *a.* anferth
month *n.* mis *m.*
monthly 1 *n.* misolyn *m.* **2** *a.*

misol
mood *n.* tymer, hwyl *f.*
moon *n.* lleuad, lloer *f.*
moonlight golau leuad
moor *n.* rhos *f*, rhostir *m*, gwaun *f.*
moral *a.* moesol
morals *n.* moesau *pl.*
more 1 *n.* rhagor, ychwaneg, chwaneg *m.* 2 *a* & *ad.* mwy, mwyach. **more than** mwy na
morning 1 *n.* bore *m.* 2 *a.* bore, boreol. **Monday morning** bore dydd Llun: **every morning** bob bore; **Morning Service** Gwasanaeth Boreol; **next morning** bore trannoeth
morrow *ad.* trannoeth
mortal 1 *n.* dyn; un marwol *m.* 2 *a.* marwol
mortgage *n.* morgais *m.*
most *a.* mwyaf, amlaf
mostly *ad.* gan mwyaf
moth *n.* gwyfyn *m.*
mother *n.* mam *f.* **mother-in-law** mam-yng-nghyfraith
mother tongue *n.* mamiaith *f.*
motor *n.* modur, car *m.* **motor bike** beic modur
motorist *n.* modurwr *m.*
motorway *n.* traffordd *f.*
mountain *n.* mynydd *m.*
mountaineer *n.* mynyddwr *m.*
mountainous *a.* mynyddig
mourn *v.* galaru
mourning *n.* galar *m.*
mouse *n.* llygoden *f.*
moustache *n.* mwstash *m.*
mouth *n.* ceg *f*, genau *pl.m.*
move *v.* symud
movement *n.* mudiad;

symudiad, symud *m.*
moving *a.* yn symud, cyffrous
mow *v.* lladd gwair
much 1 *n.* llawer. 2 *a.* llawer, mawr. 3 *ad.* yn fawr, llawer *(with comparative a.)*: **much better** llawer gwell: **too much** gormod
mud *n.* llacs *m.*
muddy *a.* llacsog
multiply *v.* lluosi
multitude *n.* llu *m*, torf, tyrfa *f.*
munch *v.* cnoi
murder 1 *n.* llofruddiaeth *f.* 2 *v.* llofruddio
murderer *n.* llofrudd *m.*
muscular *a.* cyhyrog
museum *n.* amgueddfa *f.*
mushroom *n.* madarchen *f.*; 'magic mushroom(s)' madarch hudol
music *n.* cerddoriaeth, cerdd, caniadaeth, alaw, miwsig *f.*
musical *a.* cerddorol
musician *n.* cerddor *m.*
must *n.* & *v.* rhaid *m.*
mutate *v.* treiglo
mutation *n.* treiglad, cyfnewidiad *m.*
mute *a.* mud, distaw
mutilate *v.* anafu, llurgunio
mutiny *n.* gwrthryfel, terfysg *m.*
mutton *n.* cig dafad, cig gwedder *m.*
my *pn.* fy; 'm
myrrh *n.* myrr *m.*
myself *pn.* fy hunan, mi fy hunan, myfi fy hun
mysterious *a.* rhyfedd, dirgel
mystery *n.* dirgelwch
myth *n.* chwedl, dameg, myth *f.*

N

nail 1 *n.* ewin *mf;* hoel, hoelen *f.* 2 *a.* hoelio.

naked *a.* noeth; llwm: **stark naked** noethlymun, porcyn

name 1 *n.* enw *m.* 2 *v.* enwi, galw

namely *ad.* sef

nape *n.* gwar *m.*

napkin *n.* cewyn, clwt *m.*

narrate *v.* adrodd (hanes)

narration *n.* adroddiad *m.*

narrative *n.* chwedl *f,* hanes *m,* stori *f.*

narrow 1 *a.* cul, cyfyng. 2 *v.* cyfyngu

narrow-minded *a.* cul

nasal *a.* trwynol

nasty *a.* cas, brwnt, budr, ffiaidd

nation *n.* cenedl *f.*

national *a.* cenedlaethol; gwladol. **National Assistance** Cymorth Gwladol: **National Museum** Amgueddfa Genedlaethol

nationalism *n.* cenedlaetholdeb *m.*

nationalist *n.* cenedlaetholwr *m.*

nationality *n.* cenedligrwydd *m.*

native 1 *n.* brodor *m.* 2 *a.* brodorol

nativity *n.* genedigaeth *f.*

natural *a.* naturiol

nature *n.* natur, naws *f.*

naught *n.* dim; sero *m.*

naughtiness *n.* drygioni *m.*

naughty *a.* drwg, drygionus

navy *n.* llynges *f.* **navy blue** glasddu

near 1 *a.* agos. 2 *ad.* yn agos, braidd. 3 *v.* agosáu, nesáu. 4 *prp.* ger, yn agos at

nearby *a.* & *ad.* yn ymyl, gerllaw

nearly *ad.* bron

neat *a.* twt, del, taclus, trefnus

Neath *n.* Castell-nedd *f.*

necessary *a.* angenrheidiol; **necessitate** gwneud yn angenrheidiol, gorfodi

necessity *n.* anghenraid, rhaid *m.*

neck *n.* gwddf, gwddwg *m.*

necklace *n.* neclis *f.* mwclis *pl.*

née *a.* gynt, cyn priodi. **Mair Puw, née Rhys** Mair Puw, gynt Rhys

need *n.* eisiau, rhaid. *m.*

needle *n.* nodwydd; gwaell *f.*

needy *a.* tlawd

negative *a.* negyddol

neglect *v.* esgeuluso

negligence *n.* esgeulustod *m.*

negligent *a.* esgeulus

negotiate *v.* trafod, trefnu

negro *n.* dyn du, negro *m.*

neighbour *n.* cymydog *m.*

neighbouring *a.* cyfagos

neither 1 *ad.* & *c.* na, nac, chwaith, ychwaith. 2 *pn.* nid y naill na'r llall, nid un o'r ddau

nephew *n.* nai *m.*

nerve *n.* gewyn, nerf *m.*

nervous *a.* nerfus, ofnus

nest *n.* nyth *mf.*

nestle *v.* nythu

nestling *n.* aderyn bach, cyw *m.*

net *n.* rhwyd *f.*
netball *n.* pêl rwyd *f.*
Netherlands, The *n.* Yr Iseldiroedd *f.*
never *ad.* byth, erioed
nevertheless *ad.* er hynny, eto
new *a.* newydd. **New Year** Blwyddyn Newydd; **New York** Efrog Newydd; **New Zealand** Seland Newydd; **brand new** newydd sbon
newcomer *n.* newydd-ddyfodiad *m.*
Newport (Pembs.) *n.* Trefdraeth *f.*
Newport (Mon.) *n.* Casnewydd *f.*
Newquay *n.* Ceinewydd *f.*
news *n.pl.* newyddion *pl.* newydd, hanes *m.* **good news** newyddion da; **six o'clock news** newyddion chwech
newspaper *n.* papur newydd. *m.*
next 1 *a.* nesaf. 2 *prp.* nesaf at. **next door** y drws nesaf; **Next, please** Y nesaf, os gwelwch yn dda; **next week** wythnos nesaf; **next year** y flwyddyn nesaf
nice *a.* braf, hyfryd, neis, dymunol
nickname 1 *n.* llysenw *m.* 2 *v.* llysenwi
niece *n.* nith *f.*
nigh *a, ad* & *prp.* agos, gerllaw, yn agos
night *n.* nos; noson, noswaith *f.* **night and day** nos a dydd; **night before last** echnos; **last night** neithiwr; **the last night** y noson olaf; **Good night!**

Nos Da!
night-dress *n.* gŵn nos, coban *f.*
night-gown *n.* gŵn nos, coban *f.*
nightingale *n.* eos *f.*
nightmare *n.* hunllef *f.*
nil *n.* dim *m.*
nimble *a.* heini, sionc, ystwyth
nine *n.* & *a.* naw *m.*
nineteen *n.* & *a.* pedwar ar bymtheg, un deg naw *m.*
ninety *n.* & *a.* naw deg *m.*
ninth *n.* & *a.* nawfed *m.*
no 1 *a.* ni, nid, neb, dim. 2 *ad.* na, nad, ni, nid, nac oes, naddo, nage, nac ydy ... *(Welsh uses the verb forms to answer yes/no) e.g.* **Nia? No.** Nia? Nage. **Was she there? No** Oedd hi yno? Nac oedd. **Is Non at home? No** Ydy Non gartre? Nac ydy. **Is there food here? No** Oes bwyd yma? Nac oes. **Will they be out? No** Fyddan nhw allan? Na fyddan
noble *a.* bonheddig, ardderchog
nobleman *n.* bonheddwr, uchelwr *m.*
nobody *n.* neb *m.*
noise *n.* sŵn, mwstwr, stŵr, sain, twrw *m.*
noisy *a.* swnllyd, stwrllyd
nom de plume *n.* ffugenw *m.*
none *pn.* neb, dim, dim un
nonsense *n.* lol *f.*
nook *n.* cornel, congl *f.*
noon *n.* hanner dydd, canol dydd *m.*

no one *pn.* neb

nor *ad.* & *c.* na, nac

Norman 1 *n.* Norman *m.*
2 *a.* Normanaidd: **Norman church** eglwys Normanaidd

north 1 *n.* gogledd *m.* 2 *a.* gogleddol. **North Pole** Pegwn y Gogledd: **North Wales** Gogledd Cymru

northerly *a.* gogleddol

northern *a.* gogleddol. **Northern Ireland** Gogledd Iwerddon

Northerner *n.* Gogleddwr *m.*

nose 1 *n.* trwyn *m.* 2 *v.* trwyno

nostalgia *n.* hiraeth *m.*

nostril *n.* ffroen *f.*

not *ad.* na, nac, nad, ni, nid

notable *a.* hynod, enwog, nodedig

note 1 *n.* nodyn, nod *m.* 2 *v.* nodi, sylwi. **ten pound note** papur decpunt

noted *a.* nodedig, enwog, hynod

nothing *n.* dim *m.* **nothing at all** dim byd, dim o gwbl, dim yn y byd

notice 1 *n.* rhybudd, hysbysebiad, sylw *m.* 2 *v.* sylwi.

notion *n.* syniad, amcan *m.*

notwithstanding 1 *ad.* er hynny. 2 *prp.* er, er gwaethaf, serch

noun *n.* enw *m.* **collective noun** enw torfol; **common noun** enw cyffredin; **plural noun** enw lluosog

novel 1 *n.* nofel *f.* 2 *a.* newydd

novelist *n.* nofelwr, nofelydd *m.*

November *n.* Tachwedd *m.*

now *ad.* yn awr, nawr, rŵan, bellach, y pryd hwn. **now and again** nawr ac yn y man. **nowadays** *ad.* yn y dyddiau hyn. **nowhere** *ad.* dim yn unlle

nuance *n.* naws *f.*

nuclear *a.* niwclear. **nuclear energy** egni niwclear: **nuclear power station** atomfa

numb *a.* cwsg

number 1 *n.* nifer *mf*, rhif; rhifyn *m.* 2 *v.* rhifo, cyfrif

numeral *n.* rhifol, rhifnod *m.*

numerous *a.* lluosog, niferus; aml

nun *n.* lleian *f.*

nurse 1 *n.* gweinyddes, nyrs *f.* 2 *v.* magu, nyrsio, meithrin

nursery *n.* meithrinfa *f.* **nursery class** dosbarth meithrin; **nursery nurse** gweinyddes feithrin; **nursery school** ysgol feithrin

nurseryman *n.* garddwr *m.*

nursery-rhyme *n.* hwiangerdd *f.*

nurture *v.* meithrin

nut *n.* cneuen; nyten *f.* **coconut** cneuen goco; **hazelnuts** cnau cyll; **monkey nuts** cnau mwnci; **walnut** cneuen ffrengig; **hexagonal nut** nyten hecsagonal; **square nut** nyten sgwâr; **nut and bolt** nyten a bollt

O

oak 1 *n.* derwen *f.* **2** *a.* derw.
 oak-trees derw, deri
oath *n.* llw *m.*
obedient *a.* ufudd
obey *v.* ufuddhau
object 1 *n.* gwrthrych, nod,
 amcan *m.* **2** *v.* gwrthwynebu
objective 1 *n.* amcan, nod *m.*
 2 *a.* gwrthrychol
objector *n.* gwrthwynebwr *m.*
obligation *n.* dyletswydd,
 gorfodaeth *f.*
oblige *v.* gorfodi
obscene *a.* serth, brwnt
obscure 1 *a.* aneglur, tywyll
 2. *v.* tywyllu
observation *n.* sylw *m.*
observe *v.* sylwi, edrych;
 cadw
obstacle *n.* rhwystr, maen
 tramgwydd *m.*
obstruct *v.* cau, tagu;
 rhwystro
obtain *v.* cael, ennill
obvious *a.* eglur, amlwg
occasion 1 *n.* achlysur, achos
 m, adeg *f.* **2** *v.* achosi, peri
occasional *a.* ambell
occasionally *ad.* ambell waith
occupation *n.* gwaith *m,*
 galwedigaeth *f.*
occur *v.* digwydd, taro
occurrence *n.* digwyddiad,
 achlysur *m.*
ocean *n.* môr, cefnfor, eigion
 m.
o'clock *ad.* o'r gloch
octagon *n.* wythongl *f,*
 octagon *m.*
octave *n.* wythawd *m.*

octet *n.* wythawd *m.*
October *n.* Hydref *m.*
octogenarian *n.* person
 pedwar ugain mlwydd oed *m.*
odd *a.* od, hynod, rhyfedd
ode *n.* cerdd, awdl *f.*
odious *a.* cas, ffiaidd
of *prp.* o, gan, am, ynghylch.
 of course wrth gwrs
off 1 *a.* tu allan, tu faes. **2** *ad.*
 ymaith, i ffwrdd. **3** *prp.* oddi
 ar, oddi am, oddi wrth
offence *n.* trosedd *f.*
offend *v.* troseddu
offender *n.* troseddwr *m.*
offer *n.* & *v.* cynnig *m.*
office *n.* swydd; swyddfa *f.*
officer *n.* swyddog *m.*
official 1 *n.* swyddog *m.* **2** *a.*
 swyddogol
offspring *n.* hil *f,* plant *pl.*
often *ad.* yn aml
oil 1 *n.* olew, oel *m.* **2** *v.* iro,
 oelio. **oil field** maes olew; **oil
 rig** llwyfan olew
old *a.* hen, oedrannus. **old
 age** henoed, henaint; **old
 fashioned** henffasiwn; **old
 man** hen ŵr, henwr; **of old**
 gynt
omelette *n.* omled *m.*
on 1 *ad.* ymlaen. **2** *prp.* ar
once *ad.* unwaith, un tro,
 gynt. **at once** ar unwaith
one 1 *n.* rhywun *m.* **2** *a.* un,
 naill, unig. **3** *pn.* naill: **one
 by one** bob yn un
one-way *a.* un-ffordd,
 unffordd. **one-way street**
 heol unffordd
onion *n.* winwnsyn, nionyn
 m.

only 1 *a.* unig. **2** *ad.* yn unig,
dim ond. **the only one** yr
unig un; **one only** un yn unig

open 1 *a.* agored, ar agor.
2 *v.* agor; **open air** awyr
agored; **wide open** lled y pen

opening *n.* agoriad *m.*

opera *n.* opera *f.*

operate *v.* gweithredu,
gweithio

operation *n.* gweithred *f.*,
gweithrediad *m;* triniaeth
lawfeddygol *f.*

opinion *n.* barn *f,* meddwl *m.*

opponent *n.* gwrthwynebwr,
gwrthwynebydd *m.*

opportunity *n.* achlysur, cyfle
m, siawns *f.*

oppose *v.* gwrthwynebu

opposite *a.* & *prp.* cyferbyn,
cyferbyniol

opposition *n.* gwrthwyneb,
gwrthwynebiad *m;*
gwrthblaid *f.*

optician *n.* optegwr, optegydd
m.

option *n.* dewis, dewisiad *m.*

or *c.* neu, ynte, ynteu, ai, naill
ai

oral *a.* llafar. **oral examination**
arholiad llafar

orally *ad.* ar lafar

orange *n.* & *a.* oren *mf.*

orchard *n.* perllan *f.*

orchestra *n.* cerddorfa *f.*

ordain *v.* ordeinio, urddo;
penderfynu

ordeal *n.* prawf llym *m.*

order 1 *n.* trefn; urdd; rheol *f,*
gorchymyn *m;* archeb *f.* **2** *v.*
trefnu; gorchymyn; archebu

orderly *a.* rheolaidd, trefnus

ordinarily *ad.* fel rheol

ordinary *a.* cyffredin, arferol

ore *n.* mwyn *m.*

organ *n.* organ *f,* offeryn *m.*

organic *a.* organig

organist *n.* organydd *m.*

organization *n.* trefn;
cyfundrefn *f.*

organize *v.* trefnu

organizer *n.* trefnydd *m.*

origin *n.* ffynnon, ffynhonnell
f, dechreuad *m.*

original *a.* gwreiddiol

originate *v.* dechrau, tarddu,
hannu

other 1 *a.* arall, eraill. **2** *pn.*
arall, y llall. **each other** ei
gilydd

our *pn.* ein, ein – ni; 'n. **Our
Father** Ein Tad. **our house**
ein tŷ, ein tŷ ni

ours *pn.* eiddom ni, yr
eiddom

out *ad.* allan

outcrop *n.* brig *m.*

outdoor *a.* yn yr awyr agored

outline *n.* braslun *m.*

outside 1 *n.* tu allan, tu faes.
mf. **2** *a.* & *ad.* allan, oddi
allan. **3** *prp.* tu allan i, tu
faes i

outside-half *n.* maswr *m.*

outskirts *n.* cyrrau, cyrion *pl.*

outward *a.* allanol

oven *n.* ffwrn *f,* popty *m.*
electric oven ffwrn drydan;
gas oven ffwrn nwy;
microwave oven ffwrn ficrodon

over 1 *n.* pelawd *m.* *(criced).*
2 *ad.* dros ben, drosodd.
3 *prp.* dros, uwch, uwchben

over- *px,* gor-, rhag-, rhy-, tra-
overcast *a.* cymylog
overcoat *n.* cot fawr, cot
uchaf *f.*
overcome *v.* gorchfygu,
trechu, cael y gorau ar
overcrowded *a.* gorlawn
overdo *v.* gor-wneud
overdraw *v.* gordynnu
overflow 1 *n.* gorlif *m.* **2** *v.*
gorlifo
overflowing *a.* gorlawn
overhead *a.* & *ad.* uwchben
overjoyed *a.* llawen iawn
overlook *v.* esgeuluso; edrych
dros
overnight *ad.* dros nos
overpower *v.* trechu
overseas *ad.* dros y môr,
tramor
overshadow *v.* cysgodi
overweight *a.* gor-drwm
overwork *v.* gorweithio
owe *v.* bod mewn dyled
owing *a.* dyledus
owl *n.* gwdihŵ *m,* tylluan *f.*
barn owl, white owl tylluan
wen; **little owl** tylluan
fechan; **long-eared owl**
tylluan glustiog
own 1 *a.* eiddo dyn ei hun,
priod. **2** *v.* meddu (ar)
owner *n.* perchen, perchennog
m.
Oxford *n.* Rhydychen *f.*
oxygen *n.* ocsigen *m.*

P

pace 1 *n.* cam *m.* **2** *v.* camu,
cerdded

Pacific Ocean *n.* Môr Tawel
m.
pack 1 *n.* pac *m.* **2** *v.* pacio
package *n.* paced, pecyn *m.*
packet *n.* paced, pecyn *m.*
pact *n.* cytundeb, cynghrair
m.
padlock *n.* clo *m.*
pagan *n.* pagan *m.*
page *n.* tudalen *mf.*; gwas
bach *m.*
pageant *n.* pasiant *m.*
pail *n.* bwced *m.*
pain 1 *n.* poen *mf,* dolur *m.*
2 *v.* poeni
painful *a.* poenus
painstaking *a.* gofalus
paint 1 *n.* paent, lliw *m.* **2** *v.*
peintio, lliwo
painter *n.* peintiwr, arlunydd
m.
painting *n.* llun, darlun *m.*
pair *n.* pâr, dau, cwpl *m.*
palace *n.* llys, plas, palas,
plasty *m.*
pale *a.* llwyd, glas, gwelw
Palestine *n.* Palestina *f.*
palm *n.* palmwydden *f.* **Palm
Sunday** Sul y Blodau, Sul y
Palmwydd
pamper *v.* maldodi, anwesu
pampering *n.* maldod, anwes
m.
pamphlet *n.* pamffled, llyfryn
m.
pan *n.* padell *f.*
pancake *n.* crempog, ffroesen
f.
pane *n.* cwarel, chwarel *mf.*
panel *n.* panel *m.*
paper 1 *n.* papur *m.* **2** *v.*
papuro. **newspaper** papur

newydd; **toilet paper** papur
toiled, papur tŷ bach;
wallpaper papur wal; **writing
paper** papur ysgrifennu
paperbacks *n.* llyfrau clawr
meddal *m.pl.*
papist *n.* pabydd *m.*
parable *n.* dameg *f.*
paradise *n.* gwynfa, gwynfyd
m, paradwys *f.*
paragraph *n.* paragraff *m.*
paramount *a.* pen, pennaf,
prif
parcel *n.* parsel *m.*
parch *v.* crasu, sychu
parched *a.* cras, crasboeth;
sychedig
pardon 1 *n.* pardwn,
maddeuant *m.* **2** *v.* maddau.
parent *n.* tad neu fam, rhiant
mf.
parish *n.* plwyf *m.*
park 1 *n.* parc *m.* **2** *v.* parcio.
car park maes parcio;
caravan park maes
carafanau
parliament *n.* senedd *f.*
Member of Parliament Aelod
Seneddol (A.S.)
parsley *n.* persli *m.*
parsnip *n.* panasen *f.*
parson *n.* offeiriad, person *m.*
part 1 *n.* darn *m*, rhan *f*; peth
m. **2** *v.* rhannu; gwahanu;
ymadael
particular *a.* neilltuol
particularize *v.* manylu
parting *n.* ymadael *m.*
partner *n.* cymar *m.*
party *n.* parti *m*; plaid *f.*
birthday party parti pen-
blwydd; **Christmas party**

parti Nadolig; **Conservative
Party** Plaid Geidwadol;
Green Party Plaid Werdd;
Labour Party Plaid Lafur
pass 1 *n.* bwlch; caniatâd,
pás *m.* **2** *v.* mynd heibio (i);
llwyddo
passion *n.* dioddefaint; nwyd
m.
past 1 *n.* & *a.* gorffennol *m.*
2 *ad.* heibio
pastor *n.* bugail *(eglwys)*,
gweinidog *m.*
pasture *n.* porfa *f.*
path *n.* llwybr *m*; **public
footpath** llwybr cyhoeddus
patience *n.* amynedd *m.* **the
patience of Job** amynedd
Job
patient 1 *n.* claf *m.* **2** *a.*
amyneddgar
patriot *n.* gwladgarwr *m.*
patron *n.* noddwr *m.*
patronage *n.* nawdd *m.*
pattern *n.* patrwm, patrwn *m.*
pause 1 *n.* hoe *f*, saib,
seibiant *m.* **2** *v.* pwyllo, aros,
gorffwys
pavement *n.* pafin *m.*
pavilion *n.* pabell *f*, pafiliwn
m.
paw *n.* pawen *f.*
pay 1 *n.* cyflog *mf*, tâl *m.* **2** *v.*
talu
payee *n.* talai *m.*
payer *n.* talwr *m.*
payment *n.* tâl, taliad *m.*
pea *n.* pysen *f.*
peace *n.* hedd, heddwch,
llonyddwch *m*; tangnefedd
mf.
peaceful *a.* tawel, llonydd,

tangnefeddus
peak *n.* brig, copa *m.*
pear *n.* peren *f.*
pearl *n.* perl *m.*
peasant *n.* gwerinwr *m.*
peasantry *n.* y werin *f.*
peat *n.* mawn *m.*
peck 1 *n.* pigiad *m.* **2** *v.* pigo
peculiar *a.* od, hynod,
arbennig
pedestrian 1 *n.* cerddwr *m.*
2 *a.* ar draed. **pedestrian**
crossing croesfan *f.*
peel 1 *n.* croen, pil *m.* **2** *v.*
pilio
peep 1 *n.* cipolwg, cip.
2 *v.* cipedrych, sbïo
peg *n.* peg *m.*
pen *n.* pin ysgrifennu *m.*
penalize *v.* cosbi
penalty *n.* cosb *f.*
pence *n.* ceiniogau *pl.*
pencil *n.* pensil *m.*
pendulum *n.* pendil *m.*
penitent *a.* edifar, edifeiriol
penknife *n.* cyllell boced *f.*
penniless *a.* heb geiniog
penny *n.* ceiniog *f.*
pension *n.* pensiwn *m.*
pensioner *n.* pensiynwr *m.*
pensive *a.* meddylgar
people *n.* pobl, gwerin *f.*
pepper *n.* pupur *m.*
per *prp.* trwy, wrth, yn ôl
perceive *n.* deall, gweld,
gweled
percentage *n.* hyn a hyn y
cant, canran *m.*
perfect 1 *a.* perffaith. **2** *v.*
perffeithio
perfection *n.* perffeithrwydd
m.

perfectly *ad.* yn berffaith
perforate *v.* tyllu
perforated *a.* tyllog
perforation *n.* twll *m.*
perfume *n.* arogl; persawr *m.*
perhaps *ad.* efallai, hwyrach
period *n.* adeg *f*, amser;
misglwyf, cyfnod *m.*
permanent *a.* sefydlog,
parhaol
permission *n.* caniatâd *m*,
hawl *f.*
permit *v.* caniatáu
perpetuate *v.* parhau
persecute *v.* erlid
person *n.* person *m.*
personal *a.* personol
personality *n.* personoliaeth *f.*
perspective *n.* safbwynt,
persbectif *m.*
perspiration *n.* chwys *m.*
perspire *v.* chwysu
pester *v.* blino, poeni
pet *n.* anifail anwes *m.*
petite *a.* bychan, bechan
petition *n.* deiseb *f.*
petrol *n.* petrol *m.* **petrol**
pump pwmp petrol; **petrol**
station gorsaf betrol;
unleaded petrol petrol
di-blwm
petticoat *n.* pais *f.*
petty *a.* bach, bychan, mân,
gwael
pew *n.* sedd, sêt *f*, côr *m.*
pharmacist *n.* fferyllydd *m.*
pharmacy *n.* fferyllfa *f.*
phone 1 *n.* ffôn. teleffon *m.*
2 *v.* ffonio. **phone call**
galwad ffôn
photocopier *n.* llungopïydd,
ffotogopïydd *m.*

photocopy *n.* llungopi, ffotogopi *m.*

photograph *n.* llun, ffotograff *m.*

photographer *n.* ffotograffydd *m.*

phrase 1 *n.* cymal, ymadrodd *m.* **2** *v.* geirio, mynegi

physical *a.* corfforol, materol. **physical education** addysg gorfforol

physics *n.* ffiseg *f.*

pianist *n.* pianydd *m.*

piano *n.* piano *mf.*

pick *v.* dewis, pigo, casglu (blodau/ ffrwythau)

pick up *v.* codi

picture *n.* darlun, llun, pictiwr *m.*

piece *n.* darn, pisyn *m*, rhan *f*, tamaid *m.*

pig *n.* mochyn *m.* **piglet** mochyn bach

pile *n* . pentwr *m.*

pilgrim *n.* pererin *m.*

pill *n.* pilsen *f.*

pillar *n.* colofn *f.* piler *m.*

pillow *n.* clustog *f*, gobennydd *m.*

pilot *n.* peilot *m.*

pimple *n.* tosyn, ploryn *m.*

pin 1 *n.* pin *m.* **drawing pin** pin bawd. **2** *v.* pinio, hoelio

pinch 1 *n.* pinsiad *m.* gwasgfa *f.* **2** *v.* pinsio, gwasgu

pine *n.* ffynidwydden *f*, ffynidwydd *pl;* pinwydden *f*, pinwydd *pl;* **red pine** ffynidwydd coch

pineapple *n.* afal pîn, pîn-afal *m.*

pine-end *n.* talcen tŷ *m.*

pink *n.* & *a.* pinc *m.*

pint *n.* peint *m.* **pint of milk** peint o laeth

pious *a.* duwiol, crefyddol

pipe *n.* pib, piben, pibell *f.*

pirate *n.* môr-leidr *m.*

pit *n.* pwll *m.* **coal-pit** pwll glo

pity *n.* trueni, gresyn, piti *m.* **to take pity** trugarhau

place 1 *n.* lle, llecyn, man *m.* **2** *v.* dodi, gosod, lleoli

plague *n.* haint *f*, pla *m.*

plain 1 *a.* amlwg; eglur. **2** *n.* gwastad *m.*

plan 1 *n.* cynllun, plan *m.* **2** *v.* cynllunio

planet *n.* planed *f.*

planner *n.* cynlluniwr, cynllunydd *m.*

planning *n.* cynllunio *m.*

plant 1 *n.* planhigyn *m;* offer *pl.* **2** *v.* plannu; gosod

plate *n.* plât *m.*

platform *n.* llwyfan, platfform *m.*

play 1 *n.* chwarae *m*, drama *f.* **play group** grŵp chwarae. **fair play** chwarae teg. **playtime** amser chwarae. **2** *v.* chwarae, canu *(offeryn).*

player *n.* chwaraewr *m.*

plaything *n.* tegan *m.*

pleasant *a.* pleserus, dymunol, hyfryd, serchus, siriol; braf

please *v.* bodloni, plesio. **if you please** os gwelwch yn dda

pleased *a.* bodlon, hapus

pleasurable *a.* pleserus,

dymunol
pleasure *n.* pleser, boddhad *m.*
pledge 1 *n.* addewid *mf;* ernes *f.* 2 *v.* addo
plentiful *a.* helaeth
plenty *n.* digonedd, digon *m.*
pliable *a.* hyblyg
pliant *a.* ystwyth
plot 1 *n.* cynllun; cynllwyn; darn o dir *m.* 2 *v.* cynllunio; cynllwynio
plough *v.* aredig, troi
plum *n.* eirinen *f.*
plumage *n.* plu *pl.*
plume 1 *n.* pluen *f,* plufyn *m.* 2 *v.* pluo, plufio
plural *n.* lluosog *m.*
pocket 1 *n.* poced *mf.* **pocket money** arian poced. 2 *v.* pocedu
pod *n.* plisgyn *m,* coden *f.*
poem *n.* cerdd, cân *f.*
poet *n.* bardd *m.*
poetry *n.* barddoniaeth *f.*
point 1 *n.* pwynt, blaen *m.* 2 *v.* dangos
pointless *a.* dibwynt
poison 1 *n.* gwenwyn *m.* 2 *v.* gwenwyno
poisonous *a.* gwenwynig, gwenwynol
Poland *n.* Gwlad Pwyl *f.*
pole *n.* polyn; pegwn *m.* **Pole Star** Seren y Gogledd
police *n.* heddlu *m.*
policeman *n.* heddwas, plisman, plismon
policewoman *n.* heddferch, pliswraig, plismones *f.*
Polish 1 *n.* Pwyleg *f.* 2 *a.* Pwylaidd

polish 1 *n.* cwyr *m.* 2 *v.* cwyro
political *a.* gwleidyddol, politicaidd
politician *n.* gwleidydd *m.*
politics *n.* gwleidyddiaeth *f.*
pollute *v.* llygru
polluted *a.* llygredig
pollution *n.* llygredd *m.*
pond *n.* pwll, pwllyn, pownd *m.*
Pontypool *n.* Pont-y-pŵl *f.*
pony *n.* merlyn *m,* merlen *f.* **pony-trekking** merlota; **pony-trekker** merlotwr
pool *n.* pwll, pwllyn *m.* **swimming pool** pwll nofio
poor *a.* gwael, llwm, tlawd
poorly *a.* gwael, sâl, tost
Pope *n.* Pab *m.*
poppy *n.* pabi *f.*
popular *a.* poblogaidd
population *n.* poblogaeth *f.*
porch *n.* cyntedd, porth *m.*
porridge *n.* uwd *m.*
port *n.* porth, porthladd *m.*
portable *a.* symudol
portrait *n.* llun, darlun, portread *m.*
portrayal *n.* portread *m.*
pose *v.* sefyll, ymddangos, cymryd ar
position *n.* safle *m,* sefyllfa, swydd *f.*
positive *a.* pendant, cadarnhaol
possess *v.* meddu
possession *n.* eiddo, meddiant *m.*
possessor *n.* perchen, perchennog *m.*
possibility *n.* posibilrwydd *m.*

possible a. posibl
possibly ad. efallai
post 1 n. post; postyn m;
swydd f. **postcode** côd post.
2 v. postio
postal a. post. **postal order**
archeb bost
posthumous a. ar ôl marw
postman n. postman,
postmon m.
postmaster n. postfeistr m.
post office n. swyddfa'r post
f, llythyrdy m.
postpone v. oedi
postscript n. ôl-nodiad m.
potato n. taten f.
pound n. punt f. (£); pwys m.
(lb.); ffald m.
pour v. arllwys; bwrw
pout v. pwdu
poverty n. tlodi, eisiau m.
poverty-stricken a. tlawd,
llwm
powder n. llwch, powdr,
powdwr m.
power n. gallu, nerth, pŵer,
grym m.
powerful a. cryf, galluog,
grymus, nerthol
powerless a. dirym
power station n. pwerdy
pox n. brech f. **chicken pox**
brech yr ieir
practical a. ymarferol
practice n. ymarfer f,
ymarferiad, practis m, arfer
mf.
practise v. arfer, ymarfer
practising a. ymarferol
praise 1 n. canmoliaeth f,
clod, mawl m. **2** v. canmol,
clodfori, moli

pram n. pram m.
pray v. gweddïo
prayer n. gweddi f.
preach v. pregethu
preacher n. pregethwr
precarious a. ansicr, peryglus
precious a. gwerthfawr, drud,
prid; annwyl
precis n. crynodeb mf.
precise a. manwl
preface n. rhagair,
rhagymadrodd m.
preference n. dewis m,
ffafriaeth f.
preferential a. ffafriol
prefix n. rhagddodiad m.
pregnant a. beichiog
prejudice 1 n. rhagfarn f;
niwed m. **2** v. rhagfarnu;
niweidio
prejudiced a. rhagfarnllyd
premier 1 n. prif weinidog m.
2 a. prif, pennaf, blaenaf
premium n. gwobr f, tâl,
taliad m.
preparation n. paratoad m.
prepare v. paratoi m.
prepared a. parod
preposition n. arddodiad m.
prescription n. presgripsiwn,
rysáit m.
presence n. presenoldeb,
gŵydd m.
present 1 n. anrheg, rhodd f;
presennol m. **2** v. anrhegu,
cyflwyno, dangos. **at present**
ar hyn o bryd, yn awr, nawr,
rŵan
presently ad. yn y man, yn
union
preserve 1 n. jam m. **2** v.
cadw

preside *v.* llywyddu
president *n.* llywydd,
 arlywydd *m.*
press 1 *n.* gwasg *f.* **2** *v.*
 gwasgu
pressure *n.* gwasgiad,
 pwysedd *m.*
presumably *ad.* yn ôl pob
 tebyg
presume *v.* tybio; beiddio
pretence *n.* esgus *m.*
pretend *v.* ffugio, cymryd ar;
 honni
pretext *n.* esgus *m.*
prevent *v.* atal, rhwystro
 (rhag)
preview *n.* rhagolwg *m.*
previous *a.* cynt; diwethaf
price 1 *n.* pris *m.* **price list**
 rhestr prisoedd. **2** *v.* prisio
prick 1 *n.* pigiad *m.* **2** *v.* pigo
prickly *a.* pigog
pride *n.* balchder *m.*
priest *n.* offeiriad *m.*
primary *a.* cynradd; prif.
 primary education addysg
 gynradd; **primary school**
 ysgol gynradd
prime *a.* prif, cyntaf; gorau
prince *n.* tywysog *m.*
princess *n.* tywysoges *f.*
principal 1 *n.* pen, prifathro
 m, prifathrawes *f.* **2** *a.* prif
principle *n.* egwyddor *f.*
print 1 *n.* argraff *f,* print, ôl *m.*
 2 *v.* argraffu, printio
printing-press *n.* gwasg
 argraffu
prison *n.* carchar *m.*
prisoner *n.* carcharor *m.*
private *a.* cyfrinachol, preifat
privilege *n.* braint *f.*

prize *n.* gwobr *f.*
probable *a.* tebyg, tebygol
probation *n.* prawf *m.*
 probation officer swyddog
 prawf; **probation service**
 gwasanaeth prawf
problem *n.* problem *f.*
procedure *n.* trefn *f,* arfer *mf,*
 dull *m.*
proceed *v.* mynd ymlaen
proceeds *n.* enillion *pl,* elw
 m.
procession *n.* gorymdaith *f.*
proclaim *v.* cyhoeddi, datgan
 m.
proclamation *n.* cyhoeddiad
 m.
prodigious *a.* anferth
produce *n.* cynnyrch *m.*
professor *n.* athro *m.*
profit 1 *n.* elw, ennill,
 enillion, proffid *m.* **2** *v.*
 elwa, ennill, manteisio
profitable *a.* proffidiol
profound *a.* dwfn, dwys
programme *n.* rhaglen *f.*
prohibit *v.* gwahardd
project 1 *n.* bwriad, cynllun;
 cywaith; prosiect, project *m.*
 2 *v.* bwriadu; ymestyn
proletariat *n.* y werin *f.*
prologue *n.* rhagair, prolog
 m.
prominent *a.* amlwg
promise 1 *n.* addewid *mf.*
 2 *v.* addo
promontory *n.* penrhyn,
 pentir *m.*
proneness *n.* tueddiad *m.*
pronoun *n.* rhagenw *m.*
pronounce *v.* cyhoeddi,
 datgan

pronouncement *n.*
cyhoeddiad, datganiad *m.*
proof *n.* prawf *m.*
proper *a.* addas, priod,
priodol, rheolaidd
property *n.* eiddo *m.*
prophesy *v.* proffwydo
prophet *n.* proffwyd *m.*
proportional *a.* cyfrannol.
Proportional Representation
Cynrychiolaeth Gyfrannol
proposal *n.* cynnig *m.*
propose *v.* cynnig, bwriadu
proposition *n.* cynigiad;
gosodiad *m.*
proprietor *n.* perchennog *m.*
prose *n.* rhyddiaith *f.*
prosecute *v.* erlyn
prosecution *n.* erlyniad *m.*
prosecutor *n.* erlynydd *m.*
prospect *n.* golwg *mf,* golyfga
f, rhagolwg *m.*
prosper *v.* llwyddo
prosperity *n.* llwyddiant *m.*
prosperous *a.* llwyddiannus,
llewyrchus
protect *v.* amddiffyn
protest *v.* gwrthdystio
Protestant 1 *n.* Protestant *m.*
2 *a.* Protestannaidd
proud *a.* balch
prove *v.* profi
proverb *n.* dihareb *f.*
province *n.* talaith *f;* cylch,
maes *m.*
proviso *n.* amod *mf.*
provoke *v.* profocio, pryfocio,
procio
proxy *n.* dirprwy *m.*
prudent *a.* call, doeth,
synhwyrol
pry *v.* chwilota, busnesa

psalm *n.* salm *f.*
psalter *n.* llyfr salmau *m,*
sallwyr *f.*
pseudonym *n.* ffugenw *m.*
psychologist *n.* seicolegwr *m.*
psychology *n.* seicoleg *f.*
public 1 *n.* y cyhoedd *m.*
2 *a.* cyhoeddus. **public hall**
neuadd gyhoeddus; **public
house** tŷ tafarn; **public place**
man cyhoeddus
publican *n* tafarnwr *m.*
publication *n.* cyhoeddiad *m.*
publicity *n.* cyhoeddusrwydd
m.
publicly *ad.* yn gyhoeddus
publish *v.* cyhoeddi
publisher *n.* cyhoeddwr *m.*
pudding *n.* pwdin *m.*
Christmas pudding pwdin
Nadolig
puddle *n.* pwllyn *m.*
pull 1 *n.* plwc; tynfa *f.* 2 *v.*
tynnu
pulpit *n.* pulpud *m.*
pulse *n.* curiad *m.*
pump 1 *n.* pwmp *m.* 2 *v.*
pwmpio
punctual *a.* prydlon
punctuality *n.* prydlondeb *m.*
puncture 1 *n.* twll *m.* 2 *v.*
tyllu
punish *v.* cosbi; poeni
punishment *n.* cosb,
cosbedigaeth *f.*
pup *n.* ci bach; cenau *m.*
pupil *n.* disgybl *m;* cannwyll
llygad *f.*
puppet *n.* pyped *m.*
purchase 1 *n.* pryniant *m.* 2
v. prynu
pure *a.* pur, glân, gwir

purge *v.* puro, glanhau
purify *v.* puro
purple *n.* & *a.* porffor, piws
m.
purpose *n.* bwriad, pwrpas,
amcan, diben *m.*
purr *v.* canu grwndi, canu
crwth; grwnan
purse *n.* cwd, cwdyn, pwrs
m.
pursue *v.* dilyn, erlid, erlyn,
hel, hela
pursuer *n.* erlidiwr *m.*
puffin *n.* pâl *m.*
push 1 *n.* gwthiad, hwp *m.*
2 *v.* gwthio, hwpio
pusher *n.* gwthiwr
put *v.* dodi, gosod, rhoddi,
rhoi; mynegi
puzzle *n.* pos *m.* **crossword
puzzle** pos croeseiriau
pyjamas *n.pl.* pyjamas *pl,*
gwisg nos *f.*

Q

quagmire *n.* siglen, cors *f.*
quaint *a.* od, henffasiwn
quake *v.* crynu, ysgwyd
Quaker *n.* Crynwr *m.*
Quakers Yard Mynwent y
Crynwyr
qualification *n.* cymhwyster
m.
qualified *a.* cymwys
quality *n.* rhinwedd *mf,*
ansawdd *m.*
quantity *n.* swm *m,* nifer *mf,*
maint, mesur *m.*
quarrel 1 *n.* cweryl, ffrae *f.*
2 *v.* cweryla, ffraeo

quarry *n.* chwarel *f,* cwar *m.*
quarryman chwarelwr
quart *n.* chwart, cwart *m.*
quarter *n.* chwarter, cwarter;
cwr, man *m.* **quarter of an
hour** chwarter awr
quay *n.* cei *m.* **New Quay
(Ceredigion)** Ceinewydd
queen *n.* brenhines *f.*
queer *a.* od, hynod, ysmala
quench *v.* diffodd; torri
(syched)
query 1 *n.* cwestiwn,
ymholiad *m.* 2 *v.* holi,
ymholi, amau
quest *n.* ymchwil *f,* cwest *m.*
question 1 *n.* cwestiwn *m.*
question mark gofynnod 2 *v.*
cwestiyna, holi
questioner *n.* holwr *m.*
questionnaire *n.* holiadur *m.*
queue 1 *n.* ciw *m;* cwt *mf.*
2 *v.* ciwio
quick *a.* cyflym, buan, byw.
to the quick i'r byw
quickly *ad.* yn fuan
quiet 1 *n.* tawelwch,
llonyddwch *m.* 2 *a.* tawel,
distaw, llonydd. 3 *v.* tawelu
quietness *n.* tawelwch *m.*
quilt 1 *n.* cwilt, cwrlid *m.*
2 *v.* cwiltio
quintet *n.* pumawd *m.*
quit *v.* gadael, symud,
ymadael
quite *ad.* hollol, llwyr, eithaf
quiver *ad.* crynu
quiz 1 *n.* pos, cwis *m.* 2 *v.*
holi, profocio
quotation *n.* dyfyniad *m.*
quotation marks dyfynodau

R

rabbit *n.* cwningen *f.*

race *n.* gyrfa, ras; hil *f.*

racial *a.* hiliol

racket *n.* raced *mf.*

radiator *n.* rheiddiadur *m.*

radio *n.* radio *m.* **radio programme** rhaglen radio; **radio station** gorsaf radio

rag *n.* clwtyn, rhecsyn *m.* **rag doll** doli glwt *f.*

rail *n.* cledr, cledren, rheilen; canllaw *f.* **rails (of railway)** cledrau

railway *n.* rheilffordd *f.* **railway station** gorsaf reilffordd

raiment *n.* dillad *m.* gwisg *f.*

rain 1 *n.* glaw *m.* 2 *v.* glawio, bwrw glaw

rainbow *n.* enfys *f.*

raincoat *n.* cot law *f.*

rainy *a.* glawog, glawiog

rake 1 *n.* rhaca *mf.* 2 *v.* crafu, rhacanu

ram *n.* hwrdd, maharen *m.*

range *n.* amrediad; cwmpas; ystod *f.* **range of temperature** amrediad tymheredd: **age range** ystod oed

rank *n.* rhes, rhestr, rheng, gradd *f.*

ransom *n.* pridwerth *m.*

rape 1 *n.* trais *m.* 2 *v.* treisio

rapid *a.* cyflym, buan, gwyllt

rare *a.* prin; anaml

raspberry *n.* afanen, afansen, mafonen *f.*

rat *n.* llygoden fawr, llygoden Ffrengig *f.*

rate 1 *n.* treth *f*, tâl; cyflymder; cyfradd *m.* 2 *v.* trethu

ratepayer *n.* trethdalwr *m.*

rather *ad.* braidd, go, lled, yn hytrach

raw *a.* noeth, garw; amrwd

ray *n.* pelydr, pelydryn *m.*

re *prp.* ynglŷn â, mewn perthynas â

re- *px.* ail-; eto

reach 1 *n.* cyrraedd *m.* 2 *v.* cyrraedd, estyn, hercyd

reaction *n.* ymateb, adwaith *m.*

read *v.* darllen

re-address *v.* ailgyfeirio

reader *n.* darllenwr, darllenydd; llyfr darllen *m.*

readily *ad.* yn barod, yn union, yn rhwydd

reading *n.* darllen *m.*

reading-room *n.* ystafell ddarllen *f.*

ready *a.* parod, rhwydd

real *a.* gwir, real, go-iawn

reality *n.* gwirionedd, realiti *m.*

realize *v.* sylweddoli; gwerthu

really *ad.* yn wir, mewn gwirionedd

realm *n.* teyrnas, gwlad, bro *f.*

reap *v.* medi, cywain

rear 1 *n.* cefn, pen ôl, y tu ôl *m.* 2 *v.* codi, magu, meithrin

reason 1 *n.* rheswm, achos *m.* 2 *v.* rhesymu

reasonably *a.* rhesymol

rebel 1 *n.* gwrthryfelwr *m.* 2 *v.* gwrth ryfela

rebellion *n.* gwrthryfel *m.*

rebuke 1 *n.* cerydd *m*, sen *f.* 2 *v.* ceryddu

recall *v.* galw yn ôl, galw i gof, cofio
receipt *n.* derbynneb, taleb *f.*
receive *v.* derbyn
receiver *n.* derbynnydd *m.*
recent *a.* diweddar
receptionist *n.* derbynnydd *m.*
receptive *a.* derbyniol
recipe *n.* rysáit *f.*
recitation *n.* adroddiad *m.*
recite *v.* adrodd, datgan
reckon *v.* cyfrif, rhifo; barnu
recline *v.* gorwedd, gorffwys
recluse *n.* meudwy *m.*
recognize *v.* adnabod
recollect *v.* galw i gof, cofio
record 1 *n.* record *f.* 2 *v.* cofnodi, recordio
recording *n.* recordiad *m.*
re-count *v.* ailgyfrif
recreation *n.* adloniant *m.*
rectify *v.* unioni, cywiro
recurrence *n.* ailddigwyddiad, ailymddangosiad *m.*
recycle *v.* ailgylchu
red *n.* & *a.* coch *m.*
redeem *v.* gwaredu, achub, prynu (yn ôl)
redeemer *n.* prynwr, gwaredwr *m.*
reduce *v.* gostwng
reduction *n.* gostyngiad *m.*
redundant *a.* di-swydd
refer *v.* cyfeirio, cyfarwyddo
referee 1 *n.* canolwr, rheolwr *m.* 2 *v.* dyfarnu
reference *n.* cyfeiriad; geirda *m.*
refine *v.* puro
refinery *n.* purfa *f.*
reflect *v.* meddwl, myfyrio, ystyried

reform 1 *n.* diwygiad *m.*
2 *v.* diwygio, gwella
reformation *n.* diwygiad *m;*
Protestant Reformation
Diwygiad Protestannaidd
refresh *v.* adfywio
refrigerator *n.* oergell *f.*
refuge *n.* lloches, noddfa *f.*
refugee *n.* ffoadur *m.*
refuse *n.* ysbwriel, sothach *m.*
   refuse bin   bin ysbwriel
refuse *v.* gwrthod, pallu
region *n.* ardal, cylch; rhanbarth *f;* rhandir *m.*
register 1 *n.* cofrestr *f.* 2 *v.* cofrestru
registrar *n.* cofrestrydd *m.*
regular *a.* rheolaidd, cyson
rehearsal *n.* rihyrsal, practis *m.*
reimburse *v.* talu yn ôl, ad-dalu
rejoice *v.* llawenhau
rejoicing *n.* llawenydd *m.*
relate *v.* adrodd, mynegi; perthyn
related *a.* yn perthyn; wedi ei ddweud
relating to *prp.* yn ymwneud â
relation *n.* perthynas *mf.*
relationship *n.* perthynas *mf.*
relative 1 *n.* perthynas *mf.*
2 *a.* perthynol; cymharol:
   relative pronoun rhagenw perthynol
relax *v.* llacio, llaesu, ymlacio
release *v.* gollwng, rhyddhau
relevant *a.* perthnasol
religion *n.* crefydd *f.*
religious *a.* crefyddol
relish 1 *n.* blas *m.* 2 *v.* blasu, hoffi, mwynhau

rely v. dibynnu (ar)
remain v. aros, bod ar ôl
remainder n. gweddill m.
remains n. olion, gweddillion pl.
remark 1 n. sylw m. 2 v. sylwi, dweud
remarkable a. hynod, nodedig; rhyfedd, od
remedy 1 n. meddyginiaeth f. 2 v. gwella
remember v. cofio
remembrance n. cof, coffa m.
remind v. atgoffa, atgofio, cofio
remiss a. esgeulus, diofal
remnant n. gweddill m.
remote a. pell, diarffordd, anghysbell
remotely ad. o bell
removal n. symudiad m.
remove v. symud
remunerate v. talu, gwobrwyo; cydnabod
rendering n. datganiad; trosiad m.
rendezvous n. man cyfarfod m.
renowned a. enwog, adnabyddus
repairer n. trwsiwr, cyweiriwr m.
repeat v. ailadrodd
reply 1 n. ateb, atebiad m. 2 v. ateb
report 1 n. adroddiad; sŵn ergyd m. 2 v. adrodd
reporter n. gohebydd m.
representation n. cynrychiolaeth f. **Proportional Representation** Cynrychiolaeth Gyfrannol

republic n. gweriniaeth f.
reputed a. honedig
request 1 n. cais, dymuniad m, arch f. 2 v. ceisio, dymuno
require v. ceisio, gofyn
requirements n. gofynion pl.
rescue v. achub
research 1 n. ymchwil f. **research work** gwaith ymchwil. 2 v. ymchwilio
researcher n. chwilotwr m.
resemblance n. tebygrwydd m.
reserve v. neilltuo, cadw wrth gefn
reserved a. swil; wedi ei gadw. **reserved seats** seddau cadw
reservoir n. cronfa f.
reside v. trigo, byw, preswylio
resident n. preswylydd m.
residential a. preswyl. **residential school** ysgol breswyl
residue n. gweddill m.
resign v. ymddiswyddo
resignation n. ymddiswyddiad m.
resist v. gwrthwynebu, gwrthsefyll
resolute a. penderfynol
resolution n. penderfyniad m.
resolve 1 n. penderfyniad m. 2 v. penderfynu
resources n. adnoddau pl.
respect 1 n. parch m. 2 v. parchu
respectable a. parchus
respectful a. boneddigaidd
respectfully ad. yn barchus

respiration *n.* anadliad *m.*
respire *v.* anadlu
respite *n.* egwyl *f,* seibiant *m,* hoe *f.*
respond *v.* ateb, ymateb
response *n.* ateb, atebiad *m.*
responsibility *n.* cyfrifoldeb *m*
responsible *a.* cyfrifol
rest 1 *n.* gorffwys, saib *m,* hoe *f;* gweddill *m.* **2** *v.* gorffwyso, pwyso
restaurant *n.* tŷ bwyta; bwyty *m.*
restless *a.* rhwyfus, aflonydd
restore *v.* adfer
restrict *v.* cyfyngu
result *n.* canlyniad, ateb *m.*
retain *v.* cadw, dal; llogi
retard *v.* arafu
retire *v.* ymddeol
retired *a.* wedi ymddeol
retirement *n.* ymddeoliad *m.*
retiring *a.* swil
return *v.* dychwelyd
returns *n.* enillion *pl.*
reveal *v.* datguddio, dangos, egluro, datgelu
revenge *n.* & *v.* dial *m.*
reverend *a.* parchedig: **Revd Ifan Puw** Parchg Ifan Puw
revise *v.* diwygio, cywiro
revival *n.* diwygiad *m.*
revive *v.* adfer
revolution *n.* chwyldro, chwyldroad *m.*
revolve *v.* troi
reward 1 *n.* gwobr *f,* tâl *m.* **2** *v.* gwobrwyo
rheumatism *n.* gwynegon, cryd cymalau *m.*
rhyme 1 *n.* odl *f;* rhigwm *m.* **2** *v.* odli; rhigymu

ribbon *n.* ruban *m.*
rice *n.* reis *m.*
rich *a.* cyfoethog, bras, ffrwythlon
riches *n.* cyfoeth, golud *pl.*
rickety *a.* simsan, sigledig
rid *v.* gwaredu, cael gwared o
riddle *n.* pos *m.*
ridge *n.* crib *mf,* cefn *m.*
rifle *n.* dryll, reiffl *m.*
right 1 *n.* hawl, iawn *m.* braint *f.* **2** *a.* iawn, cywir; de. **3** *ad.* yn gywir, yn iawn.
right angle ongl sgwâr; **right hand** llaw dde
righteous *a.* cyfiawn
righteousness *n.* cyfiawnder *m.*
rim *n.* ymyl *mf.*
ring 1 *n.* cylch *m;* modrwy *f;* caniad *(ffôn) m.* **wedding ring** modrwy briodas. **2** *v.* canu cloch
rinse *v.* golchi
riot *n.* terfysg *m.*
rip *v.* rhwygo
ripe *a.* aeddfed
rise 1 *n.* codiad *m.* **2** *v.* codi
river *n.* afon *f.* **River Severn** Afon Hafren; **River Tawe** Afon Tawe; **River Wye** Afon Gwy
road *n.* ffordd, heol, hewl *f.* **main road** ffordd fawr, heol fawr; **narrow road** ffordd gul, heol gul; **straight road** heol syth; **winding road** heol droellog; **bypass** ffordd osgoi
roar *v.* rhuo
roast 1 *n.* rhost. **roast potatoes** tatws rhost. **2** *v.* rhostio

rob *v.* lladrata, dwyn, dwgyd
robber *n.* lleidr *m.*
robbery *n.* lladrad *m.*
robe *n.* gwisg, gŵn *f.*
robin *n.* robin goch *m.*
rock 1 *n.* craig *f;* roc *m.* **2** *v.*
siglo
rocky *a.* creigiog
rôle *n.* rhan, rôl *f.*
roll 1 *n.* rhôl, rhestr *f.* **2** *v.*
rholio, treiglo
Roman 1 *n.* Rhufeiniwr *m.*
2 *a.* Rhufeinig. **Roman
Catholic** Pabydd *n.*
romance *n.* carwriaeth *f.*
romantic *a.* rhamantus,
rhamantaidd
Rome *n.* Rhufain *f.*
roof *n.* to *m,* nen *f.*
room *n.* lle *m,* ystafell, stafell
f.
rooster *n.* ceiliog *m.*
root *n.* gwreiddyn *m.*
rope 1 *n.* rhaff *f.* **2** *v.* rhaffu,
rhwymo
rose *n.* rhosyn *m.*
rosy-cheeked *a.* gwridog
rot *v.* pydru
rotten *a.* pwdr, drwg, sâl
rough *a.* garw, bras
round *a.* cron *f,* crwn *m.*
roundabout 1 *n.* cylchfan *f,*
trogylch *m.* **2** *a.* o amgylch
route *n.* llwybr *m,* taith,
ffordd *f.*
row 1 *n.* rhes, rhestr *f.* **2** *v.*
rhwyfo. **rowing boat** cwch
rhwyfo
row *n.* ffrae *f,* terfysg *m.*
royal *a.* brenhinol
rub *v.* rhwbio

rubber *n.* rwber *m.*
rubbish *n.* ysbwriel, sothach
coll, lol *f;* **rubbish bin** bin
ysbwriel
rudder *n.* llyw *m.*
ruddy *a.* coch, gwridog
rude *a.* anfoesgar, haerllug
rudiment *n.* egwyddor,
gwyddor, elfen *f.*
rudimentary *a.* elfennol
rugby *n.* rygbi *m.* **rugby ball**
pêl rygbi; **rugby match** gêm
rygbi
rugged *a.* garw
ruin 1 *n.* dinistr *m;* adfail *mf.*
2 *v.* dinistrio, difetha
rule 1 *n.* llywodraeth; rheol *f;*
arfer *mf;* riwl, riwler *m.* **2** *v.*
llywodraethu, rheoli
ruler *n.* llywodrodaethwr,
llyw, rheolwr; riwl, riwler,
pren mesur *m.*
ruling *n.* dyfarniad *m.*
rummage *v.* chwilota
rummager *n.* chwilotwr *m.*
rumour *n.* & *v.* si, su, *m,* sôn
mf, chwedl *f.*
run 1 *n.* rhediad *m.* **2** *v.*
rhedeg, rheoli. **Run!** Rhed!
(*singular*); Rhedwch! (*plural*)
runaway *n.* ffoadur *m.*
runner *n.* rhedwr *m.*
running *n.* rhediad *m.*
rural *a.* gwledig. **Rural Wales**
Cymru Wledig
rush 1 *n.* rhuthr *m.* **2** *v.*
rhuthro
Russia *n.* Rwsia *f.*
Russian 1 *n.* Rwsiad *m*
(*person*); Rwsieg *f* (*iaith*).
2 *a.* Rwsiaidd

S

Sabbath *n.* Sabath, Saboth *m.*

sack *n.* cwd, cwdyn *m*, sach *f.*

sacred *a.* sanctaidd, glân

sacrifice 1 *n.* aberth *mf.* 2 *v.* aberthu

sad *a.* trist, blin, truenus, trwm, prudd

sadly *ad.* yn drist, yn flin, yn brudd

sadness *n.* tristwch, trymder *m.*

safe 1 *n.* cist, cell *f.* 2 *a.* diogel, saff

sail 1 *n.* hwyl *f.* 2 *v.* hwylio, morio

sailing *n.* hwylio *m.* **sailing boat** llong hwylio

sailor *n.* llongwr, morwr *m.*

saint *n.* sant *m*; santes *f.* **Saint David** Dewi Sant; **Saint John** Sant Ioan; **Saint Mary** y Santes Fair; **Saint David's** Tyddewi

sake *n.* mwyn *m.* **for the sake of** er mwyn

salary *n.* cyflog *mf.*

sale *n.* gwerthiant *m*; sâl, sêl *f*, arwerthiant *m.* **For Sale** Ar Werth

salesman *n.* gwerthwr *m.*

saliva *n.* poer, poeri *m.*

salt 1 *n.* halen *m.* **saltcellar** llestr halen. 2 *a.* hallt. **saltwater** dŵr hallt; dŵr y môr. 3 *v.* halltu

salvation *n.* iachawdwriaeth *f.* **Salvation Army** Byddin yr Iachawdwriaeth

same *a.* yr un, yr unrhyw, yr un fath

sand *n.* tywod *m.* **sand castles** cestyll tywod

sandwich 1 *n.* brechdan *f.* 2 *v.* gwthio rhwng

Santa Claus *n.* Siôn Corn *m.*

sap 1 *n.* sudd. 2 *v.* sugno; tanseilio

satellite *n.* lloeren *f.*

satisfaction *n.* boddhad *m.*

satisfy *v.* bodloni

Saturday *n.* dydd Sadwrn *m.*

Saturn *n.* Sadwrn *m.*

sauce *n.* saws *m.*

saucepan *n.* sosban *f.* **small saucepan** sosban fach; **big saucepan** sosban fawr

saucer *n.* soser *f.*

savage 1 *n.* dyn gwyllt *m.* 2 *a.* ffyrnig, gwyllt

save 1 *v.* achub, arbed, gwaredu; cynilo. 2 *prp.* & *c.* ond

savings *n.* cynilion *pl.*

saviour *n.* gwaredwr, iachawdwr *m.*

savoury *a.* blasus

saw 1 *n.* llif *f.* **sawdust** blawd llif; **hand-saw** llawlif. 2 *v.* llifio

say *v.* dweud (wrth). **to tell someone** dweud wrth rywun

saying *n.* dywediad, ymadrodd *m.*

scale *n.* graddfa; clorian, tafol *f.* **Celsius scale** graddfa Celsius

scales *n.* clorian, tafol *f.*

scarce *a.* prin, anaml

scarcely *ad.* braidd, prin, o'r braidd

scarcity *n.* prinder *m.*

scare 1 *n.* braw, ofn *m.* 2 *v.*

ofni, dychryn
scarf *n.* sgarff *f.*
scatter *v.* chwalu
scene *n.* lle, man *m.* golygfa *f.*
scenery *n.* golygfa *f.*
scent 1 *n.* arogl, aroglau; gwynt; trywydd *m.* 2 *v.* arogli; gwynto; sawru
scheme 1 *n.* cynllun *m.* 2 *v.* cynllunio
scholar *n.* ysgolhaig, ysgolor *m.*
scholarship *n.* ysgoloriaeth *f.*
school *n.* ysgol *f.* **bilingual school** ysgol ddwyieithog; **local school** ysgol leol; **night-school** ysgol nos; **summer school** ysgol haf; **Welsh school** ysgol Gymraeg; **primary school** ysgol gynradd; **comprehensive school** ysgol gyfun
schoolboy *n*. bachgen ysgol *m.*
schooldays *n.* dyddiau ysgol *pl.*
schoolgirl *n.* merch ysgol *f.*
schoolhouse *n.* tŷ ysgol *m.*
schoolmaster *n.* athro ysgol, ysgolfeistr *m.*
schoolmistress *n.* athrawes, ysgolfeistres *f.*
science *n.* gwyddoniaeth, gwyddor *f.* **science fiction** ffuglen wyddonol
scientific *a.* gwyddonol
scientist *n.* gwyddonydd *m.*
scissors *n.* siswrn *m.*
scorch *v.* crasu; rhuddo
scorched *a.* cras

score 1 *n.* sgôr; ugain *m.* 2 *v.* sgorio
scorn 1 *n.* gwawd *m.* 2 *v.* gwawdio
Scotland *n.* Yr Alban *f.*
scowl 1 *n.* gwg *m.* 2 *v.* gwgu
scratch 1 *n.* crafiad *m.* 2 *v.* crafu
scream 1 *n.* sgrech, ysgrech *f.* 2 *v.* sgrechian, sgrechain
screw 1 *n.* sgriw *f.* 2 *v.* sgriwio
script *n.* sgript *f.*
scripture *n.* ysgrythur *f,* y Beibl *m.*
scrum 1 *n.* sgrym *f.* 2 *v.* sgrymio
scrum-half *n.* mewnwr *m.*
sea *n.* môr *m.* **sea-level** lefel y môr; **sea trip** mordaith; **sea water** dŵr y môr
seagull *See* gull
seal *n.* morlo *m;* sêl *f.*
seaman *n.* morwr, llongwr *m.*
sea-marsh *n.* morfa *m.*
seamstress *n.* gwniadyddes, gwniyddes *f.*
search 1 *n.* ymchwil *f.* 2 *v.* chwilio, edrych, ymchwilio
searcher *n.* chwiliwr *m.*
sea-shore *n.* glan y môr *f.*
seasickness *n.* salwch (y) môr. *m.*
season *n.* adeg *f,* amser, pryd, tymor *m.* **season ticket** tocyn tymor
seat 1 *n.* sedd, sêt *f.* 2 *v.* eistedd
seaweed *n.* gwymon *m.*
second 1 *n.* ail *m;* eiliad *f.* 2 *a.* ail. **second class** ail ddosbarth; isradd; **second-**

hand ail-law
secret 1 *n.* cyfrinach *f.*
2 *a.* cyfrinachol
secretary *n.* ysgrifennydd *m,*
ysgrifenyddes *f.* **Secretary of**
State Ysgrifennydd Gwladol
section *n.* adran, rhan *f.*
secure 1 *a.* diogel, sicr, siŵr.
2 *v.* sicrhau
security *n.* sicrwydd,
diogelwch; ernes. **Social**
Security Nawdd
Cymdeithasol
sediment *n.* gwaelodion,
gwaddod *m.*
see 1 *n.* esgobaeth *f.* 2 *v.*
gweld, gweled.
seed 1 *n.* had *coll,* hadyn,
hedyn *m.* 2 *v.* hadu
seek *v.* ceisio, chwilio
seem *v.* ymddangos
seemly *a.* addas
seething *n.* & *a.* berw *m.*
seize *v.* gafael, dal. **to seize**
the opportunity achub y cyfle
seldom *ad.* anaml.
select *a.* & *v.* dewis, dethol
selection *n.* detholiad *m.*
self *pn.* & *n.* hun, hunan *m.*
self-catering *a.* hunan arlwyol
self-cleaning *a.* hunan
lanhaol.
self-confident *a.* hunan
hyderus
selfish *a.* hunanol
self-respect *n.* hunan-barch
m.
sell *v.* gwerthu
seller *n.* gwerthwr *m.*
semi- *px.* hanner-, go-, lled-
semicircle *n.* hanner cylch *m.*
semi-final *a.* cynderfynol

senate *n.* senedd *f.*
send *v.* anfon, danfon, gyrru,
hala
sender *n.* gyrrwr *m.*
senile *a.* oedrannus, hen
senility *n.* henaint *m.*
senior *a.* hŷn, uwch, uchaf
sense 1 *n.* synnwyr, pwyll *m.*
ystyr *mf.* 2 *v.* synhwyro
sensible *a.* synhwyrol, call
sentence 1 *n.* brawddeg; barn
f. 2 *v.* dedfrydu
sentry *n.* gwyliwr *m.*
separate 1 *a.* ar wahân. 2 *v.*
gwahanu
separately *ad.* ar wahân
separation *n.* gwahaniad *m.*
September *n.* Medi *m.*
serenity *n.* tawelwch, hedd,
heddwch *m.*
serial 1 *n.* cyfres *f.* 2 *a.*
cyfresol
series *n.* cyfres, rhes *f.*
serious *a.* difrifol, prudd,
prysur
seriously *ad.* yn ddifrifol
sermon *n.* pregeth *f.*
serpent *n.* sarff *f.*
servant *n.* gwas *m,* morwyn *f.*
civil servant gwas sifil
serve *v.* gwasanaethu
service *n.* gwasanaeth *m;*
oedfa *f.*
set 1 *n.* set; *f.* 2 *v.* trefnu,
gosod, dodi
setting *n.* machlud; lleoliad
m.
settle 1 *n.* sgiw, setl *f.* 2 *v.*
sefydlu; penderfynu; talu,
cytuno, setlo
settled *a.* sefydlog
settlement *n.* gwladfa *f.*

seven *n.* & *a.* saith *m.*

seventeen *n.* & *a.* dau ar bymtheg, un deg saith *m.*

seventh *n.* & *a.* seithfed *m.*

seventy *n.* & *a.* deg a thrigain, saith deg *m.*

sever *v.* torri

several *a.* amryw

severe *a.* caled, llym, hallt, tost

severity *n.* caledi *m.*

Severn *n.* Afon Hafren *f.*

sew *v.* gwnïo, pwytho

sewing machine *n.* periant gwnïo *m.*

sex *n.* rhyw *m.*

sexual *a.* rhywiol

shade 1 *n.* cysgod *m.* 2 *v.* cysgodi

shadow *n.* cysgod *m.*

shady *a.* cysgodol

shake *v.* ysgwyd, siglo, crynu

shaking *n.* ysgytwad *m.*

shaky *a.* sigledig

shallow *a.* bas

sham *a.* ffug, gau

shame *n.* cywilydd

shameful *a.* gwarthus, cywilyddus

shape 1 *n.* ffurf *f*, llun *m*, siâp *f.* 2 *v.* ffurfio, llunio

shapely *a.* lluniaidd

share 1 *n.* rhan, siâr *f.* 2 *v.* rhannu

sharp *a.* llym, miniog, siarp

shawl *n.* siôl *f.*

she *pn.* hi, hithau, hyhi

shed *n.* sied, cwts *m.*

sheep 1 *n.* dafad *f.* 2 *n.* defaid *pl.*

sheer *a.* pur; glân; noeth

sheet *n.* llen *f*, lliain *m*. dalen *f*, taflen *f.*

shelf *n.* silff *f.*

shell *n.* cragen *f*; plisgyn *m.*

shelter 1 *n.* cysgod *m*, lloches *f.* 2 *v.* cysgodi, llochesu

shepherd 1 *n.* bugail *m.* 2 *v.* bugeilio

shield 1 *n.* tarian *f.* 2 *v.* cysgodi; amddiffyn

shift 1 *n.* newid, symudiad; tro *m*; shifft *f.* 2 *v.* newid, symud

shine *v.* disgleirio, llewyrchu

shiny *a.* gloyw, disglair

ship *n.* llong *f.*

shipshape *a.* taclus, trefnus, twt

shire *n.* sir (Wales), swydd (England) *f.* **Pembrokeshire** Sir Benfro (Cymru); **Gloucestershire** Swydd Gaerloyw (Lloegr)

shirk *v.* osgoi

shirt *n.* crys *m.*

shiver *v.* crynu

shivering *n.* cryd *m.*

shoal *n.* haig *f.*

shock *n.* ysgytwad, sioc *m.*

shoe *n.* esgid *f.* **pair of shoes** pâr o esgidiau

shoot 1 *n.* eginyn *m.* 2 *v.* saethu

shooter *n.* saethwr *m.*

shooting *n.* saethu

shop 1 *n.* siop *f.* 2 *v.* siopa

shopkeeper *n.* siopwr *m.*

shopper *n.* prynwr *m.*

shopping *n.* siopa *m.*

shore *n.* glan *f*, traeth *f.*

short *a.* byr, cwta, prin

shot *n.* ergyd *mf.*

shoulder *n.* ysgwydd *f.*

shout 1 *n.* bloedd *m.* gwaedd *f.* **2** *v.* bloeddio, crio, gweiddi

shove 1 *n.* hwp *m.* **2** *v.* gwthio

shovel *n.* rhaw *f.*

show 1 *n.* sioe *f.* **2** *v.* dangos, arddangos

shower *n.* cawod *f.*

shriek 1 *n.* sgrech, ysgrech *f.* **2** *v.* sgrechian, sgrechain

shrill *a.* main, llym

shut *v.* cau

shy *a.* swil

sick 1 *n.pl.* cleifion *m.* **2** *a.* claf, gwael, sâl, tost

sickness *n.* afiechyd, clefyd, dolur, anhwyldeb, anhwylder, tostrwydd *m.*

side 1 *n.* ochr *f,* ymyl, ystlys; tu *mf,* plaid *f.* **2** *v.* ochri

sidesman *n.* ystlyswr *m.*

sideways *ad.* tua'r ochr

sigh 1 *n.* ochenaid *f.* **2** *v.* ochneidio

sight 1 *n.* golwg *mf,* golygfa *f.* **2** *v.* gweld, gweled

sign 1 *n.* arwydd *m.* **2** *v.* arwyddo, llofnodi

signal *n.* arwydd *m.*

signature *n.* llofnod *m.*

silage *n.* silwair *m.*

silence 1 *n.* distawrwydd, tawelwch *m.* **2** *v.* distewi

silencer *n.* distewydd *m.*

silent *a.* distaw, tawel

silk *n.* sidan *m.*

silly *a.* ffôl, dwl, twp

silver *n.* arian *m.* **silversmith** gof arian; **silver wedding** priodas arian

similar *a.* tebyg

similarity *n.* tebygrwydd *m.*

simple *a.* syml; diniwed

sin 1 *n.* pechod *m.* **2** *v.* pechu

since 1 *c.* am, gan, oherwydd. **2** *prp.* er, ers, er pan

sincere *a.* diffuant, cywir, pur

sinew *n.* gewyn *m.*

sing *v.* canu

singer *n.* canwr, cantwr, cantor *m;* cantores *f.*

singing *n.* caniad, caniadaeth *f,* canu *m.*

single *a.* sengl, un; dibriod

singular *a.* unigol; hynod

sink 1 *n.* sinc *m.* **2** *v.* suddo

sinner *n.* pechadur *m.*

sir *n.* syr *m.*

sister *n.* chwaer *f.*

sister-in-law *n.* chwaer-yng-nghyfraith *f.*

sit *v.* eistedd

situation *n.* lle, safle *m;* sefyllfa *f.*

six *n.* & *a.* chwe, chwech *m.*

sixteen *n.* & *a.* un ar bymtheg, un deg chwech *m.*

sixth *n.* & *a* chweched *m.*

sixty *n.* & *a.* trigain, chwe deg *m.*

size *n.* maint *m.*

skate 1 *n.* sgêt *f.* **2** *v.* sglefrio. **skateboard** bwrdd sglefrio

sketch 1 *n.* llun, braslun *m;* sgets *f.* **2** *v.* braslunio

ski 1 *n.* sgi *f.* **2** *v.* sgïo

skier *n.* sgîwr *m.*

skilful *a.* medrus

skill *n.* sgil *m,* crefft *f.*

skim *v.* tynnu, codi (hufen)

skimmed milk *n.* llaeth glas *m.*

skin 1 *n.* croen *m.* **2** *v.* blingo
skip *v.* sgipio
skirt *n.* sgert, sgyrt *f.*
sky *n.* wybren, awyr, ffurfafen, nen *f.*
skylark *n.* ehedydd, uchedydd, hedydd *m.*
slack 1 *n.* glo mân *m.* **2** *a.* llac, diofal, esgeulus
slacken *v.* llacio, llaesu
slate *n.* llechen *f.*
slaughter *v.* lladd
slaughterhouse *n.* lladd-dy *m.*
slave *n.* caethwas *m.*
slay *v.* lladd
sleek *a.* llyfn
sleep 1 *n.* cwsg *m.* **2** *v.* cysgu, huno. **sleeping bag** sach gysgu
sleepy *a.* cysglyd
sleet *n.* eirlaw *m.*
sleeve *n.* llawes *f.*
slender *a.* main, tenau
slice *n.* tafell, sleisen *f.* **slice of bread and butter** tafell o fara menyn; **slice of bacon** sleisen o gig moch
slide 1 *n.* llithren *f.* **2** *v.* llithro, sglefrio
slim *a.* main
slip 1 *n.* llithriad *m.* **2** *v.* llithro dros
slipper *n.* sliper *f.*
slippery *a.* llithrig, slic
slipshod *a.* anniben
slovenly *a.* anniben
slope *n.* rhiw *f,* tyle, llethr *m.*
slow 1 *a.* araf. **2** *v.* arafu
slug *n.* malwoden *f.* slyg *m.*
sluggard *n.* diogyn, pwdryn *m.*

sluggish *a.* diog, dioglyd
slumber 1 *n.* cwsg *m.* **2** *v.* cysgu
slur 1 *n.* llithriad *m.* **2** *v.* llithro dros
sly *a.* cyfrwys
small *a.* bach, mân, bychan *m.* bechan *f.*
smallest *a.* lleiaf; see **bach**
smallholder *n.* tyddynnwr *m.*
smallholding *n.* tyddyn *m.*
smash *v.* malu
smell 1 *n.* arogl *m,* aroglau *pl,* gwynt *m.* **2** *v.* arogli, clywed arogl, gwynto
smile 1 *n.* gwên *f.* **2** *v.* gwenu
smith *n.* gof *m.* **smithy** gefail
smoke 1 *n.* mwg *m.* **2** *v.* mygu, ysmygu
smoky *a.* myglyd
smooth *a.* llyfn; esmwyth
smother *v.* mogi, mygu
snack *n.* byrbryd *m.*
snag *n.* rhwystr *m.*
snail *n.* malwoden *f.*
snake *n.* neidr *f.*
snarl *v.* chwyrnu
sneeze *v.* tisian
snobs *n.pl.* crachach *m.*
snore *v.* chwyrnu
snout *n.* trwyn *m.*
snow *n.* eira *m.* **snowball** pelen eira; **snowdrift** lluwch, lluwchfa, lluchfa; **snowflake** pluen eira
Snowdon *n.* Yr Wyddfa *f.*
Snowdonia *n.* Eryri *f.*
snowdrop *n.* eirlys, tlws yr eira, lili wen fach *m.*
snub *n.* sen *f.*
so *ad.* & *c.* fel, felly, mor

soap n. sebon m. **soap powder** powdr golchi

soccer n. pêl-droed f.

socialism n. sosialaeth f.

socialist 1 n. sosialydd m. **2** a. sosialaidd

society n. cymdeithas f.

sociology n. cymdeithaseg f.

sock n. hosan f.

soft a. meddal. **soft drinks** diodydd ysgafn

soften v. meddalu

software n. meddalwedd f.

soil 1 n. pridd m; daear f. **2** v. trochi, sarnu

soldier n. milwr m.

sole 1 n. gwadn m. **2** a. unig, unigol, un

solemn a. difrifol, dwys

solicitor n. cyfreithiwr m.

solo 1 n. unawd m. **2** a. unigol

soloist n. unawdwr, unawdydd m.

solve v. datrys, datod

some 1 a. rhyw, rhai, peth, ychydig. **2** pn. rhai, rhywrai, rhywfaint. **3** ad. rhyw, tua, ynghylch

somebody n. & pn. rhywun m.

someone n. & pn. rhywun m.

Somerset n. Gwlad yr Haf f.

something n. rhywbeth m.

sometime ad. rhywbryd, rhywdro, gynt

sometimes ad. weithiau, ambell waith, ar brydiau

somewhat ad. go, lled, braidd

somewhere ad. rhywle

son n. mab m.

son-in-law n. mab-yng-nghyfraith m.

soon ad. yn fuan, ar fyr o dro

sooner ad. yn gynt

soot n. huddygl m.

sore a. blin, tost

sorrow 1 n. gofid, tristwch, galar m. **2** v. gofidio, hiraethu

sorrowful a. trist.

sorry a. blin, drwg gan, edifar, trist

sort 1 n. math, modd, dosbarth m. **2** v. dosbarthu, trefnu

soul n. enaid m.

sound 1 n. sain f, swn m. **2** a. iach; cyfan. **3** v. swnio, seinio

soup n. cawl m.

sour 1 a. sur. **2** v. suro

source n. ffynhonnell f, tarddiad m.

south 1 n. & a. de mf, deau m; **South Wales** De Cymru. **2** ad. tua'r de

southern a. deheuol

sow n. hwch f.

sow v. hau

sower n. heuwr m.

space n. gofod, gwagle, bwlch m.

spaceman n. gofodwr m.

spaceship n. llong ofod f.

spade n. pâl, rhaw f.

Spain n. Sbaen f.

Spaniard n. Sbaenwr m.

Spanish 1 n. Sbaeneg f. (iaith). **2** a. Sbaenaidd

spare 1 a. sbâr. **2** v. arbed

spark n. gwreichionen f.

speak v. llefaru, siarad

speaker n. llefarwr, llefarydd, siaradwr m.

special *a.* arbennig, neilltuol

species *n.* math *m.*

specified *a.* nodedig

specify *v.* enwi

spectacle *n.* golygfa *f.*

spectacles *n.* sbectol *pl.*

speech *n.* araith *f;* llafar *m,* ymadrodd *m.*

speechless *a.* mud

speed *n.* cyflymder *m.*

speedy *a.* buan, cyflym

spell 1 *n.* egwyl, hoe, sbel *f;* hud, swyn *m.* 2 *v.* cael hoe; sillafu. **to cast a spell** swyno

spend *v.* gwario, hala *(arian);* treulio *(amser).*

spiced *a.* llysieuol

spider *n.* corryn, pryf copyn *m.*

spill *v.* colli

spine *n.* asgwrn cefn *m.*

spirit *n.* ysbryd *m.*

spirited *a.* ysbrydol, nwyfus

spiritual *a.* ysbrydol

spiritualize *v.* ysbrydoli

spit *n.* & *v.* poeri *m.*

spittle *n.* poer, poeri *m.*

splash *v.* tasgu

splendid *a.* rhagorol, ardderchog, penigamp, campus, gwych

splendour *n.* ysblander *m.*

split 1 *n.* hollt; rhaniad; rhwyg *m.* 2 *a.* hollt; rhanedig. 3 *v.* hollti

spokesman *n.* llefarwr, llefarydd *m.*

spoon 1 *n.* llwy *f.* 2 *v.* llwyo

spoonful *n.* llwyaid *f.*

sport *n.* sbort *f.* chwarae *m,* hwyl *f.*

sports *n.* mabolgampau *pl,* chwaraeon

spot 1 *n.* man *mf,* lle, llecyn, sbot, sbotyn, smotyn *m.* 2 *v.* adnabod; smotio

spread *v.* lledu

spring 1 *n.* ffynnon, ffynhonnell; sbring; gwanwyn; neidio *f.* 2 *v.* tarddu; neidio

sprout *n.* eginyn *m,* egin *pl.*

Brussels sprouts ysgewyll Brwsel

spur *n.* ysbardun; clogwyn *m.*

sputnik *n.* lloeren *f.*

spy 1 *n.* ysbïwr *m.* 2 *v.* ysbïo

square *n.* sgwâr *f.*

squash 1 *n.* sboncen *f.* 2 *v.* gwasgu

squirrel *n.* gwiwer *f.*

stable 1 *n.* stabl *f.* 2 *a.* sefydlog, diogel

staff *n.* ffon; staff *f.*

stag *n.* hydd *f.*

stage 1 *n.* llwyfan *m;* lefel *f.* 2 *v.* llwyfannu

stair *n.* gris *m,* staer *f.*

stall *n.* stondin *f;* côr *m.*

stamp 1 *n.* stamp *m.* 2 *v.* stampio

stand 1 *n.* stondin *f.* 2 *v.* sefyll

standard 1 *n.* safon; baner *f.* 2 *a.* safonol

standpoint *n.* safbwynt *m.*

stanza *n.* pennill *m.*

star 1 *n.* seren *f.* 2 *v.* serennu

starlight *n.* golau'r sêr

starling *n.* drudwy *m.*

starry *a.* serennog

start *n.* & *v.* cychwyn, dechrau *m.*

starve *v.* llwgu

state 1 *n.* cyflwr *m*, ffurf;
talaith *f.* 2 *v.* mynegi, dweud

statesman *n.* gwleidydd *m.*

station *n.* gorsaf *f.* safle *m*,
sefyllfa *f.* **railway station**
gorsaf reilffordd

stationary *a.* sefydlog

stationer *n.* gwerthwr
papurau *m.*

stationery *n.* papur ysgrifennu
m.

statistics *n.pl.* ystadegau

statue *n.* cerflun *m*, delw *f.*

statute *n.* deddf, cyfraith, act
f.

stay 1 *n.* arhosiad *m.* 2 *v.*
aros, oedi, sefyll

steal *v.* lladrata, dwyn

steel *n.* dur *m.*

steep *a.* serth

steer *v.* llywio; cyfeirio

stench *n.* drewdod, drewi *m.*

step 1 *n.* cam, gris 2 *v.* camu

step- *px.* llys-

stepdaughter *n.* llysferch *f.*

stepfather *n.* llystad *m.*

stepmother *n.* llysfam *f.*

stepsister *n.* llyschwaer *f.*

stepson *n.* llysfab *f.*

steward 1 *n.* stiward *m.* 2 *v.*
stiwardio

stick 1 *n.* ffon, gwialen *f*,
pren *m.* 2 *v.* glynu

stiff *a.* syth

stiffen *v.* sythu

still 1 *a.* llonydd, tawel. 2 *ad.*
eto, er hynny; byth

stillness *n.* tawelwch,
heddwch, llonyddwch *m.*

sting 1 *n.* pigiad *m.* 2 *v.* pigo

stink 1 *n.* drewdod, drewi *m.*
2 *v.* drewi

stitch 1 *n.* pwyth *m;*
2 *v.* pwytho, gwnïo

stocking *n.* hosan *f.*

stoke *v.* tanio, gofalu am dân

stomach 1 *n.* stumog *f*, bol *m.*
2 *v.* stumogi

stone *n.* carreg *f.*

stool *n.* stôl *f.*

stoop *v.* plygu, ymostwng

stop 1 atalfa *f*, stop *m.* **full
stop** atalnod llawn. 2 *v.*
atal; stopio; cau; aros, sefyll;
peidio (â)

storage *n.* stôr *m*, storfa *f.*

store 1 *n.* stôr *m*, storfa *f.*
2 *v.* storio

storehouse *n.* stordy *m.*

storm *n.* storm, tymestl *f.*

stormy *a.* stormus,
tymhestlog

story *n.* stori *f*, hanes,
hanesyn *m*, chwedl *f.*

stove *n.* ffwrn, stof *f.*

straight *a.* syth, union

straighten *v.* sythu, unioni

straightway *ad.* yn y man, yn
syth

strange *a.* dieithr, rhyfedd,
rhyfeddol, od, estron

stranger *n.* dieithryn, estron
m.

strangle *v.* tagu

straw *n.* gwelltyn; gwellt *m.*

strawberry *n.* mefusen *f.*

stream 1 *n.* ffrwd *f*, llif *m*,
nant *f.* 2 *v.* llifo

streamer *n.* ruban *m*, baner *f.*

street *n.* stryd, heol, hewl,
ffordd *f.*

strength *n.* nerth, grym *m.*

stretch *v.* estyn, ymestyn

strict *a.* cyfyng, llym, manwl

stride 1 *n.* cam *m.* **2** *v.* camu
strife *n.* ymryson *m.*
strike 1 *n.* streic *f.* **2** *v.* streicio; taro
striker *n.* streiciwr *m.*
strip *n.* llain *f.* **landing strip, airstrip** llain lanio
string *n.* cordyn, llinyn; tant *m.*
strive *v.* ymdrechu
strong *a.* cryf, grymus
structure 1 *n.* adeilad; strwythur *m.* **2** *v.* strwythuro
struggle 1 *n.* ymdrech *f.* **2** *v.* ymdrechu
student *n.* myfyriwr *m.*
study *v.* myfyrio, astudio
stump *n.* bôn *m.*
stunning *a.* syfrdanol
stupefying *a.* syfrdanol
stupid *a.* twp, dwl, hurt. **stupid person** twpsyn, hurtyn
sty *n.* twlc *m.* **pigsty** twlc mochyn
stye *n.* llefelyn, llyfelyn *m,* llefrithen *f.*
subconscious 1 *n.* isymwybod *m.* **2** *a.* isymwybodol
subjective *a.* goddrychol
submarine 1 *n.* llong danfor *f.* **2** *a.* tanfor, tanforol
submit *v.* ymostwng; anfon; cyflwyno
subordinate *a.* israddol
substance *n.* sylwedd *m.*
substantial *a.* sylweddol
substantiate *v.* profi
substitute *n.* dirprwy, un yn lle arall *m.*
subterranean *a.* tanddaear, tanddaearol

suburb *n.* maestref *f.*
subway *n.* isffordd *f,* tanlwybr *m.*
succeed *v.* llwyddo; dilyn, canlyn
success *n.* llwydd, llwyddiant *m.*
successful *a.* llwyddiannus
succour *n.* ymgeledd, swcwr *m.*
such *a.* y fath, cyfryw
suck *v.* sugno
sudden *a.* sydyn
sue *v.* erlyn
suffer *v.* dioddef, caniatáu, goddef
suffering *n.* dioddef *m,* poen *mf.*
sufficient 1 *n.* digon *m.* **2** *a.* digon, digonol
sufficiently *ad.* digon
suffocate *v.* mogi, mygu, tagu
sugar 1 *n.* siwgr *m.* **2** *v.* siwgro
suggest *v.* awgrymu
suggestion *n.* awgrym, awgrymiad *m.*
suicide *n.* hunanladdiad *m.*
suitable *a.* addas, priodol
suite *n.* cyfres *f.*
sulk *v.* pwdu
sultry *a.* clòs, trymaidd
sum 1 *n.* swm *m.* **2** *v.* crynhoi
summarize *v.* crynhoi
summary *n.* crynodeb *mf.*
summer *n.* haf *m.* **midsummer** canol haf; **a summer's day** hafddydd; **summer dwelling** hafdy, hafod; tŷ haf
summery *a.* hafaidd

summit *n.* brig, pen *m,* ban *mf,* copa *m.*

summon *v.* galw, gwysio

summons *n.* gwŷs *f.*

sumptuous *a.* moethus

sun *n.* haul *m.*

sunbathe *v.* torheulo

sunburn *n.* llosg haul *m.*

Sunday *n.* dydd Sul *m.*

sunflower *n.* blodyn yr haul *m.*

sunglasses *n.* sbectol haul *f.*

sunny *a.* heulog

sunrise *n.* codiad haul *m.*

sunset *n.* machlud haul *m.*

sunshine *n.* heulwen *f.*

superb *a.* ardderchog, rhagorol

superior *a.* uwch, gwell

supermarket *n.* archfarchnad *f.*

supernatural *a.* goruwchnaturiol

superstition *n.* ofergoel, ofergoeledd, ofergoeliaeth *f.*

superstitious *a.* ofergoelus

supper *n.* swper *m.* **the Last Supper** y Swper Olaf

supple *a.* ystwyth, hyblyg

supplement 1 *n.* atodiad *m.* 2 *v.* ychwanegu

supplementary *a.* atodol, ychwanegol

support *v.* cynnal, cefnogi

suppose *v.* tybied, tybio

supreme *a.* goruchaf, prif, pennaf

sure *a.* sicr, siŵr

suretyship *n.* mechnïaeth *f.*

surface *n.* wyneb, arwyneb, arwynebedd *m.*

surfeit 1 *n.* syrffed *m.* 2 *v.* syrffedu

surgeon *n.* llawfeddyg *m.*

surgery *n.* llawfeddygaeth, llawdriniaeth; meddygfa *f.*

surgical *a.* llawfeddygol

surname 1 *n.* cyfenw *m.* 2 *v.* cyfenwi

surpass *v.* rhagori ar, trechu

surprise 1 *n.* rhyfeddod, syndod *m.* 2 *v.* synnu

surprising *a.* rhyfedd, rhyfeddol, syn

surround *v.* amgylchynu

suspect *v.* amau

suspend *v.* crogi; atal

suspension bridge *n.* pont grog *f.*

swallow 1 *n.* llwnc *m;* gwennol *f.* 2 *v.* llyncu

swamp 1 *n.* siglen, cors *f.* 2 *v.* gorlifo

swan *n.* alarch *m.*

swarm 1 *n.* haid, torf *f.* 2 *v.* heidio, tyrru

swathe 1 *n.* ystod *f.* 2 *v.* rhwymo

sway *v.* siglo

swear *v.* tyngu, rhegi

sweat 1 *n.* chwys *m.* 2 *v.* chwysu

swede *n.* erfinen, sweden, meipen *f.*

Swede *n.* Swediad *m.*

Sweden *n.* Sweden *f.*

Swedish *a.* Swedaidd

sweep 1 *n.* ysgubwr, sgubwr *f.* 2 *v.* ysgubo, sgubo, brwsio, brwshio

sweet 1 *n.* losinen, losen *f.* 2 *a.* melys

sweetheart *n.* cariad *mf.*

sweets *n.* losin *pl.*

swell *v.* chwyddo

swerve *v.* osgoi, gwyro, troi

swift 1 *n.* gwennol ddu *f.* **2** *a.* buan, cyflym

swiftness *n.* cyflymder *m.*

swim 1 *n.* nofiad *m.* **2** *v.* nofio

swimmer *n.* nofiwr *m.*

swimming *n.* nofio *m.*

swimming pool *n.* pwll nofio *m.*

swimsuit *n.* gwisg nofio *f.*

swing 1 *n.* siglen *f.* **2** *v.* siglo

switch *n.* troswr *f. (trydan),* swits *mf.*

Switzerland *n.* Y Swistir *f.*

swoon *v.* llewygu

syllable *n.* sillaf *f.*

syllabus *n.* maes llafur *m.*

sympathy *n.* cydymdeimlad *m.*

symptom *n.* arwydd *m.*

synonym *n.* cyfystyr *m.*

synonymous *a.* cyfystyr (â)

system *a.* cyfundrefn; trefn, system *f.*

T

tabernacle *n.* tabernacl *m,* pabell *f.*

table *n.* bord *f,* bwrdd; tabl *m;* taflen *f.* **tableful** bordaid, byrddaid

tablecloth *n.* lliain bord, lliain bwrdd *m.*

tablespoon *n.* llwy fawr, llwy fwrdd *f.*

tablet *n.* tabled *m.*

tackle 1 *n.* offer *pl,* gêr, tacl *m.* **2** *v.* taclo

tackler *n.* taclwr *m.*

tail *n.* cynffon *f.*

tailback *n.* tagfa *f.*

tailor *n.* teiliwr *m.*

tailoress *n.* teilwres *f.*

take *v.* cymryd, cael, dwyn, dal

take hold *v.* cydio

tale *n.* chwedl *f,* hanes, hanesyn *m,* stori *f.*

talent 1 *n.* talent, dawn *f.* **2** *a.* talentog, dawnus

talk 1 *n.* sgwrs *f,* siarad *m.* sôn *mf.* **2** *v.* sgwrsio, siarad, sôn

talker *n.* siaradwr *m.*

tall *a.* tal, uchel

tallow *n.* gwêr *m.*

talon *n.* ewin *mf,* crafanc *f.*

tame 1 *n.* dof. **2** *v.* dofi

tang *n.* tafod *m.*

tank *n.* tanc *m.*

tanker *n.* tancer *m;* llong olew *f.*

tap 1 *n.* tap *m.* **2** *v.* taro, tapio

tape *n.* tâp, incil *m.*

tape measure *n.* tâp mesur *m.*

tape-recorder *n.* recordydd tâp *m.*

tapering *a.* pigfain

target *n.* targed, nod *m.*

tart *n.* tarten, pastai *f.* **apple tart** pastai afalau; **jam tart** pastai jam

task *n.* tasg *m.*

taste 1 *n.* blas *m.* **2** *v.* blasu, clywed, profi

tasty *a.* blasus

tavern *n.* tafarn *mf,* tŷ tafarn *m.*

tax 1 *n.* treth *f.* **Income tax** Treth Incwm; **Value Added Tax** Treth Ar Werth. **2** *v.* trethu

taxi *n.* tacsi *m.*

tea *n.* te *m.* **tea bags** cydau te; **teacup** cwpan te, dysgl de; **tea leaves** dail te

teach *v.* dysgu

teacher *n.* athro *m;* athrawes *f.*

team *n.* tîm *m.*

tea party *n.* téparti *m.*

teapot *n.* tebot *m.*

tear *n.* deigryn *m.*

tear 1 *n.* rhwyg *m.* **2** *v.* rhwygo

tease *v.* poeni

teaspoon *n.* llwy de *f.*

teaspoonful *n.* llond llwy de *m.*

technical *a.* technegol

technician *n.* technegwr *m.*

technique *n.* techneg *m.*

technology *n.* technoleg *f.*

teddy bear *n.* tedi *m.*

teenager *n.* un yn yr arddegau *mf.*

teens *n.pl.* arddegau

teetotaller *n.* llwyrymwrthodwr *m.*

telecast *n.* telediad *m.*

telephone 1 *n.* teleffon, ffôn *m.* **telephone call** galwad ffôn. **2** *v.* teleffonio, ffonio

television *n.* teledu *m.*

tell *v.* dweud (wrth), mynegi. **to tell the truth** dweud y gwir

temper *n.* tymer, natur *m.*

temperature *n.* tymheredd *m.*

tempest *n.* tymestl *f.*

tempestuous *a.* tymhestlog

temple *n.* teml; arlais *f.*

ten *n.* & *a.* deg, deng *m.*

tendency *n.* tueddiad *m.*

tender *a.* tyner, mwyn, meddal, tirion

tenderness *n.* tynerwch *m.*

tendon *n.* gewyn, tendon *m.*

tennis *n.* tenis *m.* **tennis ball** pêl denis; **tennis court** cwrt tenis; **tennis racket** raced denis

tense 1 *n.* amser *m. (gramadeg).* **2** *v.* tyn, tynn

tent *n.* pabell *f.*

tenth *n.* & *a.* degfed *m.*

term 1 *n.* tymor; term; amod *m.* **2** *v.* enwi, galw

terminus *n.* terfyn *m.*

terrace *n.* rhes dai *f,* teras *m.*

terrible *a.* dychrynllyd, ofnadwy, erchyll

terrifying *a.* dychrynllyd

territory *n.* tir *m.*

terror *n.* braw, ofn *m.*

terrorism *n.* terfysgaeth *f.*

terrorist *n.* terfysgwr *m.*

tertiary *a.* trydyddol. **tertiary college** coleg trydyddol

test 1 *n.* prawf *m.*; **reading test** prawf darllen; **spelling test** prawf sillafu **2** *v.* profi

testament *n.* testament *m.* **New Testament** Testament Newydd

testify *v.* tystio

testimony *n.* tystiolaeth *f.*

text *n.* testun *m.* **textbook** gwerslyfr

than *c.* na, nag

thank *v.* diolch. **Thanks** Diolch! **Thanks very much** Diolch yn fawr

thankful *a.* diolchgar

thankfulness *n.* diolchgarwch *m.*

thankless *a.* diddiolch

thanksgiving *n.* diolchgarwch *m.* **Thanksgiving Service** Gwasanaeth Diolchgarwch

that 1 *a.* hwnnw, honno, hynny, yna, acw. 2 *pn.* hwn, hon, yna, hwn acw, hon acw, dyna, dacw; a, y, yr. 3 *c.* mai, taw, fel y, fel yr

thaw *v.* toddi, meddalu, meirioli, dadmer, dadlaith

the *def. art.* y, yr, 'r

theatre *n.* theatr *f.*

thee *pn.* ti, tydi, tithau

theft *n.* lladrad *m.*

their *pn.* eu

theirs *pn.* eiddynt, yr eiddynt

them *pn.* hwy, hwynt, hwythau, nhw

themselves *pn.* eu hunain

then 1 *ad.* wedyn, yna, y pryd hwnnw. 2 *c.* yna, ynte, ynteu.

thereafter *ad.* wedyn

thereat *ad.* ar hynny, yna

thereby *ad.* trwy hynny

therefore *c.* am hynny, gan hynny, felly

therefrom *ad.* oddi yno

therein *ad.* yno, ynddo, yn hynny

thereupon *ad.* ar hynny

therewith *ad.* gyda hynny

thermometer *n.* thermomedr *f.*

these *pn.* & *a.* y rhai hyn, y rhain

they *pn.* hwy, hwynt, hwythau, nhw

thick *a.* tew, trwchus

thief *n.* lleidr *m.*

thieve *v.* lladrata, dwyn, dwgyd

thigh *n.* clun, morddwyd *f.*

thin *a.* main, tenau, cul

thing *n.* peth, gwrthrych *m.*

think *v.* meddwl, tybied, tybio

third *n.* & *a.* trydydd *m;* trydedd *f.*

thirst 1 *n.* syched *m.* 2 *v.* sychedu

thirsty *a.* sychedig

thirteen *n.* & *a.* tri ar ddeg, un deg tri *m.*

thirty *n.* & *a.* deg ar hugain, tri deg *m.*

this *a.* & *pn.* hwn, hon, hyn; yma. **this minute** y funud hon, y funud yma; **this hour, (now, at present)** yr awr hon, **this day** y dydd hwn; **this week** yr wythnos hon; **this month** y mis hwn; **this year** eleni

thistle *n.* ysgallen *f.*

thorn *n.* draen, draenen *f;* **thorns** drain

those 1 *pn.* hynny, y rhai hynny, y rheini, y rheiny. 2 *a.* hynny, yna

though 1 *ad.* er, serch hynny. 2 *prp.* er, pe, cyd

thought *n.* meddwl, syniad *m.*

thoughtful *a.* meddylgar

thousand *n.* & *a.* mil *f.*

thread *n.* edau *f,* llinyn *m.*

three *n.* & *a.* tri *m,* tair *f.* **three times** teirgwaith

threesome *n.* triawd *m.*

threshold *n.* trothwy *m.* rhiniog *f.*

thrill *n.* ias *f.*

thrilling *a.* iasol

throat *n.* gwddf, gwddwg, llwnc *m.*

throne *n.* gorsedd *f.*

through 1 *ad.* trwodd. **2** *prp*
drwy, trwy
throw 1 *n.* tafliad *m.* **2** *v.*
taflu
thrush *n.* bronfraith *f.*
thrust 1 *n.* gwthiad, hwp *m.*
2 *v.* gwthio
thumb 1 *n.* bawd *m.* **2** *v.*
bodio
thunder 1 *n.* taran *f*, tyrfau
pl. **2** *v.* taranu
thunderbolt *n.* bollt *m*,
mellten, llucheden *f.*
thunderclap *n.* taran *f.*
thunderstorm *n.* storm fellt a
tharanau *f.*
Thursday *n.* dydd Iau
thus *ad.* fel hyn, felly
thy *pn.* dy, 'th
ticket *n.* tocyn, ticed *m.* **ticket
collector** tocynnwr; **ticket
office** swyddfa docynnau
tide *n.* llanw *m:* **high tide**
penllanw; **ebb tide** trai
tidy 1 *a.* cryno, taclus, twt.
2 *v.* tacluso
tie 1 *n.* tei; clwm, cwlwm *m.*
2 *v.* clymu, rhwymo
tiger *n.* teigr *m.*
tight *a.* tyn, tynn; cyfyng
tile *n.* teilsen *f.*
timber *n.* coed, pren *m.*
time *n.* adeg *f*, oed; amser,
pryd *m.* **at times** ar adegau,
ar brydiau; **in time** mewn
pryd
timetable *n.* amserlen *f.*
timid *a.* llwfr, ofnus
tin *n.* tun; alcam *m.* **tin of
paint** tun o baent; **tin of peas**
tun o bys
tinge *n.* naws, gwawr *f.*

tinted *a.* lliwiog
tiny *a.* bach, bychan, bitw,
mân
tip *n.* tip *m*, tomen *f;* cyngor
m; gwobr *f;* cil-dwrn *m.*
rubbish tip tomen ysbwriel,
tip ysbwriel
tire *v.* blino
tired *a.* blinedig, blin
title *n.* teitl, enw *m;* hawl *f.*
title-page wyneb ddalen
to *prp.* at, hyd at, i, er mwyn,
tua, wrth, yn
toad *n.* llyffant *m.*
toadstool(s) *n.* madarch, caws
llyffant, bwyd y boda *pl. coll.*
See **madarch**
toast 1 *n.* tost; llwncdestun
m. **2** *v.* tostio; cynnig
llwncdestun
today *ad.* heddiw
together *ad.* gyda'i gilydd,
ynghyd
toil 1 *n.* llafur *m.* **2** *v.* llafurio
toilet *n.* toiled, tŷ-bach, lle
chwech, jeriw *m.*
token *n.* arwydd; tocyn *m.*
tolerate *v.* goddef, caniatáu
toll 1 *n.* toll, treth *f.* **2** *v.* canu
cloch
tollgate *n.* tollborth *m*,
tollglwyd *f.*
tomato *n.* tomato *m.*
tomb *n.* bedd, beddrod *m.*
tomcat *n.* cwrcath, gwrcath,
cwrcyn, gwrcyn *m.*
tomorrow *ad.* fory, yfory
ton *n.* tunnell *f.* **tonne** tunnell
fetrig
tone *n.* tôn; naws *f.*
tongue *n.* tafod *m;* tafodiaith,
iaith *f.*

tonight *ad.* heno

too *ad.* hefyd; rhy. **too much**
gormod; **too little** rhy fach;
too late rhy hwyr

tool *n.* arf, erfyn, offeryn *m.*

tooth *n.* dant *m.*

toothache *n.* dannoedd *f.*

toothbrush *n.* brwsh dannedd
m.

toothpaste *n.* sebon dannedd,
past dannedd *m.*

top *n.* pen, brig, copa, top *m.*

topic *n.* pwnc, testun *m.*

torch *n.* tors *m.*

torch-light *n.* golau tors *m.*

torment *v.* poeni, poenydio

tormentor *n.* poenydiwr *m.*

torque *n.* torch *m.*

torrid *a.* cras, poeth,
crasboeth

tortoise *n.* crwban *m.*

torture *v.* poenydio

Tory 1 *n.* Tori, Ceidwadwr
m. 2 *a.* Torïaidd

total 1 *n.* cyfanswm, y cyfan
m. 2 *a.* cyfan, hollol, llwyr

tottering *a.* sigledig, simsan

touch 1 *n.* teimlad *m.* 2 *v.*
cyffwrdd (â), teimlo

touch judge *n.* ystlyswr *m.*

touchline *n.* llinell ystlys *f.*

tour 1 *n.* taith *f,* tro *m.* 2 *v.*
teithio

tourism *n.* twristiaeth *f.*

tourist 1 *n.* teithiwr,
ymwelwr, ymwelydd *m.* 2 *a.*
twristaidd. **Tourist Board**
Bwrdd Croeso

towards *prp.* tua, at, tuag at

towel *n.* lliain, tywel *m.*

tower *n.* twr *m.*

town *n.* tref, tre *f.* **Carmarthen**

Town Tre Caerfyrddin; **town
centre** canol y dre; **town
council** cyngor y dre; **town
hall** neuadd y dre

toy 1 *n.* tegan *m.* 2 *v.*
chwarae

trace *v.* olrhain

track 1 *n.* llwybr, ôl, trac *m.*
2 *v.* olrhain

tracksuit *n.* tracwisg *f.*

trade *n.* masnach; crefft *f.*

tradesman *n.* masnachwr,
siopwr; crefftwr

tradition *n.* traddodiad *m.*

traditional *a.* traddodiadol

traffic *n.* trafnidiaeth, traffig
f. **traffic jam** tagfa

trail 1 *n.* trywydd *m.* 2 *v.*
llusgo

train 1 *n.* trên *m.* 2 *v.*
hyfforddi; ymarfer

trainer *n.* hyfforddwr

training *n.* hyfforddiant *m,*
ymarfer *f.* **in-service training**
hyfforddiant mewn swydd

tramp 1 *n.* crwydryn *m.*
2 *v.* crwydro

trample *v.* sathru, sarnu

tranquillity *n.* hedd, heddwch,
tawelwch, llonyddwch *m.*

tranquillizer *n.* tawelyn *m.*

transact *v.* trafod, trin,
gwneud

transfer *v.* trosglwyddo

transfusion *n.* trallwysiad *m.*
blood transfusion
trallwysiad gwaed

transgress *v.* troseddu

transgression *n.* trosedd *f.*

transgressor *n.* troseddwr *m.*

translate *v.* cyfieithu, trosi

translation *n.* cyfieithiad,

trosiad *m.*
translator *n.* cyfieithydd *m.*
transparent *a.* tryloyw
transplant *v.* trawsblannu
trap 1 *n.* trap *m.* **2** *v.* dal, trapio
trash *n.* sothach, ysbwriel *m.*
travel *v.* teithio
traveller *n.* teithiwr *m.*
travelling *a.* teithiol
treachery *n.* brad, twyll *m.*
treasure 1 *n.* trysor *m.* **2** *v.* trysori
treasurer *n.* trysorydd *m.*
treasury *n.* trysorfa *f.* **the Treasury** y Trysorlys
treat 1 *n.* gwledd *m.* **2** *v.* trin
treatise *n.* traethawd *m.*
tree *n.* coeden *f,* pren *m.*
tremendous *a.* dychrynllyd, ofnadwy, anferth
trench *n.* ffos *f.*
triad *n.* tri *m.*
triads *n.* trioedd *pl.*
trial *n.* prawf; treial *m.* **sheepdog trials** treialon cŵn defaid
triangle *n.* triongl *mf.*
triangular *a.* trionglog
tribe *n.* llwyth, tylwyth *m.*
tribulation *n.* trallod *m.*
trick *n.* tric *m.*
trickery *n.* twyll *m.*
tricky *a.* anodd
trim *v.* tacluso, trwsio
trinity *n.* trindod *f.*
trio *n.* triawd *m.*
triplet *n.* tripled *m;* triban *f.*
trouble 1 *n.* gofid *m,* helynt *f,* picil, picl, trafferth, trallod, trwbl *m.* **2** *v.* blino, gofidio, trafferthu

troublesome *a.* trafferthus
trousers *n.* trowsus, trwser *pl.*
trowel *n.* trywel *m.*
trudge *v.* troedio, cerdded
true *a.* gwir, cywir, iawn
truly *ad.* yn wir, yn gywir. **Yours truly** Yr eiddoch yn gywir
trunk *n.* bôn *m;* cist *f;* trwnc *m.*
trust 1 *n.* ymddiriedaeth, ymddiriedolaeth *f.* **2** *v.* ymddiried (yn); **National Trust** Ymddiriedolaeth Genedlaethol
trustee *n.* ymddiriedolwr *m.*
trusteeship *n.* ymddiriedolaeth *f.*
trusty *a.* ffyddlon, cywir
truth *n.* gwirionedd, gwir, iawn *m.*
try 1 *n.* cais *(mewn rygbi),* cynnig *m.* **converted try** trosgais. **2** *v.* ceisio, cynnig, profi
T-shirt *n.* crys-T *m.*
Tuesday *n.* dydd Mawrth *m.*
tug 1 *n.* plwc; tynfa *m.* **2** *v.* llusgo, tynnu
tuition *n.* addysg *f,* hyfforddiant *m.*
tumble 1 *n.* cwymp *m.* **2** *v.* cwympo
tumbler *n.* gwydryn *m.*
tummy *n.* bola *m.*
tumult *n.* twrw, mwstwr, terfysg, cythrwfl *m.*
tune *n.* alaw, tôn *f.*
tunnel *n.* twnnel *m.*
turkey *n.* twrci *m.*
Turkey *n.* Twrci *f.*

Turkish *a.* Twrcaidd
turmoil *n.* berw, trafferth *m.*
turn 1 *n.* tro *m.* 2 *v.* troi
turning *n.* tro *m.* tröedigaeth *m.*
turning-point *n.* trobwynt *m.*
turnip *n.* erfinen, meipen *f.*
tutor 1 *n.* athro, tiwtor, hyfforddwr *m.* 2 *v.* dysgu, hyfforddi
twelfth *n.* & *a.* deuddegfed *m.*
twelve *n.* & *a.* deuddeg, un deg dau *m.*
twentieth *n.* & *a.* ugeinfed *m.*
twenty *n.* & *a.* ugain, dau ddeg *m.*
twice *ad.* dwywaith
twig *n.* brigyn, brig *m.*
twilight *n.* cyfnos, cyfddydd *m.*
twin 1 *n.* gefell *m.* gefeilles *f.* 2 *v.* gefeillio
twine *n.* llinyn *m.*
twist 1 *n.* tro *m.* 2 *v.* troi
two *n.* & *a.* dau *m:* dwy *f;* pâr *m.* **in twos, two by two** yn ddeuoedd, yn ddau a dau
typescript *n.* teipysgrif *f.*
typewriter *n.* teipiadur *m.*
typhoon *n.* corwynt *m.*
typist *n.* teipydd *m.*
tyre *n.* teiar *m.*

U

ubiquitous *a.* ym mhob man
ugliness *n.* hagrwch *m.*
ugly *a.* hagr, hyll, salw
ultra 1 *a.* eithafol. 2 *px.* gor-, dros ben, tu hwnt i
ultra-modern *a.* tra modern, modern iawn

umbrella *n.* ambarél, ymbarél, ymbrelo *m.*
umpire 1 *n.* dyfarnwr, canolwr *m.* 2 *v.* dyfarnu
unaccompanied *a.* heb gwmni; heb gyfeiliant
unaccustomed *a.* anghyfarwydd
unacquainted *a.* anghyfarwydd
unanimous *a.* unfryd, unfrydol, unfarn
unanimously *ad.* yn ynfryd
unceasing *a.* di-baid, diddiwedd
uncertain *a.* ansicr
uncivil *a.* anfoesgar
unclad *a.* noeth
uncle *n.* ewyrth, ewythr *m.*
unclean *a.* aflan, brwnt, budr
uncommon *a.* anghyffredin
uncover *v.* datguddio
uncultivated *a.* heb ei drin
under 1 *prp.* dan, tan, o dan, is, islaw. 2 *ad.* danodd, oddi tanodd. 3 *px.* is-, tan-
underclothing *n.* dillad isaf *m.*
undercurrent *n.* islif *m.*
undergo *v.* dioddef
underground *a.* tanddaear, tanddaearol
underline *v.* tanlinellu, pwysleisio
undermine *v.* tanseilio
underneath 1 *prp.* dan, tan, oddi tan. 2 *ad.* oddi tanodd
underpass *n.* tanffordd *f.*
underskirt *n.* sgert isaf, sgyrt isaf, pais *f.*
understand *v.* deall
understanding *n.* deall, dealltwriaeth

undertake v. ymgymryd (â)
undertaker n. trefnydd
angladdau m.
undo v. datod; difetha
undress v. dadwisgo
unearned a. heb ei ennill
uneasy a. anesmwyth,
pryderus
unemployed 1 n. y di-waith
m. 2 a. di-waith, segur
unemployment n. diweithdra
m; **unemployment benefit**
budd-dâl di-waith
unending a. diddiwedd,
diderfyn
unfair a. annheg
unfaithful a, anffyddlon
unfamiliar a. anghyfarwydd,
dieithr
unfasten v. datod
unfit a. anaddas, anghymwys
unfortunate a. anffodus
unfortunately ad. yn anffodus
unhappy a. anhapus, trist
unhealthy a. afiach
uniform 1 n. gwisg swyddogol
f. 2 a. unffurf
unimportant a. dibwys
uninteresting a. anniddorol
union n. undeb m.
unionist n. undebwr m.
unique a. unigryw
unit n. uned f; un, rhif un;
undod m.
Unitarian n. Undodwr m.
unite v. uno, cysylltu, cyfuno
united a. unedig, unol. **the
United Kingdom** y Deyrnas
Unedig; **United States of
America** Unol Daleithiau
America
unity n. undod m.

universe n. bydysawd,
cyfanfyd, yr hollfyd m
university n. prifysgol f.
University of Wales Prifysgol
Cymru
unjust a. anghyfiawn
unjustly ad. ar gam
unkind a. angharedig
unleaded a. di-blwm.
unleaded petrol petrol di-
blwm
unless c. oni, onid
unlike a. annhebyg
unlimited a. diderfyn
unlucky a. anffodus, anlwcus
unmannerly a. anfoesgar
unmarried a. dibriod
unnatural a. annaturiol
unoccupied a. gwag, segur
unopened a. heb ei agor
unprepared a. amharod
unravel v. datod, datrys
unready a. amharod
unreasonable a. afresymol
unsatisfied a. anfodlon
unseen a. anweledig
unsightly a. diolwg, hyll, salw
unsteady a. simsan
unsuitable a. anaddas,
anghymwys
untidy a. anniben
untie v. datod
until prp. & c. hyd, hyd oni,
nes, tan
untrue a. celwyddog
untruth n. celwydd, anwiredd
m.
untruthful a. celwyddog
unusual a. anarferol
unwell a. anhwylus, afiach,
claf
unwholesome a. afiach

unwilling *a.* anfodlon

unwise *a.* annoeth, ffôl

unworthy *a.* annheilwng

up *ad.* & *prp.* i fyny

uphill *ad.* i fyny

uphold *v.* cynnal

upon *prp.* ar, ar warthaf, ar uchaf

upper *a.* uwch, uchaf

uppermost *a.* & *ad.* uchaf

upright *a.* syth, union, unionsyth; onest, cywir

upside-down *ad.* wyneb i waered

upstairs 1 *n.* llofft *f.* **2** *ad.* ar y llofft

up-to-date *a.* cyfoes, hyd yn hyn

upwards *ad.* i fyny

urban *a.* trefol

urge *v.* argymell

urgency *n.* brys *m.*

us *pn.* ni, ninnau, nyni, 'n

usage *n.* arfer *mf,* defnydd *m.*

use 1 *n.* arfer *mf,* defnydd, gwasanaeth, iws. **2** *v.* arfer, defnyddio

useful *a.* defnyddiol

useless *a.* diwerth

user *n.* defnyddiwr *m.*

Usk *n.* Wysg *(river);* Brynbuga *(town) f.*

usual *a.* arferol. **as usual** fel arfer

utilize *v.* defnyddio

utmost *a.* eithaf, pellaf

U-turn *n.* tro pedol *m.*

V

vacancy *n.* lle gwag *m,* swydd wag *f.*

vacant *a.* gwag

vacation *n.* gwyliau *pl.*

vaccination *n.* brechiad *m,* brech *f.*

vacuum *n.* gwagle *m.*

vain *a.* balch; ofer

vale *n.* bro *f,* cwm, dyffryn, glyn *m.* **Vale of Glamorgan** Bro Morgannwg

valiant *a.* dewr

valley *n.* cwm, dyffryn, glyn *m.*

valuable *a.* drud, gwerthfawr

value *n* gwerth *m.* **Value Added Tax (VAT)** Treth Ar Werth

van *n.* fan, men; y rheng flaenaf *f.*

vandal *n.* fandal *m.*

vandalize *v.* fandaleiddio

vandalism *n.* fandaliaeth *f.*

vanish *v.* diflannu

vanity *n.* gwagedd, oferedd *m.*

various *a.* amryw, gwahanol

vary *v.* newid

vast *a.* eang, enfawr, anferth

veal *n.* cig llo *m.*

vegetable *n.* llysieuyn *m.*

vegetarian *n.* llysfwytäwr *m.* llysfwytäwraig *f.*

vehicle *n.* cerbyd; cyfrwng *m.*

veil *n.* llen *f.*

velocity *n.* cyflymder *m.*

vengeance *n.* dial, dialedd *m.*

venom *n.* gwenwyn *m.*

venture 1 *n.* antur *m,* menter *f.* **2** *v.* mentro, beiddio, meiddio

venturesome *a.* mentrus, anturus

Venus *n.* Gwener *m.*

verb *n.* berf *f.*
verbally *ad.* mewn geiriau
verb-noun *n.* berfenw *m.*
verdict *n.* dyfarniad, dedfryd *m.*
vermin *n.* pryfed, llygod ... *pl.*
verse *n.* adnod *f,* pennill *m;* barddoniaeth *f.*
version *n.* fersiwn *m.*
versus *ad.* yn erbyn
vertical *a.* syth, unionsyth, plwm
very *a.* & *ad.* gwir, iawn, i'r dim
vessel *n.* llestr; llong *m.*
vestry *n.* festri *f.*
veterinary surgeon *n.* milfeddyg *m.*
vex *v.* blino, gofidio, poeni, becso
vexation *n.* blinder, gofid *m.*
via *prp.* trwy, ar hyd
vicar *n.* ficer *m.*
vicarage *n.* ficerdy *m.*
vice *n.* drygioni *m;* gwasg, feis *f.*
vice- *px,* is-, rhag-
vice-chairman *n.* is-gadeirydd *m.*
vice-president *n.* is-lywydd *m.*
victor *n.* buddugwr, y buddugol, enillwr, enillydd *m.*
victory *n.* buddugoliaeth *f.*
view 1 *n.* golygfa *f,* golwg *mf;* barn *f.* 2 *v.* edrych, gweld
viewer *n.* gwyliwr *m, (teledu).*
viewpoint *n.* safbwynt *m.*
vigil *n.* gwylnos, noswyl *f.*
vigour *n.* grym, nerth, egni, ynni

vigorous *a.* egnïol
vile *a.* ffiaidd, gwael, salw
village *n.* pentref *m.*
villager *n.* pentrefwr *m.*
vinegar *n.* finegr *m.*
viola *n.* fiola *f.*
violate *v.* treisio, troseddu
violence *n.* trais *m.*
violent *a.* treisiol, gwyllt. **non-violent** di-drais
violet 1 *n.* fioled *f.* 2 *a.* dulas
violin *n.* ffidil *f.*
virgin *n.* morwyn, gwyryf *f.* **the Virgin Mary** y Forwyn Fair
virtually *ad.* i bob pwrpas
virtue *n.* rhinwedd *f.*
virus *n.* firws *m.*
vision *n.* gweledigaeth *f;* golwg *mf;* gweled *m.*
visit 1 *n.* ymweliad *m.* 2 *v.* ymweld (â), galw
visitor *n.* ymwelwr, ymwelydd *m.*
vitamin *n.* fitamin *m.*
vivacious *a.* bywiog, heini
vivid *a.* byw, clir, llachar
vixen *n.* cadnawes, cadnöes, llwynoges *f.*
vocabulary *n.* geirfa *f.*
vocal *a.* llafar; lleisiol
vocalist *n.* cantor *m,* cantores *f,* canwr *m.*
vocally *ad.* â'r llais.
vocation *n.* galwedigaeth *f.*
vogue *n.* ffasiwn *m,* arfer *mf.*
voice 1 *n.* llais *m,* llef *f.* 2 *v.* lleisio, mynegi
void 1 *n.* gwagle *m.* 2 *a.* di-rym. 3 *v.* gwacáu
volcano *n.* llosgfynydd, folcano *m.*

vole *n.* llygoden y maes *f.*
volume *n.* cyfrol *f;* cyfaint;
llais, swn; foliwm *m.*
voluntary *a.* gwirfoddol
volunteer 1 *n.* gwirfoddolwr
m. 2 *v.* gwirfoddoli
vomit *v.* chwydu
vote 1 *n.* pleidlais *f.* 2 *v.*
pleidleisio
voter *n.* pleidleisiwr *m.*
vowel *n.* llafariad *f.*
voyage 1 *n.* mordaith *f.*
2 *v.* mordeithio, mordwyo,
morio. **Bon voyage** Hwyl
dda! Sirwrnai dda!
vulgar *a.* cyffredin; isel,
brwnt; aflednais; gwerinol
vulgarity *n.* diffyg moes *m.*

W

wag *v.* ysgwyd, siglo
wage *n.* cyflog *mf.*
waist *n.* gwasg *mf,* canol *m.*
waistcoat *n.* gwasgod *f.*
wait *v.* aros, disgwyl; gweini
waiter *n.* gweinydd *m.*
waitress *n.* gweinyddes *f.*
wake *v.* dihuno, deffro
Wales *n.* Cymru *f.*
walk 1 *n.* tro *m.* 2 *v.*
cerdded, mynd am dro
walker *n.* cerddwr *m.*
walking-stick *n.* ffon *f.*
wall *n.* gwal, wal *f,* mur *m.*
wallflowers *n.* blodau mam-gu
pl.
wallpaper *n.* papur wal *m.*
want 1 *n.* eisiau, diffyg *m.*
2 *v.* bod mewn eisiau
wanting *a.* yn eisiau

war 1 *n.* rhyfel *mf.* 2 *v.*
rhyfela
warehouse *n.* storfa, stôr *f,*
ystordy *m.*
warfare *n.* rhyfel *mf.*
warm 1 *n.* cynnes, gwresog,
twym. 2 *v.* cynhesu,
twymo
warmth *n.* gwres,
cynhesrwydd *m.*
warn *v.* rhybuddio
warning *n.* rhybudd *m.*
warship *n.* llong ryfel *f.*
wart *n.* dafaden, dafad *f.*
was, I *v.* bues i, bûm, fues i,
fûm, roeddwn; *see* bod
wash 1 *n.* golch, golchiad *m.*
2 *v.* golchi, ymolch, ymolchi
washer *n.* golchydd *m. see*
washing machine.
washing machine *n* peiriant
golchi *m.*
washing powder *n.* powdr
golchi *m.*
wash-house *n.* golchdy *m.*
wasp *n.* cacynen, picwnen *f.*
wasps' nest nyth cacwn
waste 1 *n.* gwastraff *m.*
nuclear waste gwastraff
niwclear. 2 *v.* gwastraffu
wasteful *a.* gwastraffus
watch 1 *n.* wats *f.* 2 *v.*
gwarchod, gwylio
watchful *a.* gwyliadwrus
watchman *n.* gwyliwr *m.*
watchnight *n.* gwylnos *f.*
water *n.* dŵr *m.*
waterfall *n.* rhaeadr, sgwd *f,*
pistyll *m.*
wave 1 *n.* ton *f.* 2 *v.* chwifio,
codi llaw
wavelength *n.* tonfedd *f.*

wax 1 *n.* cwyr *m.* **2** *v.* cwyro;
cynyddu, tyfu
way *n.* ffordd, heol, hewl *f,*
llwybr *m;* hynt *f;* arfer *fm,*
modd *m.*
wayside *n.* ymyl y ffordd *mf.*
we *pn.* ni, ninnau, nyni
weak *a.* gwan
weaken *v.* gwanhau
weakness *n.* gwendid *m.*
wealth *n.* cyfoeth, golud, da,
modd *m.*
wealthy *a.* cyfoethog, cefnog
weapon *n.* arf, erfyn *m.*
 nuclear weapons arfau
 niwclear
wear 1 *n.* gwisg; traul *f.* **2** *v.*
gwisgo; treulio
weariness *n.* blinder *m.*
wearisome *a.* blinedig, blin,
poenus
weary 1 *a.* blinedig, blin. **2** *v.*
blino, diflasu
weather *n.* tywydd *m,* hin *f.*
 fine weather tywydd teg,
 hindda; **tempestuous weather**
 tywydd mawr
weave *v.* gwau, gweu
web *n.* gwe *f.*
wed *v.* priodi
wedding *n.* priodas *f.*
Wednesday *n.* dydd Mercher *m.*
weed 1 *n.* chwynnyn *m* **2** *v.*
chwynnu
weeds *n.* chwyn *pl.*
week *n.* wythnos *f.* **the first**
 week yr wythnos gyntaf; **the**
 second week yr ail wythnos;
 the third week y drydedd
 wythnos; **the last week** yr
 wythnos diwethaf; **the final**
 week yr wythnos olaf

weekend *n.* penwythnos *m.*
weekly *a.* wythnosol
weep *v.* crio, wylo, llefain
weigh *v.* pwyso
weight *n.* pwys, pwysau *m.*
weighty *a.* pwysig; trwm
welcome 1 *n.* croeso *m.* **2** *v.*
croesawu
welfare *n.* lles, budd *m.*
welfare state *n.* gwladwriaeth
les *f.*
well 1 *n.* ffynnon *f.* **2** *a.* iach,
da, iawn. **3** *v.* llifo, cronni. **4**
ad., yn dda. **5** *i.* wel! **fairly**
well yn lled dda; **very well**
o'r gorau
Welsh *a.* Cymraeg; Cymreig:
 Welsh affairs materion
 Cymreig, **Welsh books**
 llyfrau Cymraeg; **Welsh**
 cakes picau ar y maen;
 Welsh office Swyddfa
 Gymreig; **Welsh schools**
 ysgolion Cymraeg; **Welsh**
 water dŵr Cymru
Welsh (language) *n.* Cymraeg
f.
Welsh (people) *n.* Cymry *pl.*
Welshman *n.* Cymro *m.*
Welshness *n.* Cymreictod *m.*
Welshwoman *n.* Cymraes *f.*
west 1 *n.* gorllewin *m.* **West**
 Wales Gorllewin Cymru;
 west or westerly wind gwynt
 y gorllewin
western *a.* gorllewinol
wet 1 *n.* gwlybaniaeth *f.* **2** *a.*
gwlyb. **3** *v.* gwlychu.
 wetland tir gwlyb
whale *n.* morfil *m.*
what 1 *a.* pa. **2** *pn.* pa beth.
 3 *i.* beth!

whatever *pn.* beth bynnag

wheat *n.* gwenith *m.*

wheel *n.* olwyn *f.* **front wheel** olwyn flaen; **rear wheel** olwyn gefn; **spare wheel** olwyn sbâr

wheelbarrow *n.* berfa, whilber *f.*

wheelchair *n.* cadair olwyn/ olwynion *f.*

when *ad., pn & c.* pan, pa bryd

whenever *ad.* pa bryd bynnag

where *ad.* ym mha le; yn y lle, lle

whereabouts *ad.* ymhle

whereas *c.* gan, yn gymaint â

whereby *ad.* trwy yr hyn

wherefore *ad.* paham, am hynny

wherein *ad.* yn yr hyn

wherever *ad.* ble bynnag

which 1 *rel.pn.* a; y, yr. 2 *int.pn.* pa un? p'un? 3 *a.* pa

whichever *a.* & *pn.* pa un bynnag

whilst *ad.* cyhyd, tra

whip 1 *n.* chwip *f.* 2 *v.* chwipio

whirlpool *n.* pwll tro, trobwll *m.*

whisper 1 *n.* sisial *m.* 2 *v.* sisial, sibrwd

whistle 1 *n.* chwiban *m.* 2 *v.* chwiban, chwibanu

white *a.* gwyn, gwen, can

white-lime *n.* gwyngalch *m.*

whiten *v.* gwynnu

whitewash 1 *n.* gwyngalch *m.* 2 *v.* gwyngalchu

Whitsunday *n.* Sulgwyn *m.*

whittle *v.* naddu

whiz 1 *n.* si, su *m.* 2 *v.* sio, suo

who *pn.* a, pwy; y, yr

whole 1 *n.* cwbl, cyfan, holl *m.* 2 *a.* cyfan, holl; iach, holliach

wholesome *a.* iach, iachus

wholly *ad.* yn hollol, yn gyfan gwbl, yn llwyr

whom *rel.pn.* a; y, yr

whose *pn.* eiddo pwy? pwy biau?

whosoever *pn.* pwy bynnag

why *ad.* paham, pam

wicked *a.* drwg, drygionus

wickedness *n.* drwg, drygioni *m.*

wicket *n.* wiced; clwyd *f.* **wicket-keeper** wicedwr

wide *a.* llydan, eang

wide-awake *a.* effro, ar ddihun

widely *ad.* yn eang

widen *v.* lledu, llydanu

widow *n.* gweddw, gwidw *f.*

widower *n.* gwidman *m.*

width *n.* lled *m.*

wife *n.* gwraig, gwraig briod, priod *f.*

wild *a.* gwyllt, ffyrnig

wilderness *n.* anialwch, diffeithwch *m.*

wildfire *n.* tân gwyllt *m.*

will 1 *n.* ewyllys *m.* 2 *v.* mynnu

will be, he/she/it *v.* bydd; *see* bod

willing *a.* bodlon, parod

willow *n.* helygen *f.*

win *v.* ennill. **to win the day** cario'r dydd

wind *n.* gwynt *m*; anadl *mf.*

cold wind gwynt oer; **the north wind** gwynt y gogledd
wind *v.* troi, dirwyn
windmill *n.* melin wynt *f.*
window *n.* ffenestr *f.* **window pane** cwarel
windy *a.* gwyntog
wine *n.* gwin *m.* **dry red wine** gwin coch sych; **sweet white wine** gwin gwyn melys
wineglass *n.* gwydr gwin *m.*
wing *n.* adain, aden, asgell *f;* asgellwr *m.*
winner *n.* enillwr, enillydd, y buddugol *m.*
winning *a.* buddugol
winnings *n.* enillion *pl.*
winter *n.* gaeaf *m.* **winter dwelling** hendref, hendre
wintry *a.* gaeafol
wipe *v.* sychu
wire *n.* gwifren *f.*
wisdom *n.* doethineb *m.*
wise *a.* call, doeth. **the Wise Men** y Doethion
wish 1 *n.* dymuniad, ewyllys *m.* 2 *v.* dymuno
witch *n.* gwrach *f.*
with *prp.* â, ag, gyda, gydag, efo, gan
withdraw *v.* tynnu yn ôl; cilio; codi arian
wither *v.* gwywo
withhold *v.* atal, dal yn ôl
within 1 *prp.* i mewn, o fewn, yn. 2 *ad.* tu mewn
without 1 *prp.* heb 2 *a.* tu allan
witness 1 *n.* tyst *m.* 2 *v.* tystio
wits *n.* synhwyrau *pl.*
witticism *n.* jôc, ffraethineb *f.*

witty *a.* doniol, ffraeth
wizard *n.* dewin *m.*
wolf *n.* blaidd *m.*
woman *n.* merch, menyw, gwraig, llances, dynes *f.*
wonder 1 *n.* rhyfeddod *m.* 2 *v.* rhyfeddu, synnu. **I wonder** tybed
wonderful *a.* rhyfedd, rhyfeddol
wood *n.* coed *pl,* coedwig *f.* pren *m.*
wooden *a.* o goed, o bren
woodwork *n.* gwaith coed, gwaith saer *m.*
wool *n.* gwlân *m.*
woollen *a.* gwlân, gwlanog.
woollen industry diwydiant gwlân
word *n.* gair *m.* **a good word** gair da; **the last word** y gair olaf; **word for word** gair am air
work 1 *n.* gwaith, llafur *m.* 2 *v.* gweithio, llafurio
worker *n.* gweithiwr *m.*
working *a.* gwaith, yn gweithio. **working class** dosbarth gweithiol; **working clothes** dillad gwaith; **working party** gweithgor
workpeople *n.* gweithwyr *pl.*
workshop *n.* gweithdy *m,* siop waith *f.*
world *n.* byd *m.*
worldly *a.* bydol
worldwide *a.* byd-eang
worm *n.* mwydyn, pryfyn *m.*
worried *a.* gofidus, pryderus
worry 1 *n.* gofid *m,* helynt *f,* pryder *m.* 2 *v.* gofidio, poeni, pryderu blino

worse *a.* gwaeth
worsen *v.* gwaethygu
worship *n.* addoliad *m.*
worth *n.* gwerth *m.*
worthiness *n.* teilyngdod, gwerth *m.*
worthless *a.* diwerth
worthy *a.* teilwng
wound 1 *n.* clwyf, anaf *m.* 2 *v.* clwyfo, anafu
wrap *v.* lapio, rhwymo.
 wrapping paper papur lapio
wrath *n.* llid *m.*
wreath *n.* torch *f.*
wren *n.* dryw *m.*
wretch *n.* truan *m.*
wretched *a.* truan, truenus
wretchedness *n.* trueni, trallod *m.*
wright *n.* crefftwr, saer *m.*
 cartwright saer certiau;
 wheelwright saer olwynion *(pren).*
wrist *n.* arddwrn *m.*
write *v.* sgrifennu, ysgrifennu.
 to write a name torri enw
writer *n.* ysgrifennwr, awdur *m,* awdures *f.*
writing *n.* ysgrifen, ysgrifennu *f.*
wrong 1 *n.* cam, bai *m.* 2 *a.* anghywir, rong. 3 *v.* gwneud cam â
wrongdoer *n.* troseddwr *m.*
wrongdoing *n.* trosedd *f.*
www. *n.* (y)we byd-eang *f.*

X

X-ray *n.* pelydr X, pelydryn X *m.*
X-rays pelydrau X
xylophone *n.* seiloffon *f.*

Y

yard *n.* buarth *m*, iard *f*, clos, cwrt *m;* llathen *f.*
yarn *n.* chwedl, stori; edau *f.*
year *n.* blwyddyn; blwydd (oed) *f;* blynedd *pl (after numerals).* **the first year** y flwyddyn gyntaf; **the second year** yr ail flwyddyn; **three years old** tair blwydd oed; **four years old** pedair blwydd oed; **for five years** am bum mlynedd; **for six years** am chwe blynedd; **last year** y llynedd; **leap year** blwyddyn naid; **this year** eleni; **next year** y flwyddyn nesaf
yearly *a.* blynyddol
yearn *v.* hiraethu, dyheu
yearning *n.* hiraeth *m.*
yell 1 *n.* sgrech, gwaedd *f.* 2 *v.* sgrechian, sgrechain, gweiddi
yellow *a.* melyn *m.*, melen *f.* **the yellow apple** yr afal melyn; **the yellow dress** y wisg felen
yes *ad.* ie, byddaf, byddan, do, oes, oedd, oeddwn, ydw, ydy, ydyn . . . *(Welsh uses the verb forms to answer yes/no)* **Tom? Yes** Tom? Ie. **Was he there? Yes** Oedd e yno? Oedd. **Is Huw late? Yes** Ydy Huw'n hwyr? Ydy. **Are there dogs here? Yes** Oes cŵn yma? Oes. **Will they be cold? Yes** Fyddan nhw'n oer? Byddan
yesterday *n.* & *ad.* doe, ddoe. **the day before yesterday** echdoe

yet *ad.* eto, er hynny
yew *n.* ywen *f.*
yield *v.* ildio, rhoddi
yoke *n.* iau *f.*
yolk *n.* melyn wy, melynwy *m*
yonder *ad.* acw, draw
York *n.* Efrog *f.*
you *pn.* ti; chi, chwi. **you also** tithau, chithau, chwithau; **you yourself** tydi
young *a.* ieuanc, ifanc
younger *a.* iau
youngest *a.* ifancaf
youngster *n.* crwt, hogyn, plentyn *m.*
your *pn.* dy, 'th; eich, 'ch
yours *pn.* eiddoch, yr eiddoch. **yours faithfully** yr eiddoch yn ffyddlon; **yours truly** yr eiddoch yn gywir

yourself *pn.* eich hun, eich hunan
yourselves *pn.* eich hunain
youth *n.* llanc; ieuenctid *m.*
youthful *a.* ieuanc, ifanc
Yuletide *n.* adeg y Nadolig *f.*

Z

zeal *n.* sêl *f.*
zero *n.* dim, sero *m.*
zigzag *a.* igam-ogam
zinc *n.* sinc *m.*
Zion *n.* Seion *f.*
zip 1 *n.* sip *m.* **2** *v.* sipio
zone *n.* cylch, rhanbarth *m.*
zoo *n.* sŵ *m.*
zoologist *n.* söolegwr *m.*
zoology *n.* söoleg *mf.*

supplement

verbs

In this short introduction to the study of Welsh verbs, the irregular verb **bod** (*to be*) is conjugated in the present, imperfect, future and past tenses only. A fuller discussion of the subject may be found in contemporary books on Welsh grammar.

Present tense (bod *to be*)

Affirmative form

	Singular		Plural	
1	*Rydw i	*I am*	Rydyn ni	*We are*
2	Rwyt ti	*You are*	Rydych chi	*You are*
3	Mae e/o	*He/It is*	Maen nhw	*They are*
	Mae hi	*She is*		

Note: 3rd Person

	Singular		
	mae, oes, sy,	*is, there is*
	yw, ydyw	*are, there are*
	Oes . . .?	*Is there . . .?*
		Are there . . .?

*Literary Form: **Yr wyf i**, **'Rwyf i**. In spoken Welsh one hears **Rw i/Dw i** and also **Ryn ni/Dyn ni; Rych chi/Dych chi** (see overleaf).

Interrogative form

	Singular		Plural	
1	Ydw i?	*Am I?*	Ydyn ni?	*Are we?*
2	Wyt ti?	*Are you?*	Ydych chi?	*Are you?*
3	Ydy e/o?	*Is he/it?*	Ydyn nhw?	*Are they?*
	Ydy hi?	*Is she?*		

Negative form

	Singular		Plural	
1	Dydw i ddim	*I am not*	Dydyn ni ddim	*We are not*
2	Dwyt ti ddim	*You are not*	Dydych chi ddim	*You are not*
3	Dydy e/o ddim	*He/It is not*	Dydyn nhw ddim	*They are not*
	Dydy hi ddim	*She is not*		

Learners (**Dysgwyr**) of the spoken language are introduced to the following **affirmative**, **interrogative** and **negative forms** of the above when they first encounter the verb **bod**:

Affirmative form

Singular		Plural	
1 Dw i	*I am*	Dyn ni	*We are*
2 Rwyt ti	*You are*	Dych chi	*You are*
3 Mae e/hi	*He/She/It is*	Maen nhw	*They are*

Interrogative form

Singular		Plural	
1 Ydw i?	*Am I?*	Dyn ni?	*Are we?*
2 Wyt ti?	*Are you?*	Dych chi?	*Are you?*
3 Ydy e/hi?	*Is he/she/it?*	Dyn nhw?	*Are they?*

Negative form

Singular		Plural	
1 Dw i ddim	*I'm not*	Dyn ni ddim	*We're not*
2 Dwyt ti ddim	*You're not*	Dych chi ddim	*You're not*
3 Dydy e/hi ddim	*He's/She's/It's not*	Dyn nhw ddim	*They're not*

Imperfect tense (bod *to be*)

Affirmative form

Singular		Plural	
1 *Roeddwn i	*I was/used to*	Roedden ni	*We were/used to*
2 Roeddet ti	*You were/used to*	Roeddech chi	*You were/used to*
3 Roedd e/o	*He/It was/used to*	Roedden nhw	*They are/used to*
Roedd hi	*She was/used to*		

Note: 3rd Person Singular **roedd** *was, there was*
were, there were

*Also heard in spoken Welsh: **Rown i, Roen i; Rot ti; Roedd e/hi; Ron ni; Roch chi; Ron nhw.**

Interrogative form

Singular		Plural	
1 Oeddwn i?	*Was I?*	1 Oedden ni?	*Were we?*
2 Oeddet ti?	*Were you?*	2 Oeddech chi?	*Were you?*
3 Oedd e/o?	*Was he/it?*	3 Oedden nhw?	*Were they?*
Oedd hi?	*Was she?*		

Note: 3rd person singular **Oedd . . .?** *Was there . . .?*
Were there . . .?

Negative form

Singular
1 Doeddwn i ddim   *I wasn't/I used not to*
2 Doeddet ti ddim   *You weren't/You used not to*
3 Doedd e/o ddim   *He/It wasn't/It used not to*
   Doedd hi ddim   *She wasn't/She used not to*

Plural
1 Doedden ni ddim   *We weren't/We used not to*
2 Doeddech chi ddim   *You weren't/You used not to*
3 Doedden nhw ddim   *They weren't/They used not to*

Future tense (bod *to be*)

Affirmative form

	Singular		Plural	
1	Bydda i	*I shall be*	Byddwn ni	*We shall be*
2	Byddi di	*You will be*	Byddwch chi	*You will be*
3	Bydd e/o	*He/It will be*	Byddan nhw	*They will be*
	Bydd hi	*She will be*		

Note: 3rd person singular **bydd** *will be*

Interrogative form

	Singular		Plural	
1	Fydda i?	*Shall I be?*	Fyddwn ni?	*Shall we be?*
2	Fyddi di?	*Will you be?*	Fyddwch chi?	*Will you be?*
3	Fydd e/o?	*Will he/she be?*	Fyddan nhw?	*Will they be?*
	Fydd hi?	*Will she be?*		

Negative form

	Singular		Plural	
1	Fydda i ddim	*I shall not be*	Fyddwn ni ddim	*We shall not be*
2	Fyddi di ddim	*You will not be*	Fyddwch chi ddim	*You will not be*
3	Fydd e/o ddim	*He/It will not be*	Fyddan nhw ddim	*They will not be*
	Fydd hi ddim	*She will not be*		

Imperative tense (bod *to be*)

Bydd! Bydda! (singular); **Byddwch!** (plural) *Be!*

Past tense (bod *to be*)

Affirmative form

	Singular		Plural	
1	*Bues i	*I was*	Buon ni	*We were*
2	Buest ti	*You were*	Buoch chi	*You were*
3	Buodd e/o	*He/It was*	Buon nhw	*They were*
	Buodd hi	*She was*		

*Literary form of 1st person singular past tense: **Bûm i**

Interrogative form

	Singular			Plural	
1	Fues i?	*Was I?*	Fuon ni?	*Were we?*
2	Fuest ti?	*Were you?*	Fuoch chi?	*Were you?*
3	Fuodd e/o?	*Was he/it?*	Fuon nhw?	*Were they?*
	Fuodd hi?	*Was she?*		

Negative form

	Singular			Plural	
1	Fues i ddim	*I wasn't*	Fuon ni ddim	*We weren't*
2	Fuest ti ddim	*You weren't*	Fuoch chi ddim	*You weren't*
3	Fuodd e/o ddim	*He/It wasn't*	Fuon nhw ddim	*They weren't*
	Fuodd hi ddim	*She wasn't*		

Affirmative and negative answers – *yes* and *no*

The entries shown in the English–Welsh section of the dictionary under **yes** and **no** may be further supplemented:

Present tense

	Singular		Plural	
1	Ydw/Nag ydw	*Yes/No*	Ydyn/Nag ydyn	*Yes/No*
2	Wyt/Nag wyt	*Yes/No*	Ydych/Nag ydych	*Yes/No*
3	Ydy/Nag ydy	*Yes/No*	Ydyn/Nag ydyn	*Yes/No*
	Oes/Nag oes	*Yes/No*		

Imperfect tense

	Singular		Plural	
1	Oeddwn/Nag oeddwn	*Yes/No*	Oedden/Nag oedden	*Yes/No*
2	Oeddet/Nag oeddet	*Yes/No*	Oeddech/Nag oeddech	*Yes/No*
3	Oedd/Nag oedd	*Yes/No*	Oedden/Nag oedden	*Yes/No*

Future tense

	Singular		Plural	
1	Bydda/Na fydda	*Yes/No*	Byddwn/Na fyddwn	*Yes/No*
2	Byddi/Na fyddi	*Yes/No*	Byddwch/Na fyddwch	*Yes/No*
3	Bydd/Na fydd	*Yes/No*	Byddan/Na fyddan	*Yes/No*

With the past tense **do** *yes* and **naddo** *no* are the forms relating to both singular and plural usages.

For forms such as the pluperfect **Buaswn i, Fe/Mi faswn i** *I would (be)*, see further works on contemporary Welsh grammar.

Regular verbs

Welsh verbs have inflected tenses, that is, the tenses have their own endings. These endings are added to the stem of the verbs. Most verbs follow a regular pattern but there are some irregular verbs.

In the Welsh–English section of this dictionary an entry for a verb is shown as follows:

canu *be.* **(canaf)** to sing, to play.

The stem derived from the verb-noun **canu** is **can-**. The present tense ending for the 1st person singular is **-af**, and when the ending is added to the stem, **can + af** becomes **canaf**, which is the form shown in the brackets, frequently written and pronounced **cana**.

The verb **bod** (*to be*) is used as an auxiliary in forming tenses of regular verbs such as **canu, bwyta, cysgu** . . . The present tense of **canu** is formed by using the present tense of the verb **bod**, that is, **Rydw i, Rwyt ti, Mae e** . . . followed by **yn + canu**. It also exists in compact form as shown below.

Note: **Rydw i yn canu** becomes **Rydw i'n canu/Dw i'n canu**
       Rwyt ti yn canu becomes **Rwyt ti'n canu**
       Mae e yn canu becomes **Mae e'n canu** . . .

Present tense (canu *to sing*)

Singular
1	Rydw/Dw i'n canu	*I sing, I am singing*
2	Rwyt ti'n canu	*You sing, You are singing*
3	Mae e/o'n canu	*He/It sings, He/It is singing*
	Mae hi'n canu	*She sings, She is singing*

Plural
1	Rydyn/Dyn ni'n canu	*We sing, We are singing*
2	Rydych/Dych chi'n canu	*You sing, You are singing*
3	Maen nhw'n canu	*They sing, They are singing*

The imperfect tense is formed by using the imperfect tense of **bod**, that is, **Roeddwn i, Roeddet ti, Roedd e** . . . followed by **yn canu**.

Imperfect tense (canu *to sing*)

Singular
1	Roeddwn i'n canu	*I was singing*
2	Roeddet ti'n canu	*You were singing*
3	Roedd e/o'n canu	*He/It was singing*
	Roedd hi'n canu	*She was singing*

Plural
1	Roedden ni'n canu	*We were singing*
2	Roeddech chi'n canu	*You were singing*
3	Roedden nhw'n canu	*They were singing*

The imperfect tense also conveys the meaning of continuous action. **Roedd hi'n canu** means not only *She was singing*, but also *She was going on singing*. **Roedd hi'n arfer canu** *She used to sing*.

The future tense is formed by using the future tense of **bod**, that is, **Bydda i, Byddi di, Bydd e** . . . followed by **yn + canu**.

Future tense (canu *to sing*)

Singular
1 Bydda i'n canu — *I shall be singing*
2 Byddi di'n canu — *You will be singing*
3 Bydd e/o'n canu — *He/It will be singing*
  Bydd hi'n canu — *She will be singing*

Plural
1 Byddwn ni'n canu — *We shall be singing*
2 Byddwch chi'n canu — *You will be singing*
3 Byddan nhw'n canu — *They will be singing*

Imperative (canu *to sing*)

Cana! (singular); **Canwch!** (plural) *Sing!*

The past tense of **canu** is formed by adding -ais, -aist, -odd, -on, -och, -on to the stem **can-**, and is used to convey completed action in the past.

Past tense (canu *to sing*)

Singular		Plural	
1 *Cenais i	*I sang*	Canon ni	*We sang*
2 *Cenaist ti	*You sang*	Canoch chi	*You sang*
3 Canodd e/o	*He/It sang*	Canon nhw	*They sang*
Canodd hi	*She sang*		

*In those verbs which have 'a' in the stem it is usual in literary Welsh for a > e in the 1st and 2nd person singular past tense and in the 2nd person singular present and future tenses.

The particle Fe (S.W.)/Mi (N.W.)

The verb is placed as the first word in the normal construction of the Welsh sentence:

Cerddodd Siôn i'r siop. — *Siôn walked to the shop.*
Rydw i'n darllen llyfr. — *I'm reading a book.*
Mae ci yn y cae. — *There's a dog in the field.*
Dydyn nhw ddim yma. — *They're not here.*

Usually the particle **Fe/Mi** is placed in front of the verb merely to indicate that the verb is affirmative.

Note: The particle **Fe/Mi** is not translated, and is not placed before **mae** or **maen** but may occur before other persons of the verb in speech or informal texts. Both particles are followed by soft mutation.

Golchodd Mair y dillad.
Fe olchodd Mair y dillad. — *Mair washed the clothes.*

Byddan nhw'n canu heno.
Fe fyddan nhw'n canu heno. — *They will be singing tonight.*

Canon ni yn yr eisteddfod.
Fe ganon ni yn yr eisteddfod. — *We sang in the eisteddfod.*

Compact form of verbs

The future and imperfect tenses of the verb **canu** referred to above also exist in their compact forms. These inflected verb forms are more likely to be found in formal texts than in current conversational Welsh, though they may well appear in both.

The endings for the future tense of **canu** are **-af/-a, -i, -iff/ith, -wn, -wch, -an** and are added to the stem *can-*.

Present and future tenses (compact form) (canu *to sing*)

Singular

1 Fe/Mi ganaf/gana i   *I shall sing*
2 Fe/Mi geni di/geni   *You will sing*
3 Fe/Mi gân/ganiff/ganith e/o   *He/It will sing*
  Fe/Mi gân/ganiff/ganith hi   *She will sing*

Plural

1 Fe/Mi ganwn ni   *We shall sing*
2 Fe/Mi ganwch chi   *You will sing*
3 Fe/Mi ganan nhw   *They will sing*

The endings for the imperfect tense of **canu** are **-wn, -it, -ai, -en, -ech, -en** and are added to the stem **can-**.

Imperfect tense (compact form) (canu *to sing*)

Singular

1 Canwn i   *I was singing*
2 Canit ti   *You were singing*
3 Canai e/o . . . *He/It was singing . . .*

Plural

1 Canen ni   *We were singing*
2 Canech chi   *You were singing*
3 Canen nhw   *They were singing*

Regular verbs follow the same pattern as **canu**. The present, imperfect, future and past tenses of **bwyta** are shown below.

Present tense (bwyta *to eat*)

Singular

1 Rydw i'n bwyta   *I am eating, I eat*
2 Rwy ti'n bwyta   *You are eating*
3 Mae e'n bwyta . . . *He/It is eating . . . etc.*

Imperfect tense (bwyta *to eat*)

Singular

1 Roeddwn i'n bwyta   *I was eating*
2 Roeddet ti'n bwyta   *You are eating*
3 Roedd e'n bwyta . . . *He/It was eating . . . etc.*

Future tense (bwyta *to eat*)

Singular

1 Fe/Mi fydda(f) i'n bwyta   *I shall be eating*
2 Fe/Mi fyddi di'n bwyta   *You will be eating*
3 Fe/Mi fydd e'n bwyta . . .   *He/It will be eating . . . etc.*

Past tense (compact form) (bwyta *to eat*)

Singular		*Plural*	
1 Fe/Mi fwytais i	*I ate*	Fe/Mi fwyton ni	*We ate*
2 Fe/Mi fwytaist ti	*You ate*	Fe/Mi fwytoch chi	*You ate*
3 Fe/Mi fwytodd e/o	*He/It ate*	Fe/Mi fwyton nhw	*They ate*
Fe/Mi fwytodd hi	*She ate*		

Future tense (compact form) (bwyta *to eat*)

Singular		*Plural*	
1 Fe/Mi fwyta(f) i	*I shall eat*	Fe/Mi fwytwn ni	*We shall eat*
2 Fe/Mi fwyti di	*You will eat*	Fe/Mi fwytwch chi	*You will eat*
3 Fe/Mi fwytiff e/o	*He/It will eat*	Fe/Mi fwytan nhw	*They will eat*
Fe/Mi fwytiff hi	*She will eat*		

Imperative (bwyta *to eat*)

Bwyta! (singular); Bwyt(e)wch! (plural) *Eat!*

Irregular verbs

Irregular verbs do not follow the same pattern as **canu** and have to be treated separately. Included below are: **cael, dod, gwneud, gwybod, mynd, rhoddi** and **troi**.

Present tense (cael *to have*)

Singular

1 Rydw i'n cael   *I am having, I have*
2 Rwyt ti'n cael   *You are having, You have*
3 Mae e'n cael . . .   *He/It is having . . . etc.*

Imperfect tense (cael *to have*)

Singular

1 Roeddwn i'n cael   *I was having*
2 Roeddet ti'n cael   *You were having*
3 Roedd e'n cael . . .   *He/It was having . . . etc.*

Future tense (cael *to have*)

Singular		*Plural*	
1 Fe/Mi ga(f) i	*I shall have*	Fe/Mi gawn ni	*We shall have*
2 Fe/Mi gei di	*You will have*	Fe/Mi gewch chi	*You will have*
3 Fe/Mi gaiff e/o	*He/It will have*	Fe/Mi gân nhw	*They will have*
Fe/Mi gaiff hi	*She will have*		

Past tense (cael *to have*)

	Singular			Plural	
1	Fe/Mi ges i	*I had*		Fe/Mi gawson ni	*We had*
2	Fe/Mi gest ti	*You had*		Fe/Mi gawsoch chi	*You had*
3	Fe/Mi gafodd/gas e/o	*He/It had*		Fe/Mi gawson nhw	*They had*
	Fe/Mi gafodd/gas hi	*She had*			

Imperative (cael *to have*)

Cymera! (singular); **Cymerwch!** (plural) *Have!*

Present tense (dod *to come*)

	Singular	
1	Rydw i'n dod	*I am coming*
2	Rwyt ti'n dod	*You are coming*
3	Mae e'n dod . . .	*He/It is coming . . .* etc.

Imperfect tense (dod *to come*)

	Singular	
1	Roeddwn i'n dod	*I was coming*
2	Roeddet ti'n dod	*You were coming*
3	Roedd e'n dod . . .	*He/It was coming . . .* etc.

Future tense (dod *to come*)

	Singular	
1	Fe/Mi ddeuaf/ddo(f) i	*I shall come*
2	Fe/Mi ddoi di	*You will come*
3	Fe/Mi ddaw e/o	*He/It will come*
	Fe/Mi ddaw hi	*She will come*

	Plural	
1	Fe/Mi ddown ni	*We shall come*
2	Fe/Mi ddewch/ddowch chi	*You will come*
3	Fe/Mi ddôn nhw	*They will come*

Past tense (dod *to come*)

	Singular	
1	Fe/Mi ddes i	*I came*
2	Fe/Mi ddest ti	*You came*
3	Fe/Mi ddaeth e/o, hi	*He/It came, She came*

	Plural	
1	Fe/Mi ddaethon ni	*We came*
2	Fe/Mi ddaethoch chi	*You came*
3	Fe/Mi ddaethon nhw	*They came*

Imperative (dod *to come*)

Tyrd! *(N.W.)*/**Dere!** *(S.W.)* (singular); **Dewch!** *(S.W.)*/**Dowch!** *(N.W.)* (plural) *Come!*

Present tense (gwneud to make, to do)

Singular
1 Rydw i'n gwneud   *I am making, I make*
2 Rwyt ti'n gwneud   *You are making, You make*
3 Mae e'n gwneud . . .   *He/It is making . . . etc.*

Imperfect tense (gwneud to make, to do)

Singular
1 Roeddwn i'n gwneud   *I was making*
2 Roeddet ti'n gwneud   *You were making*
3 Roedd e'n gwneud . . .   *He/It was making . . . etc.*

Future tense (gwneud to make, to do)

Singular
1 Fe/lMi wna(f) i   *I shall make*
2 Fe/Mi wnei di   *You will make*
3 Fe/Mi wnaiff e/o   *He/It will make*
   Fe/Mi wnaiff hi   *She will make*

Plural
1 Fe/Mi wnawn ni   *We shall make*
2 Fe/Mi wnewch chi   *You will make*
3 Fe/Mi wnân nhw   *They will make*

Past tense (gwneud to make, to do)

	Singular			Plural	
1	Fe/Mi wnes i	*I made*	Fe/Mi wnaethon ni	*We made*
2	Fe/Mi wnest ti	*You made*	Fe/Mi wnaethoch chi	*You made*
3	Fe/Mi wnaeth e/o	*He/It made*	Fe/Mi wnaethon nhw	*They made*
	Fe/Mi wnaeth hi	*She made*		

Imperative (cael to have)

Gwna! (singular); **Gwnewch!** (plural) *Do! Make!*

Present tense (gwybod to know)

Singular
1 Rydw i'n gwybod   *I know*
2 Rwyt ti'n gwybod   *You know*
3 Mae e/o'n gwybod . . .   *He/It knows . . . etc.*

Present tense (compact form) (gwybod to know)

	Singular		Plural	
1	Fe/Mi wn i	*I know*	Fe/Mi wyddon ni	*We know*
2	Fe/Mi wyddost ti	*You know*	Fe/Mi wyddoch chi	*You know*
3	Fe/Mi ŵyr e/o	*He/It knows*	Fe/Mi wyddan nhw	*They know*
	Fe/Mi ŵyr hi	*She knows*		

Imperfect tense (gwybod *to know*)

Singular
1 Roeddwn i'n gwybod   *I knew*
2 Roeddet ti'n gwybod   *You knew*
3 Roedd e'n gwybod . . .   *He/It knows . . .* etc.

Future tense (gwybod *to know*)

Singular
1 Bydda i'n gwybod   *I shall know*
2 Byddi di'n gwybod   *You will know*
3 Bydd e'n gwybod . . .   *He/It will know . . .* etc.

The compact form of the future and past tenses are seldom used in conversation.

Present tense (mynd *to go*)

Singular
1 Rydw i'n mynd   *I go, I am going*
2 Rwyt ti'n mynd   *You go, You are going*
3 Mae e'n mynd . . .   *He/It goes, He/It is going . . .* etc.

Present tense (compact form) (**mynd** *to go*)

Singular
1   Af/Â i   *I go, I am going*
2   Ei di   *You go, You are going*
3   *Aiff e/o   *He/It goes, He/It is going*
   *Aiff hi   *She goes, She is going . . .* etc.

The present tense follows the same pattern as the compact form of the future tense below.

Imperfect tense (mynd *to go*)

Singular
1 Roeddwn i'n mynd   *I was going*
2 Roeddet ti'n mynd   *You were going*
3 **Roedd e'n mynd . . .   *He/It was going . . .* etc.

Future tense (mynd *to go*)

Singular		*Plural*	
1 Fe/Mi af/â i	*I shall go*	Fe/Mi awn ni	*We shall go*
2 Fe/Mi ei di	*You will go*	Fe/Mi ewch chi	*You will go*
3 *Fe/Mi aiff e/o	*He/It will go*	Fe/Mi ân nhw	*They will go*
*Fe/Mi aiff hi	*She will go*		

*Literary form: **Â ef/hi** **Literary form: **Âi ef/hi**

Past tense (mynd *to go*)

Singular		*Plural*	
1 Fe/Mi es i	*I went*	Fe/Mi aethon ni	*We went*
2 Fe/Mi est ti	*You went*	Fe/Me aethoch chi	*You went*
3 Fe/Mi aeth e/o	*He/It went*	Fe/Mi aethon nhw	*They went*
Fe/Mi aeth hi	*She went*		

Imperative (mynd *to go*)

Dos! *(N.W.)*/Cer! *(S.W.)* (singular); Ewch!/Cerwch! *(S.W.)* (plural) *Go!*

Present tense (rhoi/rhoddi *to give*)

Singular

1	Rydw i'n rhoi/rhoddi	*I am giving, I give*
2	Rwyt ti'n rhoi	*You are giving, You give*
3	Mae e'n rhoi . . .	*He/It is giving, He/It gives . . .* etc.

Imperfect tense (rhoi/rhoddi *to give*)

Singular

1	Roeddwn i'n rhoi/rhoddi	*I was giving*
2	Roeddet ti'n rhoi	*You were giving*
3	Roedd e'n rhoi . . .	*He/It was giving . . .* etc.

Future tense (rhoi/rhoddi *to give*)

Singular

1	Fe/Mi roia/rodda(f) i	*I shall give*
2	Fe/Mi roddi di	*You will give*
3	Fe/Mi roddiff/rydd e/o	*He/It will give*
	Fe/Mi roddiff/rydd hi	*She will give*

Plural

1	Fe/Mi roddwn ni	*We shall give*
2	Fe/Mi roddech chi	*You will give*
3	Fe/Mi roddan nhw	*They will give*

Past tense (rhoi/rhoddi *to give*)

	Singular			*Plural*	
1	Fe/Mi roiais i/roddais i	*I gave*	Fe/Mi roddon ni	*We gave*
2	Fe/Mi roddaist ti	*You gave*	Fe/Mi roddoch chi	*You gave*
3	Fe/Mi roddodd e/o	*He/It gave*	Fe/Mi roddon nhw	*They gave*
	Fe/Mi roddodd hi	*She gave*		

Imperative (rhoi/rhoddi *to give*)

Rhodda! Rho! (singular); Rhoddwch! (plural) *Give!*

Present tense (troi *to turn*)

Singular

1	Rydw i'n troi	*I am turning, I turn*
2	Rwyt ti'n troi	*You are turning, You turn*
3	Mae e'n troi . . .	*He/It is turning, He/It turns . . .* etc.

Imperfect tense (troi *to turn*)

Singular

1	Roeddwn i'n troi	*I was turning*
2	Roeddet ti'n troi	*You were turning*
3	Roedd e'n troi	*He/It was turning . . .* etc.

Future tense (troi *to turn*)

Singular		*Plural*	
1 Fe/Mi droaf/droia i	*I shall turn*	Fe/Mi droiwn ni	*We shall turn*
2 Fe/Mi droi-i di	*You will turn*	Fe/Mi droiwch chi	*You will turn*
3 Fe/Mi dröiff e/o	*He/It will turn*	Fe/Mi droian nhw	*They will turn*
Fe/Mi dröiff hi	*She will turn*		

Past tense (troi *to turn*)

Singular		*Plural*	
1 Fe/Mi droais i	*I turned*	Fe/Mi droeson ni	*We turned*
2 Fe/Mi droaist ti	*You turned*	Fe/Mi droesoch chi	*You turned*
3 Fe/Mi droiodd e/o	*He/It turned*	Fe/Mi droeson nhw	*They turned*
Fe/Mi droiodd hi	*She turned*		

Imperative (troi *to turn*)

Tro!/Troia! (singular); Trowch!/Troiwch! (plural) *Turn!*

cloi, **paratoi** and **rhoi** follow a similar pattern.

Imperative mood

Commands – 2nd person singular and 2nd person plural

The 2nd person singular is formed by adding **-a** to the stem of the verb-noun, while the 2nd person plural is formed by adding **-wch** to the stem:

Cysga! (2nd person singular);
Cysgwch! (2nd person plural) *Sleep!*
Brysia! (2nd person singular);
Brysiwch! (2nd person plural) *Hurry!*

Commands – other persons

The forms **Gadewch i-** *Allow-/Let* is usually used to express commands in the other persons of the verb:

Gadewch i fi weithio!	(1st person singular)	*Let me work!*
Gadewch iddo fe weithio!	(3rd person singular)	*Let him work!*
Gadewch iddi hi weithio!	(3rd person singular)	*Let her work!*
Gadewch i ni weithio!	(1st person plural)	*Let us work!*
Gadewch iddyn nhw weithio!	(3rd person plural)	*Let them work!*

Verbs and mutations

The direct object of a verb in compact form takes a soft mutation:

Fe welodd e geffyl.   *He saw a horse.*
Fe brynon nhw fwyd.   *They bought food.*
Mi gana i garolau 'fory. *I'll sing carols tomorrow.*
Rhoddaf bunt iddi.   *I'll give her a pound.*

Note: When the periphrastic form of the verb (**bod** + **yn** + verb-noun) is used *no*
mutation of the object occurs, as is shown in the following sentences:

Mae e'n darllen llyfr.   *He is reading a book.*
Mae nhw'n chwarae pêl-droed.   *They are playing football.*
Roedd Siân yn golchi llestri.   *Siân was washing dishes.*
Rydw i'n rhoddi punt iddo.   *I am giving him a pound.*

For examples involving the mutation of verbs following the particles **Fe** and **Mi**,
the relative pronoun **a**, and the personal pronouns **mi, ti, ef** . . . see the section
entitled **A summary of the main rules of mutation.**

Prepositions are followed by nouns or pronouns, for example:

gyda *with*	**gyda Mam** *with Mother;* **gyda ni** *with us*
i fyny *up*	**i fyny'r bryn** *up the hill;* **i fyny'r ysgol** *up the ladder*
i lawr *down*	**i lawr y cwm** *down the valley;* **i lawr y pwll** *down the pit*
mewn *in a*	**mewn cwpan** *in a cup;* **mewn munud** *in a minute*

Some prepositions are conjugated and have personal forms:

at *to, towards* (stem **at-**)

Singular		Plural	
1 ata i	*to me*	aton ni	*to us*
2 atat ti	*to you*	atoch chi	*to you*
3 ato fe/fo	*to him/it*	atyn nhw	*to them*
ati hi	*to her/it*		

dan *under* (stem **dan-**)

Singular		Plural	
1 dana i	*under me*	danon ni	*under us*
2 danat ti	*under you*	danoch chi	*under you*
3 dano fe/fo	*under him/it*	danyn nhw	*under them*
dani hi	*under her/it*		

am *around* (stem **amdan-**)

Singular		Plural	
1 amdana i	*around me*	amdanon ni	*around us*
2 amdanat ti	*around you*	amdanoch chi	*around you*
3 amdano fe/fo	*around him/it*	amdanyn nhw	*around them*
amdani hi	*around her/it*		

ar *on* (stem **arn-**)

Singular		Plural	
1 arna i	*on me*	arnon ni	*on us*
2 arnat ti	*on you*	arnoch chi	*on you*
3 arno fe/fo	*on him/it*	arnyn nhw	*on them*
arni hi	*on her/it*		

wrth *by* (stem **wrth-**)

Singular		Plural	
1 wrtho i	*by me*	wrthon ni	*by us*
2 wrthot ti	*by you*	wrthoch chi	*by you*
3 wrtho fe/fo	*by him/it*	wrthyn nhw	*by them*
wrthi hi	*by her/it*		

drwy *and* **heb** share a similar pattern:

drwy *through* (stem **drwydd-**)

	Singular			Plural	
1	drwyddo i	*through me*	drwyddon ni	*through us*
2	drwyddot ti	*through you*	drwyddoch chi	*through you*
3	drwyddo fe/fo	*through him/it*	drwyddyn nhw	*through them*
	drwyddi hi	*through her/it*		

heb *without* (stem **hebdd-**)

	Singular			Plural	
1	hebddo i	*without me*	hebddon ni	*without us*
2	hebddot ti	*without you*	hebddoch chi	*without you*
3	hebddo fe/fo	*without him/it*	hebddyn nhw	*without them*
	hebddi hi	*without her/it*		

yn *in* (stem **yn-**)

	Singular			Plural	
1	yno i	*in me*	ynon ni	*in us*
2	ynot ti	*in you*	ynoch chi	*in you*
3	ynddo fe/fo	*in him/it*	ynddyn nhw	*in them*
	ynddi hi	*in her/it*		

i *to, for*

	Singular			Plural	
1	i fi/mi	*to me, for me*	i ni	*to us, for us*
2	i ti	*to you . . .*	i chi	*to you . . .*
3	iddo fe/fo	*to him/it . . .*	iddyn nhw	*to them . . .*
	iddi hi	*to her . . .*		

o *from* (stem **ohon-**)

	Singular			Plural	
1	ohono i	*from me*	ohonon ni	*from us*
2	ohonot ti	*from you*	ohonoch chi	*from you*
3	ohono fe/fo	*from him/it*	ohonyn nhw	*from them*
	ohoni hi	*from her/it*		

rhwng *between* (stem **rhyng-**)

	Singular			Plural	
1	rhyngo i	*between us*	rhyngon ni	*between us*
2	rhyngot ti	*between you*	rhyngoch chi	*between you*
3	rhyngddo fe/fo	*between him/it*	rhyngddyn nhw	*between them*
	rhyngddi hi	*between her/it*		

dros *over, for*

	Singular	
1	drosto/droso i	*over me, for me*
2	drostot/drosot ti	*over you, for you*
3	drosto fe/fo	*over him/it, for him*
	drosti hi	*over her/it, for her/it*

	Plural	
1	droston/droson ni	*over us, for us*
2	drostoch/drosoch chi	*over you, for you*
3	drostyn nhw	*over them, for them*

gan *with*

Singular		*Plural*	
1 gen i	*with me*	gennyn/gynnon ni	*with us*
2 gen ti	*with you*	gennych/gynnoch chi	*with you*
3 ganddo fe/fo	*with him/it*	ganddyn nhw	*with them*
ganddi hi	*with her/it*		

Sometimes the preposition **gyda** is used instead of the conjugated preposition **gan** in South Wales.

The conjugated prepositions **am, ar, at, dan, dros, drwy/trwy, gan, heb, i, o, wrth** are used in their simple form when the object governed by the preposition is a noun or verb-noun. Soft mutation follows these prepositions:

> am dro; ar bapur; at drwyn; dan wely; dros frawd; drwy fôr; heb ddiolch; i regi; o freuddwydio; wrth lusgo.

See section **Treiglad meddal – Soft mutation.**

The conjugated preposition **rhwng** is **not** followed by mutation:

rhwng cyfeillion da	*between good friends*
rhwng dau frawd	*between two brothers*
rhwng gŵr a gwraig	*between husband and wife*

The conjugated preposition **yn** in its simple form is followed by nasal mutation. It becomes **yng** before **c** and **g**, and **ym** before **p** and **b**:

yng nghornel yr ystafell	*in the corner of the room*
yng nghwrs y flwyddyn	*in the course of the year*
yng Nghorwen	*in Corwen*
yng ngardd yr ysgol	*in the school's garden*
yng nglaw mis Ebrill	*in the April rain*
yng Nglanaman	*in Glanaman*
ym mhoced y bachgen	*in the boy's pocket*
ym mhrofiad y dyn	*in the man's experience*
ym Mhorthaethwy	*in Porthaethwy (Menai Bridge)*
ym mwyd y plant	*in the children's food*
ym masged y fenyw	*in the woman's basket*
ym Mangor	*in Bangor*

yn also becomes *ym* before *m*:

ym Môn; ym Mynwy; ym Môr y Gogledd; ym mynwent y plwyf

For examples of **yn** followed by soft mutation or by non-mutation, see section entitled **A summary of the main rules of mutation.**

adjectives

In the Welsh language the adjective usually comes after the noun:

afal **sur**	*a bitter apple*
blodyn **hyfryd**	*a beautiful flower*
cadair **uchel**	*a high chair*
siwrnai **hir**	*a long journey*

When the adjective follows a singular masculine noun no mutation occurs but when the adjective follows the singular feminine noun it takes soft mutation:

bachgen bach	*a small boy*
merch fach	*a small girl*
brawd cariadus	*a loving brother*
chwaer gariadus	*a loving sister*
dyn mawr	*a big man*
menyw fawr	*a big woman*
gŵr tenau	*a thin man/husband*
gwraig denau	*a thin woman/wife*
tarw du	*a black bull*
buwch ddu	*a black cow*

Note: Adjectives do not mutate when they follow *plural* nouns.

When an adjective precedes a noun the noun is mutated whether it be masculine or feminine:

hen **ŵr**	*an old man*
hen **wraig**	*an old woman*
annwyl **dad**	*a dear father*
annwyl **fam**	*a dear mother*

The noun takes a soft mutation on each occasion.

The feminine form of a few adjectives is still used in everyday speech. Some are listed below:

Masculine	*Feminine*	
gwyn	gwen	*white*
melyn	melen	*yellow*
tlws	tlos	*pretty*
bychan	bechan	*little*
byr	ber	*short*

e.g. cot **wen**; ffrog **felen**; merch **dlos**; ynys **fechan**; stori **fer**.

The comparison of adjectives

There are three degrees of comparison of adjectives in Welsh. These are: equative, comparative and superlative. Adjectives may be compared by two methods:

1 Using **mor, mwy, mwya(f)** before the adjective. Adjectives of more than two syllables are also compared in this manner. Irregular adjectives, some of which are listed below, are an exception.

ffôl *(foolish)*	**mor ffôl**	**mwy ffôl**	**mwyaf ffôl**
cryno *(tidy)*	**mor *gryno**	**mwy cryno**	**mwyaf cryno**
rhesymol *(reasonable)*	**mor rhesymol**	**mwy rhesymol**	**mwyaf rhesymol**

Positive	Equative	Comparative	Superlative
amlwg	mor amlwg	mwy amlwg	mwya(f) amlwg
evident	*as evident*	*more evident*	*most evident*
amyneddgar	mor amyneddgar	mwy amyneddgar	mwya(f) amyneddgar
patient	*as patient*	*more patient*	*most patient*
blasus	mor *flasus	mwy blasus	mwya(f) blasus
tasty	*as tasty*	*more tasty*	*most tasty*
cyfeillgar	mor *gyfeillgar	mwy cyfeillgar	mwya(f) cyfeillgar
friendly	*as friendly*	*more friendly*	*most friendly*
diolchgar	mor *ddiolchgar	mwy diolchgar	mwya(f) diolchgar
thankful	*as thankful*	*more thankful*	*most thankful*
doniol	mor *ddoniol	mwy doniol	mwya(f) doniol
witty	*as witty*	*more witty*	*most witty*
dyledus	mor *ddyledus	mwy dyledus	mwya(f) dyledus
indebted	*as indebted*	*more indebted*	*most indebted*
dymunol	mor *ddymuol	mwy dymunol	mwya(f) dymunol
desirable	*as desirable*	*more desirable*	*most desirable*
gwerthfawr	mor *werthfawr	mwy gwerthfawr	mwya(f) gwerthfawr
valuable	*as valuable*	*more valuable*	*most valuable*
peryglus	mor *beryglus	mwy peryglus	mwya(f) peryglus
dangerous	*as dangerous*	*more dangerous*	*most dangerous*
llawen	mor **llawen	mwy llawen	mwya(f) llawen
cheerful	*as cheerful*	*more cheerful*	*most cheerful*

*Note: **mor** *(as, so, how)* is followed by soft mutation. An alternative translation in the above context would read:
> **mor amlwg** *so evident*; **mor amyneddgar** *so patient*; **mor flasus** *so tasty*; **mor gyfeillgar** *so friendly* . . .

ll and rh do not mutate after **mor.

2 With regular adjectives the endings **-ed, -ach, -af** are added respectively to the adjective in its positive form in order to form the other degrees:

Positive	Equative	Comparative	Superlative
*agos *near*	agosed *as near*	agosach *nearer*	agosa(f) *nearest*
caled *hard*	caleted *as hard*	caletach *harder*	caleta(f) *hardest*
call *wise*	called *as wise*	callach *wiser*	calla(f) *wisest*
coch *red*	coched *as red*	cochach *redder*	cocha(f) *reddest*
cryf *strong*	cryfed *as strong*	cryfach *stronger*	cryfa(f) *strongest*
cyflym *quick*	cyflymed *as quick*	cyflymach *quicker*	cyflyma(f) *quickest*
eglur *clear*	eglured *as clear*	eglurach *clearer*	eglura(f) *clearest*
glân *clean*	glaned *as clean*	glanach *cleaner*	glana(f) *cleanest*
glas *blue*	glased *as blue*	glasach *bluer*	glasa(f) *bluest*
hapus *happy*	hapused *as happy*	hapusach *happier*	hapusa(f) *happiest*
oer *cold*	oered *as cold*	oerach *colder*	oera(f) *coldest*
pell *far*	pelled *as far*	pellach *further*	pella(f) *furthest*
tawel *quiet*	taweled *as quiet*	tawelach *quieter*	tawela(f) *quietest*
trwm *heavy*	trymed *as heavy*	trymach *heavier*	tryma(f) *heaviest*
tywyll *dark*	tywylled *as dark*	tywyllach *darker*	tywylla(f) *darkest*

Note: The final **f** of the superlative is often omitted in spelling and pronunciation.

*See end of section on adjectives for alternative forms.

cyn is used to compare adjectives which in their positive forms do not contain more than two syllables and do not end in **-en**, **-gar**, **-og**, **-ol** or **-us**.

cyn and **mor** are both followed by soft mutation, except when the adjective begins with **ll** or **rh**.

cyn agosed â/ag *as near as*	yn agosach na(g) *nearer than*	yr agosa(f) *the nearest*
cyn belled â/ag *as far as*	yn bellach na(g) *further than*	y pella(f) *the furthest*

cyn goched â/ag	yn gochach na(g)	y cocha(f)
as red as	*redder than*	*the reddest*
cyn hapused â/ag	yn hapusach na(g)	yr hapusa(f)
as happy as	*happier than*	*the happiest*
cyn llawned â/ag	yn llawnach na(g)	y llawna(f)
as full as	*fuller than*	*the fullest*

When the adjective in its positive form ends in -g, -b or -d these letters harden to -c-, -p- and -t- when the adjective is compared, as is shown below with **caled, teg, gwlyb, rhad**:

cyn galeted â/ag	yn galetach na(g)	y caleta(f)
as hard as	*harder than*	*the hardest*
cyn deced â/ag	yn decach na(g)	y teca(f)
as fair as	*fairer than*	*the fairest*
cyn wlyped â/ag	yn wlypach na(g)	y gwlypa(f)
as wet as	*wetter than*	*the wettest*
cyn rhated â/ag	yn rhatach na(g)	y rhata(f)
as cheap/free as	*cheaper/freer than*	*the cheapest/freest*

â in the equative degree and **na** in the comparative degree are used when the following word begins with a consonant, and both cause spirant mutation.

ag and **nag** are used when the following word begins with a vowel:

cyn goched â thân	*as red as fire*
yn drymach na phlwm	*heavier than lead*
cyn wynned ag eira	*whiter than snow*
yn dywyllach nag uffern	*darker than hell*

Irregular adjectives

There are only a few irregular adjectives in Welsh and the most important of them are listed below:

Positive	Equative	Comparative	Superlative
bach/bychan *small*	mor fach/fychan cyn lleied	llai	lleia(f)
buan/cynnar *swift/early*	mor fuan cynt	cynted	cynta(f)
da *good*	mor dda cystal	gwell	gorau
drwg *bad*	mor ddrwg cynddrwg	gwaeth	gwaetha(f)
hawdd *easy*	mor hawdd cyn hawsed	haws	hawsa(f)
hen *old*	mor hen cyn hyned	hŷn	hyna(f)
hir *long*	mor hir cyn hired	hirach	hira(f)
ifanc/ieuanc *young*	mor ifanc cyn ieuanged	ifancach ieuangach	ifanca(f) ieuanga(f)

Positive	Equative	Comparative	Superlative
isel *low*	mor isel cyn ised	is	isa(f)
llawer/mawr *many/big*	mor fawr cymaint	mwy	mwya(f)
uchel *high*	mor uchel cyn uched	uwch	ucha(f)

Note: **cyn** *(as)* is also used in the equative degree of comparison with the appropriate **-ed** ending. (It is already contained in such forms as **cynt**, **cystal**, **cynddrwg** and **cymaint**.) **cyn** is followed by soft mutation.

Exception: **ll** and **rh** do not mutate after **mor** and **cyn**.

The adjective **agos** also has irregular equative, comparative and superlative forms:

| agos *near* | cyn nesed â *as near as* | yn nes na *nearer than* | y nesaf *the nearest* |

There are two classes of personal pronouns in Welsh: independent and dependent.

Independent personal pronouns

These pronouns are not dependent on any other word in a sentence and may stand entirely alone.

Simple

	Singular		*Plural*	
1	fi, mi	*I, me*	ni	*we, us*
2	ti, di	*you*	chi	*you*
3	fe/e, fo/o	*he, him*	nhw	*they, them*
	hi	*she, her*		

Reduplicated

Singular

1	myfi, y fi	*I, I myself*
2	tydi, y chdi (G.C.)	*you, you yourself*
3	efe, efô, y fe, y fo	*he*
	hyhi, y hi	*she, it, she herself, it itself*

Plural

1	nyni, y ni	*we, we ourselves*
2	chychi, y chi	*you, you yourselves*
3	y nhw	*they, them, they themselves*

The reduplicated forms are often placed at the beginning of a sentence for emphasis:

Myfi sy'n magu'r baban.	*It is I who nurses the baby.*
Tydi, O Dduw, sy'n maddau.	*It is You, O Lord, who forgives.*
Nyni sy'n troi y meysydd.	*It is we who plough the fields.*

Conjunctive

	Singular		*Plural*	
1	finnau, minnau	*I, me*	ninnau	*we, us*
2	tithau	*you*	chithau	*you*
3	yntau	*he, him*	nhwthau	*they, them*
	hithau	*she, her*		

The conjunctive forms frequently possess an extra meaning beyond that of the mere pronoun, the additional meaning being expressed in English by a conjunction:

minnau may mean *I (me) also; even I (me); I (me) on the other hand; I (me) for my part; then I; but I . . .*

ninnau may mean *we (us) too, we (us) also; even we (us); we (us) on the other hand; we (us) on the contrary; we (us) for our part . . .*

Dependent personal pronouns

These pronouns are dependent on either a noun, another pronoun or personal ending of a verb or preposition, or a verb-noun.

Prefixed

	Singular		*Plural*	
1	fy, f'	*my*	ein	*our*
2	dy, d'	*your*	eich	*your*
3	ei	*his/her*	eu	*their*

The prefixed forms, which are always in the genitive case, are used before nouns and verb-nouns:

Darllenodd y bachgen ei lyfr. *The boy read his book.*
Clywais fy nhad yn galw. *I heard my father calling.*
Cafodd y gân ei chanu ar y radio. *The song was sung on the radio.*

Affixed

	Singular		*Plural*	
1	i, fi	*I, me*	ni	*we, us*
2	di, ti	*you*	chi	*you*
3	e, fe, o, fo	*he, him*	nhw	*they, them*
	hi	*she, her*		

For examples of affixed forms and a fuller discussion of the subject of Welsh pronouns the reader is referred to specific works on Welsh grammar.

Words beginning with the vowels **a, e, i, o, u w** and **y** are aspirated and acquire an initial **h** when preceded by the following pronouns (or their abbreviated forms):

1	ei, 'i, 'w	*her (feminine singular)*
2	eu, 'u, 'w	*their*
3	ein, 'n	*our*

ysgol > ei hysgol (hi) *her school;*
Dyma 'i hysgol *Here is her school;*
dewch i'w hysgol *Come to her school.*

ardal > eu hardal (nhw) *their district;*
Dyna'u hardal *That is their district;*
Mi af i'w hardal *I shall go to their district.*

ewyllys > ein hewyllys *our will;* a'n hewyllys da *and our goodwill.*

annwyl > ein hannwyl blentyn *our dear child;* eu hannwyl wlad *their dear country;* ei hannwyl fam *her dear mother.*

For the mutations after the dependent personal pronouns:
  fy, dy, ei (masculine) and ei (feminine)
see the section entitled **A summary of the main rules of mutation.**

rules of mutation

Nine initial consonants mutate. They are:
  c, p, t, g, b, d, ll, m, rh.
They mutate in the manner shown in the box below:

Initial consonant	Soft	Nasal	Spirant
cath *cat*	dy gath di *your cat*	fy nghath i *my cat*	ei chath hi *her cat*
pen *head*	dy ben di *your head*	fy mhen i *my head*	ei phen hi *her head*
tad *father*	dy dad di *your father*	fy nhad i *my father*	ei thad hi *her father*
*gardd *garden*	dy ardd di *your garden*	fy ngardd i *my garden*	
bys *finger*	dy fys di *your finger*	fy mys i *my finger*	
dant *tooth*	dy ddant di *your tooth*	fy nant i *my tooth*	
llyfr *book*	dy lyfr di *your book*		
mam *mother*	dy fam di *your mother*		
rhaff *rope*	dy raff di *your rope*		

*The consonant **g** disappears when soft mutation occurs, leaving the next letter (vowel or consonant) as the initial letter of the mutated word, as in: gair > air; glo > lo; gwair > wair; gwddf > wddf; gwyrdd > wyrdd . . .

Soft mutation

Nine consonants are affected by soft mutation:

c > g; p > b; t > d; g > (disappears); b > f; d > dd; ll > l; m > f; rh > r.

Nouns

1 Feminine singular nouns after the definite article y, yr, 'r:
   y got, y bêl, y daith, yr ardd, y fraich, o'r ddafad, i'r fam.
   ll and rh do not mutate after the definite article:
   y llaw, y llwy, y rhaglen, y rhaff, i'r rhos.

2 Nouns when preceded by adjectives:
   hen ŵr *(an old man)*; annwyl frawd *(a dear brother)*; hoff le *(a favourite place)*; unig ferch *(an only daughter)*.

3 Nouns and verb-nouns after the prepositions am, ar, at, dan, dros, drwy, gan, heb, hyd, i, o, wrth:
   am flwyddyn *(for a year)*; ar fwrdd *(on a table)*; at ddrws *(towards a door)*; dan goeden *(under a tree)*; dros Gymru *(for/over Wales)*; drwy ddŵr *(through water)*; gan ddweud *(by saying)*; heb gysgu *(without sleeping)*; wrth ganu *(by singing)*. The verb-nouns dweud, cysgu and canu mutate as nouns in this context.

4 Nouns after dyma, dyna, dacw, wele:
   Dyma le da *(Here's a good place)*. Dyna dŷ hyfryd *(There's a beautiful house)*. Dacw gi defaid *(There's a sheepdog yonder)*. Wele faban! *(Behold a babe!)*

5 Feminine singular nouns after the numeral un except those nouns beginning in ll and rh; nouns after the numerals dau and dwy; and nouns after the numerals saith and wyth beginning in c, p, t, ll and rh:
   un ferch *(one girl)*; un wraig *(one woman)*; un gadair *(one chair)*; dau fachgen *(two boys)*; dau gae *(two fields)*; dwy gath *(two cats)*; dwy dref *(two towns)*; saith gant *(seven hundred)*; wyth dudalen *(eight pages)*. Exceptions remain: un llaw *(one hand)*; un llong *(one ship)*; un rhwyd *(one net)*; un rhaw *(one shovel)*.

6 A noun when it is the direct object of an inflected verb (compact form):

Prynais lyfr.	*I bought a book.*
Gwelaf gastell.	*I see a castle.*
Agorodd ddrysau'r car.	*He opened the car's doors.*
Fe ganon nhw gân hapus.	*They sang a happy song.*

   When the verb is in a periphrastic form the object does *not* mutate:

Mae Siôn yn canu cân.	*Siôn is singing a song.*
Rydw i'n ysgrifennu llythyr.	*I'm writing a letter.*

7 Nouns after the predicative yn:

Mae Siân yn ferch hyfryd.	*Siân is a lovely girl.*
Mae'r gwaith yn fraint.	*The work is a privilege.*
Bydd hwn yn drysor am byth.	*This will be a treasure for ever.*

   Exceptions: Nouns beginning in ll and rh.

Roedd Alun yn llawen.	*Alun was happy.*

8 Nouns after the personal pronouns dy and ei (masculine) together with 'i (masculine) and 'w (masculine):
   dy got *(your coat)*; dy boced *(your pocket)*; dy dafod *(your tongue)*; ei olwg *(his sight)*; ei fraich *(his arm)*; Dyma Ifan a'i gŵn. *(Here is Ifan and his dogs)*; Collodd ei frawd a'i dad. *(He lost his brother and his father)*;

Aeth e i'w dŷ. *(He went to his house)*; Chwythodd y llwch i'w lygaid. *(The dust blew into his eyes)*.

9 Nouns and verb-nouns after the conjunction **neu** *(or)*:
   te neu goffi *(tea or coffee)*; mab neu ferch *(a son or daughter)*; ci neu gath *(a dog or cat)*; ennill neu golli *(win or lose)*. Inflected verbs (compact forms) are not mutated after **neu**.

10 Feminine singular nouns after ordinal numerals:
   y drydedd ferch *(the third girl)*; y chweched bennod *(the sixth chapter)*; y nawfed gyfrol *(the ninth volume)*; y ddegfed wers *(the tenth lesson)*.

11 The numerals **dau** and **dwy** after the definite article **y**:
   y ddau fachgen *(the two boys)*; y ddwy ferch *(the two girls)*.

12 Nouns used as adjectives after feminine singular nouns:
   llwy de *(teaspoon)*; gwisg briodas *(wedding-dress)*; gardd lysiau *(a vegetable garden)*; cadair freichiau *(an armchair)*.

13 Nouns in the vocative case:
   Fam annwyl! *(Mother dear!)*; Frodyr a chwiorydd! *(Brothers and sisters!)*; Lowyr, gwrandewch! *(Miners, listen!)*; Weithwyr y byd! *(Workers of the world!)*.

14 After a break in the normal order of words:
   Roedd croeso yno.   Roedd yno groeso.
   Mae merch newydd yn yr ysgol.   Mae yna ferch newydd yn yr ysgol.

15 Nouns after **amryw, cyfryw, pa, pa fath, pa ryw, rhyw, unrhyw**:
   amryw liwiau *(several colours)*; cyfryw bethau *(such things)*; Pa le? *(What place?)*; Pa fath fachgen ydy e? *(What kind of a boy is he?)*.

16 Nouns after **ambell, aml, holl, naill, ychydig, y fath**:
   ambell waith *(sometimes)*; aml dro *(frequently)*; yr holl bentref *(the whole village)*; y naill gynllun *(the one plan)*; ychydig fwyd *(a little food)*; y fath ddyn *(such a man)*.

17 Nouns after the prefix **cyn(-)** *(former, past, ex-, pre-)*:
   cyn-brifathro *(former headteacher)*; cyn-lywydd *(past president)*; cyn-weinidog *(former minister)*; cyn-löwr *(ex-miner)*.

Adjectives

1 Adjectives after feminine singular nouns:
   cadair fach *(a small chair)*; ffordd gul *(a narrow way)*; heol fawr *(a big road)*; merch denau *(a thin girl)*; stori dda *(a good story)*.

2 Adjectives after the predicative **yn**:
   Mae Nia yn garedig.   *Nia is kind.*
   Roedd y saer yn dda.   *The carpenter was good.*
   Mae'r bwyd yn ddiflas.   *The food is distasteful.*
   ll and rh do *not* mutate after **yn**.

3 Adjectives in comparison after **cyn** and **mor**:
   cyn gyflymed â *(as fast as)*; mor gyfeillgar â *(as friendly as)*; cyn wynned â *(as white as)*; mor dyner â *(as tender as)*. ll and rh do not mutate after **cyn** and **mor**:
   cyn llawned â *(as full as)*; mor rhad â *(as cheap as)*; mor llawen â'r gog *(as happy as the cuckoo)*.

4 Adjectives after the conjunction **neu**:
   da neu ddrwg *(good or bad)*; gwyn neu ddu *(white or black)*.

5 Adjectives after the adverbs **go, gweddol, lled, mor, rhy**:

go ddrwg	*quite/fairly bad*
gweddol dawel	*fairly quiet*
lled dda	*quite good/fairly well*
mor bwysig	*so important*
rhy lawen	*too merry*

   ll and **rh** do *not* mutate after **mor**:

mor llwyddiannus	*so successful*
mor rhwydd	*so easy*

Verbs

1 Interrogative forms of inflected verbs (compact forms):

Weloch chi'r papur?	*Did you see the paper?*
Fuest ti allan heddiw?	*Were you out today?*
Ddaeth e i'r ysgol mewn pryd?	*Did he come to school in time?*

2 Verbs after the particles **Fe**(S.W.) and **Mi**(N.W.):

Fe ganodd gân.	*He sang a song.*
Mi glywais ei llais hi.	*I heard her voice.*
Fe lanwon nhw'r car.	*They filled the car.*
Mi glywson ni'r newyddion.	*We heard the news.*

3 Verbs after the relative pronoun **a** and the negative relative pronoun **na**:

   Dyma'r ferch **a dd**aeth i'r parti.   *Here's the girl who came to the party.*

   The relative pronoun **a** *is frequently omitted in conversational Welsh but the mutation caused by it is retained:*

   Dyna'r dyn (**a**) welais i.   *There's the man whom I saw.*

   The negative relative pronoun **na** causes soft mutation with verbs beginning in **g, b, d, ll, m, rh** and spirant mutation with verbs beginning in **c, p, t**:

   Dyna'r ferch **na dd**aeth i'r parti.   *There's the girl who did not come to the party.*

   Dyma'r dyn **na ch**anodd.   *Here's the man who did not sing.*

4 After the conjunction **pan**:

Pan **dd**aeth Guto i'r tŷ . . .	*When Guto came to the house . . .*
Bydda i'n hapus pan **dd**aw'r haf.	*I'll be happy when summer comes.*

5 Negative forms of inflected verbs (compact forms):

Ddarllenodd e ddim o'r Beibl.	*He didn't read the Bible.*
Welais i ddim yno.	*I didn't see anything there.*

   In written Welsh, the negative particle **ni** precedes these forms, as in '**Ni ddarllenodd e ddim o'r Beibl**' and '**Ni welais i ddim yno**', and causes soft mutation with verbs beginning in **g, b, d, ll, m, rh**. Inflected verbs beginning in **c, p, t** undergo spirant mutation.

6 Verbs after the interrogative pronouns **Beth** and **Pwy**:

Beth weloch chi?	*What did you see?*
Pwy brynodd y tocyn?	*Who bought the ticket?*

Nasal mutation

Six consonants are affected by Nasal Mutation:

c > ngh; p > mh; t > nh; g > ng; b > m; d > n.

1 After the personal pronoun **fy**:
  fy **ngh**artref *(my home)*; fy **mh**oced *(my pocket)*; fy **nh**afod *(my tongue)*; fy **ng**obaith *(my hope)*; fy **mr**awd *(my brother)*; fy **nr**ws *(my door)*.
2 After the preposition **yn**:
  (In certain instances **yn** itself changes to **yng** or **ym**
  yn + c > yng ngh-
  yn + g > yng ng-
  yn + p > ym mh-
  yn + b > ym m-
  When **yn** precedes **m** it changes to **ym** even though there is no mutation.)
  yng **ngh**orff y dyn *(in the man's body)*; ym **mh**lwyf Llangyfelach *(in the parish of Llangyfelach)*; yn **nh**re Caerfyrddin *(in Carmarthen town)*; yng **ng**olau'r gannwyll *(in the candlelight)*; ym **mr**eichiau Myfanwy *(in Myfanwy's arms)*; yn **nh**ywyllwch y nos *(in the darkness of the night)*; yng **Ngh**aerdydd; ym **Mh**ontyberem; yn **Nh**reorci; yng **Ng**orseinon; ym Miwmares; yn Ninbych; ym Mynwy; ym Maesteg; ym mis Mai.
3 **blwydd** *(a year old)*, **blynedd** *(a year)*, and **diwrnod** *(a day)* all mutate after the cardinal numbers **pum, saith, wyth, naw, deng, deuddeng, ugain** (and numbers incorporating **ugain**, such as **trigain**), and **can**.
  pum **ml**wydd oed *(five years old)*; saith **ml**ynedd *(seven years)*; wyth **n**iwrnod *(eight days)*; deng **ml**wydd oed; deuddeng **ml**ynedd; ugain **n**iwrnod; can **ml**ynedd.
  Note: Mae Siôn yn **ddwy** flwydd oed.   *Siôn is two years old.*
    Roedd Nia yma am **ddwy** flynedd.   *Nia was here for two years.*
    Mae **dau dd**iwrnod cyn y parti.   *There are two days before the party.*
  See **soft mutation** – *treiglad meddal.*

Spirant mutation

Three consonants are affected by spirant mutation:

c > ch; p > ph; t > th.

1 After the personal pronouns **ei** (feminine), **'i** (feminine) and **'w** (feminine):
  ei **ch**aws *(her cheese)*; ei **ph**en-blwydd *(her birthday)*; ei **th**ad-cu *(her grandfather)*; o'i **ch**artref *(from her home)*; o'i **ph**en i'w **th**raed *(from her head to her feet)*.

2 After the cardinal numbers **tri, chwe**:
  tri **ch**wpan *(three cups)*; tri **ph**erson *(three persons)*; chwe **ph**lentyn *(six children)*; chwe **th**estun *(six subjects)*.

3 After the prepositions **â, gyda, tua**:

torri bara â **ch**yllell	*cutting bread with a knife*
cerdded gyda **th**ad y ferch	*walking with the girl's father*
gweithio gyda **ch**yfaill	*working with a friend*
mynd tua **Ph**entre-Bach	*going towards Pentre-Bach*
aros tua **th**ymor	*waiting about a term*

4 After the conjunctions **a** *(and)*, **na** *(nor, than)*, **oni** *(until, unless)*:

dŵr a **th**an *(water and fire)*; ci a **ch**ath *(a dog and a cat)*; na **ph**en na **ch**wt *(nor head nor tail)*; yn fwy na **ph**unt *(more than a pound)*; yn gochach na **th**ân *(redder than fire)*; oni **ch**lywaf *(unless I shall hear)*.

5 After the adverbs **â** *(as)*, **tra** *(very/exceedingly)*:

cyn drymed â **ph**lwm	*as heavy as lead*
cyn oered â **ch**lai	*as cold as clay*
tra **ch**aredig	*very kind*
tra **th**ywyll	*exceedingly dark*

6 After the negative form of the relative pronoun **na**:

Dyma'r ferch na **th**alodd am ei llyfr. *This is the girl who did not pay for her book.*

Only verbs beginning in **c**, **p**, **t** and following **na** in this context are affected by spirant mutation. For verbs beginning in **g**, **b**, **d**, **ll**, **m**, **rh** after the negative pronoun **na** see **soft mutation** – *treiglad meddal*.

7 Negative forms of inflected verbs (compact forms):

Chlywais i ddim sŵn.	*I didn't hear a sound.*
Thalodd e ddim.	*He didn't pay.*
Phrynais i ddim o'r esgidiau	*I didn't buy the shoes.*

In written Welsh, the negative particle **ni** precedes these forms, as in 'Ni **ch**lywais i ddim sŵn' and 'Ni **th**alodd e ddim', and causes spirant mutation with verbs beginning in **c**, **p**, **t**. Inflected verbs beginning in **g**, **b**, **d**, **ll**, **m** and **rh** undergo soft mutation.

pronunciation

As Welsh is a vibrant phonetic language, learners who master the basic sounds early find that they are able to pronounce Welsh words right from the start. Of the 29 letters in the Welsh alphabet, nine share the same sound value as their counterparts in English, these are: **b, d, j, l, m, n, p, s, t.**

Vowels

a   as the **a** sound in **a**pple, **a**nt, **A**rthur
e   as the e sound in **e**lf, **e**nd, **e**mpty
i   as the **ee** sound in d**ee**p, k**ee**p
o   as the **o** sound in **o**il, **o**range, n**o**t
u   as for the sound in **i** above
w   as the **w** sound in **w**illow, **w**ood
y   (i) as for the sound in **i** above. It occurs in monosyllables and in the
      final syllable of polysyllables, as in bys, crys, dyn, diferyn
   (ii) as the e sound in **e**rr, th**e** land. It occurs in polysyllables (except for
      final syllables) and in such words as y, yng, ym, yn, dy, fy.
      Additional examples: dyma, dynion, ysgolion, drygioni

Consonants

a   see **Vowels**
b   as in English
c   as in **c**ap, **c**o**c**onut
ch   as in German A**ch**tung!, J.S. Ba**ch**, lo**ch**
d   as in English
dd   as the **th** sound in brea**the**, **th**is
e   see **Vowels**
f   as in the **v** sound in **v**iola, **v**ideo, **v**iew
ff   as in the **f** sound in **f**ury, **f**right, of**f**
g   as in the **g** sound in **g**ift, **g**ood, **g**reat
ng   as the **ng** sound in cli**ng**, wi**ng**
h   as in the **h** sound in **h**elp, **h**ooray
i   see **Vowels**
j   as in English
l   as in English
ll   Place tongue as though to sound **l** emitting only breath. Try these
      words: **llo, lli, llw, Llanelli**

m	as in English
n	as in English
o	see **Vowels**
p	as in English
ph	as the **ph** sound in trium<u>ph</u>, So<u>ph</u>ia, <u>Ph</u>iladel<u>ph</u>ia
r	as in <u>r</u>ed, <u>r</u>ich, <u>r</u>obin
rh	with greater expulsion of breath and rolled, as by the Scots
s	as in English
t	as in English
th	as the **th** sound in brea<u>th</u>, dea<u>th</u>, hea<u>th</u>
u	see **Vowels**
w	see **Vowels**
y	see **Vowels**

Ideally, the learner should practise pronunciation regularly with a native Welsh speaker. Welsh communities in town and country districts abound with such possibilities. Weekly programmes for learners are broadcast by Radio Cymru, Radio Wales and by local radio stations. The Welsh television channel S4C adds daily to the Welsh environment. Groups of Welsh-speaking walkers invite learners to join them on their walks. Welsh language courses at all levels of ability are comprehensively organized throughout each local education authority. The University is interested and involved in every aspect of the work. Competitions are arranged, new course-books are published, **Twmpath** dancing is celebrated and **Cymanfaoedd Canu** are joyfully attended. Facilities at the annual National and Urdd **Eisteddfodau** attract learners worldwide. **Nosweithiau llawen, Dawnsio gwerin**, CDs, tapes, records, videos, the Web. . . The list is endless as is the energy and enthusiasm of specialist teachers who devise these enjoyable events in order that learners may experience at first hand the joy of speaking their new language in as natural an environment as possible. For our children, Welsh-medium education from nursery group to degree level is flourishing.

Croeso i'n plith!   (Welcome to our midst!)